P9-DHT-247

Southern Living BOOKS

OUR
BEST
RECIPES

by Lena E. Sturges

Library of Congress Catalog Number 70-140493
Copyright © 1970

Southern Living BOOKS

Book Division of The Progressive Farmer Company
P.O. Box 2463, Birmingham, Alabama 35202

Printed in the United States of America

Fourth Printing 1973

PREFACE

Southern Living is pleased to present the first of a series of major cookbooks on the foods of the region we serve—the South.

Since we began publication, we have received from our readers more than 50,000 recipes. The most promising of these have been tested in our test kitchens; and those that proved most original and appetizing have been published in the magazine. From that number, we have chosen 1,500 recipes which, we believe, represent all that is excellent in Southern cooking.

If you are a reader of *Southern Living*, we hope this volume will serve to replace the recipes you have from time to time clipped from the pages of the magazine. So far as we know, no major magazine publisher has heretofore been able to offer its readers this special service. Nothing is more frustrating to the conscientious cook than to misplace or lose a favorite recipe. However, a hardbound collection of recipes—weighing over two pounds—will, we hope, be easily recognized and frequently turned to as a permanent addition in your kitchen.

If you are not acquainted with our magazine, what awaits you in these pages is what many people have told us is the most thorough, best organized, most easily readable collection of Southern recipes ever published.

A number of talented writers, editors, artists, and cooks on our staff have contributed their considerable skills to kitchen-test, edit, proofread, and illustrate the recipes that appear in this volume.

We join them in welcoming you to these pages.

SECRETS FOR COOKING SUCCESS

When trying a new recipe or using an old one, there are some rules that must be followed to insure a good finished food product. Here are some points that will apply to almost any recipe in this book:

Read recipe carefully. Read the recipe word for word before starting. This will help you find out whether you have all of the ingredients needed, the right size pans, and enough time to prepare the recipe.

It will also allow you to do some of the preparations ahead of time: Set butter and eggs out to reach room temperature, chop the dates or nuts, melt the chocolate, and turn on the oven so it will be the right temperature when you are ready to bake.

Use right size utensils. Recipes in this book will give the correct size pans; do not make substitutions and expect the best results.

Measure accurately. Accurate measurements are important. To measure dry ingredients, you will need a set of measuring cups (¼, ⅓, ½, and 1 cup). For measuring liquids, you will need a cup with measurements marked on the side and a lip for easy pouring.

Measuring spoon sets include ¼ teaspoon, ½ teaspoon, 1 teaspoon, and 1 tablespoon. All measurements in the recipes are level.

Make recipe alterations with caution. Do not make alterations in the basic ingredients—flour, sugar, eggs, milk, leavening, or butter or shortening. Do not substitute salad oil for shortening. Unless the recipe states otherwise, you may substitute margarine for butter.

You may make changes in some of the seasoning items. If your family does not care for onions or green pepper and the recipe calls for only a small amount, these may be omitted. You may also leave out spices without ruining the recipe; however, you may need to add a flavoring of some kind in place of the spices.

Check temperature and timing. Be sure that your oven registers the correct temperature. Always preheat oven (unless recipe tells you to place food in a cold oven); do not wait until food is ready to cook before turning on oven. If you don't have a timer on the oven, a minute minder is a good purchase.

COOKING TERMS

A LA MODE . . . . Served with a topping of ice cream.

BAKE . . . . To cook foods in the oven at a set temperature.

BARBECUE . . . . To cook in a highly seasoned sauce.

BASTE . . . . To spread, brush, or pour water, melted fat, or other liquid over food.

BEAT . . . . To make a mixture smooth or to introduce air by using brisk, regular motion that lifts the mixture over and over.

BEAT LIGHTLY . . . . To stir with a fork to mix. This process usually applies to mixing the whites or yolks of eggs.

BIND . . . . To hold foods together with a sauce or other ingredients.

BLANCH . . . . To boil in water for a short time, or to pour boiling water over food, then drain it almost immediately.

BLEND . . . . To combine two or more ingredients by mixing thoroughly.

BOIL . . . . To cook in boiling water or liquid.

BREAD . . . . To roll or coat with breadcrumbs. Often the food is first dipped into beaten egg and then rolled in crumbs.

BROIL . . . . To cook by direct heat.

BRUSH . . . . To spread or brush with melted fat or other liquid to coat.

CARAMELIZE . . . . To heat dry sugar or food containing sugar until light brown and caramel flavored.

CHILL . . . . To cool in the refrigerator or other cold place.

CHOP . . . . To cut into small pieces with a sharp knife.

COAT THE SPOON . . . . To cook until a mixture adheres to the stirring spoon in a thin layer.

CREAM . . . . To work one or more foods until mixture is soft and creamy or fluffy.

CUBE . . . . To cut into small squares of equal size.

CUT IN SHORTENING . . . . . To combine shortening with flour and other dry ingredients by chopping it into the mixture with two knives or spatulas.

DICE . . . . To cut into small cubes.

DOT . . . . To scatter small pieces of butter or other fat over food before cooking.

DREDGE . . . . To coat or sprinkle lightly with flour, sugar, etc., until food is well covered.

DUST . . . . To sprinkle food lightly with a dry ingredient such as paprika.

FOLD	To combine by using two motions, cutting vertically through the mixture and turning over and over by sliding the implement across the bottom of the mixing bowl with each turn.
GARNISH	To decorate foods, usually with other foods.
GLAZE	To brush or pour a shiny coating over foods.
GRATE	To cut food into minute particles by rubbing on a grater.
GREASE	To rub lightly with shortening.
GRIND	To cut food into tiny particles by putting through a food grinder.
KNEAD	To fold, turn, and press down on dough with the hands until it becomes smooth and elastic.
MARINATE	To let foods stand in an acid-oil mixture.
MINCE	To cut or chop into very small pieces.
MIX	To combine ingredients in any way that evenly distributes them.
PANBROIL	To cook in a skillet kept dry by pouring off accumulated fat.
PANFRY	To cook in a small amount of fat in a skillet.
PEEL	To strip off the outside covering.
POACH	To cook in water just below the boiling point.
PREHEAT	To heat oven to desired temperature before putting food in oven.
PUNCH DOWN	To strike down risen dough with the fist to allow gas to escape
(Yeast Breads)	and fresh oxygen to reach the yeast.
ROAST	To cook by dry heat in the oven.
ROUX	A smooth blend of fat and flour used for thickening.
SAUTE	To cook in a small amount of fat.
SCALD	To heat milk to just below the boiling point.
SEAR	To brown surface quickly over high heat, as in a hot skillet.
SHRED	To cut fine with a knife or sharp instrument.
SIFT	To put dry ingredients through a sieve or sifter.
SIMMER	To cook by moist heat at a low temperature.
SLIVER	To slice into long, thin strips.
SOFT PEAKS	To beat egg whites or whipping cream until peaks are formed when beaters are lifted, but tips curl over.
STEEP	Let stand in hot liquid.
STEW	To cook slowly in liquid.
STIR	To mix foods with a circular motion for the purpose of blending or obtaining uniform consistency.
TOSS	Lightly blend food ingredients.

CONTENTS

INTRODUCTION

Nobody ever told me so, but I must have cut my teeth on a wooden mixing spoon. Mixing bowls, cakepans, egg beaters, and rolling pins have always held a fascination for me. When I go back through my pack-rat accumulation of miscellany, the vinegar-spotted recipe for relish brings back memories of the hours I spent chopping vegetables, mixing, cooking, stirring, and putting the varicolored mixture into jars. And then the family didn't like it!

Home economics training in high school and college taught me to follow a recipe. I served the family broiled bananas ("why not put them in banana pudding?"), French toast ("why don't we have Mamma's biscuits today?"), and angel food cake whipped with a wire beater ("now, that's a good cake!"). Hitting one out of three isn't too bad, and from then on I was off on a cooking spree.

I cooked everything from goat chili (chili powder again), yeast breads by the oven-full, cakes with creamy frosting, and even a relish that my family would eat! And I begged for the recipe of every dish I particularly liked at anyone's house. Some of those recipes are still in that box of miscellany, and I still haven't had a chance to try them. I worry sometimes that my life will be over before I've had a chance to read all the cookbooks I want to read and to test all the recipes that sound appealing.

When *Southern Living* started four years ago, you've never seen such correspondence from readers, all wanting to share their recipes. We still have a file cabinet full of them, and someday we'll get to try them all.

It was a real fun time when we started assembling the recipes for our first *Southern Living* cookbook, with most of the recipes from the first 47 issues of the magazine (the first issue was February 1966).

During this assembling, I had a chance to reminisce on the reaction of the taste panel to the recipes I tested and served. There's not an inhibited one in the crowd, and some recipes I thought pretty good were turned down flat!

But we are most grateful to the readers of *Southern Living* for their generosity in sharing the time-tested, handed-down recipes. The least we can do is compile all these recipes into a single book that contains favorites of yours and mine.

And now that it's done, we're proud. We hope you will enjoy using the book. For my part, I'll just put on my apron and start testing recipes; who knows, we may want another cookbook soon!

Lena E. Sturges

Lena E. Sturges, Food Editor

Appetizers, Snacks, And Sandwiches

Appetizers and snacks are not generally meant to be a full meal, but merely a preview to the meal itself. Sandwiches, on the other hand, may be a light meal; it is often a soup and sandwich or sandwich and salad combination.

The cocktail hour, preceding a dinner, calls for beverages (alcoholic or non-alcoholic) plus "finger foods." These foods should merely pique the appetite. They may consist of small sandwiches and dips or spreads to be served with crackers, corn chips, or party bread slices.

Appetizers, or hors d'oeuvres, help guests ease comfortably into a social hour before the meal is announced.

Foods with a distinctive Southern flavor have always been popular as hors d'oeuvres: salted peanuts, boiled shrimp with a spicy sauce, small ham biscuits, peanut butter dips, or a tangy dip with the Southwestern flavor of hot peppers.

Ham has always been a Southern favorite for sandwiches, and left-over sliced chicken or turkey, with the addition of mayonnaise or mustard, is also popular. Seafood, found in such abundance off Southern shores, is used in sandwiches both hearty and party.

Anchovy Roll-Ups

1 (3-ounce) package cream cheese
1 tablespoon milk
1½ to 2 teaspoons anchovy paste
1 teaspoon Worcestershire sauce
Bread
3 tablespoons melted butter

Soften cream cheese with milk until creamy (add more milk if necessary). Blend in anchovy paste and Worcestershire sauce. Trim crusts from bread. Spread on mixture, and roll up. Wrap in waxed paper and store in refrigerator until ready to serve. The rolls may also be frozen. To serve, sauté rolls in melted butter. Rolls may be cut in half, if desired. Stick toothpicks in them and serve hot. Yield: 10 servings.

Avocado Fingers

1 ripe avocado
¼ teaspoon salt
⅛ teaspoon paprika
1 teaspoon lemon juice
Toast strips
Bacon strips

Mash avocado; add salt, paprika, and lemon juice. Spread on 1- x 3-inch toast strips. Place narrow strips of bacon over avocado. Broil until bacon crisps. Yield: 24 servings.

Sandwiches are in the cards for you, whether they be the two-hands, full-meal kind, or the dainty one-bite tea-size.

Hot Bacon Appetizers

½ *pound bacon, cooked*
¾ *cup (3 ounces) shredded American*
  process cheese
¼ *cup butter, softened*
2 *teaspoons caraway seed*
  Melba toast rounds

Crumble bacon. Mix well with cheese, butter, and caraway seed. Spread on melba toast rounds. Place on cookie sheet and broil about 4 inches from source of heat until cheese is melted and bubbling hot. Remove from broiler and serve immediately. Yield: about 50 appetizers.

Blue Cheese Hors d'Oeuvres

3 *ounces cream cheese*
3 *tablespoons blue cheese*
¼ *cup chopped pecans*

Mix together and spread on bread. Top with another slice of bread and toast on electric grill.

Canapés

1 *(8-ounce) package cream cheese*
1 *egg yolk*
1 *teaspoon grated onion*

Combine all ingredients and mix well. Spread on crackers and broil. The canapés puff up and turn golden brown. Yield: enough for 2 dozen crackers.

Cheesies

3 *sticks margarine*
24 *ounces sharp Cheddar cheese,*
  shredded
3 *cups flour*
1½ *teaspoons salt*
¾ *teaspoon Tabasco sauce*
4½ *cups crushed corn flakes*

Cream margarine, add shredded cheese, and

then work in the flour to which salt has been added. Add Tabasco and mix in corn flakes (mixture will be crumbly). Form into small balls and place on lightly greased cookie sheet. Bake at 350 degrees F. about 15 to 20 minutes, or until dry and lightly browned.

Cheese Log

1 *(8-ounce) package cream cheese,*
  softened
1 *(4-ounce) roll bacon and horseradish*
  cheese spread
1 *package onion dry soup mix*
1 *teaspoon chili powder*
¼ *teaspoon garlic powder*
½ *cup chopped peanuts*

Blend all ingredients except peanuts. Shape into 10- x 2½-inch roll; wrap in waxed paper and chill 4 hours. Remove paper, roll in peanuts, and serve with rye bread. Yield: 12 to 15 servings.

Cheese Snappy Wafers

2 *sticks butter*
2 *cups all-purpose flour*
8 *ounces sharp cheese, shredded*
½ *teaspoon cayenne*
½ *teaspoon salt*
2 *cups Rice Krispies*

Cut butter into flour until texture resembles coarse meal. Mix in cheese, cayenne, and salt. Fold in Rice Krispies. Pinch off small pieces, place on ungreased cookie sheet, and pat flat. Bake at 350 degrees F. for 15 minutes.

London Cheese Roll

11 *ounces cream cheese (1 large and 1*
  small package)
4 *ounces blue cheese*
2 *cups coarsely chopped nuts (walnuts*
  or pecans), divided
1 *cup thinly sliced ripe olives*

Have cheeses at room temperature. Blend thoroughly with electric mixer. Stir in 1 cup of the nuts and the olives. Spread remaining nuts on sheet of waxed paper. Flour hands lightly and shape mixture into 1 long or 2 short rolls about the size of a silver dollar. Roll back and forth in nuts until well coated; wrap in waxed paper and refrigerate several hours before using. Freezes well. Yield: 1 long or 2 short rolls.

Shrimp-Cheese Puffs

- ½ cup butter
- 2 cups shredded Cheddar cheese
- 1 egg yolk
- 1 egg white, stiffly beaten
- 30 bread squares
- 30 shrimp, cooked and cleaned

Cream butter and cheese. Blend in egg yolk. Fold in stiffly beaten egg white. Arrange bread squares on ungreased cookie sheet. Top each with a shrimp and cover with rounded teaspoonful of cheese mixture. Bake at 350 degrees F. for 15 to 18 minutes, or until golden brown. This may be refrigerated up to 24 hours before baking.

Buoy Cheese Ball

- 6 (3-ounce) packages cream cheese
- ½ pound sharp cheese
- 2 teaspoons grated onion
- 2 teaspoons Worcestershire sauce
- 2 teaspoons finely minced garlic (dried onion flakes and garlic powder may be substituted)
- Finely chopped nuts (pecan or peanut)

Put all ingredients except nuts in a mixer and blend well. Refrigerate until firm and shape like whistling buoy or a spar buoy. Roll in chopped nuts until well coated. Wrap in plastic or foil and let ripen in refrigerator for at least 24 hours. Leave out of refrigerator at least 2 hours before serving. Accompany with crisp crackers.

Curry-Coconut Cheese Balls

- 2 (8-ounce) packages cream cheese
- 1⅓ cups (about) flaked coconut
- 1½ teaspoons curry powder

Form 64 small cheese balls; set aside. Toss coconut with curry powder until well mixed; spread in a thin layer in shallow baking pan. Toast in a 350-degree F. oven 8 to 12 minutes, or until delicately browned. Stir or shake pan often to brown coconut evenly. Cool. Roll cream cheese balls in curry-coconut. Chill until firm. Yield: 64 cocktail-size cheese balls.

Ginger Ball

- 3 (8-ounce) packages cream cheese
- 1 (4-ounce) package candied or preserved ginger, coarsely chopped
- 2 or more teaspoons ground ginger
- 1 cup finely chopped pecans

In a large bowl mix cream cheese and ginger until thoroughly blended. Shape into a ball and store in refrigerator at least 24 hours before serving. About half an hour before serving, roll ball in chopped pecans and allow to come to room temperature. Serve with crackers, potato chips, or with crisp vegetable wedges.

Olive-Cheese Tidbits

- 1 stick butter
- 1 (5-ounce) glass English Cheddar cheese
- 1¼ cups flour
- Dash salt
- 48 olives, medium size, drained and dried

Cut butter and cheese into flour. Add salt. Form into small balls. Form around olives and seal well. Let stand in refrigerator overnight. Bake at 400 degrees F. about 15 minutes or until brown. Yield: 48 balls.

Gulfport Cheese Balls

¾ pound extra-sharp Cheddar cheese
3 egg whites
⅓ cup flour
4 dashes Tabasco sauce
Dash salt
1 teaspoon parsley flakes
Paprika
Cornmeal
Hot melted shortening or oil

Shred cheese. Beat egg whites very stiff. To egg whites add shredded cheese. Then add flour, Tabasco sauce, salt, parsley flakes, and paprika (for color). Roll mixture into small balls and roll in cornmeal. Place balls in skillet with about ¼-inch hot melted shortening or oil. Cook until golden brown. Turn constantly with long fork.

Cheese-Rice Crispy

2 cups shredded cheese
2 sticks margarine, softened
2 cups flour
2 cups crisp rice cereal

Mix shredded cheese and margarine. Add flour and mix well. Add crisp cereal and mix well. Shape into small balls and place on ungreased cookie sheets. Flatten each ball with a fork and bake at 375 degrees F. about 10 minutes.

Cheese Sticks

1 cup flour
½ teaspoon salt
⅛ teaspoon cayenne
1½ teaspoons baking powder
4 tablespoons butter or margarine
½ cup shredded Cheddar cheese
3 tablespoons commercial sour cream

Combine dry ingredients. Cut in butter and cheese with pastry blender or forks; stir in sour cream. Shape into a ball and chill 2 hours. On lightly floured board, roll out dough ⅛ inch thick. Cut into strips 3 x ¼ inches. Bake at 425 degrees F. for 8 minutes.

Chicken Balls

1 pound uncooked chicken breasts
3 tablespoons chopped onion
10 water chestnuts
Small can mushrooms, drained
2 tablespoons cornstarch
½ teaspoon salt
2 tablespoons soy sauce
1 tablespoon sherry
2 egg whites, stiffly beaten

Bone chicken breasts and put through food grinder with onion, water chestnuts, and mushrooms. Add cornstarch, salt, soy sauce, sherry, and beaten egg whites. Form into small balls and fry in deep hot fat. Drain and serve with toothpicks. Yield: about 50 small balls.

Cocktail Chicken Livers With Ginger

1 pound chicken livers
¼ cup butter
Salt and freshly ground pepper
Ginger

Cut livers in half. Melt butter in large skillet over moderate heat and sauté livers, shaking pan to brown lightly and evenly. If necessary, use a pair of tongs to turn the individual pieces. (A fork will pierce the livers, causing vital juices to escape.) Do not crowd the livers. Sauté in batches or use two frying pans.

When livers are barely done—a trace of pink may remain—season with salt and pepper and transfer with pan juices to a chafing dish or candle-warmed serving dish. A little widemouth pot or relish dish filled with ginger goes to the side of the livers. Guests spear chicken livers with toothpicks or cocktail forks and dip them in ginger.

Luau Bits
(Chicken Livers)

    10 *canned water chestnuts, cut in halves*
     5 *chicken livers, cut in quarters*
    10 *slices bacon, cut in halves*
    ¼ *cup soy sauce*
     2 *tablespoons brown sugar*

Wrap water chestnuts and chicken livers in bacon slices. Secure bacon slices with toothpicks. Marinate in mixture of soy sauce and brown sugar for 4 hours. Broil about 3 inches from heat until bacon is crisp.

Carrot Dip

     3 *medium carrots*
     3 *medium dill pickles*
     1 *small jar pimientos*
     2 *green peppers*
     1 *small onion*
     3 *hard-cooked eggs, chopped*
    Salt and pepper to taste
    Mayonnaise

Grind together carrots, pickles, pimientos, peppers, and onion. Drain on paper towels. Add eggs, salt and pepper, and enough mayonnaise to hold mixture together.

Deviled Crab Dip

     1 *(7¾-ounce) can crabmeat, drained*
        and flaked
     1 *hard-cooked egg, chopped*
    ½ *cup mayonnaise*
     1 *tablespoon lemon juice*
    ½ *teaspoon powdered mustard*
    ½ *teaspoon onion salt*
    ⅛ *teaspoon black pepper*

Combine ingredients; mix well. Cover and chill. Serve with assorted snack crackers. Yield: 2 cups dip.

Chili con Queso Dip

     1 *onion, minced*
     1 *clove garlic, minced*
     2 *tablespoons shortening*
     4 *to 6 tablespoons chili powder*
    ½ *teaspoon oregano*
     1 *teaspoon cumin*
     1 *teaspoon sugar*
     1 *teaspoon salt*
    1½ *cups water*
     2 *tablespoons flour*
    ¼ *cup water*
    2½ *cups shredded processed yellow*
        cheese

Sauté onion and garlic in shortening in a deep skillet. Stir in chili powder, oregano, cumin, sugar, and salt. Carefully stir in the 1½ cups water. Cover the skillet and simmer sauce 15 minutes. Thicken with the flour blended with ¼ cup water. (The foregoing can be done several days in advance.)
  Shortly before serving, reheat the sauce in the top of a double boiler. Then gradually stir in the shredded cheese. Serve hot or cold with corn chips or tostados (pieces of tortillas fried until crisp).

Jalapeño-Cheese Dip

     2 *tablespoons flour*
    ¾ *cup cream*
     3 *tablespoons margarine*
     2 *pounds processed cheese, cut up*
     1 *pint cottage cheese*
     1 *medium onion, finely chopped*
     1 *medium green pepper, finely*
        chopped
     1 *pod garlic, minced*
     4 *jalapeño peppers*

Mix flour and cream in double boiler. Add margarine and cheeses; melt. Add remaining ingredients and simmer 10 to 15 minutes or until thick, stirring occasionally. If desired, serve warm as a dip or as a spread for crackers and sandwiches.

Fruit Sticks With Curry Dip Gregnon

Cut into finger-size pieces any firm fruit, such as melon, pineapple, apples, or pears. Chill thoroughly and place on platter around Curry Dip Gregnon. Strawberries may be used with toothpicks inserted.

Curry Dip Gregnon:

> 1 *cup mayonnaise*
> 4 *tablespoons curry powder*
> 3 *tablespoons lemon juice*
> 1 *tablespoon chutney*
> *Dash Tabasco sauce*

Mix all ingredients thoroughly in blender. Chill well. For small amount, use ¼ cup mayonnaise, 1 scant tablespoon curry powder, the rest to taste. Yield: 1½ cups dip.

Shrimp Dip

> 2 *(8-ounce) packages cream cheese*
> 1 *(3-ounce) package cream cheese with chives*
> 1 *can frozen cream of shrimp soup, thawed*
> 1½ *cups chopped cooked shrimp*
> 1 *teaspoon dry mustard*
> 1 *teaspoon Worcestershire sauce*
> ¼ *teaspoon garlic powder*
> ½ to 1 *teaspoon paprika*
> *Salt and pepper to taste*
> ¾ to 1 *cup mayonnaise*
> 1 *cup drained, cooked crabmeat (optional)*

Mix ingredients thoroughly in large bowl at least 2 hours before serving. Chill well before serving. Yield: 25 to 30 servings.

"Souper" Shrimp Dip

> 1 *can frozen cream of shrimp soup*
> 1 *(8-ounce) package cream cheese, softened*
> 1 *teaspoon lemon juice*
> *Dash garlic powder*
> *Dash paprika*

To thaw, place can of soup in hot water for about 30 minutes. With an electric mixer or rotary beater, gradually blend soup and other ingredients; beat just until smooth. (Overbeating will make dip too thin.) Chill. Serve as a dip with crackers, potato chips, corn chips, celery sticks, etc. Yield: about 2 cups.

Shrimp Chip Dip

> 1 *(5-ounce) can shrimp*
> 1 *cup commercial sour cream*
> ¼ *cup chili sauce*
> 2 *teaspoons lemon juice*
> ½ *teaspoon salt*
> ⅛ *teaspoon pepper*
> 1 *teaspoon prepared horseradish*
> *Dash Tabasco sauce*

Cut the shrimp into very small pieces and mix well with other ingredients. Chill. Yield: 1½ cups.

Peanut Butter-Cheese Dip

> ½ *cup chopped onion*
> 1 *cup chopped green pepper*
> 1 *clove garlic, chopped*
> 2 *tablespoons peanut oil*
> 2 *tomatoes, peeled and chopped*
> ¾ *cup tomato juice*
> ¼ *teaspoon thyme*
> ¼ *teaspoon oregano*
> ½ *bay leaf*
> ½ *pound American Cheddar cheese, shredded*
> ¾ *cup peanut butter (smooth or crunchy)*
> ½ *teaspoon salt*
> ⅛ *teaspoon pepper*

Cook onion, green pepper, and garlic in peanut oil until tender, but not browned. Add tomatoes, tomato juice, and seasonings; cover and cook over low heat 10 minutes. Stir once or twice. Put in top of double boiler and add cheese and peanut butter, salt, and pepper. Cook and stir over boiling water until cheese is melted and mixture blended. Serve in chafing dish with corn or potato chips. Yield: 1 quart dip.

Tuna Dip

  ½ *cup commercial sour cream*
  1 *(7-ounce) can tuna*
  1 *tablespoon horseradish*
  1 *teaspoon Worcestershire sauce*
  1 *(8-ounce) package cream cheese, broken in pieces*
  ½ *small onion, sliced*
  1 *clove garlic*
  ½ *teaspoon salt*
     Dash of pepper

Place all ingredients in blender container. Blend only until smooth. Chill for several hours. Serve with crisp crackers or potato chips. Yield: 3 cups.

Tuna-Cream Dip

  1 *(6½- or 7-ounce) can tuna*
  1 *tablespoon horseradish*
  1½ *teaspoons onion salt*
  1 *teaspoon Worcestershire sauce*
  1 *cup commercial sour cream*
  2 *teaspoons chopped parsley*
     Potato chips

Drain tuna. Flake. Blend in horseradish, onion salt, and Worcestershire sauce. Fold in sour cream. Chill. Garnish with parsley and serve with potato chips. Yield: about 1½ cups of dip.

Tuna-Pineapple Dip

  1 *(6½- or 7-ounce) can tuna*
  1 *(9-ounce) can crushed pineapple*
  1 *(8-ounce) package cream cheese*
  3 *tablespoons pineapple juice*
     Dash salt
     Dash nutmeg
     Potato chips

Drain tuna. Flake. Drain pineapple and save liquid. Soften cheese at room temperature. Combine all ingredients except potato chips; blend into a paste. Chill. Serve in a bowl surrounded by potato chips. Yield: about 1 pint of dip.

Peanut Butter Meatballs

  ½ *cup peanut butter (smooth or crunchy)*
  ½ *pound ground beef*
  ¼ *cup finely chopped onion or 2 teaspoons instant minced onion*
  2 *tablespoons chili sauce*
  1 *teaspoon salt*
  ⅛ *teaspoon pepper*
  1 *egg, beaten*
  2 *tablespoons peanut oil*

Mix peanut butter lightly with beef, onion, chili sauce, salt, pepper, and egg. Form into 3 dozen small meatballs. Fry in hot peanut oil, turning to brown on all sides. Serve hot with toothpicks.

Fritosburgers

  2 *eggs, beaten*
  2 *tablespoons cornstarch*
  1 *tablespoon soy sauce*
  1 *medium onion, finely chopped or grated*
  ⅛ *teaspoon pepper*
  3 *cups corn chips, crumbled*
  1 *pound lean ground beef*

In a bowl, beat the eggs well. Add cornstarch, soy sauce, onion, and pepper, and mix well. Add the corn chips; stir and allow to stand for 20 minutes. Prepare the beef by breaking apart with two forks. Add to egg mixture and mix, using two forks. Shape into 1-inch balls, place on a foil-covered cookie sheet, and broil at 450 degrees F. until brown. Remove from heat, top with toothpicks, and let guests serve themselves. Yield: 6 to 8 servings.

Burgundy Meatballs

   1 *pound ground chuck*
  ½ *cup cornflake crumbs*
   1 *small onion, minced*
  ¾ *teaspoon cornstarch*
    Dash ground allspice
   1 *egg, beaten*
   1 *tablespoon Worcestershire sauce*
  ¼ *cup chili sauce*
  ½ *cup evaporated milk*
   1 *teaspoon salt*

Combine all ingredients; mix well and shape into teaspoon-size balls. Place on cookie sheet with sides and bake at 400 degrees F. for 10 to 15 minutes. May be baked ahead; freeze well. To serve, make Sauce and simmer in top of chafing dish. Yield: about 40.

    Sauce:

2¼ *tablespoons cornstarch*
   1 *cup water*
   2 *beef bouillon cubes*
  ¾ *cup Burgundy*
  ½ *teaspoon salt*
  ⅛ *teaspoon pepper*

Combine ingredients and cook, stirring constantly, over medium heat until mixture is thick.

"Nuts and Bolts" or Party Fare

   4 *cups shredded rice cereal*
   4 *cups bite-size shredded wheat cereal*
   4 *cups oat puffs*
   1 *(7½-ounce) can salted peanuts*
    Nuts as desired (pecans and cashews
     are especially good)
   1 *small box pretzel sticks, broken*
  ½ *pound melted margarine*
   2 *tablespoons Worcestershire sauce*
   2 *tablespoons garlic salt*
   2 *teaspoons curry powder*
    Salt to taste

Mix cereals, nuts, and pretzels in a large shallow baking pan. Combine remaining ingredients and pour evenly over cereal mixture. Heat in oven set at 250 degrees F., stirring over and under every 15 minutes for 2 hours. Cool thoroughly and store in moistureproof containers.

Consommé Pâté Mold

   1 *tablespoon unflavored gelatin*
   1 *pint canned beef consommé*
   2 *(3-ounce) packages cream cheese*
   2 *tablespoons cream*
  ⅛ *teaspoon garlic powder*
  ⅛ *teaspoon Beau Monde seasoning*
    Sliced green olives
    Pimiento strips
  ½ *cup mashed cooked chicken livers*

Dissolve gelatin in ¼ cup consommé. Heat the remaining consommé to boiling and add dissolved gelatin. Soften cream cheese with the cream; add garlic powder and Beau Monde. Arrange sliced green olives and pimiento strips in bottom of round mold, and spoon ⅛ cup of consommé mixture carefully into mold. Place in refrigerator until set, then add the remainder and return to refrigerator. Add mashed livers to cream cheese mixture and spread over congealed consommé (may be made the day before). To prepare chicken livers, lightly dust with flour, salt, and pepper. Sauté in ¼ cup butter and cook until done. Yield: 10 to 12 servings.

Corn Flings

   1 *(8-ounce) package corn muffin mix*
   4 *wieners, sliced thin*
   2 *teaspoons oregano*
1½ *cups shredded Cheddar cheese*

Prepare corn muffin mix according to package directions. Spread in a greased 10½- x 15-inch pan and arrange sliced wieners over the mix. Top with oregano and bake in a preheated 400-degree F. oven for 15 minutes.

Sprinkle cheese over hot bread and place under broiler until cheese bubbles, about 3 minutes. Cut into squares to serve. Yield: about 25 servings.

Nachos

- 1 *large package corn chips or 1 package of 10 corn tortillas*
- 1 *pound Cheddar or Longhorn cheese, cut in slices, then in ½-inch-square pieces*
- 1 *small can jalapeño peppers cut into thin strips*

Cut tortillas into triangles and fry until crisp in ½ inch hot cooking oil. Prepare ahead and store in airtight container. Heat oven to 400 degrees F. Place corn chips or tortilla triangles on cookie sheets. On each chip or tortilla place a piece of cheese topped with a jalapeño strip. Place in oven until cheese melts, about 2 to 3 minutes. Serve hot. Yield: about 20 servings.

Parched Peanuts

Put 3 quarts dried peanuts in hulls in shallow pan. Place in a 350-degree F. oven. Bake for 30 minutes, stirring occasionally. To test to see if they are parched, remove one from oven. Let cool; if crunchy, peanuts are ready. Different size nuts vary a little in time of cooking.

Peanut Butter-Bacon Spread

- 4 *slices bacon*
- ½ *cup peanut butter (smooth or crunchy)*
- ½ *cup finely chopped dill pickle*
- 2 *tablespoons dill pickle juice*
- ¼ *teaspoon salt*
- *Dash Tabasco sauce*

Cook bacon until crisp. Drain on paper towels. Crumble into small pieces. Mix with peanut butter, dill pickles, juice, and seasonings. Serve on crackers. Yield: about 1 cup.

Deviled Peanut Spread

- ½ *cup peanut butter (smooth or crunchy)*
- 1 *(2¼-ounce) can deviled ham*
- ½ *teaspoon celery salt*

Mix all ingredients lightly. Serve on crackers. Yield: ¾ cup spread.

Harris Canapé Spread

- 1 *(3-ounce) package cream cheese, softened*
- 1 *(7-ounce) can tuna fish*
- *Mayonnaise*
- *Worcestershire sauce*
- *Tabasco sauce*

Stir cream cheese until smooth; add tuna and mix well. Add just enough mayonnaise to make spreading consistency, and add seasonings to taste. Serve with crackers. Yield: about 6 to 8 servings.

Canapé Spread

- 1 *(8-ounce) package cream cheese*
- ¼ *cup mayonnaise*
- 1 *teaspoon prepared mustard*
- 1 *teaspoon Worcestershire sauce*
- *Few drops Tabasco sauce*
- 1 *teaspoon prepared horseradish*
- 1 *hard-cooked egg, minced*
- 2 *tablespoons minced stuffed olives*
- 1 *(4½-ounce) can deviled ham*

Soften cream cheese. Add mayonnaise, mustard, Worcestershire sauce, and Tabasco sauce and whip until fluffy. Blend in other ingredients and chill. Serve on crisp crackers. Yield: about 2 cups spread.

Popcorn Crumble

2 *quarts unsalted popped corn*
1⅓ *cups pecan halves*
⅔ *cup sliced almonds*
1⅓ *cups sugar*
1 *cup margarine*
½ *cup white corn syrup*
2 *teaspoons vanilla extract*

Mix popcorn and nuts in large bowl and set aside. Combine sugar, margarine, and corn syrup in heavy saucepan. Bring to a boil; stir constantly and cook to 300 degrees F. using a candy thermometer.

Next, add vanilla and very quickly pour over popcorn and nut mixture. Stir to coat well and spread on a greased cookie sheet to harden.

When mixture has cooled, break into serving-size pieces. Yield: about 1 pound.

Pumpkin Chips

Cut pumpkin in sections about 1 or 1½ inches wide. Remove rind and inside pulp until solid fruit is left; then slice in thin chips. Weigh and put in large kettle. To each pound of chips, add ¾ pound granulated sugar. Shake sugar down through chips. Set aside overnight. The next morning add 1 lemon for every 3 pounds of pumpkin chips. Cut lemons in thin strips. Cook until chips are clear and rather crisp. If pumpkin has not dried before using, it may be necessary to lift fruit from syrup and boil syrup down a little before finishing the cooking. Let come to a boil after fruit has been added to thickened syrup. Put in sterile jars and seal.

Ribbon Bologna Wedges

1 *(5-ounce) jar cheese spread with olives and pimiento*
12 *thin slices bologna*
¼ *cup finely chopped nuts*
Parsley flakes or chopped fresh parsley

Have cheese at room temperature. Spread evenly over the sliced bologna and sprinkle each piece with chopped nuts. Divide bologna into two stacks of 6 slices. Garnish tops with parsley.

Cover both rolls with plastic wrap and chill. At serving time, cut each stack into 16 wedges and insert a colored toothpick in each wedge. Yield: 32 wedges.

Braunschweiger Mold

½ *pound Braunschweiger (liver sausage)*
1 *(3-ounce) package cream cheese*
4 *tablespoons mayonnaise*
1 *to 2 tablespoons cream*
1 *tablespoon melted butter*
1 *tablespoon dry sherry*
½ *teaspoon curry powder (or more, to taste)*
¼ *teaspoon salt*
¼ *teaspoon pepper*
Pinch cayenne
Pinch nutmeg
1 *tablespoon Worcestershire sauce*

In small bowl of electric mixer beat sausage, cheese, mayonnaise, and cream. When blended, beat in remaining ingredients; turn into lightly oiled mold or bowl in which spread is to be served. Chill until ready to serve. (May be made day before serving.) Surround bowl with small rounds of rye bread. Yield: about 2 cups.

Adam and Eve Sandwich

1 *package (4) English muffins*
4 *slices boiled ham*
4 *hard-cooked eggs, sliced thin*
¾ *to 1 pound shredded Cheddar cheese*
½ *teaspoon prepared mustard*
1 *teaspoon Worcestershire sauce*
½ *cup cream*

Toast English muffins and butter immediately. Place a slice of ham on 4 muffin halves. Place sliced eggs on top of ham. Make sauce of cheese, mustard, Worcestershire, and cream. Mix all together and cook slowly until cheese melts. Pour over sandwich. Top with other half of muffin. Yield: 4 servings.

Tiny Apricot Bread Sandwiches

  ⅔ *cup dried apricots*
1⅓ *cups milk, scalded*
  ⅔ *cup Grape Nuts*
  1 *egg, well beaten*
  3 *tablespoons shortening, melted and
      cooled*
  2 *cups sifted all-purpose flour*
2½ *teaspoons double-acting baking
      powder*
  1 *teaspoon salt*
  ⅔ *cup firmly packed light brown sugar
      Softened cream cheese*

Prepare apricots as directed on package, but cook in only half the time indicated. (This will prevent apricots from being too soft in bread.) Drain, cool, and cut into pieces. Pour scalded milk over cereal in mixing bowl; stir in apricots. Let stand to cool. Add egg and shortening; mix well. Combine sifted flour, baking powder, salt, and sugar; add to cereal mixture. Stir just until moistened. Pour into a greased 8- x 4-inch loafpan. Bake at 350 degrees F. for 1 hour, or until cake tester inserted into center comes out clean. Cool in pan 10 minutes; remove from pan and finish cooling on rack. Wrap in waxed paper, plastic wrap, or aluminum foil. To serve, slice and fill with softened cream cheese. Yield: 1 loaf.

Apricot-Cream Cheese Dreams

  1 *(3-ounce) package cream cheese,
      softened*
    Butter or margarine, softened
  8 *slices sandwich bread*
  ⅓ *cup cooked dried apricots, sweetened
      to taste*

Let cream cheese soften at room temperature. Spread softened butter or margarine on bread slices. Spread mashed cream cheese on 4 slices of bread; spread other 4 slices with mashed apricots. Put slices together and cut sandwiches in rectangles or circles. Yield: about 16 small sandwiches.

Asparagus Sandwiches

  1 *small can green asparagus*
  2 *hard-cooked eggs, minced*
  3 *small pickles*
  4 *slices crisp bacon, crumbled*
    Chopped parsley
    Salt and pepper
    Mayonnaise
    Sandwich bread cut in small squares

Mash asparagus well, pouring off all liquid. Add minced eggs, pickles, bacon, and parsley. Add salt and pepper and sufficient mayonnaise to make correct consistency to spread. Spread between small squares of sandwich bread. Yield: 8 to 10 servings.

Baked Chicken or Turkey Sandwiches

1½ *cups cooked, chopped chicken or
      turkey*
  1 *can cream of mushroom soup*
  1 *can chicken gravy*
  2 *tablespoons chopped pimiento*
  2 *tablespoons chopped onion*
  1 *cup sliced water chestnuts*
20 *slices bread*
  4 *eggs, beaten*
  2 *tablespoons milk*
    Crushed potato chips

Mix the chicken, mushroom soup, gravy, pimiento, onion, and water chestnuts. Cut crusts from bread for 10 sandwiches. Spread mixture on bread and cover with a slice of bread. Wrap individual sandwiches in plastic wrap or waxed paper and freeze.

Dip the sandwiches, still frozen, in mixture of beaten eggs and milk. Coat with crushed potato chips and place on buttered cookie sheet. Bake at 300 degrees F. for 1 hour. Yield: 10 sandwiches.

Blue Cheese-Asparagus Sandwiches

1 *(10-ounce) package frozen asparagus*
  spears
1 *can condensed cream of mushroom*
  soup
6 *slices pumpernickel bread*
Softened butter or margarine
4 *hard-cooked eggs, sliced*
½ *cup crumbled blue cheese*

Cook asparagus according to package directions; drain. Heat soup; toast bread and spread with softened butter. Place toast on baking sheet; divide asparagus spears evenly on toast. Spoon soup over sandwiches. Top each with egg slices and equal amounts of cheese. Broil 3 minutes or until cheese starts to melt. Yield: 6 sandwiches.

Crunchy Cheese Sandwiches

1 *(8-ounce) package softened cream*
  cheese
3 *tablespoons mayonnaise*
2 *teaspoons prepared mustard*
1 *cup chopped ripe olives*
1 *cup diced celery*
1 *cup chopped almonds*
8 *slices brown bread*
Soft butter

Mix cheese, mayonnaise, and mustard in bowl. Stir in olives, celery, and almonds. Spread bread with butter, spread 4 slices with filling, and top each with another slice. Yield: 4 generous sandwiches.

Cucumber Party Sandwiches

Cut rounds of thin-sliced bread with cutter; lightly spread with mayonnaise. Upon each sandwich place a slice of cucumber which has been peeled. On top of that, put a very thin slice of radish, and ring the vegetables with hard-cooked egg yolk moistened with mayonnaise and squeezed through a pastry bag. Salt.

Cherry-Cheese Sandwich Spread

1 *(4-ounce) jar maraschino cherries*
  (red or green)
1 *(3-ounce) package cream cheese,*
  softened

Drain cherries and dice very fine. Add to softened cream cheese and mix well. This filling may be used for open-faced sandwiches or made into 3-layered ribbon sandwiches. Yield: about 1½ cups filling.

Broiled Chickenburgers

12 *round buns*
  Butter or margarine
1 *(1-pound) can jellied cranberry*
  sauce, cut into 12 slices
3 *cups chopped cooked chicken or*
  turkey
⅔ *cup mayonnaise or salad dressing*
½ *cup pickle relish*
¾ *teaspoon salt*
  Dash pepper

Split buns and spread with butter or margarine. Place slice of cranberry sauce on bottom half of each bun. Mix chicken or turkey, mayonnaise or salad dressing, pickle relish, salt, and pepper. Spread on top of cranberry sauce. Place under broiler until mixture is hot and bubbly, about 2 to 3 minutes. Cover with bun tops. Yield: 12 sandwiches.

Curried Chicken Sandwiches

3 *cups diced cooked chicken*
½ *cup diced celery*
½ *cup diced, unpeeled apple*
⅓ *cup mayonnaise*
½ *teaspoon salt*
1 *teaspoon curry powder*
1 *tablespoon lemon juice*
White pepper to taste
16 *slices buttered bread*

Combine the first 8 ingredients and mix well. Spread on 8 slices of the buttered bread; top with remaining slices. Yield: 8 sandwiches.

Corned Beef and Swiss Cheese on Rye

2 *tablespoons commercial sour cream*
1 *teaspoon horseradish*
1 *teaspoon chili sauce*
Rye bread
3 *large stuffed olives, sliced*
Sauerkraut Relish
Thinly sliced corned beef
Swiss cheese
Butter or margarine

Combine sour cream, horseradish, and chili sauce; mix well. Spread a slice of rye bread generously with mixture. Arrange layer of olives over sour cream mixture; then spread with layer of Sauerkraut Relish. Cover this generously with corned beef slices and sliced Swiss cheese. Top with another slice of rye bread. Butter and grill.

Sauerkraut Relish:

1 *(1-pound) can sauerkraut,*
thoroughly drained
1 *large onion, coarsely chopped*
½ *cup chopped green pepper*
1 *(2-ounce) jar pimientos, drained and*
chopped
1 *cup sugar*
1 *cup cider vinegar*

Combine all ingredients in a bowl and toss lightly until well blended. Store mixture in tightly covered jar in refrigerator at least 24 hours before serving. Yield: 4 cups.

St. John's Grilled Dogs

Hot dogs
Sharp cheese
Thin slices bacon strips
Hot dog buns

Slit dogs down the middle and place slices of sharp cheese in slits. Curl a strip of bacon

around each dog and cook slowly in electric frypan. Serve on heated buns.

Surprise Dogs

1 *pound ground beef*
¾ *cup soft breadcrumbs*
¼ *cup milk*
2 *tablespoons chopped onion*
1 *egg, slightly beaten*
½ *teaspoon salt*
Dash pepper
6 *frankfurters*
1 *cup catsup*
¼ *cup margarine*
¼ *cup molasses*
2 *tablespoons vinegar*
6 *slices bacon*
Hot dog buns

Combine ground beef with breadcrumbs, milk, onion, egg, salt, and pepper. Mix lightly and divide into six portions. Shape beef mixture around frankfurters to cover completely; wrap in waxed paper, and chill.

For sauce, combine catsup, margarine, molasses, and vinegar. Insert skewers lengthwise through frankfurters; wrap each frankfurter with a slice of bacon, and secure with toothpicks. Brush with sauce, and broil 3 inches from heat for about 15 minutes. Turn as needed to cook bacon. Simmer sauce while kabobs are cooking. Brush sauce on kabobs just before serving. Serve in toasted buns. Yield: 6 servings.

Egg-Peanut Spread

     6 *hard-cooked eggs, finely chopped*
    ½ *cup finely chopped roasted peanuts*
     2 *tablespoons finely chopped pimiento*
     2 *tablespoons finely chopped olives*
     1 *tablespoon finely chopped chives*
    ¾ *teaspoon salt*
    ¼ *cup mayonnaise*
    ¼ *cup milk*
    ¼ *teaspoon Worcestershire sauce*

Combine all finely chopped ingredients and salt. Stir mayonnaise, milk, and Worcestershire sauce together. Blend with eggs and other ingredients. Stir well. Serve with crackers and potato chips. Yield: 2 cups.

Chopped Ham Sandwiches

    ½ *cup chopped or ground cooked ham*
     1 *hard-cooked egg, chopped*
    ½ *teaspoon lemon juice*
    ½ *teaspoon prepared mustard*
    ⅛ *teaspoon Worcestershire sauce*
    ½ *teaspoon salt*
     1 *tablespoon chopped green pepper*
     1 *tablespoon chopped sour or dill*
        pickles
     Mayonnaise
     8 *slices bread*
     1 *egg*
    ¼ *cup milk*
     Butter

Mix first 8 ingredients together; moisten with enough mayonnaise to make spreading consistency. Spread mixture on bread. Beat egg with milk and dip sandwich in mixture. Brown in hot, melted butter. Yield: about 4 generous sandwiches.

Hawaiian Ham Sandwiches

     8 *slices whole wheat bread*
     Softened butter or margarine
     1 *cup ground cooked ham*
    ½ *cup drained crushed pineapple*
    ½ *tablespoon brown sugar*

Spread bread with butter or margarine. Blend together all other ingredients, and spread on 4 slices of bread. Top with remaining bread. Yield: 4 sandwiches.

Ham Cornucopias

     1 *cup ground cooked ham*
     1 *tablespoon finely chopped parsley*
     2 *tablespoons mayonnaise*
     8 *thin slices whole wheat bread*
     Soft butter or margarine

Combine ham, parsley, and mayonnaise. Remove crusts from bread; roll lightly with a rolling pin. Spread with butter. Cut each slice in quarters. Place ¼ teaspoon of the ham mixture diagonally on each square of bread. Fold two opposite corners over and fasten with a toothpick. Place on a cookie sheet, cover with waxed paper and a damp cloth, and chill 30 minutes. Remove toothpicks before serving. Yield: 32 sandwiches.

Toasted Ham Sandwiches

    ½ *pound chopped ham (canned is fine)*
    ¼ *pound American cheese, cut in small*
        squares
     Small bottle stuffed olives, chopped
     1 *green pepper, chopped*
     1 *small onion, chopped*
    ½ *cup mayonnaise*
    ½ *cup catsup*
     Hamburger buns

Mix first 7 ingredients and put on halves of hamburger buns. Broil 10 to 15 minutes and serve hot. Yield: 8 sandwiches.

Pineapple Sandwich Mixture

    15 *large marshmallows*
     Juice of one lemon
     1 *small can crushed pineapple*
     1 *package dates, chopped*
     1 *cup chopped nuts*
     1 *cup mayonnaise*

Put marshmallows, lemon juice, and pineapple in double boiler or heavy pan, and heat until marshmallows are melted. Let cool; then add chopped dates and nuts. Add mayonnaise last. Yield: about 2 cups.

Hoot Owl Sandwiches

  ½ *cup flaked tuna*
  ¾ *cup chopped hard-cooked eggs*
  ¼ *cup diced celery*
  2 *tablespoons chopped green pepper*
  1 *tablespoon lemon juice*
  Few drops Tabasco sauce
  1 *tablespoon mayonnaise or salad dressing*
  ½ *teaspoon salt*
  32 *slices bread*
  32 *small stuffed olive slices*
  2 *tablespoons slivered almonds*
  Raisins
  Pimiento strips

Combine tuna, eggs, celery, green pepper, lemon juice, Tabasco, mayonnaise, and salt. Cut a 2½-inch circle and a 1¾-inch circle from each slice of bread. On half of the circles, spread the filling and top with circle of the same size. Put on small paper plates, placing a small circle (head) against the large circle (body). Prepare olive-slice eyes, beaks and feet of slivered almonds, raisin ears, and collars and ties made of pimiento strips. Yield: 16 sandwiches.

Toasted Crabmeat Sandwiches

  1 *cup flaked crabmeat*
  3 *hard-cooked eggs, chopped*
  1 *teaspoon minced onion*
  1 *teaspoon Worcestershire sauce*
  4 *tablespoons mayonnaise*
  ½ *teaspoon salt*
  ⅛ *teaspoon pepper*
  6 *slices bread*
  ¼ *cup shredded cheese*
  Paprika

Mix crabmeat, egg, onion, Worcestershire sauce, mayonnaise, salt, and pepper. Toast one side of bread. Spread mixture on untoasted side of bread. Sprinkle with cheese, then with paprika. Broil 4 inches from unit until cheese has melted. Serve at once. Yield: 6 sandwiches.

Monte Cristo Sandwich

  2 *eggs, well beaten*
  1 *cup milk*
  Black pepper to taste
  ¼ *cup butter*
  8 *bread slices (day old)*
  4 *ham slices*
  4 *cheese slices (American, Swiss, or brick)*
  4 *slices chicken or turkey (optional)*
  Butter

To beaten eggs, add milk and pepper. Butter bread; cover half of slices with ham and cheese. (Add chicken or turkey, if desired.) Top with another slice of bread and press tightly together.

Dip sandwich in egg and milk mixture and sauté in butter until golden brown on both sides. Cheese should be melted. Drain on absorbent paper and serve hot with jam, jelly, or maple syrup. Yield: 4 sandwiches.

Pizza Sandwiches

  4 *English muffins, split*
  Softened butter
  1 *pound mild Italian sausage*
  1 *(8-ounce) can tomato sauce*
  ½ *pound Cheddar cheese, cut in strips*

Toast cut side of muffins; spread with softened butter. In a skillet, slowly fry the sausage until browned and thoroughly cooked; drain on absorbent paper towels. Place muffins on broiler pan; spread each with 1 tablespoon tomato sauce. Spread muffins with cooked sausage; top with cheese slices, crisscross fashion. Spoon 1 tablespoon tomato sauce over each. Broil until cheese is melted. Yield: 8 small pizzas.

Open-Face Turkey Sandwiches

    1 *small can deviled ham*
    4 *slices bread, toasted*
    4 *large slices cooked white meat of*
        turkey
    1 *can cream of mushroom soup*
    3 *tablespoons mayonnaise*
  ¼ *cup dry sherry*
      Paprika

Spread deviled ham on toast; top with slice of turkey and place in shallow baking dish. Combine soup, mayonnaise, and sherry; heat to simmering and spoon over sandwiches. Bake at 400 degrees F. about 10 minutes. Dust with paprika and serve immediately. Yield: 4 servings.

Shrimp Sandwich Filling

    2 *cups boiled and peeled shrimp*
    2 *hard-cooked eggs*
    1 *whole dill pickle*
    1 *small onion*
    1 *teaspoon lemon juice*
    1 *cup mayonnaise*
      Salt and pepper to taste

Chop shrimp, eggs, pickle, and onion with a blender (high speed for 5 seconds) or a food chopper. Combine with other ingredients; mix well and spread on mayonnaise-coated bread slices.

Festive Seafood Sandwiches

  ¼ *cup chopped olives*
  ¼ *cup chopped celery*
  ¼ *cup chopped green peppers*
  ¼ *cup chopped pimiento*
    1 *(7½-ounce) can crabmeat or tuna*
  ½ *cup mayonnaise*
    6 *slices whole wheat bread, toasted*
    2 *tablespoons butter*

Fold chopped olives, celery, green peppers, and pimiento into crabmeat or tuna. Fold in mayonnaise. Spread bread slices with butter; fill with seafood. Yield: 6 servings.

Shrimp Sandwich

    1 *pound cooked shrimp, deveined*
    1 *small green pepper, chopped*
  ½ *cup chopped celery*
  ¼ *teaspoon ground mace*
      Few drops of red pepper sauce to taste
      Salt and black pepper to taste
      Mayonnaise

Grind (or chop fine) shrimp, green pepper, and celery together. Add other ingredients except mayonnaise and mix well. Add enough mayonnaise to spread. Refrigerate. Yield: about 2½ cups.

Shrimp Sandwiches

    2 *(3-ounce) packages cream cheese,*
        softened
    4 *tablespoons mayonnaise*
    2 *tablespoons catsup*
    2 *teaspoons prepared mustard*
      Dash garlic powder
    2 *cups finely chopped cooked shrimp*
  ½ *cup finely chopped celery*
    2 *teaspoons finely chopped onion*
  ½ *teaspoon salt*
      Buttered bread

Blend cheese with mayonnaise. Mix in catsup, mustard, and garlic powder. Stir in shrimp, celery, onion, and salt. Spread lightly on buttered bread. This amount will use a whole loaf of bread. Yield: filling for 10 to 12 sandwiches.

Reuben Sandwich

    Using pumpernickel bread, spread mayonnaise lightly over each slice. Cover bottom slice with drained sauerkraut, using scantily or generously according to taste.

    Over this place a slice of corned beef, then a slice of Swiss cheese, and top with the other slice of bread. Spread outside top and bottom of sandwich lightly with softened butter or margarine. Toast on each side over charcoal or on grill.

Turnip Sandwich

  2 *slices three-day-old rye bread*
     Mayonnaise
     Soft butter
     Turnip
     Salt
     Horseradish
  1 *thin slice boiled ham*
     Onion
     Bahamian mustard
     Sliced cooked breast of turkey
     Black pepper

Place bread face up on work table; spread one piece generously with mayonnaise, the other with soft butter.

Bread spread with mayonnaise: Choose a turnip, nice size; wash in cold water, but do not peel. Slice ¼ inch thick and cover bread; salt generously. Then over turnip, spread a light portion of prepared horseradish; add a slice of ham.

Buttered Bread: Cover with raw onion, sliced ¼ inch thick. Spread onion with Bahamian mustard; add sliced turkey. Spread turkey lightly with soft butter. Add black pepper to taste. Cut sandwich in half.

Serve on a 9-inch dinner plate garnished with raw radishes, turnip tops, and hot green pepper.

Western Burgers

  3 *pounds ground steak*
  ½ *cup cooking wine*
  1 *teaspoon salt*
  ⅛ *teaspoon freshly ground black*
      pepper
  ¼ *pound margarine*
12 *hamburger buns (split)*
  1 *large Spanish onion*
  ¼ *cup chili sauce*

Combine meat, wine, salt, and pepper. Mix well and form into 12 patties. Broil for 3 minutes on each side (longer if you want them well done). Butter buns and toast them. Serve a patty on bun with an onion slice and chili sauce. Yield: 6 servings.

Rolled Sandwiches

  1 *(3-ounce) package cream cheese*
  1 *teaspoon lemon juice*
  ⅓ *cup commercial sour cream*
  ⅛ *teaspoon salt*
  1 *teaspoon snipped chives*
  1 *cup chopped watercress*
18 *slices white bread*
  2 *tablespoons soft butter*
     Sprigs watercress

In a bowl blend cream cheese, lemon juice, sour cream, salt, and chives. Stir in chopped watercress. Trim crusts from bread and roll slices lightly with a rolling pin to make them more pliable. Spread bread with soft butter, then with watercress mixture. Roll like a jelly roll.

Arrange close together, seam side down, in a shallow pan. Cover with plastic wrap or foil and chill at least 1 hour.

To serve, slice each roll-up crosswise into two lengths (each about 1½ inches long). Stand them upright and insert sprigs of watercress in top. Yield: 36 party sandwiches.

notes

Beverages

No Southern cookbook would be complete without a recipe for eggnog. For no particular reason, this is primarily a Christmas beverage. We offer you some choice eggnog recipes, many of which were handed down on bits of browned paper bearing the heading "Eggnog Receipt."

Many recipes for other beverages have been passed down in similar ways and have become cherished treasures. Apple cider has long been a favorite beverage and is still sold at country art shows by the gallons. Using bottled apple cider, the modern homemaker can add cinnamon and cloves to turn it into a party drink. The same is true of the citrus "ades" or punches.

It's easy to tell when it's summertime down South, for that's the time for lemonade and iced tea (with lemon or home-grown mint).

Lemon-Orange Drink

    1 *(6-ounce) can frozen orange juice*
       concentrate
    Cold water
  ½ *cup fresh or bottled lemon juice*
    Cracked ice
    Lemon slices
    Maraschino cherries

Combine concentrate with ½ can less water than called for in directions on can. Add ½ cup lemon juice, mixing well. Pour into glasses filled with cracked ice. Garnish each glass with a lemon slice and a maraschino cherry. Yield: 3 to 4 servings.

Raspberry Delight

    1 *(6-ounce) can frozen pink lemonade*
       concentrate
    Cold water
    1 *pint raspberry sherbet*
    Whipped topping
    Cherries

Fruit juice coolers are popular thirst-quenchers before, between, and with meals.

Mix lemonade with cold water as directed on can, and chill until very cold. Spoon one or two scoops raspberry sherbet in tall glasses and pour lemonade over. Just before serving, add whipped topping, and top with a cherry. (Best serve this with a straw and a parfait spoon!) Yield: 4 servings.

Lime Sparkle

    1 *(6-ounce) can frozen lime juice*
       concentrate
    Soda water
    Watermelon juice
    Small watermelon wedges, peeled
    Orange slices

Reconstitute lime juice concentrate according to directions on can, substituting soda water for tap water. Sweeten with a little watermelon juice (a piece of watermelon in a pie plate is easily "juiced" with a potato masher—then strain). *Note:* Watermelon juice is extremely sweet, so add it sparingly until sweet enough to suit your own family. A small wedge of peeled watermelon in the drinks and an orange slice on each glass completes the picture. Yield: 3 to 4 servings.

Apple Blossom Punch

    3 *quarts apple juice*
    3 *quarts ginger ale*
    3 *(12-ounce) cans frozen orange juice*
       concentrate
      Fresh orange slices

Combine fruit juices and ginger ale. Pour over block of ice. Float orange slices on top of punch. Yield: 50 servings.

Golden Apricot Shake

 1½ *cups apricot nectar*
   1 *cup milk*
   1 *teaspoon lemon juice*
   1 *pint vanilla ice cream*

Put all ingredients in blender. Cover and blend until smooth. Yield: 4 servings.

Mock Pink Champagne

  ½ *cup sugar*
 1½ *cups water*
   2 *cups cranberry juice*
   1 *cup pineapple juice*
  ½ *cup orange juice*
   2 *(7-ounce) bottles lemon-lime*
     carbonated beverage

Boil sugar and water until sugar dissolves; cool. Stir in cranberry, pineapple, and orange juices. Chill. Just before serving add carbonated beverage. Yield: 14 servings.

Spider Cider

   2 *quarts apple cider*
 12 *whole cloves*
   4 *sticks cinnamon*
     Rind of 4 lemons
   2 *lemons, peeled and thinly sliced*
  ¼ *teaspoon ground nutmeg*

Combine cider, cloves, cinnamon sticks, thinly peeled rind of 4 lemons, 2 lemons

peeled and thinly sliced, and the nutmeg. Cover and heat to boiling. Reduce heat and simmer for about 15 minutes. Allow to cool; then strain. Discard spices. Chill overnight in refrigerator to allow flavors to blend. Heat when ready to serve. Yield: 8 to 10 servings.

Holiday Orange Eggnog

   6 *eggs*
  ¾ *cup sugar*
  ¼ *teaspoon cinnamon*
  ½ *teaspoon nutmeg*
   1 *cup chilled evaporated milk*
   3 *cups cold milk*
   1 *cup chilled fresh orange juice*
     Grated orange peel
     Nutmeg

In large bowl beat eggs until light and fluffy; add sugar, cinnamon, and nutmeg. Stir in milk, blending well. Gradually stir in orange juice. Serve in small mugs or cups; sprinkle each serving with a little grated orange peel and a dash of nutmeg. Yield: 24 cups.

Frozen Eggnog for Twelve

 12 *egg yolks*
   1 *cup sugar*
  ½ *cup brandy*
   1 *quart whipping cream*
   1 *cup whiskey*

Beat yolks until light. Add sugar gradually. Add brandy slowly. Beat cream until stiff. Add yolks and whiskey. Pack in ice and ice cream salt till frozen.

Banana Eggnog

   2 *eggs, separated*
   3 *cups milk*
   3 *medium-size ripe bananas*
     Dash salt
     Dash nutmeg

Separate eggs. Beat yolks with milk. Mash bananas through food mill or blender. Add egg-milk mixture, salt, and nutmeg. Beat egg whites until stiff but not dry. Add to banana mixture and beat until frothy. Serve immediately. Yield: Four 8-ounce servings.

Party Perfect Eggnog

   6 *eggs*
  ½ *cup white corn syrup*
  ¼ *teaspoon ground ginger*
  ¼ *teaspoon ground cloves*
  ¼ *teaspoon ground cinnamon*
  ¼ *teaspoon ground nutmeg*
   2 *quarts orange juice, chilled*
  ½ *cup lemon juice, chilled*
   1 *quart vanilla ice cream*
   1 *quart ginger ale, chilled*
  Nutmeg

Beat eggs well. Mix in syrup, ginger, cloves, cinnamon, and nutmeg. Stir in orange juice and lemon juice. Cut ice cream into chunks the size of small eggs; put into large punch bowl.

Pour ginger ale over ice cream. Stir in egg mixture. Sprinkle with nutmeg. Yield: 6 quarts.

Great-Granddaddy's Eggnog

  24 *egg yolks*
  2½ *cups bourbon*
   2 *quarts whipping cream*
   6 *tablespoons sugar*
  24 *egg whites*
  18 *tablespoons sugar (1 cup plus 2*
       tablespoons)
  Nutmeg to taste

Beat egg yolks for 20 minutes at medium speed on electric mixer until they are a light lemon color and are very fluffy. Continue beating and add bourbon, a drop at a time. (This part of the mixing may be done the night before and mixture placed in covered container in refrigerator.)

Whip cream until it stands in peaks. Add 6 tablespoons sugar, and fold egg yolks into whipped cream.

Beat egg whites until they are dry and have completely lost their gloss before you start adding the 18 tablespoons sugar. (This step is very important; it is the secret of the eggnog's "standing up" quality.) Add sugar to egg whites a tablespoon at a time. Continue beating for about 10 minutes after all sugar has been added.

Fold the egg whites into the cream and egg yolk mixture, continuing to blend with a folding motion until it is well mixed and smooth.

Ladle from silver or crystal bowl into tall glasses and eat with iced-tea spoon. Top each glass with a dash of nutmeg. Yield: 25 servings.

Overnight Eggnog

  12 *egg yolks*
  1½ *cups bourbon*
  ¾ *cup sugar*
   2 *quarts milk*
  12 *egg whites*
   1 *quart whipping cream*
  Nutmeg

Beat egg yolks until lemon colored. Add bourbon slowly, a jigger at a time. Add sugar slowly; then add milk and beat well.

Cover bowl and set in refrigerator overnight. Just before serving, beat egg whites until stiff and fold into yolk-milk mixture. Beat cream until stiff and add nutmeg. Pour over mixture. Ladle into cups so that each cup is topped with a layer of whipped cream and nutmeg. Yield: 30 servings.

Christmas Eggnog

1 *cup sugar*
1 *quart light cream*
8 *eggs, separated*
1 *to 1½ pints bourbon, rum, or brandy*
1 *tablespoon ground nutmeg*
Whipped cream

Prepare at least a day before you plan to serve. Mix sugar and cream. Beat egg whites and add to sugar-cream mixture. Stir until egg whites cannot be seen. Add beaten egg yolks and mix well. Slowly stir in bourbon, rum, or brandy. Cover and put in refrigerator. To serve, ladle into cups, sprinkle with nutmeg, and add a spoon of whipped cream to each cup. Yield: 15 to 20 servings.

Westmoreland Club Eggnog

Beat the yolks of 12 eggs until thick, adding gradually 12 tablespoons of powdered sugar. When lemon colored, add 3 pints of good brandy (or bourbon) and ½ cup of Jamaica rum. The liquors must be added slowly, not more than half a cup at a time, for they "cook" the eggs.

Beat 12 egg whites stiff and fold half of them into the eggnog along with 1 quart of cream, either coffee cream or whipping cream. (If an eggnog less rich is preferred, use milk.) Chill overnight.

When ready to serve, add the remaining egg whites, sweetened very slightly, and sprinkle with nutmeg. Whipped cream on top is optional. Yield: 12 to 15 servings.

Tom and Jerry

12 *egg yolks*
1 *cup sugar*
1 *cup rum*
12 *egg whites*
Bourbon whiskey
Cinnamon

Beat egg yolks until light and lemon colored. Then add, gradually, sugar and rum alter-

nately until the batter is thick. Fold in the egg whites, beaten to a meringue.

When ready to serve, ladle approximately ⅓ cup of this batter into a warm mug. Add one jigger (2 ounces for the men, 1 ounce for the ladies) of bourbon. Fill the mug with hot water. Sprinkle each cup with cinnamon. Yield: about 16 servings.

Citronade
(French Lemonade)

1 *lemon*
¾ *cup sugar*
1 *cup water*
3½ *cups water*
Maraschino cherries
Lemon slices

Wash lemon; cut into small pieces and remove seeds. Place in electric blender, with sugar and 1 cup water. Blend until smooth. Add blended mixture to 3½ cups water, mixing well. Pour into ice-filled 8- to 10-ounce glasses; garnish with the cherries and lemon slices. Yield: 5 to 6 servings.

Florida Citrus Punch

2 *(6-ounce) cans Florida frozen orange*
  juice concentrate
1 *(6-ounce) can Florida frozen*
  grapefruit juice concentrate
1 *(6-ounce) can Florida frozen limeade*
  concentrate
1 *quart ginger ale*
Orange and lime sherbet

Reconstitute the orange and grapefruit concentrates according to directions on the cans. Combine with undiluted limeade and mix well. Add the ginger ale just before serving. Scoops of orange and lime sherbet added just before serving give the finishing touches. Yield: 25 servings.

Citrus Punch

¼ *teaspoon ground nutmeg*
½ *teaspoon cinnamon*
½ *teaspoon allspice*
2 *cups cider*
¼ *cup sugar*
6 *cups orange juice*
Orange slices
Cloves

Heat spices and cider to boiling point. Remove from heat. Stir in sugar if desired. Cool. Add orange juice. Serve chilled with ice cubes and use clove-studded orange slices as decoration. Yield: 2 quarts (16 one-half cup servings).

Lemonade

2½ *to 3 cups sugar*
4¾ *cups lemon juice*
20 *cups water, divided*
Ice
Lemon slices
Sprigs of mint

Combine sugar and juice with 4 cups water. Boil for 5 minutes or until sugar is completely dissolved. Remove from heat. Add remaining water and cool. Just before serving, add ice. Garnish with lemon slices and mint. Yield: 25 servings.

Old-Fashioned Lemonade

4 *lemons*
2 *cups sugar*
½ *cup water*
Maraschino cherries
Lemon slices

Cut lemons in thin slices, place in a bowl, and cover with sugar. Mash thoroughly until all juice is extracted. Add water. Let stand 1 hour. Strain. Allow 1 or 2 tablespoons of the strained lemon juice for each serving. Pour into glass filled with shaved ice and add water. Garnish with maraschino cherry and slice of lemon. Yield: 3 to 4 servings.

Irish Coffee

It has been said that Irish coffee traveled from Shannon, Ireland, straight to San Francisco and from there to the rest of the United States. Southerners have never been averse to mixing "a little something" with their coffee, and Irish coffee is one of their favorites. This is the way we make it:

For each serving, place 2 teaspoons of sugar, or less, according to taste, into a warmed cup. Fill about two-thirds full with strong hot coffee. Mix well. Then add 2 tablespoons of Irish whiskey, topping with whipped cream, as much or as little as you like. That's it! And back for refills!

Mocha-Cocoa for Eight

¼ *cup sugar*
¼ *cup cocoa*
1 *teaspoon instant coffee*
¼ *teaspoon salt*
2 *cloves*
¾ *cup water*
4¾ *cups milk*
2 *teaspoons vanilla extract*
Cinnamon stick
Whipped cream (optional)

Mix sugar, cocoa, coffee, salt, cloves, and ¾ cup of water in a saucepan. Bring to a boil. Add milk and heat until hot. Stir to keep a skim of milk from forming on the top. Add vanilla and cinnamon stick; mix well. Serve hot, topped with whipped cream if desired. Yield: 8 servings.

Plantation Coffee Punch

  ¼ cup sugar
  ⅓ cup instant coffee
     Dash of salt
  1 teaspoon vanilla extract
  5 cups whole milk
  1 pint vanilla or coffee ice cream
     Whipped cream for garnish
     Ground nutmeg

Combine sugar, coffee, salt, vanilla, and milk. Stir until sugar dissolves. Chill until serving time. Then ladle ice cream by large spoonfuls into punch bowl; pour chilled coffee mixture over this. Top with puffs of whipped cream and sprinkle with a little nutmeg. Serve in punch cups. Yield: 12 servings.

Rum-Flavored Coffee for A Crowd
(Café Rhum)

  48 cups strong black coffee
   1 cup granulated sugar
   3 cups heavy cream
   3 cups light rum

Prepare coffee. While still hot add sugar. Let cool; then add heavy cream and rum. Beat well with a rotary beater, in batches of 1 or 2 quarts at a time (since 48 cups equal nearly 2 gallons you can't beat all of it at the same time).

  Before serving, bring the mixture to a boil and serve hot.

Cranberry Punch

   6 pints cranberry juice cocktail
  1½ quarts strained orange juice
  1½ cups water
  2½ cups strained lemon juice
   3 cups pineapple juice
   3 cups sugar

Combine ingredients and blend well. Chill in refrigerator. Pour into a punch bowl with an ice ring and lemon slices. Yield: about 50 servings.

Cranberry Cooler

  ½ cup fresh lemon juice
  1 cup fresh orange juice
  1 pint bottle cranberry juice cocktail
  1¼ cups sugar
  4 cups ice water or chilled sparkling
       water
     Lemon slices

Combine lemon juice, orange juice, cranberry juice, and sugar; stir until sugar is dissolved. Add ice water or chilled sparkling water. Pour in ice-filled pitcher or punch bowl; garnish with lemon slices. Yield: 16 4-ounce servings.

Pineapple-Cranberry Punch

  2 pints cranberry juice
  2 cups orange juice
  ¼ cup lemon juice
  1 quart pineapple sherbet
  1 quart sparkling water or ginger ale

Combine cranberry juice, orange juice, and lemon juice; beat in pineapple sherbet; then chill. Just before serving, slowly pour in sparkling water. Pour over cracked ice and serve immediately. Yield: 14 to 16 servings.

Ruby Red Frost

   1 pint bottle cranberry juice cocktail
  1½ cups fresh lemon juice
   1 cup sugar
   2 (28-ounce) bottles chilled ginger ale
   1 pint raspberry sherbet
      Lemon slices

Combine cranberry juice cocktail, fresh lemon juice, and sugar, blending well. Chill. To serve, pour over ice in punch bowl. Add chilled ginger ale and sherbet. Garnish with lemon slices. Serve at once. Yield: 24 cups.

Cranberry Punch

    4 *cups cranberry juice cocktail*
1½ *cups sugar*
    4 *cups pineapple-grapefruit juice*
    2 *quarts ginger ale*

Slowly add cranberry juice to sugar; stir until sugar dissolves. Add pineapple-grapefruit juice; chill. Pour into punch bowl; add the chilled ginger ale. Yield: about 32 punch-cup servings.

Fruit Punch

    2 *(6-ounce) cans frozen orange juice*
    1 *(6-ounce) can frozen lemonade*
    1 *cup pineapple juice*
  ¼ *cup cherry juice (optional)*
    2 *quarts pale dry ginger ale*

Mix fruit juices; cover and let stand 12 hours or more in refrigerator. Add cold ginger ale to juices just before serving. Serve over crushed ice or freeze half the ginger ale in refrigerator trays. Yield: 24 servings.

Fruit Punch

    1 *(6-ounce) can frozen orange juice concentrate*
    2 *(6-ounce) cans frozen limeade concentrate*
    1 *(6-ounce) can frozen lemonade concentrate*
    1 *(1-pound 14-ounce) can pineapple juice*
    1 *pint cranberry juice cocktail*
    4 *cups cold water*
    2 *quarts ginger ale, chilled*
    1 *pint club soda, chilled*
Fruit Ice Ring
Fruits and mint for garnish

Empty frozen concentrates, pineapple and cranberry juices, and water into a large container. Let stand until frozen juice is thawed; stir well. Pour mixture into punch bowl; add ice cubes. Just before serving, gently pour in ginger ale and club soda. Garnish with Fruit Ice Ring and fruits and mint leaves. Yield: 25 to 30 servings.

Fruit Ice Ring: Use any combination of lime, lemon, or orange slices. Arrange in a pattern in the bottom of an 8-inch ring mold. Add water to cover fruit. Freeze. To unmold, loosen ring by dipping bottom of mold in warm water. Float on top of punch.

Golden Gate Punch

2½ *cups sugar*
    1 *cup water*
    2 *(No. 2) cans (4½ cups) pineapple juice*
    2 *cups strained lime juice*
    1 *quart strained orange juice*
1¼ *cups strained lemon juice*
    2 *quarts chilled ginger ale*
Colored ice cubes

Make syrup by combining sugar and water. Heat to boiling. Cool. Combine fruit juices. Add cooled sugar syrup. Chill. Just before serving, add ginger ale and colored ice cubes. To make colored cubes, blend vegetable food coloring with water before freezing. Yield: 5 quarts.

Golden Punch

    2 *large cans pineapple juice*
    1 *large can sweetened orange juice*
    1 *large can unsweetened orange juice*
    1 *can fresh frozen lemon juice*
    1 *quart water*
    3 *bananas, sliced*
    2 *large bottles ginger ale*
    1 *quart lime or pineapple sherbet*

Mix juices and water and chill. When ready to serve, add bananas, ginger ale, and sherbet. Yield: 40 servings.

Cherry Punch

   2 *(3-ounce) packages cherry-flavored*
      gelatin
   4 *cups boiling water*
   1 *cup sugar*
   1 *quart chilled pineapple juice*
   1 *quart orange juice*
   1 *quart ginger ale*

Dissolve gelatin in boiling water; add sugar and stir until dissolved. Cool to room temperature. (This is very important. Do not chill in refrigerator.) Add fruit juices. Just before serving add ginger ale. Yield: 25 to 30 servings.

Golden Punch

   2 *(6-ounce) cans frozen orange*
      juice concentrate
  ½ *cup lemon juice*
   1 *cup canned pineapple juice*
  ¼ *cup maraschino cherry juice*
   2 *quarts ginger ale*

Combine orange juice concentrate, lemon juice, pineapple juice, and cherry juice; mix well. Pour over ice in punch bowl. Add cold ginger ale. Garnish with berries and pineapple spears if desired. Yield: 25 punch-cup servings.

Grape Punch

   2 *cups grape juice*
 1½ *cups orange juice*
  ¾ *cup sugar*
   1 *cup water*
    Ice cubes
   3 *(7-ounce) bottles ginger ale*
   1 *lemon, sliced*

Pour fruit juices into 2-quart pitcher. Add sugar and stir until dissolved. Add water and ice cubes. Let stand for a few minutes in refrigerator. Pour equal amounts into 16 tall glasses in which there are a couple of ice cubes. Then fill to top with ginger ale and garnish with lemon slices.

Holiday Fruit Punch

   2 *quarts boiling water*
  ¼ *cup loose tea*
   2 *cups sugar*
   2 *cups lemon juice*
   4 *cups orange juice*
 1½ *quarts cranberry juice*
   1 *quart water*
   1 *quart ginger ale*
   1 *lemon, sliced*
   2 *limes, sliced*
    Maraschino cherries

Bring 2 quarts of water to a full rolling boil. Immediately pour over the tea. Brew 5 minutes. Strain. Set aside to cool at room temperature. Combine with sugar, fruit juices, and 1 quart water. Chill. Just before serving, pour over large piece of ice or ice cubes; then add ginger ale. Garnish with lemon and lime slices and cherries. Yield: 25 servings.

Party Punch

   1 *quart pineapple juice, chilled*
   1 *quart orange juice, chilled*
   1 *quart apple juice, chilled*
   2 *quarts ginger ale, chilled*
   2 *quarts pineapple sherbet*

Pour chilled juices and ginger ale into punch bowl. Top with scoops of sherbet. Yield: 15 servings.

Holiday Punch

    Juice of 2 limes
    Juice of 1 lemon
   3 *(6-ounce) cans frozen orange juice*
   1 *(6-ounce) can frozen lemon juice*
   1 *(6-ounce) can frozen lime juice*
   1 *(No. 2) can pineapple juice*
  ½ *teaspoon salt*
 1½ *quarts water*
   1 *quart chilled ginger ale*
   1 *pint vodka*
    Red food coloring, if desired

Several hours ahead mix together the fruit juices, salt, and water, and place in covered container in refrigerator to chill.

At serving time, combine above mixture with ginger ale and vodka. Stir in food coloring, if desired. Serve over a block of ice in punch bowl. Yield: 25 generous servings.

Patio Punch

> 1 *cup strong tea*
> 2 *(6-ounce) cans frozen orange juice concentrate, thawed, undiluted*
> 1 *(6-ounce) can frozen grapefruit juice concentrate, thawed, undiluted*
> 1 *(12-ounce) can apricot nectar*
> ½ *cup sugar*
> *Ice cubes*
> 1 *quart carbonated water or ginger ale*
> *Strawberries*
> *Mint sprigs*

Prepare tea and chill, or use instant tea. Combine tea, undiluted orange concentrate, undiluted grapefruit concentrate, apricot nectar, and sugar in punch bowl or pitcher. Stir until sugar is dissolved. Add ice. Just before serving, add carbonated water or ginger ale. Garnish with strawberries and mint sprigs.

Punchmelon

> 1 *large watermelon*
> 2 *cups orange juice*
> 2 *cups lemon juice*
> 1 *(6-ounce) bottle grenadine syrup*
> 2 *quarts bottled lemon-lime beverage, chilled*
> 1 *orange, sliced*
> 1 *lemon, sliced*

With melon standing on end, cut a thin slice off side so it will sit level. Remove top third of melon. Using a coffee cup as a guide, trace scallops around top outside edge. With a sharp knife, carve scalloped edge, following tracing; scoop out fruit, leaving just a trace of red showing in bowl of melon; use scraped-out melon as desired. Chill melon bowl and serve cold.

Combine orange juice, lemon juice, and grenadine; chill. When ready to serve, place a small block of ice, or ice cubes, in melon bowl. Pour juices over ice; pour lemon-lime beverage down side of melon bowl into juice mixture. Float orange and lime slices on top of punch. Yield: 3½ quarts.

Pineapple Punch

> *Measure into each glass:*
>
> 2 *tablespoons pineapple juice*
> 1 *tablespoon lemon juice*
> 2 *to 3 tablespoons sugar*
> ¾ *cup cooled, prepared tea*
> *Ice cubes*

Stir well. Garnish with thin slices of lemon and sprig of mint.

Seafoam Punch

> ½ *cup sugar*
> 1 *quart cold water*
> 1 *(½-ounce) envelope unsweetened lemon-lime soft drink powder*
> 1 *pint vanilla ice cream*
> 2 *(7-ounce) bottles lemon-lime carbonated beverage, chilled*

Place sugar and water in large punch bowl. Add soft drink powder and stir until powder dissolves. Add vanilla ice cream, one spoonful at a time. Pour in the carbonated beverage, resting the bottle on rim of bowl. Serve immediately. Yield: about 16 servings.

Red Velvet Punch

  8 *cups cranberry juice cocktail*
  1 *(6-ounce) can frozen orange juice*
  1 *(6-ounce) can frozen pineapple juice*
  1 *(6-ounce) can frozen lemon juice*
  2 *cups brandy*
  2 *fifths white champagne*

Combine juices and brandy; mix well and pour over a block of ice in punch bowl. Add champagne. Yield: about 30 servings.

Golden Tea Punch

   3 *cups boiling water*
 10 *tea bags or 10 teaspoons tea leaves*
 24 *whole cloves*
   1 *(3-inch) stick cinnamon, crumbled*
 2¼ *cups fresh lemon juice*
 1¼ *cups fresh orange juice*
   3 *cups sugar*
   4 *quarts cold water*
     Orange and lemon slices

Pour boiling water over tea bags, whole cloves, and crumbled stick cinnamon. Cover; steep 5 minutes. Strain and cool. Add lemon juice, orange juice, and sugar, stirring until sugar is dissolved. Add cold water. Pour into ice-filled punch bowl. Garnish with orange and lemon slices. Yield: 50 punch-cup servings.

Instant Spiced Tea Mix

 ½ *cup instant tea*
 2 *cups orange-flavored instant*
    breakfast drink
 1 *package sweetened lemonade mix*
 1 *teaspoon ground cloves*
 1 *teaspoon ground cinnamon*
 2 *cups sugar*

Combine ingredients in large bowl and mix well. Spoon into jars and seal. To serve, add 2 teaspoons to a cup of boiling water. Yield: about 40 cups.

Hospitality Tea Punch

 15 *tea bags or 5 tablespoons loose tea*
  2 *quarts boiling water*
  2 *cups lemon juice*
  1 *quart orange juice*
 1½ *quarts grape juice*
  2 *cups sugar*
  2 *quarts cold water*
  1 *quart ginger ale*
    Ice cubes

Pour boiling water over tea. Steep 3 to 5 minutes and strain or remove tea bags. Cool tea. Stir in remaining ingredients except ginger ale. Add ginger ale and ice cubes just before serving. Yield: 2 gallons.

Russian Tea

 1 *stick cinnamon*
 1 *tablespoon whole cloves*
 1 *cup sugar*
 1 *quart water*
   Juice of 3 lemons
   Juice of 3 oranges
 1 *(No. 2) can pineapple juice*
 2 *cups strong tea*

Put cinnamon stick and whole cloves in a cheesecloth bag. Place in saucepan with sugar and water. Bring to a boil and boil for 15 minutes. Remove spices and add remaining ingredients. Heat and serve. Yield: 2 quarts.

Minted Pineapple Tea

  1 *quart boiling water*
 15 *tea bags or ⅓ cup loose tea*
  4 *tablespoons chopped fresh mint*
    leaves
  1 *quart cold water*
  1 *cup lemon juice*
 ⅔ *cup sugar*
 ¾ *cup (6-ounce can) pineapple juice*
    Ice cubes
    Lemon wedges

Pour 1 quart boiling water over tea and mint leaves. Cover and let stand for 5 minutes.

Strain the tea into a pitcher holding 1 quart cold water. Add lemon juice, sugar, and pineapple juice. Stir to dissolve sugar, and chill.

To serve, pour the minted tea over ice cubes. Garnish with lemon wedges. Yield: about 2½ quarts.

Mrs. Graham's Russian Tea

1 *gallon weak tea*
Juice of 6 oranges
Juice of 5 lemons
½ *bottle cinnamon red hots*
Sugar to taste
1 *small bottle ginger ale*

Mix tea, fruit juices, red candies, and sugar to taste. Heat to serving temperature. Add ginger ale. Yield: about 25 cups.

Spiced Tea

1 *gallon boiling water*
1 *or 2 sticks cinnamon*
1 *teaspoon whole cloves*
1 *teaspoon whole allspice*
¼ *cup (4 ounces) dry tea*
3 *cups sugar*
2 *cups orange juice*
1 *cup lemon juice*

Pour boiling water over spices and tea. Let steep 15 minutes. Remove tea and spices. Add sugar and fruit juices. Serve hot.

Wassail Punch

1 *gallon apple cider*
1 *quart orange juice*
1 *cup lemon juice*
1 *quart pineapple juice*
24 *whole cloves*
4 *sticks cinnamon*
1 *cup sugar*

Mix all ingredients and simmer for 10 minutes. Remove cinnamon and cloves. Serve warm in punch cups. Yield: 1½ gallons.

For a festive punch bowl, float small oranges that have been precooked about 10 minutes. Stick several cloves in each orange.

notes

Breads

Corn has long been one of the staples of Southern farms, and most Southerners grow up with a liking for cornbread. The first settlers found the Indians raising patches of corn and learned from them the rudiments of making bread from home-ground corn. Hoecakes, corn dodgers, and corn pone were generally served at least once and usually twice each day. Even today, most Southerners feel that fresh vegetables are most enjoyable when cornbread is served with them.

When eggs became more plentiful, the early settlers added them to the cornmeal mixture to make spoonbread, which remains the ultimate in the gourmet line of cornbread. The South takes second place to no other section of the country in the preparation of this soufflé-type dish.

Biscuits continue to be the mainstay of many Southern breakfasts, and biscuit dough has been used to make a light dessert known as Stickies, rich with butter and sugar.

Yeast bread, or "light bread," has been another Southern favorite, and the present-day sourdough bread had its start when early homemakers kept a pat of leftover yeast dough in a jar of buttermilk until the next baking.

Pancakes, battercakes, or hotcakes have also been more or less regular fare, although not served as frequently as biscuits for breakfast. These breads remain popular with all ages.

Basic Sweet Dough

    2   cups all-purpose flour
    ½   cup sugar
    2   packages dry yeast
    2   teaspoons salt
    1¼ cups milk
    ¼   cup butter or margarine
    2   eggs
    About 3 cups all-purpose flour

In a large bowl thoroughly mix 2 cups flour, sugar, yeast, and salt. Combine milk and butter in a small saucepan. Heat over low heat until liquid is warm. (Butter does not need to melt.) Gradually add to dry ingredients and beat 2 minutes at medium speed of electric mixer, scraping bowl often. Add eggs and beat well.

Beat in additional flour to make a soft dough (do this with wooden spoon if you do not have a heavy-duty mixer). Turn out on lightly floured board; knead until smooth and elastic, about 10 minutes. Place in a greased bowl, turning to grease top. Cover and let rise in a warm place, free from draft, until doubled in bulk, about 1 hour.

Punch dough down, and let rest about 10 minutes. Shape into tea rings, coffeecakes, cinnamon rolls, kolaches, or sweet rolls. Place in greased pans and let rise until doubled in bulk, about 1 hour. Bake coffeecakes and small loaves at 350 degrees F. for 30 minutes; 25 minutes for pan rolls. Yield: enough dough to make 3 coffeecakes or about 3½ dozen rolls.

Yeast breads, clockwise from upper left: Swedish Rye Bread, Cinnamon Loaf, Kolaches, Stickies, Cinnamon Rolls, Shaped Sweet Rolls.

Cinnamon Rolls: Divide Basic Sweet Dough into halves. Roll each half into a rectangle about ½ inch thick and brush with melted butter. Combine 1½ cups sugar, ⅔ cup seedless raisins, and 2 teaspoons ground cinnamon. Sprinkle half of this mixture over each piece of dough. Roll each up as for a jellyroll to make 18-inch rolls. Seal edges firmly. Cut each roll into 1½-inch slices and place, cut side down, in greased pans. Cover; let rise in warm place until doubled in bulk, about 1 hour. Bake at 350 degrees F. about 25 minutes or until done. Remove from pans and cool on wire racks. Serve plain or frost with a mixture of 1 cup powdered sugar mixed with about 3 tablespoons milk. Yield: 3 to 4 dozen.

Cinnamon Loaf: Divide Basic Sweet Dough in half. Roll each half about ½ inch thick and brush with melted butter. Combine 1 cup sugar and 2 teaspoons cinnamon; spread over each piece of dough. Roll in jelly roll fashion, and place in greased loafpans to rise. Bake at 350 degrees F. about 30 minutes.

Shaped Sweet Rolls: Divide dough into halves. Roll one piece about ½ inch thick. Cut into 3- or 4-inch squares; place a teaspoon of your favorite preserves in center and seal. Place on greased baking sheets and let rise. Bake at 350 degrees F. about 20 minutes.

With the other half of the dough, roll into pencil-shaped pieces. Hold one end of each strip firmly and wind dough loosely to form a coil. Top with preserves; let rise and bake at 350 degrees F. about 20 minutes.

Kolaches: Work with ½ recipe of Basic Sweet Dough at a time. Roll on floured board to ½ inch thickness. Cut circles with a 2½-inch biscuit cutter. Place about 2 inches apart on greased baking sheets. Cover; let rise in a warm place until doubled in bulk, about 1 hour.

Press an indentation in center of each bun, leaving a rim about ¼ inch wide. Fill with preserves. Bake at 350 degrees F. about 20 minutes.

Stickies: To make 1½ dozen Stickies, use ½ recipe of Basic Sweet Dough. After it has risen the first time, punch down, and shape into 18 balls. Place ½ teaspoon butter in 18 muffin cups; add about 1 teaspoon white or brown sugar and 1 tablespoon finely chopped pecans. Place balls of dough in cups; cover; let rise until doubled in bulk. Bake at 350 degrees F. about 20 minutes.

Swedish Rye Bread

　2　*packages dry yeast*
　¼　*cup very warm water*
　½　*cup molasses*
　⅓　*cup butter*
1¾　*cups beer*
　2　*teaspoons salt*
　1　*tablespoon caraway seed*
　3　*cups rye flour*
　　About 3 cups white all-purpose flour
　2　*tablespoons melted butter*

Dissolve yeast in water. Put molasses and butter in saucepan and heat until butter has melted; stir in beer. Add dissolved yeast, salt, and caraway seed. Add rye flour and mix well. Stir in enough white flour to make a soft dough. Brush top of dough with melted butter, cover bowl, and let dough rise until doubled in bulk.

Punch down, turn onto a floured board, and knead thoroughly about 7 or 8 minutes. Stir in white flour as needed, but be careful not to add too much. Shape into two loaves and place in greased loafpans. Cover and let rise until doubled in bulk. Bake at 350 degrees F. for 35 to 45 minutes or until loaves sound hollow when rapped with knuckles. Yield: 2 loaves.

CoolRise White Bread

4½ to 6½ *cups flour (regular or instant blending)*
  2 *packages or cakes yeast, active dry or compressed*
  ½ *cup warm water (105 to 115 degrees F.)*
1¾ *cups warm milk (105 to 115 degrees F.)*
  2 *tablespoons sugar*
  1 *tablespoon salt*
  3 *tablespoons margarine or shortening*
  Cooking oil

Measure flour. Crumble or sprinkle yeast into warm water in a warm bowl. Stir until dissolved. Add milk, sugar, salt, and margarine. Add 2 cups flour and beat with a rotary beater. Then add 1 cup flour and beat with a spoon vigorously for 150 strokes. (This is a very important step since it strengthens the dough and makes high, light loaves.)

Mix in remaining flour gradually, adding enough to make a soft dough that leaves the sides of the bowl. Turn out onto floured board. Shape dough into a ball and then knead for about 5 to 10 minutes until smooth and springy. To check, press finger firmly into dough. If kneaded sufficiently, the dough will spring back.

Cover the roll of dough with plastic wrap and then a towel. Let dough rest for 20 minutes.

Punch dough down and divide in half. Roll each half into an 8- x 12-inch rectangle. Beginning with upper 8-inch, roll toward you; seal with thumbs or heel of hand. Seal ends and fold sealed ends under. Do not tear dough. Place loaves seam side down in center of greased 8½- x 4½- x 2⅝-inch loafpans. Brush with oil. Cover loosely with oiled waxed paper and plastic wrap, but be sure that waxed paper and plastic wrap are not tucked under the pans. They should be loose to allow dough to rise. Place in refrigerator on a shelf which allows room for dough to rise. The space between shelves should be about 5 inches.

Refrigerate 2 to 24 hours. Remove from refrigerator and uncover. Let stand at room temperature for 10 minutes. Preheat oven to 400 degrees F. Bake 30 to 40 minutes. Remove from pans immediately and brush with margarine. Cool slightly before slicing. Yield: 2 loaves.

Hot Cross Buns

  1 *package dry yeast*
  ¼ *cup very warm water*
  ¾ *cup milk*
  1 *stick (½ cup) margarine*
  ⅓ *cup sugar*
  ½ *teaspoon salt*
  4 *cups sifted flour*
  1 *teaspoon ground cinnamon*
  ¼ *teaspoon ground allspice*
  ¼ *teaspoon ground cardamom (optional)*
  1 *egg*
  ½ *cup currants*

Soften yeast in very warm water. Heat milk in a 3-quart saucepan until bubbling at edges. Add margarine, sugar, and salt. Cool to lukewarm. Stir in yeast mixture.

Sift together flour, cinnamon, allspice, and cardamom. Add half of flour to margarine mixture. Beat well. Blend in egg and currants. Add remaining flour and stir to make a soft dough.

Turn dough onto a lightly floured pastry cloth or board. Knead until smooth and elastic. Place in a bowl or saucepan rubbed with margarine. Twirl dough to grease surface.

Cover and let rise until double in bulk. Punch down, turn, and let rise again.

Divide dough into 24 pieces. Form each into a round bun, tucking edges underneath. Place on a baking sheet which has been rubbed with margarine. Brush surfaces of buns with slightly beaten egg white. If desired, cut crosses with knife or scissors. Let rise until double in bulk.

Bake at 400 degrees F. for 12 to 15 minutes.

Frosting Crosses: Add enough sifted powdered sugar (about 1½ cups) to remaining egg white to make a thick frosting. Pipe crosses onto warm buns. Yield: 2 dozen.

Sourdough Starter

1 *package dry yeast*
½ *cup very warm water*
2 *cups lukewarm water*
1 *tablespoon sugar*
1 *tablespoon salt*
2 *cups flour*

Dissolve yeast in ½ cup very warm water. Stir well; then add 2 cups lukewarm water, sugar, and salt. Stir well. Stir in flour and mix well. Place mixture in a jar, cover with cheesecloth, and leave at room temperature for 2 or 3 days until mixture begins to ferment. When it foams and bubbles, it is ready to use. It may be used immediately or stored (as explained above) in the refrigerator until ready for use.

After starter has been removed for baking, add 1 cup lukewarm water, ½ cup flour, and 3 teaspoons sugar for each cup starter removed. Mix well, cover jar, and let it stand until ready to make bread again.

Sourdough Biscuits

½ *cup Sourdough Starter*
1 *cup milk*
2½ *cups flour, divided*
¾ *teaspoon salt*
2 *teaspoons sugar*
1 *teaspoon baking powder*
½ *teaspoon soda*
About ½ cup salad oil

Mix the Sourdough Starter, milk, and 1 cup of the flour in a large bowl from 8 to 12 hours before you plan to serve biscuits. Cover the bowl and keep at room temperature. When ready to make biscuits, stir in 1 cup flour. Combine salt, sugar, baking powder, and soda with ½ cup flour and sift over the top. Mix well by hand; then knead on a lightly floured board. Roll out to ½-inch thickness; cut out biscuits with a 2½-inch cutter. Dip each biscuit in salad oil and place close together in a 9-inch-square pan. Let set in warm place to rise for about 30 minutes. Bake at 375 degrees F. for 30 to 35 minutes. Yield: about 16 biscuits.

Sourdough Loaf Bread

1 *cup Sourdough Starter*
2½ *cups water*
5 *cups flour*
3 *tablespoons melted shortening*
2 *tablespoons sugar*
1 *tablespoon salt*
½ *to 1 teaspoon soda (depending on sourness of starter)*
Melted butter or margarine

In a large bowl combine the Sourdough Starter, water, and flour. Cover and leave overnight at room temperature. The next day add shortening, sugar, salt, and soda and stir until well blended.

Turn out dough on a well-floured board; knead thoroughly, adding more flour as needed. Divide dough in half; shape into 2 loaves. Place each in a 9- x 5- x 3-inch greased loafpan; let rise until nearly doubled (as long as 3 hours, since this bread rises more slowly than regular bread).

Brush the loaves with melted butter; bake at 400 degrees F. for 40 minutes. Turn out of pans to cool.

Sourdough Flapjacks

1 *package active dry yeast*
1 *cup very warm water*
Flour
1 *or 2 eggs, unbeaten*
¼ *teaspoon soda*
¾ *teaspoon salt*
6 *tablespoons sugar*

Dissolve yeast in very warm water; stir well. Add enough flour to make batter as stiff as waffle batter. Cover; let stand overnight at room temperature.

The next morning add 1 egg for thick batter or 2 eggs for a thin batter. Add soda, salt, and sugar. Mix well and cook in same way as other pancakes. Yield: 8 servings.

To have an additional breakfast from the sourdough, set aside 3 tablespoons of original mixture after it has set overnight. This will be used in place of the yeast cake. Add water and flour and let stand for next day's baking.

Sourdough French Bread

    1 *package dry yeast*
  1½ *cups very warm water*
    1 *cup Sourdough Starter*
    2 *teaspoons salt*
    2 *teaspoons sugar*
      About 6 cups flour, divided
    ½ *teaspoon soda*

Dissolve yeast in very warm water. Add Sourdough Starter, salt, and sugar; stir in about 4 cups flour to make a fairly stiff dough. Beat vigorously. Turn dough into a large greased bowl, cover with a damp towel, and let rise in warm place until doubled in bulk (may double in 1½ to 2 hours).

Stir soda into 1 cup flour and stir into dough, which will be very stiff. Turn dough onto floured board and begin kneading, adding 1 cup or more flour so dough does not stick to board. Knead until dough is satiny.

Shape into 2 long loaves and place on a lightly greased flat cookie sheet that has been sprinkled lightly with cornmeal. Cover and let rise until doubled in bulk. Just before baking, brush loaves with water and make slashes on top of loaf.

Place a shallow pan of hot water in bottom of oven and place baking sheet on rack in center of oven. Bake bread at 400 degrees F. for 45 minutes. Brush often with hot water. To make a very heavy, tough crust, remove loaves from oven about 10 minutes before they are done, brush with salted water, and return to oven. Raise temperature to 425 degrees F. and bake remaining time.

Spoon Rolls

    1 *package dry yeast*
    2 *cups very warm water*
  1½ *sticks margarine, melted*
    ¼ *cup sugar*
    1 *egg*
    4 *cups self-rising flour*

Place yeast in 2 cups warm water. Melt butter; cream with sugar in a large bowl; then add beaten egg. Add dissolved yeast to creamed mixture. Then add the flour and stir until well mixed. Place in airtight bowl and keep in refrigerator. To cook, drop by spoonfuls into well-greased 2½-inch muffin tins and bake at 350 degrees F. about 20 minutes or until browned. This dough keeps for several days. Yield: 2 dozen.

Raisin Coffeebreak Crescents

    2 *cups sifted flour*
    3 *teaspoons baking powder*
    1 *teaspoon salt*
    1 *tablespoon sugar*
    ½ *cup shortening*
    1 *egg*
    ½ *cup milk*
    3 *tablespoons melted butter or*
        margarine
    ¼ *cup brown sugar, firmly packed*
    1 *cup dark or golden raisins*

Resift flour with baking powder, salt, and sugar. Cut in shortening. Add beaten egg and milk, stirring to a moderately soft dough. Divide in half and roll each to an 8- or 9-inch round. Spread rounds with melted butter; then sprinkle with brown sugar and raisins. With a sharp knife cut each circle into 8 wedges. Starting from outside edge, roll up each triangle to its point. Place on greased baking sheets, curving pointed ends into crescent shape. Bake at 425 degrees F. about 15 minutes. Remove from oven and frost with Coffee Glaze. Yield: 16 raisin crescents.

Coffee Glaze: Combine 1 cup sifted powdered sugar with ½ teaspoon instant coffee powder. Add a few drops of water to make moderately thin glaze.

Holiday Fruit Bread

½ cup milk
2 packages or cakes yeast, active dry or
      compressed
½ cup very warm, not hot, water
      (lukewarm for compressed yeast)
4 cups sifted all-purpose flour, divided
½ cup margarine or butter, softened
½ cup sugar
3 tablespoons lemon juice
1 tablespoon grated lemon peel
1 teaspoon salt
3 eggs
1½ cups seedless raisins
1 (3-ounce) can citron, chopped
1 (3-ounce) can orange peel, chopped

Scald milk. Pour into large mixing bowl and cool to lukewarm. Sprinkle or crumble yeast into water (very warm, not hot, water for active dry yeast; lukewarm water for compressed yeast). Stir until dissolved. Add to lukewarm milk in bowl. Stir in 1½ cups of the sifted flour. Beat until smooth.

In another bowl, blend together softened margarine or butter, sugar, lemon juice, grated lemon peel, and salt. Add eggs, one at a time, beating well after each addition. Stir in remaining flour. Mix with yeast batter. Beat thoroughly until smooth. Stir in raisins, citron, and orange peel. Cover and let rise in a warm place free from draft until doubled in bulk (about 3 hours).

Beat dough down; pour into well-greased and lightly floured fancy 2-quart tube mold. Cover and let rise in a warm place, free from draft, until doubled in bulk (about 1½ hours). Bake at 350 degrees F. for 50 to 60 minutes or until a toothpick inserted in center comes out clean.

Stickies

Make dough as for biscuits and roll thin. Spread with a mixture of butter, sugar, and cinnamon. This should be only thin enough to spread. Roll up and slice. Place slices close together on pan or cookie sheet. Bake at 400 degrees F. until light brown on top. Watch carefully to prevent burning.

Granny's Texas Bran Bread

1½ cups boiling water
3 tablespoons butter
3 tablespoons dark brown sugar
2 teaspoons salt
2 tablespoons molasses
1 cup whole bran cereal
1 package active dry yeast
½ cup very warm water
5 to 5½ cups (or more) sifted flour
Melted butter

Pour boiling water over butter, sugar, salt, molasses, and bran in a large bowl. Blend well and set aside; cool to lukewarm.

Meanwhile, soften yeast in warm water and let stand 5 to 10 minutes. Beat 1 cup of the flour into the bran mixture. Add softened yeast and beat until smooth. Continue beating while adding half of the remaining flour. Beat in enough of the remaining flour to make a soft, smooth dough. Turn into a greased bowl and lightly grease surface of dough. Cover with waxed paper and a damp towel. Let rise in a warm place until doubled (about 2 hours).

Turn out on lightly floured surface, divide into 2 portions, and shape dough into loaves. Put in two greased 8½- x 4½- x 2½-inch loafpans. Cover and let rise in warm place until almost doubled.

Bake at 325 degrees F. for 50 to 55 minutes. Remove from oven and lightly brush tops of loaves with melted butter. Yield: 2 loaves.

Doughnut Goblins

1 dozen small round gumdrops
½ dozen plain doughnuts
3 ring gumdrops

Cut 6 round gumdrops in half and arrange as eyes on the doughnuts. Place a whole round gumdrop over center of each doughnut for the nose. Cut ring gumdrops in half and then cut jagged edge with paring knife or scissors to represent teeth; place on doughnuts in position of mouth.

Caraway Sticks

>   2 *cups self-rising flour*
>   4 *tablespoons sugar*
>   ½ *cup shortening*
>   1 *tablespoon caraway seed*
>   ¾ *cup milk (about)*
>   *Granulated sugar*

Mix flour and sugar; cut in shortening until mixture is consistency of cornmeal. Add caraway seed and enough milk to make mixture consistency of biscuit dough. Roll out thin, about ¼ inch. Cut with case knife in strips. 4 inches long and about ¼ inch wide. Place on lightly oiled cookie sheet; bake at 375 degrees F. about 10 minutes or until light brown. Sprinkle with granulated sugar.

Corn Sticks

>   ⅓ *cup butter*
>   ⅓ *cup sugar*
> 1½ *teaspoons salt*
>   3 *whole eggs*
> 2⅓ *cups milk*
>   1 *pound cornmeal*
>   ½ *pound cake flour*
>   2 *tablespoons baking powder*

Cream butter, sugar, salt, and eggs. Add gradually milk, cornmeal, cake flour, and baking powder. Pour mixture into well-greased corn-stick pan and bake 20 minutes in 400-degree oven. Yield: 2 dozen corn sticks.

Fungi

>   4 *cups water*
>   ½ *teaspoon salt*
>   2 *cups cornmeal*
>   1 *tablespoon butter*

Bring to a boil 4 cups water. Add salt. Slowly stir in cornmeal. Stir in butter and cook the mixture over a gentle fire, stirring constantly, until it runs from side of pan. Remove from fire and serve hot or cold.

South Carolina Awendaw Cornbread

>   1 *cup boiled big-grain hominy*
>   2 *egg yolks, lightly beaten*
>   ½ *teaspoon butter or margarine*
>   1 *cup milk*
>   1 *cup cornmeal*
>   ¾ *teaspoon salt*
>   2 *egg whites, stiffly beaten*

Stir hominy into egg yolks; add butter or margarine, then milk. Gradually stir in cornmeal and salt; fold in stiffly beaten egg whites. Batter should resemble a custard at this point. Pour into a buttered 1½-quart baking pan and bake at 325 degrees F. for 45 minutes to 1 hour. Yield: 4 servings.

Buttered Cornbread Squares

>   2 *cups water-ground white cornmeal*
>   3 *teaspoons baking powder*
>   2 *teaspoons flour*
> 2½ *teaspoons salt*
> 3½ *teaspoons sugar*
>   2 *eggs*
>   2 *cups buttermilk*
>   5 *tablespoons vegetable shortening*

Sift all dry ingredients together; beat eggs and add to buttermilk and mix well, but do not overbeat. Combine the two mixtures. Melt shortening in bottom of a 13- x 9- x 2-inch pan in which bread is to be baked. Pour melted shortening into cornbread mixture, leaving enough to coat pan; then pour mixture into pan. Bake cornbread at 425 degrees F. about 15 minutes.

Remove bread from oven, cut into squares, split squares, and butter while still warm. Place in a warming oven on low heat until ready to serve.

If a hot plate is to be used, place cornbread squares carefully in aluminum foil and put on hot buffet tray to keep warm while meal is being served. Yield: 8 to 10 servings.

Outer Banks Cornbread

½ *stick butter*
1 *cup yellow cornmeal*
1 *tablespoon flour*
2 *teaspoons baking powder*
Pinch of salt
2 *teaspoons sugar*
1 *cup cold milk*
1 *egg*

Preheat oven to 425 degrees F. Place ½ stick of butter in 9- x 5-inch oblong pan. Put in oven to melt butter and heat pan.

Mix meal, flour, baking powder, salt, and sugar in bowl; add cold milk and egg—just beat together for a minute. Pour into hot pan (with butter). Bake at 425 degrees F. for 20 minutes.

Crackling Cornbread

1 *quart sifted cornmeal*
1 *teaspoon salt*
1 *cup crushed cracklings*
About 2 cups warm water

Mix meal, salt, and crushed cracklings thoroughly in mixing bowl. Add sufficient warm water to make a stiff dough that can be handled. Shape into pones and bake on a greased baking sheet or iron griddle at 350 degrees F. until a golden brown.

Science Hill Hot Water Cornbread

2 *cups water-ground cornmeal*
½ *teaspoon salt*
1½ *tablespoons bacon drippings*
1 *teaspoon sugar*
Enough boiling water to make a stiff batter that can be formed
Bacon drippings or shortening for frying

Mix first 5 ingredients together, pat into thin cakes, and fry in hot fat until brown on both sides. These cakes have a firmer consistency than the usual cornbread cakes, which are usually dropped as batter from a spoon. Yield: about 8 servings.

Southern Cornbread

1½ *cups cornmeal*
½ *teaspoon soda*
1½ *teaspoons salt*
1 *teaspoon baking powder*
2 *eggs, slightly beaten*
1¼ *cups buttermilk*
2 *tablespoons melted shortening*

Mix dry ingredients. Beat eggs and add to dry ingredients along with buttermilk. Add shortening and mix well. Pour into a greased, hot skillet. If using an iron skillet, bake at 450 degrees F. for 15 to 30 minutes; aluminum at 400 degrees F. for 20 minutes.

Cracklings can be added.

Corn Crisps

1 *cup cornmeal*
1 *teaspoon salt*
Scant 1 cup boiling water
5 *or 6 egg whites, stiffly beaten*

Scald cornmeal to which salt has been added by pouring boiling water over it. Stir well. Mixture will be crumbly moist rather than mushy. Fold stiffly beaten egg whites into cooled cornmeal mixture. Drop by teaspoonfuls at once onto a greased cookie sheet. Make indentation in top of each. Bake at 250 to 300 degrees F. about 30 minutes. The bread will be crisp, dry, tender, and lightly browned. It may be necessary to remove from cookie sheet with a spatula. Yield: 30.

Corn Pone
(Hot Water Cornbread)

1 *tablespoon shortening*
¾ *cup boiling water*
1 *cup cornmeal*
1 *teaspoon salt*

Melt shortening in heavy 8- or 9-inch skillet in which pones will be cooked. Heat water to boiling point and pour immediately over meal and salt. Add melted shortening; stir to blend well. As soon as mixture has cooled enough to handle, divide into four equal portions. Shape each portion into a pone about ¾ inch thick by patting between the hands. Place in pan and bake at 450 degrees F. about 50 minutes or until golden brown. Yield: 4 servings.

Crackling Bread

 2 *cups cornmeal*
 ¼ *teaspoon salt*
 ½ *teaspoon soda*
 1 *cup sour milk or buttermilk*
 1 *cup cracklings, diced*

Sift cornmeal, salt, and soda together. Add milk and stir in cracklings. Form into oblong cakes and place on greased baking sheets. Bake at 450 degrees F. for 30 minutes. Yield: 3 to 4 servings.

Crackling Cornbread

 2 *cups cracklings*
 1 *teaspoon salt*
 2 *cups cornmeal*
 Hot water

Cube cracklings in small pieces and pour the salt over them. Add meal and mix well. Add enough hot water to make a stiff paste. Make 2 pones and bake at 400 degrees F. about 30 minutes. Yield: 6 servings.

Johnny Cake

 1 *cup cornmeal*
 1 *cup flour*
 ½ *teaspoon salt*
 ½ *teaspoon soda*
 2 *cups sour milk*
 2 *tablespoons molasses*
 2 *eggs*

Mix the cornmeal, flour, and salt together. Add soda to sour milk and stir until it foams; then add to the meal and flour. Add molasses and unbeaten eggs and mix well.

Pour into a 13- x 9- x 2-inch oiled baking pan. Bake at 400 degrees F. for 20 minutes. Yield: 8 to 10 servings.

Hoe Cake

 2 *cups cornmeal (plain)*
 1 *teaspoon salt*
 Hot water

Put cornmeal and salt in bowl and mix well. Moisten with hot water till dough can be handled. Let stand an hour. Shape by spoonfuls into flat cakes about ½ inch thick. Fry on hot greased griddle or skillet until golden brown, turning to brown both sides. Serve piping hot. Yield: 4 to 6 servings.

Jalapeño Cornbread

 3 *cups cornbread mix*
 2½ *cups milk*
 ½ *cup salad oil*
 3 *eggs, beaten*
 1 *large onion, grated*
 2 *tablespoons sugar*
 1 *cup cream-style corn*
 ½ *cup very finely chopped jalapeño*
   peppers (fresh or canned)
 1½ *cups sharp cheese, shredded*
 ¼ *pound bacon, cooked and crumbled*
 ¼ *cup chopped pimientos*
 ½ *clove garlic, crushed (optional)*

Put cornbread mix in large bowl; add milk and stir. Add other ingredients in order given. Bake in three greased 8- x 8- x 2-inch pans at 400 degrees F. about 35 minutes or until done. Yield: 12 to 16 servings.

(This freezes well and is excellent served with vegetables or as base for chili shortcake.)

Victorian Buttermilk Cornbread

    1 *cup yellow cornmeal (coarse ground*
       meal if available)
  ½ *teaspoon soda*
  ¼ *teaspoon baking powder*
  ½ *teaspoon salt*
    3 *tablespoons vegetable shortening*
    1 *cup buttermilk*
    1 *egg, slightly beaten*

Sift dry ingredients into large bowl. Place shortening in 8-inch iron skillet and heat. Add buttermilk and egg to dry ingredients and mix well. Pour hot shortening into cornbread and stir well.

    Pour into hot skillet; bake at 425 degrees F. for 25 minutes. Yield: 6 servings.

Mexican Cornbread

    1 *cup yellow cornmeal*
  ½ *teaspoon salt*
  ½ *teaspoon soda*
  ⅓ *cup melted shortening*
    2 *eggs, beaten*
    1 *cup cream-style corn*
  ⅔ *cup buttermilk or small carton*
      commercial sour cream
    1 *cup shredded cheese*
    1 *small can green chili peppers,*
      drained and finely chopped

Combine cornmeal, salt, and soda and mix well. Stir in melted shortening. Add eggs and mix well. Stir in corn and buttermilk and mix well. Spoon one-half the mixture into a greased 12-inch heavy skillet. Sprinkle cheese and chopped peppers over mixture and cover with other half of cornmeal mixture. Bake at 275 degrees F. for 30 to 40 minutes.

Spoonbread

    1 *cup cornmeal*
    1 *quart whole milk*
    3 *tablespoons melted butter*
 1½ *teaspoons salt*
  ½ *teaspoon baking powder*
    4 *eggs, beaten*

Blend cornmeal with 1 cup milk. Then add the remaining 3 cups milk. Cook at medium temperature, stirring constantly. Add melted butter, salt, and baking powder. Fold in well-beaten eggs. Pour into a greased 1½-quart baking dish. Bake at 350 degrees F. for 45 to 50 minutes.

Campbell's Tavern Spoonbread

 1⅓ *teaspoons sugar*
 1½ *teaspoons salt*
    1 *cup cornmeal*
 1⅓ *cups boiling water*
    3 *whole eggs*
    1 *tablespoon baking powder*
 1⅓ *cups fresh milk*
     Butter or oleo

Mix sugar and salt with cornmeal and blend well. Pour boiling water over meal, stirring constantly. Let stand until cool. Beat eggs until light; add eggs and baking powder to mixture. Add milk and pour mixture into a 2-quart buttered pan or baking dish. Then dot with butter or oleo. Place in shallow pan of hot water in 350-degree oven. Bake about 35 minutes. Yield: 8 servings.

Southern Spoonbread

    4 *cups milk*
    1 *cup cornmeal*
    2 *teaspoons baking powder*
    1 *teaspoon salt*
    2 *tablespoons butter or margarine*
    4 *eggs, well beaten*

Mix 1 cup milk with cornmeal. Scald 3 cups milk in top of double boiler. Add hot milk to cornmeal mixture; then cook in top of double boiler about 10 minutes or until mixture is consistency of thin mush. Add baking powder, salt, and butter. Remove from double boiler and fold beaten eggs slowly into mixture. (Whites and yolks may be beaten separately and folded into mixture if desired. This produces a lighter bread, more like a soufflé.) Pour into buttered 1½-quart baking dish. Bake at 400 degrees F. for 45 minutes. Serve at once from dish in which it was cooked. Yield: 4 to 5 servings.

Corn Muffins

       1   *cup cornmeal*
       ½   *cup flour*
       1   *tablespoon baking powder*
       1   *teaspoon salt*
       1   *tablespoon sugar*
       1   *cup niblet corn, drained*
       ¾   *cup milk*
       1   *egg, slightly beaten*
       2   *tablespoons butter or margarine*

Sift dry ingredients together; add corn and mix well. Add milk, egg, and butter and blend well. Pour into greased muffin tins and bake at 450 degrees F. about 20 minutes. Yield: 12 muffins.

Cornbread Waffles

    1½   *cups cornmeal*
       ¾   *cup sifted all-purpose flour*
       2   *teaspoons baking powder*
       ½   *teaspoon soda*
       1   *teaspoon salt*
       2   *tablespoons sugar*
       2   *egg yolks*
    1½   *cups buttermilk*
       4   *tablespoons melted butter*
       2   *egg whites, beaten*

Sift dry ingredients together 3 times. Beat egg yolks and add to dry ingredients alternately with milk. Stir in melted butter and then fold in stiffly beaten egg whites. Bake in preheated waffle iron. Serve hot, topped with turkey hash. Yield: 8 waffles.

Texas Orange Muffins

       ⅓   *cup shortening*
       ½   *cup sugar*
       1   *egg*
       ½   *cup whole bran cereal*
       1   *teaspoon grated orange rind*
       ½   *cup orange juice*
       ¼   *cup milk*
    1¾   *cups flour*
       2   *teaspoons baking powder*
       ¼   *teaspoon soda*
       ½   *teaspoon salt*

Cream shortening and sugar thoroughly; add egg and beat until creamy. Add bran cereal, orange rind, orange juice, and milk. Sift flour with baking powder, soda, and salt; add to first mixture and stir only until flour disappears. Fill greased muffin pans two-thirds full and bake at 400 degrees F. about 30 minutes. Yield: 8 large muffins 3 inches in diameter or 12 small muffins 2¼ inches in diameter.

Corn Muffins or Corn Sticks

       2   *cups cornmeal*
       3   *teaspoons baking powder*
       1   *teaspoon salt*
       1   *tablespoon sugar (optional)*
       1   *egg, beaten*
    1¼   *cups milk*
       3   *tablespoons soft or melted
           shortening*

Sift together cornmeal, baking powder, salt, and sugar. Mix together beaten egg, milk, and shortening; add all at once to the dry ingredients. Stir just to moisten and blend all ingredients. Pour batter into hot greased muffin or corn-stick pans, filling about two-thirds full. Bake at 450 degrees F. about 15 to 20 minutes. Yield: 6 servings.

Cornmeal-Peanut Butter Muffins

       2   *cups cornmeal (yellow is preferred)*
       4   *teaspoons baking powder*
    1½   *teaspoons salt*
       1   *egg, slightly beaten*
    1½   *cups milk*
       2   *tablespoons melted shortening or
           cooking oil*
       ½   *cup crunchy peanut butter*

Mix ingredients in order given, stirring just to moisten dry ingredients. Do not beat. Lightly oil large muffin tins and preheat greased tins. Spoon batter into tins, and bake at 450 degrees F. for 15 to 20 minutes. Yield: 12 large muffins.

Best Ever Muffins

2 *cups sifted all-purpose flour*
3 *teaspoons baking powder*
¼ *teaspoon soda*
½ *teaspoon ground ginger*
½ *teaspoon salt*
1 *egg, well beaten*
½ *cup milk*
½ *cup molasses*
4 *tablespoons melted shortening*
¾ *cup shredded cheese*

Sift flour and measure; then sift with baking powder, soda, ginger, and salt. Combine egg, milk, and molasses. Add to the dry ingredients, stirring just enough to mix. Do not beat. Add shortening and fold in shredded cheese. Fill oiled muffin tins two-thirds full. Bake at 375 degrees F. for 15 to 20 minutes. Yield: 16 muffins.

Cheese and Corn Muffins

½ *cup cornmeal*
1 *cup flour*
3 *teaspoons baking powder*
1 *tablespoon sugar*
½ *teaspoon salt*
¾ *cup milk*
1 *egg, well beaten*
1 *tablespoon melted butter*
1 *tablespoon chopped green pepper*
1 *teaspoon chopped onion*
½ *cup shredded cheese*

Combine dry ingredients. Add milk gradually and mix well. Add other ingredients. Turn into greased muffin pans and bake at 375 degrees F. for 25 minutes.

Chili-Cheese Muffins

2 *cups biscuit mix*
1 *cup shredded sharp Cheddar cheese*
1 *teaspoon chili con carne seasoning*
½ *teaspoon oregano*
2 *teaspoons chervil*
¾ *cup milk*
1 *egg, slightly beaten*

Combine biscuit mix, cheese, chili con carne seasoning, oregano, and chervil. Beat milk and egg together until well blended; then add, all at once, to dry ingredients. Stir until just blended. Spoon into 12 greased, medium-size muffin cups. Bake at 400 degrees F. for 25 to 30 minutes or until golden brown. Turn out onto a rack to cool. Yield: 12 medium-size muffins.

Creole Corn Muffins

2 *eggs, well beaten*
1½ *cups milk*
¾ *cup shortening, melted*
2 *tablespoons chopped green pepper*
2 *tablespoons chopped onion*
2 *tablespoons chopped pimiento*
¾ *cup shredded American cheese*
2½ *cups flour*
1 *teaspoon salt*
2 *tablespoons baking powder*
4 *tablespoons plus 1 teaspoon sugar*
4 *tablespoons plus 1 teaspoon cornmeal*
¼ *teaspoon red pepper*

Mix the egg, milk, and shortening. Add the green pepper, onion, pimiento, and cheese to the flour, salt, baking powder, sugar, cornmeal, and red pepper. Add the milk mixture and stir only enough to mix. Bake in greased muffin pans at 400 degrees F. for 25 to 30 minutes. Yield: about 2 dozen 2-inch muffins.

Fresh Lemon Muffins

2 *lemons*
1 *cup unsifted flour*
1 *teaspoon baking powder*
¼ *teaspoon salt*
½ *cup butter or margarine*
½ *cup sugar*
2 *eggs, separated*
2 *tablespoons sugar*
¼ *teaspoon ground cinnamon* .

Grate lemon peel to yield 1 tablespoon peel; ream lemons to yield 3 tablespoons juice; set aside. Sift together flour, baking powder, and salt. Cream butter thoroughly; gradually add sugar, beating until light and fluffy. Beat egg yolks until lemon colored; add to butter-sugar mixture, blending well. Add flour mixture alternately with lemon juice. Do not overmix. Beat egg whites until stiff, but not dry. Carefully fold whites and grated lemon peel into batter. Fill lightly greased muffin pan three-fourths full. Combine sugar and cinnamon; mix well and sprinkle about ½ teaspoon over each muffin. Bake at 375 degrees F. about 25 minutes or until done. Excellent served as an accompaniment for salads—particularly fruit salads. Also serve leftover muffins halved, toasted, and buttered. Yield: about ten 2½-inch muffins.

Orange-Cornmeal Muffins

1 *cup yellow cornmeal*
1 *cup flour*
2 *tablespoons sugar*
3 *tablespoons baking powder*
½ *teaspoon salt*
1 *egg, slightly beaten*
1 *cup milk*
¼ *cup vegetable shortening, melted*
1 *jar orange marmalade (about ½ cup)*

Sift together cornmeal, flour, sugar, baking powder, and salt. To beaten egg add milk and shortening; add to dry ingredients, stirring enough to moisten. Fill greased muffin pans (use paper fillers in pans if desired) about one-third full, and put 1 teaspoon orange marmalade in each section. Add remaining batter. Bake at 400 degrees F. for 25 minutes. Yield: 12 large muffins.

Blueberry-Orange Muffins

1 *(13-ounce) package blueberry muffin mix*
1 *egg*
¼ *cup orange juice*
¼ *cup water*
1 *tablespoon grated orange rind*

Prepare blueberry muffin mix according to package directions, reserving blueberries. Set aside. Combine egg, orange juice, and water in medium bowl until well mixed. Add muffin mix and rind. Stir until ingredients are moistened. Do not overmix; batter will be slightly lumpy. Gently fold in blueberries. Spoon into 12 lightly greased medium muffin cups, filling about one-half full. If desired, sprinkle with a combination of 2 tablespoons sugar and 1½ teaspoons grated rind. Bake in a 400-degree F. oven for 20 minutes or until golden brown. Serve warm. Yield: 1 dozen.

Light-Hearted Hotcakes

1 *package dry yeast*
¼ *cup very warm water*
1 *cup milk*
1 *egg*
1 *tablespoon peanut oil*
1 *cup pancake mix*

Sprinkle yeast into very warm water. Stir until dissolved. Add remaining ingredients and beat with rotary beater until smooth. Grease griddle lightly. For each pancake pour ¼ cup onto moderately hot griddle and turn when tops are covered with bubbles and edges are cooked. Turn only once. Yield: 8 to 10 servings.

Cola Pancakes

2 *egg yolks*
2 *small bottles cola drink*
1 *teaspoon salt*
2 *cups flour*
½ *stick butter or margarine, melted*
2 *egg whites, beaten stiff*

Beat egg yolks into cola drinks. Add salt to flour; stir in cola and egg and beat well. Add melted butter. Fold in egg whites and add more cola as needed to make a very thin batter. The secret of good pancakes is to make them very thin (not over ⅛ inch thick). Cook on hot griddle, turning only once.

Battercakes

  1 *cup white cornmeal*
  ½ *teaspoon soda*
  ½ *teaspoon salt*
  1 *egg*
 1¼ *cups buttermilk*

Sift together cornmeal, soda, and salt. Beat egg into buttermilk and add to dry mixture. Mix well. Pour by spoonfuls onto hot greased skillet or griddle. Turn battercakes as soon as they are brown. Butter, and cover with syrup.

Buttermilk Pancakes

  2 *cups sifted all-purpose flour*
  1 *teaspoon baking powder*
  ½ *teaspoon salt*
  ½ *teaspoon soda*
  1 *egg, slightly beaten*
 1½ *cups buttermilk*
  2 *tablespoons melted butter*

Sift flour, baking powder, salt, and soda together into bowl. Combine egg and buttermilk and add to flour mixture, mixing only until smooth. Blend in butter. Bake on a hot, lightly greased griddle, using ¼ cup of batter for each pancake. Turn only once. Yield: 4 servings.

Cloud-Light Pancakes

  1 *cup plain flour*
  2 *tablespoons sugar*
  2 *tablespoons baking powder (yes,*
     tablespoons!)
  ½ *teaspoon salt*
  1 *egg*
  2 *tablespoons cooking oil*
    Milk (enough to make the batter pour
     easily)

Combine dry ingredients. Add egg, oil, and enough milk for mixture to pour easily. Mix lightly—mixture will be bubbly and foamy. Bake on well-greased griddle. Yield: 2 to 3 servings.

Oatmeal Pancakes

  2 *cups uncooked oatmeal*
  2 *cups scalded milk*
  2 *egg yolks*
  ½ *cup melted butter*
  ½ *cup all-purpose flour*
  1 *tablespoon sugar*
  2 *teaspoons baking powder*
  ½ *teaspoon salt*
  2 *egg whites, beaten*

Stir oatmeal into scalded milk and mix well; let stand until cool. Beat egg yolks; gradually add melted butter, stirring constantly. Stir this mixture into oatmeal. Sift dry ingredients together and add to oatmeal. Mix lightly but thoroughly. Beat egg whites until stiff; fold into mixture. Cook as regular pancakes. Yield: 1 dozen 3-inch pancakes.

Sour Cream Pancakes

  2 *eggs, separated*
  2 *tablespoons sugar*
  ½ *teaspoon salt*
  ½ *teaspoon soda*
  1 *cup commercial sour cream*
  1 *cup sifted all-purpose flour*

Mix well-beaten egg yolks, sugar, salt, soda, and sour cream. Add flour and stir until smooth. Fold in stiffly beaten egg whites. Drop by tablespoonfuls onto hot, ungreased griddle. Turn only once. Yield: 6 servings.

Plain Pancakes

  2 *cups sifted all-purpose flour*
 2½ *teaspoons baking powder*
  ½ *teaspoon salt*
  1 *egg, slightly beaten*
 1½ *cups milk*
  2 *tablespoons melted butter*

Sift flour, baking powder, and salt together into bowl. Combine egg and milk and add to flour mixture, mixing only until smooth. Blend in butter. Bake on a hot, lightly greased griddle, using ¼ cup batter for each pancake. Turn only once. Yield: 4 servings.

Butter-Raisin Fritters

Dough:

   1 *cup (2 sticks) butter*
   4 *cups flour*
   ¼ *teaspoon salt*
   ¾ *cup (approximately) ice water*

Cut butter into flour mixed with salt until mixture resembles cornmeal. Mix in enough of the water to make a firm dough. Cover and chill until ready to use.

Filling:

   ½ *cup chopped raisins*
   ¼ *cup orange juice*
   1 *egg white*
   1 *cup chopped walnuts*
   1 *cup sugar*
   ½ *cup dried cookie, cake, or bread crumbs*
   1 *egg yolk*
      Powdered sugar

Marinate raisins in orange juice several hours or overnight; then mix with egg white, walnuts, sugar, and crumbs. Roll dough on lightly floured board until thin; cut into 4-inch rounds. Place about 1 tablespoon of filling in center of each; brush edges with egg yolk, fold in half, and press together firmly. Fry a few at a time in deep fat (375 degrees) until golden. Dust with powdered sugar while still warm. *Note:* Butter-Raisin Turnovers may be made exactly the same as the fritters, only instead of deep-fat frying, place turnovers on a cookie sheet and bake at 400 degrees F. for 25 minutes. While turnovers are still warm, drizzle on a glaze made by blending 1 cup powdered sugar with 2 tablespoons orange juice. Serve warm. Yield: 28 to 30 fritters.

Lemon Toast

      Juice and grated rind of 2 lemons
   ½ *cup sugar*
   4 *teaspoons butter or margarine, melted*
   8 *slices toast*

Combine lemon juice, grated rind, and sugar. Cook until it comes to a hard boil; add melted butter and reheat, stirring constantly. Spread on toast and place under broiler for 1 or 2 minutes. Yield: 8 servings.

Oven French Toast

   2 *teaspoons sugar*
   ¼ *teaspoon salt*
   2 *eggs, unbeaten*
   1 *cup milk*
   ¼ *cup salad oil*
   8 *slices of bread*

Add sugar and salt to unbeaten eggs in shallow dish and stir until well mixed. Stir in milk and melted fat. Dip bread in mixture and place in well-greased pan. Bake at 450 degrees F. for about 10 minutes until brown. This is much easier than French toast fried in deep fat, is not nearly as fattening, and is just as good.

Spicy Raisin Biscuits

   ½ *cup seedless raisins*
      Boiling water
   1½ *cups biscuit mix*
   ¼ *teaspoon ground cinnamon*
   ¼ *teaspoon ground nutmeg*
   2 *tablespoons sugar*
   1 *egg, beaten*
   ½ *cup coffee*
   2 *tablespoons heavy cream*
   2 *tablespoons sugar*

Cover raisins with boiling water. Let stand for 5 minutes. Drain and cool. Combine biscuit mix, spices, and 2 tablespoons sugar. Combine beaten egg and coffee; add to biscuit mix. Add raisins. Pat out ½ inch thick on lightly floured board. Cut with small biscuit cutter; place on greased cookie sheet. Bake at 450 degrees F. for 10 to 12 minutes. Whip cream with fork; add remaining sugar and brush over biscuits. Put under broiler to brown and glaze. Yield: 18 biscuits.

Ham Biscuits

   2 *cups flour*
   2 *teaspoons baking powder*
   ¼ *teaspoon soda*
   1 *teaspoon salt*
   6 *tablespoons shortening*
   ⅔ *cup buttermilk*
     Slivers of baked ham

Sift together flour, baking powder, soda, and salt. Cut in shortening until mixture is consistency of cornmeal. Stir in milk. Form mixture into a ball. Place on flour-covered board and knead lightly. Roll or pat to ¼-inch thickness. Cut with a small biscuit cutter. Place on ungreased baking sheet and bake at 450 degrees F. about 8 to 10 minutes, or until browned. Open biscuits and spread with butter if desired. Place slivers of baked ham in biscuit. Serve hot. Yield: about 24 small biscuits.

Almond Popovers

   2 *eggs, beaten*
   1 *cup milk*
   1 *tablespoon melted shortening or oil*
   ½ *teaspoon salt*
   1 *cup sifted flour*
   1 *tablespoon finely chopped blanched almonds*

Grease popover pan or 6 custard cups. Preheat oven to 425 degrees F. In medium-size mixing bowl blend together eggs, milk, shortening or oil, and salt. Blend in flour until smooth; beat at least 1 minute on electric mixer or 3 minutes with rotary beater. Fill popover pan or custard cups half full. Sprinkle almonds over tops. Bake 40 to 45 minutes or until brown and firm to touch. For crisper popovers, prick the side of each popover with a fork, reduce oven temperature to 350 degrees F., and bake 20 minutes longer. Serve hot. Yield: 6 large or 11 small popovers.

Bacon Popovers: Cook 3 strips of bacon until crisp. Drain. Substitute 1 tablespoon bacon drippings for shortening or oil in popover recipe. Substitute finely crumbled bacon for almonds. To serve, fill baked popovers with scrambled eggs.

Pecan Popovers: Substitute 2 tablespoons finely chopped pecans for almonds. To serve, fill baked popovers with creamed chicken.

Parsley Popovers: Blend 1 tablespoon dried parsley flakes into egg mixture and omit almonds. To serve, fill baked popovers with shrimp salad.

Chili Popovers: Blend 2 teaspoons chili powder into egg mixture and omit almonds. To serve, fill baked popovers with chili con carne.

Cheese Popovers: Blend ¼ cup grated Parmesan cheese or shredded American cheese into egg mixture and omit almonds. To serve, fill baked popovers with applesauce or cooked apple slices.

Note: Preheat pans for a crisper crust. Baking time remains the same.

Popovers

   2 *eggs, well beaten*
   1 *cup flour*
   1 *cup milk*
   ½ *teaspoon salt*

Combine all ingredients and beat until batter is very smooth, but do not beat more than enough to remove lumps. Pour into well-greased popover pan. Fill each cup three-fourths full. Put into cold oven, set at 450 degrees F., and bake 30 minutes. Don't peep! Yield: 12 popovers.

Patricia Murphy's Popovers

   2 *teaspoons butter or vegetable shortening*
   1 *cup flour*
   ¼ *teaspoon salt*
   2 *eggs*
   1 *cup milk*
   1 *tablespoon melted butter or vegetable shortening*

Divide the 2 teaspoons butter and put in 6

muffin pans or custard cups. Heat in oven 5 minutes while you are mixing batter.

Sift flour and salt into a bowl. Beat eggs with rotary beater; add milk and 1 tablespoon melted butter. Sift in the flour, beating only enough to make a smooth batter. Fill hot muffin pans (or custard cups) one-third full of the mixture. Bake at 450 degrees F. for 30 minutes, then at 250 degrees F. for 15 minutes or until firm, brown, and popped. Keep oven door closed while baking. Yield: 6 large popovers or 9 small ones.

Pumpkin-Nut Bread

 1½ cups sifted flour
 1¼ teaspoons soda
  1 teaspoon salt
  1 teaspoon ground cinnamon
  ½ teaspoon ground nutmeg
  1 cup pumpkin, canned or fresh
  1 cup sugar
  ½ cup buttermilk
  1 egg
  2 tablespoons soft butter
  1 cup chopped pecans

Sift together flour, soda, salt, and spices. Combine pumpkin, sugar, buttermilk, and egg in mixing bowl. Add dry ingredients and butter; beat until well blended. Stir in nuts. Spread in well-greased loafpan. Bake

at 350 degrees F. for 1 hour or until toothpick inserted in center comes out clean.

Oatmeal Yeast Bread

  2 packages dry yeast
  ½ cup very warm water
  3 cups milk, scalded
  ⅔ cup shortening
  ½ cup sugar
  2 tablespoons salt
 6½ to 7 cups sifted all-purpose flour
  3 cups oatmeal (quick or old-fashioned, uncooked)
   Melted shortening

Soften yeast in very warm water. Pour scalded milk over shortening, sugar, and salt. Cool to lukewarm. Stir in 1 cup flour; add softened yeast and oatmeal. Stir in additional flour to make a soft dough.

Turn out on lightly floured board or canvas; knead until smooth and satiny, about 10 minutes. Round dough into ball; place in greased bowl; brush lightly with melted shortening. Cover and let rise in warm place until double in size, about 1 hour. Punch dough down; cover; let rest 10 minutes. Divide dough into 3 equal parts. Shape to form regular, twin, round, or slash-topped loaves.

For each twin loaf, cut one part of dough in half. Shape each half to form a ball. Place the two balls of dough in greased 8½- x 4½- x 2½-inch loafpan. Brush lightly with melted shortening. For each round loaf, shape one part of dough to form ball about 6 inches in diameter. Place in greased 8-inch round baking pan. Brush lightly with melted shortening. For each slash-topped loaf, shape one part of dough to form a regular loaf. Place in greased 8½- x 4½- x 2½-inch loafpan. Cut diagonal slashes, about 1 inch apart and ¼ inch deep. Brush with melted shortening. Sprinkle with sesame seed.

Cover; let rise until nearly double in size, about 45 minutes. Bake at 375 degrees F. about 50 minutes or until golden brown. Remove from pans; brush with melted butter. Yield: 3 loaves.

Cakes and Frostings

In no other aspect of culinary excellence does the Southern homemaker shine more brightly than with her cakes. Each area of the South has its own specialty, but many cake recipes have Southwide reputations.

The rich pound cake may well have the longest uninterrupted record of popularity. Oldtime recipes were literally "pound" cakes, and ingredients were listed as a pound of flour, butter, sugar, etc.

And the things that a homemaker can still do with pound cake: use it as a base for fruit cakes; cover it with a soft custard and berries; serve it as the base for shortcakes; and give it a complete character change with the addition of chocolate.

Lane cake is another cake that is truly Southern, although the origin might be debatable. Both Georgia and Alabama lay claim to this cake, which is a favorite at Christmas.

Kentucky has its bourbon cake, Texas its pecan cake, and Kentucky, Arkansas, and Tennessee claim the jam cake as one of their favorites.

Southwide though, few can match the popularity of a fresh coconut cake. Although it might appear on all tables at Christmas, it is served year-round, with packaged or canned coconut replacing the fresh coconut.

Coconut Cake

  1 *cup butter*
  2 *cups sugar*
  5 *eggs*
  1 *teaspoon soda*
  Dash salt
2¾ *cups cake flour*
  1 *teaspoon baking powder*
  1 *cup buttermilk*
  1 *teaspoon vanilla extract*
½ *to ¾ teaspoon coconut flavoring*
  2 *recipes Never Fail Frosting*
  2 *cups fresh grated coconut*

Cream butter and sugar until perfectly smooth (about 15 minutes on electric mixer). Add eggs, beating well after each addition. Sift dry ingredients together and add to creamed mixture alternately with buttermilk. Stir in vanilla and coconut flavoring. Bake in 3 or 4 greased and floured round 9-inch layer cake pans (number you use will depend on whether you like 3 thick layers or 4 thinner ones). Bake at 350 degrees F. for about 25 minutes or until layers test done. Cool and frost. Sprinkle with coconut.

Never Fail Frosting:

  1 *cup sugar*
¼ *teaspoon salt*
½ *teaspoon cream of tartar*
  2 *unbeaten egg whites*
  3 *tablespoons water*
  1 *teaspoon vanilla extract*

Combine all ingredients except vanilla in top of double boiler. Use mixer to stir. Beat briskly for 3 minutes or until frosting is fluffy and holds its shape. Remove and add vanilla. Yield: enough for two 9-inch layers.

A fruitcake full of fruits and pecans has been a longtime favorite in Southern homes at Christmas.

Applesauce-Nut Cake

¾ *cup butter*
1 *cup granulated sugar*
1 *cup brown sugar*
3 *eggs*
3 *cups applesauce*
3½ *cups sifted flour*
2 *teaspoons baking powder*
1 *teaspoon salt*
¾ *teaspoon ground cloves*
1 *teaspoon ground nutmeg*
3 *teaspoons ground cinnamon*
1 *pound seedless raisins*
1½ *cups pecans*

Cream butter and sugar. Add eggs and applesauce and beat well. Combine dry ingredients and stir in. Add raisins and pecans and mix well. Pour into greased 13- x 9- x 2-inch cakepan. Bake at 325 degrees F. for 2 hours.

Dutch-Apple Cake

⅓ *cup milk*
¼ *cup sugar*
½ *teaspoon salt*
4 *tablespoons margarine or butter*
1 *package dry yeast*
¼ *cup warm, not hot, water*
1 *egg, well beaten*
1⅓ *cups sifted flour*
1½ *cups canned apples sliced, drained*
2 *tablespoons brown sugar*
¼ *teaspoon ground cinnamon*
¼ *teaspoon ground nutmeg*

Scald milk. Stir in sugar, salt, and 2 table-spoons of margarine. Cool to lukewarm. Dissolve yeast in warm water. Stir in luke-warm milk mixture. Add egg and flour. Beat until smooth. Spread dough evenly in greased 9- x 9- x 2-inch pan. Arrange apple slices on top. Sprinkle with mixture of brown sugar, cinnamon, and nutmeg. Dot with remaining margarine. Cover and let rise in warm place, free from draft, until doubled in bulk, about 40 minutes. Bake at 400 degrees F. for 25 minutes.

Apple-Cherry-Nut Bread

4 *cups sifted all-purpose flour*
2 *teaspoons baking powder*
1 *teaspoon soda*
1 *teaspoon salt*
1¼ *cups sugar*
⅔ *cup shortening*
3 *eggs*
1 *jar or can applesauce*
1 *cup chopped nuts*
½ *cup maraschino cherries, drained*
2 *tablespoons grated lemon peel*

Sift flour, baking powder, soda, and salt together. Beat sugar and shortening until fluffy. Add eggs and beat until smooth. Beat in flour mixture alternately with applesauce. Stir in nuts, chopped cherries, and lemon peel. Pour into two greased 9- x 5- x 3-inch loafpans. Bake at 350 degrees F. for 50 minutes until lightly browned. Take from pans while warm and when slightly cool spread with Vanilla Glaze.

Vanilla Glaze:

1 *cup powdered sugar*
2 *tablespoons evaporated milk*
1 *teaspoon vanilla extract*

Blend sugar and milk until smooth, add vanilla, and spread on Nut Bread loaves.

Apricot Braid

2½ *to 3 cups unsifted flour*
¼ *cup sugar*
1 *teaspoon salt*
1 *package dry yeast*
¾ *cup milk*
¼ *cup (½ stick) margarine, divided*
1 *egg (at room temperature)*
1½ *cups dried apricots*
1 *cup boiling water*
1 *cup firmly packed light brown sugar*
⅓ *cup unsifted flour*
2 *tablespoons sugar*
½ *teaspoon ground cinnamon*
1 *egg yolk*
2 *tablespoons milk*

In a large bowl thoroughly mix ¾ cup flour, ¼ cup sugar, salt, and undissolved dry yeast.

Combine ¾ cup milk and 2 tablespoons margarine in a saucepan. Heat over low heat until liquid is warm. (Margarine does not need to melt.) Gradually add to dry ingredients and beat 2 minutes at medium speed of electric mixer, scraping bowl occasionally. Add egg and ¼ cup flour, or enough flour to make a thick batter. Beat at high speed 2 minutes, scraping bowl occasionally. Stir in enough additional flour to make a soft dough. Turn out onto lightly floured board; knead until smooth and elastic, about 8 to 10 minutes. Place in greased bowl, turning to grease top. Cover; let rise in warm place, free from draft, until doubled in bulk, about 1 hour.

Meanwhile, combine apricots and boiling water in a saucepan. Bring to a boil. Reduce heat and simmer, uncovered, until liquid is absorbed and apricots are tender, about 25 minutes; sieve. Stir in brown sugar until dissolved. Cool.

Punch dough down; turn out onto lightly floured board. Divide in half. Roll out each half into a 14- x 8-inch rectangle. Place on greased baking sheets. Spread one-half of the apricot filling down the center third of each rectangle. Slit dough at 1-inch intervals along each side of filling. Fold strips at an angle across filling, alternating from side to

side. Cover; let rise in warm place, free from draft, until doubled in bulk, about 1 hour.

Combine ⅓ cup flour, 2 tablespoons sugar, and cinnamon. Cut in remaining 2 tablespoons margarine until mixture is crumbly. Brush cakes with combined egg yolk and 2 tablespoons milk. Sprinkle each with crumbly mixture.

Bake at 350 degrees F. about 20 minutes or until done. Remove from baking sheets and cool on wire racks. Yield: 2 coffeecakes.

Banana-Nut Spice Cake

      6 *very ripe bananas*
      ½ *cup vegetable oil*
      ¼ *pound butter*
      2 *cups sugar*
      4 *eggs*
      3 *cups flour*
      2 *teaspoons soda*
    2½ *teaspoons ground cinnamon*
    1½ *teaspoons ground cloves*
      ½ *teaspoon salt*
    1½ *cups seedless raisins*
    1½ *cups chopped pecans*

Mash bananas; pour vegetable oil over bananas and let stand while mixing cake. Cream butter and sugar; add eggs, one at a time, beating well after each addition. Stir in banana mixture and mix well. Add dry ingredients, which have been combined. Stir in raisins and pecans and mix thoroughly. Spoon mixture into 3 greased loafpans and bake at 250 degrees F. for 1½ hours.

Favorite Banana-Nut Bread

      1 *cup butter or margarine*
      2 *cups sugar*
      4 *eggs*
      ¼ *teaspoon salt*
      2 *teaspoons soda*
      4 *cups flour*
      6 *large, very ripe bananas, mashed*
      1 *cup finely chopped pecans*

Cream together butter and sugar. Add eggs, one at a time, beating well after each addition. Sift dry ingredients together and add to creamed mixture. Add bananas and nuts. Pour into two well-greased loafpans, and bake at 250 or 300 degrees F. from 1 to 2 hours. A few of the pecans may be saved for sprinkling over the top of each loaf before baking. Yield: 2 loaves.

Banana-Nut Cake

- 1 *cup soft vegetable shortening*
- 2½ *cups sugar*
- 3 *cups sifted flour*
- 1½ *teaspoons soda*
- 1 *teaspoon salt*
- 4 *egg yolks, beaten*
- 6 *tablespoons buttermilk*
- 2 *teaspoons vanilla extract*
- 2 *cups mashed ripe bananas*
- 1 *cup chopped pecans*
- 4 *egg whites, beaten*

Cream shortening and sugar. Combine dry ingredients and add to creamed mixture alternately with beaten egg yolks and buttermilk. Add vanilla, mashed bananas, and pecans. Fold in beaten egg whites. Bake in large greased tube pan at 325 degrees F. for about 1½ hours.

Banana Bread

- ½ *cup butter or margarine*
- 1 *cup sugar*
- 2 *eggs*
- 3 *bananas*
- 2 *cups all-purpose flour*
- ½ *teaspoon salt*
- 1 *teaspoon soda dissolved in*
- 2 *tablespoons buttermilk*
- ½ *cup finely chopped nuts (optional)*

Cream together butter and sugar; add other ingredients. Mix well, pour into greased and floured loafpan. Bake at 325 degrees F. for 50 minutes.

Caramel-Nut Ring

- 2 *tablespoons melted butter or margarine*
- 2 *tablespoons water*
- ½ *cup brown sugar*
- ¼ *cup sliced filberts or other nuts*
- 10 *or 12 brown-and-serve dinner rolls*

Combine butter, water, brown sugar, and filberts. Spread this mixture on bottom and sides of a 5-cup ring mold. Press rolls, close together with tops down, over sugar mixture in mold. Bake at 400 degrees F. for 15 minutes. Let rolls stand in pan 1 minute or longer after removing from oven. Invert mold and remove rolls in one complete ring. Caramel nut mixture will be on top. Serve immediately. Yield: 5 or 6 servings.

Bishop's Bread

- 3 *cups packaged biscuit mix*
- 1 *cup sugar*
- ½ *cup wheat germ*
- 1½ *cups orange juice*
- 3 *tablespoons cooking oil*
- 1 *egg*
- 1 *tablespoon grated orange peel*
- 1 *(6-ounce) package chocolate chips, divided*
- ¼ *cup seedless raisins*
- ¼ *cup halved candied cherries*
- ¼ *cup chopped walnuts or pecans*

Measure biscuit mix, sugar, and wheat germ into mixing bowl. Stir well to blend. Combine orange juice, oil, egg, and orange peel in small bowl. Add to flour mixture; stir until all ingredients are moistened. Stir in ⅔ cup of chocolate chips, raisins, cherries, and walnuts or pecans. Pour into greased, paper-lined loafpan. Sprinkle remaining ⅓ cup chocolate chips on top. Bake at 350 degrees F. for 45 to 55 minutes or until toothpick inserted comes out clean. Cool on rack 10 minutes before removing from pan.

Bishop's Bread

- 2 *cups sifted flour**
- 1 *tablespoon baking powder*
- 1 *teaspoon salt*
- 1 *cup chopped walnuts*
- 1 *cup chopped maraschino cherries, well drained*
- ½ *cup chopped candied citron*
- ⅔ *cup semisweet chocolate pieces*
- 4 *eggs, separated*
- 1 *cup sugar*

Sift together flour, baking powder, and salt. Combine walnuts, cherries, citron, and chocolate. Coat with ½ cup flour mixture. Beat egg yolks until light; then gradually beat in sugar. Stir in fruit mixture. Mix in remaining 1½ cups flour. Beat egg whites until stiff, but not dry, and peaks are formed. Fold into mixture. Turn into well-greased, waxed paper-lined 9¼- x 5¼-inch loafpan. Bake at 325 degrees F. for 1 hour and 20 minutes or until cake tester inserted in center comes out clean. Yield: 1 loaf.

*If you don't sift and in the absence of other directions, spoon flour directly from container into dry measuring cup, level off, then remove 2 level tablespoons, according to USDA recommendations. If self-rising flour is used, omit baking powder and salt.

Broken Glass Cake

  3 *(3-ounce) packages fruit-flavored*
     gelatin (assorted)
  2 *cups vanilla wafer or graham cracker*
     crumbs
  ½ *cup sugar*
  1 *stick margarine, melted*
  1 *envelope unflavored gelatin*
  2 *tablespoons cold water*
  ½ *cup hot fruit juice*
  2 *packages whipped topping*
  1 *teaspoon vanilla extract*
  ¼ *cup sugar*
  1 *cup milk*
  Chopped nuts, if desired

Prepare the three fruit gelatins according to package directions (select assorted colors and flavors). Pour into three shallow pans and keep in refrigerator overnight. Mix 1¾ cups of the crumbs with ½ cup sugar and melted margarine; use to line bottom and sides of a 13- x 9- x 2-inch pan. Dissolve unflavored gelatin in cold water; let stand 5 minutes. Add hot juice and heat until gelatin is dissolved; cool. Whip packaged topping with vanilla, ¼ cup sugar, and 1 cup milk. Fold unflavored gelatin mixture into this mixture.

Cut fruit gelatin into small cubes and fold into topping mixture. This dessert gives the appearance of colored glass cubes. Pour into crumb-lined pan and sprinkle with remainder of crumbs and nuts. Chill and serve. Yield: 12 to 16 servings.

Carrot Cake

  2 *cups sugar*
  3 *cups flour*
  1 *teaspoon soda*
  ½ *teaspoon salt*
  1 *teaspoon ground cinnamon*
  2 *cups coarsely grated carrots*
1⅓ *cups salad oil*
  2 *eggs, beaten*
  1 *cup chopped nuts*
  1 *cup crushed pineapple, drained*
  1 *teaspoon vanilla extract*
  1 *teaspoon lemon extract*
  ½ *teaspoon almond extract*

Combine dry ingredients in large mixing bowl. Add carrots, salad oil, and eggs. Beat until well mixed. Add other ingredients and stir. Put batter in two large or three small loafpans which have been oiled and floured. Bake at 350 degrees F. for 1 hour.

Chantilly Cake

  1 *angelfood cake ring*
  ½ *pint whipping cream, whipped stiff*
  5 *or 6 tablespoons sugar*
  ½ *teaspoon vanilla extract*
  1 *(10-ounce) package frozen*
     strawberries, thawed, or 2 cups
     crushed fresh strawberries
  1 *(8½-ounce) can crushed pineapple,*
     drained
12 *large marshmallows, cut in small*
     pieces
  Toasted coconut

Cut angelfood cake in two layers. To whipped cream add sugar, vanilla, strawberries, pineapple, and marshmallows. Mix well, then cover bottom and top layers of cake. Sprinkle top and sides generously with toasted coconut. Keep in refrigerator.

Butter Bottom Camp Cake for Six

> 1 *box yellow cake mix, the one-layer size*
> ⅓ *stick butter or margarine*
> *Juice of ½ lemon*
> 1 *cup apricot preserves plus ½ cup chopped pecans or 1 cup plum preserves plus ½ cup chopped black walnuts*

If you have a camp oven: Mix the cake according to package directions. Melt butter in 9-inch skillet. Add lemon juice to the butter and spoon the preserves onto the butter-lemon juice mixture. Sprinkle chopped nuts on the preserves. Spoon cake batter over this mixture in the skillet and bake in 350-degree F. oven for 30 to 40 minutes, or until done and lightly browned. Turn out of skillet immediately, or it will stick. It is gooey and will break up somewhat, but who cares? It's delicious!

If you have no camp oven: Make up the cake batter, but fry it like small pancakes in well-oiled skillet, turning once. Put the little cakes together in pairs with preserves and chopped nuts. Another tasty variation: Put pairs of cakes together, while hot, with pieces of chocolate bars.

Appetizer Cheesecake

> *Melted butter*
> 1 *(6-ounce) box cheese crackers, crushed*
> ½ *cup finely chopped stuffed olives*
> 1 *cup finely chopped celery*
> 1 *medium green pepper, finely chopped*
> 1 *small onion, finely chopped*
> 2 *tablespoons lemon juice*
> 1 *teaspoon salt*
> 1 *teaspoon Worcestershire sauce*
> ¼ *teaspoon paprika*
> *Dash liquid hot pepper*
> 2 *cups thick commercial sour cream*
> *Ripe olives, cut in rings*
> *Pimiento strips*

Brush sides and bottom of 9-inch springform pan with melted butter and press half the crushed cracker crumbs on bottom to form base. Combine chopped olives, celery, green pepper, onion, lemon juice, salt, Worcestershire sauce, paprika, and liquid hot pepper with sour cream; blend well. Spread this mixture over cracker base. Scatter remainder of crumbs over top. Cover with waxed paper and refrigerate for at least 24 hours. Remove pan side and place cake (still on pan bottom) on serving platter. Garnish top with ripe olive rings and pimiento strips. Cut in 10 or 12 wedges.

Tangy Lemon Cheesecake

> 2 *tablespoons unflavored gelatin*
> 1 *cup sugar*
> ¼ *teaspoon salt*
> 2 *egg yolks*
> ¾ *cup milk*
> 3 *cups cottage cheese, beaten until almost smooth*
> 2 *tablespoons grated lemon rind*
> 2 *tablespoons lemon juice*
> ½ *cup graham cracker crumbs*
> ¼ *teaspoon ground cinnamon*
> ½ *teaspoon grated lemon rind*
> 1 *tablespoon sugar*
> 2 *tablespoons melted butter*
> 2 *egg whites*
> 1 *cup cream, whipped*

Mix gelatin, 1 cup sugar, and salt in top of double boiler. Beat together egg yolks and milk; stir into gelatin mixture. Cook over boiling water, stirring constantly, about 10 minutes, or until gelatin is dissolved and mixture is slightly thickened. Remove from heat. Mix cottage cheese, 2 tablespoons lemon rind, and lemon juice. Gradually add and stir in gelatin mixture. Mix until blended. Chill, stirring occasionally, until mixture mounds slightly when dropped from spoon.

Mix graham cracker crumbs, cinnamon, ½ teaspoon lemon rind, 1 tablespoon sugar, and butter; reserve as topping for cake.

Beat egg whites until stiff, but not dry. Gently fold with whipped cream into cheese mixture. Pour into 8-inch springform pan and sprinkle top with crumbs. Chill until firm. Garnish with pineapple and maraschino cherries.

Chess Cake

        2 *sticks margarine*
        1 *box brown sugar*
        1 *cup granulated sugar*
        4 *egg yolks*
        2 *cups all-purpose flour*
        2 *teaspoons baking powder*
      ¼ *teaspoon salt*
        1 *cup broken nuts (optional)*
     1½ *teaspoons vanilla extract*
        4 *egg whites*
           Powdered sugar

Melt margarine, add both sugars, and blend well. Add egg yolks and beat well. Sift flour, baking powder, and salt; add to creamed mixture. Fold in nuts and vanilla. Beat egg whites until stiff; fold into creamed mixture. Spread batter in greased and floured 13- x 9-inch pan and bake at 350 degrees F. for 30 to 45 minutes. When done, sprinkle with powdered sugar.

Devil's Food Cake

      ⅔ *cup shortening*
      ⅔ *cup sugar*
        1 *teaspoon soda*
        1 *teaspoon salt*
        1 *teaspoon vanilla extract*
      ⅔ *cup unsulphured molasses*
        3 *squares bitter chocolate or 9 tablespoons cocoa*
        2 *eggs*
      ¾ *cup sour milk*
     1½ *cups sifted all-purpose flour*

Cream together shortening, sugar, soda, salt, and vanilla. Stir in molasses. Melt chocolate over hot water; add to shortening-sugar mixture. Beat in eggs. Add sour milk alternately with flour (about ½ cup at each time). Put batter in two well-greased and lightly floured 8-inch layer cake pans. Bake at 375 degrees F. for 25 minutes or until cake tests done. Cool and frost as desired. Yield: 10 to 12 servings.

"White Chocolate" Cake

      ⅓ *cup "white chocolate," cut in small pieces*
      ½ *cup hot water*
        1 *cup butter*
     1½ *cups sugar*
        4 *egg yolks, unbeaten*
        1 *teaspoon vanilla extract*
     2½ *cups sifted cake flour*
        1 *teaspoon baking soda*
        1 *cup buttermilk*
        4 *egg whites, stiffly beaten*

Melt "white chocolate" in hot water; allow to cool. Cream butter and sugar together until light and fluffy. Add egg yolks, one at a time, beating well after each addition. Add melted "white chocolate" and vanilla.

Sift flour and baking soda together and add alternately with buttermilk to creamed mixture. Gently fold in stiffly beaten egg whites. Pour into 3 greased and floured 9-inch layer pans. Bake 30 to 35 minutes in preheated 350-degree F. oven. Cool.

    "White Chocolate" Frosting:

      ½ *cup plus 2 tablespoons sugar*
        6 *tablespoons evaporated milk*
      ¼ *cup butter or margarine*
        2 *cups "white chocolate," cut into small pieces*
     1½ *teaspoons vanilla extract*
           Slivered toasted almonds or other nuts for garnish

Combine sugar, milk, and butter in a saucepan. Bring mixture to full rolling boil and boil 1 minute. Remove from heat and add "white chocolate" and vanilla. Stir until candy is melted; beat until smooth and of spreading consistency. Frost cake and garnish with nuts.

Chocolate Yeast Cake

½ *package yeast*
3 *tablespoons lukewarm water*
1⅓ *cups plus ½ teaspoon sugar*
½ *cup butter*
½ *teaspoon salt*
2 *eggs, well beaten*
½ *cup cocoa*
⅔ *cup sweet milk*
1 *teaspoon vanilla extract*
2 *cups flour*
¾ *teaspoon baking soda*
2 *tablespoons warm water*

Stir yeast in 3 tablespoons lukewarm water. Add ½ teaspoon sugar. Let stand for 5 minutes. Cream butter, 1 cup sugar, and salt. Add eggs and then add cocoa mixed with ⅓ cup sugar. Stir in milk, vanilla, and flour alternately. Add softened yeast; mix well. Cover batter; let stand in a cool place overnight.

Dissolve soda in 2 tablespoons warm water; stir into batter. Pour in two greased layer cake pans. Bake at once in 350-degree F. oven about 25 minutes or until cake tests done.

Frost cake with your favorite kind of white frosting.

Red Cake

½ *cup vegetable shortening*
1½ *cups sugar*
2 *whole eggs*
1½ *ounces red food coloring*
2 *level tablespoons cocoa*
1 *scant teaspoon salt*
1 *teaspoon soda*
2½ *cups cake flour*
1 *cup buttermilk*
2 *tablespoons vanilla extract*

Cream the shortening and sugar; add the eggs, and cream until well blended. Mix the food coloring and cocoa and add to the creamed mixture. Sift salt, soda, and cake flour. Add dry ingredients and liquids alternately to creamed mixture. Fold; do not

beat. Bake in three greased 9-inch cakepans at 350 degrees F. for 30 to 35 minutes. Serve as a three-layer cake, frosted with White Icing. Recipe below is suggested.

White Icing:

6 *tablespoons flour*
1 *cup water*
1 *cup butter*
1 *cup granulated sugar*
1 *teaspoon vanilla extract*

Cook the flour and water until slightly clear. Cool for at least 2 hours. Cream the butter, sugar, and vanilla, and add to cool flour mixture. Beat with electric beater until light and fluffy.

Fresh Coconut Cake

1 *cup butter*
2 *cups sugar*
3½ *cups flour*
3½ *teaspoons baking powder*
1 *cup milk*
8 *egg whites, beaten*
½ *teaspoon vanilla extract*
½ *teaspoon lemon extract*

Cream the butter; add sugar gradually, continuing to cream well. Combine flour and baking powder and add to creamed mixture alternately with milk. Beat egg whites until stiff, but not dry. Fold into creamed mixture. Add flavorings. Bake in three greased and floured 9-inch cakepans at 375 degrees F. about 30 to 35 minutes or until browned. Cool before icing.

Icing:

3 *cups granulated sugar*
1 *cup water*
2 *teaspoons vinegar*
3 *egg whites, beaten*
½ *teaspoon cream of tartar*
1 *teaspoon lemon extract*
1 *teaspoon vanilla extract*
1½ *cups freshly grated coconut*

Stir together the sugar, water, and vinegar.

Cook until it spins a fine hairlike thread. Beat egg whites with cream of tartar. Gradually add sugar mixture, beating constantly. Add lemon and vanilla extracts and mix well. Stir in coconut and spread on cooled cake layers.

Heavenly Coconut Cake

    1 *cup vegetable shortening*
    2 *cups sugar*
    1 *teaspoon vanilla extract*
    6 *eggs*
    2 *cups flour*
    1 *teaspoon salt*
    1 *can flaked coconut*

Cream shortening and sugar; add vanilla and beat well. Add eggs, one at a time, beating well after each addition. Combine flour and salt and add to creamed mixture. Fold in coconut. Pour batter into a greased and floured 10-inch tube pan and bake at 325 degrees F. for 1 hour and 20 minutes or until cake tests done.

Cola Cake

    2 *cups flour*
    2 *cups sugar*
    1½ *cups chopped marshmallows*
    ½ *cup shortening*
    ½ *cup margarine*
    3 *tablespoons cocoa*
    1 *cup cola drink*
    ½ *cup buttermilk*
    1 *teaspoon soda*
    2 *eggs, beaten*

Sift together flour and sugar and stir in marshmallows; set aside. In a saucepan, put the shortening, margarine, cocoa, and cola. Bring to a boil and heat just until shortening and margarine melt. Remove from heat and pour over flour mixture. Stir in buttermilk, soda, and eggs.

Pour into a greased tube pan and bake at 350 degrees F. for 45 minutes, or until cake tests done. Remove from oven and cool in

pan. Cake may crumble slightly. Cake may be baked in a 9- x 9- x 2-inch pan or a loaf-pan, but it will take slightly longer to bake. Cover with Icing.

Note that you do not beat the mixture.

Icing:

    ½ *cup margarine*
    3 *tablespoons cocoa*
    6 *tablespoons cola drink*
    1 *box powdered sugar*
    1 *cup chopped pecans*

Put margarine, cocoa, and cola in saucepan and bring to a boil. When margarine has melted, remove from heat and add sugar and pecans. Spread on cake. (If frosting is too stiff, add a few drops of hot water.)

Honey-Crisp Coffeecake

    1½ *cups flour*
    2 *teaspoons baking powder*
    ½ *teaspoon salt*
    ½ *cup sugar*
    1 *egg, beaten*
    ½ *cup milk*
    3 *tablespoons melted shortening*
    Honey-Crisp Topping

Sift together flour, baking powder, salt, and sugar. Combine egg, milk, and melted shortening; add to flour mixture, stirring until mixture is smooth. Pour into greased 8- or 9-inch cakepan. Top with Honey-Crisp Topping and bake at 400 degrees F. about 25 minutes.

Honey-Crisp Topping:

    3 *tablespoons softened butter or*
        margarine
    ⅓ *cup honey*
    ¼ *cup shredded or flaked coconut*
    ½ *cup crushed corn flakes*
    ½ *cup drained crushed pineapple*

Cream together butter or margarine and honey until light and fluffy. Add remaining ingredients; mix thoroughly. Spread on coffeecake before baking.

Apple Coffeecake

½ *cup shortening*
1 *cup sugar*
1 *teaspoon vanilla extract*
1 *teaspoon salt*
2 *eggs*
2½ *cups flour*
1 *teaspoon baking powder*
1 *teaspoon soda*
1 *cup commercial sour cream*
2 *cups peeled, chopped apples*
½ *cup chopped black walnuts*
½ *cup brown sugar*
1 *teaspoon ground cinnamon*

Cream together shortening, sugar, vanilla, and salt. Add eggs and beat well. Sift together flour, baking powder, and soda; add to creamed mixture alternately with sour cream. Fold in chopped apples.

Pour batter into a greased 13- x 9- x 2-inch pan. Sprinkle top evenly with chopped black walnuts. Combine brown sugar and cinnamon and sprinkle over nuts. Bake at 350 degrees F. for 25 to 30 minutes. Yield: 12 servings.

Daisy Coffeecake

2 *packages dry yeast*
¼ *cup very warm water*
1 *cup milk*
½ *cup sugar*
¼ *cup shortening or oil*
2 *teaspoons salt*
5 *cups sifted flour*
2 *eggs*
2 *tablespoons melted butter or margarine*
¼ *cup sugar*
½ *teaspoon ground cinnamon*
   Powdered sugar icing (optional)

Soften yeast in water. Scald milk. Combine ½ cup sugar, shortening or oil, and salt in large bowl. Add hot milk, stirring until sugar dissolves and shortening is melted. Cool to lukewarm. Stir in about 1½ cups flour and beat well. Beat in softened yeast

and eggs. Stir in enough additional flour to make a soft dough. Turn out on lightly floured board or pastry cloth and knead until smooth and satiny, 5 to 8 minutes.

Shape into ball and place in lightly greased bowl, turning to grease surface of ball. Cover and let rise in warm place (80 to 85 degrees F.) until doubled, about 1½ hours. Punch down. Divide dough in half. Wait 10 minutes; then roll each half of dough to a 12-inch square about ¼ inch thick. Brush half of square with melted butter or margarine. Combine ¼ cup sugar and cinnamon. Sprinkle 4 teaspoons of this mixture over buttered half of dough. Fold unbuttered half over buttered half, sealing edges. Brush half of dough with butter or margarine and sprinkle with 2 teaspoons cinnamon-sugar. Fold in half again, sealing edges. Roll out to 12-inch circle. Place on greased baking sheet.

With scissors or sharp knife cut into 16 wedges, cutting to 1 inch of center. Twist each wedge three times in same direction.

Let rise in warm place until doubled, about 45 minutes.

Bake at 350 degrees F. for 20 to 25 minutes or until golden brown. Brush with powdered sugar icing, if desired. Make icing by adding soft butter and a little cream to powdered sugar to make a thin mixture. Yield: 2 coffeecakes.

Lightly Lemon Coffeecake

2 *tablespoons vinegar*
⅞ *cup canned evaporated milk*
1 *teaspoon soda*
½ *cup soft butter or margarine*
1 *cup sugar*
2 *eggs, well beaten*
1 *teaspoon grated lemon rind*
1¾ *cups unsifted cake flour*
2 *teaspoons baking powder*
½ *teaspoon salt*
½ *cup brown sugar*
1 *tablespoon ground cinnamon*
2 *tablespoons lemon juice*
1 *cup sifted powdered sugar*
   Lemon peel, nuts, cherries (optional)

Combine vinegar and evaporated milk in small bowl; stir in soda. Cream butter and sugar together until fluffy; add eggs and lemon rind, and beat well. Sift flour, baking powder, and salt together; add alternately with milk mixture to creamed mixture, beating well. Mix brown sugar and cinnamon. Spread half of batter in greased, floured 10-inch tube pan; sprinkle with half the cinnamon-sugar. Add remaining batter; sprinkle with rest of cinnamon-sugar. Bake at 350 degrees F. for about 45 to 50 minutes. Cool in pan 5 minutes; remove from pan. Mix lemon juice and powdered sugar, spoon over cake. Garnish with peel, nuts, or cherries. Serve warm. Yield: 16 servings.

Prune and Apricot Coffeecake

    ¾ cup dried prunes
    ¾ cup dried apricots
    ¾ cup shortening
    ¾ cup sugar
    2 eggs
    2 cups flour
    2 teaspoons baking powder
    ½ teaspoon salt
    ¾ cup milk
    1 teaspoon vanilla extract
    ⅔ cup brown sugar
    1 tablespoon flour
    1 tablespoon ground cinnamon
    6 tablespoons melted butter or
          margarine
    ⅓ cup chopped walnuts

Soak fruit in hot water for 5 minutes. Drain and chop fine. Cream shortening and sugar; add eggs, one at a time, beating well after each addition. Sift together dry ingredients; add alternately with milk and vanilla to creamed mixture. Fold in chopped fruit.

Combine brown sugar, flour, and cinnamon. Pour one-third of fruit mixture into oiled and floured 9-inch tube pan. Sprinkle with one-third of brown sugar mixture and one-third of melted butter. Repeat twice. Sprinkle with nuts. Bake at 350 degrees F. for 55 minutes. Cool in pan 25 minutes. Yield: 8 servings.

Peach Skillet Coffeecake

    1 (1-pound) can sliced peaches
    ¼ teaspoon yellow food coloring
    ½ cup sugar
    ¾ cup butter
    1½ cups sugar
    1 egg
    1½ teaspoons vanilla extract
    2½ cups all-purpose flour
    2 teaspoons baking powder
    ½ teaspoon salt
    1 can evaporated milk

Topping:

    ½ cup flour
    ½ cup firmly packed brown sugar
    1 teaspoon ground cinnamon
    ¼ cup butter
    ¼ cup sliced, blanched almonds

Combine peaches, food coloring, and ½ cup sugar in saucepan. Heat to dissolve sugar, stirring occasionally. Keep mixture warm while preparing batter.

Cream butter with 1½ cups sugar until light and fluffy. Beat in egg and vanilla. Combine flour, baking powder, and salt. Add dry ingredients to creamed mixture alternately with milk, beginning and ending with dry ingredients. Beat well after each addition. Spread batter evenly in the bottom of a well-greased, large electric frypan which has been preheated to 280 degrees F.

Carefully spoon peaches over batter. Cover pan tightly with vent closed and bake 20 minutes. Open vent and continue baking 10 minutes longer.

Prepare Topping by combining ½ cup flour with brown sugar and cinnamon. Cut in ¼ cup butter until mixture resembles coarse cornmeal. When cake is done, sprinkle with Topping, then with nuts. Cover pan again, turn off heat and let stand 10 minutes before removing cover.

Sour Cream Coffeecake

  2 *sticks butter or margarine*
1½ *cups sugar*
  1 *cup commercial sour cream*
  2 *eggs, well beaten*
  1 *teaspoon vanilla extract*
  2 *cups all-purpose flour*
  1 *teaspoon baking powder*
  ¼ *teaspoon salt*
  ½ *teaspoon soda*
  1 *cup finely chopped nuts*
1½ *teaspoons sugar*
2½ *teaspoons ground cinnamon*

Cream butter, sugar, and sour cream; add eggs and vanilla and beat well. Combine dry ingredients and add to creamed mixture; beat well. Thoroughly grease a 10-inch tube pan.

Make topping by combining chopped nuts, sugar, and cinnamon. In bottom of the well-greased tube pan put a third of topping mixture; alternate layers of batter and topping, ending with batter. Bake at 350 degrees F. for 45 minutes.

Quick Coffeecake

  1 *package white cake mix*
  6 *tablespoons butter, melted*
  ½ *cup sugar*
  1 *tablespoon dry instant coffee*
  ½ *teaspoon ground cinnamon*
  ½ *cup chopped nuts (optional)*

Prepare cake mix according to directions on package. Pour batter into two greased 9- x 9- x 2-inch pans, and bake at 350 degrees F. for 30 to 35 minutes.

Dribble melted butter over warm cake. Combine sugar, instant coffee, and cinnamon and sprinkle over cake. Chopped nuts may be added if desired. Yield: about 12 servings.

Cupcakes

  1 *cup butter*
  2 *cups sugar*
  4 *eggs*
Flour enough to make mixture as thick as pound cake (about 4 cups sifted flour)
  1 *teaspoon ground nutmeg*
  ½ *teaspoon soda*
  1 *cup milk*

Cream butter and sugar until well blended. Add eggs one at a time and beat well. Sift flour and add nutmeg and soda. Add to mixture alternately with milk. Bake in cupcake pans at 350 degrees F. for 35 to 40 minutes. Yield: about 3 dozen 2-inch cupcakes.

Orange Cupcakes

  ½ *cup shortening or butter*
  1 *cup sugar*
  2 *eggs*
  1 *teaspoon soda*
  ⅔ *cup buttermilk*
  2 *cups flour*
  ½ *teaspoon salt*
  1 *cup raisins or dates*
  1 *cup chopped pecans*
Orange Syrup

Cream shortening or butter with sugar. Add eggs and beat. Add soda to buttermilk and stir well. Add dry ingredients to creamed mixture alternately with buttermilk. Add fruit and nuts. Put in small baking cups and bake at 375 degrees F. for about 12 minutes. Pour Orange Syrup over each cupcake.

Orange Syrup:

>   1 *cup sugar*
>   1 *cup orange juice*
>   1 *tablespoon grated orange rind*

Add sugar to orange juice and grated orange rind. Bring to a boil and pour a tablespoon (or less) over each cooked cupcake.

Truly Different Cupcakes

>   4 *squares unsweetened chocolate*
>   2 *sticks margarine*
>   ¼ *teaspoon butter flavoring*
>   1½ *cups broken pecan meats*
>   1¾ *cups sugar*
>   1 *cup flour*
>   4 *large eggs*
>   1 *teaspoon vanilla extract*

Melt chocolate and margarine in a heavy pan. Add butter flavoring and pecans and stir to coat pecans. Remove from heat.

Combine sugar, flour, eggs, and vanilla and mix only until blended. Do not beat. Add chocolate-nut mixture and again mix carefully, but do not beat. Put into 18 baking cups set in muffin pans. Bake at 325 degrees F. about 30 to 35 minutes.

Easy Cake-Pineapple Filling

>   ⅔ *cup shortening*
>   2 *cups sugar*
>   4 *eggs*
>   3 *cups flour*
>   3 *teaspoons baking powder*
>   ⅛ *teaspoon salt*
>   1 *cup water*
>   1 *teaspoon vanilla extract*
>   1 *teaspoon lemon juice*
>   *Pineapple Filling*
>   *White frosting*

Cream shortening and sugar until smooth. Add eggs, one at a time, beating after each addition. Sift dry ingredients together and add to creamed mixture alternately with water. Stir in vanilla and lemon juice. Bake in 3 greased and floured 8-inch pans at 350 degrees F. 25 minutes or until cake tests done. Cool. Put Pineapple Filling between layers; frost with favorite white frosting.

Pineapple Filling:

>   1 *tall can crushed pineapple, drained*
>   ½ *cup sugar*
>   2 *tablespoons flour*

Combine ingredients in a saucepan. Cook until thick; stir constantly. Cool; spread between layers.

Four-Egg-Rich Cake

>   1 *cup butter*
>   1½ *cups sugar*
>   4 *egg yolks*
>   2 *cups flour*
>   3 *teaspoons baking powder*
>   ¼ *teaspoon salt*
>   1 *cup light cream*
>   1 *teaspoon vanilla extract*
>   4 *egg whites, beaten*

Cream butter and sugar and add 1 unbeaten egg yolk at a time. Mix well; combine flour, baking powder, and salt, and add to creamed mixture alternately with the cream and vanilla. Fold in stiffly beaten egg whites. Bake in two greased 8- or 9-inch cakepans at 350 degrees F. for 25 to 30 minutes. Frost with Easy Chocolate Frosting.

Easy Chocolate Frosting:

>   1 *stick butter or margarine*
>   ⅓ *cup cocoa*
>   2 *cups sugar*
>   ¼ *teaspoon salt*
>   ⅔ *cup evaporated milk*
>   1 *teaspoon vanilla extract*

Melt butter slowly in heavy saucepan. Add other ingredients except vanilla and boil 3 minutes. Add vanilla and cool. Beat to spreading consistency and spread between layers and on top of cake.

Gingerbread

  2   *eggs, beaten*
  ¾   *cup brown sugar*
  ¾   *cup molasses*
  ¾   *cup cooking oil*
2½   *cups flour*
  2   *teaspoons soda*
  2   *teaspoons ground ginger*
1½   *teaspoons ground cinnamon*
  ½   *teaspoon ground cloves*
  ½   *teaspoon ground nutmeg*
  ½   *teaspoon baking powder*
  1   *cup boiling water*

Add beaten eggs to brown sugar, molasses, and oil. Combine dry ingredients and sift; add to egg mixture. Stir in boiling water. Bake in a greased 13- x 9- x 2-inch pan at 350 degrees F. for 25 minutes or until cake is springy to the touch. Yield: 16 servings.

Old-Fashioned Gingerbread

  ⅓   *cup shortening*
  1   *cup sugar*
  2   *eggs*
  ½   *cup molasses*
  1   *cup commercial sour cream*
  2   *cups sifted flour*
  1   *teaspoon soda*
  ½   *teaspoon salt*
1½   *teaspoons ground ginger*
  ¼   *teaspoon ground cloves*

Cream shortening and sugar; add eggs, one at a time, beating well after each addition. Stir in molasses and sour cream. Blend sifted dry ingredients into creamed mixture; beat 2 minutes at medium speed. Bake in greased 13- x 9- x 2-inch pan at 350 degrees F. for 35 minutes, or until cake tests done.

Hot Water Gingerbread

  2   *cups sifted cake flour*
  2   *teaspoons soda*
  1   *teaspoon ground nutmeg*
  2   *teaspoons ground ginger*
  ½   *teaspoon ground cloves*
  ½   *teaspoon ground cinnamon*
  ½   *teaspoon salt*
  ½   *cup shortening*
  1   *cup brown sugar*
  2   *eggs*
  ½   *cup boiling water*
  ½   *cup molasses*

Sift all dry ingredients together three times. Cream shortening; add sugar and unbeaten eggs; beat all thoroughly. Add to dry ingredients, mixing thoroughly; add boiling water and molasses mixed together. (Will be a rather thin batter.) Bake in greased paper-lined 11- x 8-inch pan at 350 degrees F. about 30 minutes, or until done. Allow to remain in pan 5 minutes after removing from oven; then cool on wire rack.

Whole Wheat Gingerbread

  ¼   *cup butter*
  ½   *cup sugar*
  1   *egg, well beaten*
  ½   *cup molasses*
  ½   *cup sour milk*
1¾   *cups whole wheat flour*
  ½   *teaspoon soda*
  2   *teaspoons baking powder*
1½   *teaspoons cinnamon or allspice*
  1   *teaspoon ground ginger*
  ¼   *teaspoon salt*

Cream butter and sugar until smooth. Add well-beaten egg. Mix molasses and milk together. Mix flour with soda, baking powder, spices, and salt. Add dry ingredients to creamed mixture alternately with liquid, adding flour first and last. Bake in a greased 9-inch pan at 350 degrees F. for 35 to 40 minutes.

Lane Cake

  1 *cup butter*
  2 *cups sugar*
  1 *teaspoon vanilla extract*
3¼ *cups all-purpose flour*
3½ *teaspoons baking powder*
 ¾ *teaspoon salt*
  1 *cup milk*
  8 *egg whites, beaten*

Cream butter until smooth; add sugar gradually and beat until light and fluffy. Add vanilla. Combine dry ingredients and add to creamed mixture alternately with milk, beating until smooth. Fold in beaten egg whites. Pour batter into four round 9-inch cakepans greased and lined with paper that has been greased. Bake at 375 degrees F. for about 20 minutes. (If you have only two pans, bake half the batter at a time.) After removing cakes from oven, let stand 5 minutes; then turn out on racks to cool. Spread Lane Frosting between layers and on top and sides of cake. Cake is best if stored for several days before serving.

Lane Frosting:

  8 *egg yolks*
1¼ *cups sugar*
 ½ *cup butter or margarine*
  1 *cup chopped pecans*
  1 *cup finely chopped seedless raisins*
  1 *cup flaked or fresh grated coconut*
  1 *cup finely cut candied cherries*
 ¼ *teaspoon salt*
 ⅓ *cup whiskey or fruit juice*

Beat egg yolks slightly; add sugar and butter. Place in saucepan and cook over medium heat, stirring constantly, for about 5 minutes or until sugar is dissolved and mixture is slightly thickened. (Do not overcook or let egg yolks become scrambled in appearance. Mixture should be almost transparent.) Remove from heat and add remaining ingredients. Let cool before spreading.

Pineapple Loaf Cake

  3 *sticks margarine*
1½ *boxes powdered sugar*
  6 *eggs*
  1 *teaspoon vanilla extract*
  1 *teaspoon lemon juice*
  1 *sugar box of flour*
  1 *large can crushed pineapple (well drained)*

Cream margarine; add sugar and beat well. Add eggs, one at a time, beating well after each addition. Add vanilla and lemon juice. Stir in flour and mix well. Add pineapple (be sure that all juice has been drained). Spoon batter into a greased and floured 10-inch tube pan. Bake at 350 degrees F. for 1½ hours or until cake tests done. No frosting is needed for this cake; it keeps well.

Mary Dawson Ware's White Fruitcake

  1 *pound butter*
  1 *pound sugar*
16 *egg whites*
  1 *pound flour*
  2 *teaspoons baking powder*
  1 *grated coconut*
 ¼ *pound light citron, chopped*
 ½ *pound crystallized cherries, chopped*
 ¼ *pound crystallized pineapple, chopped*
  1 *pound blanched almonds, chopped*
 ½ *pound English walnuts, chopped*

Cream butter and sugar. Beat egg whites well. Mix flour and well-beaten whites of eggs alternately with creamed mixture, reserving a little flour for coating fruits. Add baking powder, then the grated coconut and beat well. Stir in fruits and mix thoroughly. Add nuts last.

Pour into a greased and floured large tube pan or several loafpans and bake at 350 degrees F. for 4 or 5 hours or until an inserted straw comes out clean. Temperature of oven may be reduced after 10 minutes. Yield: about 6 pounds.

Lemon-Pecan Fruitcake

    1   *box brown sugar*
    1   *pound margarine*
    6   *egg yolks, beaten*
    2   *cups flour*
    1   *teaspoon baking powder*
    2-ounce bottle lemon extract
    1   *quart chopped pecans*
    ½   *pound candied pineapple, chopped*
    ½   *pound candied cherries, chopped*
    2   *cups flour*
    6   *egg whites, beaten*

Cream together sugar and margarine until smooth; add beaten egg yolks and mix well. Combine 2 cups flour and baking powder and add to creamed mixture. Add lemon extract. Coat pecans, pineapple, and cherries with 2 cups flour and add to creamed mixture. Fold in beaten egg whites. Cover and let stand overnight.

The next day, put mixture into a greased tube pan and bake at 250 degrees F. for 2½ hours, or until cake tests done.

Japanese Fruitcake

    1   *cup butter or margarine*
    2½   *cups sugar*
    ½   *cup milk*
    6   *eggs, beaten*
    4   *cups flour*
    ¼   *teaspoon salt*
    1   *teaspoon ground cloves*
    1   *teaspoon ground allspice*
    1   *teaspoon ground cinnamon*
    2   *teaspoons baking powder*
    1   *cup chopped nuts*
    1   *cup seedless raisins*

Cream butter or margarine and sugar; add milk. Beat well. Add beaten eggs. Combine dry ingredients; mix into batter and add

nuts and raisins. Reserve 1¾ cups of batter for Filling. Bake in three greased 8-inch cakepans at 375 degrees F. about 25 minutes.

Filling:

    2   *cups sugar*
    1   *cup water or coconut milk*
    1¾   *cups cake batter*
         Juice and grated rind of 2 lemons
    1   *large grated coconut or 2 cans*
         coconut
    1   *cup chopped nuts*
    3   *tablespoons melted butter or*
         margarine
    ¼   *cup green candied cherries*
    ¼   *cup candied pineapple*

Combine sugar and water or coconut milk, and boil until slightly syrupy. Add the reserved cake batter, lemon juice, and rind. Cook until thickened, stirring constantly. Then add coconut, nuts, melted butter or margarine, and chopped candied fruits. Spread between layers and on cake.

Kentucky Bourbon Cake

    ¾   *pound butter*
    2   *cups sugar*
    6   *eggs*
    ½   *cup molasses*
    4   *cups all-purpose flour*
    1   *heaping teaspoon baking powder*
    2   *teaspoons ground nutmeg*
    1   *pound raisins*
    1   *cup chopped candied pineapple*
    1   *cup chopped candied cherries*
    1   *cup orange marmalade*
    2   *pounds shelled pecans, chopped*
    1   *large cup bourbon*
         Apple slices

Cream butter and sugar; add eggs, one at a time, beating well after each addition. Add molasses and mix well. Sift together flour, baking powder, and ground nutmeg. Put fruits, marmalade, and nuts in large bowl. Add about 1 cup of flour mixture and stir to coat fruit. Add remainder of flour to creamed mixture alternately with whiskey. Stir in fruits and nuts.

Grease 1 large mold or two smaller ones (two large loafpans are right size); line with heavy brown paper which has been greased. Spoon batter into pans and cover with greased brown paper. Bake at 250 degrees F. until toothpick or cake tester inserted in center comes out clean (about 2½ to 3 hours).

Wrap cake in cloth which has been dampened with whiskey; place in a tin container. Add apple slices and cover container. Let sit until cake has "ripened." A month would not be too long to let ripen.

Italian Cream Cake

  1 *stick margarine*
  ½ *cup vegetable shortening*
  2 *cups sugar*
  5 *egg yolks*
  2 *cups flour*
  1 *teaspoon soda*
  1 *cup buttermilk*
  1 *teaspoon vanilla extract*
  1 *small can angel flake coconut*
  1 *cup chopped nuts*
  5 *egg whites, stiffly beaten*
  Cream Cheese Frosting

Cream margarine and shortening; add sugar and beat until mixture is smooth. Add egg yolks and beat well. Combine flour and soda and add to creamed mixture alternately with buttermilk. Stir in vanilla. Add coconut and chopped nuts. Fold in stiffly beaten egg whites. Pour batter into three greased and floured 8-inch cakepans. Bake at 350 degrees F. for 25 minutes or until cake tests done; cool. Frost with Cream Cheese Frosting.

Cream Cheese Frosting:

  1 *(8-ounce) package cream cheese, softened*
  ½ *stick margarine*
  1 *box powdered sugar*
  1 *teaspoon vanilla extract*
  Chopped pecans

Beat cream cheese and margarine until smooth; add sugar and mix well. Add vanilla and beat until smooth. Spread between layers and on top and sides of cake. Sprinkle top with pecans. Yield: enough for three 8-inch layers.

Molasses Layer Cake

  ½ *cup butter or margarine*
  ½ *cup sugar*
  1 *cup unsulphured molasses*
  2 *egg yolks*
  2½ *cups self-rising flour*
  ½ *teaspoon salt*
  ¼ *teaspoon ground allspice*
  1 *teaspoon ground cinnamon*
  ¼ *teaspoon ground cloves*
  ½ *cup milk*
  ½ *cup raisins*
  ¾ *cup chopped nuts*
  2 *egg whites, stiffly beaten*
  Molasses-Mocha Icing

Cream butter and sugar; add molasses and egg yolks and beat well. Combine flour, salt, and spices and add to creamed mixture alternately with milk, putting raisins and nuts in the last addition of flour mixture. Fold in stiffly beaten egg whites.

Put batter into three greased and floured 8-inch layer cake pans and bake at 350 degrees F. about 25 minutes or until cake tests done. Put layers together with Molasses-Mocha Icing. If icing is desired for sides of cake, make 1½ times the recipe.

Molasses-Mocha Icing:

  3 *tablespoons molasses*
  3 *tablespoons evaporated milk*
  3 *teaspoons boiled coffee*
  4 *tablespoons soft butter or margarine*
  1 *teaspoon vanilla extract*
  About 2 cups powdered sugar
  Chopped nuts

Combine all ingredients except powdered sugar and nuts. Sift sugar into liquid and beat well. Add enough sugar to make icing the consistency to spread. Sprinkle with chopped nuts. Yield: enough to ice between 3 (8-inch) layers.

Arkansas Blackberry Jam Cake

    3 cups sifted flour
    1 teaspoon soda
    ¼ teaspoon salt
    1 teaspoon each: allspice, cloves,
          cinnamon, nutmeg
    1 cup chopped pecans
    1 cup candied citron or drained
          watermelon rind preserves,
          chopped
    1 cup butter
    1½ cups sugar
    3 eggs, well beaten
    1 cup blackberry jam
    1 cup buttermilk

Sift together flour, soda, salt, and spices. Sift a little of the flour mixture over the nuts and citron. Cream butter until soft and smooth. Gradually add sugar and beat until light and fluffy. Beat in eggs and jam. Add flour mixture alternately with buttermilk. Beat until smooth after each addition. Fold in nuts and citron or watermelon rind. Pour into three 9-inch layer pans and bake at 350 degrees F. for 20 to 25 minutes. Spread butter-sugar icing between layers and over cake.

Kiss Cakes

    4 egg whites
    2 cups fine, granulated sugar
    1 tablespoon cornstarch
    Dash of salt
    1 teaspoon vanilla extract
    3 drops almond extract
    1 cup broken pecan meats

Beat the egg whites very stiff; add sugar a little at a time, stirring in with a fork. It is very important to add only a little bit of sugar at a time, beginning as the eggs pile up and taking plenty of time and thought as you go. Sprinkle in the cornstarch and the salt. Add the flavorings. Next add the pecans, sprinkling in a few at a time. Drop mixture by the tablespoonfuls on brown paper; place on a cookie sheet and bake at

350 degrees F. for 45 minutes. They are done when you can lift them from the paper. This is a famous party cookie, served often with fruit punch at large gatherings. Yield: 2½ dozen cookies.

Orange Slice Cake

    1 cup butter or margarine
    2 cups sugar
    4 eggs
    1 teaspoon soda
    ½ cup buttermilk
    3½ cups all-purpose flour
    1 pound dates, chopped
    1 pound candy orange slices, chopped
    2 cups chopped nuts
    1 can flaked coconut
    1 cup fresh orange juice
    2 cups powdered sugar

Cream butter or margarine and sugar until smooth. Add eggs, one at a time, and beat well after each addition. Dissolve soda in buttermilk and add to creamed mixture. Place flour in large bowl and add dates, orange slices, and nuts. Stir to coat each piece.

Add flour mixture and coconut to creamed mixture. This makes a very stiff dough that should be mixed with the hands. Put in a greased and floured 13- x 9- x 2-inch cakepan. Bake at 250 degrees F. for 2½ to 3 hours. Combine orange juice and powdered sugar and pour over hot cake. Let stand in pan overnight.

Peach Tart Viennese

    ¼ cup butter or margarine
    ¼ cup powdered sugar
    1 cup sifted flour
    1 tablespoon cornstarch
    2 tablespoons sugar
    ¼ teaspoon ground mace
    ½ cup orange juice
    ½ cup currant jelly, melted
    8 large fresh peaches
    Whipped cream

Cream butter and powdered sugar (adding sugar gradually and creaming constantly); then add flour, mixing to form soft dough. Pat on bottom and sides of a 12-inch pizza pan. Bake in 350-degree F. oven for 20 minutes.

Combine cornstarch, sugar, mace, and orange juice in a saucepan. Cook over very low heat until thick and clear, stirring constantly. Stir in melted currant jelly. Allow to cool slightly. While glaze is cooling, peel, slice, and arrange peaches in a single layer in the baked pie shell. Spoon the glaze evenly over the peaches. Chill in refrigerator. Garnish with whipped cream before serving. Yield: 6 to 8 servings.

Easter Dawn Cake

⅔ *cup soft butter*
1¾ *cups sugar*
2 *eggs*
1½ *teaspoons vanilla extract*
3 *cups sifted cake flour*
2½ *teaspoons baking powder*
1 *teaspoon salt*
1¼ *cups milk*
  Red food coloring
¼ *teaspoon peppermint flavoring, if desired*
1 *(6½-ounce) package fluffy white frosting mix*

Beat butter, sugar, eggs, and vanilla 5 minutes at high speed on mixer or by hand until fluffy. Sift dry ingredients together. Add to creamed mixture, 4 tablespoons at a time, alternately with milk (start and end with dry ingredients). Blend on low speed just until smooth.

Put two-thirds of the batter into three greased and floured 8- or 9-inch round or square layer pans. To rest of batter add food coloring and peppermint flavoring. Pour here and there over plain batter in pans. Cut through batter with knife several times for marbled effect. Bake at 350 degrees F. for 30 to 35 minutes or until toothpick inserted in center of cake comes out clean. Frost with fluffy white frosting mix, lightly tinted with red food coloring. For lots of frosting, use 2 packages frosting.

Pecan Cake

1 *stick butter or margarine*
2 *cups sugar*
4 *eggs*
2 *squares unsweetened chocolate, melted and cooled*
2 *cups sifted all-purpose flour*
1½ *pounds (6 cups) shelled pecans*

Cream butter; add sugar and beat until smooth. Add eggs, one at a time, beating well after each addition. Add cooled chocolate and mix well. Sift flour and mix with pecans. Pour batter into flour and pecans and mix well.

Grease tube pan and line with heavy brown paper that has been oiled (this is the secret of the cake; paper must be very heavy). Cover top of cake with oiled paper. Bake at 250 degrees F. 2 to 3 hours, or until cake tests done.

Cake may also be baked in large loafpan and two smaller ones; doubled recipe will fill three large loafpans.

Pearl McGinley's Pecan Cake

1 *cup butter*
2½ *cups sugar*
3½ *cups flour*
2 *teaspoons baking powder*
1 *teaspoon salt*
1 *cup sweet milk or whiskey or some of each*
1 *quart pecan meats*
1 *pound raisins*
  Spices to suit

Cream butter and sugar. Add dry ingredients alternately with milk. Stir in pecans, raisins, and spices. Put in greased and floured tube pan and bake at 275 degrees F. for 3 to 4 hours or until done. Ice with caramel icing.

Jet Prune Cake

    4 cups sifted cake flour
    2 teaspoons soda
    3 cups sugar
    6 eggs
    2 cups vegetable oil
    2 cups buttermilk
    2 teaspoons ground nutmeg
    2 teaspoons ground cinnamon
    1 teaspoon salt
    2 cups chopped, cooked prunes

Sift cake flour, soda, and sugar together. Beat eggs for 1 minute. Add eggs and remaining ingredients to flour mixture and beat 3 minutes. Pour into 3 greased and floured 9-inch pans. Bake in moderate (350-degree) oven for 35 to 40 minutes.

Icing:

    Whites of 3½ eggs
    4 cups powdered sugar
    3 cups soft butter
    1 teaspoon vanilla extract
    1 teaspoon lemon extract
    Dash of salt
    ½ cup chopped nuts (optional)

For the Icing, beat egg whites; add sugar gradually, then add butter, vanilla extract, and lemon extract. Add salt. Mix thoroughly. If desired, sprinkle top of iced cake with chopped nuts.

Pound Cake

    4½ cups sifted cake flour
     2 teaspoons double-acting baking
           powder
     1 teaspoon salt
     2 cups butter
    2½ cups sugar
    2½ teaspoons vanilla extract
     ¼ teaspoon ground mace
     8 eggs
     ½ cup milk
        Orange Butter Glaze
        Flaked coconut

Sift flour with baking powder and salt. Cream butter 10 minutes or until *very soft and fluffy.* Add sugar, 2 tablespoons at a time, creaming thoroughly after each addition. Blend in vanilla and mace. Thoroughly beat in eggs, one at a time. Add flour mixture alternately with milk, beginning and ending with flour and beating after each addition until smooth. Bake in a greased and floured 10-inch tube pan at 325 degrees F. for about 1 hour and 30 minutes or until cake tester inserted into cake comes out clean. Cool in pan 15 minutes; remove and finish cooling on rack. Glaze top and drizzle down sides of cake with Orange Butter Glaze. Sprinkle with flaked coconut. *Note:* Cake is easier to slice when wrapped tightly in plastic wrap or aluminum foil and stored overnight.

Orange Butter Glaze:

    2 tablespoons orange juice
    1 tablespoon milk
    1 tablespoon butter
    2½ cups sifted powdered sugar
    ½ teaspoon grated orange rind (op-
           tional)

Heat orange juice, milk, and butter until butter melts. Add to sugar in a small bowl; then beat until smooth. Add rind. (Increase liquid if thinner consistency is desired.) Yield: ¾ cup.

Brown Sugar Pound Cake

    1 cup shortening
    1 stick margarine
    1 box light brown sugar, sifted
    5 eggs
    3 cups flour
    ½ teaspoon salt
    ½ teaspoon baking powder
    1 cup evaporated milk
    2 teaspoons maple flavoring
       Brown Sugar Frosting

Cream shortening, margarine, and sifted brown sugar. Add eggs, one at a time, beating well after each addition. Sift dry ingredients and add them alternately with milk. Add flavoring. Pour mixture into greased and floured tube pan; bake at 300 degrees F. for 1½ hours. Cover with Brown Sugar Frosting.

Brown Sugar Frosting:

     1 *stick margarine*
     1 *cup brown sugar*
    ¼ *cup milk*
     3 *cups powdered sugar*
     1 *teaspoon vanilla extract*

Melt margarine on medium heat. Add brown sugar and stir 1 minute. Add milk, powdered sugar, and vanilla and blend until creamy.

Pineapple Pound Cake

    ½ *cup vegetable shortening*
    ½ *pound butter or margarine (2 sticks)*
   2¾ *cups sugar*
     6 *large eggs*
     3 *cups sifted all-purpose flour*
     1 *teaspoon baking powder*
    ¼ *cup milk*
     1 *teaspoon vanilla extract*
    ¾ *cup undrained crushed pineapple and juice*
    ¼ *cup butter or margarine (½ stick)*
   1½ *cups powdered sugar*
     1 *cup crushed pineapple, drained*

Cream shortening, butter, and sugar. Add eggs, one at a time, beating thoroughly after each addition. Add flour sifted with baking powder, 1 spoonful at a time, alternately with milk.

Add vanilla; stir in crushed pineapple and juice and blend well. Pour batter into well-greased 10-inch tube pan.

Place in cold oven. Turn oven to 325 degrees F. and bake for 1½ hours or until top springs back when touched lightly. Let stand for few minutes in pan. Run knife around edges and remove carefully to rack.

Combine butter, powdered sugar, and about 1 cup drained pineapple. Pour over cake while hot.

One-Two-Three-Four Pound Cake

     1 *cup shortening*
     2 *cups sugar*
     4 *eggs*
     2 *teaspoons vanilla extract*
     3 *cups flour*
    ½ *teaspoon soda*
    ½ *teaspoon salt*
     1 *cup buttermilk*

Cream shortening and sugar. Add eggs one at a time and beat between each addition. Add vanilla and then alternately add the dry ingredients and buttermilk. Put batter in a greased tube pan. Bake at 325 degrees F. until light golden brown, about an hour and 15 minutes.

Chocolate Pound Cake

     1 *cup butter or margarine*
    ½ *cup shortening*
     3 *cups sugar*
     5 *eggs*
     1 *teaspoon vanilla extract*
     3 *cups flour*
    ½ *teaspoon baking powder*
    ½ *teaspoon salt*
     4 *tablespoons cocoa (may be heaping if desired)*
     1 *cup milk*

Cream together butter and shortening. Add sugar and mix well. Add eggs, one at a time, beating after each addition. Add vanilla. Combine dry ingredients and add alternately with milk to creamed mixture. Bake in greased 10-inch tube pan at 325 degrees F. for 80 minutes.

Infallible Pound Cake

1½ *cups vegetable shortening*
2½ *cups sugar*
  8 *eggs*
  3 *cups flour, sifted*
  1 *teaspoon lemon extract*
  1 *teaspoon vanilla extract*
  1 *teaspoon almond extract*

Cream shortening and sugar until smooth. Add eggs, one at a time, beating well after each addition. Add flour, stir well, then add flavorings. Bake in a greased tube pan at 325 degrees F. for 1½ hours.

Coconut Pound Cake

  2 *sticks butter or margarine*
 ½ *cup vegetable shortening*
  3 *cups sugar*
  6 *eggs*
 ½ *teaspoon almond flavoring*
  1 *teaspoon coconut flavoring*
  3 *cups all-purpose flour*
  1 *cup milk*
  1 *can flaked coconut*

Cream butter, shortening, and sugar until light and fluffy. Add eggs, one at a time, beating well after each addition. Add flavorings and mix well. Alternately add flour and milk, beating after each addition. Stir in coconut. Spoon batter into 10-inch greased tube pan or Bundt pan. Bake at 350 degrees F. for 1 hour and 15 minutes.

Dolley Madison Pound Cake

  1 *pound butter*
  1 *pound granulated sugar*
 12 *eggs, separated and beaten*
  1 *pound flour, sifted twice*
 ½ *pound pitted dates*
 12 *almonds, skinned*
  6 *tablespoons honey*

Cream the butter and sugar together. Add well-beaten egg yolks and stiffly beaten egg whites alternately with flour to the creamed sugar-butter mixture. Beat. When very light, pour into a well-greased and floured round pan. The pan should be large enough to hold the entire mixture plus an inch or more at the top of the pan. Bake in a moderate oven (350 degrees) until golden brown. Baking should be slow and watched carefully. Allow to cool while in the pan. When cooled, remove from pan and decorate with dates and almonds. Pour honey over the top for glaze.

Raisin Cake

  1 *cup raisins*
  2 *cups water*
 ½ *cup shortening*
  1 *cup sugar*
1⅓ *cups all-purpose flour*
  1 *teaspoon soda*
  1 *teaspoon ground cloves*
  1 *teaspoon ground cinnamon*
  1 *teaspoon ground nutmeg*
 ½ *cup finely chopped nuts*

Simmer raisins in the water for 10 minutes. Remove from heat; add shortening and stir till melted. Cool. Combine dry ingredients; add nuts and add this mixture to the raisin mixture. Put into a greased loafpan and bake at 350 degrees F. for 35 to 40 minutes.

Raisin-Pecan Cake

  1 *cup butter*
  2 *cups sugar*
  6 *eggs, beaten*
 ½ *cup molasses*
  2 *teaspoons soda*
  3 *cups all-purpose flour*
 ½ *teaspoon salt*
  2 *pounds seedless raisins*
  1 *pound (4 cups) chopped pecans*
 ½ *cup flour*

Cream butter and sugar until smooth. Add beaten eggs and mix well. Stir in molasses, to which soda has been added. Combine 3 cups flour and salt and add to creamed mixture. Coat raisins and pecans with ½ cup flour and stir into batter, which will be very stiff. Place batter in a 10-inch tube pan, which has been lined with well-oiled heavy brown paper. Bake at 250 degrees F. for 4 hours. Cool in pan; then turn out on cake rack and remove brown paper. Wrap in a cloth that has been dampened with grape juice. Store several days before serving. Yield: 16 to 20 servings.

Raisin-Nut Cake

(100-year-old German-originated recipe)

½ cup shortening
1 cup white sugar
¾ cup brown sugar (packed)
3 egg yolks
2 cups plus 2 teaspoons flour
1 teaspoon baking powder
¾ teaspoon soda
1 teaspoon salt
1 cup buttermilk
½ cup chopped pecans
½ cup dark or light seedless raisins
1 tablespoon maple flavoring
3 egg whites, beaten stiff

Cream shortening and sugars; add egg yolks, one at a time, beating well after each addition. Sift dry ingredients together. Put buttermilk, nuts, and raisins in blender, or chop very fine. Add this mixture alternately with dry ingredients to creamed mixture. Add flavoring; fold in stiffly beaten egg whites. Put batter in two 9-inch layers, three 8-inch layers, or a 13- x 9- x 2-inch pan. Grease pans before adding batter. Bake at 350 degrees F. about 25 to 35 minutes. When cool, cover with Icing.

Icing:

½ cup butter
1 cup brown sugar (packed)
¼ cup milk
1¾ cups powdered sugar

Combine butter, brown sugar, and milk. Boil over low heat for 2 to 4 minutes. Remove from heat and beat thoroughly. Cool. Add powdered sugar and beat well. Chopped nuts, coconut, or maple flavoring may be added. Spread between layers and on top of cake.

Pumpkin-Raisin-Nut Cake

2 cups sugar
1 cup cooking oil
4 eggs
2 cups self-rising flour
2 teaspoons ground cinnamon
½ teaspoon ground nutmeg
1 (No. 2) can pumpkin or 2 cups fresh, cooked pumpkin
¾ cup seedless raisins
1 cup nuts (your choice)
¼ cup cooking oil
¼ cup self-rising flour

Using medium speed of electric mixer, cream sugar and cooking oil until smooth. Add eggs one at a time, mixing thoroughly after each addition. Sift flour with spices three times. Add to creamed mixture and mix until smooth. Add pumpkin and mix thoroughly. Mix the raisins and nuts with the ¼ cup cooking oil and the ¼ cup flour. Using low speed of mixer add mixture to cake batter. Pour into 2 greased and floured 9-inch layer cake pans (round or square). Bake at 325 degrees F. for 30 to 35 minutes or until cake is done.

While cake is warm, ice with Lemon-Cheese Icing or your own favorite icing.

Lemon-Cheese Icing:

¾ box powdered sugar
1 (8-ounce) package cream cheese
Pinch of salt
Juice and rind of one lemon
2 tablespoons evaporated milk

Mix all ingredients and heat until of spreading consistency.

Raisin-Date-Pecan Cake

> 1   *cup butter*
> 2   *cups sugar*
> 4   *eggs*
> 1⅓   *cups buttermilk*
> 1   *teaspoon soda*
> 4   *cups all-purpose flour, divided*
> 1   *cup seedless raisins*
> 1   *cup finely chopped pecans*
> 1   *(1-pound) box pitted dates, chopped*
> 4   *tablespoons grated orange peel*

Cream butter and sugar until light and fluffy. Add eggs one at a time, beating well after each addition. Add buttermilk and mixture of soda and 3 cups flour and mix well. Mix 1 cup flour with raisins, pecans, and dates. Stir until all pieces are coated; then add to creamed mixture. Add orange peel and mix well. Put batter in a greased 10-inch tube pan and bake at 350 degrees F. about 1½ hours.

South Carolina Sally White Cake

> 2   *large coconuts, grated*
> 2   *pounds citron, finely cut*
> 2   *pounds almonds, blanched*
> 1   *pound butter*
> 2½   *cups sugar*
> 12   *egg yolks*
> 1   *teaspoon each: mace, cinnamon, and*
>   *nutmeg*
> 1   *cup sherry or brandy*
> 4   *cups sifted all-purpose flour*
> 12   *egg whites, beaten*

Prepare coconuts, citron, and almonds a day ahead. Cream butter, add sugar, and cream thoroughly together. Add well-beaten egg yolks and spices mixed with wine. Combine flour with coconut, citron, and almonds. Beat egg whites until stiff, and add alternately with floured fruits to creamed mixture. If batter is too stiff, add more wine. Bake in greased, paper-lined pans at 325 degrees F. for 2 hours. Yield: a 10-pound cake.

White Cake

> 1   *cup butter*
> 2   *cups sugar, sifted*
> 3½   *cups cake flour*
> ½   *teaspoon salt*
> 4   *teaspoons baking powder*
> 1   *cup milk*
> 1   *teaspoon vanilla extract*
> ¼   *teaspoon almond extract*
> 7   *or 8 egg whites*
> ⅛   *teaspoon salt*

Cream butter until soft. Sift in sugar gradually. Blend these ingredients until they are very light and creamy. Sift cake flour before measuring. After measuring, resift it twice with the ½ teaspoon salt and baking powder. Add flour in three parts alternately with milk divided into three parts. Beat the batter until it is smooth after each addition. Add vanilla and almond extract. Whip egg whites until stiff but not dry. Add ⅛ teaspoon salt. Fold egg whites lightly into cake batter. Bake in a greased 13- x 9-inch pan at 350 degrees F. about 40 minutes, or in three 8-inch pans for 25 minutes at 375 degrees F.

> *Decorating Butter Cream:*
> *(For icing cake and for making*
> *decorations)*
>
> 2   *cups vegetable shortening*
> 1   *cup powdered sugar*
> ½   *cup egg whites*
> 1   *cup granulated sugar*

Cream shortening and powdered sugar in electric mixer until light and fluffy; remove to largest bowl of mixer. Heat egg whites and granulated sugar in double boiler to 150 degrees F. (be sure to use candy thermometer; exact temperature is important). Then whip for several minutes on medium-high speed to make a thick meringue. Add half of meringue to first mixture and beat for about 10 minutes. Add rest of meringue and beat at medium-high speed until icing holds its shape. Add flavoring and coloring as desired. Keep stored in covered container in refrigerator until ready for use.

Buttermilk White Cake

¾ *cup vegetable shortening*
2¼ *cups sugar*
8 *egg whites*
3 *cups all-purpose flour*
¼ *teaspoon salt*
¾ *teaspoon cream of tartar*
¾ *cup buttermilk*
1 *teaspoon vanilla extract*
⅜ *teaspoon soda*
2 *tablespoons warm water*

Cream shortening and sugar. Add egg whites (unbeaten) alternately with flour, salt, and cream of tartar which have been sifted together. Add all of buttermilk at one time before adding last portion of dry ingredients. Stir in vanilla and beat well. Dissolve soda in warm water and add last; stir well. Bake in three oiled 8-inch layer cake pans at 350 degrees F. from 20 to 25 minutes or until cake pulls away from sides of pan. This cake can also be baked in a large tube pan (about 1 hour) or a 13- x 9-inch pan (about 40 to 45 minutes). Frost, if desired.

Irish Potato Cake

1 *cup butter*
2 *cups sugar*
2 *cups cooked mashed potatoes*
1 *teaspoon vanilla extract*
1 *teaspoon lemon extract*
1 *teaspoon ground cloves*
1 *teaspoon ground allspice*
1 *teaspoon ground cinnamon*
1 *teaspoon ground nutmeg*
½ *cup milk*
2 *cups flour*
1 *tablespoon soda*
½ *cup cocoa*
4 *eggs, well beaten*
1 *cup chopped nuts*
1 *cup raisins*
¼ *cup flour*

Cream butter and sugar. Add potatoes, ex-

tracts, and spices and mix well. Add milk. Combine flour, soda, and cocoa and add to creamed mixture. Add well-beaten eggs. Dredge nuts and raisins with ¼ cup flour and add to batter. Pour into a greased 10-inch tube pan and bake at 300 degrees F. for 2 hours.

French Pecan Torte

1 *heaping tablespoon breadcrumbs*
4 *cups finely ground pecans*
1 *grated lemon rind*
8 *egg whites*
1 *cup sugar*
8 *egg yolks, beaten*
Juice of ½ lemon
2 *cups cream*
Pecan halves, garnish

Combine breadcrumbs, ground pecans, and lemon rind in a large mixing bowl. Place the 8 egg whites in another mixing bowl and beat until stiff, gradually adding the sugar.

In still another installment beat the already beaten egg yolks with lemon juice until thick and lemon-creamy.

Now pour the egg whites over the pecan mixture. Then very carefully fold ingredients together, now pouring the egg yolk mixture over and into the egg whites. *Do not stir mixture or cake will fall!* Careful folding of ingredients is absolutely essential.

When properly folded together, pour the whole mixture into a greased 12-inch spring-form pan and bake in a moderate (375-degree) oven. Bake 45 minutes. Remove from oven and cool in the pan. Remove cooled cake from pan and slice in half, side to side, making two layers.

Whip the heavy cream until thick. Spread bottom half with whipped cream, and replace top layer.

Frost the top and sides of cake with remaining whipped cream. Garnish artistically with pecan halves.

This flamboyant delicacy should be served with a flair—gourmet style.

Huguenot Torte

4 *eggs*
3 *cups sugar*
8 *tablespoons flour*
5 *teaspoons baking powder*
2 *cups chopped tart apples*
2 *cups chopped pecans*

Beat whole eggs until very frothy and lemon colored. Add other ingredients and mix well; pour into two 12- x 8-inch well-buttered pans. Bake at 350 degrees F. about 45 minutes or until crusty and brown. Let cool. Cut in squares; lift with pancake turner, keeping crusty part on top. Serve with whipped cream.

Black Forest Torte

1¾ *cups all-purpose flour*
1¾ *cups sugar*
1¼ *teaspoons soda*
1 *teaspoon salt*
¼ *teaspoon baking powder*
⅔ *cup soft margarine or butter*
4 *(1 ounce each) squares unsweetened chocolate, melted and cooled*
1¼ *cups water*
1 *teaspoon vanilla extract*
3 *eggs*
Chocolate Filling
Cream Filling
½ *of 4-ounce sweet chocolate bar*

Measure into a large mixing bowl flour, sugar, soda, salt, baking powder, margarine, melted chocolate, water, and vanilla. Beat at low speed to blend. Then beat at medium speed for 2 minutes, scraping sides and bottom of bowl frequently. Then add eggs and beat for an additional 2 minutes.

Spoon into four 9-inch round layer cake pans which have been greased (approximately 1¼ cups batter in each). Layers will be very thin. If preferred, only two layers may be baked at a time. Bake at 350 degrees F. from 15 to 18 minutes or until wooden pick inserted in center comes out clean. Cool

slightly; then remove from pans. Cool thoroughly before adding filling.

Place bottom layer of cake on serving plate and spread with half of Chocolate Filling. Add another layer and spread with half of Cream Filling. Repeat layers, having Cream Filling on top. Using a vegetable peeler, make chocolate curls with the ½ bar of sweet chocolate. Decorate top completely. Sides of torte do not have frosting. Wrap with plastic wrap and refrigerate until ready to serve. Yield: 12 servings.

Chocolate Filling: Melt 1½ sweet chocolate bars (4 ounces each) over hot water. Cool; blend in ¾ cup margarine. Stir in ½ cup chopped almonds or pecans.

Cream Filling: Whip together 2 cups whipping cream with 1 tablespoon sugar and 1 teaspoon vanilla; do not overbeat.

Special Cake

2 *cups crushed pineapple and juice*
1½ *cups grated coconut*
1 *cup pecans, if desired*
1 *box yellow cake mix*
2 *sticks margarine, sliced in ¼-inch squares*

Pour crushed pineapple and juice into a greased 14- x 10-inch pan (or two 8-inch pans). Cover with coconut and pecans (if desired). Spread dry cake mix over mixture. Place squares of margarine over entire top of cake. Bake at 350 degrees F. for about 25 minutes or until brown. Serve with ice cream or whipped cream. Yield: about 12 to 15 servings.

Old Virginia Rocky Mountain Cake

1 *cup butter*
2 *cups sugar*
3 *cups flour*
3 *teaspoons baking powder*
4 *eggs, beaten*

Cream butter and sugar together; work in

flour that has been sifted with baking powder. Beat eggs until lemon colored and mix well with batter. Pour into two greased and floured 8-inch round cakepans and bake at 375 degrees F. for about 25 minutes or until cake begins to come away from the sides of pans. Cool for about 15 minutes on racks before removing from pans.

Filling:

Boiled icing
½ *pound currants*
1 *pound seedless raisins, chopped*
¼ *pound blanched almonds, chopped*
½ *pound fresh grated coconut*
¼ *pound blanched almonds, whole*

Make boiled icing and mix currants, raisins, and chopped almonds with it when it is of spreading consistency. Spread Filling between layers and on top and sides of cake. Sprinkle coconut over cake and decorate top with whole almonds.

Pecan-Date Loaf

1 *pound whole pitted dates*
1 *pound pecan halves*
1 *cup sifted all-purpose flour*
½ *teaspoon salt*
2 *teaspoons baking powder*
4 *egg yolks*
½ *cup sugar*
½ *cup dark corn syrup*
4 *egg whites*
2 *teaspoons vanilla extract*

In a large bowl place whole dates, pecan halves, flour, salt, and baking powder. Mix together with a spoon so that dates and nuts are well coated.

In a smaller bowl beat egg yolks until creamy, add sugar, beat until thick, and stir in corn syrup. Pour into date-pecan mixture and stir well. Fold in stiffly beaten egg whites. Add vanilla and spoon into well-greased, floured 9½- x 5½- x 2½-inch loaf-pan.

Bake at 325 degrees F. for 1 to 1¼ hours or until cake tester is clean.

Rum Cake

1 *cup butter*
2 *cups sugar*
3½ *cups sifted cake flour*
8 *egg whites, stiffly beaten*
1 *cup milk*
3½ *teaspoons baking powder*
1 *teaspoon vanilla extract*
Pinch salt

Cream butter; gradually add sugar and continue creaming until smooth. Sift flour; measure and keep out 2 tablespoons. To the creamed mixture, add rest of flour, egg whites, and milk alternately in thirds. Beat well after each addition.

Next mix the baking powder with the 2 tablespoons flour and add after the cake is thoroughly mixed. Beat vigorously. Add vanilla and salt last. Bake in two greased 8- x 8- x 2-inch layer cake pans at 350 degrees F. about 20 to 30 minutes.

Filling:

⅔ *cup butter*
½ *cup rum*
2½ *cups sifted powdered sugar*

Mix all ingredients thoroughly and set in refrigerator to thicken. Put between layers and put cake in refrigerator to set Filling before frosting. Frost with your favorite frosting, using rum for flavoring.

Yellow Mold Cake

3 *sticks butter*
1 *(1-pound) box powdered sugar*
6 *eggs*
2½ *cups flour*
½ *teaspoon salt*
1 *teaspoon vanilla extract*
1 *teaspoon lemon extract*

Cream butter and sugar until smooth. Add eggs, one at a time, beating well after each addition. Add flour, salt, vanilla and lemon extracts, and beat well. Bake in greased 10-inch tube pan at 325 degrees F. for 1 hour.

Tutti-Frutti Loaf Cake

    2¼ cups flour
    1¼ cups sugar
    1½ teaspoons baking powder
     1 teaspoon salt
     ½ cup soft shortening
     ½ cup milk
     1 teaspoon vanilla extract
     4 egg whites (½ cup), beaten
     ¼ cup chopped nuts
     1 cup chopped mixed candied fruit
     2 tablespoons flour

Combine dry ingredients in large bowl. Add shortening, milk, and vanilla; beat well. Add egg whites and beat an additional 2 minutes. Fold in nuts and fruits which have been coated with 2 tablespoons flour. Bake in a large greased loafpan at 350 degrees F. for 60 to 65 minutes or until cake tests done.

Meringue Spice Cake

     ¾ cup shortening
     2 cups brown sugar
     2 beaten egg yolks
    2⅓ cups flour
     ¾ teaspoon salt
     1 teaspoon baking powder
     1 teaspoon ground cinnamon
     1 teaspoon ground cloves
     1 teaspoon soda in 1¼ cups buttermilk
     1 teaspoon vanilla extract

Cream shortening and sugar. Add egg yolks and beat until fluffy. Sift dry ingredients together; add to creamed mixture alternately with milk, beating after each addition. Add vanilla. Pour into greased and floured pan, about 13 x 9 x 2 inches.

Meringue:

     2 egg whites
     1 cup brown sugar
     ½ cup chopped nuts

Beat egg whites; add sugar gradually as in other meringues. Spread over batter. Sprinkle with nuts. Bake at 325 degrees about 50 minutes. Cut in squares to serve.

Black Walnut Cake

     ½ cup butter
     2 cups brown sugar
     3 egg yolks, beaten
     2 cups flour
     3 teaspoons baking powder
     ½ teaspoon salt
    ⅔ cup milk
     1 teaspoon vanilla extract
     1 cup black walnuts, chopped fine or
        ground
     3 egg whites, beaten

Cream butter; add sugar and beat until smooth. Add beaten egg yolks and mix well. Combine dry ingredients and add to creamed mixture alternately with milk. Add vanilla and walnuts and mix well. Fold in stiffly beaten egg whites.

Bake in greased tube pan at 350 degrees F. for 45 minutes.

Strawberry Shortcake

     2 cups all-purpose flour
     3 teaspoons baking powder
     ¾ teaspoon salt
     3 tablespoons sugar
     1 (3-ounce) package cream cheese,
        softened
     3 tablespoons softened butter or
        margarine
     1 egg, beaten
    About ½ cup milk
    Melted butter
    Sweetened strawberries
    Whipped cream

Sift together flour, baking powder, salt, and sugar. Cut in cream cheese and butter. Pour beaten egg into measuring cup and add enough milk to measure ¾ cup. Gradually stir into the flour mixture. Knead dough about 20 seconds. Divide dough into two parts; roll each part ½ inch thick. Cut 6 circles from each half of dough. Spread one circle with melted butter and place another circle on top. Bake at 425 degrees F. about 15 minutes.

When done, separate layers. Spread each

layer with butter. Put sweetened berries on one circle and top with other circle. Add strawberries and top with whipped cream. Continue until all circles have been used. Yield: 6 servings.

Strawberry Shortcake

  2 *cups flour*
  3 *teaspoons baking powder*
 ½ *teaspoon salt*
  2 *tablespoons sugar*
 ⅓ *cup shortening*
 ⅔ *cup milk*
   Melted butter
  1 *quart strawberries*
1½ *cups sugar*
   Whipped cream

Sift flour, baking powder, salt, and 2 tablespoons sugar. Add shortening and cut in until mixture resembles coarse crumbs. Add milk and mix well. Divide dough and pat into two round 8-inch cakepans. Brush with melted butter and bake at 450 degrees F. for 15 to 18 minutes.

Prepare strawberries and mix with 1½ cups sugar. Reserve some whole berries for garnish and crush the other berries with a fork. Let sit until sugar is melted and syrup forms. Spread berries between layers of shortcake and on top. Serve with whipped cream, garnished with whole berries.

Strawberry Refrigerator Cake

  6 *ladyfingers or 1 small sponge cake*
  3 *tablespoons sugar*
1¼ *cups crushed strawberries*
 ⅓ *cup heavy cream*
 ¼ *teaspoon vanilla extract*
  1 *tablespoon chopped nuts*

Line springform pan with split ladyfingers or sliced sponge cake. Add sugar to strawberries. Whip cream with vanilla. Cover cake with berries, then a layer of whipped cream. Repeat in layers until all material is used, saving part of cream for top of cake.

Sprinkle with nuts and chill for 8 hours. Yield: 2 servings.

Holiday Jam Cake

2 *cups sugar*
1 *cup butter or vegetable shortening*
3 *eggs*
1 *cup buttermilk*
1 *cup jam (any kind)*
3 *cups sifted cake flour*
1 *teaspoon soda*
1 *cup chopped nuts*
1 *cup chopped dates*
1 *cup raisins*
1 *apple, grated*

Cream sugar and butter; add eggs and mix well. Combine buttermilk and jam. Add alternately with combined dry ingredients to the creamed mixture. Add nuts and fruits. Mix well. Bake in three greased 9-inch cakepans at 350 degrees F. for 30 minutes. Turn out on racks to cool before icing the cake.

  Filling:

2 *cups sugar*
2 *tablespoons flour*
1½ *cups milk*
1 *cup butter*
1 *cup chopped nuts*
1 *cup cookie coconut*
1 *cup chopped dates*
1 *cup raisins*
1 *apple, grated*

Mix sugar and flour; add milk and butter. Cook until mixture thickens, stirring occasionally. Remove from heat and stir in nuts, coconut, dates, raisins, and apple. Spread Filling between layers and over top of cake.

Candies and Confections

Visitors to New Orleans always feel it's a *must* to carry back a box of pralines to the folks at home. This thin, sweet wafer of candy loaded with pecans (and calories) is a rare treat unmatched in any other area of the South.

Peanuts and pecans, grown abundantly in the South, are staple ingredients of favorite candies. Peanut brittle and peanut butter fudge are two of the more popular candies using peanuts in some form. As for pecans, if they are not stirred into a candy itself, we manage some way to press a pecan half into shaped candy rolls. And Texas shares the south-of-the-border flavor with a special Mexican pecan candy.

Divinity, fudge, and penuche are candies that have long been favored for Christmas-giving.

Divinity

    2 cups sugar
    ½ cup white corn syrup
    ½ cup water
       Dash of salt
    2 egg whites, stiffly beaten
    1 teaspoon vanilla extract
    ¾ cup broken pecans

In a saucepan over low heat place the sugar, corn syrup, water, and salt. Stir until sugar is dissolved; then cook without stirring to 252 degrees F. (hard ball stage). Remove from heat and pour into stiffly beaten egg whites, beating constantly. Continue beating until mixture loses its gloss. Add vanilla and pecans and drop quickly from tip of spoon onto waxed paper, or spread in greased pan and cut in squares when cold. Yield: 18 to 24 pieces.

All the Christmas decorations are not on the Christmas tree; artist-cooks throughout the South take pride in their colorful cakes, cookies, and candies.

Ripple Divinity

    3 cups sugar
    ½ cup water
    ½ cup white corn syrup
    2 egg whites, stiffly beaten
    1 teaspoon vanilla extract
    1 cup chocolate pieces

Combine sugar, water, and corn syrup in a 2-quart saucepan. Cook over high heat to boiling stage; reduce heat and continue cooking until mixture reaches 240 degrees F. Slowly pour one-third of the mixture over the egg whites, beating constantly. Cook remaining syrup to 265 degrees F.; then gradually add to first mixture. Beat until mixture will hold its shape when dropped from a spoon. Add vanilla and fold in chocolate pieces. (Since the mixture is warm, the chocolate pieces will partially melt and give a rippled appearance to the divinity.) Drop from teaspoon onto a greased baking sheet. Yield: about 4 dozen.

Note: Black walnuts or shredded coconut may be substituted for chocolate pieces.

Brown Sugar-Cocoa Fudge

   1 *pound light brown sugar*
   2 *cups white sugar*
   Dash of salt
   6 *tablespoons cocoa*
  ¼ *teaspoon cream of tartar*
   3 *tablespoons light corn syrup*
   1 *cup milk*
   3 *tablespoons butter or margarine*
   2 *teaspoons vanilla extract*

Mix brown sugar, white sugar, salt, cocoa, and cream of tartar in a heavy aluminum 4-quart saucepan. Add corn syrup and milk. Stir well until sugar dissolves. Bring to boil and cook to soft ball stage (234 degrees F.), stirring constantly. Remove from heat. Add butter and vanilla extract. Beat until glossy and beginning to thicken. Pour into a buttered 11- x 7- x 1½-inch pan to cool. Cut into squares. Yield: 2½ to 3 pounds.

Chocolate Fudge

  ¾ *cup milk*
   2 *squares unsweetened chocolate or 4*
       tablespoons cocoa
   2 *cups sugar*
   Dash of salt
   2 *tablespoons white corn syrup*
   2 *tablespoons butter*
   1 *teaspoon vanilla extract*
  ¾ *cup chopped pecans*

Cook milk and unsweetened chocolate in heavy saucepan over low heat until blended, stirring constantly. Do not let boil. Stir in sugar, salt, and corn syrup and cook without stirring to 234 degrees F. (soft ball stage). Remove from heat and add butter, vanilla, and pecans. Cool to lukewarm and then beat until it holds its shape. Pour into a greased 8- x 8- x 2-inch pan and cut in squares. Yield: about 18 large pieces.

Hawaiian Fudge

 2½ *cups sugar*
   1 *cup rich milk or cream*
   1 *small can crushed pineapple, drained*
   1 *cup pecans*
   Few drops green food coloring

Combine sugar, milk or cream, and well-drained pineapple. Bring to a boil over medium heat and cook until mixture reaches the soft ball stage. Remove from heat and add pecans and coloring. Let cool slightly and then beat until creamy. Pour into a greased loafpan, cool, and cut into squares. Yield: 18 squares.

Opera Fudge Log

   2 *cups sugar*
  ¾ *cup heavy or light cream*
  ½ *cup milk*
   1 *tablespoon light corn syrup*
  ⅛ *teaspoon salt*
   1 *teaspoon vanilla extract*
  ¾ *cup chopped walnuts*
   6 *squares semisweet chocolate*

Combine sugar, cream, milk, corn syrup, and salt in heavy saucepan. Place over low heat and stir until mixture begins to boil. Continue boiling, stirring frequently to prevent scorching, until mixture will form a soft ball in cold water (or to a temperature of 234 degrees F.). Remove from heat. Wipe pouring edge of saucepan with damp cloth; then pour mixture into clean pan. Cool until lukewarm (110 degrees F.) without stirring. Add vanilla; beat until candy loses its gloss. Add nuts and continue stirring until candy can be handled. Place on foil or waxed paper; knead and shape into a log 7 inches long. Cool.

    Partially melt chocolate over hot water. Remove from water; stir rapidly until entirely melted. Spread some of the melted chocolate over top and sides of log. Turn log when firm, and coat bottom with remaining chocolate. Slice the log crosswise. Yield: about 1½ pounds.

Crunchy Peanut Butter Fudge

2 *cups sugar*
1 *cup milk*
2 *cups marshmallow cream*
1 *(12-ounce) jar crunchy peanut butter*
1 *teaspoon vanilla extract*

Combine sugar and milk. Bring to a boil; stir and cook over medium heat to soft ball stage (234 degrees on candy thermometer). Remove from heat. Stir in marshmallow cream, peanut butter, and vanilla. Beat until well blended and spread into a greased 9-inch square pan. Cool and cut in squares. Yield: about 2 pounds.

Peanut Butter Fudge

2 *cups sugar*
⅔ *cup milk*
½ *pint jar marshmallow cream*
1 *cup chunk-style peanut butter*
1 *(6-ounce) package semisweet chocolate pieces*
1 *teaspoon vanilla extract*

Butter sides of heavy 2-quart saucepan. In saucepan combine sugar and milk. Heat and stir over medium heat until sugar dissolves and mixture comes to boil; cook to soft ball stage (234 degrees F.). Remove from heat and add other ingredients. Stir until blended. Pour into buttered 9-inch square pan. Score in squares while warm.

Raisin Snacks

⅓ *cup margarine*
4 *cups miniature marshmallows*
5½ *cups crisp rice cereal*
1½ *cups currants or raisins*
1 *cup roasted peanuts*

Melt margarine and marshmallows in large pan. Stir constantly. Remove from heat and add cereal, raisins, and peanuts; stir until well coated. Press into greased 13- x 9-inch pan. Cool. Cut into squares.

Pecan Pralines

2 *cups granulated sugar*
1 *teaspoon soda*
1 *cup buttermilk*
⅛ *teaspoon salt*
2 *tablespoons butter*
2½ *cups broken pecans*
1 *teaspoon vanilla extract*

In large heavy saucepan combine sugar, soda, buttermilk, and salt. Cook over high heat for 5 minutes, stirring often. Scrape bottom of pan; add butter and pecans and continue cooking, about 5 minutes, until candy reaches soft ball stage. Remove from heat and add vanilla; cool slightly. Beat until creamy. Quickly drop by tablespoonfuls onto waxed paper and let cool.

Pralines

1 *box brown sugar*
1 *cup white sugar*
¼ *pound butter*
2 *cups broken pecans*
4 *tablespoons white corn syrup*
⅔ *cup water*
Pinch of salt
1 *teaspoon vanilla extract*

Combine all ingredients except vanilla in a heavy saucepan. Cook until syrup reaches the soft ball stage. Remove from heat and cool slightly. Add vanilla and beat until it begins to thicken. Drop by spoonfuls onto waxed paper. Yield: about 18 pralines.

Cobblestone Candy

3 *cups semisweet chocolate pieces*
2 *cups miniature marshmallows*
1 *cup coarsely chopped walnuts*

Melt chocolate pieces over hot, not boiling, water. Stir until smooth. Add marshmallows and walnuts. Line 8-inch square pan with aluminum foil. Turn chocolate mixture into foil-lined pan and let stand until firm. Cut into squares. Yield: 1⅔ pounds.

Leche Quemada

2½ *cups sugar*
1 *small can evaporated milk*
Water
2 *tablespoons butter or margarine*
2 *tablespoons light corn syrup*
½ *cup sugar*
1 *tablespoon butter or margarine*
2 *cups coarsely chopped pecans*

Put sugar in heavy saucepan. Measure evaporated milk into measuring cup; add water to make 1 cup. To the sugar add milk, 2 tablespoons margarine, and corn syrup. Bring to a boil; add the additional ½ cup sugar and 1 tablespoon margarine. Add pecans and cook to the soft ball stage. Remove from heat; beat until creamy. Drop by spoonfuls onto greased cookie sheets or a marble slab.

Mexican Pecan Candy

2 *cups sugar*
1 *cup milk*
2 *tablespoons butter*
2 *tablespoons white corn syrup*
½ *teaspoon salt*
¼ *teaspoon soda*
1 *cup chopped pecans*
1 *teaspoon vanilla extract*

Mix all ingredients except pecans and vanilla in a large saucepan and bring to a boil. When mixture comes to a boil, add pecans and cook until it reaches 234 degrees F. or until it forms a soft ball when dropped in cold water. Add vanilla and beat until creamy. Drop by spoonfuls on waxed paper, or spread in buttered pan and cut in squares. Yield: about 24 pieces.

Date and Nut Roll

2 *cups fine vanilla wafer crumbs*
1 *cup coarsely cut dried dates*
½ *cup coarsely chopped pecans*
½ *cup sweetened condensed milk*
2 *teaspoons lemon juice*
Whipped cream

In medium-size mixing bowl combine vanilla wafer crumbs, dates, and pecans. In measuring cup combine condensed milk and lemon juice; pour into crumb mixture and knead well. Form into a roll about 3 inches thick and 3½ inches long. Wrap and refrigerate at least 12 hours. Slice and serve with whipped cream.

Marzipan

1 *(7-ounce) package flaked coconut*
1 *(3-ounce) package fruit-flavored gelatin (dry)*
1 *cup finely chopped nuts*
⅔ *cup sweetened condensed milk*
1½ *teaspoons sugar*
1 *teaspoon almond extract*

Mix coconut, gelatin, nuts, condensed milk, sugar and almond extract together. Chill and shape as desired. Chill until dry and then store covered at room temperature. Yield: about 3 dozen candies.

Peanut Brittle

2 *cups sugar*
1 *cup light corn syrup*
½ *cup water*
2 *cups broken peanuts*
1 *tablespoon butter*
1 *teaspoon vanilla extract*
1 *teaspoon soda*

In a large saucepan cook sugar, syrup, and water until it reaches hard ball stage when dropped in a cup of water. Add peanuts and cook until golden brown. Add butter and vanilla; stir until well mixed. Add soda and stir well. Do not stir too long after adding soda. (This is the secret of this candy.) Pour into buttered pan or onto a marble slab. Yield: 2 pounds.

Iced Almonds

  1 *cup whole blanched almonds*
  ½ *cup sugar*
  2 *tablespoons butter or margarine*
  ½ *teaspoon vanilla extract*
  ¾ *teaspoon salt*

Heat almonds, sugar, and butter in heavy skillet over medium heat, stirring constantly, until almonds are toasted and sugar is golden brown (about 15 minutes). Stir in vanilla. Spread almond mixture on a sheet of aluminum foil; sprinkle with salt. Cool; break into 2- or 3-nut clusters.

Prissy Pecans

  2 *teaspoons powdered instant coffee*
  ¼ *cup sugar*
  ¼ *teaspoon ground cinnamon*
  2 *tablespoons water*
  Dash salt
  2 *cups pecan halves*

Combine all ingredients in saucepan. Bring to a boil over medium heat and boil 3 minutes, stirring constantly. Spread on waxed paper and separate pecan halves as they cool. Pecans will be sugar coated, but not sticky.

Chocolate Fondant

  2 *cups sugar*
  Dash salt
1¼ *cups water*
  2 *tablespoons light corn syrup*
  2 *tablespoons butter*
  1 *teaspoon vanilla extract*
  4 *squares semisweet chocolate, melted*

Combine sugar, salt, water, and corn syrup. Place over low heat and stir constantly until sugar is dissolved and mixture boils. Cover and cook 3 minutes; then remove cover and continue boiling without stirring. Wipe down sides of pan occasionally with damp cloth. Cook until a small amount of syrup forms a soft ball in cold water (or to a temperature of 234 degrees F.).

Remove from heat. Add butter and pour out on cold, wet platter or on greased surface. Cool to lukewarm (110 degrees F.). Work with paddle or spatula until white and creamy. Add vanilla and knead until smooth. Shape into ball; make indentation in top and pour about one-fourth of chocolate into it. Knead until chocolate is blended. Repeat until all chocolate is used.

Store in tightly covered jar to ripen for several days. If fondant begins to dry out, cover with damp cloth. Yield: 1⅛ pounds.

Chocolate Balls: Prepare Chocolate Fondant as directed. Add 1 cup finely cut raisins to ripened fondant. Knead and shape into small balls. Roll in tinted flaked coconut. (Raisins may be omitted.) Yield: 6 dozen balls.

Chocolate Coconut Drops: Prepare Chocolate Fondant as directed. Melt ripened fondant in top of double boiler, keeping water in lower part just below boiling point. Add 1 cup flaked coconut, mixing well. Drop from teaspoon onto waxed paper. (If mixture is not stiff enough to hold its shape, cool a little before dropping.) Yield: 3 dozen drops.

Chocolate Coconut Slices: Prepare Chocolate Fondant as directed. Add ¾ cup finely cut raisins and ¾ cup flaked coconut to ripened fondant and knead. Shape into rolls 1 inch in diameter. Wrap in waxed paper and chill. When firm, cut in ¼-inch slices. Yield: about 1¾ pounds candy.

Black Cat Popcorn Balls

1½ *cups light, mild molasses*
½ *cup sugar*
¼ *cup water*
2 *teaspoons cider vinegar*
½ *teaspoon salt*
5 *tablespoons vegetable shortening*
2 *teaspoons vanilla extract*
3 *quarts popped corn*

Combine molasses, sugar, water, vinegar, and salt; cook slowly, stirring constantly, to 270 degrees F. (hard ball stage). Remove from heat; add shortening and vanilla, stirring just to mix. Pour over popcorn, stirring constantly. Grease hands; quickly shape popcorn into balls. Cool. Wrap in transparent plastic wrap, if desired. Yield: 24 medium-size balls.

Peanut Popcorn Balls

2 *quarts popped corn*
⅔ *cup corn syrup*
⅔ *cup sugar*
½ *teaspoon salt*
1 *cup roasted peanuts*

Put popped corn in deep kettle. Mix syrup, sugar, and salt in heavy saucepan. Cook 2 minutes, stirring constantly. Pour over popped corn and stir over medium heat 3 to 5 minutes. Add peanuts gradually to this mixture. Remove from heat. Rub hands in butter and shape popcorn mixture into balls. Work as quickly as possible. Wrap popcorn balls in plastic wrap. Yield: 20 balls.

Apricot-Coconut Balls

1½ *cups dried apricots, ground*
2 *cups moist, shredded coconut*
½ *cup ground pecans*
1 *can sweetened condensed milk*
Colored coconut

In a large mixing bowl blend together apricots, coconut, and ground pecans. Stir in condensed milk. Shape into small balls and roll in colored coconut. Let stand in air until firm.

Chocolate Balls

2 *sticks margarine*
1½ *cups graham cracker crumbs*
½ *cup chopped pecans*
1 *cup freshly grated coconut*
1 *box powdered sugar*
1 *tablespoon vanilla extract*
1 *(12-ounce) jar crunchy peanut butter*
1 *(6-ounce) package semisweet chocolate bits*
½ *cake paraffin wax (half of ¼-pound size)*

Melt margarine in large container. Stir in graham cracker crumbs, pecans, coconut, powdered sugar, and vanilla; add peanut butter and mix well. Roll into walnut-size balls and lay out on waxed paper. Melt chocolate and paraffin together over hot water. Using 2 teaspoons (or any method you prefer), dip each ball into mixture, returning to waxed paper. The balls will cool quickly and be pretty and glossy. Yield: 6 dozen balls.

Bourbon Balls

3 *cups vanilla wafers, rolled to a dust*
3 *tablespoons corn syrup*
1 *cup powdered sugar*
½ *cup powdered cocoa*
1 *cup finely chopped pecans*
½ *cup bourbon*

Mix all ingredients together. Shape into small balls (about ½ inch in diameter). Roll balls in powdered sugar, cocoa, or finely shredded coconut. Rum may be substituted for bourbon. Yield: about 50 balls.

Ringa-Lings

  1 *(6-ounce) package semisweet*
      chocolate pieces
  1 *cup corn flakes*
  ½ *cup shredded or flaked coconut*
  1 *teaspoon vanilla extract*
  1 *cup salted peanuts*

Melt chocolate over hot, not boiling, water. Stir in corn flakes, coconut, vanilla, and peanuts. Drop by teaspoonfuls onto waxed paper and put in refrigerator until firm. Yield: 2 dozen.

Penuche

  1 *pound light brown sugar*
  ¾ *cup light cream or half-and-half*
  1 *tablespoon light corn syrup*
  2 *tablespoons butter*
  1 *teaspoon vanilla extract*
  1 *cup coarsely chopped walnuts or*
      pecans

Into large saucepan measure all ingredients except vanilla and nuts. Heat to boiling, stirring constantly, and boil gently to 234 degrees F. or until a few drops in cold water form a soft ball. (Don't worry if mixture curdles; beating will make it smooth.) Remove from heat and let stand without stirring until bottom of pan feels lukewarm; then stir in flavoring and nuts, and beat with spoon until thick and creamy and mixture begins to lose its gloss. Pour into buttered 8-inch square pan. Cut into squares while warm. Yield: about 1 pound.

Coconut-Stuffed Prunes

  1 *cup flaked coconut*
  1 *cup walnuts*
  ¼ *cup honey*
  2 *teaspoons lemon juice*
  3 *dozen drained cooked, pitted prunes*

Grind coconut and walnuts in food chopper; mix well. Add honey and lemon juice, mixing thoroughly. Fill prune centers with mixture. Yield: 3 dozen stuffed prunes.

Tiny Tim's Tree

  1 *(4¼-ounce) package puffed rice*
  1 *cup small gumdrops*
  1 *(3-ounce) jar red cinnamon candies*
  ½ *cup butter or margarine*
  1 *pound fresh marshmallows (about*
      64)
    Few drops green food coloring

Using heavy brown paper, make large cone about 15 inches tall and 7 inches in diameter at the base.

  Heat puffed rice in 350-degree F. oven for 10 minutes. Pour into large greased bowl; add gumdrops and red candies. Melt butter and marshmallows in top of double boiler over boiling water; stir until smooth. Add food coloring. Pour over puffed rice; stir until evenly coated.

  With greased hands pack mixture into cone, reserving 1 cup for base of tree. Pack the 1 cup into greased custard cup. Cool 2 hours or longer. Carefully unwrap paper from tree. Using spatula, loosen base from cup. With 4 toothpicks attach base to tree.

Coconut-Candied Apples

12 *medium apples*
2 *cups firmly packed brown sugar*
1 *cup granulated sugar*
1 *cup light corn syrup*
1 *cup water*
2 *tablespoons butter*
2 *teaspoons vanilla extract*
3 *cups shredded coconut*

Wash and dry apples; remove stems. Stick wooden skewers into stem ends. Combine sugars, corn syrup, water, and butter in deep, small saucepan. Cook over low heat until sugar is dissolved, stirring constantly. Continue cooking, without stirring, until a few drops poured into a cup of cold water become slightly brittle (or to a temperature of 272 degrees F.). Remove from heat. Add vanilla. Dip apples quickly, one at a time, into hot syrup, until they are coated. Roll in shredded coconut and place apples upright on well-greased cookie sheet to cool. Apples may be wrapped in plastic wrap.

No-Bake Crunchies

¼ *cup peanut butter*
1 *(6-ounce) package butterscotch chips*
4 *cups corn flakes, crushed*

Slowly melt peanut butter and butterscotch chips. Place crushed corn flakes in large bowl; pour peanut butter mixture over corn flakes and stir until well mixed. Drop by teaspoonfuls onto waxed paper and let cool. Yield: 24 pieces.

Apples-on-a-Stick

8 *medium red apples*
3 *cups sugar*
½ *cup light corn syrup*
½ *cup water*
1 *drop oil of cinnamon*
1 *teaspoon red vegetable coloring*

Wash and dry apples; remove stems. Insert wooden skewers in stem end of apples. Combine sugar, corn syrup, and water in heavy deep saucepan. Cook over medium heat, stirring constantly until mixture boils. Then cook without stirring to soft crack stage (285 degrees F.) or until a small amount separates into threads which are hard but not brittle when tested in very cold water. Remove from heat; add flavoring and coloring and stir only to mix. Hold each apple by skewer end and quickly twirl it in syrup, tilting pan to cover apple with syrup. Allow excess to drip off; then twirl to spread syrup smoothly over apple. Place on lightly buttered baking sheet to cool. Store in cool place. Yield: 8 apples.

Goblin Treats

⅓ *cup margarine or butter*
1 *pint marshmallow cream*
½ *teaspoon vanilla extract*
6 *cups (6-ounce package) bite-size shredded rice biscuits*
½ *cup chopped peanuts*

Heat margarine and marshmallow cream over hot water until thin and syrupy. Do not let water boil. Stir occasionally. Add vanilla and beat thoroughly. Put rice biscuits and peanuts into a large greased bowl. Pour on marshmallow mixture. Stir briskly until bite-size biscuits are well coated. Let stand 5 minutes before shaping into balls. Wrap and tie on wreath. Yield: 18 (2-inch) balls.

Variation: Dissolve 1 cup semisweet chocolate bits in marshmallow mixture before pouring over cereal.

Directions for Making Wreath: Bend a wire coathanger into a circle. Wrap hanger with tissue paper. Padding should be about 2 inches in diameter. Fasten with tape wherever needed. Cover padding with orange crepe paper. Using 8- to 9-inch pieces of string, tie balls onto wreath. Form two rows of balls. Fill center space with a picture or cutout of a jack-o-lantern. Attach plastic scissors and a bow.

Note: For a 13-inch wreath, about 36 balls (2 recipes) are needed.

Peanut Butter-Fruit Squares

 1 *cup pitted, dried dates*
 ½ *cup seedless raisins*
 ½ *cup currants*
 ¼ *cup sweetened condensed milk*
 1 *cup peanut butter*
 Powdered sugar

Put fruits through food chopper into medium-size mixing bowl. Add condensed milk and peanut butter; stir until blended. Sprinkle bottom of 8- x 8- x 2-inch pan with sugar. Turn mixture into pan and press evenly on bottom. Sprinkle top with sugar. Refrigerate until firm. Cut into 1-inch squares with sharp knife.

Cereals

Two cereals that are most popular in the South are grits and rice. Grits actually is another name for a coarsely ground hominy (in some sections called hominy grits).

Grits, customarily served at breakfast, may be used as a basis for casserole dishes. Cold grits, sliced and fried, make "second go-round" servings just as popular as the first.

Arkansas, Louisiana, Mississippi, and Texas are the largest rice-producing states in the country, and more rice probably is consumed in our Southern region than in any other. Rice can be served with butter or with cream gravy. It can be used as a basis for many regional stews and served with many dishes, such as Shrimp Creole (recipe below). Rice pudding probably was developed in some Southern kitchen from leftover rice with the addition of eggs, cream, butter, and raisins. In Charleston, tomato sauce may be added to the basic ingredients to make red rice, and in Louisiana cooked rice and red beans are often combined.

Macaroni, noodles, and spaghetti are other cereals used extensively, especially in casserole dishes. These cereals are used a great deal in vegetable soup, a hearty dish that is almost a meal in itself.

Shrimp Creole

  1½ *pounds shrimp, fresh or frozen*
  ¼ *cup chopped onion*
  ¼ *cup chopped green pepper*
  1 *clove garlic, finely chopped*
  ¼ *cup butter or other fat, melted*
  3 *tablespoons flour*
  1 *teaspoon chili powder*
Dash pepper
  1 *teaspoon salt*
  2 *cups canned tomatoes*
Cooked rice

Peel shrimp, remove sand veins, and wash. Cut large shrimp in half. Cook onion, green pepper, and garlic in butter until tender; blend in flour and seasonings. Add tomatoes

and cook until thick, stirring constantly. Add shrimp and simmer uncovered about 20 minutes. Serve over rice. Yield: 6 servings.

Cheese Grits

  4 *cups boiling water*
  1 *teaspoon salt*
  1 *cup instant grits*
  1 *stick butter or margarine*
  1 *roll garlic cheese*
  2 *eggs*
Milk

Bring salted water to rolling boil and slowly stir in grits. Cook 3 minutes, stirring constantly. Remove from heat and stir in margarine and garlic cheese. Put eggs in cup and add milk to make 1-cup measure. Beat well and add to grits mixture.

Bake in greased, 2-quart casserole at 300 degrees F. for 1 hour. Yield: 6 servings.

Rice is a popular Southern cereal. In Louisiana, Shrimp Creole is served on a mound of rice.

Grits and Sausage

    4 *cups water*
    1 *teaspoon salt*
    1 *cup grits*
  ½ *cup cornmeal*
      Black pepper to taste
    1 *pound tenderloin pork sausage*

Bring to a boil 4 cups salted water; add grits and cook about 3½ minutes. Add ½ cup cornmeal and black pepper and mix thoroughly. Cut up the pork sausage; add and mix with grits and cornmeal mixture. Put in loafpan and chill overnight in refrigerator. Cut in slices about ¾ inch thick and fry on both sides until brown. Yield: about 8 servings.

Tomato-Grits Casserole

  ½ *cup quick-cooking grits*
    2 *cups boiling water*
    1 *teaspoon salt*
    1 *quart stewed tomatoes (fresh or*
        canned)
  ¾ *cup sugar*
  ¼ *cup butter*

Add grits to rapidly boiling water to which salt has been added; stir well and cook until thick, stirring often. Combine tomatoes, sugar, and butter; heat. Combine with grits, blending well. Simmer gently for 5 minutes. Yield: 6 to 8 servings.

Glorified Grits

 1½ *cups quick-cooking grits*
   6 *ounces coarsely shredded American*
      cheese
   2 *tablespoons Worcestershire sauce*
   1 *tablespoon Tabasco sauce*
  ½ *teaspoon garlic powder*
  ½ *stick margarine or butter*
   1 *egg, beaten*
      Paprika

Cook grits as directed on the package. While grits are hot, add the other ingredients. Place in a 2-quart baking dish. Sprinkle paprika on top for color. Bake at 300 degrees F. for about 40 minutes or until firm but not too dry. Yield: 4 to 6 servings.

Grits With Summer Sausage

Cook grits for 6 according to package directions. Five minutes before grits are done, add 1 pound summer sausage, skinned, split lengthwise twice, and cut into ⅛-inch chunks. Serve with a generous pat of butter. With fruit juice, toast and coffee, this makes a breakfast that will stick to the ribs.

Cheese-Stuffed Manicotti With Meat Sauce

  ½ *pound ground beef*
  ⅓ *cup chopped green pepper*
   1 *large clove garlic, minced*
   1 *teaspoon Italian seasoning, crushed*
   2 *(10¾-ounce) cans condensed tomato*
      soup
  ½ *cup water*
   4 *cups (2 pounds) creamed cottage*
      cheese
   2 *eggs, slightly beaten*
  ½ *cup grated Parmesan cheese*
  ½ *cup chopped parsley*
   1 *package (5 to 8 ounces) manicotti*
      macaroni, cooked
   3 *slices (3 ounces) mozzarella cheese,*
      cut in half

In saucepan, brown meat and cook green pepper, garlic, and Italian seasoning until green pepper is tender. Stir in soup and water. Meanwhile, combine cottage cheese, eggs, Parmesan, and parsley; use to fill manicotti macaroni. Arrange manicotti in a shallow baking dish (16 x 10 x 2 inches); cover with sauce. Bake at 350 degrees F. for 45 minutes. Top with mozzarella. Bake until cheese melts. Yield: 4 to 6 servings.

Macaroni Loaf

4½ cups uncooked elbow macaroni
5 teaspoons salt
9 quarts boiling water
1 cup butter
1 cup chopped pimiento
1 cup minced parsley
3 teaspoons pepper
9 cups milk
6 cups soft breadcrumbs
9 cups shredded Cheddar cheese
¾ cup minced onion
18 eggs, beaten

Cook macaroni in salted water for 12 minutes. Drain and cool macaroni. Mix all ingredients in a large bowl. Place in 3 loaf-pans and bake at 350 degrees F. about 40 minutes. Yield: 24 servings.

Skip's Tuesday Night Macaroni

1 pound ground beef
Salt and pepper
1 (10½-ounce) can beef bouillon
1 (10½-ounce) can onion soup
1 (10¾-ounce) can tomato soup
1 (4-ounce) can mushrooms in butter, undrained
1 chicken bouillon cube
8 ounces cut macaroni
3 tablespoons butter or salad oil
Grated Romano or Parmesan cheese

Season ground beef with salt and pepper; brown in heavy skillet without additional fat. Add soups, mushrooms, and bouillon cube; simmer until well blended.

In a large heavy saucepan sauté macaroni in butter or salad oil until macaroni turns slightly yellow. Pour beef mixture into saucepan with macaroni, mix well, and bring to a boil. Cover and cook over lowest possible heat for about 20 minutes. Remove from heat, stir in cheese, and serve immediately. Yield: 4 to 6 servings.

Italian Delight

½ pound shell macaroni
2 pounds chuck beef, ground
3 medium onions, chopped
1 medium green pepper, minced
1 bud garlic, minced (optional)
¼ pound butter or margarine
4 (8-ounce) cans tomato sauce
1 (No. 2) can whole-kernel corn
3 (3-ounce) cans mushrooms and liquid
1 tablespoon brown sugar
1 tablespoon Worcestershire sauce
2 tablespoons chili powder
2 teaspoons salt
¼ teaspoon pepper
1 cup shredded Cheddar cheese

Cook macaroni according to package directions; drain and set aside. Brown meat, onion, green pepper, and garlic in butter or margarine. Transfer to a 6-quart casserole dish and thoroughly stir in all ingredients; add cooked macaroni and mix well.

Refrigerate overnight or cool and freeze.

The next day (or when ready to serve) heat oven to 350 degrees F. Cover casserole dish and bake for 2 hours or until it bubbles. Yield: about 8 to 10 servings.

Macaroni and Broccoli Casserole

> 3 *tablespoons butter or margarine*
> 3 *tablespoons flour*
> 1½ *teaspoons salt*
> ⅛ *teaspoon pepper*
> 1½ *cups milk*
> ¼ *to ½ cup shredded cheese*
> ¾ *cup mayonnaise*
> 1 *(8-ounce) package cut macaroni*
> 2 *cups chopped, cooked broccoli*

Melt butter; stir in flour, salt, and pepper. Add milk gradually, stirring constantly. Cook until thickened, stirring often. Remove from heat and stir in cheese and mayonnaise. Cook macaroni in boiling, salted water according to package directions. Cook just until tender; do not overcook. Drain, rinse, and drain again. Place a layer of macaroni, then a layer of chopped, cooked broccoli in greased 1½-quart casserole. Pour sauce over broccoli. Repeat layers, ending with sauce. Bake at 350 degrees F. about 20 minutes, or until thoroughly heated. Yield: 6 to 8 servings.

Beef and Noodles in Sour Cream

> 1 *cup chopped onion*
> 2 *tablespoons shortening*
> 1 *pound ground chuck*
> 3 *cups noodles, uncooked*
> 3 *cups tomato juice*
> 2 *teaspoons salt*
> 1 *teaspoon celery salt*
> *Dash pepper*
> 2 *teaspoons Worcestershire sauce*
> 1 *cup commercial sour cream*

Cook onion in melted shortening until onion is transparent. Add meat and brown lightly. Put in a large saucepan and add noodles, tomato juice, salt, celery salt, pepper, and Worcestershire sauce. Bring to a boil over low heat (mixture will burn easily). Cover and simmer until noodles are tender (about 30 minutes). Stir in 1 cup sour cream; heat gently to boiling. Add more seasoning if desired. Serve hot. Yield: 6 servings.

Thomas Jefferson's Noodles à la Macaroni

> 6 *eggs*
> 1 *cup milk*
> ½ *teaspoon salt*
> 4 *cups flour*
> *Salted, boiling water*

Beat the eggs until light, and add milk and salt. Add flour until you have a thick dough. Roll, using a rolling pin, to thickness of about ⅛ inch—about the thickness of macaroni. Cut into small pieces and roll around between your hands to get long strips—about the size of macaroni. Now cut them to length of 4 or 5 inches. Drop into salted, boiling water. Cook briskly for about 15 minutes. Serve as you would macaroni, with butter, shredded cheese, or cream sauce. These Noodles à la Macaroni are delicious served in hot soup.

Hamburger-Noodle Casserole

> 2 *tablespoons butter*
> 1 *pound ground beef*
> 1 *clove garlic, minced*
> 1 *tablespoon salt*
> ½ *teaspoon pepper*
> 1 *tablespoon sugar*
> 2 *(8-ounce) cans tomato sauce*
> 1 *(8-ounce) package noodles*
> 6 *scallions*
> 1 *(3-ounce) package cream cheese*
> 1 *cup commercial sour cream*
> ½ *cup shredded Cheddar cheese*

Combine first six ingredients and sauté until meat is done. Then add tomato sauce and simmer 20 minutes. Cook noodles according to directions on package. Cut up scallions; add them to the blended cream cheese and sour cream. In a slightly greased casserole, place ⅓ of noodles, then ⅓ of scallion mixture, then ⅓ of meat sauce; continue this two more times. Top casserole with the shredded cheese and bake at 350 degrees F. for 20 minutes or until thoroughly heated.

Sour Cream-Noodle Casserole

  1 *(8-ounce) package medium noodles*
  1 *pound ground beef*
  2 *tablespoons butter*
  1 *teaspoon salt*
 ⅛ *teaspoon pepper*
 ¼ *teaspoon garlic salt*
  1 *(8-ounce) can tomato sauce*
  1 *cup creamed cottage cheese*
  1 *cup commercial sour cream*
 ½ *cup chopped green onions*
 ¾ *cup shredded sharp Cheddar cheese*

Cook noodles in boiling salted water according to package directions. Rinse and drain. In skillet brown meat in butter. Add salt, pepper, and garlic salt, then tomato sauce. Simmer for 5 minutes.

Combine cottage cheese, sour cream, chopped onion, and noodles. Alternate layers of noodle mixture and meat mixture in a 2-quart casserole, beginning with noodles and ending with meat. Top with shredded Cheddar cheese. Bake at 350 degrees F. for 25 to 30 minutes or until cheese is melted and browned. Yield: 8 servings.

Delicious Lasagna

  1 *(8-ounce) package lasagna noodles*
  1 *tablespoon salad oil*
  2 *bay leaves*
  1 *recipe Savory Meat Sauce*
  1 *pound cottage cheese*
 ¼ *cup Parmesan cheese*
  6 *to 8 ounces mozzarella cheese, thinly*
     sliced

Cook noodles according to package directions, adding the oil and bay leaves to the boiling water. Drain. Oil a 12- x 18-inch baking dish. Starting with noodles, make layers of noodles and one-third of Savory Meat Sauce, dot with half the cottage cheese, sprinkle with Parmesan, and add a few slices of mozzarella cheese. Repeat layers. Make top layers of noodles and meat sauce. Decorate with strips of mozzarella cheese. Bake at 350 degrees F. for 30 minutes. Let stand 15 minutes. Yield: 6 servings. (This recipe is even better when prepared a day ahead.)

Savory Meat Sauce:

  1 *pound ground beef*
  1 *tablespoon salad oil*
  1 *(1-pound) can tomatoes*
 ½ *cup water*
  1 *(6-ounce) can tomato paste*
 ½ *cup diced celery*
  1 *(1½-ounce) package spaghetti sauce*
     mix
   Salt to taste
  1 *tablespoon sugar*
  1 *tablespoon prepared mustard*

Brown meat in hot oil; break it apart as it browns. Add remaining ingredients. Bring to boil; reduce heat and simmer 15 to 20 minutes, or until thick. Stir frequently.

Yankee Doodle Dandy

1½ *cups diagonally cut sliced celery*
 ¼ *cup butter or margarine*
  2 *tablespoons flour*
 ½ *teaspoon salt*
  1 *cup milk*
  1 *(17-ounce) can cream-style corn*
  1 *(8-ounce) package noodles, cooked*
     and drained
  1 *cup shredded sharp Cheddar cheese*
 ¼ *pound shredded dried beef*

Sauté celery in melted butter until just tender. Stir in flour and salt; gradually blend in milk. Add corn, and combine mixture with cooked noodles. Add shredded cheese and shredded dried beef. Mix well and place in greased 2½-quart casserole. Bake at 350 degrees F. about 30 minutes. Yield: 6 to 8 servings.

Spaghetti and Oysters With Cheese

2 *cups spaghetti*
1 *pint oysters, drained*
1 *cup shredded cheese*
Butter
Salt and pepper
½ *cup milk*

Cook spaghetti according to directions on package; drain. Butter 1½-quart baking dish. Place a layer of drained spaghetti in dish, then oysters, shredded cheese, salt, and pepper. Continue layers until all are used. Add milk. Bake at 350 degrees F. for about 30 minutes, or until oysters curl. Yield: 6 servings.

Baked Rice

2 *tablespoons salad oil*
1 *cup rice*
¼ *cup chopped onion*
1½ *cups hot chicken stock (with fat removed)*
¾ *cup sautéed sliced mushrooms (optional)*
1 *cup cooked wild rice*

In a heavy skillet heat oil till hot and add rice and onion. Stir till they are very light brown. Add chicken stock and mushrooms and place in 350-degree oven uncovered for approximately 30 minutes. Stir during cooking time and add more liquid if necessary. (Never let any rice overcook; grains should be tender and stand apart.) Add 1 cup of cooked wild rice; stir and season to taste.

Browned Rice With Pork Chops

4 *pork chops*
1 *cup uncooked rice*
1 *(1-pound) can tomatoes*
1½ *cups water*
⅔ *cup chopped green pepper*
⅓ *cup chopped onion*
Salt and pepper to taste

Brown the chops in large, deep skillet or Dutch oven. Remove from skillet. Put rice into drippings in skillet and cook, stirring constantly, until brown. Add remaining ingredients. Lay chops on top. Cover and cook on low heat 20 to 30 minutes, or until liquid is absorbed. Turn off heat and leave on range about 20 minutes longer. Yield: 4 servings.

Baked Rice and Cheese

3 *cups cooked rice*
2 *cups shredded cheese*
2 *tablespoons finely chopped green pepper*
2 *eggs, beaten*
1¼ *cups milk*
1 *teaspoon salt*
Cayenne pepper to taste
½ *cup coarse breadcrumbs*
1 *tablespoon melted butter*

Arrange alternate layers of cooked rice, cheese, and green pepper in buttered baking dish. Combine beaten eggs, milk, salt, and pepper. Pour over rice and cheese mixture. Toss breadcrumbs with melted butter. Sprinkle over top of casserole. Bake at 350 degrees F. about 45 minutes or until set. Yield: 6 servings.

Easy Rice Casserole

½ *stick butter or margarine*
1 *medium onion, chopped*
1 *cup uncooked rice*
1 *(10½-ounce) can consommé*
1 *(10¾-ounce) can beef bouillon*

Melt butter or margarine in skillet; add onion and sauté. In a greased 1½-quart casserole add uncooked rice. Over this pour the consommé and bouillon; stir in onion and butter. Bake, covered, at 350 degrees F. about 30 minutes or longer. Uncover last few minutes for rice to brown.

Curried Rice With Raisins Indienne

    2 tablespoons butter, divided
    1 teaspoon curry powder
    1 cup rice
    2 cups rich chicken broth
    ⅔ cup seedless raisins
    ⅓ cup chopped green onion
    ⅓ cup chopped green pepper
    ⅓ cup chopped celery
    ½ teaspoon seasoned salt
    1 tablespoon chutney
    2 tablespoons chopped pimiento
    2 tablespoons pine nuts (optional)
    1 tablespoon vinegar
    1 tablespoon brown sugar

Combine 1 tablespoon butter with curry powder and rice. Cook, stirring over low heat, 5 minutes. Add chicken broth and heat to boiling. Stir, cover tightly, and cook over low heat about 15 minutes or until liquid is absorbed. Meanwhile, sauté raisins, onion, green pepper, and celery in remaining tablespoon butter only until vegetables begin to soften but do not lose their color. Add remaining ingredients; toss lightly together. Pile hot rice on serving platter. Spoon raisin mixture over top. Yield: 4 servings.

Huhn Fricassee mit Reis
(Gourmet Chicken With Rice)

    1 cup uncooked rice
    1 (10½-ounce) can mushroom soup
    1 (10½-ounce) can onion soup
    1 can water
    1 frying-size chicken
    Salt and pepper

Place uncooked rice in bottom of 9- x 12-inch pan; pour mushroom and onion soups and water over rice. Mix slightly. Cut up chicken as for frying. Salt and pepper pieces generously and place on top of rice mixture. Bake at 325 degrees F. for about 1 hour and 15 minutes (depending on size of chicken). When chicken has browned on one side, turn and allow to brown on other side.

Charleston Red Rice

    2 cups raw, long grain rice
    6 cups boiling water
    3 teaspoons salt
    6 slices lean bacon
    2 medium onions, chopped fine
    1 (8-ounce) can tomato sauce
    1 (6-ounce) can tomato paste
    3 teaspoons sugar
    2 teaspoons Worcestershire sauce
    Dash red-hot pepper sauce

Cook the rice in 6 cups salted water until light and fluffy—not soft and sticky. Fry bacon until brown and crisp; remove from fat and reserve for garnishing rice. Sauté chopped onions in 4 tablespoons of the bacon fat until clear. Add tomato sauce and paste, sugar, Worcestershire sauce, and hot sauce, and cook slowly for 10 minutes. Place the cooked rice in a buttered 2-quart baking dish and stir all of the seasonings into the dry, fluffy rice with a fork. Place in oven and bake at 325 degrees F. for 45 minutes, or until rice has absorbed all of the liquid. Crumble bacon over top and serve hot. Yield: 10 to 12 servings.

Chinese Fried Rice

    2 eggs, beaten
    1 tablespoon butter or margarine
    3 tablespoons cooking oil
    ½ cup sliced scallions (include green part)
    4 cups cold cooked rice
    2 tablespoons soy sauce
    ½ teaspoon sugar
    1 cup diced cooked ham

Scramble beaten eggs in butter and set aside. In a large skillet heat cooking oil and stir in sliced scallions and cooked rice; stir quickly to coat rice with the oil. Mix in the soy sauce, sugar, and cooked ham. Stir in scrambled eggs which have been cut into small pieces. Heat for about 5 minutes, stirring frequently. Serve immediately. Yield: 4 servings.

Chinese Fried Rice

1 *cup diced cooked shrimp, chicken,*
ham, or pork
Cooking oil
1 *(3-ounce) can broiled, sliced*
mushrooms, drained
1 *(1-pound) can bean sprouts, drained*
1 *green onion, finely chopped*
½ *medium green pepper, chopped*
2 *tablespoons soy sauce, or more to*
taste
3 *cups day-old cooked rice*
Salt and pepper to taste
1 *egg, well beaten*

Cut meat in thin strips; lightly brown in hot cooking oil. Add mushrooms, bean sprouts, onion, green pepper, and soy sauce and cook 5 minutes. Add rice and continue to cook over low heat another 10 minutes, stirring frequently. Add salt and a little pepper; add beaten egg and continue to stir while cooking an additional 5 minutes, or until mixture is fluffy. Add more soy sauce, if desired. Serve hot. Yield: 6 to 8 servings.

Fried Rice

1½ *cups uncooked rice*
1 *cup cooked pork*
2 *tablespoons shortening*
2 *eggs, beaten*
1 *cup cooked shrimp, cut in small*
pieces
2 *tablespoons soy sauce*
1 *cup green onion tops, cut in small*
pieces

Cook rice early in the day according to package directions (do not use instant rice). Let sit in pan until ready to use; rice must be cold.

Cut fresh pork into narrow strips. Fry in skillet until brown. Remove from pan. Add shortening to pan and scramble eggs, stirring with a fork. Add rice, pork, and shrimp. Cook for 5 minutes, stirring often. Add soy sauce and mix well. Add onion greens and serve. Yield: 4 to 6 servings.

Chicken Fried Rice

1 *cup long-grain rice*
4 *tablespoons vegetable oil*
2 *cups chicken broth*
Chopped chives or green onion tops

Place rice and vegetable oil in a saucepan. Set over medium heat until grains "pop" or become opaque and slightly browned. Add chicken broth, turn heat to lowest setting, cover, and simmer until all liquids are absorbed (an asbestos pad helps here). This should end up rather on the dry side. Do not stir while cooking. Garnish with chopped chives or green onion tops. Yield: 4 servings.

(This is a versatile recipe; one may add a few chopped onions and ground chicken gizzards and livers and it becomes the "dirty rice" of the Louisiana Cajun country.)

The General's Rice

1 *cup raw rice*
2 *(10½-ounce) cans bouillon*
½ *stick margarine*

Combine all the ingredients in a large baking dish and bake uncovered at 425 degrees F. for 45 minutes. Voila! Golden brown and delicious rice—ready to accompany steaks, beef roasts, or chicken entrées.

Rice With Rib Meat Creole

1 *cup rice*
1 *cup water*
1 *teaspoon salt*
8 *slices streak o' lean meat*
1 *medium onion, chopped*
1 *(No. 2) can tomatoes*
1 *(6-ounce) can tomato paste*
1 *green pepper, minced*

Put rice, water, and salt in top of double boiler; steam-cook for 45 minutes. Do not stir. Will be light and fluffy. Brown meat and onion; add other ingredients. Cook at 350 degrees F. for 2 hours. Serve over hot rice.

Armenian Rice Pilaf

  1 *cup thin egg noodles*
  ½ *stick butter or margarine*
  1 *cup long-grain rice*
2½ *cups boiling water*
  1 *teaspoon salt*
    Pepper to taste

Sauté noodles in butter or margarine over low heat until noodles are golden brown; add rice, stirring constantly until rice is coated with butter. Add boiling water, salt, and pepper. Cover with a tight-fitting lid and simmer over low heat for 15 to 20 minutes.

Let mixture sit for 20 minutes after heat has been cut off; do not disturb or stir during this time. Before serving, stir rice and noodles (noodles tend to come to the top during cooking). Yield: 4 to 6 servings.

Ravishing Rice

   1 *pound bulk hot sausage*
   1 *large Spanish onion, chopped*
   1 *large green pepper, chopped*
   1 *cup chopped celery*
 4½ *cups boiling water*
   2 *envelopes chicken-noodle soup mix*
   ½ *cup raw rice*
     Slivered almonds
     Chopped parsley

First, put the sausage on to cook over low heat in a large skillet, pouring off the grease now and then and stirring to crumble the meat. Combine the chopped onion, green pepper, and celery and set aside.

In 4½ cups of boiling water, boil the soup mix and rice for 7 minutes. Do not drain.

Combine soup mixture, vegetables, and sausage and mix well. Pour into a large (2-quart) casserole. Sprinkle top with slivered almonds and chopped parsley. If you are serving it with the Chicken Cornelia (page 279), substitute paprika for the parsley, for you don't want parsley on everything, good as it is. Yield: 10 to 12 servings.

Rice à la Grecque

  3 *tablespoons butter or margarine*
  1 *onion, chopped*
  1 *small clove garlic, crushed*
  3 *or 4 leaves green lettuce, shredded*
  2 *fresh pork sausages, sliced*
  3 *mushrooms, sliced*
  3 *tomatoes, peeled, seeded, and diced*
  1 *cup raw rice*
  2 *cups boiling water or chicken broth*
  1 *teaspoon salt*
    Dash pepper
  ½ *cup cooked peas*
  1 *diced pimiento*
  2 *tablespoons raisins*
    Butter or margarine

Melt butter or margarine over low heat and add onion. When onion is brown, add garlic, lettuce, sausages, mushrooms, tomatoes, and raw rice. Mix well. Add boiling water or chicken broth, salt, and pepper. Cover tightly and continue cooking for 20 minutes. Mix well with fork. Add peas, pimiento, and raisins (which have been sautéed in butter or margarine). Yield: approximately 4 cups.

Mock Wild Rice

  ¼ *cup butter or margarine*
 1⅓ *cups packaged precooked rice*
  1 *cup finely chopped celery*
  ¼ *cup chopped celery leaves*
  ¼ *cup finely chopped onion*
    Dash of salt
    Dash of pepper
 1⅓ *cups water*

Melt butter in saucepan. Add rice, celery, celery leaves, onion, salt, and pepper. Cook and stir over medium heat until onion is tender, but not browned, and rice is partially browned—about 8 minutes. Stir in water and bring quickly to a boil over high heat. Then cover, remove from heat, and let stand 5 minutes, or until all liquid is absorbed. Fluff rice with a fork. Yield: 3 cups, or 4 servings.

Wild Rice

1½　cups wild rice
　4　(10½-ounce) cans undiluted
　　　bouillon or beef broth
　1　cup chopped onion
　1　cup chopped green pepper
　1　cup mushrooms
　¼　cup soft butter
　1　cup thick cream
　Salt and pepper to taste

Wash rice, then cook in bouillon or beef broth until most of the liquid has been absorbed. Sauté onion, pepper, and mushrooms in butter. Add cream, and salt and pepper to taste. Add to cooked rice and put into a casserole dish. Bake at 350 degrees F. for 20 minutes.

Sausage-Rice Yum Yum

　1　pound smoked sausage, cut in ½-
　　　inch rounds
　1　large onion, chopped
　1　tablespoon bacon drippings
　1　cup regular rice
　1　(1-pound) can tomatoes
　1　(8-ounce) can tomato sauce
　½　cup water
　1　teaspoon salt
　1　large bay leaf
　¼　teaspoon dried thyme

In a large iron skillet sauté smoked sausage and chopped onion in bacon drippings. Add rice and cook over medium heat, stirring frequently, until onions are transparent and rice is golden.

Add tomatoes, which have been sieved or mashed, tomato sauce, and water. Season with salt, bay leaf, and dried thyme. Bring to a boil, cover, and reduce heat to low. Cook 15 minutes or until rice swells. Remove cover and lift rice from bottom of skillet often with a spoon to keep it from sticking. Cook uncovered until done. Yield: 4 to 6 servings.

Note: The sausage used in above recipe is the ordinary type, smoked in casings and sometimes in links, that can be found at any self-service meat counter. For a special flair, substitute pepperoni for the sausage. Those cooks living in Florida near a Latin American community will find chorizo, a Spanish sausage, ideally suited for this dish; omit the thyme and bay leaf as chorizos are highly seasoned.

Franks and Rice Bake

　1　pound frankfurters, cut in thirds
　⅓　cup chopped onion
　1　tablespoon butter or margarine
　1　(10¾-ounce) can condensed
　　　Cheddar cheese soup
　2　cups cooked rice
　1　(8-ounce) can tomatoes, chopped
　1　teaspoon Worcestershire sauce

In saucepan, brown frankfurters and cook onion in butter until tender. Stir in soup; add remaining ingredients. Pour into shallow baking dish (12 x 8 x 2 inches). Bake at 350 degrees F. for 30 minutes or until hot. Yield: 4 servings.

White Rice Casserole

1½　cups uncooked rice
　1　teaspoon basil
　1　teaspoon thyme
　Salt and pepper
　1　pound processed cheese, shredded
　1　cup chopped parsley
　3　green onions and tops, chopped fine
　½　cup chopped green pepper
　½　cup salad oil
　2　eggs, beaten
　1　cup milk

Cook rice according to package directions, making sure it is not cooked too dry. Add basil, thyme, salt, and pepper. Stir in shredded cheese while rice is hot. Add other ingredients and mix well. Put into 1½-quart casserole dish and bake at 325 degrees F. for 45 minutes. Yield: 6 to 8 servings.

Herbed Rice à la Willis

1½ *sweet green peppers, cut in thin*
 slices
2½ *cups beef bouillon*
1 *package herb rice*
½ *of 5-ounce can slivered almonds,*
 toasted

Cook the sliced peppers in beef bouillon for 8 minutes. Add rice and cook according to package directions. Stir with a fork. Place rice in hot baking dish and cover with toasted almonds. Yield: 4 servings.

Spanish Rice-Meat

1 *pound ground chuck*
2 *tablespoons bacon drippings*
1 *medium onion, chopped*
3 *tablespoons diced green pepper*
1 *(3½-ounce) can mushrooms*
1 *(6-ounce) can tomato sauce*
½ *cup water*
 Salt
2 *cups instant rice*

Sear ground beef in bacon drippings. Add chopped onion, green pepper, mushrooms, tomato sauce, water, and salt to taste. Simmer this mixture at least 2 hours or longer. When ready to serve, add rice; cover and cook for 15 minutes. Yield: 4 to 6 servings.

Spanish Rice With Shrimp

2 *tablespoons butter or margarine*
3 *tablespoons finely chopped onion*
4 *tablespoons finely chopped green*
 pepper
2 *cups shrimp, boiled and peeled*
1½ *cups cooked rice*
1½ *cups canned tomatoes*
1 *cup fresh mushrooms*
½ *teaspoon salt, or to taste*
¼ *teaspoon pepper*

Melt butter; add onion and green pepper and cook on moderate heat for 3 minutes. Add shrimp and cook 3 minutes. Add rice, tomatoes, mushrooms, salt, and pepper. Cook, stirring, for 2 or 3 minutes. Cover and simmer 10 minutes. Yield: 6 servings.

Saffron Rice

 Dash powdered saffron
½ *cup hot water*
¼ *cup butter or margarine, melted*
1½ *cups uncooked rice*
¼ *cup chopped onion*
½ *teaspoon salt*
2½ *cups hot water*

Dissolve saffron in ½ cup hot water. Combine the dissolved saffron, butter, rice, onion, salt, and 1 cup of the water in a 1½-quart casserole. Bake uncovered in hot oven (450 degrees) for 20 minutes or until rice is very dry, stirring at the end of 10 minutes. Stir in remaining 1½ cups hot water; cover and return to hot oven for 15 minutes. Uncover and cook 5 minutes longer. Fluff with fork before serving. Yield: 8 to 12 servings.

Rice With Almonds

½ *cup uncooked rice*
2 *cups milk*
1½ *packages unflavored gelatin*
1 *cup sherry*
1 *teaspoon vanilla extract*
½ *teaspoon almond extract*
6 *tablespoons sugar*
½ *cup almonds, blanched and chopped*
½ *pint whipping cream*

Cook rice and milk in top of double boiler until rice is tender. Dissolve gelatin in sherry. Add extracts and sugar to cooked rice. Add gelatin and almonds to rice and set aside until gelatin has melted. Then with a fork break rice apart and stir in whipped cream. Top with Raspberry Sauce.

Raspberry Sauce: Crush frozen raspberries (one 10-ounce box) and add 1 teaspoon cornstarch. Cook over low heat, stirring often, until sauce is slightly thickened. If desired, add a little sugar.

Cheese and Eggs

Early settlers of the South produced a surplus of milk and milk products. Much of this soured milk, called clabber, was made into cottage cheese; a softer cheese, resembling Neufchâtel, also found favor among these pioneers.

French settlers brought to the South many recipes which called for the fine imported cheeses of their homeland; however, as better grades of American cheeses were developed, they found ready acceptance in cherished recipes. Of course, imported cheeses still hold an important place in gourmet meals.

Eggs, too, have been plentiful in our heritage. Family histories show that the pioneer cook searched for cake recipes that called for at least a dozen eggs. Deviled or stuffed eggs have always been popular picnic fare. And an early-morning breakfast of scrambled eggs, sausage, grits, and hot biscuits has been the mainstay of hunters and fishermen, enabling many a master of reel and rifle to get his limit of fin, fur, or feathers.

Cheese-Noodle Casserole

    3 cups uncooked noodles
    ¼ cup butter (½ stick)
    3 tablespoon flour
    ¾ teaspoon salt
    ¼ teaspoon garlic salt
    ⅛ teaspoon white pepper
       Dash ground nutmeg
    2 cups milk
    ½ cup dry white cooking wine
    1 (8-ounce) package pasteurized
          process Swiss cheese, shredded
    2 tablespoons sliced green onion
    2 tablespoons diced pimiento
    ½ cup grated Parmesan cheese

Cook noodles according to package directions; drain and set aside. Melt butter; blend in flour, salt, garlic salt, pepper, and nutmeg. Add milk and cook, stirring constantly, until sauce is smooth and thickened. Add wine and Swiss cheese; stir until cheese is melted. Fold in cooked noodles, green onion, pimiento, and ¼ cup Parmesan cheese. Pour mixture into 1½-quart shallow casserole. Sprinkle with remaining Parmesan cheese. Bake in moderate oven, 350 degrees F., for 25 minutes or until hot and bubbly around the edges. Yield: 6 servings.

Cheese and Beef Casserole

    2 eggs, slightly beaten
    1 cup milk
    2 tablespoons Worcestershire sauce
    2 teaspoons salt
       Pepper to taste
    1 teaspoon dry mustard
    2 cups dry breadcrumbs
    2 pounds ground beef
    4 tablespoons minced onion
    ¼ pound sharp Cheddar cheese, sliced

Combine eggs, milk, Worcestershire sauce, salt, pepper, mustard, and breadcrumbs. Allow to stand 5 minutes. Then add ground beef and onion and mix well. Place half the mixture in bottom of greased, 8- x 8-inch baking dish. Arrange slices of cheese evenly on top. Cover with remainder of meat mixture. Bake at 350 degrees F. for 40 to 50 minutes. Yield: 9 servings.

Cheese comes in a variety of colors and flavors, and is served in any course from appetizers to desserts.

Cheese and Ham Casserole

    1 *tablespoon butter*
    1 *tablespoon flour*
    2 *cups milk, divided*
    ¼ *pound shredded Cheddar cheese*
    4 *eggs, well beaten*
    *Salt and cayenne or black pepper to
        taste*
    2 *tablespoons minced stuffed olives*
    1 *tablespoon minced parsley*
    1 *tablespoon minced green onion tops*
    ½ *cup chopped ham*
    ½ *cup mushroom pieces*
    Sliced olives or parsley for garnish

Melt butter in a small pan; add flour and cook until flour has darkened. Gradually add 1 cup of the milk, stirring constantly. Stir in shredded cheese and cook over low heat until cheese has melted. Remove from heat and add 1 cup milk, the well-beaten eggs, and salt and pepper. Add minced olives, parsley, green onions, chopped ham, and mushroom pieces. Spoon into 6 or 8 well-greased individual baking dishes.

Place baking dishes in a pan, with about 1 inch cold water in pan. For earthenware dishes bake at 375 degrees F., and for glass dishes bake at 350 degrees F. from 20 to 30 minutes or until mixture is done. Insert knife blade into center of dishes, and if blade comes out clean, mixture is done. Serve hot, garnished with sliced olives or parsley sprigs. Yield: 6 to 8 servings.

Curried Hominy Casserole

    2 *cups cream sauce*
    2 *cups Cheddar cheese, shredded*
    1 *teaspoon curry powder*
    1 *teaspoon salt*
    ½ *teaspoon white pepper*
    3 *(No. 2) cans white hominy, drained*

Make cream sauce and add shredded cheese, curry powder, salt, and pepper. Put hominy into buttered 3-quart casserole in alternate layers with cream sauce. Bake at 350 degrees F. for 30 minutes. Yield: 12 servings.

Cheese Chops

    1 *pound coarsely shredded American
        cheese*
    4 *tablespoons softened butter or
        margarine*
    2 *teaspoons prepared mustard*
    ⅛ *teaspoon pepper*
    1 *teaspoon salt*
    1 *tablespoon finely chopped parsley or
        chives, or both*
    2 *eggs, beaten*
    1⅔ *cups cracker crumbs*
    4 *to 6 tablespoons shortening*

Combine the ingredients in order listed. Shape mixture to look like meat chops. Fry in hot shortening over low heat until golden brown on both sides. Serve with Creole Sauce. Yield: 4 to 6 servings.

Creole Sauce:

    ½ *cup chopped onion*
    ¼ *cup chopped green pepper*
    2 *tablespoons salad oil*
    1½ *cups canned tomatoes*
    2 *tablespoons chopped pimiento*
    2 *tablespoons sugar*
    ½ *teaspoon salt*
    Dash cayenne pepper
    1 *tablespoon vinegar*
    1 *tablespoon catsup*
    1 *tablespoon Worcestershire sauce*

Brown onion and green pepper in hot salad oil. Add other ingredients; bring to boiling point; simmer for 20 minutes.

Gouda Luncheon Supreme

    4 *Gouda cheese balls*
    1 *cup baked or boiled ham, diced*
    1 *cup chicken or turkey, cooked and
        diced*
    ¼ *cup onion, minced very fine*
    ¼ *cup celery, minced very fine*
    ½ *cup French dressing*
    Salt and pepper to taste
    1 *head lettuce*
    2 *tomatoes cut into wedges*

Core out each of the cheese balls, leaving a thickness of about ¼ inch. Also trim away the red cover surrounding balls. Mix in a bowl the diced ham, diced chicken or turkey, onion, celery, French dressing, and salt and pepper. Stuff each of the Gouda balls with the ham-chicken mixture. Place the filled cheese balls onto a lightly greased cookie sheet and into a preheated, 375-degree oven. Bake until the cheese balls are melted through, but not out of shape. Remove balls and serve on a large leaf of lettuce. Place tomato wedges into cheese for garnish. Each cheese ball serves one person.

Baked Cheese and Ham Puff

1 *cup milk*
1 *cup fine, soft, enriched breadcrumbs*
1 *tablespoon butter or margarine*
½ *teaspoon salt*
⅛ *teaspoon pepper*
¼ *teaspoon dry mustard*
  Few grains cayenne pepper
½ *cup diced Cheddar cheese*
½ *cup minced ham, bologna, or tongue*
3 *eggs, separated*

Scald milk in a double boiler. Add breadcrumbs, butter or margarine, seasonings, and cheese; cook until cheese melts. Stir occasionally. Add the meat. Beat egg yolks. Slowly stir in a little of the cheese mixture; then pour into the cooking cheese mixture. Cook and stir over hot water for 2 minutes, or until mixture thickens. Then cool. When tepid, beat egg whites stiff and fold in. Pour into 1½-quart buttered casserole. Bake at 325 degrees F. for 50 minutes. Serve at once. Yield: 4 servings.

Cheese and Nut Puff

8 *(½-inch) slices day-old white bread*
2 *cups shredded sharp American cheese*
¾ *cup ground Brazil nuts*
½ *teaspoon salt*
¼ *teaspoon dry mustard*
½ *teaspoon paprika*
2 *eggs*
2 *cups milk*

Remove bread crusts; cut slices in half diagonally. Place half in a 2½-inch-deep, 10-inch, heatproof dish. Strew the bread with half the cheese and ½ cup nuts; cover with second layer of bread and cheese. Add seasonings to eggs; beat until blended. Stir in milk and pour over bread and cheese. Sprinkle nuts over top. Bake at 325 degrees F. 45 minutes. Serve at once. Yield: 6 to 8 servings.

Cheese Strata

3 *eggs, beaten slightly*
1¼ *cups milk*
½ *teaspoon brown sugar*
⅛ *teaspoon paprika*
1 *small onion, minced*
¼ *teaspoon dry mustard*
¼ *teaspoon salt*
¼ *teaspoon black pepper*
¼ *teaspoon Worcestershire sauce*
¼ *teaspoon red pepper*
  Soft butter or margarine
4 *slices bread*
¾ *pound shredded Cheddar cheese*

Combine eggs, milk, brown sugar, paprika, onion, mustard, salt, pepper, Worcestershire sauce, and red pepper. Set aside. Butter bread; cut off crusts and cut each slice into small squares. Put a layer of bread squares in a baking dish; top with shredded cheese, and repeat layers until all bread and cheese are used. Pour egg-milk mixture over all. Cover and place in refrigerator for 4 hours or overnight. Take out of refrigerator 30 minutes before time for baking. Bake at 300 degrees F. for 1 hour. Yield: 8 servings.

Cheese Soufflé

1½ *cups milk*
1 *cup coarse breadcrumbs*
1 *tablespoon butter or margarine*
½ *pound shredded cheese (about 2 cups)*
4 *egg yolks, well beaten*
¾ *teaspoon salt*
   White pepper to taste
4 *egg whites, stiffly beaten*

Heat milk, breadcrumbs, and butter in top of a double boiler. Add cheese to the hot mixture; stir until cheese has melted. Add this mixture to well-beaten egg yolks; season with salt and pepper. Fold this mixture into beaten egg whites. Pour into a 2½-quart greased casserole and bake at 475 degrees F. for 10 minutes; reduce heat and bake at 400 degrees F. for 20 to 25 minutes longer. Serve immediately. Yield: 4 to 6 servings.

Savory Eggs

1 *cup shredded American cheese*
2 *tablespoons butter or margarine*
½ *cup cream*
¼ *teaspoon salt*
¼ *teaspoon pepper*
1 *teaspoon prepared mustard*
6 *eggs, beaten slightly*

Spread cheese in greased shallow 8-inch round or square baking dish. Dot with butter. Combine cream, salt, pepper, and mustard. Pour half this mixture over cheese. Pour eggs into baking dish. Add remaining cream mixture. Bake at 325 degrees F. about 25 minutes. Yield: 6 servings.

Swiss Eggs

1 *tablespoon butter*
4 *very thin slices cheese*
4 *eggs*
   Salt and pepper to taste
3 *tablespoons cream*
2 *tablespoons shredded cheese*

Melt butter in a shallow baking dish. Cut the slices of cheese in pieces of convenient size to cover bottom of dish. Break the eggs and drop them into the dish over cheese. Season to taste and pour the cream over the eggs. Sprinkle the shredded cheese on top and bake at 300 degrees F. till the eggs are set and the cheese is a delicate brown (about 15 to 20 minutes). Yield: 4 servings.

Casserole of Eggs And Asparagus

1 *large can green asparagus spears*
4 *hard-cooked eggs, sliced*
   Salt and pepper to taste
2 *canned pimientos, sliced*
1 *cup hot, medium white sauce*
½ *cup shredded American cheese*
½ *cup buttered, toasted breadcrumbs*

Arrange half of asparagus on bottom of a buttered, 1½-quart casserole. Top with slices of 2 eggs, add salt and pepper and 1 sliced pimiento. Add more asparagus and repeat. Add white sauce and shredded cheese. Top with breadcrumbs. Bake at 325 degrees F. for about 30 minutes. Yield: 6 servings.

Eggs and Broccoli Bake

1 *(10-ounce) package frozen broccoli, cooked and drained*
6 *hard-cooked eggs, halved lengthwise*
2 *(10¾-ounce) cans condensed Cheddar cheese soup*
1 *cup milk*
¼ *cup melted butter or margarine*
¼ *cup water*
2 *cups herb-seasoned stuffing mix*

Arrange broccoli and eggs in shallow baking dish (12 x 8 x 2 inches). Stir soup until smooth; gradually blend in milk. Pour over broccoli and eggs. In bowl, combine butter and water; stir in stuffing mix. Sprinkle over casserole. Bake at 400 degrees F. for 30 minutes. Yield: 4 servings.

Omelet Parisienne

8 *eggs*
Sugar
3 *tablespoons butter*
1 *tablespoon peanut oil*
3 *tablespoon Cointreau or Grand Marnier*
Orange or banana slices or diced pineapple
Butter
2 *teaspoons sugar*
4 *tablespoons Cognac, Armagnac, or rum*

Separate eggs. Whisk yolks until frothy; whisk whites until very stiff. Fold yolks into beaten whites and add sugar to taste. Heat butter and oil in an omelet pan, and when very hot, pour in omelet mixture. Spoon Cointreau or Grand Marnier over mixture and cook until omelet is done but still moist. Place slices of orange, banana, or pineapple, which you have heated in a little butter, in the center of the egg mixture. Fold over. Place on a hot platter. Sprinkle with sugar and glaze under a hot grill. Flame with Cognac, Armagnac, or rum and serve immediately. Yield: 6 servings.

Confetti Omelet
(Big Daddy Style)

8 *eggs*
½ *cup milk*
1 *teaspoon salt*
⅛ *teaspoon pepper*
2 *tablespoons butter*
1 *to 2 slices crisp bacon, crumbled*
10 *suffed olives, sliced*
¼ *cup shredded cheese*

Beat eggs slightly; add milk, salt, and pepper, and mix well. Melt butter over low heat in skillet or frying pan, tilting pan to distribute butter evenly over bottom and sides. Pour egg mixture into pan and cook over low heat. As omelet cooks, lift edges with a spatula and tilt pan to allow uncooked portion to flow underneath.

Continue cooking until whole omelet is set. Loosen edges with spatula and crease omelet. Add crisp bacon and olives and fold omelet in half. Sprinkle with shredded cheese and serve hot. Yield: 4 to 6 servings.

Scrambled Eggs à la Asparagus

10 *to 12 eggs*
1 *cup milk*
Salt
Pepper
½ *cup butter or margarine*
1 *cup shredded or cubed American cheese*
1 *large can asparagus spears, drained*
Slices of hard-cooked eggs

Blend together eggs, milk, salt, and pepper. Melt butter or margarine in skillet and add egg mixture and cheese. Cook slowly, stirring constantly, to desired doneness of eggs. Pour into serving dish. Arrange asparagus spears on top. Garnish with slices of hard-cooked eggs. Sprinkle lightly with paprika and parsley flakes, if desired. Yield: 4 to 6 servings.

Scrambled Eggs And Mushrooms

2 *dozen eggs*
1 *cup light cream*
2 *teaspoons salt*
¼ *teaspoon pepper*
⅛ *teaspoon paprika*
3 *tablespoons butter or margarine*
1 *cup medium white sauce*
1 *(4-ounce) can sliced mushrooms, drained*
Parsley flakes

Beat eggs slightly; add cream, salt, pepper, and paprika. Cook slowly in the butter; fold in white sauce and mushrooms while eggs are still creamy. Garnish with additional mushrooms and parsley flakes. Yield: 12 servings.

Cookies and Small Cakes

Sugar cookies, or tea cakes as grandma called them, would probably take honors for the cookie recipe that has had the longest reign of popularity in our area. Made with fresh butter, eggs, and flour, they needed no liquid to hold ingredients together. Rolled thin as paper, they were, and are, cut with favorite cookie cutters. These cookies were often used originally to decorate the family Christmas tree.

Peanut butter, ginger, oatmeal, and lemon cookies have held their place in the cookie kingdom of the South.

Changes in conditions, cooks, and creative abilities have brought forth cookies with names that echo the 20th-century flavor: Ranger Cookies, Forever Ambers, Chocolate Jet Refrigerator Cookies, and Seven-Layer Cookies.

Cookies can be small enough to serve at a formal tea or large enough to satisfy the taste of a hungry Little Leaguer. Cookie jars are standard equipment for Southern kitchens and most of the time are filled with creative works of the cook.

Fruitcake Bars

     1 *cup brown sugar (packed)*
  1¼ *cups water*
    ⅓ *cup shortening*
     2 *cups raisins*
     2 *cups flour*
     1 *teaspoon salt*
     1 *teaspoon soda*
     1 *teaspoon baking powder*
    ½ *teaspoon ground nutmeg*
     1 *teaspoon ground cloves*
     2 *teaspoons ground cinnamon*
    ½ *cup chopped nuts*

Heat oven to 350 degrees. Mix brown sugar, water, shortening, and raisins in saucepan and bring to a boil; remove from heat and cool. Sift flour; blend dry ingredients; stir into cooled mixture. Mix in nuts. Spread dough evenly in greased pan, 13 x 9 x 2 inches. Bake at 350 degrees F. for 35 to 40 minutes or until no imprint remains when touched. Cool and cut into 2- x 1½-inch bars.

Seven-Layer Cookies

    ½ *stick butter*
     1 *cup graham cracker crumbs*
     1 *(7-ounce) can flaked coconut*
     1 *(6-ounce) package chocolate chips*
     1 *(6-ounce) package butterscotch chips*
     1 *can sweetened condensed milk*
     1 *cup chopped pecans*

Melt butter in a 9- x 12-inch baking pan. Add ingredients by layers, in order listed. Bake at 325 degrees F. about 30 minutes. Let cool in pan, then cut into small squares.

Christmas is something sweet . . . and there's no better way to express this than with a gift-wrapped package of homemade cookies.

Choco-Chewy Scotch Bars

1 *(12-ounce) package or 2 cups*
   semisweet chocolate pieces
1 *(15-ounce) can sweetened condensed*
   milk
2 *tablespoons butter or margarine*
1 *cup butter or margarine, melted*
1 *(1-pound) box or 2¼ cups firmly*
   packed brown sugar
2 *eggs*
2 *cups all-purpose flour*
1 *teaspoon salt*
1 *teaspoon vanilla extract*
½ *cup chopped pecans*
½ *cup flaked coconut*

In top of double boiler, over boiling water, melt chocolate pieces with condensed milk and 2 tablespoons butter; blend until smooth. Set aside.

In large mixing bowl combine 1 cup melted butter, brown sugar, and eggs. No need to sift flour; measure by lightly spooning into cup and leveling off. Add flour and salt; blend well. (*Note:* If self-rising flour is used, omit salt.) Stir in vanilla, pecans, and coconut; mix well. Spread half of dough in ungreased 15- x 10-inch jellyroll pan. Drizzle chocolate mixture over dough in pan. Dot top of chocolate mixture with remaining dough. Swirl slightly with tip of knife. Bake at 350 degrees F. for 30 to 35 minutes or until golden brown. Cool; cut into bars. Yield: about 48 bars.

Date-Pecan Bars

1 *cup butter or margarine*
2 *cups sugar*
3 *eggs*
1 *teaspoon soda*
2 *teaspoons water*
Dash of salt
1 *teaspoon vanilla extract*
1 *(8-ounce) package dates, chopped*
½ *pound candied cherries, chopped*
2 *cups chopped pecans*
3 *cups sifted flour*
Colored sugar or dragées

Cream together butter and sugar until light and fluffy. Add eggs, one at a time, beating well after each addition. Combine soda and water and blend into creamed mixture. Add salt and vanilla.

Add dates, cherries, and pecans and mix. Stir in flour and mix well. Press dough into a greased jellyroll pan. Sprinkle sugar or dragées over top (or press cut fruit and nuts into top of dough). Bake at 300 degrees F. for 25 to 30 minutes. Cut into bars and allow to cool in pan. When cool, remove to cake racks. Yield: 6 or 7 dozen bars.

Sugared Cranberry-Chocolate Bars

1 *(4-ounce) package sweet cooking*
   chocolate
2 *cups sifted cake flour*
½ *teaspoon baking soda*
¾ *teaspoon ground ginger*
¾ *teaspoon ground cinnamon*
½ *teaspoon ground cloves*
1 *cup butter or margarine*
1½ *cups granulated sugar*
2 *eggs*
1 *teaspoon vanilla extract*
1 *cup whole-berry cranberry sauce*
½ *cup buttermilk*
Powdered sugar

Melt chocolate over low heat; cool. Sift flour with baking soda and spices. Cream butter. Gradually add sugar; cream until light and fluffy. Add eggs, one at a time, beating well after each. Blend in melted chocolate, vanilla, and cranberry sauce. Add flour mixture alternately with buttermilk, beating after each addition until smooth. Pour into oiled paper-lined 13- x 9-inch pan. Bake at 350 degrees F. for about 40 minutes or until cake just begins to pull away from sides of pan. Cool 10 minutes. Remove from pan. Sprinkle top with powdered sugar. Cut into bars. Yield: 30 bars.

Self-Frosted Fudge Brownies

　1　(21½-ounce) package brownie mix
　1　egg
　⅓　cup plus 1 tablespoon water
　2　tablespoons butter or margarine,
　　　softened
　2　tablespoons lukewarm water
　1　(6¼-ounce) package buttercream
　　　fudge frosting mix*
　3　tablespoons hot coffee
　½　cup commercial sour cream
　1　(6-ounce) package or 1 cup
　　　semisweet chocolate pieces

Prepare brownies, using egg and ⅓ cup plus 1 tablespoon water, as directed on package. Spread in 13- x 9-inch pan which has been generously greased on bottom only.

In small mixer bowl blend butter, 2 tablespoons lukewarm water, dry frosting mix, and coffee at low speed until dry ingredients are moistened. Beat at medium speed until creamy, about 1 minute. Stir in sour cream. Pour over brownie mix, spreading to cover. Sprinkle with chocolate pieces.

Bake at 375 degrees F. for 25 to 30 minutes. Brownies will be soft to the touch and puffy and will begin to pull away from the edges of the pan. Cool completely; cut into bars. Yield: about 36 bars.

*Or use 1⅔ cups dry frosting mix from a 12½-ounce package. Measure by lightly spooning into cup and leveling off.

Cream Cheese Brownies

　1　(4-ounce) package German's Sweet
　　　Chocolate
　5　tablespoons butter or margarine
　1　(3-ounce) package cream cheese
　1　cup sugar
　3　eggs
　½　cup plus 1 tablespoon unsifted flour
　1½　teaspoons vanilla extract
　½　teaspoon baking powder
　¼　teaspoon salt
　½　cup chopped nuts
　¼　teaspoon almond extract

Melt chocolate and 3 tablespoons butter over very low heat. Stir; then cool. Cream 2 tablespoons butter with cream cheese. Gradually add ¼ cup sugar, creaming until fluffy. Blend in 1 egg, 1 tablespoon flour, and ½ teaspoon vanilla. Set aside.

Beat 2 eggs until lemon colored. Slowly beat in remaining ¾ cup sugar until mixture thickens. Add baking powder, salt, and ½ cup flour. Blend in chocolate mixture, 1 teaspoon vanilla, nuts, and almond extract.

Spread half of the chocolate batter in greased 8- or 9-inch square pan. Top with cream cheese mixture. Spoon remaining chocolate batter over top. Then zigzag knife through batter to obtain marble effect. Bake at 350 degrees F. about 35 to 40 minutes. Let cool. Cut in 20 bars or 16 squares.

Cherry-Coconut Squares

These delightful squares are extra rich, moist, and chewy.

　2　cups flour
　1　cup shortening
　6　tablespoons powdered sugar
　4　eggs, slightly beaten
　2　cups sugar
　½　cup flour
　1　teaspoon baking powder
　½　teaspoon salt
　2　teaspoons vanilla extract
　1½　cups coarsely chopped pecans
　1　cup shredded or flaked coconut
　1　cup maraschino cherries, cut in
　　　quarters

Combine flour, shortening, and powdered sugar. Mix well and pat firmly into bottom of ungreased 13- x 9-inch pan. Bake at 350 degrees F. about 20 to 25 minutes. Do not brown.

While pastry is baking, combine slightly beaten eggs and sugar. Add flour, baking powder, salt, vanilla, pecans, coconut, and cherries. Spread mixture over top of baked pastry. Bake at 350 degrees F. about 25 minutes.

Cut in small squares to serve. If stored, keep in a tightly covered container to conserve moisture. Yield: about 3 dozen.

Coconut-Orange Squares

⅔ cup sifted all-purpose flour
½ teaspoon baking powder
½ teaspoon salt
¼ cup butter
1 cup sugar
1 egg
1 tablespoon milk
1 teaspoon grated orange rind
1 cup flaked coconut
½ package (4 squares) semisweet
    chocolate, melted

Sift flour with baking powder and salt. Cream butter. Gradually add sugar; cream until light and fluffy. Add egg, milk, and orange rind; beat well. Add flour mixture and coconut, mixing only enough to blend. Place in an 8-inch square pan which has been lined with paper and then greased. Bake at 350 degrees F. for 25 minutes. Remove from pan and trim off edges. Spread with melted chocolate. Cool. Cut into squares. Yield: 12 servings.

Alternate baking pan: This may also be baked in a 9- x 5-inch loafpan. Increase baking time to 30 minutes. Cool. Cut into bars. Yield: 12 servings.

Congo Squares

⅔ cup shortening
1 box light brown sugar
3 eggs
2¾ cups flour
2½ teaspoons baking powder
½ teaspoon salt
1 cup chopped nuts
1 (6-ounce) package chocolate bits

Melt shortening over low heat; add brown sugar and beat well. Let cool. Add eggs and blend. Combine flour, baking powder, and salt and add to sugar mixture. Mix well. Add nuts and chocolate bits. Spread in a greased 15- x 12- x 1-inch pan and bake at 325 degrees F. for 30 minutes. Cool and cut into squares. Yield: about 4 dozen.

Fig-Nut Squares

2 eggs
½ cup sugar
½ teaspoon vanilla extract
½ cup flour
½ teaspoon baking powder
½ teaspoon salt
1½ cups finely cut dried figs
1 cup chopped nuts

Beat eggs until foamy. Beat in sugar and vanilla. Sift dry ingredients together; stir into egg mixture. Add figs and nuts (2 cups finely cut dates may be used in place of the figs); spread in greased square pan, 9 x 9 x 1¾ inches. Bake at 350 degrees F. for 25 to 30 minutes. Yield: 24 squares.

Butter Pecan Cookies

1 cup butter or margarine
¾ cup brown sugar
¾ cup granulated sugar
2 eggs
1 teaspoon vanilla extract
2¼ cups sifted flour
1 teaspoon soda
½ teaspoon salt
1 cup chopped pecans

Cream butter and sugars until light and fluffy. Beat in eggs and vanilla. Combine dry ingredients; add to creamed mixture and mix well. Stir in pecans. Drop from teaspoon onto ungreased cookie sheets. Bake at 375 degrees F. about 10 minutes or until lightly browned. Yield: about 48.

Swiss Almond Drops

3 eggs
1½ cups sugar
½ cup sifted flour
⅛ teaspoon salt
2 cups toasted almonds, finely chopped
1 (6-ounce) package semisweet
    chocolate pieces
1½ teaspoons vanilla extract

Beat eggs until thick; add sugar and continue beating until very thick. Add other ingredients and mix well. Chill until dough has stiffened (about 15 minutes). Drop by half teaspoonfuls onto greased cookie sheets. Bake at 325 degrees F. for 25 minutes. Yield: about 7 dozen.

Old-Fashioned German Cookies

    1 *pound salted red Spanish peanuts*
    3 *egg whites, beaten very stiff*
    3 *tablespoons flour*
    1 *cup sugar*

Grind peanuts in food chopper. Add stiffly beaten egg whites, flour, and sugar; stir to mix well. Drop by teaspoonfuls onto greased and floured cookie sheets. Bake at 300 degrees F. for 15 minutes. Let cool before storing in cardboard boxes, where they will keep indefinitely (do not store in canisters or cookie jar). Yield: 5 dozen.

Forgotten Cookies

    2 *egg whites*
    ⅔ *cup sugar*
      Pinch salt
    1 *teaspoon vanilla extract*
    1 *cup chopped pecans*
    1 *cup chocolate bits or corn flakes or*
        crisp rice cereal
    1 *cup coconut, if desired*

Beat egg whites until foamy (be sure that eggs are at room temperature before using). Gradually add sugar and continue beating until stiff. Add salt and vanilla, and mix well. Add pecans and choice of other ingredients.

Preheat oven to 350 degrees F. Drop cookies by teaspoonfuls onto ungreased foil-covered cookie sheet. Place cookies in oven and immediately turn oven off. Leave cookies in closed oven overnight. Yield: 2 dozen cookies.

Fruitcake Cookies

    ½ *cup butter or margarine*
    1 *cup light brown sugar*
    4 *eggs, beaten*
    2½ *cups flour*
    2 *cups chopped pecans*
    ½ *pound candied pineapple, chopped*
    ½ *pound candied cherries, chopped*
    ¼ *pound candied orange peel, chopped*
    ¼ *pound candied lemon peel, chopped*
    1 *teaspoon soda*
    ¾ *teaspoon ground cardamom*
    ½ *cup flour*

Cream butter and sugar. Add beaten eggs and mix well. Add 2½ cups flour and mix. Combine chopped nuts and fruits. Add soda and cardamom to the ½ cup flour. Add to chopped nut-fruit mixture and stir to coat. Add to creamed mixture and mix well. Drop by teaspoonfuls on greased cookie sheets and bake at 275 degrees F. for 12 to 15 minutes. Yield: 6 to 8 dozen.

Cherry Drop Cakes

    ½ *cup butter or margarine*
    1 *(3-ounce) package cream cheese*
    1 *cup sugar*
    2 *eggs*
    1 *teaspoon vanilla extract*
    1 *teaspoon almond extract*
    2¼ *cups all-purpose flour*
    2 *teaspoons baking powder*
    1 *teaspoon soda*
    ½ *teaspoon salt*
    1 *(8½-ounce) can crushed pineapple,*
        well drained
    ½ *cup chopped maraschino cherries*
    1 *cup chopped pecans (optional)*

Blend the butter and cream cheese together. Gradually add sugar; cream well. Add eggs one at a time, beating well after each addition. Add flavorings. Add combined dry ingredients gradually; mix thoroughly. Stir in pineapple, chopped cherries, and pecans. Drop by large rounded tablespoonfuls onto unoiled cookie sheets. Bake at 375 degrees F. for 12 minutes. Yield: 2 dozen.

Chocolate-Nut Drops

⅔ cup soft shortening
1 cup brown sugar, firmly packed
1 egg
2 squares unsweetened chocolate,
  melted and cooled
1¾ cups sifted flour
½ teaspoon salt
½ teaspoon soda
½ cup milk (sweet or sour)
½ cup chopped pecans

Cream shortening and sugar; add egg and beat well. Stir in melted chocolate. Sift dry ingredients and add to creamed mixture alternately with milk. Stir in pecans and drop by spoonfuls on greased cookie sheet. Bake at 350 degrees F. for 12 to 15 minutes. Top with powdered sugar frosting, if desired. Yield: about 5 dozen.

Lemon-Date Cookies

½ cup finely chopped pitted dates
3 (¾-ounce) packages instant lemon
  pudding mix
1 cup biscuit mix
⅓ cup shortening
1 egg
1 tablespoon fresh lemon juice

Chop dates and set aside. Blend the pudding mix and biscuit mix. Cut in shortening; mix in egg, lemon juice, and dates. Drop by spoonfuls onto ungreased baking sheet. Flatten with the bottom of a glass dipped in sugar. Bake at 375 degrees F. for 10 minutes. Cool on rack. Yield: 2½ dozen cookies.

Almond Macaroons

½ pound almond paste
3 egg whites, slightly beaten
½ cup sifted all-purpose flour
½ cup fine granulated sugar
½ cup powdered sugar

Work the almond paste with a wooden spoon until it is smooth. Add the slightly beaten egg whites and blend thoroughly. Add flour, resifted with the granulated and powdered sugar. Cover cookie sheets with ungreased white paper. Drop cookie mixture from tip of a teaspoon or press through a cookie press. Bake at 300 degrees F. about 30 minutes. Remove macaroons from paper with spatula while warm. Yield: about 30.

Date-Nut Cookies

2 teaspoons soda
2 cups chopped dates
½ cup boiling water
1 cup butter
1½ cups sugar
2 eggs, beaten
1 cup coconut or raisins
1 cup chopped nuts
1 teaspoon vanilla extract
3¼ cups flour

Sprinkle soda over chopped dates. Add boiling water, stir well, and set aside.

Cream butter and sugar; add eggs and beat well. Stir in dates, coconut, nuts, and vanilla and mix well. Add flour and mix well (batter will be very stiff).

Drop by teaspoonfuls onto greased cookie sheets and bake at 375 degrees F. about 12 minutes or until browned. Yield: about 7 dozen cookies.

Holiday Fruit Cookies

1 pound candied cherries
1 pound candied pineapple
5 (8-ounce) packages dates
1 pound (4 cups) shelled pecans
3 cups flour
½ teaspoon soda
½ teaspoon salt
½ cup butter
1½ cups sugar
3 eggs, well beaten
1 teaspoon vanilla extract
1 teaspoon lemon extract
2 teaspoons ground cinnamon

Cut fruit in small pieces; leave pecans in halves. Sift flour, soda, and salt together and sift over chopped fruit and pecans. Cream butter and sugar until light; add beaten eggs and mix well. Stir in vanilla, lemon, and cinnamon. Stir in flour-covered fruit. Drop by teaspoonfuls onto greased cookie sheets and bake at 300 degrees F. for about 25 minutes. Yield: 150 small cookies.

Fruit Cookies

1 *cup shortening*
2 *cups brown sugar, packed*
2 *eggs*
½ *cup buttermilk*
3½ *cups flour*
1½ *teaspoons soda*
1 *teaspoon salt*
2 *cups broken pecans*
2 *cups chopped candied cherries*
2 *cups chopped dates*

Combine shortening, sugar, eggs, and buttermilk and beat well. Sift dry ingredients together; stir into shortening mixture. Mix in pecans, cherries, and dates. Drop by teaspoonfuls onto greased cookie sheets, spacing about an inch apart. Bake in preheated 300-degree F. oven for 10 to 15 minutes. Cool on cake rack and store in tight container. Cookies keep well for several weeks. Yield: 6 or 7 dozen, according to size desired.

Hawaiian Drop Cookies

2 *cups sifted flour*
2 *teaspoons baking powder*
½ *teaspoon salt*
⅔ *cup shortening*
1¼ *cups sugar*
½ *teaspoon vanilla extract*
½ *teaspoon almond extract*
1 *egg*
¾ *cup well-drained crushed pineapple*
½ *cup chopped pecans, if desired*
½ *cup finely grated coconut*

Sift together flour, baking powder, and salt

and set aside. Cream shortening; add sugar and flavorings and beat until smooth. Add egg and beat until mixture is fluffy. Blend in pineapple (and nuts if desired) and the dry ingredients. Drop by teaspoonfuls on ungreased cookie sheets about 3 inches apart. Sprinkle with coconut and bake at 325 degrees F. about 20 minutes.

Honey Drops

¼ *cup shortening*
½ *cup honey*
1 *egg*
1 *cup oatmeal*
1 *tablespoon milk*
1 *cup sifted flour*
3 *teaspoons baking powder*
½ *teaspoon salt*
½ *teaspoon ground cinnamon*
½ *cup chopped raisins*

Cream shortening and honey together. Add egg and beat until blended. Stir in oatmeal and milk. Sift dry ingredients; add with raisins and mix well. Drop from teaspoon onto greased baking sheet. Bake at 400 degrees F. about 18 to 20 minutes. Yield: 2½ dozen.

French Almond Meringues

1 *(6-ounce) package semisweet chopped chocolate pieces*
3 *egg whites*
½ *teaspoon vanilla extract*
1 *cup sugar*
⅓ *cup blanched almonds, finely chopped*

Melt chocolate pieces over hot, not boiling, water. Remove from heat, and cool about 5 minutes. Combine egg whites and vanilla and beat until stiff but not dry. Gradually add sugar and beat until very stiff. Fold in finely chopped almonds and cooled melted chocolate. Drop by teaspoonfuls onto greased cookie sheet. Bake at 350 degrees F. about 10 to 12 minutes. Yield: 4 dozen.

Fudge-Oatmeal Cookies

2 *cups sugar*
½ *cup evaporated milk*
2 *tablespoons cocoa*
1 *stick butter*
½ *teaspoon vanilla extract*
½ *cup chopped nuts*
2½ *cups quick-cooking oatmeal*

Combine sugar, milk, cocoa, and butter in saucepan. Cook over medium heat for 2 minutes, stirring constantly to prevent sticking. Remove from heat.

Add vanilla and nuts and mix well. Add oatmeal and blend thoroughly. (*Note:* Do not use instant oatmeal.) Drop by teaspoonfuls onto waxed paper. Do not bake; these are ready to eat. Yield: 4 dozen.

Holiday Lizzies

½ *cup sugar*
⅓ *cup butter*
2 *eggs, well beaten*
1½ *cups flour*
1½ *teaspoons soda*
1½ *tablespoons milk*
1 *pound candied cherries, chopped*
1 *pound dates, chopped*
1 *pound chopped pecans*
1 *pound candied pineapple, chopped*
Whiskey (wine glass full)

Cream together sugar, butter, and eggs. Sift flour and soda together and add to egg mixture; stir in milk. Add rest of ingredients and mix well. Drop by spoonfuls onto greased cookie sheet. Bake at 325 degrees F. for about 12 to 15 minutes. Yield: 80 or 90 cookies.

Meringue Cookies

½ *teaspoon cream of tartar*
6 *egg whites*
2 *cups sugar*
1 *pound chopped walnuts or pecans*

Add cream of tartar to egg whites and beat until stiff. Add sugar and beat with electric mixer for 20 minutes or by hand for 30 minutes. Stir in nuts and drop by teaspoonfuls onto greased cookie sheet.

Bake at 300 degrees F. for approximately 7 minutes. (*Note:* As ovens vary, it is advisable to bake a few test cookies when trying this recipe for the first time. An adjustment of baking time and oven temperature is sometimes necessary.) Placing the cookie sheet on a wet cloth after removing it from the oven makes it easier to remove the cookies without breaking them. They should be removed immediately and carefully, using a spatula, and placed on a rack until cool. Yield: 4 dozen.

Oatmeal Cookies

1 *cup granulated sugar*
½ *cup shortening*
1 *egg*
½ *cup molasses*
2 *cups sifted flour*
1 *teaspoon salt*
1½ *teaspoons soda*
1 *teaspoon vanilla extract*
1 *cup quick-cooking oatmeal*

Cream sugar and shortening. Add egg and molasses; beat well. Add sifted dry ingredients and mix well. Add vanilla and stir in oatmeal. Drop from teaspoon onto greased baking sheet. Bake at 375 degrees F. for 10 to 12 minutes. Yield: approximately 48 cookies.

Note: Chopped pecans or chocolate chips may be added if desired.

Tots and Teens

½ *package cake mix (any flavor)*
1 *egg*
1 *cup corn flakes*
½ *cup chopped nuts*
½ *cup finely shredded coconut*
1 *teaspoon flavoring (vanilla, lemon, almond, or mixed)*

Orange Gumdrop Cookies

  1 *cup shortening*
  1 *cup granulated sugar*
  1 *cup brown sugar*
  2 *eggs*
  1 *teaspoon vanilla extract*
  2 *cups flour*
  1 *teaspoon baking powder*
  1 *teaspoon baking soda*
 ½ *teaspoon salt*
  2 *cups quick-cooking oatmeal*
  1 *cup chopped pecans*
  1 *cup flaked coconut*
  1 *cup chopped orange slices*
    (gumdrops)

Cream shortening and sugars together. Add eggs one at a time, blending well. Add vanilla. Add sifted dry ingredients. Add remaining ingredients. Drop by teaspoonfuls on greased cookie sheet. Bake at 325 degrees F. for 10 to 12 minutes. Let cool slightly before removing from cookie sheet. Yield: 6 to 8 dozen small cookies.

Jumbo Raisin Cookies

  2 *cups raisins*
  1 *cup boiling water*
  1 *cup vegetable shortening*
  2 *cups sugar*
  3 *eggs*
  1 *teaspoon vanilla extract*
  4 *cups flour*
  1 *teaspoon baking powder*
  1 *teaspoon soda*
  1 *teaspoon salt*
 1½ *teaspoons ground cinnamon*
 ½ *teaspoon ground allspice*

Cook raisins in boiling water for 5 minutes. Cool. Cream shortening; add sugar and beat well. Add eggs and beat until well blended. Add vanilla and cooled raisins.

Combine flour, baking powder, soda, salt, and spices. Add to the creamed mixture and mix well. Drop by spoonfuls on greased cookie sheet. Bake at 325 degrees F. for 10 to 15 minutes. Yield: about 6 dozen.

Ambrosia Cookies

  2 *cups flour*
 ½ *teaspoon baking powder*
 ½ *teaspoon salt*
  1 *teaspoon soda*
  1 *cup shortening*
  1 *cup white sugar*
  1 *cup brown sugar*
  2 *eggs*
  1 *teaspoon vanilla extract*
 1½ *cups uncooked oatmeal*
  1 *cup coconut*
  1 *cup raisins*
  1 *cup chopped dates*
  1 *cup chopped nuts*

Combine dry ingredients. Cream shortening and sugar until light. Add eggs, one at a time, beating well after each addition. Add vanilla. Stir in dry ingredients.

Combine oatmeal, coconut, raisins, dates, and nuts; stir into creamed mixture. Shape into small balls and place on greased cookie sheets. Bake at 375 degrees F. about 12 to 14 minutes. Yield: about 5 dozen cookies.

Butter-Roll Cookies

  2 *sticks butter*
 ½ *cup sugar*
  2 *cups flour*
  1 *teaspoon ground cinnamon*
  1 *tablespoon vanilla extract*
  2 *cups corn flakes, crushed*
  1 *cup chopped pecans*
 ¼ *cup powdered sugar*

Combine all ingredients except powdered sugar and mix well. Form into balls and bake on greased cookie sheets at 325 degrees F. for 30 minutes. Roll in powdered sugar while still warm. Yield: 4 dozen.

Brandy Balls

1 (12-ounce) package crushed vanilla
    wafers
½ cup rum
½ cup brandy
½ cup honey
1 pound ground walnuts
Powdered sugar

Mix first five ingredients together well. Roll into small balls. Gently roll in powdered sugar and store in tightly covered container in the refrigerator. These will keep for 5 weeks. Yield: about 50 balls.

Butterscotch Crisps

½ cup butter or shortening
½ cup firmly packed brown sugar
1 (4-ounce) package butterscotch
    pudding mix
1 egg
1½ cups sifted all-purpose flour
1 teaspoon soda
1 teaspoon cream of tartar

Cream butter, sugar, and pudding mix together. Add egg and blend well. Sift dry ingredients together and add to creamed mixture. Blend well and roll into small balls about the size of walnuts. Place on greased cookie sheets. Press with fork that has been dipped in flour. Bake at 350 degrees F. for 10 to 12 minutes. Yield: 4 dozen.

Vanilla-Cocoa Balls

1 cup vanilla wafer crumbs
2½ tablespoons cocoa
1 cup powdered sugar
¾ cup finely chopped pecans
1½ tablespoons white corn syrup
3 to 5 tablespoons cream, rum, or
    brandy

Mix the crumbs, cocoa, sugar, and pecans together. Add syrup slowly and blend. Add cream or flavoring last, using only enough

so that the balls will hold their shape. With your fingers, form into balls the size of a walnut. Yield: 2 dozen balls.

Christmas Puffs

1 stick butter or margarine
½ cup sifted powdered sugar
1 egg yolk
½ teaspoon vanilla extract
1½ cups sifted all-purpose flour
¼ teaspoon salt
1 egg white
2 tablespoons granulated sugar
½ cup finely chopped pecans
Candied red cherries

Cream butter with powdered sugar until light and fluffy. Beat in egg yolk and vanilla. Gradually sift in flour and salt, blending well to make a stiff dough. Form into small balls and place on ungreased cookie sheets. Make a well in center of each with tip of a wooden spoon handle. Chill while making meringue filling. Beat egg white until foamy; add sugar and beat until meringue stands in stiff peaks. Fold in pecans and spoon generous amount of mixture into wells in cookies. Bake at 350 degrees F. for 15 minutes. Top with half a candied cherry after baking. Yield: 2 dozen.

Forever Ambers

1 pound candy orange slices, cut fine
2 (3½-ounce) cans flaked coconut
1 teaspoon orange flavoring
2 cans sweetened condensed milk
1 cup finely chopped pecans
1 teaspoon vanilla extract
Powdered sugar

Combine all ingredients except powdered sugar, and mix well. Spread mixture in a lightly oiled 15- x 10- x 1½-inch baking pan and bake at 275 degrees F. for 30 minutes. Remove from oven, and while still hot spoon mixture into bowl of sifted powdered sugar. Roll into balls the size of small walnuts and place on cake racks to cool. Yield: 72 cookies.

Date-Nut Balls

  1 *(8-ounce) package dates, chopped*
  ¾ *cup sugar*
  1 *stick margarine*
  1 *cup chopped pecans or walnuts*
2½ *cups crisp rice cereal*
    Powdered sugar

Cook dates, sugar, and margarine, stirring constantly until margarine is absorbed. Add nuts and pour hot mixture over rice cereal in a large bowl; mix well. Form into small balls and dust with powdered sugar. Put several small balls in a paper bag with powdered sugar; shake until balls are coated. Yield: about 4 dozen.

Coconut Butterballs

½ *cup butter*
2 *tablespoons unsifted powdered sugar*
½ *teaspoon vanilla extract*
1 *cup unsifted all-purpose flour*
¾ *cup flaked coconut*
  Additional unsifted powdered sugar

Cream butter. Add 2 tablespoons sugar and the vanilla; cream until light and fluffy. Add flour, all at once, and blend well. Mix in coconut. Shape into ¾-inch balls and place on ungreased baking sheets. Chill 15 minutes. Bake at 350 degrees F. for 15 minutes, or until lightly browned. Roll in additional powdered sugar while still warm. Yield: 3 dozen.

Mincemeat Ball Cookies

  1 *cup butter*
  ¼ *cup sugar*
  2 *egg yolks*
2⅔ *cups flour*
    Mincemeat

Cream butter and sugar. Add egg yolks and beat until fluffy. Add flour and mix well. Shape into small balls and place on greased cookie sheets. Press thumb in center of each cookie and fill center with mincemeat. Bake at 350 degrees F. about 10 to 12 minutes.

Quick Cookies

¾ *cup biscuit mix*
1 *package instant pudding mix (any flavor)*
¼ *cup cooking oil*
1 *egg*

Combine ingredients, and mix until dough forms a ball. Shape into balls, using 1 teaspoon dough for each ball. Place on ungreased baking sheet. Flatten to about 2-inch size with hand. Bake at 350 degrees F. for 8 minutes. Yield: 24 cookies.

Cookie Jar Gingersnaps

2 *cups sifted flour*
1 *tablespoon ground ginger*
2 *teaspoons baking soda*
1 *teaspoon ground cinnamon*
½ *teaspoon salt*
¾ *cup shortening*
1 *cup sugar*
1 *egg, unbeaten*
¼ *cup molasses*

Measure flour, ginger, baking soda, cinnamon, and salt; sift twice onto waxed paper and return to sifter. Cream shortening until soft; add sugar gradually, creaming after each addition until mixture is well blended. Beat in egg and molasses. Sift dry ingredients over creamed mixture; blend well. Form teaspoonfuls of dough into small balls by rolling lightly between palms of hands; roll dough balls in additional sugar to cover entirely. Place 2 inches apart on ungreased cookie sheet. Bake at 350 degrees for 12 to 15 minutes or until tops are slightly rounded and cracked.

Nutty Nuggets

½ *cup butter or margarine*
2 *tablespoons sugar*
1 *cup enriched flour less 2 tablespoons*
⅛ *teaspoon salt*
1 *cup chopped pecans*
1 *teaspoon vanilla extract*
Powdered sugar

Cream the butter and sugar. Combine the flour and salt and add to the creamed mixture. Add pecans and vanilla. Form into ¾-inch balls and place on oiled cookie sheet. Bake at 350 degrees F. for 15 minutes. Remove from oven; cool slightly and roll in a generous amount of powdered sugar. When cold, roll again in powdered sugar. Yield: 3 dozen.

Frost 'n Bake Cookies

1 *cup butter or margarine, softened*
1 *(8¼-ounce) package coconut-almond frosting mix*
2 *teaspoons vanilla extract*
1 *teaspoon coconut flavoring, if desired*
1 *teaspoon rum flavoring, if desired*
1½ *cups all-purpose flour*
½ *cup raisins*
¼ *teaspoon salt*
Fudge Frosting
Pecan halves for garnish
Powdered sugar, if desired

In large mixing bowl cream butter, frosting mix, and flavorings. No need to sift flour; measure by lightly spooning into cup and leveling off. Blend in flour, raisins, and salt; mix until a soft dough forms. (*Note:* If self-rising flour is used, omit salt.) Shape into 1-inch balls (or drop by spoonfuls). Place 1½ inches apart on ungreased cookie sheets. Flatten with fork. Spread 1 teaspoon Fudge Frosting on each cookie. Top with a pecan half. Bake at 300 degrees F. for 15 to 18 minutes or until edges are lightly browned. If desired, dip slightly cooled cookies in powdered sugar. Yield: about 56 cookies.

Fudge Frosting:

5 *(1 ounce each) squares semisweet chocolate*
½ *cup sweetened condensed milk*
¼ *teaspoon salt*
1 *teaspoon vanilla extract*
¼ *teaspoon almond extract*
¼ *teaspoon coconut flavoring, if desired*

In small saucepan melt chocolate in condensed milk over low heat. Remove from heat. Add salt and flavorings; blend until smooth.

Coconut Butterballs

1 *cup soft butter or margarine*
¼ *cup sifted powdered sugar*
1 *teaspoon vanilla extract*
2 *cups all-purpose flour*
1½ *cups flaked coconut*
Sifted powdered sugar

Cream butter or margarine until light and fluffy; gradually add sugar and vanilla and mix well. Blend in flour, then coconut. Roll into 1-inch balls and place on ungreased cookie sheet. Place cookie sheet in refrigerator for about 15 minutes. Bake at 350 degrees F. about 15 minutes or until delicately browned. While still warm, roll in powdered sugar. Yield: 4 dozen.

Molasses-Coconut Lace Wafers

¼ *cup unsifted cake flour*
¼ *teaspoon double-acting baking powder*
⅛ *teaspoon baking soda*
¼ *cup unsulphured or light molasses*
¼ *cup sugar*
¼ *cup butter*
⅔ *cup flaked coconut*

Mix flour, baking powder, and soda; set aside. Combine molasses, sugar, and butter in saucepan. Bring to a full boil and cook 1 minute. Remove from heat. Add flour mixture and coconut; mix well. Drop by ½ teaspoonfuls on a lightly greased baking sheet. (Bake only about 9 at a time for ease in handling cookies.) Bake at 350 degrees F. for 5 to 8 minutes. Cool slightly; remove each wafer carefully from baking sheet while still warm and roll quickly over handle of wooden spoon. Place on rack to cool. If wafer hardens on pan, return to oven for a few minutes. Yield: about 2½ dozen wafers.

Poppyseed Cookies

  ½ *cup butter or margarine*
  ⅓ *cup sugar*
  2 *egg yolks*
  1 *cup flour*
  ⅓ *teaspoon salt*
  ¼ *teaspoon grated lemon rind*
  ½ *teaspoon vanilla extract*
  2 *teaspoons poppy seed*

Cream butter and sugar. Beat in egg yolks and other ingredients. Mix well, cover bowl, and chill at least 2 hours. Shape dough into 1-inch balls, place on greased cookie sheets, and flatten with a fork. Bake at 375 degrees F. for 10 minutes. Yield: 24 cookies.

Yeast Cookie Butterfingers

  1 *pound butter, softened*
  1 *cup sugar*
  1 *cake, compressed, or 1 package*
       dry yeast
  ¼ *cup very warm water*
  2 *eggs, separated*
  4 *cups sifted flour*
  ½ *cup finely chopped nuts*
  ½ *cup chocolate shot or toasted*
       coconut

Cream butter and sugar until fluffy. Dissolve yeast in water and add with egg yolks to creamed mixture. Gradually beat in flour, mixing thoroughly. Chill dough for easier handling. To form cookies, roll about 1 tablespoon dough into a finger shape. Dip in egg whites, then roll in nuts and chocolate

or coconut. Place on greased cookie sheet and bake at 375 degrees F. for 10 to 12 minutes. Cool and store in covered container. The cookies keep well. They may be frozen, or the dough may be frozen.

Swedish Pecan Balls

  1 *cup ground pecans*
  2 *tablespoons sugar*
  ½ *cup butter or margarine*
  1 *cup flour*
  1 *teaspoon vanilla extract*
  ⅛ *teaspoon salt*
     Powdered sugar

Combine all ingredients except powdered sugar and mix well. Shape dough into balls the size of walnuts. Place on ungreased cookie sheet and bake at 275 degrees F. about 30 minutes or until light brown. Roll in powdered sugar while hot and again after cookies have cooled. Yield: 2 dozen.

Praline Cookies

  ¾ *cup shortening*
  ¾ *cup sugar*
  ½ *cup unsulphured molasses*
  1 *egg*
  2¼ *cups sifted all-purpose flour*
  1 *teaspoon ground cinnamon*
  1½ *teaspoons baking soda*
  ½ *teaspoon salt*
  ½ *teaspoon ground ginger*
  1 *(6-ounce) package butterscotch-*
       flavored morsels
     Pecan halves

Cream together shortening and sugar until light and fluffy. Add molasses and egg; mix well. Sift in dry ingredients; mix thoroughly. Stir in butterscotch morsels. Chill in refrigerator 2 hours. Form into approximately 1-inch balls; roll in granulated sugar. Place on greased baking sheets. Top each with a pecan half. Bake in a 375-degree F. oven for 10 to 12 minutes. Yield: approximately 5 dozen cookies.

Gingersnaps

  ¾ *cup soft shortening*
   1 *cup sugar*
   1 *egg*
  ½ *cup molasses*
2¼ *cups all-purpose flour*
   2 *teaspoons soda*
  ½ *teaspoon salt*
  ½ *teaspoon ground cloves*
  ½ *teaspoon ground cinnamon*
   1 *teaspoon ground ginger*
   Pinch ground cardamom, if desired
  ¼ *cup sugar*
  ½ *teaspoon ground cinnamon*

Cream shortening, sugar, egg, and molasses. Combine flour, soda, salt, and the next 4 spices; add to creamed mixture. Chill dough thoroughly. Roll into balls the size of small walnuts. Dip tops in mixture of ¼ cup sugar and ½ teaspoon ground cinnamon. Place, sugar side up, about 3 inches apart on a greased cookie sheet. Sprinkle each cookie with two or three drops of water to produce a crackled surface. Do not flatten cookies. Bake at 375 degrees F. about 10 to 12 minutes or until cookies are just set, but not hard.

Although cookies will puff up in baking, they flatten when removed from the oven. Yield: 4½ dozen.

Lollipop Cookies

   1 *cup sifted flour*
  ½ *cup granulated sugar*
   1 *teaspoon baking powder*
  ¼ *teaspoon salt*
  ½ *cup brown sugar*
  ½ *cup soft shortening*
   1 *egg*
   1 *teaspoon vanilla extract*
   1 *teaspoon water*
   1 *cup oatmeal, quick-cooking or*
     regular
   Powdered sugar frosting
   Semisweet chocolate pieces, gumdrops,
     cinnamon candies, colored coconut

Sift together first four ingredients. Add brown sugar, shortening, egg, vanilla, and water. Beat until smooth, about 2 minutes. Stir in oatmeal.

Shape into 24 balls; place on ungreased cookie sheets. Flatten with bottom of glass dipped in flour. Insert wooden skewers into each. Bake at 350 degrees F. for 11 to 12 minutes. Remove from cookie sheets; cool. Using powdered sugar frosting, attach semi-sweet chocolate pieces for eyes, gumdrops for nose, cinnamon candies for mouth, and colored coconut for hair. Yield: 24 cookies.

Molasses Krinkles

  ¾ *cup shortening*
   1 *cup light brown sugar*
   1 *egg, beaten*
  ¼ *cup sorghum molasses*
2¼ *cups all-purpose flour*
   2 *teaspoons soda*
  ¼ *teaspoon salt*
  ½ *teaspoon ground cloves*
   1 *teaspoon ground ginger*
   1 *teaspoon ground cinnamon*
   Sugar
   3 *tablespoons firm jelly*

Cream shortening and sugar. Add egg and molasses and beat well. Combine flour, soda, salt, and spices and add to creamed mixture. Chill overnight in refrigerator.

Roll dough into balls the size of walnuts and dip tops in sugar. Place, sugar side up, on greased cookie sheets. Make indentation in top of each cookie and fill with a little jelly. Bake at 375 degrees F. about 10 to 12 minutes. Yield: 4½ dozen.

Oatmeal Cookies

1 *cup shortening*
1 *cup brown sugar*
1 *cup white sugar*
2 *eggs, beaten*
1 *teaspoon vanilla extract*
1½ *cups flour*
1 *teaspoon soda*
1 *teaspoon ground nutmeg*
1 *teaspoon ground cinnamon*
1 *teaspoon salt*
1 *cup chopped pecans*
3 *cups uncooked oatmeal*

Cream shortening and sugar. Add eggs and vanilla and beat well. Combine flour, soda, nutmeg, cinnamon, and salt and add to creamed mixture, a small amount at a time. Add nuts and oatmeal and mix well. Divide mixture into three parts and shape into rolls. Wrap in waxed paper and foil and freeze until needed. Slice thin and place on greased cookie sheet. Bake at 350 degrees F. for 8 to 10 minutes. Yield: 4 dozen.

Butterscotch Cookies

2 *cups brown sugar*
3 *cups flour*
1½ *teaspoons soda*
1⅓ *teaspoons cream of tartar*
½ *cup melted butter or margarine*
2 *eggs, beaten*

Combine sugar, flour, soda, and cream of tartar together. Add melted butter or margarine and beaten eggs. Turn onto a lightly floured board and knead. Shape into small rolls and wrap in waxed paper. Refrigerate overnight. Slice and bake on a greased cookie sheet at 350 degrees F. for 12 minutes. Yield: about 7 dozen.

Fresh Orange Butter Cookies

1 *tablespoon grated orange rind*
1 *teaspoon grated lemon rind*
1 *cup (2 sticks) butter or margarine*
¼ *teaspoon salt*
1 *cup sugar*
1 *large egg*
¼ *cup fresh orange juice*
2 *cups sifted all-purpose flour*

Blend orange and lemon rinds with softened butter or margarine. Mix in salt and sugar. Beat in egg and orange juice. Stir in flour. Mix well. Chill dough until stiff enough to handle; then shape into 1-inch balls. Place 2 inches apart on ungreased cookie sheets. Bake in a preheated moderate oven (375 degrees F.) 10 to 12 minutes or until done. Cool on wire racks. Store in airtight container. Yield: about 4 dozen.

Chocolate Jet Refrigerator Cookies

½ *cup butter*
1 *cup sugar*
1 *egg*
1 *teaspoon vanilla extract*
2 *cups sifted all-purpose flour*
1 *teaspoon baking powder*
½ *teaspoon salt*
1 *tablespoon milk*
2 *squares unsweetened chocolate, melted and cooled*

Cream butter, sugar, and egg together until smooth. Add vanilla. Add flour slowly, then baking powder and salt. Stir in milk and melted chocolate. Shape into rolls and cover with plastic wrap. Refrigerate 5 hours or overnight. Slice; place on greased baking sheet and bake at 375 degrees F. about 10 minutes. Yield: 50 cookies.

Cookie dough may also be rolled after chilling. Cut with cookie cutter, brush with beaten egg white, and sprinkle with dry strawberry-flavored gelatin.

Peanut Butter Pinwheel Cookies

 ½ cup shortening
 1 cup sugar (may be half brown)
 ½ cup peanut butter
 1 egg
 2 tablespoons milk
 1¼ cups sifted flour
 ½ teaspoon soda
 ½ teaspoon salt
 1 (6-ounce) package chocolate chips

Cream shortening and sugar until light and fluffy. Beat in peanut butter, egg, and milk. Sift dry ingredients together and stir into creamed mixture. Place dough on lightly floured waxed paper and roll into a 15- x 8-inch rectangle. Melt chocolate chips over hot water; cool slightly and spread over dough. Roll jellyroll fashion and chill 20 to 30 minutes. Slice ¼ inch thick. Bake on ungreased cookie sheet at 375 degrees F. for 8 to 10 minutes. Yield: about 4 dozen.

Ribbon Cookies

 1 cup butter or other shortening
 1½ cups sugar
 1 egg, beaten
 1 teaspoon vanilla extract
 2½ cups flour
 ½ teaspoon salt
 1½ teaspoons baking powder
 ¼ cup chopped candied cherries
 ¼ cup chopped pecans
 1 ounce semisweet chocolate, melted
 2 tablespoons poppy seed

Cream butter and sugar. Add egg and vanilla; beat thoroughly. Add flour combined with salt and baking powder. Mix well. Divide dough into three parts. Add cherries to one part, nutmeats and chocolate to another, and poppy seed to the third. Line a small, narrow loafpan with waxed paper; pack chocolate-nut dough into the bottom. Over this pack cherry dough, then the poppyseed mixture. Cover with waxed paper and place in refrigerator to harden. When

ready to bake, turn out of pan and slice thin. Place on an oiled cookie sheet and bake at 400 degrees F. for 10 minutes. Yield: 6 to 8 dozen cookies.

Christmas Cookies

 ½ cup butter
 ½ cup shortening
 1 cup sugar
 3 eggs
 3½ cups all-purpose flour
 1 teaspoon soda
 2 teaspoons cream of tartar
 1½ teaspoons vanilla extract
 Colored sugar

Cream together butter, shortening, and sugar; add the eggs and blend well. Sift together flour, soda, and cream of tartar; add to the creamed mixture. Stir in vanilla.

Chill the dough; then roll it out on floured pastry cloth and cut with cookie cutters. Place on ungreased cookie sheets, sprinkle with the colored sugar, and bake at 425 degrees F. for 6 to 8 minutes. Yield: 5 to 7 dozen.

Tea Cakes

 3 cups flour
 2 teaspoons cream of tartar
 1 teaspoon soda
 ½ teaspoon salt
 1 cup sugar
 1 cup shortening
 2 eggs
 1 teaspoon vanilla extract

Sift dry ingredients together. Cut in shortening, add eggs and vanilla, and mix well.

Drop by rounded teaspoontuls onto greased baking sheet. Bake at 425 degrees F. until edges are golden. Yield: 4 dozen.

Peanut Blossoms

½ cup shortening
½ cup peanut butter
½ cup granulated sugar
½ cup brown sugar
 1 egg
 2 tablespoons milk
 1 teaspoon vanilla extract
1¾ cups all-purpose flour
 1 teaspoon soda
½ teaspoon salt
    Powdered sugar
48 chocolate candy kisses

Cream shortening and peanut butter; add sugars and beat thoroughly. Stir in egg, milk, and vanilla and beat well. Combine flour, soda, and salt; add to creamed mixture. The dough will be very stiff.

Shape dough into balls, using a round teaspoon for each. Roll balls in powdered sugar and place on a lightly greased cookie sheet. Bake at 375 degrees F. for 10 to 12 minutes. After removing from oven, top each with a candy kiss, and press down firmly. Yield: 4 dozen.

Starlight Sugar Crisps

 1 package dry yeast
¼ cup very warm water
3¾ cups all-purpose flour
1½ teaspoons salt
 1 cup butter or margarine
 2 eggs, beaten
½ cup commercial sour cream
 1 teaspoon vanilla extract
1½ cups sugar
 2 teaspoons vanilla extract

Soften yeast in very warm water. Sift the flour and salt together into a large mixing bowl. Cut in butter or margarine until particles are size of small peas. Blend in beaten

eggs, sour cream, softened yeast, and 1 teaspoon vanilla; mix thoroughly. Cover and chill at least 2 hours or overnight.

Combine 1½ cups sugar and 2 teaspoons vanilla. Sprinkle about ½ cup of sugar-vanilla mixture on cloth or board. Roll out half of the dough into a 16- x 8-inch rectangle. Sprinkle with about 1 tablespoon sugar-vanilla mixture.

Fold one end of dough over center; fold other end over to make three layers. Turn one-fourth way around and repeat, rolling out to 16- x 8-inch rectangle and folding, with the final rolling to about ¼-inch thickness. Cut into 4- x 1-inch strips; twist each 2 or 3 times and place on lightly greased cookie sheets. Bake at 375 degrees F. about 15 to 20 minutes or until cookies are a light brown. Repeat procedure for other half of dough and sugar-vanilla mixture. Yield: about 4 dozen.

Christmas Tea Cakes

½ cup soft butter
 1 cup sugar
 2 eggs, well beaten
2½ cups all-purpose flour
½ teaspoon baking powder
¼ teaspoon salt
 1 teaspoon vanilla extract
 1 tablespoon milk
    Thin powdered sugar frosting
    Colored sugar or decorating candies

Cream butter and sugar until light and fluffy; add eggs and beat well. Combine dry ingredients and stir into creamed mixture; add vanilla and milk and mix well. Chill several hours. Roll out on lightly floured board to less than ⅛-inch thickness. Cut with floured Christmas cutters and place on lightly greased cookie sheets. Bake at 325 degrees F. about 8 minutes. Cool. Spread with thin powdered sugar frosting (made by adding small amount water to powdered sugar) and sprinkle with red or green sugar or decorating candies; let stand until firm. Store in airtight containers. Yield: about 6 dozen.

Rolled Molasses Cookies

  ½ cup shortening
  1 cup molasses
  2½ cups all-purpose flour
  1½ teaspoons soda
  1 teaspoon salt
  2 teaspoons grated lemon rind
  1 teaspoon ground cinnamon

Put shortening and molasses in small saucepan and bring to a boil. Remove from heat and cool. Combine remaining ingredients and stir in the cooled molasses mixture. Mix well. Cover container and chill in refrigerator for 3 hours.

Roll dough on lightly floured board to about ¼ inch thickness. Cut in desired shapes and place cookies about 2 inches apart on ungreased shiny cookie sheets. Work quickly because the dough softens as it warms. Bake at 350 degrees F. about 8 to 10 minutes. Yield: about 3½ dozen (2-inch) cookies.

Sherry Christmas Cookies

  2 cups sifted all-purpose flour
  ¾ teaspoon baking powder
  ½ teaspoon salt
  1 cup finely diced assorted candied
      fruits
  1 cup chopped nuts
  ⅔ cup shortening
  ½ cup sugar
  ⅔ cup white corn syrup
  2 eggs
  ⅔ cup sweet cooking sherry

Sift together flour, baking powder, and salt. Dredge fruit and nuts with ½ cup of flour mixture and set aside. Cream shortening and sugar; add corn syrup and mix well. Add eggs and beat until smooth. Add dry ingredients alternately with sherry, mixing well after each addition. Gently fold in fruit mixture.

Turn batter into small greased cupcake pans. Bake at 325 degrees F. for 25 to 30 minutes. When cakes are cool, frost with a thin powdered sugar frosting, if desired. Store in covered container. Yield: 4 dozen cookies.

Date-Nut Tarts

Pastry:
  1 stick butter or margarine
  1 (8-ounce) package cream cheese
  2 cups flour
  Cold water

Cream butter and cream cheese; stir in flour. Add enough cold water to hold mixture together. Refrigerate 1 hour.

Filling:

  1 stick butter or margarine
  2 egg yolks
  1 cup sugar
  1 teaspoon vanilla extract
  2 cups chopped nuts
  2 cups chopped dates
  2 egg whites, stiffly beaten
  Powdered sugar

Mix butter and egg yolks; add sugar and vanilla and beat well. Add nuts and dates and mix well. Fold in beaten egg whites.

Roll chilled pastry on lightly floured board or cloth. Cut with small cookie cutter and line small muffin pans with pastry circles. Put 1 teaspoon filling on each tart. Bake at 375 degrees F. for 20 minutes. Dust with powdered sugar. Yield: about 6 dozen tarts.

Christmas Nut and Date Roll

  1 pint whipping cream
  1 large package miniature
      marshmallows
  1 (1-pound) package graham crackers
  1 (1-pound) package pitted dates,
      chopped
  1 cup chopped nuts

Combine whipping cream and marshmallows in a large bowl and let sit 1 hour, stirring occasionally. Crush graham crackers into fine crumbs. Divide crumbs in half.

At the end of 1 hour add chopped dates, nuts, and half the graham cracker mixture to cream-marshmallow mixture; stir well. Put remainder of cracker crumbs on large sheet of waxed paper. Roll the date-nut mixture in crumbs, completely covering roll with crumbs. Wrap in waxed paper and aluminum foil and refrigerate. The longer it is kept properly wrapped, the better it is. Serve in thin slices.

Teatime Tassies

> 1 *(3-ounce) package cream cheese*
> ½ *cup butter or margarine*
> 1 *cup all-purpose flour*
> 2 *eggs*
> 1 *cup light brown sugar*
> 2 *tablespoons butter or margarine, melted*
> 1 *teaspoon vanilla extract*
> *Pinch of salt*
> 1 *cup chopped nuts*

Soften cream cheese and butter. Stir in flour and mix well. Chill 1 hour or longer. Shape into 24 balls; press in muffin tins and shape to look like piecrust ½ inch high. Beat eggs slightly; add brown sugar and butter; mix well. Add other ingredients and blend. Put tablespoon of filling into each piecrust. Bake at 325 degrees F. for 20 to 30 minutes.

Dated-Up Cookie Cakes

> 1 *(15.3-ounce) roll refrigerated butterscotch-nut slice 'n bake cookies, softened to room temperature*
> ⅔ *cup butterscotch ice cream topping*
> 2 *eggs, separated*
> 1 *cup chopped dates*
> 1 *cup commercial sour cream*
> *Coconut Topping*

In large mixing bowl break cookie dough into smaller pieces. Add ice cream topping, 1 whole egg plus 1 egg yolk (reserve egg white for Coconut Topping). Stir until blended. Stir in dates and sour cream. Spoon into 18 to 20 paper-lined muffin cups, filling cups two-thirds full. Bake at 325 degrees F. for 30 to 35 minutes or until golden brown. Remove from oven; spread each cupcake with Coconut Topping. Bake an additional 10 to 15 minutes or until Coconut Topping is golden brown. Yield: 18 to 20 cupcakes.

> *Coconut Topping:*
>
> *Reserved egg white*
> ⅛ *teaspoon salt*
> 1 *cup powdered sugar*
> 1 *(3½-ounce) can or about 1⅓ cups flaked coconut*

In small mixer bowl beat egg white and salt until soft peaks form. Add powdered sugar and continue beating until well blended. Stir in coconut.

notes

Desserts

It's an old Southern custom to serve desserts, and a hospitable custom it is. Custards and puddings, ice creams and sherbets, and a veritable smorgasbord of other desserts merit a chapter in themselves, apart from cakes and pies.

The old-fashioned egg custard takes on a new and regal aspect when served as the basis for Queen of Puddings. Rice, peaches, sweet potatoes, apples, bananas, and even cornmeal go into making some of the South's most cherished desserts.

The hand-cranked ice cream freezer may have been replaced by one that is electric-motor driven, but the same tried and true, handed-down recipes for the "custard" of the ice cream still rate raves from the interplanetary generation. Ice cream festivals in the South are almost a thing of the past, but the appetites for homemade ice cream are just as strong as ever.

Apples form the basis of many desserts. Perhaps the oldest and most regional one is fried apples, which probably had its beginning in Virginia.

Cobblers, in all their simplicity, are favorites if there's a crowd to feed, especially when berries and peaches are in season. With a dollop of whipped cream, even this most plebian offering becomes a royal dessert.

Peach Ice Cream

    10 egg yolks
     3 cups sugar
    ½ teaspoon salt
     1 teaspoon vanilla extract
     1 can evaporated milk
     1 quart mashed fresh peaches
     4 envelopes unflavored gelatin
    ¼ cup water
     2 cups milk

Put egg yolks, sugar, salt, and vanilla in large mixer bowl. Beat at high speed until mixture is very thick. Add evaporated milk and peaches and mix well. Sprinkle gelatin over water to soften. Add to 2 cups milk and heat at low temperature to dissolve gelatin. Combine peach and gelatin mixtures and put in freezer can immediately. Add additional milk if needed and start freezing at once. All ingredients except gelatin may be refrigerated beforehand. Yield: 1 gallon.

Homemade Peach Ice Cream

    1½ cups sugar
     2 tablespoons flour
    ½ teaspoon salt
     3 eggs, beaten
     1 quart whole milk
    ½ pint whipping cream
     1 tablespoon vanilla extract
     6 cups chopped peaches
     1 cup sugar

Combine the sugar, flour, and salt; add eggs and blend well. Add milk and cook slowly until slightly thickened. Let cool. Add the whipping cream, vanilla, and sweetened peaches. Pour into freezer and freeze. Yield: 1 gallon.

Watch the eyes of the kids (and grown-ups) light up when there's a freezer of homemade ice cream in the making. Peach Ice Cream is a favorite.

Avocado Ice Cream

½ cup orange juice
½ cup lemon juice
1 (14½-ounce) can evaporated milk, chilled well
1 cup mashed ripe avocados
1½ cups sugar

Mix juices. Beat milk in chilled bowl until almost doubled in volume. Add all ingredients. Blend well. Freeze.

Buttermilk Ice Cream

Juice of 1 lemon
1 cup sugar
2 (14½-ounce) cans evaporated milk
1 quart buttermilk
4 egg whites, beaten

Mix the lemon juice and sugar, then slowly add the evaporated milk, next buttermilk, and lastly the beaten egg whites. Freeze.

Fresh Fig Ice Cream

1 quart fresh, peeled pink figs (Celeste variety)
1 pint whole milk
1 pint heavy cream
6 egg yolks
1¼ cups fine, granulated sugar
6 egg whites, stiffly beaten
3 tablespoons cream sherry wine

Crush peeled figs with a wooden spoon. Scald the milk and cream, but do not boil; skim. Beat egg yolks and sugar together until very light. Pour the hot milk over the egg yolk mixture, stirring constantly. Add the stiffly beaten egg whites and stir in the wine. Cool, then start freezing. When slightly frozen, add the crushed figs and stir well. Return to freezer and finish freezing. Allow to ripen a few hours before serving. Yield: 6 to 8 servings.

Coconut Ice Cream

3 eggs
Grated rind of 1 lemon
1 pint milk
1 cup shredded coconut (fresh or canned)
1½ cups sugar
Juice of 1 lemon
1 quart cream

Beat together eggs, grated lemon rind, and milk. Place in double boiler and heat, stirring constantly, until mixture begins to thicken (approximately 2 minutes). Add coconut and set aside to cool. When cool add sugar, lemon juice, and cream. Mix thoroughly and freeze in 2-quart hand freezer. Yield: 2 quarts.

Blueberry Ice Cream

2 cups fresh blueberries
½ cup sugar
⅛ teaspoon salt
½ cup half-and-half
1 cup heavy cream, whipped

Crush berries and combine with sugar. Cook for 5 minutes; then put through a fine sieve or food mill. Add salt and allow to cool; strain again when cool. Add half-and-half and put into refrigerator tray, stirring when mixture is frozen to a mush. Fold in whipped cream and freeze for about 3 hours. Yield: 4 to 6 servings.

Mango Ice Cream

3 cups whole milk
3 eggs, slightly beaten
1 cup sugar
3 cups thin cream
2 cups ripe mango pulp

Cook milk, eggs, and sugar in double boiler until of custard consistency. Cool thoroughly; then add cream and mango pulp. Freeze. Yield: 2 quarts.

Chocolate Ice Cream

1½ squares unsweetened chocolate or ¼
     cup cocoa
1 cup sugar
⅓ cup hot water
   Dash salt
1 tablespoon vanilla extract
1 quart thin cream

Melt chocolate. Combine melted chocolate
(or cocoa), sugar, and water and cook until
smooth and sugar is dissolved. Add salt and
vanilla and cool. Add to cream and freeze.

Chocolate Ice Cream

1¼ cups sugar
  8 egg yolks, beaten
  4 ounces sweet chocolate, grated
  1 quart milk, scalded
  1 teaspoon vanilla extract
  1 cup heavy cream

Mix the sugar, egg yolks, and chocolate in
top of double boiler. Add milk and cook,
stirring constantly, about 3 to 5 minutes.
Cool. Add vanilla and cream. Chill. Pour
into chilled freezer can and freeze. Yield: ½
gallon.

Tutti-Frutti Ice Cream

20 marshmallows
  1 cup hot milk
  1 cup cream, whipped
 ¼ cup chopped pecans
  1 teaspoon vanilla extract
    Small can crushed pineapple, drained
 ¼ cup chopped red maraschino
      cherries, drained

Dissolve marshmallows in hot milk. When
cool, add whipped cream and other
ingredients. Do not use any juice from cherries and pineapple. Pour into tray and freeze,
stirring occasionally. When frozen, cover
with aluminum foil or freezing paper.
Yield: 4 servings.

Cranberry Ice Cream

1 (1 pound) can cranberry sauce
1 tablespoon lemon juice
1 cup heavy cream, whipped

Break up the cranberry sauce with a fork
and beat with a rotary beater until all lumps
are gone. Blend in the lemon juice. Put in
refrigerator tray and freeze to a mush. Blend
in the whipped cream and beat until smooth.
Return to freezing tray and freeze. For added
smoothness, remove and beat a second time
before final freezing.

Fruit Ice Cream

1½ cups honey
  4 eggs, slightly beaten
  3 cups heavy cream
  2 teaspoons lemon juice or extract
  3 cups milk
  1 (3½-ounce) can coconut
  2 (8½-ounce) cans crushed pineapple
 ½ teaspoon salt

Combine all ingredients. Pour into manual
or electric gallon ice cream freezer can. Use
one part ice cream salt for every eight parts
crushed ice. Crank for about 15 minutes or
until ice cream becomes firm. Yield: 1
gallon.

Raspberry-Vanilla Cream

1 family-size (6-ounce) package rasp-
     berry-flavored gelatin
2½ cups boiling water
  2 medium bananas
 ¼ cup lemon juice
  1 quart vanilla ice cream

Mix gelatin with boiling water; cool slightly. Mash bananas and sprinkle lemon juice
over them. Stir bananas and ice cream into
the gelatin and stir until ice cream is melted.
Pour into individual molds, serving dishes,
or a large (2-quart) mold. Chill until set.
Yield: 12 servings.

Fresh Orange Juice Crush

    2 *cups fresh orange juice*
    2 *tablespoons fresh lemon juice*
    ½ *cup sugar*
    1 *teaspoon grated orange rind*
    ½ *teaspoon grated lemon rind*
    1 *egg white, unbeaten*
    Dash salt

Combine orange juice, lemon juice, sugar, orange rind, and lemon rind. Turn into refrigerator trays and freeze until crystals form around the edges, about 1 hour and 15 minutes. Remove from freezer and place in a mixing bowl. Add egg white and salt. Beat with an electric or rotary beater until fluffy. Return to freezer and freeze until firm, stirring 3 or 4 times. Yield: 6 servings.

Italian Ice Cream
(Gelato)

    2 *envelopes unflavored gelatin*
    ½ *cup cold water*
    1 *quart whole milk*
    2 *cups dry milk solids*
    1 *cup sugar*
    Pinch salt
    1 *to 2 teaspoons vanilla extract*

Sprinkle gelatin over cold water and set aside. In a saucepan put other ingredients. Add gelatin and cook over medium heat until gelatin dissolves. Let cool.

Freeze in refrigerator trays to mushy stage. Remove and beat with mixer. Return to trays and freeze until firm.

Pineapple Ice Cream

    2 *cups commercial sour cream*
    2 *(15-ounce) cans sweetened*
        condensed milk
    4 *cups whole milk*
    1 *(No. 2) can crushed pineapple*

Combine sour cream and sweetened condensed milk; add whole milk. Pour into gallon freezer can and freeze, using 6 parts ice to 1 part ice cream salt, until mixture is partially frozen. Add pineapple (don't drain); freeze until firm.

Peppermint Ice Cream

    6 *eggs, beaten*
    1 *package vanilla ice cream powder*
    1 *can sweetened condensed milk*
    1 *(15-ounce) can sweetened condensed*
        milk
    1 *(14½-ounce) can evaporated milk*
    1 *tablespoon vanilla extract*
    **About 3 cups crushed hard*
        peppermint candy
    Milk

Beat eggs well; add ice cream powder and stir well. Stir in other ingredients, adding the peppermint candy last. Add enough whole milk to mixture to fill gallon ice cream freezer about ⅔ full. Freeze.

*For an ice cream not quite as sweet, use less crushed candy and add peppermint flavoring.

Peppermint Ice Cream

    2 *cups sugar*
    4 *eggs*
    1 *quart milk*
    1 *pint whipping cream*
    1 *pound peppermint stick candy, finely*
        crushed* (about 20 sticks)
    1 *teaspoon (about) peppermint extract*
        or oil of peppermint

Mix well sugar, eggs, and milk. Cook over medium heat, stirring often, until mixture begins to thicken and coats spoon. Cool. This is basic boiled custard mixture for ice cream. When ready to freeze, combine remaining ingredients; add to custard. Pour into freezer can; add additional milk to fill can. Freeze. Yield: 1 gallon.

*Candy may be pounded in heavy cloth bag with wooden mallet.

Strawberry Ice Cream

    4 *eggs*
2½ *cups sugar*
    1 *pint half-and-half*
    3 *cups pureed fresh strawberries*
    2 *teaspoons vanilla extract*
    1 *quart milk*

Beat eggs until frothy. Gradually add the sugar and beat well. Stir in the half-and-half and strawberries (put strawberries through blender to make puree). Add vanilla extract and milk and pour into ice cream freezer. Freeze. Yield: 1 gallon.

Strawberry Ice Cream

1½ *cups evaporated milk*
    Scant ½ cup sugar
    2 *tablespoons cornstarch*
  ½ *cup water*
    1 *(10-ounce) package frozen*
      strawberries, partially thawed

Chill 1 cup of the evaporated milk in refrigerator tray until milk starts to freeze around the edges of tray.

Mix sugar and cornstarch together. Combine remaining ½ cup of evaporated milk and the water. Add gradually to the cornstarch mixture.

Cook over moderate heat, stirring constantly, until thick. Then chill thoroughly. Place chilled milk in the glass container of blender. Mix until stiff. Stop blender motor. Add the chilled custard and mix until well blended, stopping and starting motor as needed to scrape mixture from the sides of container. Add strawberries and mix for 1 second.

Put into freezing compartment of the refrigerator. Set temperature control at coldest point and freeze to desired serving consistency.

Strawberry Milk Mallobet

16 *large marshmallows*
  1 *cup milk, chilled*
  ¾ *cup crushed, fresh strawberries*
  1 *tablespoon lemon juice*

Heat marshmallows and 2 tablespoons milk in top of a double boiler. Stir carefully until marshmallows are about half melted. Remove from heat and continue stirring until the mixture is smooth and spongy. Cool to lukewarm and then blend in remaining milk, crushed strawberries, and lemon juice. Pour into freezing trays of refrigerator and freeze, stirring several times. Yield: 4 servings.

Fresh Strawberry Ice Cream

  1 *cup commercial sour cream*
  ½ *teaspoon baking soda*
  2 *cups milk*
  1 *(15-ounce) can sweetened condensed*
      milk
  1 *cup crushed fresh strawberries*

In large bowl combine sour cream and baking soda. Beat together well. Add milk and the sweetened condensed milk. Beat well, pour into two freezer trays, and freeze until partially frozen. Pour frozen cream into chilled bowl and stir in the crushed strawberries. Return to refrigerator trays and freeze. Stir mixture once during freezing. Yield: about 1½ quarts.

Pumpkin Ice Cream Squares

   1 *cup fine gingersnap crumbs*
  ¼ *cup sugar*
  ¼ *cup butter or margarine, melted*
   1 *envelope unflavored gelatin*
  ¼ *cup cold water*
  ½ *cup cooked pumpkin*
  ½ *teaspoon salt*
   1 *teaspoon ground cinnamon*
  ¼ *teaspoon ground ginger*
  ¼ *teaspoon ground nutmeg*
   1 *teaspoon vanilla extract*
   1 *quart vanilla ice cream*

Combine crumbs, sugar, and butter; reserve ⅓ cup mixture. Press into bottom of 8- x 8- x 2-inch baking pan. Soften gelatin in cold water; combine in a saucepan with next six ingredients. Stir over low heat until gelatin dissolves; cool. In chilled bowl, stir ice cream to soften; fold in pumpkin mixture. Spoon over crust; sprinkle reserved crumbs over top. Freeze firm. Cut into squares.

Ice Cream-Macaroon Loaf

  2 *cups coconut macaroon cookie*
     crumbs
  ½ *cup chopped black walnuts*
  2 *pints chocolate ice cream*
  3 *pints cherry-nut brick ice cream*
Maraschino cherries
Whipping cream, whipped

Blend crumbs and nuts into softened chocolate ice cream. Set in freezer while preparing mold. Working with one brick of ice cream at a time, line bottom and sides of chilled 9- x 5- x 3-inch loafpan with slices of cherry-nut ice cream. Cut each brick into four crosswise slices; place three slices in bottom of pan, two slices on each side, and one slice at each end. Cut off any ice cream extending over top edge of pan and use to fill in corners. Spoon in chocolate-macaroon mixture. Place remaining three slices of ice cream on top of chocolate and smooth top. Wrap and freeze. Garnish with maraschino cherries and whipped cream. Yield: 8 servings.

Vanilla Ice Cream
(Custard)

  2 *cups sugar*
  4 *tablespoons flour*
  ¼ *teaspoon salt*
  3 *cups milk*
  4 *eggs, well beaten*
  3 *pints light cream*
  6 *to 8 teaspoons vanilla extract*

Mix sugar and flour. Add salt, then milk. Cook in top of double boiler about 10 minutes, stirring constantly. Add some of the cooked mixture to beaten eggs, return to double boiler, and cook an additional 2 or 3 minutes. Cool. Add cream and vanilla. Pour mixture into 1-gallon freezer. Add additional milk if needed to fill can within 3 inches of top. Freeze. Yield: 1 gallon.

Vanilla Ice Cream

  2 *cups milk*
 25 *marshmallows*
  2 *cups cream*
  1 *teaspoon vanilla extract*

Melt marshmallows in milk over low heat, stirring constantly. (Do not let milk boil.) Cool thoroughly, then add cream and vanilla. Partially freeze; remove to a chilled bowl and whip thoroughly, then return to freezer. This may be made in an ice cream freezer.

French Vanilla Ice Cream

  ½ *cup sugar*
  ¼ *teaspoon salt*
  1 *cup milk*
  3 *egg yolks, beaten*
  1 *tablespoon vanilla extract*
  1 *cup whipping cream*

Set refrigerator control for fast freezing. Blend sugar, salt, milk, and egg yolks in saucepan. Cook over medium heat, stirring constantly, until mixture comes to a boil.

Cool. Add vanilla. Pour into refrigerator tray and freeze until mixture is mushy and partly frozen. Whip cream until barely stiff. Empty partially frozen mixture into chilled bowl and beat until smooth. Fold in whipped cream. Pour into two freezer trays and freeze until firm, stirring frequently and thoroughly during first hour of freezing. It will take about 3 to 4 hours to freeze thoroughly. Yield: 1 quart.

Vanilla Ice Cream

      4 *eggs*
    2½ *cups sugar*
      6 *cups milk*
      4 *cups light cream*
      1 *tablespoon vanilla extract*
      ½ *teaspoon salt*

Beat eggs until light and fluffy. Gradually add sugar, beating until mixture is lemon-colored and thick. Beat in remaining ingredients. Pour into chilled freezer and freeze. Yield: 1 gallon.

Apricot Sherbet

      1 *(17-ounce) can apricots*
      Water
      Juice of 1 lemon
      1 *cup sugar*

Squeeze apricots through food mill (do not drain); measure. Into a saucepan, measure amount of water equal to amount of apricots. Add sugar; simmer for 10 minutes. Add to apricots and lemon juice and freeze.

Cranberry Sherbet

      4 *cups fresh cranberries*
      2 *cups water*
      3 *cups sugar*
      Juice and grated rind of 1 lemon
      2 *cups milk*

Put cranberries in water and cook for about 4 minutes. Put through food mill. Add sugar, lemon juice, grated rind, and milk. Mix well and pour into refrigerator trays to freeze. This does not require any stirring.

Fresh Blackberry Sherbet

    1½ *cups fresh blackberries*
      ⅓ *cup powdered sugar*
      ⅔ *cup sweetened condensed milk*
      2 *tablespoons lemon juice*
      2 *egg whites, beaten stiff*

Mix berries with powdered sugar. Allow to stand 15 minutes; then crush through sieve. Combine sweetened condensed milk and lemon juice with berries. Chill until mixture begins to thicken. Fold beaten egg whites into chilled mixture; place in refrigerator tray and chill until partially frozen. Remove and beat until smooth; keep in freezing unit until frozen. Yield: 3 to 4 servings.

Kumquat-Lemon (or Lime) Sherbet

      ¾ *cup kumquat sauce*
      ¼ *cup lemon or lime juice*
      ⅓ *cup sugar*
      1 *tablespoon water*
      1 *cup milk*

Blend kumquat sauce, lime juice, and sugar thoroughly. Rinse juice reamer and measuring cup with water. Add milk by drops, stirring briskly to prevent curdling. Pour into refrigerator tray and freeze, stirring occasionally. Yield: 4 to 5 servings.

Pineapple Sherbet

      1 *quart milk*
    1½ *cups sugar*
      ½ *cup lemon juice*
      1 *cup crushed pineapple*

Scald milk. Cool. Add sugar, lemon juice, and pineapple. Freeze in freezer section of refrigerator or in electric or hand-turn freezer. Yield: 2 quarts.

Spanish Caramel Custard
(Flan)

    3 *cups sugar*
    ½ *cup boiling water*
    6 *eggs*
    1 *tablespoon anisette*
    1 *teaspoon vanilla extract*
    Dash nutmeg
    Dash salt
    2 *cups scalded milk*

Melt 1 cup of the sugar in a heavy skillet over low heat, stirring constantly. When mixture is light brown, remove from heat and slowly add boiling water; stir and boil until caramel is dissolved. Pour into 8 custard cups.

Beat eggs until frothy. Add remaining sugar, anisette, vanilla, nutmeg, and salt; beat well. Add milk gradually. Pour mixture into caramel cups. Place cups in a pan of water and bake at 350 degrees F. for 30 to 40 minutes or until custard is set. Cool; then chill in refrigerator. When ready to serve, loosen edges with a spatula and turn mold upside down. The caramel tops the custard. Yield: 8 servings.

Old-Fashioned Egg Custard

    1 *cup sugar*
  2½ *tablespoons flour*
    ⅛ *teaspoon salt*
    Dash of ground nutmeg
    4 *egg yolks*
    2 *egg whites*
    1 *cup milk*
    2 *tablespoons butter or margarine,*
      melted
    2 *egg whites*
    2 *tablespoons sugar*
    1 *unbaked 9-inch piecrust*

Combine sugar, flour, salt, and nutmeg. Beat 4 egg yolks and 2 egg whites and add to dry ingredients. Beat well. Add milk gradually, then stir in melted butter. Pour in crust and bake at 400 degrees F. for 10 minutes. Reduce temperature to 325 degrees F. and bake 25 to 30 minutes longer. Beat 2 egg whites and add sugar. Spread meringue on pie and bake at 325 degrees F. for 10 to 15 minutes or until meringue is brown.

Cup Custard
(85 calories each)

    6 *tablespoons dry skim milk*
 1⅔ *cups water*
    2 *small eggs*
    3 *tablespoons sugar*
    ½ *teaspoon vanilla extract*
    Nutmeg

Mix dry skim milk and water. Set aside. Break eggs; add sugar and vanilla. Beat. Pour milk over egg mixture and beat just to mix. Pour in custard cups. Place cups in pan of water. Sprinkle with nutmeg. Bake at 325 degrees F. about 35 minutes or until done. Insert knife in center of cup—if it comes out clean, custard is done. Yield: 4 servings.

Banana Pudding

    ½ *cup sugar*
    ⅓ *cup flour*
    ¼ *teaspoon salt*
    2 *cups scalded milk*
    2 *egg yolks, beaten*
    1 *teaspoon vanilla extract*
  18 *vanilla wafers*
    3 *bananas, sliced*
    2 *egg whites*
    ¼ *cup sugar*

Blend ½ cup sugar, flour, and salt in top of double boiler. Stir in scalded milk; cover and cook until mixture thickens (do not let water boil in bottom of pot). Stir in well-beaten egg yolks, and cook until mixture is quite thick. Add vanilla. Line 1½-quart baking dish with vanilla wafers; add cooked custard and banana slices in layers. Beat egg whites until stiff, folding in ¼ cup sugar. Spread on top of pudding and bake at 325 degrees F. for approximately 20 minutes or until lightly browned. Yield: 6 to 8 servings.

Banana Pudding

½ cup sugar
2 tablespoons flour
¼ teaspoon salt
3 cups scalded milk
3 egg yolks
1 teaspoon vanilla extract
Vanilla wafers
Sliced bananas
3 egg whites
¼ cup sugar

Blend ½ cup sugar with the flour and salt. Put in top of double boiler and add scalded milk. Cook until slightly thickened, stirring constantly. Beat egg yolks; add a small amount of cooked custard and mix well. Add to custard and cook about 2 minutes, stirring until mixture is thick. Add vanilla.

Line a buttered casserole dish with vanilla wafers. Add a layer of sliced bananas. Cover with a layer of cooled custard; repeat layers until all custard is used. Make a meringue of egg whites and ¼ cup sugar. Spread over custard; bake at 325 degrees F. about 20 minutes or until meringue is browned. Yield: 6 to 8 servings.

Peach-Nut Pudding

4 cups sliced, peeled fresh peaches
⅓ cup sugar
¼ teaspoon salt
¼ cup water
5 cups soft breadcrumbs
1 cup brown sugar, firmly packed
1 cup chopped pecans
¼ cup melted butter or margarine

Combine peaches, sugar, salt, and water; cook for 15 minutes or until peaches are tender. Combine soft breadcrumbs, brown sugar, pecans, and butter. Arrange alternate layers of the peach and breadcrumb mixtures in a greased 1½-quart casserole, using crumbs on top layer. Bake at 350 degrees F. for 40 minutes. Serve either hot or cold, with cream or whipped cream as desired. Yield: 8 servings.

Apple Pudding

4 cups cooked, mashed
    apples
¼ pound butter or margarine
Sugar to taste
4 eggs, beaten
¾ cup breadcrumbs

Cook apples in small amount of water; drain, mash, and measure. To 4 cups hot, cooked apples add butter or margarine. Stir until butter is dissolved. Add sugar to taste. Cool. Add beaten eggs after apples have cooled. Butter a 1½-quart baking dish and sprinkle with breadcrumbs (reserve some for topping). Add apple mixture and top with breadcrumbs. Bake at 325 degrees F. for 1 hour. Before removing from oven, sprinkle top with sugar. Serve hot or cold. Yield: 6 to 8 servings.

Queen of Puddings

2 cups milk
⅛ teaspoon salt
1 tablespoon butter or margarine
1 teaspoon grated lemon rind
1 teaspoon vanilla extract
2 egg yolks, beaten
1½ cups vanilla wafer crumbs, finely
    rolled (about 35 cookies)
¼ cup red currant jelly
2 egg whites
¼ cup sugar

Heat milk with salt, butter or margarine, lemon rind, and vanilla. Add beaten egg yolks. Fold in vanilla wafer crumbs. Pour into 6 (6-ounce) buttered glass baking dishes. Place dishes in a baking pan. Pour in water to 1-inch depth. Bake at 325 degrees F. until set, about 35 to 40 minutes. Cool slightly. Dot surface of each pudding with red currant jelly. Beat egg whites until foamy. Gradually add sugar; beat until smooth and glossy. Spread on top of jelly. Return puddings to oven until meringue is set and lightly browned. Serve immediately. Yield: 6 servings.

Melksnysels
(Milk Pudding)

  1⅛ *cups sifted flour*
  ¼ *teaspoon salt*
  ½ *teaspoon baking powder*
  2 *quarts milk*
  3 *egg yolks*
  ¼ *cup sugar*
  ½ *teaspoon ground cinnamon*
  3 *egg whites*

Sift 1 cup of the flour with salt and baking powder into a bowl, and add gradually about ½ cup of milk—use just enough to make the dough stiff. Knead until the dough is springy. Roll out as thin as possible on a floured surface. Let the dough remain on this surface until "set"—about 15 to 20 minutes. Sprinkle top of dough with the rest of the flour and roll up carefully like a jelly roll. Cut evenly into ¼-inch slices.

Pour the remaining milk into a pan and bring to a boil. Drop the ribbons of dough into the milk and cook until they rise to the surface. Drain and keep warm. Reserve the milk.

Beat the egg yolks, sugar, and cinnamon in a bowl. Add, gradually, 1 cup of the hot milk, and beat constantly to prevent curdling. Return the contents of the bowl to the remaining milk and keep stirring. Heat, but do not allow to boil. Beat the egg whites until stiff but not dry and pour the milk mixture over them. Mix gently. Place the noodles in bowls and pour the milk mixture over them. Serve hot.

New Orleans Bread Pudding With Lemon Sauce

  4 *slices bread*
    Butter
  4 *eggs*
  ½ *cup sugar*
  2 *cups milk, scalded*
  ½ *cup white raisins*
  2 *tablespoons butter*
  1 *teaspoon vanilla extract*

Butter bread and cut into cubes. Cream eggs with sugar and add scalded milk gradually. Add bread cubes, raisins, butter, and vanilla extract. Blend well. Pour into a buttered 1½-quart baking dish. Bake in a pan of boiling water at 300 degrees F. for 1 hour, or until tester comes out clean. Cool and serve with Lemon Sauce.

Lemon Sauce:

  4 *egg yolks*
  ½ *cup sugar*
  4 *tablespoons flour*
 1½ *cups milk, scalded*
  4 *tablespoons lemon juice*

Beat yolks slightly; add sugar and flour. Gradually pour into scalded milk. Cook over low heat until thick. Remove and add lemon juice. Yield: 8 servings.

Yam Pudding

 2½ *cups milk*
  3 *medium yams*
  3 *eggs*
  2 *cups sugar*
  2 *teaspoons ground cinnamon*
  ½ *cup nuts (pecans or blanched,*
      slivered almonds)
  ½ *stick butter or margarine*
  ½ *cup pineapple juice (optional)*

Put milk into 2-quart casserole. Grate yams, adding to milk as you grate to prevent potatoes from turning dark. Beat eggs well and add sugar gradually. Add cinnamon and nuts. Pour into potato mixture and mix well. (If using pineapple juice, put this in last and fold into potato mixture.) Dot generously with butter and bake at 300 degrees F. for 2 hours.

Sweet Potato Pudding

    4 cups grated sweet potatoes
       Grated rind of 1 lemon
       Grated rind of ½ orange
    2 eggs, beaten
    ½ cup brown sugar
    ½ teaspoon ground cinnamon
    ½ teaspoon ground nutmeg
    ½ teaspoon ground cloves
    ½ cup molasses
    ⅔ cup milk
    ⅓ cup bourbon
    ½ cup melted butter

Mix sweet potatoes, lemon and orange peel. Beat eggs and sugar and stir into potato mixture; then add the spices, molasses, milk, bourbon, and butter. Mix thoroughly and put in buttered 2-quart casserole. Bake at 325 degrees F. for 1 hour. Yield: 8 servings.

Sweet Potato Pudding

    ½ cup raisins
    ½ cup warm water
    4 cups grated or shredded raw sweet
         potatoes
   1½ cups sugar
    1 cup milk
    1 teaspoon ground cinnamon
    1 teaspoon ground nutmeg
    1 teaspoon ground allspice
    2 eggs, beaten
    ½ teaspoon salt
    ½ stick melted butter or margarine
       Marshmallows, if desired

Soak raisins in warm water. Measure sweet potatoes in cup, packing well. Place in large mixing bowl and add sugar, milk, spices, eggs, salt, and melted butter; mix well. Drain raisins well and add last. Place mixture in greased 2-quart casserole and bake at 350 degrees F. for 1½ hours or until set. During last part of cooking period, marshmallows may be placed on top to brown, if desired. Yield: 4 to 6 servings.

Lemon-Almond Rice Pudding

    3 tablespoons butter
    1 cup sugar
    4 egg yolks
    3 tablespoons flour
    ⅓ cup lemon juice
    2 teaspoons grated lemon rind
    ¼ teaspoon salt
    2 cups evaporated milk
    ½ cup toasted, slivered almonds
    1 cup packaged precooked rice
    4 egg whites, beaten

Cream butter; add sugar gradually and cream together until light and fluffy. Add egg yolks and beat well. Add flour, lemon juice, rind, and salt; mix well. Stir in milk. Blend in ¼ cup almonds and 1 cup rice. Beat egg whites until stiff. Fold into mixture. Pour into greased 13- x 9-inch baking dish. Set in pan of hot water and bake at 325 degrees F. for 40 minutes. Increase to 350 degrees F. and bake until brown (about 10 minutes). Sprinkle with remaining almonds and serve hot or cold. Top with whipped cream and cherries.

Fruited Rice Pudding

    1 cup crushed pineapple, drained
    ⅔ cup packaged precooked rice
    ⅔ cup water
    ½ teaspoon salt
   1½ cups tiny marshmallows
    1 fully ripe banana, diced
    2 teaspoons lemon juice
    1 cup heavy cream, whipped (or 1
         package whipped topping mix)

Drain pineapple, reserving syrup. In saucepan combine rice, water, pineapple syrup, and salt; mix just to moisten rice. Bring quickly to boiling. Reduce heat, cover, and simmer for 5 minutes. Remove from heat and let stand for 5 minutes. Add marshmallows, pineapple, banana, and lemon juice. Cool thoroughly. Fold in whipped cream or whipped topping mix prepared according to package directions. Chill. Yield: 8 to 10 servings.

Chantilly Raisin Rice Pudding

⅔ cup seedless raisins
2½ cups half-and-half (milk and cream)
2 eggs
⅛ teaspoon ground nutmeg
⅛ teaspoon salt
3 tablespoons sugar
1 tablespoon vanilla extract
1 cup cooked rice
¼ cup chopped toasted walnuts or
    pecans

Combine raisins and half-and-half and heat slowly. Meanwhile, beat eggs with nutmeg, salt, sugar, and vanilla. Combine with cooked rice. Stir in hot half-and-half and raisins. Turn into 1-quart baking dish; set in shallow pan of hot water. Bake at 350 degrees F. for 15 minutes. Sprinkle top with nuts and continue baking 10 to 15 minutes longer until custard is barely set in center. Place pudding dish in pan of cold water to cool quickly and keep custard creamy. Serve warm or cold. May be topped with sweetened whipping cream if desired. Yield: 8 servings.

Indian Pudding

3 cups milk
⅓ cup yellow cornmeal
½ cup dark molasses
¼ cup sugar
1 teaspoon salt
½ teaspoon ground cinnamon
¼ teaspoon ground nutmeg
2 tablespoons butter or margarine
1 cup cold milk

Heat 3 cups milk in top of double boiler. Add cornmeal, molasses, sugar, salt, spices, and butter. Cook over hot water, stirring occasionally, for about 25 minutes or until mixture is slightly thickened. Pour into a 1½-quart casserole which has been rubbed with butter. Add cold milk. Do not stir. Bake at 300 degrees F. for 2½ hours. Serve warm with whipped cream or vanilla ice cream. Yield: 6 to 8 servings.

Rice Pudding

1½ cups cooked rice
¾ cup raisins
½ cup sugar
2 eggs, beaten
¼ teaspoon vanilla extract
½ teaspoon ground cinnamon
    Dash ground nutmeg
2 cups milk, scalded
2 tablespoons melted butter

Combine first 7 ingredients; add scalded milk and melted butter; mix well. Pour into 1½-quart casserole. Bake at 350 degrees F. about 1 hour or until mixture is firm. Yield: 6 servings.

Fresh Orange Bread Pudding

1 cup diced fresh orange sections
1½ cups day-old bread cubes
⅔ cup sugar
1 tablespoon cornstarch
¼ teaspoon salt
2 egg yolks
1½ cups milk, divided
2 tablespoons butter or margarine
1 teaspoon grated fresh orange peel
1 teaspoon vanilla extract
    Meringue

Place diced oranges and bread cubes in 1-quart casserole. Set aside while making custard. Combine sugar, cornstarch, and salt in saucepan. Blend in egg yolks and ¼ cup of the milk. Mix in remaining milk. Stir and cook over very low heat until custard coats a metal spoon and is slightly thickened (about 10 minutes). Add butter, orange peel, and vanilla. Pour into casserole over oranges and bread cubes. Place in pan of hot water. Bake at 325 degrees F. for 1½ hours or until pudding is firm in center.

Next, cover with Meringue. Reduce heat to 300 degrees F. Return pudding to oven, leaving it in pan of hot water. Bake 20 minutes or until the Meringue is brown. Serve warm. Yield: 6 servings.

Meringue:

  2 *egg whites*
  4 *tablespoons sugar*
  ¼ *teaspoon vanilla extract*

Beat egg whites until they stand in soft peaks. Gradually beat in sugar. Add vanilla. Spread over Fresh Orange Bread Pudding.

Woodward Pudding

  1 *cup sugar*
  ½ *cup vegetable shortening*
  3 *eggs*
  1 *cup flour*
  1 *teaspoon ground cinnamon*
  1 *teaspoon ground allspice*
  ½ *teaspoon soda*
  4 *tablespoons sweet milk*
  1 *cup drained, canned or fresh, sliced peaches*

Cream sugar and shortening until smooth; add eggs and beat until smooth. Add flour and spices and mix well. Stir soda in milk and add to mixture. Beat until smooth. Stir in sliced peaches. Baked in a greased 8- x 8- x 2-inch pan at 350 degrees F. for 35 minutes. Cut in squares to serve.

Tapioca Pudding

  2 *egg yolks*
  1 *(14½-ounce) can evaporated milk*
  ⅓ *cup quick-cooking tapioca*
  ½ *cup sugar*
  ¼ *teaspoon salt*
  2⅓ *cups water*
  2 *egg whites*
  1 *teaspoon vanilla extract*

In a saucepan mix egg yolks with a small amount of the milk. Add tapioca, sugar, salt, remaining milk, and water. Bring mixture quickly to a boil over direct heat, stirring constantly. Remove from heat. (Mixture will be thin. Do not overcook.) Beat egg whites until just stiff enough to hold shape. Fold

hot tapioca mixture into beaten egg whites. Cool. When slightly cool, stir in the vanilla. Chill. Yield: 12 servings.

Ozark Pudding

  2 *eggs*
  1¼ *cups granulated sugar*
  2 *teaspoons vanilla extract*
  2 *cups diced apples*
  ½ *cup chopped nuts*
  ⅔ *cup sifted flour*
  3 *teaspoons baking powder*
  ½ *teaspoon salt*

Beat eggs; add sugar and vanilla and mix well. Add apples and nuts and mix well. Combine flour, baking powder, and salt; add to apple mixture. Pour into greased 8- x 12-inch pan and bake at 350 degrees F. for 20 to 30 minutes, or until a rich golden brown. Yield: 10 to 12 servings.

Apple Meringue

  1 *cup sugar*
  1 *cup water*
  ⅛ *teaspoon salt*
  5 *medium tart baking apples*
  ¼ *cup fresh orange juice or red wine*
  2 *egg whites*
  ¼ *cup sugar*
  ½ *teaspoon vanilla extract*

Combine sugar, water, and salt in saucepan. Bring to boiling point. Pare, quarter, and core apples. Add to hot syrup. Cover. Bring to boiling point, reduce heat, and cook gently 15 minutes or until apples are tender. Transfer apples from syrup to a buttered 1-quart casserole. Sprinkle with orange juice or red wine. Beat egg whites until they stand in soft, stiff peaks. Gradually beat in sugar and vanilla. Spread over apples. Bake in a preheated slow oven (325 degrees F.) 15 minutes or until browned. Serve warm or cold. Yield: 6 servings.

Apple Dessert

  1 *cup sugar*
 ½ *stick margarine*
  1 *egg*
  1 *teaspoon soda*
 ¼ *teaspoon salt*
 ½ *teaspoon ground nutmeg*
  1 *teaspoon cinnamon*
  1 *cup flour*
 ½ *cup pecans*
  1 *teaspoon vanilla extract*
  3 *medium apples, diced*

Cream sugar and margarine. Add egg and beat well. Add dry ingredients and mix well. Stir in pecans, vanilla, and diced apples. Bake in a greased 9-inch pan at 300 degrees F. for 1 hour. Serve with Sauce. Yield: 8 servings.

  Sauce:

  1 *stick butter*
 ½ *pint coffee cream*
 ½ *cup brown sugar*
 ½ *cup white sugar*
  1 *teaspoon vanilla extract*

Combine ingredients; cook over low heat about 5 minutes; stir constantly.

Baked Apples

  6 *baking apples*
 ¼ *cup seedless raisins*
 ¼ *cup canned slivered blanched almonds*
  1 *tablespoon orange marmalade*
 ½ *cup sugar*
 ½ *cup water*
  1 *teaspoon grated orange peel*
 ¼ *cup orange juice*
  1 *tablespoon butter*

Core apples, being careful not to cut all the way through. Peel about one-third the way down from stem end. Combine raisins, almonds, and marmalade; fill apple centers with this mixture. Combine remaining ingredients in saucepan. Stir over low heat until sugar dissolves; let simmer 5 minutes. Place apples in baking pan; pour syrup over them.

Cover; bake at 350 degrees F. for 45 minutes to 1 hour, basting frequently with syrup in pan. When tender, baste once more and run under broiler to glaze. Serve with whipped cream. Yield: 6 servings.

Baked Apples

  6 *medium baking apples*
 ¼ *cup boiling water*
 ⅓ *cup sugar*
 ½ *teaspoon ground cinnamon*
  6 *teaspoons butter or margarine*
  6 *rounds cinnamon toast*

Wash and core unpeeled apples. Place in a buttered 8- x 2-inch round baking dish. Add ¼ cup boiling water. Mix sugar with cinnamon and spoon into cavities of apples. Add 1 teaspoon butter or margarine to each cavity. Cover. Bake in a preheated moderate oven (350 degrees F.) 20 minutes. Remove cover; baste with liquid around apples. Continue cooking 35 to 40 minutes or until apples are tender. Serve on rounds of cinnamon toast. Yield: 6 servings.

Southern Fried Apples

 ⅓ *cup sugar*
  1 *teaspoon ground nutmeg*
 ½ *teaspoon ground cinnamon*
 ⅛ *teaspoon salt*
  4 *large cooking apples*
  5 *tablespoons butter*

Mix together sugar, nutmeg, cinnamon, and salt. Wash, core, and slice apples in ½-inch slices.

Heat butter in heavy frying pan. Add apple rings and one-half the sugar mixture. Cook about 3 minutes. Turn, sprinkle with remainder of sugar mixture, and continue cooking until apples are almost transparent. Serve hot. Yield: 6 servings.

Buttered Apples

   1 *cup sugar*
   1 *cup water*
   ¼ *teaspoon salt*
   6 *medium tart baking apples*
   Butter or margarine
   Jelly (any kind)
   2 *tablespoons sugar*

Combine sugar, water, and salt in a sauce-pan. Bring to boiling point. Peel and core apples. Leave whole and place in boiling syrup. Cover and cook until half done (about 10 minutes). Transfer apples from syrup to a buttered baking dish. Fill the cavity of each apple with butter or margarine. Spread with jelly and sprinkle with sugar. Place in a preheated 375-degree F. oven and cook 30 minutes or until apples are tender. Serve topped with ½ teaspoon jelly. Yield: 6 servings.

Scheiterhaufen
(As made in Old Vienna)

   9 *to 11 ounces thinly sliced bread (not*
      quite ¾ of a pound loaf)
   ¼ *cup melted butter*
   1 *pound apples, peeled and sliced*
   4 *tablespoons chopped nuts*
   4 *tablespoons raisins*
   6 *tablespoons sugar*
   Dash of ground cinnamon
   1 *tablespoon rum*
   Chopped peel of ¼ lemon
   2 *cups milk*
   3 *eggs*
   ½ *teaspoon vanilla extract*
   Sugar

Toast the bread slices and drip the butter over them. Line the bottom of a pie plate with part of the slices. Crumble the rest and mix with the apples, nuts, raisins, sugar, cinnamon, rum, and lemon peel. Arrange loosely in the pie dish. Whisk the milk with the eggs and vanilla and pour over the mixture. Bake at 375 degrees F. about 45 minutes or until golden brown. Serve hot, sprinkled with sugar. Yield: 6 to 8 servings.

Coddled Fresh Apples

   1 *cup sugar*
   2 *cups boiling water*
   6 *fresh tart apples*
   Heavy cream (optional)

Mix sugar with water and boil 5 minutes. Peel, quarter, and core apples. Drop a few pieces at a time into syrup. Simmer until tender, 15 minutes. Lift out carefully with a slotted spoon. Drain and cool. Boil the remaining syrup until thick and pour over apples. Serve warm with heavy cream, if desired. Yield: 6 servings.

Stewed Apples With Cider

   6 *fresh apples*
   2 *tablespoons butter or margarine*
   ½ *cup sugar*
   ½ *cup apple cider*
   1 *tablespoon fresh lemon juice*
   ⅛ *teaspoon salt*

Peel apples and cut into ½-inch slices. Sauté apples in butter or margarine in a 9- or 10-inch skillet. Sprinkle with sugar. Add cider, lemon juice, and salt. Simmer, uncovered, until apples are tender (about 10 minutes). Serve with pork or poultry. Yield: 6 to 8 servings.

Dutch Apples

   3 *cups finely chopped cooking apples*
   White sugar and cinnamon (to taste)
   ¾ *cup flour*
   1 *cup brown sugar*
   ½ *cup butter*

Arrange apples in baking dish. Sprinkle with white sugar and cinnamon. In another bowl thoroughly mix flour, brown sugar, and butter. Pat into flat cake and spread over apples. Bake at 325 degrees F. until well done. Serve warm with whipped cream or vanilla ice cream. Yield: 4 to 6 servings.

Banana-Stuffed Baked Apples

    6 *large baking apples*
    2 *small bananas*
    1 *teaspoon fresh lemon juice*
    5 *tablespoons sugar*
    Dash salt
    ½ *teaspoon ground nutmeg*
    1 *cup fresh orange juice*
    Whipped cream (optional)

Wash, pare, and core apples. Place in a baking dish. Peel bananas; dice and mix with lemon juice. Spoon into cavities of apples. Combine sugar, salt, and nutmeg and sprinkle over apples. Pour orange juice over all. Cover and bake in a preheated 375-degree F. oven for 55 minutes or until apples are tender when pierced with a toothpick. Baste with orange juice 4 times while baking. Serve warm or cold with a little syrup poured over each. Top with whipped cream, if desired. Yield: 6 servings.

Southern Fried Apples

    6 *medium cooking apples*
    ⅓ *cup butter*
    ⅔ *cup sugar*
    1 *tablespoon ground cinnamon*
    Dash salt

Core but do not peel apples. Slice ½ inch thick to make perfect rings. Heat butter in heavy skillet. Fit in the apple slices to cover bottom of skillet without breaking slices. Mix sugar with cinnamon and salt and cover apples with one-half the mixture. Cook slowly for 5 minutes; turn slices with a pancake turner to avoid breaking. Cover with remaining sugar mixture and cook over low heat until apples are almost transparent. If too well-done, they will break easily. Serve hot. Yield: 6 servings.

Coeur de Crème

    2 *pounds low-calorie cottage cheese,*
        drained
    1½ *cups whipping cream*

Take one-half of the cottage cheese, put in blender, and beat until smooth. Slowly add ¾ cup whipping cream. Beat enough to blend, but do not overbeat. Repeat procedure for the other half of cottage cheese and whipping cream.

Put mixture in a heart-shaped wicker basket which has been lined with cheesecloth or tea towels. Set in a pan to catch drippings and put in the refrigerator. After a day or two the cheese will become firm.

When you are ready to serve, decorate with fresh strawberries which have been dipped in melted currant jelly, with red food coloring and water added to the jelly to thin it. Serve the cheese on 1-inch slices of French bread and pass fresh strawberry jam to each guest.

To make strawberry jam, cook 10-ounce package frozen strawberries with ¼ cup currant jelly and about ½ cup sugar.

Brown Orchid Soufflé

    ¾ *cup sugar*
    ½ *cup flour*
    ¾ *teaspoon salt*
    1⅓ *cups milk*
    1 *teaspoon vanilla extract*
    1 *(6-ounce) package chocolate pieces*
    6 *egg yolks*
    6 *egg whites*
    ¼ *teaspoon cream of tartar*

Combine sugar, flour, and salt in saucepan. Combine milk and vanilla and gradually stir into sugar mixture. Cook, stirring constantly, over medium heat until mixture thickens. Reserve ⅔ cup of mixture. To remainder of mixture in saucepan, add chocolate pieces and stir until pieces have melted.

Beat egg yolks until thick. Beat egg whites and cream of tartar until stiff but not dry. Stir half of the yolk mixture and half of the egg white mixture into the reserved custard mixture; stir other half into chocolate mixture. Spoon mixtures alternately into ungreased 2-quart casserole. Bake at 325 degrees F. for 65 to 75 minutes. Serve immediately. Yield: 8 to 10 servings.

Brennan's Bananas Foster

    2 *tablespoons butter*
    4 *small bananas*
    2 *tablespoons brown sugar*
    Dash ground cinnamon
    1 *tablespoon banana liqueur*
    ½ *cup rum*
    Ice cream

Melt butter in a small skillet. Cut bananas in half and brown them in the butter. Sprinkle with brown sugar and a dash of ground cinnamon. Add banana liqueur and rum and set aflame. Serve blazing with ice cream. Yield: 4 servings.

Banana Split

    1 *ripe banana*
    3 *scoops ice cream (preferably vanilla,*
        chocolate, and strawberry)
    2 *to 3 tablespoons chocolate sauce*
    4 *to 6 tablespoons fruit sauce, crushed*
        fruit, or preserves
    Whipped cream
    Finely chopped nuts
    Maraschino cherries

Peel banana and cut lengthwise into halves. Place halves, cut side up, side by side in a shallow dish. Place scoops of ice cream side by side on top of banana halves. Pour chocolate sauce over one portion of ice cream. Cover other scoops with fruit sauce, crushed fruit, or preserves. Garnish with whipped cream, nuts, and cherries. Yield: 1 full-size banana split.

Strawberries Romanoff

    1 *quart fresh strawberries, cleaned and*
        slightly mashed
    ½ *cup powdered sugar*
    3 *tablespoons Cointreau*
    1 *pint vanilla ice cream*
    1 *cup whipping cream, whipped*
    6 *tablespoons Cointreau*

Prepare strawberries; add sugar and 3 tablespoons Cointreau and set aside. Whip ice cream until slightly softened and fold in whipped cream and 6 tablespoons Cointreau. Fold in prepared strawberries. Blend quickly and lightly and serve in chilled stemmed glasses. Yield: 6 servings.

Strawberry Charlotte Russe

    2 *cups whipping cream*
    ⅔ *cup powdered sugar*
    1 *teaspoon vanilla extract*
    3 *egg whites, beaten until stiff*
    2 *cups crushed strawberries*
    1 *cup sugar*
    Ladyfingers or spongecake

Whip cream until stiff. Add powdered sugar, vanilla, and egg whites, beaten until stiff. Add crushed strawberries and sugar. Line a mold with slices of ladyfingers or spongecake. Fill with cream mixture. Chill and serve.

Strawberry Charlotte Russe

    2 *(3-ounce) packages strawberry-*
        flavored gelatin
    2 *cups boiling water*
 1½ *cups crushed strawberries, fresh or*
        frozen
    1 *tablespoon lemon juice*
    ½ *cup sugar*
    ⅛ *teaspoon salt*
    2 *cups heavy cream, whipped*
    Ladyfingers

Put gelatin in large bowl; add boiling water and stir until dissolved. Combine strawberries, lemon juice, sugar, and salt; stir until sugar is dissolved. Combine with gelatin mixture. Chill to consistency of beaten egg whites. Fold in whipped cream. Line side of springform pan with narrow strip of waxed paper; then line with ladyfingers. Carefully spoon mixture into pan and chill for 4 to 5 hours. Decorate top with additional strawberries and whipped cream, if desired.

Charlotte Russe

1½ *dozen ladyfingers*
2 *envelopes unflavored gelatin*
½ *cup cold water*
2 *cups milk, scalded*
6 *egg yolks, beaten*
1 *cup sugar*
Vanilla extract to taste
2 *cups whipping cream*

Line springform cakepan with ladyfingers. Soften gelatin in cold water. Scald the milk. Beat egg yolks and sugar together until smooth; stir in scalded milk; cook in top of double boiler until mixture begins to thicken. Just before removing from heat, add gelatin and stir until gelatin is dissolved. Add vanilla and cool. When thoroughly cool, fold in whipped cream and place in pan lined with ladyfingers. To serve: unmold on cake plate and slice as cake. Yield: 6 to 8 servings.

Strawberry Angelfood Dessert

1 *package angelfood cake mix*
2 *(10-ounce) boxes frozen sliced strawberries*
1 *(3-ounce) box strawberry-flavored gelatin*
½ *cup sugar*
1 *cup hot water*
1 *cup heavy cream, whipped*
Whole fresh strawberries, washed and hulled for garnish

Prepare cake mix as directed on the package, baking in a 10-inch tube pan. Cool. Thaw berries and drain, reserving syrup. Dissolve gelatin and sugar in the hot water. Add 1 cup reserved syrup. Chill until slightly thickened. Cut cake in 1-inch pieces. Arrange half in a 13- x 9- x 2-inch pan or dish. Fold drained berries into slightly thickened gelatin. Pour about half the gelatin mixture over cake in dish. Top with remaining cake, then with rest of gelatin. Chill until set. Whip cream and spread on top of dessert. Cut in 15 squares. Garnish with the fresh strawberries. Yield: 15 servings.

Baked Fruit Casserole

3 *oranges*
2 *cups water*
1 *(No. 2) can sliced pineapple, cut in quarters*
1 *(No. 2) can pear halves, cut*
1 *(No. 2) can sliced peaches*
1 *small jar maraschino cherries*
1 *stick butter or margarine*
⅔ *cup sugar*
⅓ *cup flour*
¼ *teaspoon salt*
⅓ *cup sherry*

Slice oranges very thin; cut in quarters and remove peel. Cut orange pieces small and set aside. Grind orange peel and boil about 20 minutes in about 2 cups water. Discard water. Add drained peel to the cut orange and the canned fruits.

Melt butter and make a paste with the sugar, flour, and salt. Cook until thickened and add sherry. Butter a large casserole dish and arrange fruits, mixing them as you add them. Pour sauce over fruits and bake at 375 degrees F. for 20 minutes. Serve with turkey, ham, or chicken. Yield: 10 to 12 servings.

Cranberry Fluff
In Orange Shells

2 *cups raw cranberries, ground fine or 1-pound can whole berry cranberry sauce*
¾ *cup sugar*
3 *cups miniature marshmallows*
2 *cups diced, peeled apples*
1 *cup chopped pecans*
1 *cup heavy cream, whipped*
8 *to 10 orange shells*
Salad greens
Clusters of seedless green grapes

Combine cranberries, sugar, and marshmallows. (If using cranberry sauce, omit sugar.) Cover and refrigerate several hours or overnight. Add apples and nuts; fold in whipped cream. Spoon into orange shells. Serve on a tray with salad greens and grape clusters. Yield: 8 to 10 servings.

Orange Fluff

  1 *cup white sugar*
  1 *egg, beaten*
  2 *tablespoons flour*
  1 *cup water*
  4 *oranges, sectioned*
 ½ *pint whipped cream*

Mix first three ingredients. Then add water gradually and stir until smooth. Place mixture in heavy saucepan. Stir carefully to keep from lumping. Cook until thick. Remove from heat; when almost cold, add carefully diced sections of 4 (more, if small) oranges. (In preparing oranges, remove outer peeling and all white skin; then dice each section toward the center. If sections are large, cut in bite-size pieces.) When dessert is cold, fold in whipped cream.

Fluff may be kept for several days in the refrigerator. Serve in sherbet dishes. To expand this dessert, add 10 large marshmallows and melt in cooked mixture.

Orange Mousse

  2 *envelopes unflavored gelatin*
  2 *cups cold water*
  2 *cups sugar*
  2 *cups orange juice*
    Grated peel of 2 oranges
  2 *cups heavy cream, whipped*

Sprinkle gelatin on cold water in saucepan. Add sugar and heat, stirring constantly, until gelatin and sugar are dissolved. Remove from heat; add orange juice and orange peel. Chill until mixture is consistency of unbeaten egg white. Fold in whipped cream and turn into 8 individual parfait glasses or 8 to 10 meringue shells. Chill 3 hours.

Mrs. Haney's Glazed Oranges

  6 *whole oranges*
  1 *quart water*
 1½ *cups sugar*
  2 *ounces brandy*

Peel the oranges, down to the flesh. Shred the peelings of 3 of them julienne style.

Boil the water and sugar to make a syrup; add the shredded orange peel and simmer a few minutes. Blend in the brandy and pour the syrup over the oranges in a baking dish. Place the oranges in a preheated oven, 375 degrees, and bake 5 minutes, or until glazed. Serve warm or chilled in 6 sherbet glasses.

Fruited Rum Roll

  ¼ *cup hot mashed potatoes*
  1 *teaspoon melted butter*
  2 *cups sifted powdered sugar*
  ½ *teaspoon salt*
 1½ *teaspoons rum or ½ teaspoon rum*
     extract
  ¼ *cup diced candied cherries*
  ¼ *cup diced candied pineapple*
  ¼ *cup chopped pecan meats*
  1 *cup flaked coconut*

Mix potatoes and butter together in bowl. Add sugar gradually and beat until thoroughly blended. Add salt, rum, fruits, and nuts. Shape into two rolls about 1¼ inches in diameter. Then roll in coconut. Cut crosswise in slices. Yield: 24 pieces.

Apricot Frappé

  4 *cups apricot puree*
  2 *cups apricot nectar*
  ½ *cup honey*
  1 *cup lime juice*

Combine all ingredients and freeze until hard; then beat until mushy. Return to freezer until time to serve. Serve in punch cups. Yield: 12 servings.

Blueberry Cobbler

⅔ to 1 cup sugar
 2 tablespoons cornstarch
 ¾ cup water
 3 cups fresh blueberries
 1 tablespoon butter or margarine
 1 teaspoon ground cinnamon
 1 cup all-purpose flour
1½ teaspoons baking powder
 ½ teaspoon salt
 ⅓ cup milk
 3 tablespoons salad oil

Mix sugar and cornstarch in sauce pan; stir in water and boil for 1 minute, stirring constantly. Add berries; pour into 1½-quart baking dish. Dot with butter or margarine and sprinkle cinnamon over top.

Sift together flour, baking powder, and salt. Combine milk and oil and add to dry mixture. Stir with a fork until mixture forms a ball. Drop by spoonfuls onto berries. Bake at 425 degrees F. for 25 to 30 minutes or until lightly browned. Yield: 6 servings.

Chilled Pineapple Soufflé

 4 eggs
 1 (1-pound 4½-ounce) can crushed
     pineapple
 2 envelopes unflavored gelatin
 1 teaspoon salt
 ⅓ cup sugar
 2 tablespoons lemon juice
 1 teaspoon vanilla extract
 ½ teaspoon almond extract
 1 cup whipping cream

Separate eggs. Beat yolks with undrained crushed pineapple. Add gelatin mixed with salt and 2 tablespoons sugar. Cook, stirring constantly, over medium heat until gelatin is dissolved, about 5 minutes. Remove from heat; blend in lemon juice and flavorings. Chill, stirring occasionally, until mixture mounds slightly when dropped from spoon. Beat egg whites until stiff; beat in remaining sugar. Fold in pineapple gelatin and stiffly beaten cream. Turn into 4-cup soufflé dish

with 3-inch collar.* Chill several hours or overnight. To serve, remove the collar and garnish with additional crushed pineapple and fresh mint, if desired. Yield: about 10 servings.

*Make foil collar by tying double-thick strip of foil or waxed paper around soufflé dish. Top edge should extend 3 inches above edge of dish.

Frosted Pecan-Fruit Roll

 1 cup milk
4½ cups sifted cake flour
 3 tablespoons sugar
 1 teaspoon salt
 1 cup shortening
 1 package or cake yeast, active dry or
     compressed
 ½ cup very warm water (lukewarm for
     compressed yeast)
 3 egg yolks, beaten
 1 cup golden seedless raisins
 1 cup coarsely chopped pecans
 1 cup coarsely chopped pitted dates
 1 cup sifted brown sugar, firmly
     packed
 1 teaspoon ground cinnamon
 1 cup cherry preserves
 3 egg whites

Scald milk. Cool to lukewarm. Sift flour, sugar, and salt together into large bowl. Cut in shortening, using pastry blender or two knives. Sprinkle or crumble yeast into water (very warm for active dry yeast; lukewarm for compressed yeast). Stir until dissolved. Add lukewarm milk and egg yolks. Blend into flour and shortening mixture, beating well. Add a little more cake flour if needed to make a very soft, sticky dough. Brush dough lightly with soft shortening. Cover bowl tightly and refrigerate overnight.

Turn out on lightly floured board. Knead dough lightly until smooth enough to roll. Divide into four equal pieces. Roll out each into very thin rectangle 18 x 11 inches. Combine raisins, pecans, dates, brown sugar, cinnamon, and fruit preserves. Beat egg whites until stiff but not dry. Spread each rectangle with one-fourth of the egg whites; then sprinkle with one-fourth of the fruit mixture. Roll up as for jellyroll, 11 inches long. Pinch seam together. Place rolls seam side down on greased cookie sheet. Let rise 45 minutes in warm place, free from draft. Bake at 400 degrees F. for 30 to 35 minutes or until tops are firm when tapped. Cool.

Frost with the following frosting: Blend ¼ cup margarine or butter with 2 cups sifted powdered sugar, 1 teaspoon vanilla, and as much as ⅓ cup milk, cream, or evaporated milk as needed for good spreading consistency. Sprinkle with chopped pecans. Serve warm or cold. Yield: about 30 slices.

Baked Fruit Casserole

    1 *(No. 2½) can peaches or apricots*
    1 *(No. 2½) can pears*
    1 *(No. 2½) can sliced or chunk*
        pineapple
    ¾ *cup brown sugar*
    ⅓ *cup margarine*
    1 *teaspoon ground ginger*

Drain fruit well and cut into bite-size pieces. Place in buttered 3-quart casserole.

Combine brown sugar, margarine, and ginger and stir over low heat until margarine has melted. Pour over fruit and bake at 325 degrees F. about 30 minutes or until mixture is hot and syrup bubbles. Yield: 8 servings.

Pineapple Flambée

Slice fresh pineapple in about ½-inch slices. Remove hard core from slices. Dip pineapple in flour, then in milk, and again in flour. Carefully place slices on paper towels to dry. Melt butter (about ¼ cup for 4 to 6 slices). Brown pineapple slices in butter, then place in a baking dish. Sprinkle generously with sugar and place a maraschino cherry in center of each ring. Bake at 400 degrees F. about 5 minutes. Remove from oven as soon as sugar begins to brown. Warm ¼ cup Co-gnac in silver ladle; blaze it and pour flaming over the pineapple. Serve flaming.

Blackberry Roll

    1¾ *cups all-purpose flour*
    1 *teaspoon salt*
    1 *teaspoon baking powder*
    1 *teaspoon sugar*
    4 *tablespoons shortening*
    ⅔ *to ¾ cup milk*
    2 *tablespoons melted butter*
    3 *cups blackberries*
    ½ *cup sugar*
    ½ *teaspoon ground cinnamon*
        (optional)
    3 *cups blackberries*
    ½ *cup sugar*
    Whipped cream

Combine flour, salt, baking powder, and 1 teaspoon sugar. Cut in shortening. Add milk and mix well. Turn the dough on a lightly floured board and knead. Roll to a thickness of ⅓ inch. Brush with melted butter. Sprinkle with 3 cups of berries, ½ cup sugar, and the cinnamon. Roll the dough like a jelly roll. Place in a large, well-oiled 13- x 9-inch baking pan. Surround with remainder of berries and sugar. Bake at 425 degrees F. for about 30 minutes. Slice and serve with sauce from the pan and topped with whipped cream. Yield: 6 to 8 servings.

Speed-Easy Dessert

    1 *(1-pound) can date-nut roll, chilled*
    1 *cup drained, chilled mandarin orange*
        segments
    ½ *cup whipped cream*
    2 *teaspoons powdered sugar*
    ½ *cup toasted almond slivers*

Slice chilled date-nut roll into 6 slices. Place on serving dishes and top with drained mandarin oranges. Add whipped cream, which has been sweetened with powdered sugar. Sprinkle almonds on top. Yield: 6 servings.

Fish and Seafood

From storied Chesapeake Bay, from along the Atlantic shoreline of Virginia, North and South Carolina, Georgia, and Florida, from the Gulf of Mexico lapping the shores of Florida, Alabama, Mississippi, Louisiana, and Texas come the small and great fishes and crustaceans of the sea. Whence: seafood.

Also, the rivers, lakes, and streams of the Southland make their contributions of sport and fish, with these bodies of fresh water having become a veritable fisherman's paradise.

Oysters, roasted or on the half shell; fried catfish; shrimp, plain or in Creole dishes; broiled lake trout; clams in chowder; or any number of creative mixtures in gumbo—all contribute to the South's culinary excellence.

Oysters may be used in dressing for Christmas or Thanksgiving turkeys or in creamy stew, which is standard fare for New Year's Eve.

Selected riverside restaurants serving fried catfish offer few disappointments. The same can be said for fishermen who properly cook trout, bass, or bream at the campsite.

Shrimp and Rice

1 cup rice
3 tablespoons butter or margarine
1 medium onion, chopped
1 green pepper, chopped
1 clove garlic, sliced
1½ teaspoons salt
2½ cups hot water
1½ pounds peeled and deveined shrimp
½ pound cheese, shredded
⅓ cup evaporated milk

Brown 1 cup rice in 3 tablespoons butter. Add onion, pepper, and garlic; brown. Add salt and hot water. Put shrimp on top, cover, and cook 30 to 40 minutes. Combine shredded cheese and milk in top of double boiler. Serve as a sauce over shrimp. Yield: 4 to 6 servings.

Shrimp is a favorite ingredient in many Southern dishes. Shrimp boats are a common sight in Gulf and Eastern shore waters.

Baked Stuffed Shrimp

24 jumbo shrimp, cooked and cleaned
1 medium onion, minced
1 green pepper, minced
4 tablespoons butter, divided
1 (7½-ounce) can crabmeat, flaked
1 teaspoon dry sherry
1 teaspoon dry mustard
1 teaspoon Worcestershire sauce
½ teaspoon salt
2 tablespoons mayonnaise
1 cup basic medium white sauce
Grated Parmesan cheese
Paprika

Split shrimp and open flat. Cook onion and green pepper in 2 tablespoons butter until soft but not brown. Add crabmeat, sherry, mustard, Worcestershire sauce, salt, mayonnaise, and white sauce; mix well. Stuff shrimp with crabmeat mixture. Dot with remaining butter. Sprinkle lightly with grated Parmesan cheese and paprika. Bake at 350 degrees F. for 10 minutes. Yield: 6 servings.

Shrimp-Rice Alfresco

 ¼ cup bacon drippings or butter
 1 medium onion, thinly sliced (about
    ½ cup)
 ½ medium green pepper, diced (about
    ⅓ cup)
 2 cups packaged precooked rice
 2 cups hot water
 2 (8-ounce) cans tomato sauce
 1 teaspoon salt
  Dash of pepper
 ½ teaspoon prepared mustard
    (optional)
 1½ cups canned or cooked shrimp

Heat drippings in saucepan or skillet. Add onion, green pepper, and rice. Cook and stir over high heat until lightly browned. Add remaining ingredients, mix well, and bring to a boil. Then reduce heat and simmer, uncovered, 5 minutes. Yield: 6 servings.

Shrimp Casserole for a Crowd

 1 green pepper, chopped
 2 stalks celery, chopped
 1 medium onion, chopped
 2 cups water
  Small can pimientos, chopped
 3 pounds cooked, deveined shrimp
 1 (7½-ounce) can crabmeat
 4 hard-cooked eggs, cut in thick slices
 4 tablespoons butter
 4 tablespoons flour
 2 cups light cream
 1 cup shredded sharp Cheddar cheese
 ½ teaspoon salt
 ⅛ teaspoon pepper
 ¾ cup buttered bread or cracker crumbs

Combine chopped pepper, celery, onion, and water and cook until vegetables are tender. Drain. Add pimiento, shrimp, crabmeat, and eggs.
  Make cheese sauce: melt butter and stir in flour until smooth. Gradually add cream and cook until mixture thickens, stirring constantly. Add cheese, salt, and pepper.
  Add sauce to shrimp mixture and put in a 3-quart casserole dish. Sprinkle crumbs over

top and bake at 400 degrees F. for 15 minutes. Yield: 12 to 15 servings.

Shrimp Casserole

 1 (4-ounce) can deveined shrimp,
    drained
 ¾ cup uncooked white rice
 2 tablespoons corn oil
 1 (8-ounce) can tomatoes
 1 tablespoon Worcestershire sauce
 1 teaspoon Tabasco sauce or 1
    teaspoon cayenne pepper
 1 teaspoon salt
 1 medium onion, chopped
 4 tablespoons catsup

Combine all ingredients and place in a 1½-quart casserole. Cover and bake at 300 degrees F. for 45 minutes. Yield: 2 servings.

Shrimp and Mushroom Casserole

 1½ tablespoons butter or margarine
 2 teaspoons chopped onion
 2 teaspoons chopped green pepper
 2 tablespoons flour
 ¾ cup half and half (cream and milk)
 ¼ teaspoon paprika
 ½ teaspoon salt
 ½ cup shredded cheese
 1 (6-ounce) can mushrooms, quartered
 1 pound shrimp, boiled and cleaned
  Buttered breadcrumbs

Melt butter or margarine; add onion and green pepper and cook until tender, but not brown. Add flour and blend. Next add remaining ingredients, except breadcrumbs, and pour into a buttered casserole dish. Top with buttered breadcrumbs and bake at 350 degrees F. for 20 minutes. Yield: 4 servings.

Shrimp-Rice Casserole

  1¼ *pounds shrimp*
  ½ *large onion, chopped*
  1 *tablespoon margarine*
  1 *can mushroom soup*
  ½ *tablespoon lemon juice*
     Dash of garlic salt
     Salt and pepper to taste
  ¾ *cup cooked rice*
  ½ *cup commercial sour cream*
  ¾ *cup shredded cheese*
  ½ *green pepper, sliced*

Cook and clean shrimp. Sauté onion in margarine until tender. Make a sauce by adding soup, lemon juice, and seasonings. Fold rice and shrimp into the sauce. Fold in sour cream and pour into a 1-quart buttered baking dish. Sprinkle shredded cheese on top and decorate with green pepper rings, parboiled for 2 minutes. Heat in 325-degree F. oven for 30 minutes. Yield: 6 servings.

Shrimp Curry

  1¼ *teaspoons curry powder*
  ⅛ *teaspoon sugar*
     Dash ground ginger
  1 *cup medium white sauce*
  1 *(7-ounce) package frozen shrimp,*
     cooked

Blend curry powder, sugar, and ginger with a few tablespoons of white sauce. Stir into remaining sauce. Add shrimp; heat to simmering point. Serve on rice, biscuits, toast, or English muffins. Yield: 3 to 4 servings.

Seafood-Spoonbread Casserole

  1 *cup yellow cornmeal*
  ⅔ *teaspoon salt*
  1 *cup water*
  1½ *cups milk, scalded*
  ½ *cup butter or margarine*
  1 *egg, well beaten*
  ⅛ *teaspoon pepper*
  2 *cups oysters, drained (or shrimp,*
     scallops, etc.)

Mix cornmeal, salt, and water; cook over low heat, stirring occasionally, about 15 minutes. Scald milk, add butter, and let melt; add to cornmeal mixture and stir until smooth. Slowly stir in beaten egg, pepper, and oysters; pour into well-greased 1½-quart casserole. Bake at 350 degrees F. for 40 minutes. Yield: 4 servings.

Shrimp Creole

  1 *pound peeled and deveined shrimp*
  6 *stalks celery, chopped*
  ½ *green pepper, chopped*
  1 *onion, chopped*
  1 *clove garlic, minced*
  4 *tablespoons shortening*
  1 *(No. 303) can tomatoes*
  1 *(10½-ounce) can tomato soup*
  1 *tablespoon Worcestershire sauce*
  1 *teaspoon Tabasco sauce*

Cook, clean, and devein shrimp. Cook celery, pepper, onion, and garlic in shortening until tender. Add all other ingredients except shrimp and simmer for 45 minutes. Add shrimp and simmer for 15 minutes longer. Serve hot over hot, cooked rice. Yield: 6 to 8 servings.

Shrimp Remoulade

  3 *pounds fresh or frozen small or*
     medium shrimp
  ¾ *cup mayonnaise*
  2 *teaspoons dry mustard*
  2 *stalks celery, minced*
  6 *green onions, minced*
  2 *drops Tabasco sauce*
  1 *teaspoon salt*
  1 *teaspoon paprika*
  3 *sprigs parsley*

Boil and peel shrimp; chill. Mix mayonnaise, dry mustard, celery, onion, Tabasco sauce, salt, paprika, and parsley. Let sit at least 3 hours. Pour over boiled shrimp and serve with thin, crisp party crackers.

Shrimp Dejonghe

(Jekyll Island, Georgia)

    ½ cup butter, softened
    1 teaspoon salt
    1 clove garlic, minced
    ⅔ cup fine dry breadcrumbs
    2 tablespoons finely chopped parsley
    ⅓ cup sherry
    ⅛ teaspoon cayenne pepper
    2 pounds cooked shrimp, peeled and
         deveined

Combine softened butter, salt, garlic, breadcrumbs, parsley, sherry, and cayenne. Arrange shrimp in a shallow 3- or 4-quart casserole and top with crumb mixture, spreading so it covers all the shrimp. Bake at 375 degrees F. for 20 to 25 minutes or until topping has melted over shrimp and becomes slightly brown. Do not overcook. Yield: 4 to 6 servings.

Deep Shrimp and Fish Dish With Mashed Potato Crust

    1 pound cleaned and deveined
         medium shrimp
    ½ pound fillet of flounder
    2 tablespoons butter
    1 small onion, grated
    1 small green pepper, sliced in very
         thin strips
    1 (4-ounce) can whole mushroom caps
    2 tablespoons butter
   4½ cups cooked, seasoned, mashed
         potatoes
       Salt and white pepper
       Dash celery and garlic salt
   10 stuffed olives, sliced
       Thin slices of sharp Cheddar cheese

Cook shrimp about 10 minutes in boiling water with spiced shrimp boil added. Broil flounder in 2 tablespoons butter about 7 minutes on each side. Sauté onion, pepper, and mushrooms in 2 tablespoons butter until clear and tender.

Line deep casserole pan with potatoes and bake at 350 degrees F. about 25 minutes.

Mix all other ingredients except cheese, adding fish and olives last. Spoon into potato crust and top with sliced cheese. Return to oven and bake at 300 degrees F. for about 20 to 25 minutes. Serve at once. Yield: 4 to 6 servings.

Low-Calorie Shrimp Dish

(130 calories per serving)

   1½ pounds frozen, cleaned, and deveined
         shrimp
    ¼ cup chopped green onions
    1 tablespoon cooking oil
    1 chicken bouillon cube dissolved in ½
         cup boiling water
    1 (No. 303) can cut green beans,
         drained
    ¼ teaspoon ground ginger
       Dash of garlic powder
       Freshly ground pepper
    1 tablespoon cornstarch dissolved in
         ½ cup cold water

Defrost shrimp. Combine shrimp, onions, and oil in large skillet and cook 5 to 7 minutes. Add remaining ingredients, saving the cornstarch and water mixture until last. Cook 7 to 10 minutes. Yield: 4 servings.

Shrimp Fricassee

    2 tablespoons butter or margarine
    2 tablespoons flour
   1½ cups canned tomatoes and juice
    2 tablespoons instant minced onion
    2 tablespoons sweet pepper flakes
    ¼ teaspoon garlic salt
    ⅛ teaspoon ground thyme
    ½ teaspoon parsley flakes
    1 bay leaf
    ½ teaspoon celery salt
    ⅛ teaspoon ground black pepper
    1 pound shrimp, cooked and deveined
    2 cups cooked rice

Melt butter in a frying pan. Add flour and stir constantly until slightly brown. Add tomatoes and juice, onion, sweet pepper flakes, and seasonings; stir until blended. Add shrimp. Cover and simmer gently 15 to 20 minutes. Pack cooked rice into greased cups and place in preheated moderate oven at 350 degrees F. for about 5 minutes. Unmold onto platter. Remove the bay leaf and pour shrimp mixture over hot rice. Yield: 4 servings.

Shrimp Jambalaya

- ¾ *pound cooked, peeled, cleaned shrimp, fresh or frozen, or 3 (4½-ounce) cans shrimp*
- ¼ *cup chopped bacon*
- 3 *tablespoons chopped onion*
- 3 *tablespoons chopped green pepper*
- 1 *clove garlic, finely chopped*
- 1 *tablespoon flour*
- ½ *teaspoon salt*
- ½ *teaspoon Worcestershire sauce*
- *Dash cayenne pepper*
- *Dash paprika*
- ½ *cup pitted ripe olives, sliced crosswise*
- 1 *(16-ounce) can tomatoes*
- 2 *cups cooked rice*

Thaw frozen shrimp or drain canned shrimp. Cut large shrimp in half. Fry bacon until crisp. Add onion, green pepper, and garlic; cook until tender. Blend in flour and seasonings; add olives and tomatoes and cook until thick, stirring constantly. Stir in rice and shrimp; heat. Yield: 6 servings.

Quick Shrimp Jambalaya

- 2 *pounds shrimp, peeled*
- 2 *tablespoons olive oil*
- 1 *onion, chopped*
- 1 *green pepper, chopped*
- 2 *(1-pound) cans Spanish rice*
- *Salt, black pepper, and Tabasco to taste*

Sauté shrimp in olive oil until pink. Add onion and green pepper and cook until soft. Stir in rice; add salt, pepper, and Tabasco to taste and serve hot. Yield: 4 to 6 servings.

Seafood Crêpe Flambée

(Pirate's House, Savannah, Georgia)

- 2 *cups milk*
- 3 *tablespoons butter*
- 2 *drops Tabasco sauce*
- ¼ *teaspoon salt*
- ⅛ *teaspoon pepper*
- 2 *egg yolks*
- *Pancake mix*
- ¼ *cup sherry*
- ¾ *pound cooked crabmeat*
- 1½ *pounds cooked shrimp*
- 1 *(4-ounce) can drained mushrooms*
- 1½ *ounces brandy*

Put milk in saucepan; add butter, Tabasco, salt, and pepper. Beat egg yolks and add to milk mixture. Blend until smooth and cook over low heat until mixture thickens, stirring constantly. Make four 5-inch crepes from pancake mix, following package directions. Add one-third more liquid than called for, and omit sugar.

Add sherry, seafood, and mushrooms to milk and egg mixture. Pour over crepes and fold shells around mixture. Place in individual casserole dishes and bake at 350 degrees F. for about 5 to 10 minutes. Flame with brandy and serve immediately. Yield: 4 to 6 servings.

Shrimp Seviche

- 1 *pound shrimp, cooked and deveined*
- *Juice of 4 limes or enough to cover shrimp*
- 2 *tablespoons chopped onion*
- 2 *tablespoons chopped green pepper*
- 1 *fresh tomato, chopped fine*
- ½ *cup tomato juice*
- *Salt, pepper, and hot sauce to taste*

Soak shrimp in lime juice 1 hour or more in refrigerator. Stir and drain. Combine lime juice with other ingredients. Serve in small bowls as a sauce for shrimp used as appetizers. Yield: 4 to 6 servings.

Shrimp Kabobs

  2 *pounds jumbo shrimp*
  2 *cloves minced garlic*
  1 *finely chopped medium onion*
  1 *teaspoon dried basil*
  1 *teaspoon powdered mustard*
  1 *teaspoon salt*
  ½ *cup olive or salad oil*
  4 *tablespoons lemon juice*

Cut through the shell on the back of each shrimp with kitchen scissors. Wash under running water to remove vein.

Combine other ingredients to make marinade; pour over shrimp in a bowl, cover, and let stand in refrigerator several hours, turning shrimp occasionally.

When ready to cook, remove shells and thread shrimp on thin metal skewers. Grill about 5 minutes over hot coals, basting with marinade; turn once. Yield: 6 servings.

Sweet and Sour Shrimp Over Rice

  1 *(10-ounce) package frozen breaded*
    shrimp
  6 *tablespoons olive or cooking oil*
  ⅓ *cup minced onion*
  ½ *cup chopped green pepper*
  ½ *cup sugar*
  1 *tablespoon cornstarch*
  1 *teaspoon powdered mustard*
  ¼ *teaspoon salt*
  ½ *cup vinegar*
  ⅓ *cup water*
  1 *cup drained pineapple tidbits*
    Hot cooked rice

Fry shrimp in oil in skillet until they are golden brown. Remove to heated platter and keep warm. Reduce heat under skillet. Add onion and green pepper, and cook 1 minute. Combine dry ingredients. Blend in vinegar and water and stir until smooth. Add this mixture to the skillet along with the pineapple and cook until thickened and smooth. Toss shrimp lightly in sauce from skillet. Serve hot over cooked rice. Yield: 4 to 6 servings.

Pickled Shrimp

  2½ *pounds fresh shrimp*
  3 *pints water*
  ¼ *cup mixed pickling spices*
    Several celery tops with leaves
  2 *large onions, sliced*
  8 *bay leaves*
  1¼ *cups salad oil*
  2½ *teaspoons celery seed*
  2½ *teaspoons capers and juice*
  ¾ *cup white vinegar*
  2 *teaspoons salt*
  2 *dashes Tabasco sauce*

Prepare shrimp. Bring 3 pints water to a boil; add mixed pickling spices and celery. Boil 5 minutes; then add shrimp and boil 12 minutes. Pour off water. Let shrimp cool; then rinse. Arrange shrimp in a shallow container, alternating layers of shrimp and sliced onion; add bay leaves.

Mix other ingredients and pour over shrimp. Cover container and place in refrigerator. Let stand at least 24 hours before serving. Yield: 15 to 20 servings.

Shrimp Marengo

  3½ *pounds shrimp*
  7 *slices bacon*
  1 *clove garlic, crushed*
  1 *pound mushrooms, wiped and sliced,*
    or 1 (8-ounce) can mushroom
    pieces
  1 *medium onion, chopped*
  2 *(14-ounce) cans Italian tomatoes*
  1 *(6-ounce) can tomato paste*
  1 *(10½-ounce) can consommé*
  1½ *teaspoons oregano*
  1½ *teaspoons sweet basil*
  1 *tablespoon sugar*
  1 *tablespoon salt*
  ⅛ *teaspoon black pepper*
  3 *drops liquid hot pepper seasoning*
  6 *or 7 teaspoons prepared mustard*
  ¼ *cup flour*
  ½ *cup water*

Cook shrimp 7 minutes in a large amount of boiling water. Shell and devein shrimp. Cut bacon into small pieces and cook until crisp; remove bacon. Sauté shrimp in bacon drippings to which crushed garlic has been added. Add mushrooms and onion and continue to sauté for a few minutes longer. Add the tomatoes, tomato paste, bacon, and consommé.

Season with oregano, sweet basil, sugar, salt, pepper, hot pepper seasoning, and mustard. Cook 10 minutes, stirring often; taste for seasoning and correct if needed. Mix flour with water until smooth. Add to shrimp mixture, stirring briskly, and let cook about 1 minute. This dish should be prepared in advance as it improves with a stay in the refrigerator or freezer. To serve, remove from freezer or refrigerator and reheat. Yield: 2½ quarts or 10 servings.

Shrimp Toulouse

Peel and devein fresh shrimp. Sauté in fresh butter. Then add lemon juice, herbs, pimiento, green pepper, and mushrooms. It is an excellent luncheon dish served on toasted French bun, based with artichoke bottoms and flavored with white wine.

Shrimp on a Skewer

⅓ cup salad oil
⅓ cup lemon juice
3 or 4 cloves garlic, minced
1½ teaspoons salt
½ teaspoon paprika
¼ teaspoon pepper
2 pounds (about 30 large) fresh or frozen shrimp, cleaned
2 medium green peppers, cut in wedges
2 medium onions, cut in wedges
12 red cherry tomatoes or 3 medium, quartered

Combine salad oil, lemon juice, garlic, and seasonings; pour over shrimp and refrigerate at least 2 hours. Drain, reserving marinade. On 6 greased, 12-inch skewers, alternate shrimp, green pepper, and onion; brush with marinade. Broil 3 inches from heat about 13 minutes, or until shrimp are tender, turning once and brushing frequently with marinade. During last 2 or 3 minutes, place tomatoes on skewers. Serve with lemon wedges. Yield: 6 servings.

Shrimp and Peas With Rice

¼ cup salad oil
1½ pounds medium shrimp, deveined and shelled
1 clove garlic, minced
1 tablespoon soy sauce
1 tablespoon lemon juice
1½ cups hot vegetable broth
1 (10-ounce) package frozen green peas, thawed
3 tablespoons cornstarch
¼ cup cold water
1 cup water chestnuts, thinly sliced
3 cups hot cooked rice

Heat oil in a deep skillet. Add uncooked shrimp and cook gently, turning them over, until they turn pink. Add garlic, soy sauce, lemon juice, hot vegetable broth, and green peas. Simmer until peas are just tender—3 to 5 minutes. Stir together the cornstarch and cold water until smooth; add to shrimp mixture with water chestnuts. Cook and stir constantly until sauce is thickened and clear. Serve over hot rice. Yield: 6 servings.

Bass in Beer

3 *pounds bass, cleaned*
2 *large onions, chopped*
4 *tablespoons butter or margarine*
2 *tablespoons flour*
2 *cups beer*
1 *teaspoon salt*
2 *tablespoons brown sugar*
½ *teaspoon black pepper*
1 *teaspoon Worcestershire sauce*
1 *tablespoon vinegar*

Cut fish in 3-inch slices. Brown onion in butter. Add flour and cook for about 2 minutes. Add beer, salt, brown sugar, pepper, and Worcestershire sauce. Boil until sauce is thickness of thin cream. Add fish and cook until fish flakes easily (this will not take long). Add vinegar and cook an additional 2 minutes. Fish may be served in sauce, or sauce may be strained and served separately. Yield: 4 to 6 servings.

Broiled Bass

4 *pounds bass*
2 *teaspoons salt*
¼ *teaspoon pepper*
½ *cup butter*

Use whole pan-dressed fish or fillets. Sprinkle with salt and pepper. Place on foil or greased broiler pan, skin side up. Brush with butter or with half butter and half lemon juice. Place 2 to 3 inches from source of heat and broil 5 to 7 minutes or until lightly browned. Baste with butter; then turn carefully. Baste again and broil 5 to 7 minutes or until fish flakes easily when tested with a fork. Yield: 8 servings.

Note: An easy trick for turning whole fish—cut 2 pieces of paper the size of the whole fish; grease both well. In broiler pan lay fish on one piece of paper. When fish is ready to be turned, place other greased paper on top. Turn fish fillets carefully; and remove first paper and discard.

Ugnstekt Fisk Och Makaroni
(Baked Fish and Macaroni)

1¼ *cups macaroni, broken in small*
    pieces
1¾ *pounds bass or other fish*
2 *small carrots*
2 *small onions*
Salt

Sauce:

2 *tablespoons butter*
3 *tablespoons flour*
½ *teaspoon salt*
½ *teaspoon white pepper*
1½ *cups fish stock*
½ *cup heavy cream*
1 *egg yolk*
3 *tablespoons white wine*

Topping:

3 *tablespoons shredded*
    cheese
3 *tablespoons breadcrumbs*
3 *tablespoons butter*
Paprika

Cook the macaroni in salted, boiling water until tender; then drain. Clean the fish thoroughly, discarding the heads, tails, and the viscera. Cook the fish and vegetables in salted, boiling water (just enough to cover) until tender. Drain, reserving the cooking stock for the sauce. Skin the fish and fillet into small pieces. Using a large saucepan, melt the butter; stir in flour until smooth. Add salt and pepper. Gradually add the fish stock and cream, stirring until slightly thickened. Beat the egg yolk; then add to the sauce and stir. Add the wine a few drops at a time and stir. Remove the sauce from the heat. Using a large buttered baking dish, arrange a layer of cooked macaroni, then sprinkle with the cheese. Add a layer of fish, then cover with sauce. Repeat these layers reserving the top layer for macaroni. Sprinkle crumbs over the top layer and add any remaining cheese. Dot with butter and sprinkle with paprika for color. Place into a 450-degree F. oven and bake until the top browns and the mixture is thoroughly heated. Serve hot. Yield: 6 servings.

Baked Stuffed Bass

  3- to 4-*pound bass, cleaned*
  Salt and pepper to taste
  ¼ *cup butter*
  ¼ *cup chopped onion*
  ½ *cup chopped celery*
  4 *cups dry breadcrumbs*
  1 *egg, beaten (optional)*
  ¼ *teaspoon thyme*
  ½ *teaspoon sage (optional)*
  1 *teaspoon salt*
  ⅛ *teaspoon pepper*
  Melted butter or bacon strips

Dry fish and sprinkle inside with salt and pepper. Place fish on a well-greased bake-and-serve platter or baking pan. Melt butter in skillet and sauté the onion and celery in it until they are tender. Add to breadcrumbs, along with egg and the seasonings. Mix thoroughly, and add 2 tablespoons water if dressing seems dry.

Stuff fish loosely with dressing. Brush with melted butter, or cover with strips of bacon held in place with toothpicks. Bake at 350 degrees F. for 45 minutes to l hour or until fish flakes easily with a fork. Yield: 6 servings.

Barbecued Bass

  2 *pounds bass fillets*
  ½ *cup cooking oil*
  ½ *cup sesame seeds*
  ⅓ *cup lemon juice*
  ⅓ *cup cognac*
  3 *tablespoons soy sauce*
  1 *teaspoon salt*
  1 *clove garlic, crushed*

Place fillets in a single layer in shallow bowl. Combine other ingredients and pour over fish. Let stand 30 minutes, turning once. Remove fish, and reserve sauce for basting. Place fish on well-greased wire grills. Cook 8 minutes on barbecue grill about 4 inches from moderately hot coals.

Baste while fish is cooking. Turn and cook about 7 minutes on other side. Serve remaining sauce with fish. Yield: 6 servings.

Broiled Bass

Fish may be sprinkled with salt and pepper and brushed with fat before broiling. When broiler is hot, place broiler pan, with fish skin side up, about 2 inches from heat. After fish is brown, turn carefully and brown other side. Serve hot.

Bass With Oyster Stuffing

  2 (3- to 4-*pound) bass, split and boned*
  Oyster Stuffing
  ¼ *cup melted butter*
  Salt and pepper to taste

Grease shallow pan, or line with aluminum foil. Place two halves of fish, skin side down, in pan. Spread with Oyster Stuffing; place other halves, skin side up, on stuffing. Fasten with skewers. Brush with melted butter; sprinkle with salt and pepper. Bake at 350 degrees F. about 1 hour. Brush occasionally with butter. Yield: 6 servings.

  Oyster Stuffing:

  1 *cup oysters, chopped*
  3 *cups dry bread cubes*
  2 *teaspoons salt*
  ⅛ *teaspoon pepper*
  ⅛ *teaspoon sage*
  3 *tablespoons butter*
  1 *small onion, minced*
  2 *tablespoons minced parsley*
  ½ *cup minced celery*

Place oysters in skillet; sauté about 5 minutes; drain. Combine bread cubes, salt, pepper, sage, and oysters. Melt butter in another skillet; add onion, parsley, and celery, and sauté until tender. Add to oyster mixture.

Baked Fish With Dressing

  1 *whole fish (red snapper, flounder,*
      whitefish, or haddock)
Salt
  1 *medium onion, finely chopped*
  ¼ *cup butter or margarine*
  2 *cups soft breadcrumbs*
  ¼ *cup water*
  1 *egg, beaten*
  1 *tablespoon chopped green onion*
  1 *tablespoon chopped parsley*

Clean and wipe fish, and rub inside with salt. Sauté onion in melted butter. Soak breadcrumbs in water. Add to onion; add egg and cook for about 5 minutes, over low heat, stirring frequently. Remove from heat and add green onion and parsley.

    Fill fish with stuffing and tie fish. Brush outside with melted shortening. Bake at 350 degrees F., about 15 minutes to the pound. Yield: 4 to 6 servings.

Berkley Seafood Casserole

  2 *cans frozen cream of shrimp soup,*
      thawed
  2 *(4-ounce) cans mushrooms, drained*
      (reserve liquid)
  2 *tablespoons fresh lemon juice*
  2 *teaspoons soy sauce*
  2 *teaspoons celery salt*
  2 *cups shredded Swiss and Parmesan*
      cheese, mixed
  1 *pound crabmeat (fresh, frozen, or*
      canned)
  2 *pounds raw shrimp, boiled, shelled,*
      and cleaned
  1 *pound fine noodles, boiled*

Heat soup; add mushrooms, lemon juice, soy sauce, and celery salt. When thoroughly heated, stir in cheese, crabmeat, and shrimp. (Use mushroom liquid to thin mixture if it seems thick.) Spread boiled noodles in bottom of buttered casserole; pour hot mixture over, place foil loosely over top, and bake at 375 degrees F. for 25 to 30 minutes. Yield: 12 servings.

To freeze: Assemble casserole, cool quickly, and freeze. To serve, defrost and bake as directed.

Broiled Fish Supreme

  6 *or 8 fish fillets (flounder, sole, or*
      other fish)
  ¼ *cup melted shortening or butter*
  ½ *cup mayonnaise*
  2 *egg yolks*
  1 *tablespoon chopped parsley*
  1 *tablespoon chopped pimiento*
  1 *teaspoon chopped onion*
Dash cayenne pepper
  2 *egg whites*

Brush fish fillets with the shortening. Broil lightly for 2 or 3 minutes. Turn, brush other side with shortening, and broil another 2 or 3 minutes. Fillets will puff and brown lightly.

    Beat the mayonnaise; add egg yolks and beat well. Add parsley, pimiento, onion, and pepper; mix well. Beat egg whites stiff and gently fold into the mixture. Spread over broiled fish and brown lightly. The sauce mixture will puff up and make a brown cover for fish. Watch carefully. Yield: 4 to 6 servings.

Grilled Catfish

  6 *cleaned catfish (1 to 1½ pounds*
      each)
  1 *stick margarine, melted*
Juice of 6 lemons
Dash Tabasco sauce
  1 *teaspoon prepared mustard*
  2 *tablespoons Worcestershire sauce*
  1 *teaspoon salt*
  1 *teaspoon pepper*
  1 *teaspoon paprika*

After coals have burned down, place fish on grill. Combine all ingredients for basting sauce and baste frequently as fish cook. Cook for 20 minutes on one side; turn and cook an additional 15 minutes, basting often. Yield: 6 servings.

Lemonfish Casserole

1½   *cups uncooked rice*
  1   *quart water*
    Salt to taste
 ½   *pound lemonfish steak*
 ½   *stick margarine*
    Tomato Sauce
    Orange slices, lemon wedges

Pour uncooked rice into bottom of large baking dish. Add water and salt. Cut lemonfish into strips and lay strips across the rice. Add lumps of margarine; cover and bake at 400 degrees F. for 1 hour. Remove cover and brown top of fish 5 to 10 minutes. To serve, pour Tomato Sauce over fish and rice. Garnish with fruits. Yield: 4 servings.

Tomato Sauce:

  1   *medium onion, chopped*
 ½   *stick margarine*
  3   *(8-ounce) cans tomato sauce*
  1   *small green pepper, chopped*
  1   *tablespoon soy sauce*
  3   *drops liquid red pepper sauce*
    Salt to taste
  2   *cups water*

Brown onion in margarine. Add tomato sauce and other ingredients. Stir; cover. Bring mixture to boil, reduce heat, and cook slowly about an hour and a half.

Seafood Casserole

  1   *can cream of mushroom soup*
 ⅓   *cup salad dressing*
 ⅓   *cup milk*
  1   *pound fresh, boiled, and deveined shrimp or 1 (6-ounce) can, drained*
  1   *(5-ounce) can water chestnuts, drained and sliced*
  1   *cup diced celery*
  2   *tablespoons chopped parsley*
  2   *teaspoons grated onion*
  2   *cups cooked rice*
    Dash Tabasco sauce
1½   *cups fresh breadcrumbs*
  3   *tablespoons melted butter*

Combine soup, salad dressing, and milk in a 2-quart casserole. Mix in shrimp, water chestnuts, celery, parsley, onion, rice, and Tabasco. Combine breadcrumbs and butter and sprinkle over top. Bake at 350 degrees F. for 30 minutes. Yield: 4 to 6 servings.

Coquilles St. Jacques

  8   *scallops*
  1   *large tomato, peeled and sliced*
  1   *small onion, finely chopped*
  1   *(4-ounce) can finely sliced mushrooms*
    Salt and pepper to taste
 ¼   *cup butter or margarine*
 ¼   *cup Bechamel sauce (white or cream sauce)*
    Parsley for garnish

Wash the scallops and cover with cold, salted water; cook over medium heat. Bring them to a boil. (This takes about 8 minutes to cook until soft.) Drain and chop the white and red parts together. Mix with tomato, onion, mushrooms, and salt and pepper.

Now we intensify these flavors by melting the butter in a skillet and adding the scallop mixture. Cook 3 to 5 minutes. Add the Bechamel (white or cream) sauce. Stir well. Spoon the entire mixture into four scallop shells. Brown them in your broiling compartment about 3 inches away from the heat. Garnish with parsley before serving. Yield: 4 servings.

Coquilles St. Jacques is the epitome of *haute cuisine*, yet it is not difficult to prepare.

Crabmeat au Gratin

      3 tablespoons butter
    ½ green pepper, minced
    ½ onion, chopped
      3 tablespoons flour
      2 cups milk
      2 cups crabmeat
    ½ teaspoon salt
        Dash ground nutmeg
    ½ cup shredded cheese
        Buttered breadcrumbs

Melt butter; add pepper and onion and cook for 5 minutes. Add flour and milk, then crabmeat, salt, and nutmeg. Cook 10 minutes. Pour in shallow buttered baking dish or use crab shells. Sprinkle with shredded cheese and buttered breadcrumbs and bake at 350 degrees F. until cheese is brown.

Crabmeat St. Jacques

    ¼ onion, chopped
    ½ green pepper, chopped
    ½ cup mushrooms, finely chopped
        Butter
      2 cups white sauce
        Salt and pepper
        Paprika
      1 teaspoon Worcestershire sauce
      1 pound canned crabmeat
        Shredded American cheese
        Buttered breadcrumbs
        Paprika

Sauté onion, pepper, and mushrooms in a small amount of butter. Add the white sauce seasoned with salt and pepper, a generous amount of paprika, and 1 teaspoon Worcestershire sauce. Add crabmeat and stir to mix.

Put mixture into a buttered casserole and sprinkle top lightly with shredded American cheese, buttered breadcrumbs, and paprika. Bake at 450 degrees F. for 15 minutes.

Baked Crabs

      1 large onion, minced
    ½ cup minced celery
      1 small green pepper, minced
    ½ stick butter or margarine
      1 pound crabmeat (light or dark meat)
      1 cup breadcrumbs
      1 tablespoon prepared mustard
      1 tablespoon mayonnaise
      2 eggs, well beaten
      1 to 4 teaspoons garlic salt
        Salt and pepper to taste
    10 medium crab shells

Sauté minced seasonings in butter or margarine until they become glazy, but not brown. Mix crabmeat and breadcrumbs, and add cooked seasonings. Add mustard, mayonnaise, eggs, garlic salt, salt, and pepper. Mix until well blended.

Pack into well-greased shells, top lightly with breadcrumbs, and bake in hot oven at 400 degrees F. until lightly browned. Yield: 10 medium-size servings.

Crab Belvedere

      1 (1-pound) can fresh lump crab (not frozen)
        Dash ground nutmeg
      1 teaspoon dry mustard
        Dash salt
        Dash white pepper
        Dash thyme
      1 tablespoon Worcestershire sauce
    ¼ cup fresh homemade mayonnaise
        Crab shells
      1 small can anchovies
      1 small can pimiento strips

Combine crab, nutmeg, dry mustard, salt, pepper, thyme, and Worcestershire sauce. Add homemade mayonnaise, enough to hold above together. Put into crab shells; top with mayonnaise, anchovies, and pimiento; bake at 450 degrees F. for 10 to 15 minutes. Serve with potatoes, lemon, tartar sauce, and a salad. Yield: 4 to 6 servings.

Crabmeat Eleanor

    1 (4-ounce) can button mushrooms
    ¼ cup slivered, blanched almonds
    1 small green pepper, cut in 1-inch
        strips
    ¼ cup melted butter
    2 tablespoons orange juice
    1 teaspoon lemon juice
    2 cans cream of mushroom soup
    ½ teaspoon celery salt
    ¼ cup quartered ripe olives
    ¼ cup chopped pimiento
    2 tablespoons chopped parsley
    Dash of Tabasco sauce
    3 (3-ounce) cans crabmeat
    Salt and pepper to taste
    Hot, fluffy rice
    Chives

Drain mushrooms and reserve liquid. Lightly sauté mushrooms, almonds, and green pepper in melted butter. Add mushroom liquid, orange and lemon juice, mushroom soup, and celery salt. Blend well over low heat. Stir in olives, pimiento, parsley, and Tabasco sauce. Flake crabmeat and remove any shells. Add to hot mixture and season to taste with salt and pepper. Heat thoroughly, but do not boil. Hold over very low heat, if necessary, until serving time. Spoon over hot, fluffy rice tossed with chives. Yield: 8 servings.

Cruiser Crab

    Margarine
    Chopped celery leaves
    Broken bits of white bread
    Chunks of freshly boiled crabmeat
    Salt and pepper
    (The amounts depend upon the number
        to be fed.)

Let margarine and celery leaves simmer in frypan for a few minutes; toss in broken bits of bread and chunks of crabmeat. Add salt and pepper to taste and steam on low heat for ½ hour. This gets raves when served with potato chips, rolls, and a cold drink.

Justine's Crabmeat Suzette

    ⅓ cup all-purpose flour
    1 tablespoon sugar
    Dash of salt
    1 egg
    1 egg yolk
    ¾ cup milk
    1 tablespoon butter or margarine,
        melted
    1 tablespoon butter or margarine
    1 tablespoon all-purpose flour
    Dash of salt
    Dash of white pepper
    ½ cup milk
    1 cup fresh lump crabmeat or 1 (6-
        ounce) package frozen crabmeat
    1 tablespoon lemon juice
    2 tablespoons sherry
    Dash bottled hot pepper sauce
    Dash Worcestershire sauce
    ½ cup hollandaise sauce

Measure the first seven ingredients into a blender container or mixing bowl; blend or beat with an electric or rotary beater until batter is smooth. Refrigerate for several hours or until batter is thick.

In a saucepan, melt 1 tablespoon butter over low heat. Blend in flour, salt, and white pepper. Add milk all at once; cook quickly, stirring constantly, until mixture thickens and bubbles. Add crabmeat, lemon juice, sherry, hot pepper sauce, and Worcestershire sauce. Heat through and keep warm.

Heat a heavy 6-inch skillet till a drop of water will dance on the surface. Grease lightly and pour in 2 tablespoons of the chilled batter. Lift skillet off heat and tilt from side to side till batter covers the bottom of the skillet evenly. Return skillet to heat and cook till underside is slightly browned, about 1½ minutes. Remove crêpe by inverting skillet over paper towels. Cook remaining crêpes the same way, on one side only. Spread 1 tablespoon of the hot crabmeat filling across each crêpe. Place in a 400-degree F. oven and heat till edges of crêpes begin to toast. Remove from oven and spoon hollandaise sauce over crêpes. Serve as an appetizer or entrée. Yield: about 11 crêpes.

Crabmeat Soufflé

    2 *tablespoons butter*
    2 *tablespoons flour*
    ¾ *teaspoon salt*
    ⅛ *teaspoon pepper*
    1 *cup evaporated milk diluted with*
        1 *cup water*
    ½ *cup soft breadcrumbs*
    2 *cups flaked cooked crabmeat*
    3 *egg yolks, well beaten*
    2 *teaspoons minced parsley*
    3 *egg whites, stiffly beaten*

Heat butter in skillet; add flour, salt, and pepper, and mix well. Add milk gradually and bring to boiling point, stirring constantly. Add breadcrumbs and cook 2 minutes longer. Remove from heat; add crabmeat, egg yolks, and parsley. Fold in stiffly beaten egg whites. Put into a greased 2-quart baking dish and bake, uncovered, at 350 degrees F. for about 50 minutes. Serve hot. Yield: about 6 servings.

Crabmeat Lorenzo

    1 *pound crabmeat*
    2 *cloves garlic, chopped*
    ¼ *pound butter*
    ½ *bunch shallots, chopped*
    1 *green pepper, chopped*
    1 *tablespoon flour*
    1 *cup milk*
    6 *sprigs parsley, chopped*
    ½ *cup sherry*
    1 *cup breadcrumbs*
   12 *anchovy strips*
    4 *tablespoons Italian cheese*

Prepare crabmeat. Sauté garlic in butter until half brown. Add shallots and green pepper. Cook slowly until done, but not brown. Add flour and stir in well. Add milk and parsley; stir until thick. Add sherry. Fold in crabmeat. Sprinkle in breadcrumbs. Mold into balls and place on round, crisp toast. Lay 2 strips of anchovies on top of each. Sprinkle with Italian cheese. Place under broiler until brown.

Crabmeat Imperial

    1 *green pepper, finely diced*
    2 *pimientos, finely diced*
    1 *tablespoon English mustard*
    1 *teaspoon salt*
    ½ *teaspoon white pepper*
    2 *whole eggs*
    1 *cup mayonnaise*
    3 *pounds lump crabmeat*

Mix pepper and pimientos; add mustard, salt, white pepper, eggs, and mayonnaise, and mix well. Add crabmeat, mixing with fingers so lumps are not broken. Divide mixture into eight crab shells or casseroles, heaping it in lightly. Top with little coating of mayonnaise and sprinkle with paprika. Bake at 350 degrees F. for 15 minutes. Serve hot or cold. Yield: 6 to 8 servings.

Baked Crabmeat Remick

    1 *pound white crabmeat*
    6 *strips crisp bacon*
    1 *teaspoon dry mustard*
    ½ *teaspoon paprika*
    1 *teaspoon celery salt*
       Few drops Tabasco sauce
    ½ *cup chili sauce*
    1 *teaspoon tarragon vinegar*
   1¾ *cups mayonnaise*

Pile crabmeat in 6 baking casseroles. Heat in oven and top each with strip of bacon. Blend mustard, paprika, celery salt, and Tabasco. Add chili sauce and vinegar; mix well. Add mayonnaise. Spread the hot crabmeat with this sauce and glaze under broiler flame. Yield: 6 servings.

Fish in One

This is a simple way of preparing a delicious, complete meal in one package for each person being served. Prepare 14-inch squares of heavy aluminum foil for the number of servings. Place dressed fish, thinly sliced Irish potatoes, and sliced onions near the center of the square. Add salt, pepper, butter, and lemon juice. Then fold up sides into a tight envelope and place on the grill, away from the charcoal and hickory. Close hood. These cook in about an hour over a steady 30-briquette fire. Loosen envelope tops and leave in the hot smoke for 10 minutes before serving.

Escargots Bourguignonne

  48 *black snails*
  ½ *cup butter, softened*
  ½ *teaspoon salt*
  4 *to 6 tablespoons finely chopped parsley*
  2 *cloves garlic, minced*
  2 *or 3 shallots, finely chopped*
  1 *teaspoon white pepper*

Place snails in shells. Cream butter until smooth; then add salt, parsley, garlic, shallots, and white pepper. Mix well. Pack butter mixture on top of snails and place shells in shallow metal pans. Bake at 400 degrees F. until butter mixture is lightly browned. Yield: 6 to 8 servings.

Fish Fillets in a Savory Sauce

  2½ *pounds fish fillets*
      Salt and coarsely ground pepper to taste
      Margarine
  ½ *cup soy sauce*
  ¼ *cup Worcestershire sauce*
  2 *tablespoons Pickapepper sauce (optional)*
  ¼ *teaspoon garlic powder*
  ½ *teaspoon dried marjoram*
  ½ *cup chopped green onions*
  2 *tablespoons capers*
  1 *(4-ounce) can mushrooms*
      Anchovy strips

Fillet the fish, removing all bones. Skin the fillets by placing them skin side down on a cutting board; hold the very end of the tail section firmly with a fork and slide a sharp knife along the skin under the fillet, thus easily and cleanly separating skin from fillets.

Wash thoroughly and dry with paper towels. Salt and pepper fillets and place close together in a pan lined with foil which has been generously rubbed with margarine. Combine soy sauce, Worcestershire sauce, Pickapepper sauce (if used), salt and pepper, garlic powder, and marjoram. Pour mixture over the fish and dot fillets with butter. Sprinkle generously with chopped green onions, reserving some for topping.

Set broiler at 300 degrees F. and cook for 30 to 35 minutes or until fish flakes easily with fork or toothpick. If your broiler does not operate with a thermostat, cook in the oven and run under broiler at the last minute. In the last 5 minutes or so, sprinkle with capers, mushrooms, and remaining onions. Serve immediately, garnished with anchovy strips. Yield: 6 servings.

Flounder au Gratin

  1 *large flounder (about 2½ pounds)*
      Salt
      Juice of 1 lemon
  ¼ *cup fine dry breadcrumbs*
  ¼ *cup shredded cheese*
  3 *tablespoons butter or margarine*
  ½ *cup minced onion*

Have your fish dealer dress the fish for you, which means removing scales, insides, head, and tail. Sprinkle fish with salt and lemon juice. Lay fish in greased shallow baking dish. Cover with breadcrumbs, cheese, lumps of butter, and minced onion. Bake fish at 375 to 400 degrees F. for 35 to 45 minutes or until fish flakes easily when tested with a fork. Baste from time to time with juices in pan. Yield: 4 servings.

Broiled Flounder

    2 to 2½ pounds flounder
    Salt and pepper
    ½ cup mayonnaise
    ¼ cup pickle relish
    2 tablespoons chopped parsley
    1 tablespoon lemon juice
    ¼ teaspoon salt
    Dash cayenne pepper
    2 egg whites

Wipe fillets with damp cloth, and if necessary cut into serving-size pieces. Sprinkle with salt and pepper; arrange on lightly greased shallow baking pan.

Stir together all other ingredients except egg whites; then fold in egg whites which have been beaten until stiff but not dry. Broil fish 2 inches from unit or top of flame 6 to 10 minutes or until nearly cooked through. Spread sauce in even layer over top of fish; broil 3 to 5 minutes longer or until sauce is puffed and lightly browned. Serve at once with broiled tomato halves. Yield: 6 servings.

Ocracoke Grilled Flounder

    1 fresh flounder (pound or more
       dressed weight)
    Salt and pepper to taste
    2 teaspoons flour
    2 slices bacon or salt pork
    2 small potatoes, peeled and sliced thin
    2 small onions, peeled and sliced thin

Rub the dressed fish inside and out with salt, pepper, and flour. On a sheet of heavy-duty foil place 1 slice bacon and arrange half the sliced vegetables on the bacon. Place seasoned fish on vegetables; then put remaining vegetables on the fish. Sprinkle with more salt and pepper. Top with the second slice of bacon. Drugstore-wrap the pack, keeping it thin, and grill over hot coals 30 to 40 minutes, turning once. Test for doneness by opening pack carefully and testing with fork. Yield: 2 servings.

Flounder Meunière

    2 pounds flounder fillets, fresh or
       frozen
    1 teaspoon salt
    Dash pepper
    1 cup flour
    ½ cup butter
    1 tablespoon lemon juice
    1 tablespoon chopped parsley

Thaw frozen fillets; skin them if necessary. Cut into serving-size portions. Sprinkle with salt and pepper. Roll in flour. Fry in butter. When fish is brown on one side, turn carefully and brown the other side. Cooking time will be approximately 10 to 15 minutes, depending on thickness of fish. Remove fish from pan and place on a hot platter. To browned butter, add lemon juice; pour over fish. Sprinkle with parsley. Yield: 6 servings.

Flounder Kiev

    2 pounds flounder fillets, fresh or
       frozen
    ½ cup soft butter or margarine
    2 tablespoons chopped parsley
    1 tablespoon lemon juice
    ¾ teaspoon Worcestershire sauce
    ¼ teaspoon Tabasco sauce
    1 clove garlic, finely chopped
    ½ teaspoon salt
    Dash pepper
    ½ cup flour
    2 eggs, beaten
    2 tablespoons water
    Breadcrumbs

Thaw frozen fillets. Combine butter, parsley, lemon juice, Worcestershire sauce, Tabasco, and garlic. Place butter mixture on waxed paper and form into a roll. Chill until hard. Skin fillets and divide into 12 strips about 6 x 2 inches. Sprinkle fish with salt and pepper. Cut butter roll into 12 pieces. Place a piece of butter at one end of each strip of fish. Fasten with toothpicks. Roll fish in flour; dip in eggs, to which water has been added; and roll in crumbs. Chill for 1 hour. Fry in deep fat, 375 degrees F., for 2 to 3 minutes or until golden brown and fish flakes easily when tested with a fork. Drain on absorbent paper. Remove toothpicks before serving. Yield: 6 servings.

Frog Legs Roberto

     8 *pairs of frog legs*
    ½ *bottle dry wine (white Maconnais)*
        Garlic salt
        Lemon-pepper marinade
        Dash lemon juice
     1 *stick butter*
    ½ *cup olive oil*
     2 *to 4 cloves garlic*
        Pimiento strips
        Chopped parsley
     1 *(4-ounce) can sliced mushrooms*

Place frog legs in large sauté pan so they are one layer. Add the wine. Sprinkle with garlic salt, lemon-pepper marinade, and a dash of lemon juice. Cover, bring to a boil, and then simmer gently for about 5 minutes. Remove frog legs and arrange carefully in ovenproof serving dish; discard marinade.

Melt butter, add olive oil, and heat; sauté garlic for a minute or so. Pour over frog legs and garnish with pimiento, chopped parsley, and sliced mushrooms. Place in a 350-degree F. oven just long enough to heat well. Serve with generous portions of Chicken Fried Rice (page 98). Yield: 4 servings.

Fruits de Mer

On shallow baking sheet place 4-ounce fresh fillet of flounder, 2 sea squabs, 4 lobster dainties (halved), and 2 raw oysters and liquid on shell.

Sprinkle all four seafoods with melted butter, lemon juice, Spanish paprika, and freshly ground pepper. To oysters add 3 drops Worcestershire sauce and ½ strip bacon.

Cover bottom of baking sheet with water. Cook under medium broiler flame until flounder is firm, about 10 minutes. (Do not overcook. Add more water to pan, if necessary.) About 3 or 4 minutes before cooking time has elapsed, sprinkle a light coating of Grape Nuts Flakes and butter over flounder. Finish cooking.

Jambalaya

     1 *pint oysters*
     1 *cup uncooked rice*
     3 *heaping tablespoons lard or oil*
    ½ *cup minced onion*
    ½ *cup minced celery*
     1 *small green pepper, minced*
     2 *cloves garlic, minced*
     2 *cups boiling water*
    ½ *cup oyster juice, heated*
        Salt and pepper to taste

Drain oysters and keep juice. Put rice into heated fat in a heavy saucepan, stir until lightly browned. Add minced ingredients and sauté for about 1 minute. Add boiling water and juice, salt and pepper and mix thoroughly. Add oysters or other seafood, stir once, reduce heat to simmer, cover and cook for about 15 minutes or until rice is tender. If desired, after rice is done, place about four pats of real butter on top, cover, and allow to melt.

Lobster Andalouse

  4 *frozen lobster tails*
  5 *tablespoons sweet butter*
  1 *clove fresh garlic, crushed*
   Juice of 1 fresh lemon
  1 *cup finely chopped parsley*
 1½ *cups vermouth*
   Lemon slices
   Parsley

Cut lobster in 1-inch chunks. Put butter in skillet, add crushed garlic, and cook at low heat until butter is well seasoned. Remove garlic. Add lobster to garlic butter and stir until cooked (from 10 to 15 minutes). Add lemon juice and parsley and cook about 3 minutes longer. Add vermouth and set aflame. When flame dies down, serve at once. Garnish with lemon slices and parsley. Yield: 4 servings.

Sherried Lobster

  2 *tablespoons butter*
  3 *tablespoons flour*
 1½ *cups milk or 1 cup milk and ½ cup*
   light cream
  1 *small jar pimientos, chopped*
  ½ *green pepper, finely chopped*
  1 *cup tiny green peas*
  ½ *cup sherry wine*
   Salt and pepper to taste
   Cubed meat from 1 large or 2 small
   boiled lobsters
   Shredded Romano cheese
   Paprika

In top of double boiler melt butter and mix in flour. Add next six ingredients and cook over boiling water to the consistency of thick white sauce. Add lobster and put into a 2-quart casserole.
 Sprinkle with shredded Romano cheese and paprika and bake at 400 degrees F. until golden and bubbly. Serve on toast squares. Yield: 4 to 6 servings.

Lobster Gundy

  2 *cups cooked lobster meat*
  ½ *cup finely chopped onion*
  4 *ounces pimiento, drained and*
   chopped
  ¼ *cup salad oil*
  2 *tablespoons lime juice*
  ½ *teaspoon salt*
   Few drops hot pepper sauce

Put lobster through grinder. Add remaining ingredients and mix well. Chill. Place on lettuce leaves and garnish the mound with sprays of parsley, cooked carrots, and beets. Yield: 6 servings.

Oyster Bisque

(Radium Springs Inn, Albany, Georgia)

  1 *slice onion, chopped (about 1*
   tablespoon)
  1 *stalk celery, diced*
  2 *tablespoons butter*
  1 *quart oysters and juice*
  2 *cups light cream*
   Salt and white pepper to taste
   Dash Tabasco sauce
  ¼ *cup sherry*

Cook onion and celery in butter until translucent, but not brown. Chop oysters; to them add juice, onion, and celery. (If you have a blender, use it for this step instead of chopping.) Put into an enamel saucepan along with cream, salt, pepper, Tabasco, and sherry. Simmer over low heat, stirring constantly. Do not allow to boil. Yield: 4 to 6 servings.

Oysters Maryland

  3 *dozen large oysters*
   Catsup
   Cayenne pepper
   Tabasco sauce
   Sieved breadcrumbs
  6 *slices buttered toast*
  6 *slices finely chopped bacon*

Drain the oysters. Dip them into catsup seasoned with cayenne and Tabasco, then in breadcrumbs, then back into seasoned catsup, and finally back in breadcrumbs. Lay them on buttered toast. Sprinkle with chopped bacon. Broil until the bacon browns.

Oysters "Johnny Reb"

      2 *quarts oysters, drained*
    ½ *cup finely chopped parsley*
    ½ *cup finely chopped shallots or onions*
      Salt and pepper to taste
      Tabasco sauce to taste
      1 *tablespoon Worcestershire sauce*
      2 *tablespoons lemon juice*
    ½ *cup melted butter or margarine*
      2 *cups fine cracker crumbs*
      Paprika
    ¾ *cup half milk and half cream*

Place a layer of oysters in the bottom of a greased shallow 2-quart baking dish. Sprinkle with half of parsley, shallots, seasonings, lemon juice, butter, and crumbs. Make another layer of the same. Sprinkle with paprika. Just before baking pour the milk into evenly spaced holes, being very careful not to moisten crumb topping all over. Bake at 375 degrees F. about 30 minutes or until mixture is firm. Yield: 12 to 15 servings.

Oyster Casserole

      2 *cups cracker crumbs, rolled fine*
      1 *tablespoon chopped pimiento*
      1 *teaspoon salt*
    ¼ *teaspoon paprika*
    ¼ *teaspoon celery salt*
      2 *teaspoons minced parsley*
    ½ *cup melted butter or margarine*
      1 *pint oysters*
      1 *egg, slightly beaten*
    ⅔ *cup undiluted cream of mushroom
        soup*

Add the crumbs, pimiento, salt, paprika, celery salt, and minced parsley to melted butter and mix well. Line a shallow casserole with half the crumb mixture. Combine oysters, egg, and soup and pour this over the crumb mixture. Cover oysters with rest of crumb mixture. Bake at 350 degrees F. for 1 hour. Yield: 8 servings.

Escalloped Oysters

    ½ *cup butter*
    ½ *cup flour*
    ½ *teaspoon salt*
    ¼ *teaspoon pepper*
    ½ *teaspoon paprika*
      1 *onion, minced*
    ½ *green pepper, minced*
      1 *teaspoon lemon juice*
      1 *tablespoon Worcestershire sauce*
      1 *quart oysters*
    ¼ *cup cracker crumbs*

Melt butter; add flour and cook 5 minutes or until light brown. Add salt, pepper, and paprika and cook 3 minutes. Add minced onion and green pepper. Cook slowly for 5 minutes. Take from the heat. Add lemon juice, Worcestershire sauce, and oysters which have been heated in their own liquid. Pour in baking dish and sprinkle with crumbs. Bake at 400 degrees F. for 30 minutes. Yield: 8 to 10 servings.

Oven-Fried Fish

      2 *pounds pan-dressed fish*
      1 *tablespoon salt*
      1 *cup milk*
      1 *cup breadcrumbs*
      4 *tablespoons melted butter or
        margarine*

Cut fish into serving-size pieces. Add salt to milk and mix well. Dip fish in milk and roll in crumbs; place in well-greased or foil-lined baking dish. Pour melted butter over fish. Place pan on shelf near top of oven preheated to 500 degrees F. Bake 10 to 12 minutes or until fish flakes easily when tested with a fork. Serve immediately. Yield: 4 servings.

Fish Pudding

        3   pounds bluefish, boned and skinned
        ½   teaspoon garlic salt
        ½   teaspoon pepper
        ½   teaspoon ground mace
        ½   cup butter
        1   tablespoon shortening
        8   ounces tomato sauce
        1   medium onion, chopped
        1   green pepper, chopped
        ¼   cup chopped celery
       12   salty crackers, crushed
        1   cup milk
        4   eggs, beaten

Grind, or finely chop, the fish. Add garlic salt, pepper, and mace. Melt butter and shortening over medium heat; stir in tomato sauce. Add onion, pepper, and celery. Cook until onion is transparent and remove from heat. Stir in fish, crackers, milk, and eggs. Pour into a 3-quart casserole. Cover and bake at 350 degrees F. for 1 hour and 15 minutes. Yield: 8 servings.

Pompano Papillote

        ¼   pound butter
        1   onion, chopped fine
        1   cup flour
        1   pint scalded milk
            Whites of 2 eggs
            Dash ground nutmeg
            Dash Tabasco sauce
        1   ounce Sauterne wine
        ½   pound shrimp, boiled and chopped
        ½   pound crawfish, boiled and chopped
            Pompano fillets

Melt butter; add onion and cook about 5 minutes, stirring constantly. Slowly add the flour to form a paste, and cook slowly until completely dry. Add milk and let cook to a thick cream sauce. Beat egg whites with nutmeg, Tabasco, and Sauterne wine and fold into cream sauce. Add chopped, boiled shrimp and crawfish.

On buttered side of French paper, spread a part of the paste, then a slice of skinned pompano steak. Spread more paste, then another slice of pompano. Spread remaining sauce over top of pompano. Fold paper to form a bag with edges crimped. Brush melted butter over paper and bake at 350 degrees F. for 30 minutes. Yield: 4 servings.

Cheese Salmon Loaf

        1   (1-pound) can salmon, flaked
        1   egg, beaten
        ½   cup cream
        ½   teaspoon salt
        ⅛   teaspoon pepper
        3   tablespoons melted butter
        1   tablespoon lemon juice
      1¼   cups shredded cheese
        1   cup buttered breadcrumbs

Combine all ingredients except breadcrumbs and put into a greased loafpan. Top with buttered breadcrumbs and bake at 350 degrees F. for 30 minutes.

Broiled Lake Trout— Almond Sauce

        4   servings lake trout
            Pinch of salt
        ¾   cup butter, melted
            Salt and pepper
            Paprika
        ½   cup slivered almonds
            Juice and grated rind of 1 lemon

Place whole fish or fillets, cut in desired size servings, in skillet with just enough boiling water to cover. Add salt and cook for 12 minutes. Carefully remove fish to avoid breaking; place in a shallow pan. Butter fish well and sprinkle with salt and pepper. Place under broiler for 5 minutes. Baste with butter if necessary to prevent drying during broiling process. Sprinkle with paprika and additional butter near end of broiling period.

Toast almonds in remaining butter; add lemon juice and rind and pour over fish at serving time.

Picadilly Trout

  2 *pounds pan-dressed trout or other*
      small pan-dressed fish, fresh or
      frozen
1½ *teaspoons salt*
¼ *teaspoon pepper*
    Dash paprika
½ *cup butter or margarine*
  2 *teaspoons dill weed*
  3 *tablespoons lemon juice*

Thaw fish if frozen, or clean and cut the fresh catch almost through lengthwise and spread open. Sprinkle with salt and pepper. Dust with paprika. Melt butter in a 10-inch frypan; add dill weed. Place fish in a single layer, flesh side down, in the hot dill butter.

Fry at moderate heat for 2 to 3 minutes. Turn carefully. Fry 2 to 3 minutes longer or until fish flakes easily when tested with a fork. Place on a warm serving platter. Keep warm.

When all the fish have been fried, turn heat very low and stir in lemon juice. Pour sauce over fish. Delicious with hush puppies. Yield: 6 servings.

Tuna Bake

  2 *cans chunk-style tuna*
  1 *medium onion, chopped*
  1 *medium green pepper, chopped*
  2 *(No. 303) cans small English peas*
  2 *cans condensed cream of celery soup*
    Salt and pepper to taste
  2 *cans ready-to-cook biscuits*
  2 *cups shredded American cheese*

Drain small amount of oil from tuna into a skillet. Sauté chopped onion and pepper in oil until transparent. In a 2-quart casserole dish, combine onion, pepper, tuna, peas, and soup. Add salt and pepper to taste.

Flatten each biscuit; add small amount of shredded cheese and fold over, pinching edges together to form a pocket. Place on top of tuna mixture. Bake at 400 degrees F. about 15 minutes, or until biscuits are browned. Yield: 10 to 12 servings.

Crusty Tuna Pie

1½ *cups diced pared potatoes*
½ *cup diced celery*
  2 *tablespoons chopped onion*
  1 *can condensed cream of celery soup*
¼ *cup light cream or milk*
  1 *(7-ounce) can tuna*
  1 *cup canned or cooked peas, drained*
  1 *can pimientos, cut in strips*
    Cheese-Swirl Biscuits

Cook potatoes, celery, and onion in small amount of unsalted water until almost tender; drain. Add soup and cream or milk; heat. Add tuna (leave in large pieces), peas, and pimiento; bring just to boiling. Pour into a 10- x 6- x 1½-inch baking dish. Arrange Cheese-Swirl Biscuits, cut side down, on hot tuna mixture. Bake at 425 degrees F. for 15 to 20 minutes or until biscuits are lightly browned and done. Yield: 5 or 6 servings.

Cheese-Swirl Biscuits:

  1 *cup sifted flour*
  2 *teaspoons baking powder*
¼ *teaspoon salt*
  2 *tablespoons shortening*
⅓ *cup milk*
½ *cup shredded sharp processed*
    American cheese

Sift together flour, baking powder, and salt. Cut in shortening with pastry blender until mixture resembles coarse meal.

Add milk and stir until the dough follows fork around bowl. Turn out on lightly floured surface and knead gently for ½ minute. Roll in rectangle ¼ inch thick.

Sprinkle with the shredded cheese and roll as for jellyroll, starting at narrow end, and seal edge. Cut in ½-inch slices.

Tuna-Broccoli Casserole

  1 *package frozen broccoli*
  1 *(7-ounce) can tuna, flaked*
  1 *(10½-ounce) can cream of*
     mushroom soup
 ½ *can milk (soup can)*
 ½ *cup crushed potato chips*

Split broccoli stalks; cook 3 minutes; drain. Place in 1½-quart baking dish. Cover with tuna. Mix soup and milk. Pour over tuna. Sprinkle potato chips over top. Bake at 450 degrees F. for 15 minutes. Yield: 4 servings.

Tuna Quickie Casserole

  1 *(5-ounce) package broad noodles*
  2 *teaspoons salt*
  3 *cups boiling water*
  1 *can condensed mushroom soup*
 ⅓ *cup milk*
  1 *(7-ounce) can tuna*
  1 *cup cooked peas*
    Buttered breadcrumbs

Cook noodles in boiling salted water about 2 minutes. Cover, remove from heat, and let stand about 10 minutes. Meanwhile, combine mushroom soup, milk, tuna, and peas. Rinse noodles with warm water and drain well. Fold noodles into tuna mixture; pour into a greased 1-quart casserole. Sprinkle with breadcrumbs and bake at 350 degrees F. about 30 minutes. Yield: 4 servings.

Tuna-Cashew Crunch

  1 *(10-ounce) package frozen peas*
  1 *(7-ounce) can tuna*
  1 *can cream of mushroom soup*
  1 *soup can milk*
 ½ *cup cashews, chopped*
 ¼ *cup ripe olives, chopped*
  3 *cups chow mein noodles*

Cook peas according to package directions; drain. Combine with tuna (flaked and drained), mushroom soup, milk, cashews,

olives, and 2½ cups of the noodles. Spoon into buttered 1½-quart casserole and top with remaining noodles. Bake at 350 degrees F. for 30 minutes. Garnish with ripe olives.

Chopstick Tuna

  1 *can condensed cream of mushroom*
     soup
 ¼ *soup can of water*
  1 *(3-ounce) can chow mein noodles*
  1 *(7-ounce) can tuna*
  1 *cup chopped celery*
 ½ *cup salted, toasted cashews*
 ¼ *cup chopped onion*
    Dash pepper

Combine soup and water. Add 1 cup of the chow mein noodles, the tuna, celery, cashews, onion, and pepper. Toss lightly. Place in ungreased 10- x 6- x 1½-inch baking dish. Sprinkle remaining noodles over top. Bake at 375 degrees F. for 20 to 25 minutes, or until heated. Garnish with drained, canned mandarin orange slices, if desired. Yield: 4 to 5 servings.

Doodle-Noodle Casserole

  1 *(5-ounce) package noodles*
  1 *(7-ounce) can tuna, drained*
 ½ *cup mayonnaise*
  1 *cup chopped celery*
 ½ *cup chopped onions*
 ¼ *cup chopped green peppers*
 ¼ *cup chopped pimiento*
  1 *teaspoon salt*
  1 *can cream of celery soup*
  1 *cup milk*
  1 *cup sharp shredded cheese*
 ½ *cup slivered, blanched toasted*
     almonds

Cook noodles according to package directions; drain. Combine noodles and tuna; add mayonnaise, all the chopped vegetables, and the salt. Blend in the soup and the milk and stir well. Heat on top of range and add the cheese. Stir until cheese melts. Spoon into a 1½-quart casserole; top with almonds. Bake at 425 degrees F. for 20 minutes. Yield: 8 servings.

Tuna-Lima Bean Casserole

 1 *(10-ounce) package frozen lima*
   beans
1½ *cups cooked macaroni*
 ½ *cup chopped onion*
 2 *tablespoons butter or margarine*
 1 *cup milk*
 1 *can cream of celery soup*
 1 *(7-ounce) can tuna, drained*
 2 *pimientos, chopped*
 1 *tablespoon lemon juice*
 ½ *cup buttered bread or cracker crumbs*

Cook lima beans, following label directions; drain. Cook macaroni in salted water until tender; drain. Sauté onion in butter or margarine, until softened, in medium-size heavy saucepan; stir in milk and soup; heat slowly, stirring often. Stir in tuna, lima beans, pimientos, and lemon juice; simmer 10 minutes. Fold in cooked macaroni. Pour into 1½-quart casserole. Sprinkle crumbs on top. Bake at 350 degrees F. for 20 minutes or until bubbly. Yield: 6 servings.

Tuna-Egg Scallop

1 *(7-ounce) can tuna*
1 *tablespoon lemon juice*
2 *tablespoons butter or margarine*
4 *tablespoons flour*
¼ *teaspoon dry mustard*
2½ *cups milk*
3 *hard-cooked eggs, chopped*
1 *tablespoon minced parsley*
¼ *teaspoon Tabasco sauce*
1 *cup soft buttered breadcrumbs*

Drain oil from tuna. Reserve the oil. Break tuna into pieces; add lemon juice. Melt butter, add tuna oil, flour, and dry mustard; stir to a smooth paste. Add milk and cook, stirring constantly until mixture thickens and comes to a boil. Add tuna, eggs, parsley, and

Tabasco. Turn into individual casseroles. Sprinkle with buttered breadcrumbs. Bake at 375 degrees F. for 25 minutes or until crumbs are very lightly browned. Yield: 4 to 6 servings.

Deviled Tuna Casserole

2 *(7-ounce) cans tuna*
1 *tablespoon grated onion*
1 *tablespoon lemon juice*
2 *tablespoons chopped parsley*
½ *teaspoon garlic salt*
¼ *cup butter or margarine*
¼ *cup flour*
½ *teaspoon salt*
 Dash cayenne pepper
2 *cups milk*
1 *cup soft bread cubes*
½ *cup crushed potato chips*

Drain tuna; break into large pieces. Add onion, lemon juice, parsley, and garlic salt. Melt butter; blend in flour, salt, and pepper. Add milk gradually and cook until thick and smooth, stirring constantly. Fold in bread cubes and tuna mixture. Place in a well-greased 1-quart casserole, cover with potato chips, and bake at 400 degrees F. for 15 to 20 minutes. Yield: 6 servings.

Water's Edge Fish Fry

Fresh dressed fish
Salt and pepper to taste
Packaged pancake mix
1 *egg, beaten with 1 tablespoon water*
Margarine for frying
Lemon wedges for garnish

Dry fish on paper towels. Salt and pepper lightly on both sides. Coat with pancake mix; dip in egg-water mixture and then in pancake mix again. Heat margarine in skillet and fry fish until done and brown, turning once. Fish is done when it flakes easily with a fork. Serve with plenty of lemon.

Food Preservation

Times have changed since every homemaker put up jar upon jar of preserves or pickles. Although berries and fruits may now be frozen, there is still the creative challenge to make scuppernong, or muscadine, or strawberry, or peach, or pear preserves.

Berries are normally frozen for later use in the ever-popular cobbler, but a few jars of blackberry jam may be cooked up, if for no other reason than for use in Christmas baking.

Grapes are still made into butters, jams, preserves. Pear honey, preserves, or sweet pickles prolong the enjoyment of hard pears.

From the Florida and Texas citrus belts come mouth-watering recipes for marmalade and candied citrus peel.

Pickles and relishes are so easy to make that few homemakers can resist adding a few jars to their pantry. Pickled okra, considered a delicacy in gourmet food shops, takes only a few minutes of preparation and makes a very impressive gift.

1-2-3 Conserve

> 1 *pound ripe tomatoes*
> 2 *pounds peeled and sliced peaches*
> 3 *pounds granulated sugar*

Peel the tomatoes and cut fine, removing the hard core at the stem end. Put into a colander; allow to drain, but do not squeeze out any juice. Peel and slice the peaches in narrow strips. Add the sugar. Now add the drained tomato pulp to the peaches and sugar. Stir this well for 2 or 3 minutes before cooking. Boil the conserve slowly but steadily for a half hour. Cool 3 minutes before putting into the sterilized jars. For a wonderful flavor, add a half cup of chopped crystallized ginger just before sealing. Yield: about 3 pints.

All strawberries need not be served as strawberry shortcake. They make excellent preserves, and are mighty tasty with hot biscuits and butter.

Pear Conserve

> 1 *orange*
> 2 *lemons*
> 5 *cups peeled and chopped pears*
> 2 *cups raisins*
> 5 *cups sugar*

Run the orange and lemons through the food grinder, using the coarse knife. Combine ground fruit with chopped pears, raisins, and sugar. Cook slowly until thick. Pour into hot sterilized jars and seal. Yield: 3 to 4 pints.

Assorted Conserves

Use cherry, strawberry, cranberry, damson, plum, grape, peach, apricot, orange, lemon, or lime marmalade. Add ½ cup chopped pecans to 2 cups marmalade and mix well. Serve with any hot buttered bread.

Peach Chutney

  4 *pieces ginger root*
  1 *tablespoon pickling spice*
1½ *cups cider vinegar*
  2 *cups sugar*
  1 *(No. 2½) can peaches, drained and*
      cut in pieces
  1 *cup seedless raisins*
  1 *hard pear, peeled, sliced, and*
      chopped
12 *pitted dates*
  1 *hot red pepper, broken*
  1 *teaspoon turmeric*
  1 *clove garlic, minced*
  ¼ *teaspoon salt*
  ½ *pound small onions, chopped*

Pound the ginger root, combine it with the pickling spice, and tie loosely in a cheese-cloth bag. Put it in a large kettle with the vinegar and sugar and bring it to a boil. Drain the peaches. Boil the peach liquid un-til there is only ½ cup remaining. Add the fruits, red pepper, turmeric, garlic, and salt to the vinegar mixture. Simmer, without a cover, for about 1½ hours, stirring occasion-ally. Add the onions after the first hour of cooking. When it is thick, remove the spice bag. Pour into jars and seal. Yield: about 6 half pints.

Pineapple Chutney

  4 *cups (2 No. 303 cans) crushed*
      pineapple
  1 *cup cider vinegar*
  1 *cup brown sugar, firmly packed*
  2 *cups seedless raisins*
  1 *tablespoon salt*
  4 *tablespoons chopped candied ginger*
  4 *cloves garlic, finely chopped*
  ¼ *teaspoon cayenne pepper*
  ¼ *teaspoon ground cloves*
  ¼ *teaspoon ground cinnamon*
  ⅓ *cup chopped almonds*

Cook the pineapple and pineapple syrup, vinegar, sugar, raisins, salt, ginger, the finely chopped garlic, cayenne pepper, cloves, and cinnamon over low heat for about 50 minutes or until it is thick. Stir it frequently and add the almonds just before pouring into the sterilized jars. Yield: about 4 half pints.

Carrot Chutney

  4 *medium carrots*
  8 *apples*
  1 *lemon*
  1 *onion*
  2 *cups sugar or honey*
  2 *teaspoons ground cloves*
  1 *teaspoon ground ginger*
  2 *cups vinegar*
  ½ *cup water*

Put the carrots, apples, lemon, and onion through the food chopper. Add other ingredients and cook all together over low heat until thick, about 1½ hours. Seal in sterilized jars. Yield: about 2 to 3 pints.

Orange Chutney

  6 *thin-skinned oranges*
  3 *cups sugar*
  2 *cups water*
  ¾ *cup vinegar*
  1 *(1-pound) can whole cranberry sauce*
  2 *tablespoons molasses*
  ½ *cup raisins*
  1 *tablespoon salt*
1½ *teaspoons Tabasco sauce*
  1 *tablespoon curry powder*
  ½ *teaspoon whole cloves*
  3 *(3-inch) pieces stick cinnamon*
  3 *pieces whole ginger*

Put whole oranges in large saucepan; add 1½ quarts water. Bring to a boil; boil 20 minutes. Drain and cut oranges into eighths. Combine sugar, 2 cups water, and vinegar. Place over low heat and stir until sugar is dissolved. Stir in remaining ingredients. Bring to a boil. Add orange wedges and sim-mer about 20 minutes. Ladle into hot ster-ilized jars and seal. Yield: about 10 cups.

Grape Juice

Homemade grape juice is excellent for use out of season in fruit drinks, gelatin desserts, pudding sauces, fruit cocktails, and syrup for pancakes and waffles. Preserved juice can be made into jelly at your convenience.

To retain the fresh fruit flavor, use vine-ripened firm grapes, cook the fruit below the boiling point, and cool promptly. Follow these simple steps for an excellent product:

Wash the grapes in several changes of cold water and drain. Remove the grapes from the stems. Crush the grapes and add 1 pint water to 10 pounds grapes (or 1 cup water to 1 gallon grapes). Heat the grapes to 150 to 180 degrees F. Hold at this temperature 5 to 7 minutes until pulps are soft, but not broken. Remove from heat and allow to set 5 minutes to intensify the color.

Pour into a jelly bag or four layers of cheesecloth. Press or squeeze the bag to remove all juice.

Pour juice in glass container. Set in the refrigerator for 6 to 24 hours to allow tartaric acid crystals and dregs to settle in the bottom of the container.

Strain the juice through a cotton flannel cloth, jelly bag, or four thicknesses of cheesecloth. (DO NOT SQUEEZE.)

To sweeten: Add 1 cup sugar to each gallon of strained juice. Stir until all sugar is dissolved.

To can: Heat the juice to 180 degrees F., stirring constantly, and pour into preheated jars, leaving ¼-inch headspace. Adjust lids, process at simmering temperature in boiling water bath canner for 10 minutes.

To freeze: Pour the sweetened juice into rigid freezer containers, leaving headspace. Fasten airtight, label, quickfreeze, and store at zero degrees until ready to use.

Note: For jelly making, *do not* add any sugar to the juice.

Deseeding Grapes

Many products such as spiced grapes, grape preserves, jams, marmalades, grape butter, and frozen grapes are made from whole grapes with only the seed removed.

To deseed grapes, place a screen of ½-inch hardware cloth, or sheet metal with ½-inch holes, over the container. Crush and rub grapes over the screen; the pulp, which contains the seed, and the juice will pass through the screen, leaving the hulls behind. Larger pulps may be pushed through individually. To separate the seed from the pulp, heat in the juice about 5 minutes or until the pulp is broken down sufficiently to liberate the seed; force through a colander, leaving the seed to be discarded.

The pulp may be measured and frozen at this stage and used later for jams. Do not add sugar. To use, thaw and follow recipe directions.

Frozen Grape Purée

Wash the grapes in cold water; stem and drain. Place grapes in saucepan and heat 8 to 10 minutes at low temperature (not over 145 degrees F.) to loosen skins. *Do not boil.*

Put heated grapes through food mill, colander, or wide-mesh strainer. Cool the grape purée quickly. Pour the purée into glass freezer jars or other rigid freezer containers, leaving headspace; seal, label, and quickfreeze.

Spiced Grapes

> 5 *pounds deseeded grapes (pulp and hulls)*
> 4½ *pounds sugar*
> 1 *cup vinegar*
> 1½ *teaspoons ground cinnamon*
> 4 *teaspoons ground mace*

Boil deseeded grapes for 15 minutes or until hulls are tender. Add sugar and cook until thick. Add vinegar and spices and cook until the product gives a very light jell test (223 degrees F.). Pack hot in hot sterilized jars and seal. Yield: 9 to 10 pints.

Grape Butter

  5 *pounds grape pulp and ground hulls*
2½ *pounds sugar*
2½ *teaspoons ground cinnamon*
  2 *teaspoons ground mace*
  2 *drops clove oil*

Wash and crush grapes. Separate hulls and pulp. Heat pulp with juice and put through a colander to remove seeds; grind hulls in a food chopper using fine blade. Combine deseeded pulp, juice, and hulls. Cook until hulls are tender. Add sugar and spices. Cook very slowly, stirring repeatedly, until the mixture is very thick and has a jellylike consistency. Pack in hot, sterilized jars and seal. Yield: about 8 pints.

Blackberry Jam

  6 *cups crushed blackberries (about 3 quarts)*
  1 *package powdered pectin*
8½ *cups sugar*

Sort and wash fully ripe berries; remove any stems or caps. Crush berries. If they are very seedy, put part or all of them through a sieve or food mill.

Measure crushed berries into a kettle; add the pectin and stir well. Place on high heat and bring quickly to a full rolling boil, stirring constantly. Add the sugar, continue stirring, and heat again to full bubbling boil. Boil hard for 1 minute, stirring constantly.

Remove from heat; skim and stir alternately for 5 minutes. Ladle into hot containers and seal. Yield: about 14 glasses.

Paradise Pear Jam

4½ *cups prepared fruit (1 orange, 1 lemon, about 2 pounds ripe pears, ¼ cup chopped maraschino cherries, ½ cup finely chopped citron, and one 8½-ounce can crushed pineapple)*
  5 *cups (2¼ pounds) sugar*
  1 *box powdered pectin*

First, prepare the fruit. Remove rinds from orange and lemon in quarters; discard about half the white part of rinds. Slice rinds, chop orange and lemon, and discard seeds. Peel, core, and grind about 2 pounds fully ripe pears. Combine all the fruits, including cherries, citron, and pineapple. Measure 4½ cups fruit into a large saucepan.

Then make the jam. Measure sugar; set aside. Stir powdered pectin into fruit. Place over high heat; stir until mixture comes to a hard boil. Stir in sugar at once. Bring to a full rolling boil and boil hard 1 minute, stirring constantly. Remove from heat and skim. Stir and skim for 5 minutes to cool slightly and prevent floating fruit. Ladle quickly into glasses; cover at once with ⅛ inch of hot paraffin. Yield: about 9 glasses.

Strawberry and Pineapple Jam

  4 *cups prepared fruit (1 ripe pineapple and about 1 quart ripe strawberries)*
  7 *cups (3 pounds) sugar*
  ½ *bottle liquid pectin*

Pare one medium, fully ripe pineapple. Grind or chop very fine. Crush about 1 quart fully ripe strawberries. Combine fruit. Measure 4 cups into a very large saucepan.

Add sugar to fruit in saucepan and mix well. Place over high heat, bring to a full rolling boil, and boil hard for 1 minute, stirring constantly. Remove from heat and at once stir in liquid pectin. Skim off foam with metal spoon. Then stir and skim by turns for 5 minutes to cool slightly and to prevent floating fruit. Ladle quickly into glasses. Cover jam at once with ⅛ inch hot paraffin. Yield: 10 medium-size jelly glasses.

Note: If desired, substitute 1 (No. 2) can crushed pineapple for the fresh pineapple.

Orange Marmalade

  4 *medium oranges*
  3 *lemons*
  6 *cups water*
  Sugar

Lightly grate outer edge of oranges and

lemons. Remove peel and cut into thin slivers. Measure peel. To 2 cups orange peel and 1½ cups lemon peel, add 6 cups water and let stand overnight. Next day cook mixture until peel is tender. Let stand overnight. On third day add 2 cups sugar for each 2 cups of cooked peel and liquid. Cook to jelly stage (10 minutes). Let stand until it cools slightly, stirring occasionally, so that fruit will be evenly distributed. Pour into sterilized jars and seal while hot. Yield: about 2 pints.

Hot Pepper Jelly

> ¼ *cup chopped or ground red or green hot peppers*
> 1½ *cups chopped or coarsely ground sweet green peppers*
> 6½ *cups sugar*
> 1½ *cups vinegar*
> 1 *bottle liquid pectin*

Grind peppers on fine blade of food grinder. Mix peppers, sugar, and vinegar and bring to a brisk boil. Boil for 3 minutes. Add pectin and boil 1 minute longer. Remove from heat and let set 5 minutes. Put into hot, sterilized jars and seal. Jelly may be strained.

Peach Honey

> 4 *cups sliced, ripe peaches*
> 4 *cups sugar*
> *Juice of 1 lemon*

Peel and slice ripe peaches, removing bad spots. Put in large, heavy pan with sugar and cook over medium heat until it reaches a good boil, stirring constantly. Add the lemon juice. Continue cooking until thick; stir constantly. Put in sterilized jars and seal.

Pear Honey

> 1 *quart ground pears*
> 1 *(No. 2) can crushed pineapple*
> 6 *cups sugar*

Peel and grind pears. Cook until tender. Add other ingredients and cook until mixture is thick. Put in hot sterilized jars and seal.

Mincemeat

> 2 *pints lean beef, boiled and ground*
> 1 *pint suet, ground*
> 2 *pints raisins*
> 1 *pint chopped citron*
> 3 *pints chopped apples (not peeled)*
> 4 *pints (8 cups) sugar*
> 1 *pint molasses*
> 1 *pint cider vinegar or wine*
> 1 *tablespoon ground cloves*
> 2 *tablespoons ground cinnamon*
> 1 *tablespoon ground nutmeg*
> *Salt to taste*

Cut beef in 2-inch chunks and cook until tender in salted water. Remove from bones and grind in food chopper or sausage mill. (Pork may be used; omit suet if pork is used.) Grind suet, raisins, and citron. Do not grind apples. Combine with cooked, ground beef and all other ingredients. Mix well and cook very slowly (200 to 300 degrees in an electric roaster) for at least 4 to 5 hours or until apples are done. Stir often to prevent scorching. Remove cooked mincemeat to jars or crocks; cover and set in cool place until ready to use (preferably about 3 weeks). It may be kept in refrigerator if a cool storage place is not available.

Pear Mincemeat

Wash, quarter, and core enough pears to make 2 quarts after they are ground. Cover with water and boil 10 minutes. Add:

> 3 *cups brown sugar*
> 1 *cup white sugar*
> 1 *cup dark molasses*
> 1 *box raisins, ground*
> 1 *box currants*
> 3 *cups chopped apples*
> 1 *cup candied orange peel*
> ⅓ *pound beef suet, finely chopped*
> 2 *teaspoons each ground cloves, cinnamon, allspice, and nutmeg*
> 3 *lemons, grated rind and juice*
> 2 *cups fruit juice (any kind or sweet pickle juice)*

Simmer 45 minutes. Pack into sterilized jars and seal while hot. Process in hot-water bath for 20 minutes.

Preserved Oranges

If they're available, use Temple oranges in making the preserves. Any other juicy, flavorful orange will do, but there's a special piquancy to the Temples. Cover 6 to 7 scrubbed oranges with water, add a teaspoon of soda, and after the water comes to a boil, let them boil for 20 minutes. Drain fruit.

When the oranges are cool enough to handle, cut each orange into eighths. Then, with your kitchen scissors, snip out the seeds and the bit of white "rag" (that's the citrusman's expression for it) to which the seeds cling. Meanwhile, bring to a boil a syrup made of 2 cups sugar, 1½ cups water, ½ cup lemon juice, and grated rind of 1 lemon. Let syrup simmer for 5 minutes; then add the prepared oranges and cook for 20 minutes. Remove from heat; when cold, put oranges and syrup into a covered container and keep in the refrigerator.

The oranges go well with fowl of any kind or with glazed country ham. They also make a nice garnish for vanilla ice cream or tangerine sherbet. They're good, too, with luncheon popovers.

Bourbon Orange Slices

  4 *seedless oranges*
2½ *cups sugar*
  1 *cup water*
  1 *cup light corn syrup*
    Juice of 1 lemon
 ⅓ *cup bourbon*

Wash oranges and cut, rind and all, into ½-inch-thick slices. Cut each slice into halves. Combine sugar, water, corn syrup, and lemon juice. Bring to a boil and boil rapidly for 5 minutes. Add orange slices and simmer slowly for 5 minutes without stirring. Remove orange slices to jar and arrange in overlapping layers. Stir bourbon into syrup and spoon over orange slices, covering them completely. Seal and store in a cool, dry place. Serve with vanilla ice cream, over plain cake slices, as a pudding topping, or use in cocktails such as old-fashioneds and sours. Yield: about 4 cups.

Cherry-Flecked Peach Preserves

5 *pounds peaches*
3 *pounds sugar*
  Juice of 2 lemons
½ *teaspoon salt*
  Small bottle maraschino cherries

Cut peaches in small pieces. If peaches are soft, cut pieces a little larger, as you will want small chunks of peaches in the preserves when done. Cook peaches with sugar, lemon juice, and salt until clear and fruit has cooked down thick.

Drain and squeeze juice from center of each cherry. Cut in half and then cut again in small wedges like tiny slices of watermelon. Drain on paper towels.

Add the prepared cherries to the preserves and cook about five minutes longer to allow them to cook into the preserves. Seal hot in sterilized jars.

Peach Preserves

1 *quart sliced peaches*
  Juice of ½ lemon
1 *tablespoon butter*
4 *cups sugar*

Combine peaches, lemon juice, butter, and 2 cups sugar. Boil for 10 minutes, and then add 2 more cups sugar and cook for 12 minutes. Remove from heat and put in large bowl. Let stand overnight, stirring occasionally. Seal in sterilized jars the next day.

Scuppernong Preserves

5 *pounds deseeded grapes (pulp and hulls)*
5 *pounds sugar*

Cook deseeded grapes slowly until the hulls are tender (about 15 minutes, but time will vary with variety of grapes). Add the sugar directly to simmering hulls and pulp. Cook until product gives a light jell test (occurs when temperature reaches 223 degrees F.). Pack in hot jars and seal. Yield: 8 to 9 pints.

Cucumber Pickles

    8 *pounds cucumbers*
    2 *cups household lime*
    2 *gallons water*
    2 *quarts vinegar*
    9 *cups sugar*
    2 *tablespoons salt*

Slice cucumbers crosswise. Put them in a mixture of lime and water in enameled or pottery container; let stand overnight. Remove from limewater. Wash cucumbers through three changes of fresh, cold water.

   Mix vinegar, sugar, and salt and place drained cucumber slices in mixture. Let stand in sugar mixture for 3 hours. Bring to a boil and boil for 30 minutes. Place in hot sterilized jars and seal.

Pear Pickles

    1 *gallon pears*
    2 *quarts sugar*
    1 *pint water*
    1 *quart cider vinegar*
  2½ *sticks cinnamon*
    2 *tablespoons whole allspice*

Kieffer pears or firm, juicy pears are good pickling pears. Wash the pears, peel, cut in half or quarter, and core. Boil the pears for 10 minutes in water to cover. Boil water, sugar, vinegar, and spices tied loosely in cheesecloth. Add the drained pears and let stand overnight in the syrup.

   Next morning drain off syrup and boil until thick. Add pears and cook until tender. Do not stir but keep pears under syrup. Pack hot into sterilized jars. Cover with syrup, then seal and store in a cool, dry place.

Spicy Pineapple Pickles

    1 *(20-ounce) can pineapple chunks*
   ⅔ *cup sugar*
      Dash salt
   ½ *cup vinegar*
    5 *or 6 whole cloves*
    3 *or 4 whole allspice (optional)*
    2 *sticks cinnamon*
      Red and green food coloring

Drain pineapple, divide, and put into two refrigerator dishes. Combine sugar, salt, vinegar, cloves, allspice, and cinnamon and bring to a boil. Simmer about 10 minutes. Divide into 2 portions; add green coloring to one portion, red to the other. Pour over pineapple chunks in the refrigerator dishes; let cool before returning to refrigerator. Best if prepared several days in advance to allow flavors to blend. Spicy cinnamon "red hots" may be used instead of the stick cinnamon.

Sweet Pickled Peaches

    1 *cup vinegar*
    2 *cups water*
    8 *cups sugar*
    3 *teaspoons cloves and allspice*
    2 *sticks cinnamon (if desired)*
    8 *pounds peaches (clingstone are best)*

Mix vinegar, water, sugar, and spices. Bring to a boil. Drop in whole, fresh peaches which have been peeled. Simmer peaches in syrup for about 5 minutes; then pack in warm, clean jars and pour syrup over them. Seal and store in a cool place.

Pickled Okra

> Garlic (1 clove each jar)
> Hot pepper (1 for each jar)
> Okra
> Dill seed (1 teaspoon each jar)
> 1 quart white vinegar
> 1 cup water
> ½ cup salt

Place the garlic and hot pepper in the bottom of clean, hot pint jars. Pack firmly with clean, young okra pods from which only part of the stem has been removed. Stem end must be open. Add dill seed.

After packing jars, bring vinegar, water, and salt to a boil. Simmer about 5 minutes and pour, while boiling hot, over the okra. Seal the jars immediately. This amount of pickling solution will fill from 5 to 7 pint jars.

Heart of Palm Pickles

> 4 quarts of tender hearts of palm
> 2 tablespoons salt
> 1 quart cold water
> 1 ounce mustard seed
> 1¼ ounces dry mustard
> 3 cups granulated sugar
> 2 tablespoons turmeric
> 1½ cups flour
> Red pepper to taste
> 2 quarts apple cider vinegar
> Juice of 1 lemon
> Rind of 1 lemon

Be sure that all tough fiber is trimmed from heart of palm. Cut the tender white portion of heart into small strips. Place these strips to soak in salted water. Let sit in a cool place for two days.

On the morning of the third day, pour off all salt water, wash palm pieces well in clear water, and drain. Mix the mustard seed, mustard, sugar, turmeric, flour, red pepper, and vinegar. Boil slowly, stirring with a wooden spoon. Add the juice of a lemon and the rind, sliced into tiny slivers. Cook 10 minutes. Add the pieces of palm, bring to a boil, and boil 2 minutes. Fill hot, sterilized pint jars with the pickles and seal while hot. Yield: 8 pints.

Dilled Carrots

> 1 (1-pound) package frozen whole
>   baby carrots
> 2 tablespoons chopped fresh dill or ¼
>   cup dill sprigs
> 1 clove garlic, cut into quarters
> ⅓ cup olive oil
> ⅓ cup frozen lemon juice
> 1 teaspoon sugar
> 1 teaspoon salt
> ¼ teaspoon freshly ground black
>   pepper

Cook carrots in boiling salted water according to package directions. Drain and place in an earthenware or glass bowl. Add dill and garlic. Combine remaining ingredients; mix well and pour over carrots. Toss lightly to coat evenly. Let stand at room temperature at least 30 minutes, stirring occasionally. Remove garlic. Serve immediately or refrigerate until ready to serve. Yield: 6 servings.

Pumpkin Pickle

> 6-pound pumpkin (weighed before
>   preparing)
> 5 pounds sugar
> 2 cups white vinegar
> 2 tablespoons whole cloves
> 6 sticks cinnamon

Peel pumpkin and scrape away all seeds and stringy matter from the center. Cut into thin slices. Cover with sugar and let stand overnight.

Next morning, add vinegar, cloves, and cinnamon to sugared pumpkin and cook together over medium heat until pumpkin is transparent and syrup is thick, about 1 to 1½ hours. Pour into sterilized pint jars, pouring any remaining syrup over them, and seal. Yield: about 6 pints.

Chili Sauce

  1½ *cups white vinegar*
   2 *teaspoons whole cloves*
   1 *teaspoon celery seed*
   1 *teaspoon broken stick cinnamon*
  5½ *pounds (18 to 22 medium) tomatoes,*
     washed, peeled, and quartered
   1 *cup granulated sugar*
   1 *tablespoon chopped onion*
  ½ *teaspoon cayenne pepper*
   1 *tablespoon salt*

Combine first four ingredients. Bring to a boil; remove from heat. Combine half of the tomatoes, ½ cup sugar, onion, and cayenne pepper in deep kettle. Boil vigorously for 30 minutes, stirring frequently. Add remaining tomatoes and sugar; boil vigorously 30 minutes longer, stirring frequently.

Strain vinegar solution; discard spices. Add spiced vinegar and salt to boiling tomato mixture. Continue boiling (stirring constantly) 15 to 25 minutes or until desired consistency is reached. Pour immediately into hot, sterilized jars, filling to within ⅛ inch from top. Seal each jar at once. Yield: 2 pints.

Goldcoast Carrot Relish

   1 *dozen onions*
   1 *dozen carrots*
   8 *green peppers*
   2 *medium heads of cabbage*
  ⅓ *cup salt*
   3 *pints vinegar*
   6 *cups sugar*
   1 *tablespoon celery seed*
   1 *tablespoon mustard seed*

Grind vegetables through a food chopper. Add salt; let stand 3 hours, then drain, Mix vinegar, sugar, celery seed, and mustard seed. Boil 5 minutes and let cool. Stir into well-drained ground vegetables. Put in pint jars and seal. Yield: 8 pints.

Meats

Barbecue weather comes along every month of the year in the South, and almost any meat, including beef, pork, lamb, or chicken, may be found cooking over the coals.

Texas is cow country, and Texans tip their Stetsons only to well-prepared barbecue. Unlike many of their Southern neighbors, they do not serve chipped meat in barbecue sauce. They heap a plate with thin slices of the pit-cooked meat and give you a choice of eating it with or without their robust peppery sauce.

Southern ham is the elite member of the pork family. Good Southern cooks use every bit of every ham cooked: sliced ham as a main dish, slivers of ham in hot biscuits for appetizers, ground leftover ham for casseroles or salads, and ham hock for cooking with green vegetables or dried beans or peas.

Fried country ham with red-eye gravy makes any breakfast something special. And sausage found in Southern markets will range from mild to very hot, with enough takers of each variety to prove that sausage is a favorite breakfast meat.

Of course, barbecued spareribs take a back seat to nothing on any menu.

Since the South is a hunter's paradise, quail, dove, wild duck, and venison are limited only by the hunting season, or by the "ones that got away."

Hunters' Sautéed Quail

    6 club rolls
    ¾ cup butter
    6 quail, split
    1 teaspoon salt
    Freshly ground black pepper
    Fruit Sauce

Split rolls in half and hollow out centers. Toast in a low oven (325 degrees F.) until brown. Melt ¼ cup butter and brush the rolls with the butter. Sauté the quail over high heat in the remaining ½ cup butter for 10 minutes or until golden brown. Sprinkle them with salt and pepper. Arrange quail on rolls and serve with Fruit Sauce. Yield: 6 servings.

    Fruit Sauce:

        1 cup seedless white grapes
        1 cup water
        4 tablespoons butter
        ½ cup port wine
        ⅛ teaspoon ground cloves
        ½ teaspoon ground ginger
        2 tablespoons finely chopped
            mushrooms
        ½ cup finely chopped filberts

Bring grapes and 1 cup of water to a boil. Cover, reduce heat, and simmer for 5 minutes. Drain off water. Add butter, wine, cloves, and ginger. Cover and simmer for 5 minutes. Stir in mushrooms and simmer for 5 minutes. Add filberts (or hazelnuts, as they are often called) and serve immediately.

Although the South consumes a great deal of beef and pork, wild game is served in abundance during hunting season. Baked Quail is a favorite.

Quail à la Glenn

16 *quail*
   Salt and pepper
1½ *sticks butter*
½ *cup flour*

Pick birds clean and wash thoroughly. Place on a rack in a roasting pan, breasts up. Sprinkle with salt and pepper, and dot with butter. Pour enough water in pan to almost cover birds and then put rest of butter in pan. (Add water during cooking, if necessary, to maintain constant level.) Cover roaster and put in an oven preheated to 300 degrees F. Cook slowly until tender (about 3 hours). Brown ½ cup dry flour in pan under broiler, stirring occasionally. Place browned flour in bowl and add enough water to make creamy batter. Pour over birds and stir pan liquid gently to prevent tearing meat. Cook about 20 minutes longer, basting several times. Add butter to gravy if greater richness is desired. Serve quail on country ham with wild rice and cover with gravy from cooking pan.

Baked Quail

 6 *quail*
   Water
 4 *tablespoons Worcestershire sauce*
 1 *teaspoon Tabasco sauce*
 3 *tablespoons olive oil*
   Juice of 3 lemons
½ *stick butter*
 2 *tablespoons molasses*
   Salt and pepper to taste
 1 *teaspoon prepared mustard*

Put quail in roasting pan with enough water to cover bottom of the pan. Cover and place in 300-degree F. oven. Combine other ingredients and blend together over low heat. When quail have cooked for 30 minutes, remove from oven and pour sauce over birds. Return to oven, cover, and continue cooking 30 to 40 minutes longer, basting frequently. During the last 10 minutes of cooking time, remove cover to brown birds and thicken the sauce. Yield: 6 servings.

Braised Quail With Bacon

 6 *quail*
18 *strips bacon*
 2 *tablespoons butter or margarine*
½ *cup hot water*
 4 *tablespoons flour*
 6 *slices toast*

Prepare quail for cooking and let stand overnight in refrigerator. The next day, cover quail with salted water, using 1 tablespoon salt for each quart water. Let stand for 15 minutes; drain and dry inside and out with a cloth.

Place 1 strip bacon in cavity of each bird and place in shallow roasting pan. Place a strip of bacon over breast of each and a strip over the legs. Bake at 450 degrees F. for 5 minutes; reduce heat to 350 degrees and continue cooking for 40 minutes, basting frequently with a mixture of the butter and hot water. At the end of the baking time, sprinkle with flour, increase heat to 450 degrees F., and brown about 10 minutes. Serve on toast. Yield: 6 servings.

Coach Howard's Quail Pie

 6 *quail*
 2 *cups water*
 3 *cups self-rising flour*
 1 *cup shortening*
   Ice water
   Salt and pepper to taste
 3 *tablespoons melted butter*
 2 *tablespoons flour*
   Milk

Cook quail in water in a pressure cooker for about 25 minutes. Make a pastry of flour and shortening and just enough ice water to make a stiff dough. Roll out one-half the pastry to cover bottom of a large casserole. Remove quail from cooker, and save the broth. Remove bones from quail and place meat in the casserole. Sprinkle salt and pepper and pour melted butter evenly over the meat. Thicken broth with 2 tablespoons flour and pour over quail. Roll remaining pastry thin and cut into strips. All pastry strips should be well pricked. Place a few thin, pricked strips of pastry over the quail, bringing ends of strips to meet bottom pastry. Brush with milk and bake at 350 degrees F. for 40 minutes.

Quail With Wild Rice

     8 *quail*
    ½ *cup butter*
     2 *cups sliced mushrooms*
    ½ *cup chopped green onion*
     1 *cup dry white wine*
     2 *tablespoons lemon juice*
        Salt
        Freshly ground black pepper
        Cooked wild rice

Brown the quail in butter, remove, and set aside. Sauté mushrooms and onions in butter. Place quail, mushrooms, and onion in shallow pan and cover with foil. Bake at 350 degrees F. for 1 hour. The last 15 minutes of cooking time, remove foil. Combine wine, lemon juice, salt, and pepper, and baste quail often. Serve hot with wild rice.

Stuffed Quail

    1½ *pounds chicken livers*
     2 *large onions, chopped*
     1 *green pepper, chopped*
     2 *buds garlic, minced*
    1½ *sticks butter*
    2½ *cups boiled wild rice*
    10 *quail*
        Sliced oranges
        Sliced onions
        Sliced celery
     2 *cups chicken broth*
    1½ *cups port wine*

Sauté liver, onion, pepper, and garlic in butter. Do not let the vegetables brown, but cook to a clear color. Add boiled wild rice to sautéed mixture for the stuffing. Stuff quail and then wrap each one in cheesecloth and completely cover with slices of oranges, onions, and celery. Pour the chicken broth over the quail and add wine. Bake at 375 degrees F. about 30 minutes. When quail are done, take cheesecloth off quail and you will have enough gravy to pour over birds.

Smothered Baked Quail à la Rivers

    12 *plump South Carolina quail*
     6 *tablespoons butter*
     3 *tablespoons cooking oil*
        Salt and pepper to taste
        Dash of garlic salt for each bird
     2 *(4-ounce) cans sliced mushrooms, drained*
     1 *(8-ounce) can brown gravy*
        Mushroom liquid plus ½ cup water
        Cooked wild rice

Wipe quail and rub each bird with butter. Put cooking oil in a large oblong pan; place quail in pan and bake at 350 degrees F., uncovered, for about 25 minutes. When quail begin to get tender, remove and add the rest of the butter which has been melted, the salt, pepper, and garlic salt. Put pan under broiler, watching carefully until quail are browned. Remove from broiler and add sliced mushrooms, gravy, and liquid. Return to 350-degree F. oven and cook until tender, basting often. Add more salt and garlic salt if needed. Serve with cooked wild rice. Yield: 12 servings.

Stuffed Quail

Dress birds, open down the back, and refrigerate for 48 hours. At the end of this time salt and pepper inside and out.

Stuff each bird with large fresh oysters. Sew or tie openings, with wings and legs close to the body. Place in a baking dish just large enough to hold them and dot with butter. Pour liquid from oysters over quail, cover container, and bake at 350 degrees F. about 1½ hours or until tender.

Remove to serving dish, pour gravy over them, and serve hot.

Quail With Wild Rice

      10 *quail*
       1 *stick butter or margarine*
     1½ *pounds chicken livers*
       2 *large onions, chopped*
       1 *green pepper, chopped*
       2 *buds garlic, minced*
     1½ *sticks butter or margarine*
     2½ *cups cooked wild rice*
       2 *cups chicken broth*
     1½ *cups port wine*

Sew together body cavity of quail. Sauté in 1 stick butter or margarine until quail are browned. Place in baking dish. Cover dish and bake at 325 degrees F. about 30 minutes.

Sauté livers, onions, pepper, and garlic in 1½ sticks butter or margarine. Do not let vegetables brown, but cook to a clear color. Add cooked rice, chicken broth, and wine. Place mixture in 3-quart baking dish; cover and bake at 325 degrees F. about 20 minutes or until liquid is absorbed. Serve quail over rice. Yield: 8 to 10 servings.

Variation: Body cavity of quail may be sewed up and the quail lightly browned in butter and placed on top of the stuffing in baking pan. Mix chicken broth and wine and pour over quail and stuffing. Cover pan and bake at 375 degrees F. for about 30 minutes.

Smothered Quail

       6 *quail*
       6 *tablespoons butter*
       3 *tablespoons flour*
       2 *cups chicken broth*
     ½ *cup sherry*
        Salt and pepper to taste
        Cooked rice

Prepare quail; brown in heavy skillet or Dutch oven in 6 tablespoons butter. Remove quail to baking dish. Add flour to butter in skillet and stir well. Slowly add chicken broth and sherry and salt and pepper to taste; blend well and pour over quail. Cover

baking dish and bake at 350 degrees F. about 1 hour. Serve with cooked rice. Yield: 6 servings.

Roasted Quail With Mushrooms

       4 *quail*
       4 *slices bacon*
       1 *tablespoon butter or margarine*
     ¼ *cup lemon juice*
     ½ *cup hot water*
     ⅓ *cup chopped mushrooms*
        Toast or rice and gravy

Prepare quail. Wrap bacon around each quail, securing with skewers or toothpicks. Put birds in shallow buttered pan; cover and bake at 350 degrees F. about 30 minutes, basting with mixture of lemon juice and water. When birds are tender, remove from oven. Add mushrooms and heat. Serve on toast or rice with gravy. Yield: 4 servings.

Fried Quail

Place cleaned quail in solution of cold water and vinegar, using ½ cup vinegar to 1 gallon water. Let stand several hours; wash through cold water several times and dry thoroughly. Season with salt and pepper and roll in flour. Fry in deep, hot fat until well browned on all sides. Add 1 cup hot water slowly, cover, and simmer over low heat 1 hour or until pan is dry. Increase heat; cook until quail is crisp.

Barbecued Duck

(Callaway Gardens, Pine Mountain, Georgia)

Cut ducks in half. Make sauce of vinegar, butter, and lemon juice. Season with salt and pepper and place on a heated outdoor grill. Put ducks on grill and baste with sauce as ducks cook. Turn them after about 30 minutes and continue cooking and basting until the outside skin is crisp and brown.

Roast Duck

    2 *ducks, cut in half*
    Garlic
    Salt and pepper
    1 *cup chopped celery*
    1 *large onion, chopped*
    1 *or 2 buttons garlic, chopped*
    1 *cup chili sauce*
    1 *tablespoon Worcestershire sauce*
    1 *tablespoon dry mustard*
    ½ *tablespoon ground nutmeg*
    Juice of 1 small lemon
    2 *cups water*
    Paprika

Rub ducks with garlic, salt, and pepper. Place breast-side down in roaster. Combine other ingredients except paprika; pour over ducks. Bake at 325 degrees F. for 3 hours. When ducks are tender, turn breast-side up and sprinkle with paprika. Bake until golden brown. Serve gravy with ducks. If a thickened gravy is desired, add a small amount of flour to drippings and cook until thickened. Yield: 4 servings.

Caddo Wild Duck

After the duck is prepared, cleaned, singed, scrubbed with meal or soda, rub him lavishly inside and out with lemon. Salt and pepper to taste and fill each duck with a stuffing:

    ½ *apple, chopped*
    1 *teaspoon salt*
    1 *teaspoon Worcestershire sauce*
    ⅛ *teaspoon black pepper and a little*
        cayenne pepper
    1 *small onion, chopped*
    ½ *cup chopped celery*

Mix all together, stuff cavity, and pin together with toothpicks. Brown in a Dutch oven. After browning, wrap each duck with bacon and place them close together, breast-side down, in a pan they will fit. They really cook better with two or three ducks placed side by side in a Dutch oven or roaster. Choose the pan to fit the ducks. Bake at 325 degrees F. for 3 hours or until tender. The size and age of duck will govern cooking time.

Some people prefer to stuff an onion inside and nothing more; others insist a rutabaga turnip is the best.

Good accompaniments to duck are rutabagas, green beans, wild rice, or vegetables of your own taste.

Note: Many people now are skinning ducks before any other means of preparation. (This removes lots of the fat and wild taste.) Some wrap a piece of bacon around the duck and wrap in foil to bake.

Wild Duck
Caneton aux Oranges

The simplest duck recipe, and the surest one, is an old Bohemian recipe.

Save the orange peel from a half-dozen oranges and keep fresh in cool water. When ready to cook the duck, cut strips of the peel between ⅛ and ¼ inch wide and about 1 inch long. Poke small holes in the duck breast with the point of a very sharp knife every 1½ to 2 inches square (about like cloving a ham) and force the orange peel strips into the holes. Then lay the rest of the orange peel over the duck, completely covering it.

Long-grained rice stuffing is best, but saffron can be added to regular rice if no wild rice is available. Roast the duck as you would a roasting hen, with a light application of poultry spices and plenty of basting. Do not overcook.

The best plan for roasting duck, as recommended in the definitive recipe of Caneton aux Oranges, is, for a 6-pound duck, to roast it for 10 minutes at 500 degrees F., pour off fat, then prick holes in the outer skin again, and roast for 10 more minutes, again draining off fat. Reduce heat to 325 degrees F. and roast for 2½ hours, basting the ducks every 10 minutes.

Wild Duck à la Duchein

    4 *ducks*
    Salt and coarsely ground pepper, to
        taste
    4 *ribs celery*
    2 *onions, cut in halves*
    2 *turnips or apples, cut in halves*
    Hot water
    1 *(10-ounce) can beef bouillon*
    ½ *cup soy sauce*
    ¼ *cup Worcestershire sauce*
    1 *tablespoon Pickapepper sauce*
 1½ *cups red wine*
    4 *small onions (golf ball size),*
        quartered
    ⅛ *teaspoon garlic powder or 1 pod*
        garlic, mashed
    ¼ *teaspoon dried marjoram*
    ½ *cup chopped green onions*
    6 *ounces Grand Marnier, Cointreau, or*
        Triple Sec

Wash, clean, and dry ducks thoroughly. Rub inside and out with salt and pepper. Stuff each carcass with a rib of celery, half of onion, and apple or turnip. This helps remove the wild taste. Some ducks will have a wilder taste and stronger smell than others depending on whether they have fed on fish or wild rice in the marshes. To help eliminate this, remove stuffing and replace with fresh amounts halfway through the cooking process.

Place the stuffed ducks in a Dutch oven or baking pan, the more crowded the better. Pour in enough hot water to halfway cover the ducks. Add bouillon, soy sauce, Worcestershire sauce, Pickapepper sauce, 1 cup red wine, whole onions, and seasonings. Cook uncovered in an oven preheated to 550 degrees F. until sauce is bubbling strongly. Reduce temperature to 400 degrees F.

Turn ducks every half hour, basting frequently. When the sauce has been reduced by approximately one-half, or in about 2 hours, add remaining ½ cup wine, green onions, and Grand Marnier, Cointreau, or Triple Sec. Continue to cook until the sauce is reduced to about 1½ inches, or about 30 to 40 more minutes.

Remove ducks from the sauce. With paper toweling folded in half, blot all fat from the surface of the sauce. If sauce appears too thin it can be further cooked. Reheat ducks in the fat-free sauce and serve, one half to each person. Yield: 8 servings.

Roast Pheasant With Rice

    2 *pheasants, about 2½ pounds each*
    1 *tablespoon salt*
 1½ *cups long-grain rice*
    3 *cups water*
    1 *teaspoon salt*
    ½ *cup butter*
    1 *cup finely chopped celery*
    3 *tablespoons minced onion*
    ½ *cup sliced mushrooms*
    Dash crushed sage
    Dash crushed thyme
    Dash crushed savory
    1 *tablespoon butter*
    ½ *glass currant jelly*
    Juice of ½ lemon
    Dash cayenne pepper
    ½ *cup water*
    3 *whole cloves*
    Salt to taste
    ½ *cup port wine*
    Melted butter
    6 *slices bacon*

Rub cavity of pheasants with 1 tablespoon salt. Brown rice in a dry frying pan. Remove rice to a saucepan; add water and 1 teaspoon salt, and cook until tender.

Melt butter in frying pan. Add celery, onion, and mushrooms and cook until slightly wilted. Add to cooked rice; add herbs. Stuff birds lightly; sew together and truss.

Make sauce by combining 1 tablespoon butter, currant jelly, lemon juice, cayenne, ½ cup water, cloves, and salt. Simmer for a few minutes; strain and add wine. Add meat drippings, if desired.

Brush birds with butter; place strips of bacon across breasts. Roast in a covered pan at 350 degrees F. about 2 hours, or until tender, basting frequently with sauce. Yield: 2 to 4 servings.

Dove Hash à la Reith

   4 *cups diced cooked breast of doves*
   1 *can chicken consommé*
   6 *tablespoons butter*
2½ *tablespoons flour*
 ⅔ *cup cream*
 ⅔ *cup breadcrumbs*
 ⅔ *cup chopped green pepper*
 ⅔ *cup chopped onion*
   2 *tablespoons chopped parsley*
 ½ *teaspoon ground sage*
 ½ *teaspoon salt*
     Freshly ground black pepper to taste
   2 *ounces sherry wine*

Cook whole doves in chicken consommé until tender. Remove breasts and dice meat. Measure 4 cups and set aside. Take 3 tablespoons butter and blend in flour and cream. Take remaining 3 tablespoons butter and sauté breadcrumbs, green pepper, onion, parsley, and sage. Mix the sautéed ingredients, flour mixture, and dove meat. Place in skillet. Add salt, pepper, and sherry, and let cook gently for 25 to 30 minutes. Before serving, put into a casserole dish for a few minutes under the broiler. To keep right consistency while sautéing, add pot liquor left from cooking whole doves.

Doves Brazos Valley

   6 *doves*
1½ *sticks melted butter*
   1 *tablespoon Worcestershire sauce*
   1 *teaspoon garlic salt*
 ⅓ *cup cooking sherry*
   1 *cup chopped mushrooms*
 ½ *teaspoon ground nutmeg*
     Salt and pepper to taste
 ⅓ *cup flour*

Brown doves on all sides in melted butter in a large skillet. After doves become brown, add remaining ingredients except flour. Cover skillet. Allow to simmer about 20 minutes. Remove the doves from skillet; add to the sauce ⅓ cup flour, forming a roux. Place doves on toast and top with sauce. Garnish with fresh grapes. Yield: 3 servings.

Squirrel Mulligan

   3 *squirrels*
   2 *onions, chopped*
   1 *green pepper, chopped*
   2 *medium potatoes, diced*
 ¼ *cup diced celery*
   4 *tablespoons chili powder*
     Salt and pepper to taste
     Dash Louisiana hot sauce
   1 *cup cooked rice*

Stew squirrels and reserve broth. Remove meat from bones and put back into broth. Bring to a boil and add all ingredients except rice. Cook about 45 minutes or until vegetables are tender. Add cooked rice. Serve hot.

Stewed Grouse

   2 *(not too young) grouse*
   2 *tablespoons flour*
   1 *teaspoon salt*
 ¼ *teaspoon pepper*
 ¼ *teaspoon onion salt*
 ¼ *teaspoon celery salt*
   2 *tablespoons bacon drippings or*
       butter
   2 *medium onions, sliced thin*
   2 *medium carrots, scraped and sliced*
       thin
 ¼ *pound mushrooms, sliced*
   1 *bay leaf*
   6 *small link sausages*
   1 *tablespoon whiskey (optional)*
   2 *chicken bouillon cubes*
1½ *cups boiling water*

Cut grouse into quarters. Combine flour and seasonings, and sprinkle over grouse. Sauté over low heat in the drippings or butter. Line the bottom of a buttered casserole dish with the sliced onions, carrots, and mushrooms; place browned grouse on top of the vegetables. Next add the bay leaf, sausages, whiskey, and bouillon cubes dissolved in boiling water. Cover with a very tight lid. Bake at 325 degrees F. for about 2 hours. Stir well before serving. Yield: 4 to 6 servings.

Chef Alfred's Goose

    1 *wild goose, dressed (6 to 8 pounds)*
    2 *pounds potatoes*
    Goose liver, chopped fine
    2 *medium onions, chopped*
    1 *tablespoon butter*
    ½ *teaspoon thyme*
    ½ *teaspoon sage or poultry seasoning*
    1 *teaspoon salt*
    ¼ *teaspoon pepper*
    2 *tablespoons fat*
    ¼ *cup water*
    Flour for dredging

Clean and dress goose; wash in cold water, being sure that cavity is clean. Let stand in cold water for at least 1 hour before cooking. For the stuffing, boil the potatoes in salted water with their jackets on. After they have cooked, peel and mash while hot.

Lightly sauté the goose liver and chopped onion in the butter. Add to the mashed potatoes, together with the herbs, salt, and pepper. (You can be generous with the pepper as the stuffing is best if very hot.)

Spoon stuffing into the cavity of the goose and sew with cord and skewers. Do not overstuff.

Place on a rack in an uncovered baking pan and baste with the fat. Add water and bake at 350 degrees F. for 2 hours, basting frequently. In the last half hour, dredge the breast with a small amount of flour. Baste again with the hot drippings so the skin will get crisp and brown. Serve hot with applesauce. Yield: 6 servings.

Rehbraten

    4 *to 5 (½- to 1-inch) venison steaks*
    1 *box pickling spices*
    1 *(8-ounce) bottle Italian dressing*
    1 *to 2 cups tart red wine*
    Meat tenderizer
    Flour
    Margarine

Trim all cartilage from steaks (shoulder, round, or rump roasts may be used); cut steaks into "teriyaki" strips.

Make a marinade of the pickling spices, Italian dressing, and red wine. Lay venison strips in a flat shallow dish with enough marinade to cover the meat. Cover the dish with plastic wrap or aluminum foil and place in the refrigerator. The marinating process must be at cold temperature and the meat must be completely covered with the marinade at all times.

After 3 or 4 days take the meat out of the marinade, drain well, and wipe with a paper towel. Sprinkle both sides with a meat tenderizer. Flour the meat on both sides and brown in margarine in an iron skillet or Dutch oven.

Strain the marinade into a shallow baking dish. Add to meat and when it is simmering briskly, cover and continue cooking until meat is tender, about 3 hours. Peek at it occasionally and if the gravy cooks down, add more wine so that the meat is completely covered at all times.

Onions, small potatoes, scallions, carrots, and celery sticks may be added if desired. These vegetables add a special zest to the other vegetable you will have with the meal. With this dish serve a steamed green vegetable such as broccoli, asparagus, or brussels sprouts served with hollandaise sauce or hot slaw dressing. Yield: 6 to 8 servings.

Venison, Hunter's Style

    3 *pounds venison*
    Salt and pepper
    2 *tablespoons butter*
    1 *onion, chopped*
    1-*inch cube ham, minced*
    1 *clove garlic, minced*
    2 *bay leaves*
    2 *sprigs thyme, crushed*
    1 *tablespoon flour*
    2 *cups warm water*
    1 *quart consommé*
    ½ *pound fresh mushrooms, chopped*
    Grated peel of 1 lemon

Cut venison into pieces 2 inches square. Salt and pepper generously. Heat butter in skillet and brown venison slowly. When almost brown, add onion; brown slightly. Then add ham, garlic, bay leaves, and thyme. Stir and simmer for 2 minutes. Add the flour and cook a few minutes longer.

Add warm water and let cool to a good simmer. Add consommé and cook slowly for 1 hour. Season again according to taste; then add mushrooms and grated lemon peel. Let cook 30 minutes longer. Serve on a very hot plate. Yield: 8 servings.

Venison Burgers

2½ pounds ground venison
½ cup minced onion
1 clove garlic, minced
4 tablespoons chopped parsley
⅔ cup dry red wine
2 tablespoons soy sauce
Salt and pepper to taste

Mix all ingredients; form into thick patties. Cook on barbecue grill, 4 inches from coals, or broil in oven, 10 minutes on each side (less for rare burgers). Serve immediately in hot burger buns. Yield: 8 to 10 servings.

Venison Meatballs

1 pound ground venison
½ pound ground pork
½ cup fine dry breadcrumbs
1 egg, beaten
½ cup mashed potatoes
1 teaspoon seasoned salt
½ teaspoon brown sugar
¼ teaspoon pepper
¼ teaspoon ground allspice
¼ teaspoon ground nutmeg
⅛ teaspoon ground cloves
⅛ teaspoon ground ginger
3 tablespoons butter

Combine all ingredients except butter. Mix well and shape into balls about 1 inch in diameter. Melt butter in skillet over low heat. Add meatballs and brown on all sides, shaking pan now and then. Cover with tightly fitting lid and cook over low heat for 15 minutes. Serve with wild rice and gravy, hash browned or mashed potatoes, or white rice. Yield: 6 to 8 servings.

New South Venison Steak

¼ cup flour
¾ teaspoon salt
Cayenne pepper
Dash of thyme
Dash of ground nutmeg
Dash of ground cloves
3-pound steak cut from rump of venison
2 tablespoons melted beef suet
3 large onions, thinly sliced
2 cups fresh tomatoes, peeled and quartered, or 2 cups stewed tomatoes
1½ tablespoons Worcestershire sauce
4 drops Tabasco sauce
1½ cups Burgundy
1 whole clove
½ small clove garlic
Bouquet garni
Salt and pepper to taste
1 scant cup sautéed mushroom caps

Sift flour with salt, a few grains of cayenne, thyme, nutmeg, and cloves. Vigorously pound this seasoned flour into venison steak. Cut the steak into 1-inch cubes.

Heat melted beef suet in a heavy stewpot or Dutch oven and sear venison on all sides, adding thinly sliced onions to the pot. When meat and onions are well browned, add tomatoes, Worcestershire sauce, Tabasco, Burgundy, clove, garlic, and bouquet garni.

Cover pot closely, set in a moderate oven, and cook 2½ hours or until meat is tender. Add salt and pepper to taste and bring to a boil over direct heat. Stir in sautéed mushroom caps and serve with wild rice and red currant jelly.

As a variation, port may be substituted for part of the Burgundy, or 2 tablespoons red currant jelly may be stirred into the sauce.

Stegt Dyrekolle
(Roast Venison)

  1 *leg venison*
  6 *ounces fat-larding pork*
1½ *teaspoons salt*
 ¼ *teaspoon pepper*
 ½ *tablespoon ground ginger*
  2 *tablespoons olive oil*
  1 *cup butter or fat, melted*
  2 *cups meat stock (more if you want)*
  1 *cup dry sherry*
 ⅓ *cup flour*
  2 *tablespoons butter*
  5 *teaspoons cider vinegar or Chianti wine*
 ¼ *tablespoon grated orange rind*
  2 *tablespoons currant jelly*
    Bits of currant jelly

Before being cooked, venison should hang in a cool place for three or four days after the kill. Wipe it and dry well. Remove all skin, membrane, and sinews. The fat pork should be cut into strips about ⅓ inch wide and 2 inches long.

Collect the seasonings (you can also add oregano and/or marjoram leaves or powder). Then roll the pork strips in seasonings and insert them in a larding needle. Pull the strips through the meat at regular intervals, allowing the fat to show outside the meat at both ends.

Now, rub the roast with the oil and place in roasting pan, preferably with basting depression. Pour melted butter or fat over it and bake in moderate oven (325 degrees F.) 4 to 5 hours or until meat is brown and very tender. It should be basted every 10 to 15 minutes with meat stock and half of sherry. At the end of the cooking time, remove the meat from pan, and skim off the fat from natural gravy.

Make a smooth paste of flour, butter, and stock; add vinegar or wine and orange rind and stir in the natural gravy in the pan. Then cook this for about 10 minutes on low heat and add the rest of the sherry and currant jelly. Now, baste roast in slow heat, with the completed gravy, for about 15 minutes to an hour.

Serve gravy in gravy boat and garnish the venison with currant jelly or serve currant jelly with it.

If no larding needle is available, use smoke-cured bacon, slit the meat slightly under each bacon strip, and cook at 250 degrees F., 50 minutes a pound. Baste twice as often.

This venison will taste the way venison is supposed to taste.

Breast of White Guinea Hen
(May also be prepared with breast of chicken.)

For 6 breasts: (about ¾ pound each)

  3 *tablespoons butter*
    Salt to taste
  1 *teaspoon white pepper*
  2 *tablespoons flour*
 ½ *teaspoon Beau Monde seasoned salt*
  1 *garlic clove, mashed*
  1 *tablespoon parsley, chopped very fine*
  1 *tablespoon green onion (white and green part, chopped very fine)*
  3 *cups rich chicken stock (all fat removed)*
  1 *tablespoon imported Parmesan*
  1 *teaspoon Maggi Seasoning*
  2 *tablespoons dry sherry*
 ¾ *cup sliced, sautéed mushrooms*
    Cooked rice
    Hearts of artichoke
    Butter

Remove skin. Rub breasts with melted butter, salt, and pepper; brown lightly in heavy iron skillet and then place in roaster, meaty side down.

Make sauce by melting butter and flour and simmering 10 minutes, browning only very slightly. Add Beau Monde, garlic, pepper and salt to taste, parsley, onion, and chicken stock. Then add Parmesan, Maggi, and sherry and whip till smooth. This should be rather a thin sauce, so a little more chicken stock may be added if necessary. Pour over guinea breasts; cover and cook in 275-degree oven for 2 hours.

Remove breasts; strain sauce and add sautéed mushrooms. Place breasts in center of mound of rice; place hearts of artichoke on each side of guinea and glaze with sauce. Yield: 6 servings.

Hamburger Special

    1 (14-ounce) bottle catsup
 1½ cups water
    ½ cup vinegar drained from sweet
          pickles or ¼ cup plain vinegar
 1½ medium onions, chopped fine
    ¼ cup prepared mustard
    ¼ cup Worcestershire sauce
    3 pounds ground beef
    2 tablespoons salt
    1 teaspoon black pepper

Combine catsup, water, vinegar, chopped onions, mustard, and Worcestershire sauce in large saucepan. Place over low heat and cook slowly while preparing hamburgers.

Mix ground beef, salt, and pepper, and shape into 12 hamburgers. Put hamburgers in hot sauce, and cook gently for 2 hours or more. Serve with buns and coleslaw or salad, potato chips, and pickles. A light dessert of cookies or toasted marshmallows is suggested. Yield: 12 servings.

Grill Steak

Select Choice cuts of steak, about 1½ inches thick. Rub meat generously on both sides with garlic salt, pepper, and Louisiana hot sauce. The hot sauce helps to tenderize the steak, giving it flavor without making it too hot. Let sit for about 20 to 30 minutes before cooking.

Never use a fork in turning or handling steaks. The use of tongs is better because they do not puncture the steak and allow the flavorful juices to escape.

Let grill thermometer reach 500 degrees F. For rare steaks cook 4 minutes on one side, 3 minutes on the other; for medium, 5 and 4 minutes; and for well done, 6 and 5 minutes. Watch carefully during cooking.

Barbecued Round Steak

 1½ pounds round steak, 1½ inches thick
    2 tablespoons oil or shortening
    1 clove garlic, minced
    ¾ cup vinegar
    1 tablespoon sugar
    1 teaspoon paprika
    2 tablespoons Worcestershire sauce
    ½ cup catsup
    1 teaspoon salt
    1 teaspoon powdered mustard
    ½ teaspoon pepper

Cut steaks into crosswise slices 1 inch wide. Heat oil; brown steak on all sides. Remove meat to casserole. Pour off fat, then place all remaining ingredients in skillet and simmer 3 minutes. Pour over steak, cover, and bake at 350 degrees F. for 1 hour. Uncover and bake for 30 minutes. Yield: 4 servings.

Smoked Sirloin Tip

This can be one of the most tasty main courses from your covered grill. When a 30-briquette fire is glowing, add hickory. Take a sirloin tip of appropriate size and place on foil slightly larger than the flat side of the meat; place on the grill. Close hood. Cooking time depends upon the size of the cut and the fire. A 4-pound cut should be beautifully "medium" inside in about an hour.

Zesty Beef Patty

    ¼ pound ground chuck
    1 tablespoon fresh lemon juice
 1½ teaspoons melted butter
 1½ teaspoons fresh lemon juice
    ¼ teaspoon poultry seasoning

Shape meat into a 3-inch patty ½ inch thick. Roll patty in 1 tablespoon fresh lemon juice. Blend the next three ingredients and brush over meat. Broil for 6 to 7 minutes on one side. Turn, baste, and broil 3 minutes or until meat has browned. Yield: 1 serving.

Carpetbag Steaks

    4 *eye-of-round steaks, about 1½*
        inches thick
  ½ *pint oysters*
    2 *cups sherry*
  ¼ *pound butter*
     Salt and pepper to taste
     Paprika

Cut pockets into each of the steaks. Marinate oysters in 1 cup of sherry for 1 hour. Place 2 or 3 oysters into each steak with a little sherry. Place butter into a large skillet and melt. Add 1 cup of sherry to butter. Place the steaks in wine-butter sauce and steam on each side for 1 minute. Remove steaks from skillet, and salt and pepper to taste. Sprinkle paprika on steaks and place in preheated broiler. Broil desired amount of time, then baste with wine and butter sauce. Yield: 4 servings.

Beef en Casserole

    2 *pounds beef chuck, cut in 1½-inch*
        cubes
    3 *tablespoons flour*
    3 *tablespoons shortening*
  ½ *teaspoon freshly ground pepper*
    1 *teaspoon salt*
  ½ *teaspoon thyme*
    2 *teaspoons parsley flakes*
    1 *bay leaf*
    1 *cup beef bouillon*
    1 *(6-ounce) can tomato paste*
  ½ *cup red cooking wine*
    6 *small white onions, peeled and left*
        whole
    6 *medium carrots, scraped and*
        quartered
    1 *cup celery slices*

Using heavy pan, brown floured meat slowly in hot fat. Transfer meat to 3-quart casserole. Mix ground pepper, salt, thyme, and parsley flakes and sprinkle over meat. Add bay leaf. Combine beef bouillon, tomato paste, and wine and pour over meat. Cover the casserole and cook at 325

degrees F. for 1½ hours. Add vegetables, cover, and cook an additional 40 minutes. Yield: 6 servings.

Ground Beef With Eggplant
(Moussaka)

    3 *medium eggplants*
     Salt
    1 *cup salad oil*
    6 *medium potatoes*
 1½ *cups chopped onions*
    2 *cloves garlic, minced*
    6 *tablespoons butter*
    2 *pounds ground lean beef*
    1 *tablespoon salt*
    1 *teaspoon pepper*
    1 *teaspoon dried mint*
    2 *tablespoons chopped fresh parsley*
  ½ *teaspoon ground cinnamon*
    4 *tablespoons tomato paste*
     Cream Sauce

Leaving the skin on, slice the eggplant into ½-inch slices. Sprinkle well with salt, and allow to drain for about 20 minutes. Wash off this salt, and dry the eggplant on a towel. Heat the salad oil and fry the slices of eggplant, a few at a time, until brown on both sides. Peel and slice the washed potatoes into ¼-inch slices and fry these in the same manner, adding more oil if necessary. Sauté the chopped onion and minced garlic in 6 tablespoons butter, and add ground beef; cook and stir about 10 minutes.

    Next, add salt, pepper, mint, parsley, cinnamon, and tomato paste to beef mixture. Cook, uncovered, about 10 minutes to reduce the liquid.

    Arrange one-half of the eggplant in a 13- x 9- x 2-inch oiled baking dish. Top with half the potatoes and half the meat. Repeat this process with the remaining eggplant, potatoes, and meat.

    Cover evenly with Cream Sauce and bake at 375 degrees F. about 30 minutes, or until sauce is set. If not brown enough, place under the broiler for a few minutes. Yield: 6 to 8 servings.

Cream Sauce:

¼ *pound butter*
¾ *cup flour*
1 *quart warm milk*
4 *eggs, slightly beaten*
½ *teaspoon salt*

Melt butter in a saucepan. Remove from heat and stir in the flour, blending until smooth. Slowly add the warm milk, stirring constantly. Add this mixture to the slightly beaten eggs. Stir in salt. Cook over low heat until thick, being careful not to scorch. Pour sauce over the eggplant mixture.

Pronto Pups

½ *cup cornmeal*
1½ *cups flour*
¼ *cup sugar*
¼ *teaspoon pepper*
2 *teaspoons salt*
4 *teaspoons baking powder*
1 *egg, beaten*
1 *cup milk*
1 *pound frankfurters*

Mix all dry ingredients together. Add egg and milk and beat with a rotary egg beater until smooth. Dip franks in batter and fry in hot deep fat until brown on one side. Turn and brown the other side. Drain on paper towel. Serve hot with mustard. Yield: 8 to 10 servings.

Franks and Cheese Casserole

1⅔ *cups evaporated milk*
½ *teaspoon salt*
2 *cups shredded cheese*
4 *cups cooked noodles*
2 *cups sliced frankfurters*

Simmer evaporated milk and salt on low heat to just below the boiling point. Add cheese and stir until melted. Pour over cooked noodles and franks in a buttered 2-quart casserole. Bake at 350 degrees F. for 30 minutes. Yield: 4 to 6 servings.

Children's Delight Casserole

1 *pound wieners, chopped*
1 *small can evaporated milk*
1 *can cream of chicken soup*
1 *can cream of celery soup*
1 *(5-ounce) can Chinese noodles*

Mix all ingredients together. Bake in buttered 1-quart casserole at 350 degrees F. for 25 minutes. Yield: 6 servings.

Beef-Bean Casserole

1½ *pounds ground beef*
½ *cup catsup*
½ *teaspoon dry mustard*
2 *tablespoons vinegar*
3 *tablespoons dark brown sugar*
1 *small onion, minced*
1 *(No. 303) can green lima beans*
1 *(No. 303) can red kidney beans*
1 *(No. 303) can pork and beans*
½ *teaspoon salt*

Brown meat in skillet. Mix with other ingredients. Divide mixture into two 1½-quart casserole dishes. Bake at 350 degrees F. for 30 minutes. Yield: 8 servings.

Cool Casserole

2 *pounds ground meat*
1 *large onion, chopped fine*
1 *large green pepper, diced*
3 *large cans spaghetti with tomato sauce*
1 *small can mushrooms, including sauce or juice*
1 *small can tomatoes, including juice*

Brown the ground meat with the onion and pepper. Add the other ingredients. Put in a 2-quart casserole and bake at 350 degrees F. for 30 minutes. Cool and freeze, or you may freeze before baking, then pull it out of the freezer allowing enough time for it to thaw before baking. If baked first, it will have to be thawed and then warmed in the oven for serving. This improves with age. Sprinkle with oregano before serving, if desired.

Beef Casserole for a Crowd

1½ pounds ground chuck
1 cup chopped onions
1 (1-pound) can whole-kernel corn, drained
1 can cream of chicken soup
1 can cream of mushroom soup
¼ cup chopped pimiento
1½ teaspoons salt
½ teaspoon pepper
1 cup commercial sour cream
1 (10-ounce) package noodles, cooked
1 cup buttered crumbs

Brown meat and onions until meat is white and onions are tender. Add all other ingredients except crumbs and put into a 2½-quart casserole or two smaller casseroles. Top with crumbs and bake at 350 degrees F. for 30 minutes. Yield: 12 to 15 servings.

Hamburger Harvest Casserole

1 pound ground chuck
1 cup chopped onion
1 (No. 2) can tomatoes
1 tablespoon Worcestershire sauce
2 teaspoons salt
1 can whole-kernel corn
2 cups thinly sliced raw potatoes
½ cup flour
1 chopped green pepper
1½ cups shredded American cheese

Combine beef, onion, tomatoes, Worcestershire sauce, and salt. Put in layers with corn, potatoes, flour, and green pepper, which have been combined. Bake uncovered at 375 degrees F. for 45 minutes; then sprinkle with cheese and bake 30 more minutes or until vegetables are done. Yield: 6 servings.

Hamburger-Bean-Rice Casserole

1 pound dry pinto beans
1½ cups rice
2 tablespoons shortening
1 pound hamburger meat
1 tablespoon salt
½ cup chopped onion
½ teaspoon black pepper
1 (6-ounce) can tomato sauce
Chili powder, if desired
6 strips of bacon

Wash beans and place in a 4-quart, covered Dutch oven. Cover with water and cook until tender. Add more hot water if needed. Add rice and cook until rice is tender. In a skillet melt shortening, add hamburger meat, salt, onion, and pepper. Cook until brown, then add to beans and rice. Add tomato sauce (and chili powder, if desired). Mix well and place in a 2-quart casserole. Place strips of bacon over top and bake at 350 degrees F. until bacon is brown. Yield: 6 to 8 servings.

Hungarian Beef-Rice Casserole

1 pound stew beef
Bacon drippings
1 teaspoon basil
1 teaspoon paprika
1 teaspoon pepper
1 tablespoon salt
1 can tomato-rice soup plus ½ can warm water
1 tablespoon Worcestershire sauce
1 (1-pound) jar small onions, drained
2 to 3 medium potatoes, sliced
1 bay leaf
Cooked rice

Brown beef in bacon drippings. Drain off drippings and season meat with basil, paprika, pepper, and salt. Mix soup, water, and Worcestershire sauce in 2-quart casserole dish. Add drained onions, sliced potatoes, bay leaf, and beef and mix well. Cover casserole and bake at 325 degrees F. about 2 hours or until tomato sauce has thickened and potatoes are done. Serve on fluffy rice.

Casserole International

   3 *cups cooked prime rib roast cut into*
      large cubes
   1 *cup tomato juice*
   2 *small cloves garlic, minced*
  ½ *teaspoon "fines herbes"*
   1 *teaspoon curry powder*
   1 *teaspoon minced green pepper*
   1 *package frozen chow mein*
   1 *cup cooked fettucine (macaroni)*
  ½ *cup cooking sherry*
  ½ *cup shredded sharp Cheddar cheese*
   2 *tablespoons minced parsley*

Simmer the cooked roast beef for 15 minutes in tomato juice with minced garlic, herbs, curry powder, and green pepper. Add frozen chow mein and simmer until it is thawed and blended with other ingredients.

Add the cooked fettucine and cooking sherry, stirring all ingredients to distribute evenly. If more moisture is required, add tomato juice. Place in greased casserole dish and sprinkle top with shredded cheese and parsley. Warm in 300-degree F. oven for about 15 minutes. Yield: 6 servings.

Italian Rice Casserole

   1 *cup chopped onion*
  ½ *cup chopped green pepper*
  ½ *cup chopped celery*
   1 *tablespoon vegetable oil*
   1 *pound ground beef*
   1 *(18-ounce) can tomatoes*
   1 *(6-ounce) can Italian tomato paste*
   1 *(2-ounce) can mushroom pieces*
   2 *tablespoons chopped parsley*
   1 *teaspoon salt*
  ½ *teaspoon thyme*
  ½ *teaspoon black pepper*
  ¼ *teaspoon marjoram*
   1 *cup uncooked regular rice*
   1 *cup shredded Cheddar cheese*

Sauté onion, pepper, and celery in oil until they are almost transparent. Add ground beef and cook until it is brown. Add tomatoes, tomato paste, mushrooms, parsley, and seasonings. Simmer 1 hour over low heat.

Meanwhile, cook rice in boiling salted water according to package directions. Mix rice with sauce and place in shallow baking dish. Top with shredded cheese and bake at 350 degrees F. for 15 to 20 minutes. Yield: 6 servings.

Meatball Casserole

 1½ *pounds ground meat*
  ¾ *cup uncooked oatmeal*
   1 *cup evaporated milk*
   1 *tablespoon instant onion flakes*
   1 *teaspoon salt*
  ½ *teaspoon pepper*
   1 *cup catsup*
   2 *tablespoons vinegar*
  ½ *cup water*
   2 *tablespoons sugar*

Combine meat, oatmeal, milk, onion flakes, salt, and pepper. Mix well, shape into 8 large meatballs, and place in 2-quart casserole.

Combine catsup, vinegar, water, and sugar and pour over top of meatballs. Bake at 350 degrees F. for 1½ hours. Yield: 8 servings.

Mixed Vegetable Hot Dish

 1½ *pounds ground beef*
   1 *large onion, chopped*
   1 *cup diced celery*
   2 *cans cream of mushroom soup*
   1 *can chicken and rice soup*
   1 *(1-pound) can mixed chow mein*
      vegetables
   1 *(3-ounce) can mushroom slices*
   2 *to 4 tablespoons soy sauce*
   2 *cups chow mein noodles*

Brown meat, onion, and celery in large skillet over low heat. Add soups, mixed vegetables, and mushrooms (do not drain). Mix well; then add soy sauce to taste. Spoon into 6-cup casserole, sprinkle with noodles, and bake uncovered at 350 degrees F. about 30 minutes. Yield: 10 to 12 servings.

Pastitsio
(Greek Dish)

    1   *large onion, chopped very fine*
    ½   *pound butter*
    2   *pounds ground beef*
    ½   *can tomato paste*
    ½   *cup water*
    ½   *teaspoon ground cinnamon*
    ½   *teaspoon ground nutmeg*
        Salt and pepper to taste
    ½   *cup white wine*
    1   *pound elbow macaroni*
    1   *pound shredded Kefalotevi*
          (Parmesan cheese may be used)
    2   *eggs, well beaten*
    1   *cup milk*

Sauté onion in a little of the butter. Add ground beef and stir until brown. Add tomato paste thinned with ½ cup water. Add seasonings and wine and simmer slowly until thick. Cook macaroni in boiling salted water, and drain. Melt the remaining butter and pour over drained macaroni, mixing carefully. Spread half of the macaroni in the bottom of a 13- x 9-inch pan and sprinkle generously with cheese. Spread meat sauce over the bottom layer of macaroni and cover with remaining macaroni. Top with cheese.

Over this pour a sauce made of 2 eggs and 1 cup milk, mixed well. Bake at 350 degrees F. for 45 minutes. Allow to cool slightly and cut in squares to serve. Yield: 12 servings.

Ground Beef and Potato Casserole

    1   *pound ground beef*
    1   *tablespoon shortening*
    ¾   *cup boiling water*
    1   *small onion, finely chopped*
    1   *can cream of mushroom soup*
    ½   *teaspoon salt*
    ¼   *teaspoon black pepper*
    6   *medium potatoes, thinly sliced*

Brown ground beef in shortening. Drain. To the boiling water add onion and simmer for 5 minutes. Add mushroom soup, salt, and pepper to cooked onion. Cover bottom of

1½-quart casserole with layer of thinly sliced potatoes. Cover with a thin layer of ground beef. Top with onion-soup mixture. Continue alternating layers. Bake at 350 degrees F. for 40 minutes to 1 hour, or until potatoes are tender. Extra water may be added if needed. Yield: 4 to 6 servings.

Tomato-Beef Casserole

    ½   *pound ground beef*
    1   *medium onion, chopped*
    1   *can tomato soup*
    ½   *soup can water*
    1   *cup English peas*
    1   *cup cooked rice*
    ½   *cup shredded cheese*

In a skillet brown the beef and onion, stirring to separate meat. Stir in soup, water, peas, and rice. Spoon into 1½-quart casserole dish and cover with shredded cheese. Bake at 375 degrees F. about 20 or 25 minutes. Yield: 4 servings.

Layered Grecian Bake

    1½ *pounds lean ground beef*
    ½   *cup chopped onion*
    1   *egg, slightly beaten*
    ½   *cup fine, dry breadcrumbs*
    1   *teaspoon basil*
    1¼ *teaspoons salt*
    ¼   *teaspoon pepper*
    2   *(8-ounce) cans tomato sauce with
          cheese*
    1   *small eggplant, pared and sliced*
    ½   *cup commercial sour cream*
    1   *cup shredded Cheddar cheese*

Combine first 7 ingredients with 1 can tomato sauce with cheese. Pack half the meat mixture into an 8- x 8-inch square or round baking dish. Place eggplant slices on top. Combine sour cream and shredded cheese; spread over eggplant slices. Top with remaining meat mixture. Bake at 350 degrees F. for 1 hour. Drain off excess fat. Top with remaining 1 can tomato sauce.

Bake an additional 15 minutes. Yield: about 6 servings.

Beef Oriental

  1½ *pounds ground beef*
    2 *green onions with tops, sliced*
    2 *tablespoons shortening or cooking oil*
   ¾ *teaspoon salt*
   ⅛ *teaspoon pepper*
   ¼ *teaspoon ground ginger*
    1 *tablespoon soy sauce*
    2 *fresh tomatoes, peeled and cut into eighths*
    1 *can condensed mushroom soup*
    1 *(3-ounce) can chow mein noodles*

Brown the beef and onions in shortening or cooking oil. Pour off excess fat. Combine ground beef, salt, pepper, ginger, soy sauce, tomatoes, mushroom soup, and chow mein noodles, reserving ½ cup of the noodles for topping. Spoon mixture into a 2-quart casserole. Sprinkle with reserved noodles and bake, uncovered, at 375 degrees F. for 20 to 25 minutes. Yield: 6 servings.

One-Dish Meal

    1 *tablespoon shortening*
    1 *pound ground beef*
    1 *medium onion, chopped*
    2 *(1-pound) can tomatoes*
    1 *(1-pound) can whole-kernel corn*
    1 *(4-ounce) package noodles*
   ½ *cup chopped ripe olives*
    1 *small can chopped mushrooms*
      Salt to taste
   ½ *pound shredded cheese*

Melt shortening. Add meat and chopped onion and brown lightly. Add tomatoes and cook slowly in covered pan or electric frypan about 30 minutes.

    Add corn and a little water. Cook 20 minutes more. Add uncooked noodles and cook until tender. Add more liquid if needed, then olives, mushrooms, and salt. Sim-

mer 15 minutes. Add shredded cheese. Cook until melted thoroughly. Yield: 6 servings.

Beef-Potato Croquettes

    1 *pound ground lean beef*
    2 *cups grated raw potato*
   ¼ *cup grated onion*
  1½ *teaspoons salt*
   ¼ *teaspoon red pepper*
      Bacon drippings or shortening for frying

Combine first 5 ingredients and mix well. Form into 6 croquettes. Over medium heat, brown on all sides in hot shortening, turning frequently. Allow 15 to 20 minutes for cooking. Yield: 6 servings.

Orient Casserole

  1½ *pounds ground chuck beef*
    1 *small onion, chopped*
   ½ *cup chopped celery*
    1 *can water chestnuts, drained and chopped*
    1 *small can mushrooms, drained and chopped*
   ⅔ *cup uncooked rice*
    1 *teaspoon salt*
    1 *teaspoon pepper*
   ⅓ *cup soy sauce*

Brown beef, onion, and celery together. Drain chestnuts and mushrooms and reserve liquid. Add chestnuts, mushrooms, rice, salt, pepper, and soy sauce to meat. Add water to drained liquid to make 2 cups and add to mixture. Stir just to mix. Put in covered casserole dish and bake at 350 degrees F. for 1 hour. Yield: 6 to 8 servings.

Round Steak Casserole

¼ cup flour
2 pounds round steak, cut in serving
    pieces
Salt and pepper to taste
2 medium or 1 large onion, sliced
2 carrots, cubed

Pound flour into steak; sprinkle with salt and pepper. Roll up and secure with toothpicks. Alternate layers of steak, onion slices, and carrots in casserole. Repeat layers until all is used, ending with steak. Cover with boiling water. Cover pan and bake at 325 degrees F. for 3 hours. Add water as necessary. Remove cover and brown if needed. *Note:* The amount of flour used may be varied according to the desired thickness of gravy. Yield: 4 servings.

Rolled Stuffed Flank Steak

1 flank steak
½ cup finely chopped onion
1½ cups soft breadcrumbs
½ cup chopped celery
¼ cup chopped pimiento-stuffed green
    olives
1 teaspoon salt
½ teaspoon pepper
2 tablespoons lard or drippings
1 cup beef bouillon or water

Score flank steak (make light cuts ¼ to ½ inch apart across the surface of the meat). Pound steak with edge of a heavy saucer or a meat pounder to flatten somewhat. Mix onion, breadcrumbs, celery, olives, salt, and pepper, and spread evenly on one side of the steak, leaving an inch margin free of stuffing. Roll steak, beginning at narrow end, and tie with string or fasten with skewers. Brown meat roll in hot fat. Add bouillon or water, cover, and cook over low heat 1½ to 2 hours or until tender. (Meat may be cooked, covered, in a 325-degree F. oven for the same length of time.) When cooked, place on serving platter; remove strings. Cut into slices to serve. Accompany with the

cooking liquid thickened for gravy. Yield: 4 to 6 servings.

Grilled Flank Steak

2-pound flank steak
Meat tenderizer
1½ cups salad oil
¾ cup soy sauce
¼ cup Worcestershire sauce
2 teaspoons dry mustard
2¼ teaspoons salt
1 teaspoon freshly ground pepper
½ cup wine vinegar
1½ teaspoons dried parsley flakes
2 cloves garlic, crushed
⅓ cup fresh lemon juice

Score steak; sprinkle with tenderizer and let sit about 1 hour at room temperature. Combine other ingredients. Place steak in flat dish and pour marinade over. Let sit 8 hours or more.

Remove from marinade and grill about 10 to 15 minutes for each side. Slice thinly on the diagonal. Yield: 4 servings.

Filet Virginia

Salt and pepper a strip filet. Put it in a frying pan over medium heat, with a strip of bacon "for grease and flavor," and fry it on one side until it is cooked to your liking. Then turn it and pour Sauce Virginia over the cooked side, letting the sauce and the steak simmer for three minutes before serving.

Sauce Virginia:

In a skillet, pour in sufficient cooking oil to handle one sliced Bermuda onion and two minced cloves of garlic. Cook at a very low heat until the sliced onion is soft, but not browned.

Meanwhile, in a saucepan, cook the tomato part of the sauce. Start by dipping four good-sized tomatoes in boiling water and peeling and quartering them. Remove the seed and strain into the saucepan the juice from the pulp. Grind up the seeded and drained tomatoes, and put into the pan with the juice. When this starts to boil, add two cans of tomato sauce and six Mexican jalapeño peppers cut in strips. Boil just long enough to soften the peppers, not longer than three minutes. Then combine the boiling tomato mixture with the hot onion-garlic preparation, and pour over a cooking steak.

Chinese Gingered Beef

- 1 *pound beef*
- 6 *tablespoons oil*
- ½ *cup fresh, raw ginger, sliced thin, not more than ⅛ inch*
- 6 *tablespoons soy sauce*
- 4 *teaspoons sherry or sauterne*
- 4 *teaspoons sugar*
- ¼ *teaspoon garlic powder*
- 2 *tablespoons cornstarch*
- ¾ *cup water*

Slice semifrozen beef across the grain into little bite-size pieces. Into a cold iron skillet, place oil and ginger and cook over moderately high heat until very lightly browned. Add beef slices and continue stirring until the juices are evaporated. Blend in soy sauce, wine, sugar, and garlic powder. Continue to cook over high heat until the liquid is absorbed. Add the cornstarch to the water and gradually add to the meat mixture. Stirring constantly, cook several minutes more until well blended. Yield: 4 servings.

Filet de Boeuf With Béarnaise Sauce

Rub a whole filet of beef (about 5 pounds, trimmed) with butter. Baste with consommé. Bake at 350 degrees F. for 20 to 25 minutes for rare meat.

Serve on platter with canned new potatoes browned in butter, cherry tomatoes warmed in butter, and fresh string beans with brown butter.

To make brown butter, heat ¼ pound butter slowly in a skillet until it gets brown in color. Add salt and pepper and pour over beans. Make Béarnaise Sauce and pour over meat immediately before serving.

Béarnaise Sauce:
- ¾ *cup vermouth*
- 1 *tablespoon vinegar*
- 1 *chopped green onion*
- *Parsley*
- 4 *pinches tarragon*
- *Pinch of chervil*
- 2 *peppercorns*
- ½ *pound butter*
- 3 *egg yolks*
- 1 *pinch tarragon*

Combine vermouth, vinegar, onion, parsley, 4 pinches tarragon, chervil, and peppercorns and cook until the mixture is reduced to one-half volume. Cool. Melt butter and beat egg yolks. Add butter and egg yolks alternately to first mixture, stirring constantly. (Hint: Beat mixture off the heat, then return to range to thicken.) Continue beating until sauce is the consistency of whipping cream. Strain through a sieve and add a pinch of tarragon.

Green-Stick Shish Kabobs

- *Pointed green sticks, about ½-inch thick*
- 1 *pound lean round steak (¼-inch thick), cut into 1-inch pieces*
- 8 *small onions, partially cooked*
- 8 *small boiled potatoes*
- 2 *strips bacon (¼-inch thick), cut into squares*
- 8 *rolls or 16 slices of bread*

Prepare sticks by removing bark from 3 inches of pointed ends.

Skewer pieces of steak, onions, potatoes, and bacon loosely on sticks. Heat kabobs over hot coals and sear quickly, holding close to the coals and turning to seal in all juices. Then cook slowly, turning until done.

Push kabobs back on sticks to loosen. Then push pieces off the pointed ends. Serve on rolls or bread. Yield: 8 servings.

Skewered Beef and Chicken

1½ *pounds boneless tender beefsteak*
4 *large chicken breasts*
1 *crushed mint sprig*
3 *tablespoons chutney*
¼ *cup lemon juice*
¼ *cup peanut oil*
1 *mashed clove garlic*
1 *teaspoon salt*
1 *tablespoon grated onion*
1 *teaspoon finely crumbled marjoram*
1 *teaspoon finely crumbled basil*
2 *tablespoons finely chopped parsley*
¼ *cup dry sherry*

Trim any fat from beef; cut into 2-inch chunks. Bone chicken breasts; cut each breast into 4 pieces. Shake all remaining ingredients in covered jar to blend. Pour over beef and chicken. Cover and refrigerate several hours, turning meat several times in marinade. Thread beef and chicken on skewers. Broil over hot coals, basting with marinade as meat cooks. Yield: 4 servings.

Meatball Kabobs

1 *cup soft breadcrumbs*
¼ *cup warm water*
1½ *pounds ground chuck*
2 *eggs, slightly beaten*
2 *tablespoons grated Parmesan cheese*
¼ *cup finely chopped parsley*
2 *teaspoons salt*
½ *teaspoon pepper*
4 *bacon slices, cut in 1-inch pieces*
½ *cup canned mushroom caps, drained*
2 *green peppers, cut in 1-inch squares and parboiled*
3 *tomatoes, cut in wedges*
½ *cup butter, melted*
1 *envelope old-fashioned garlic salad dressing mix or 1 teaspoon garlic salt and ¼ teaspoon pepper*

Soak breadcrumbs in ¼ cup water for about 5 minutes. Squeeze out water. Then combine the soaked crumbs with the ground chuck, eggs, cheese, parsley, salt, and ½ teaspoon pepper. Mix lightly but thoroughly. Shape

mixture into 30 balls about 1 inch in diameter. Arrange meatballs, bacon slices, mushrooms, green peppers, and tomatoes alternately on ten 6-inch skewers, beginning and ending with meatballs.

Combine melted butter and salad dressing mix. Arrange kabobs in a pan and brush with the garlic-butter mixture. Broil for 5 minutes. Turn kabobs, brush again with garlic-butter, broil another 5 minutes. Yield: 10 kabobs.

Frank Kabobs

8 *frankfurters*
4 *stuffed olives*
8 *or 10 pineapple chunks*
4 *slices bacon, cut in halves*
4 *teaspoons salad oil*
4 *teaspoons soy sauce*

Cut franks into quarters; thread onto skewers along with stuffed olives and pineapple chunks wrapped with bacon. Brush with mixture of salad oil and soy sauce. Cook until bacon is crisp. Yield: 4 servings.

Chinese Hamburger Hash

1 *pound ground beef*
½ *to 1 cup chopped onion*
½ *to 1 cup chopped celery*
1 *package frozen peas, thawed*
1 *can condensed mushroom soup*
1 *can condensed chicken soup*
1 *soup can water*
½ *cup uncooked rice*
¼ *cup soy sauce*
¼ *teaspoon pepper*
1 *(3-ounce) can chow mein noodles*

Brown meat until crumbly, then add onion, celery, peas, soups, water, rice, soy sauce, and pepper. Bring to a boil. Then put into a lightly greased 1½-quart baking dish. Cover and bake at 350 degrees F. for 30 minutes. Remove cover and bake an additional 30 minutes. Top with noodles and bake for 15 minutes longer. Yield: 8 servings.

Biff à la Lindstrom
(Beef Lindstrom)

    1½ pounds boneless beef
     4 egg yolks
    ⅓ cup heavy cream
    ½ teaspoon salt
    ¼ teaspoon pepper
     2 cooked potatoes, diced fine
     4 tablespoons diced, cooked beets
     1 tablespoon minced onion
     1 tablespoon chopped capers
     1 teaspoon Worcestershire sauce
     3 tablespoons butter

Wipe the meat with a clean wet cloth; then scrape to remove any tissue. Next, pound the meat in a mortar. Mix the egg yolks with the cream and gradually add to the meat. Continue mixing and pounding. Season the meat with salt and pepper. Dice the potatoes very fine and, with the beets, onion, and chopped capers, add to the recipe. Add Worcestershire sauce and continue to mix and pound until smooth. Form this mixture into small cakes about ½-inch thick. Fry quickly in melted butter and serve hot. Yield: 4 servings.

Lemon Meatballs

     1 pound ground chuck
     1 cup soft breadcrumbs
    ⅓ cup catsup
     1 egg, beaten slightly
     1 cup shredded cheese
    ¼ cup finely chopped green pepper
     2 tablespoons chopped onion
    ¼ cup lemon juice
     1 teaspoon salt
    12 slices bacon

Put ground meat in large bowl. In a separate bowl add breadcrumbs to catsup and slightly beaten egg and mix well; add to ground meat. Add cheese, pepper, onion, lemon juice, and salt and mix well. Shape mixture into 12 balls and wrap each with a strip of bacon. Fasten bacon securely with toothpicks. Place on a rack in a shallow pan and bake at 350 degrees F. about 40 minutes, or

until bacon is cooked evenly. Turn meatballs often during baking. Yield: 4 servings.

Sweet and Sour Meatballs

     1 cup cubed breadcrumbs
     1 cup milk
    ⅓ cup finely chopped onion
    1½ pounds ground beef
    ½ pound ground pork (optional)
     1 egg
     1 teaspoon salt
    ¼ teaspoon pepper
     2 (12-ounce) bottles chili sauce
    ½ cup water
     1 (10-ounce) jar grape jelly
     1 cup commercial sour cream
        Cooked noodles

Combine breadcrumbs, milk, onion, meat, egg, salt, and pepper. Shape into balls the size of walnuts. Drop into sauce made by combining chili sauce, water, and jelly. Simmer gently for 1 hour. Just before serving, stir in sour cream. Serve over hot noodles.

Jumbo Meatballs

     1 pound ground beef
    ½ pound ground pork
    ¼ cup milk
     1 egg
    ¼ cup breadcrumbs
    ¼ cup chopped onion
     1 tablespoon catsup
     2 tablespoons chopped parsley
    1½ teaspoons salt
    ½ teaspoon pepper
    ¼ cup bacon drippings or lard
    ¼ cup bouillon or water

Mix all ingredients except bacon drippings and bouillon. Shape into 1½-inch balls. Refrigerate at least 1 hour. Brown meatballs in hot drippings, add liquid, and cover pan. Cook over low heat 45 minutes or until meat is cooked. Remove meatballs to warm dish. For gravy, thicken drippings with a paste of flour and water. Yield: 6 servings.

Porcupine Balls

  1 *pound hamburger meat*
 ¼ *cup rice, uncooked*
  1 *small onion, chopped*
     Salt and pepper
     Catsup
  1 *(6-ounce) can tomato sauce*

Mix hamburger, rice, onion, salt, and pepper. Add enough catsup to make mixture stick together. Make into balls the size of walnuts. Place in glass baking dish and pour tomato sauce over meat. Cover with foil and bake at 350 degrees F. for 1 hour.

Cheese Meat Loaf

  1 *pound ground beef*
  2 *cups corn flakes, crushed*
  1 *egg*
 ½ *cup shredded, sharp Cheddar cheese*
 ½ *cup milk*
 ¾ *teaspoon salt*
     Juice of one lemon
 ¼ *cup chopped olives or green pepper*
     (optional)
  3 *slices bacon*

Mix all ingredients except bacon. Place in 1-quart baking dish. Cool and freeze. To serve, thaw slightly and top with 3 slices bacon. Bake at 350 degrees F. for 45 minutes.

Glazed Meat Loaf

  1 *egg*
 ½ *cup milk*
 ¼ *cup fine dry breadcrumbs*
  1 *pound ground beef*
  1 *pound ground pork*
  2 *tablespoons minced onion*
  2 *tablespoons minced parsley*
1½ *cups finely chopped celery*
  1 *teaspoon salt*
 ½ *teaspoon pepper*
 ½ *teaspoon pumpkin pie spice*
  1 *tablespoon soy sauce*
  1 *(8-ounce) can whole cranberry sauce*

In a large mixing bowl beat the egg enough to combine yolk and white; add milk and beat to combine. Stir in breadcrumbs; allow to stand for about 15 minutes. With your hands or a mixing fork thoroughly mix in the beef, pork, onion, parsley, celery, salt, pepper, pumpkin pie spice, and soy sauce.

Turn into a round layer cake pan (8 x 1¼ inches); pack down. Line an oblong pan (13 x 9 x 2 inches) with foil, turning sides up; turn out meat mixture into center of oblong pan. Bake at 375 degrees F. for 1 hour.

Spread cranberry sauce over top of meat loaf; return to oven to heat cranberry sauce—about 10 minutes. Transfer to serving plate, using a large spatula or pancake turner. Loaf will look pretty ringed with watercress sprigs. Yield: 8 servings.

Joan Crawford's Meat Loaf

  2 *pounds ground sirloin*
  1 *pound ground veal*
  1 *pound bulk sausage*
  3 *raw eggs*
  1 *large onion, finely chopped*
  2 *green peppers, finely chopped*
  1 *tablespoon seasoned salt*
  1 *tablespoon Worcestershire*
     sauce
  1 *teaspoon steak sauce*
  4 *hard-cooked eggs*
  2 *tablespoons seasoned salt*
  2 *tablespoons Worcestershire sauce*
  2 *teaspoons steak sauce*
  1 *cup water*

Combine meats, unbeaten eggs, chopped onion and pepper, 1 tablespoon seasoned salt, 1 tablespoon Worcestershire sauce, and 1 teaspoon steak sauce. Mix thoroughly.

Shape mixture into oval loaf in shallow baking pan. Gently press hard-cooked eggs into loaf. Sprinkle 2 tablespoons seasoned salt, 2 tablespoons Worcestershire sauce, and 2 teaspoons steak sauce on top of loaf. Pour 1 cup water in pan. Do not pour over meat loaf after sauce has been put on.

Bake in preheated 350-degree F. oven for 30 minutes. Turn oven down to 300 degrees

F. and bake for 30 minutes; then turn oven down to 250 degrees F. and bake for 45 minutes to 1 hour, basting frequently with pan juice. Yield: 10 servings.

Lemon-Barbecued Beef Loaves

Meat Loaf Mixture:
- 1½ *pounds ground beef*
- ¼ *cup lemon juice*
- ½ *cup water*
- 1 *egg, slightly beaten*
- 4 *slices stale bread, finely diced*
- ¼ *cup finely chopped onion*
- 2 *teaspoons seasoning salt*

Topping:
- ½ *cup catsup*
- ⅓ *cup brown sugar*
- 1 *teaspoon dry mustard*
- ¼ *teaspoon ground cloves*
- ¼ *teaspoon ground allspice*
- 6 *thin slices lemon*

Combine all ingredients for meat loaves. Mix well and shape into 6 individual loaves. Place in a greased oblong baking pan. Combine ingredients for the topping, with the exception of the lemon slices. Bake loaves at 350 degrees F. for 15 minutes; then cover with topping and place a lemon slice on each loaf. Continue baking for 30 minutes, basting occasionally with sauce spooned over loaves. Yield: 6 servings.

Midget Meat Loaves

- 3 *cups corn flakes or ¾ cup packaged cornflake crumbs*
- 1½ *pounds ground beef*
- 1 *teaspoon salt*
- ⅛ *teaspoon pepper*
- 1¼ *cups (10½-ounce can) condensed onion soup*
- 3 *stuffed olives, halved*
- 6 *(¾-inch) cubes Cheddar cheese*

If using corn flakes, crush into fine crumbs. Mix together ground beef, corn flake crumbs, seasonings, and soup. Spoon mix-

ture into 12 ungreased 3-inch muffin cups; press lightly to shape. Top half of meat loaves with olive halves; press cheese cubes into remainder. Bake in moderately hot oven (400 degrees F.) about 20 minutes. Yield: 6 servings of 2 loaves each.

Try the following suggestions when serving meat loaf the second day.

Sandwich Style: Slice and serve between toasted buttered hamburger buns with catsup or pickle relish.

Spaghetti Sauce: Chop meat loaf into fine pieces and heat with tomato sauce (1 can). Season with onion, salt, pepper, Worcestershire sauce, and herbs. Serve over hot spaghetti.

Casserole: Cube the meat and alternate in layers with cooked seasoned noodles. Add some shredded cheese and a few herbs to a can of tomato soup and pour over layers, lifting layers so soup will run through. Top with buttered breadcrumbs and bake in a moderate oven until heated through.

Italian Meat Loaf

- 3 *cups soft bread cubes*
- ¾ *cup milk*
- 2 *teaspoons salt*
- ¼ *teaspoon pepper*
- ½ *teaspoon thyme*
- ¾ *teaspoon basil*
- 1 *(8-ounce) can tomato sauce*
- ½ *cup chopped onions*
- 2 *tablespoons butter or margarine*
- 2 *pounds ground beef*
- 2 *slices American cheese (2 ounces)*

Soak bread cubes in milk; add salt, pepper, thyme, ½ teaspoon basil, and ¼ cup of the tomato sauce. Stir with a fork to break up bread cubes. Cook onions in hot butter 5 minutes; add to breadcrumb mixture. Combine meat and breadcrumb mixture, mixing lightly with a fork; turn into a 2-quart loaf-pan. Bake at 350 degrees F. for 1 hour; then drain fat. Cool slightly and turn out into a shallow baking pan. Combine remaining tomato sauce and basil; spoon over loaf. Top with slices of cheese cut in half. Return to oven and bake 15 minutes. Yield: 6 servings.

Little Loaves

  1 *pound lean ground beef*
  ¼ *cup finely chopped onion*
  ¼ *cup fine dry breadcrumbs*
  1 *egg*
  ½ *(8-ounce) can tomato sauce*
  1 *teaspoon salt*
     Dash black pepper
  4 *green pepper rings*
  ¼ *cup orange marmalade*
  ½ *(8-ounce) can tomato sauce*

Combine first 7 ingredients; shape into 4 small loaves. Top each with a green pepper ring and bake at 450 degrees F. for 15 minutes. Brush with orange marmalade and pour on tomato sauce; bake 20 minutes longer. Yield: 4 servings.

Pickle Supper Loaf

  1 *pound ground beef chuck*
  ¼ *cup drained sweet pickle relish*
  ½ *cup fine dry breadcrumbs*
  ⅔ *cup milk*
  1 *egg, beaten*
  ¼ *cup chopped onion*
  1 *teaspoon salt*
  ⅛ *teaspoon pepper*
  3 *slices bacon*

Combine beef, pickle relish, breadcrumbs, milk, egg, onion, salt, and pepper; mix well. Shape into loaf; put on rack in shallow baking pan. Top with bacon. Bake at 350 degrees F. for 40 minutes or until done. Yield: 4 servings.

Cheeseburger Loaf

  ½ *cup evaporated milk*
1½ *pounds ground beef*
1½ *teaspoons salt*
  1 *tablespoon catsup*
  1 *egg, beaten*
  1 *cup cracker crumbs*
  2 *teaspoons dry mustard*
  1 *cup shredded Cheddar cheese*

Combine all ingredients except cheese, and mix well. Grease a loafpan and spread ½ cup shredded cheese evenly in bottom of pan. Cover with half the meat mixture. Repeat with remaining cheese and meat mixture. Bake at 350 degrees F. about 1 hour. Allow loaf to stand 10 minutes before removing from pan. Yield: 8 servings.

Salisbury Loaf

  2 *eggs, slightly beaten*
  1 *cup milk*
  2 *teaspoons salt*
  ⅛ *teaspoon pepper*
  1 *teaspoon Worcestershire sauce*
  ¼ *cup chopped parsley*
  1 *tablespoon chopped onion*
1¼ *pounds ground beef*
  ¼ *pound ground pork or sausage*
  4 *cups corn flakes*

Combine all ingredients, crushing corn flakes slightly before adding. Mix thoroughly. Turn into loafpan. Bake at 375 degrees F. for 45 to 50 minutes. Yield: 8 servings.

Succulent Meat Loaf

  1 *(10½-ounce) can condensed cream*
     of mushroom soup
1½ *pounds ground beef*
  ⅓ *cup uncooked oatmeal*
  1 *egg, slightly beaten*
  ¼ *cup finely chopped onion*
  2 *tablespoons chopped parsley*
  1 *tablespoon minced green pepper*
  ½ *teaspoon salt*
     Dash pepper
  ¼ *cup water*

Combine ½ can soup with all other ingredients except water; mix thoroughly. Shape firmly into a loaf; place in shallow baking pan. (Thorough mixing and firm shaping will result in a moist, easy-to-slice loaf.) Bake in a moderate oven (350 degrees F.) for 1 hour. Blend remaining soup with water and 2 tablespoons drippings from meat loaf; pour over loaf. Bake 15 minutes longer. Yield: 6 servings.

Hamburger Pie

 1 *package herb-seasoned stuffing mix*
 1 *cup boiling water*
 ½ *cup butter, melted*
 1 *pound ground beef*
 1 *cup shredded Cheddar cheese*
 1 *egg, beaten*
 ¼ *cup catsup*
 2 *teaspoons instant minced onion*
 1 *teaspoon seasoned salt*
 ½ *teaspoon sweet basil*
 ⅛ *teaspoon black pepper*

Combine stuffing, water, and melted butter; mix well. Reserve 1 cup of mixture. Press remaining stuffing into 10-inch pie plate to form pie shell.

In skillet, brown ground beef until it loses its red color; remove from heat. Stir in cheese, beaten egg, catsup, onion, salt, basil, pepper, and the cup of stuffing mixture. Spoon the mixture into pie shell and bake at 375 degrees F. for 15 minutes or longer if desired. Yield: 4 servings.

Hamburger Pie

 1 *pound ground beef*
 1 *medium onion, chopped*
 1 *teaspoon salt*
 2 *teaspoons chili powder*
 Dash Worcestershire sauce
 1 *(15½-ounce) can tomatoes*
 1 *(15½-ounce) can green peas*
 1 *(15½-ounce) can whole potatoes, diced*
 1 *(15½-ounce) can whole-kernel corn*
 1 *cup cornmeal*
 1 *cup flour*
 1 *tablespoon salt*
 1 *tablespoon baking powder*
 1 *egg, beaten*
 About 1½ cups buttermilk

Brown beef in skillet, along with onion, salt, chili powder, and Worcestershire sauce.

Drain liquid from vegetables. Spread meat mixture in bottom of an oiled 3-quart baking dish; combine drained vegetables and spread over meat layer.

Combine cornmeal, flour, salt, and baking powder. Stir in beaten egg and buttermilk. Mix well and spoon over vegetable layer. Bake at 400 degrees F. for 30 to 45 minutes, or until cornmeal topping is brown. Yield: 8 to 10 servings.

Cheeseburger Pie

 1¼ *cups soda cracker crumbs*
 ½ *stick (¼ cup) butter or margarine*
 ½ *cup chopped onion*
 1 *tablespoon shortening*
 1 *pound ground beef*
 2 *eggs, beaten*
 ¾ *cup milk*
 1½ *teaspoons salt*
 ½ *cup shredded cheese*
 ¼ *cup soda cracker crumbs*
 ½ *cup shredded cheese*

Mix crumbs with softened butter. Press firmly against bottom and sides of a 9-inch pie tin. For the filling, sauté onion in shortening until tender. Add ground beef and cook only until red is gone. Spoon evenly into crumb crust.

Beat eggs, milk, and salt. Stir in ½ cup shredded cheese. Heat, stirring constantly, until cheese melts. Pour over filling. Combine ¼ cup crumbs and ½ cup cheese. Sprinkle over the top of pie. Bake at 325 degrees F. for 45 minutes or until a knife comes out clean. Yield: 4 to 6 servings.

Mexicali Meat Pie

6 *slices bacon*
1 *pound ground beef*
1 *cup drained whole-kernel corn*
¼ *cup finely chopped green pepper*
¼ *cup finely chopped onion*
¼ *cup cornmeal*
½ *teaspoon oregano*
½ *teaspoon chili powder*
½ *teaspoon salt*
⅛ *teaspoon pepper*
1 *(8-ounce) can tomato sauce*
Piecrust
1 *egg*
¼ *cup milk*
½ *teaspoon salt*
½ *teaspoon dry mustard*
½ *teaspoon Worcestershire sauce*
1½ *cups shredded Cheddar cheese*
4 *stuffed olives, sliced*

Fry bacon until crisp; break into large pieces. Chill ⅓ cup drippings until firm and reserve for piecrust mixture. Brown ground beef in large skillet; drain. Stir in corn, green pepper, onion, cornmeal, oregano, chili powder, salt, pepper, and tomato sauce. Prepare Piecrust. Place meat mixture in pastry-lined pan. Bake at 425 degrees F. for 25 minutes. Combine egg, milk, salt, mustard, Worcestershire sauce, and cheese. Spread on pie. Top with bacon and olives. Bake 5 minutes or until cheese melts. Let stand 10 minutes before serving. If desired, serve with a tomato sauce. Yield: 6 servings.

Piecrust:

1 *cup flour*
2 *tablespoons cornmeal*
⅓ *cup firm bacon drippings*
3 *to 4 tablespoons cold water*

Combine flour and cornmeal. Cut in bacon drippings until mixture is the size of small peas. Sprinkle water over mixture, stirring with fork until dough holds together. Form into a ball. Flatten to ½ inch; smooth edge. Roll out on floured surface to a circle 1½ inches larger than inverted 9-inch piepan. Fit into pan. Fold edge to form a standing rim; flute edge of crust.

Hot Tamale Pie

1½ *pounds ground beef*
1 *onion, chopped*
½ *cup chopped green pepper*
1 *package chili seasoning mix*
1 *teaspoon salt*
1 *(1-pound) can tomatoes*
1½ *cups whole-kernel corn*
1 *(3¼-ounce) can black olives, drained and pitted*
1 *cup yellow cornmeal*
1 *teaspoon salt*
2½ *cups cold water*
¼ *cup chopped pimiento*
1 *cup shredded Cheddar cheese*

Brown beef in skillet. Add next 5 ingredients and simmer 5 minutes. Stir in corn and olives.

Combine cornmeal, salt, and water. Cook, stirring, until thick. Add the pimiento. Line greased shallow pan or 2-quart baking dish with a part of the cornmeal mixture. Pour in beef mixture and make a border of remaining cornmeal mixture around edge of baking dish.

Bake at 350 degrees F. for about 40 minutes. Sprinkle cheese over top and bake an additional 5 minutes. Yield: about 6 to 8 servings.

Chili Pie

1 *pound ground beef*
2 *tablespoons salad oil*
1 *teaspoon salt*
½ *teaspoon black pepper*
2 *teaspoons chili powder*
1 *clove garlic, minced (optional)*
1 *(8-ounce) can tomato sauce*
2 *(1-pound) cans kidney beans*
½ *cup water*
1 *(4-ounce) package corn chips, crushed*
1 *medium onion, chopped*
½ *cup shredded sharp Cheddar cheese*

Sear beef in salad oil until brown. Add salt, pepper, chili powder, garlic, tomato sauce, kidney beans, and water and simmer until mixture is thick. Stir often while mixture cooks.

Spread half of crushed corn chips in buttered 2½-quart casserole, add a layer of half the meat mixture, and sprinkle with chopped onions. Repeat layers and bake at 350 degrees F. about 20 minutes. Just before serving, sprinkle top with shredded cheese and return to oven to melt cheese. Yield: 6 servings.

Mexican Meat Pie

    2 *tablespoons butter*
 1½ *pounds ground beef*
    1 *onion, diced*
    1 *clove garlic, minced*
    2 *cups canned tomatoes*
    1 *(6-ounce) can tomato paste*
    1 *(14-ounce) can drained whole-kernel corn*
    1 *(12-ounce) package frozen lima beans*
    1 *cup chopped celery*
    1 *tablespoon chili powder*
    2 *teaspoons salt*
  ¼ *teaspoon pepper*
 1½ *cups sifted all-purpose flour*
    3 *teaspoons baking powder*
    1 *teaspoon salt*
    1 *cup cornmeal*
  ¼ *cup shortening*
    1 *cup milk*
    1 *egg yolk*
    1 *tablespoon cold water*

Heat butter in large, heavy saucepan. Add ground beef and cook gently, stirring often until crumbly and lightly browned. Add onion and garlic and continue cooking and stirring 2 minutes more. Add tomatoes, tomato paste, corn, lima beans, celery, chili powder, salt, and pepper. Cover and simmer 20 minutes, stirring occasionally. Remove from heat and let cool slightly while preparing dough.

Heat oven to 375 degrees. Sift flour, baking powder, and salt into mixing bowl. Add cornmeal and stir lightly with a fork. Add shortening and cut in coarsely. Add milk and stir lightly with a fork just until all dry ingredients are moistened. Gather into a ball and knead lightly about 6 times on floured board.

Use two-thirds of dough and roll into a round large enough to line bottom and sides of a 2-quart casserole and extend a little over the edge. Pour meat filling into casserole when it is lined in this way. Roll remaining dough quite thin and cut into strips 1 inch wide. Lay these strips in lattice fashion on top of pie, letting strips extend over edge. Turn edge of bottom lining and end of strips under and flute to make a high edge. Beat egg yolk and water together and brush over lattice. Bake at 375 degrees F. about 25 minutes or until pastry is well browned and filling is bubbly. Yield: 8 servings.

Quick Beef Stroganoff

  ¼ *cup margarine*
  ¾ *cup chopped onion*
  ¼ *cup chopped green pepper*
 1½ *pounds ground beef*
  ⅓ *cup flour*
    2 *teaspoons salt*
  ⅛ *teaspoon garlic salt*
  ¼ *teaspoon black pepper*
    1 *tablespoon Worcestershire sauce*
    1 *(6-ounce) can tomato paste*
    1 *can beef consommé*
    1 *cup evaporated milk*

Melt margarine in heavy skillet. Sauté onion and pepper in melted margarine. Cook ground beef in a separate skillet until brown. Add flour gradually, then the onion and pepper. Add other ingredients slowly, stirring to blend. Cover and cook over low heat for 30 minutes. Serve over hot noodles or fluffy rice. Yield: 6 to 8 servings.

To freeze: Let cool thoroughly before putting into moisture- and vapor-proof containers. Freeze. Remove from freezer and heat to serve.

Afrikaner Beef and Onion Pie

3 *tablespoons butter*
3 *onions, chopped*
2 *slices white bread*
1 *cup milk*
3 *pounds beef, ground twice*
2 *eggs*
2 *tablespoons curry powder*
1 *teaspoon salt*
2 *tablespoons plum jam*
3 *tablespoons lemon juice*
¼ *cup ground almonds*
3 *bay leaves*

Melt butter in a saucepan. Add the onion and sauté for 10 minutes, stirring occasionally. Soak the bread in the milk and squeeze dry, reserving the milk. Mash the bread. Combine beef, sautéed onion, mashed bread, one of the eggs, curry powder, salt, plum jam, lemon juice, and ground almonds, mixing thoroughly.

Arrange bay leaves in the bottom of a buttered baking dish and place the meat mixture over them. Beat the remaining egg with the reserved milk; pour over meat mixture. Bake in a 350-degree oven for 1¼ hours. Serve hot from the dish.

Chili-Cheeseburger Pie

1 *pound ground lean beef*
½ *cup chopped onion*
½ *cup evaporated milk*
⅓ *cup fine dry breadcrumbs*
½ *cup catsup*
1 *tablespoon chili powder*
1 *teaspoon salt*
½ *teaspoon oregano*
¼ *teaspoon pepper*
1 *unbaked 10-inch pie shell*
1½ *cups shredded processed American cheese*
1 *teaspoon Worcestershire sauce*

Preheat oven to 400 degrees F. Brown ground beef and onion in a 10-inch skillet over medium heat. Remove from heat and pour off drippings. Stir in evaporated milk, breadcrumbs, catsup, chili powder, salt,

oregano, and pepper. Spread in unbaked piecrust shell.

Place piepan on cookie sheet and bake 20 minutes. Remove from oven and top with a mixture of cheese and Worcestershire sauce. Bake 10 minutes longer. Let stand 10 minutes before serving. Yield: 6 servings.

Meatza Pie

1 *pound ground beef*
½ *to 1 teaspoon garlic salt*
½ *cup breadcrumbs*
⅔ *cup evaporated milk*
⅓ *cup tomato paste*
  Green pepper slices
2 *or 3 slices American cheese*
¼ *teaspoon oregano*

Mix beef, garlic salt, breadcrumbs, and evaporated milk. Pat this mixture in bottom of a 9-inch piepan. Spread with tomato paste and arrange green pepper slices over mixture. Place cheese slices on top and sprinkle with oregano. Bake at 400 degrees F. for 20 minutes. Yield: 4 to 6 servings.

Beef Pinwheels

¼ *cup chopped onion*
¼ *cup chopped green pepper*
1 *tablespoon shortening*
1 *pound ground beef*
1 *teaspoon salt*
¼ *teaspoon pepper*
1 *teaspoon Worcestershire sauce*
1 *tablespoon chopped parsley*
3 *tablespoons shortening*
3 *tablespoons enriched flour*
1 *cup milk*
  Biscuit dough using 3 cups flour

Sauté onion and green pepper in shortening. Add meat; cook until brown. Add seasonings and parsley. Make white sauce with shortening, flour, and milk; add to meat.

Spread meat and sauce mixture on dough rolled ¼ inch thick; roll in jellyroll fashion. Cut in 1-inch slices; place cut side down on oiled baking sheet. Bake at 400 degrees F.

for 20 minutes. Serve with tomato or cheese sauce. Yield: 6 servings.

Quick Cheese Sauce:

½ *pound process cheese, cubed*
⅔ *cup milk*
¼ *teaspoon dry mustard*
   Dash cayenne pepper

Heat all ingredients together on low heat, stirring occasionally, until cheese is melted. Yield: 1½ cups.

Pizzaburger

1 *pound ground beef*
½ *pound ground sausage meat*
¾ *cup chopped onion*
¾ *cup diced green pepper*
1 *clove garlic, crushed*
1 *large tomato, chopped*
2 *teaspoons salt*
1½ *teaspoons sugar*
¼ *teaspoon pepper*
2 *cups cooked rice*
   Biscuit Topping
   Melted butter or margarine
¾ *cup shredded sharp cheese*

Combine ground beef, sausage, onion, green pepper, and garlic. Mix well. Cook in a large skillet until meat is lightly browned. Add tomato, seasonings, and cooked rice. Continue cooking about 5 minutes, or until all the liquid is absorbed. Turn into greased 9-inch square casserole.

Place Biscuit Topping on top of meat. Brush with melted butter and bake at 450 degrees F. for 15 minutes. Remove from oven. Invert onto a serving plate. Sprinkle shredded cheese over meat and broil about 1 minute, or until cheese is melted. Yield: 6 servings.

Biscuit Topping:

2 *cups biscuit mix*
⅔ *cup milk*

Combine biscuit mix and milk. Mix only until well blended. Turn onto floured pastry cloth and roll to about ¼-inch thickness.

Meat-Vegetable Pie

1 *pound ground beef*
1 *cup soft breadcrumbs*
1 *egg, beaten*
1 *(8-ounce) can tomato sauce, divided*
1 *teaspoon salt*
1 *teaspoon chili powder*
Dash cayenne pepper
1 *package frozen mixed vegetables, thawed*
½ *cup shredded American cheese*

Combine beef, breadcrumbs, egg, ¼ cup of the tomato sauce, salt, chili powder, and cayenne. Press into a 9-inch piepan; bake at 350 degrees F. for 10 minutes. Top with the thawed mixed vegetables; add remainder of the tomato sauce and continue baking for 30 minutes longer. Sprinkle shredded cheese over top and bake until cheese melts. Yield: 4 to 6 servings.

Texas Pizza Pie

1 *pound ground beef*
1 *teaspoon salt*
2 *medium onions, chopped*
¼ *teaspoon black pepper*
3 *tablespoons Worcestershire sauce*
1 *(3-ounce) can sliced mushrooms, drained*
3 *eggs, beaten well*
1 *cup biscuit mix*
⅓ *cup evaporated milk*
1 *cup shredded Cheddar cheese*

Mix beef, salt, chopped onion, and black pepper. Put in heavy skillet and cook slowly until beef is brown. Remove from heat and add Worcestershire sauce and drained mushrooms; mix well. Stir in well-beaten eggs.

To biscuit mix add evaporated milk and mix well. Knead and roll to a 9-inch piecrust; crimp edges. Spoon meat mixture into piecrust; sprinkle top with shredded cheese and bake at 375 degrees F. for 20 minutes. Serve hot. Yield: 6 servings.

Barbecued Pot Roast

    1 *(4- to 5-pound) chuck roast, boneless*
    4 *cloves minced garlic*
    Juice of 3 lemons
    ¾ *cup olive oil*
    1 *teaspoon crushed rosemary*
    ½ *teaspoon dry mustard*
    2 *tablespoons soy sauce*
    1 *cup California red wine*

Marinate meat for two days in a mixture of the other ingredients listed. Cook until fork-tender over hot coals, basting frequently with the same marinade. Yield: 6 servings.

Pot Roast, Pappas Style

    4 *tablespoons butter*
    6 *tablespoons olive oil*
  3½ *pounds choice-quality sirloin tip or top round beef*
    1 *large onion, coarsely chopped*
    4 *cloves garlic, minced*
    2 *carrots, sliced*
    3 *sticks celery, sliced*
    1 *tablespoon pickling spices*
    1 *tablespoon salt*
    1 *teaspoon pepper*
    1 *(6-ounce) can tomato paste*
    6 *cups water*
    ¼ *cup claret wine*

Heat butter and oil in a large pot. Add meat, and brown well on all sides. Add onion and garlic; allow to brown slightly. Add other vegetables, spices, salt, pepper, and tomato paste. Cook a few minutes and add 6 cups water. Bring to a boil and add the wine. Reduce the heat and cook slowly for 2 to 2½ hours, turning the meat after it has cooked 1 hour. Test meat for doneness, as more cooking may be necessary depending on quality of meat used.

    When meat is done, remove from pot and strain the vegetables. Mash vegetables and add to the liquid. This gravy may be thickened if desired. To serve, slice meat and cover with gravy. Yield: 6 to 8 servings.

Marinated Eye of the Round Roast

    ¼ *cup soy sauce*
    1 *cup orange juice*
    2 *tablespoons wine vinegar*
  2½- *to 3-pound eye of the round roast*
    Salt and pepper

Combine soy sauce, orange juice, and vinegar. Pour over meat; cover and refrigerate overnight, basting and turning meat in marinade several times. Drain, saving marinade. Place roast in small roasting pan; sprinkle with salt and pepper. Roast uncovered at 375 degrees F. until roast begins to brown, about 30 minutes. Pour about half the marinade over meat. Cover; lower temperature to 350 degrees F. Cook until beef is tender, about 2½ to 3 hours. Baste occasionally. Yield: 6 to 8 servings.

Chuck Steak With Mushrooms

    Select Choice aged beef (preferably what is referred to as the "blade chuck") 1½ inches to 2 inches thick.

    ¼ *cup olive oil*
    ¼ *cup vegetable oil (preferably corn oil)*
    1 *teaspoon parsley flakes*
    1 *tablespoon salt*
    1 *teaspoon black pepper*
    2 *tablespoons honey*
    ½ *teaspoon dry mustard*
    ½ *teaspoon soy sauce*
    Dash Tabasco sauce
    1 *tablespoon lemon juice*
    2 *tablespoons steak sauce*
    ¼ *cup wine vinegar*
    ¼ *cup cooking sherry*
    4 *tablespoons catsup*
    2 *small cans mushroom buttons*

Mix together all the above ingredients except mushrooms. Stir well in a saucepan; heat slowly (do not boil).

    Place meat in baking pan. (A 10- x 8- x 3-inch glass pan works nicely.) Pour all of the above over meat and marinate for at least 4 hours. Hold in refrigerator while marinating and baste occasionally. Preheat oven to about 350 degrees F. Pour off most of the liquid into another container and place meat in oven. Baste occasionally with liquid that has been saved. A few minutes before meat has cooked as done as desired, place the mushroom buttons, drained, in pan around meat and sauté until brown. Then place mushrooms on top of meat and pour enough sauce over meat to heat and make desired amount of natural gravy. To serve, cut with grain of meat in size servings desired.

Sauerbraten With Gingersnap Gravy and Noodles

     6 -pound beef rump roast
     3 cups vinegar
     3 cups red wine
     3 cups water
     3 onions, sliced
     1 lemon, sliced
    12 whole cloves
     6 bay leaves
     6 whole black peppers
     3 tablespoons salt
    12 gingersnaps

Noodles:
     1 egg
    ½ teaspoon salt
     2 tablespoons milk
     1 cup flour

Place meat in a large bowl. Combine next 9 ingredients and pour over meat. Place in refrigerator and marinate 36 to 48 hours or longer (the longer the spicier), turning meat occasionally.

Remove meat and brown on all sides in hot fat. Add 1 cup of marinade mixture, cover, and cook at 300 degrees F. for 3 to 4 hours until tender.

Homemade noodles are easy: Beat egg, salt, and milk. Add flour. Combine and mix into stiff dough. Roll out on floured surface and let stand a few minutes. Roll up like a jellyroll and slice. Unroll the slices and spread the noodle strips to dry for the time it takes to cook the roast. Drop the noodle strips into salted boiling water, cook for 10 minutes, drain, and serve with meat and gravy. Yield: 6 to 8 servings.

For gingersnap gravy, remove meat from roasting pan after it is cooked. Add about a dozen crushed gingersnaps to the drippings and marinade in the pan. Use a wire whisk to stir the mixture until it is smooth. Thin with water if necessary.

Old English Prime Rib

    Prime rib or standing rib, ½ pound per
         serving
     2 *tablespoons Worcestershire sauce*
     1 *teaspoon paprika*
    Salt and pepper to taste
    Rock salt (ice cream salt)

Select Choice prime rib or standing rib. Season with Worcestershire sauce, paprika, and salt and pepper. Rub this seasoning into the meat. In a large, heavy pan, such as the bottom section of a roaster, pour a layer of rock salt (ice cream salt) until the bottom surface of the container is completely covered. Lightly dampen the rock salt with water until the salt is just moist. Place the prime rib onto the salt in a standing rib position. Then cover completely the remaining portion of the meat with rock salt and again repeat procedure of dampening all of the salt very lightly with water.

Without a cover for the roaster, place roast, covered with salt, into an oven preheated to 500 degrees F. Allow meat to roast for 15 minutes per pound. When cookingtime is completed, remove roast from the oven. The salt will be very hard and must be carefully broken away from the meat. Using a wooden mallet, gently strike the surface of the salt, creating cracks. Pull the salt sections away from the meat. This process, which doesn't impart a salt flavor, traps vital flavor juices and insures minimum shrinkage of the meat.

Cubed Steak Sauerbraten

1½   pounds round steak, ½ inch thick
 3   tablespoons shortening
 3   level tablespoons flour
 2   cups water
 2   beef bouillon cubes
1½   tablespoons instant minced onions
 2   tablespoons brown sugar
 2   tablespoons white vinegar
 ½   teaspoon salt
 ½   teaspoon pepper
 ½   teaspoon ground ginger
 1   teaspoon Worcestershire sauce
 1   (10-ounce) package noodles

Cut meat in 1-inch squares. In a large skillet, brown meat on all sides in hot shortening. Remove meat from skillet and make a thin gravy by adding the 3 tablespoons flour to the shortening remaining in skillet. Stir until the flour browns slightly. Add the 2 cups water slowly, stirring constantly. Bring to a boil and add other ingredients, except noodles. Mix well and return meat to the gravy mixture. Cover tightly and simmer for about 1½ hours, stirring occasionally. When ready to serve, pour over hot buttered noodles. Yield: 6 servings.

Marinated Chuck Roast

 ¼   cup chopped green pepper
 ¼   cup chopped onion
 ¼   cup chopped celery and celery tops
 ¼   cup vinegar
1½ to 2 teaspoons salt
 ½   teaspoon pepper
 ¼   cup salad oil
 ½   cup burgundy or grape juice
 3 -pound chuck roast

Combine all ingredients except the roast. Place roast in a flat pan. Pour marinade over roast, cover, and let marinate in refrigerator for 12 to 24 hours, turning meat occasionally to coat with marinade.

Place meat on a rack in roasting pan. Roast, uncovered, at 325 degrees F. for 2½ to 3 hours, basting occasionally with marinade. Yield: 6 servings.

Pot Roast Jardiniere

 3- to 4-pound pot roast (chuck or round)
 1   (10½-ounce) can condensed beef broth
 1   teaspoon salt
 ¼   teaspoon pepper
 ¼   teaspoon crushed rosemary
 4   small carrots, halved lengthwise
 2   medium turnips, quartered
 8   small whole white onions
     Chopped parsley
 ¼   cup water
 ¼   cup flour

In large, heavy pan, brown meat on all sides. (Use shortening if necessary.) Add soup. Cover and cook over low heat 2½ hours. Add seasonings and all vegetables except parsley. Cover and cook 1 hour more, or until meat and vegetables are done. Remove meat and vegetables to heated platter; garnish with parsley. To make gravy, gradually blend water into flour and slowly stir into liquid. Cook, stirring until thickened. Yield: 4 to 6 servings.

Creamy Beef Strips

1½   pounds round steak
 2   tablespoons shortening
     Salt and pepper to taste
 1   medium onion, sliced
 1   clove garlic, crushed
 1   (3- or 4-ounce) can or jar mushrooms
 ¼   teaspoon dry mustard
 ¾   cup canned condensed beef broth
 1   cup commercial sour cream
 1   (16-ounce) can peas
 1   tablespoon butter or margarine
 3   cups hot cooked noodles
     Parsley flakes

Cut round steak into thin strips and brown in shortening; sprinkle lightly with salt and pepper. Add sliced onion, crushed garlic, drained mushrooms, and dry mustard; cook until mushrooms are browned and onion is tender. Add beef broth; cover and simmer about an hour, or until meat is tender. Remove meat mixture from heat and add sour cream; mix well.

To serve, arrange meat on platter with heated drained peas that have been tossed with butter and noodles that have been sprinkled with parsley. Yield: 6 servings.

Braised Shortribs

    3 *pounds shortribs*
    Flour, salt, pepper
    Cooking oil
 1½ *cups water*
    1 *small can tomatoes*
    2 *medium carrots, chopped*
    2 *medium onions, chopped*
    2 *stalks celery, chopped*
    ½ *small head cabbage, chopped*

Roll ribs in flour, season with salt and pepper, and brown on both sides in cooking oil. Place ribs in baking dish; gradually blend remaining flour into drippings by adding water. Add tomatoes and other chopped vegetables and pour over ribs. Place cover on dish and simmer about 1½ hours or until ribs are tender. Serve over noodles. Yield: 4 to 6 servings

Steak à la Creole

    2 *pounds round steak*
    Salt and pepper
    2 *tablespoons shortening or bacon*
        drippings
    2 *tablespoons flour*
    1 *large onion, finely chopped*
    1 *green pepper, finely chopped*
    1 *cup water*
    2 *cups tomatoes, whole, canned or*
        fresh
    1 *clove garlic, mashed*
    1 *bay leaf*
    ½ *teaspoon dried thyme*
    ¼ *cup chopped parsley*

Salt and pepper the meat. In an iron skillet, brown the meat in the shortening or bacon drippings. Remove and set aside. Make a roux by browning flour, along with onion and green pepper, in the fat remaining in the skillet. Add water, tomatoes, and seasonings. Allow to simmer for about 30 minutes. If more liquid is needed, add water. Return the meat to gravy and cook until tender. Serve over rice. Yield: 6 servings.

Tournedos Diane

    4 *small tenderloin steaks about 2*
        inches thick
    Salt and pepper
    4 *thin slices tomato*
    4 *large mushroom crowns*
    Butter
    4 *slices truffles*
    Instant Marchand de Vin Sauce
    Parsley snips

Sear steaks 1 minute on each side in a very hot iron skillet so they are well browned, but not overcooked, even to the rare stage. Sprinkle with salt and pepper and arrange in ovenproof serving dish. On top of each filet place a thin slice of tomato and a large mushroom crown, previously browned in butter. (A layer of chopped mushrooms may be substituted for the mushroom crowns.) Top with a slice of truffle. Pour over all the Instant Marchand de Vin Sauce and place in a 350-degree F. oven to lightly brown tops for about 15 minutes (or less if there is to be a waiting period on a hot tray). Filets should be at the rare stage when removed from the oven. Garnish with parsley snips. Yield: 4 servings.

    Instant Marchand de Vin Sauce:

    1 *package mushroom gravy mix*
    ½ *cup red wine (Burgundy or claret*
        type)
    ½ *cup water*
    2 *tablespoons butter*

Combine ingredients in saucepan. Bring to a boil, reduce temperature, and simmer until thickened.

Marinated Steak

    3 -*pound boneless sirloin, about ¾*
        inch thick
  1½ *teaspoons salt*
    ¼ *teaspoon pepper*
    ½ *cup dry red wine*
    ⅛ *teaspoon garlic powder*
    2 *tablespoons chopped parsley*
    2 *tablespoons olive oil*
    ⅛ *teaspoon garlic powder*

Rub beef with salt and pepper. Mix together wine, garlic powder, and parsley. Marinate meat in wine for 12 hours, turning often.

When steak is thoroughly marinated, remove and pat dry with paper towel. The marinade is saved for the sauce.

In a hot heavy skillet, sauté steak in olive oil for 4 to 7 minutes on each side, depending on desired doneness. Remove steak to heated platter. Add remaining marinade and ⅛ teaspoon garlic powder to hot skillet. Reduce heat and stir until well blended with pan juices. More chopped parsley may be added. Pour sauce over steak. Yield: 6 to 8 servings.

Mustard Beef

  1¼ *pounds top round cut in thin strips*
    3 *tablespoons spicy brown mustard*
    3 *tablespoons butter or margarine*
    1 *onion, thinly sliced*
    1 *(15½-ounce) can spaghetti sauce*
        with mushrooms
    ¼ *teaspoon oregano*
    1 *teaspoon salt*
    ¼ *teaspoon pepper*
    3 *tablespoons commercial sour cream*
      Cooked noodles

Spread meat with mustard mixed with butter or margarine; brown meat on all sides. Add onion and cook until tender. Add spaghetti sauce and seasonings. Cover and simmer about 25 minutes or until meat is tender. Stir in sour cream and just heat through. Serve with hot cooked noodles. Yield: 4 to 6 servings.

Chinese Pepper Steak

  1½ *pounds sirloin steak*
    ¼ *cup vegetable oil*
    1 *clove garlic, crushed*
      Dash of salt
    1 *teaspoon ground ginger*
    ½ *teaspoon pepper*
    3 *green peppers, sliced*
    2 *large onions, sliced*
    ¼ *cup soy sauce*
    ½ *teaspoon sugar*
    1 *can beef bouillon*
    1 *can water chestnuts, sliced*
    1 *tablespoon cornstarch*
    ½ *to 1 cup water*
    4 *green onions, cut in pieces*

Freeze steak 1 hour to make cutting easier. Heat oil in skillet; add garlic, salt, ginger, and pepper. Sauté until garlic is golden. Add steak which has been cut in ¼-inch strips, and brown lightly. Remove meat. Add green peppers and onions, and cook approximately 3 to 5 minutes. Return beef to pan and add soy sauce, sugar, bouillon, water chestnuts, cornstarch dissolved in water, and green onions. Simmer about 15 to 20 minutes. Serve over hot rice. Yield: 6 to 8 servings.

Skillet Swiss Steak

    ⅓ *cup flour*
    2 *teaspoons salt*
    ¼ *teaspoon freshly ground pepper*
    2 *pounds round steak, about 1 inch*
        thick
    3 *tablespoons bacon drippings*
    1 *medium onion, diced*
    ¼ *cup chopped green pepper*
    1 *(No. 2) can tomatoes*
    1 *(8-ounce) can tomato sauce*

Combine flour, salt, and pepper; pound into steak. Brown steak slowly on both sides in hot drippings. Remove steak to platter and keep warm. In same pan, sauté onion and green pepper only until clear. Add canned tomatoes and cook together 5 minutes. Place steak back into pan with sauce. Add tomato sauce and mix well. Cover pan and cook slowly until tender, usually about an hour. Add small amounts of water if necessary to keep sauce from sticking to pan. This can also be baked in a covered dish at 350 degrees F. for about the same length of time. Yield: 6 servings.

Sunday Swiss Steak

- ½ cup flour
- 2 teaspoons salt
- ¼ teaspoon pepper
- 6 slices eye of round steak, 1½ inches thick
- ½ cup thinly sliced onion
- ¼ cup shortening
- 1 (8-ounce) can tomato sauce
- 1 cup pizza sauce

Combine flour, salt, and pepper; pound into meat. Brown onion lightly in hot shortening in large skillet. Remove onion; brown meat. After meat has been browned on both sides, place onion on top of meat. Add tomato and pizza sauces. Cover and simmer for 1½ to 2 hours. Serve sauce with the meat. Yield: 6 servings.

Sukiyaki

- 2 tablespoons butter
- 1½ pounds sirloin steak (cut into small cubes)
- 1 cup green onions (sliced into thin 1-inch strips)
- ⅓ cup cooking sherry
- 1 cup mushrooms
- 2 cups bamboo shoots
- 1 cup celery (sliced into thin 1-inch strips)
- ½ cup green pepper (sliced into thin 1-inch strips)
- ¼ cup beef stock (canned beef consommé may be substituted)
- ¼ cup soy sauce
- 2 tablespoons sugar
- 1 cup blanched almonds
  Salt and pepper to taste
- 2 cups cooked rice

Melt butter in skillet and sauté cubes of sirloin steak. When steak cubes are browned, add onions, wine, mushrooms, bamboo shoots, celery, green pepper, beef stock, soy sauce, sugar, almonds, and salt and pepper to taste.

Cover skillet and simmer for about 6 minutes. The items in this recipe should not be overcooked, but rather they should remain crisp. Serve on a platter over a bed of cooked rice. Yield: 6 servings.

Supper in a Skillet

- 6 slices bacon
- 1½ pounds round steak
  Salt and pepper
  Paprika
- 2 cups water
- 4 medium onions
- 3 or 4 large potatoes
- 2 carrots

Day before: Cook bacon in electric skillet and remove from drippings. Cut steak in 2-inch squares. Brown in bacon drippings (do not dredge in flour beforehand). Add salt and pepper to suit taste and a great deal of paprika to add color to the dish. Add water, cover skillet, and cook until meat is tender (about 2 hours) at 350 degrees F. Add more water if needed (you will need some liquid after meat is cooked). Cool and set in refrigerator till the next night.

Day of serving: Remove skillet from refrigerator and heat. Peel onions, potatoes, and carrots. Leave whole or cut as desired. Add vegetables to meat and cook until vegetables are tender (about 20 minutes).

Succulent Steak Roll

1 -*pound top round steak, sliced thin (5
　　slices)*
Garlic
Salt and pepper
3 *tablespoons catsup*
1 *tablespoon prepared mustard*
5 *slices bacon*
5 *olives*
1 *dill pickle, cut in 5 thick slices*
1 *onion, minced*
2 *tablespoons cooking oil*
Water
½ *cup red wine*

Rub thin slices of steak with garlic, season
with salt and pepper, and add catsup and
mustard to each slice. On each slice put 1
slice of bacon, 1 olive, 1 slice of pickle, and
sprinkle with the minced onion.

Roll up and tie with butcher string or fasten with poultry skewers. Heat cooking oil
in skillet. Add steak rolls and sauté for
about 10 minutes, turning rolls to brown
each side. Reduce heat. Add water to half-
cover steak rolls; cover and simmer for
about 30 minutes. Add wine and simmer for
an additional 5 minutes. Yield: 5 servings.

Medieval Veal Chops

2½ *pounds veal cutlet, cut ½ inch thick*
2 *teaspoons prepared mustard*
1¼ *teaspoons salt*
¼ *teaspoon white pepper*
¼ *teaspoon ground nutmeg*
½ *cup finely chopped onion*
½ *cup finely chopped dill pickles*
1 *cup crushed potato chips*
Flour
5 *slices smoked bacon*
1 *cup commercial sour cream*
1 *teaspoon dried dill weed*

Using the side of a mallet, pound cutlet to a
thickness of ¼ inch. Spread mustard evenly
over cutlet; sprinkle with salt, pepper, and
nutmeg. Spread onion, pickle, and potato
chips evenly over meat. Roll cutlet and

secure with heavy string in several places.
Dust roll of meat with flour.

In an electric skillet or heavy iron skillet,
fry bacon until it is crisp; then crumble it
and set it aside. Sauté veal roll quickly in
bacon grease until it is golden on all sides
(about 6 to 8 minutes). Cover tightly; let
simmer about 1¼ hours or until meat is
fork tender. Remove meat to a heated platter and keep hot.

Add sour cream, dill weed, and crumbled
bacon to the pan juices. Blend thoroughly
with browned bits which stick to the bottom
of the pan. Heat sour cream mixture but *do
not boil.*

Remove string from roll of meat; cut into
1-inch chops. Surround chops with watercress and chutney-filled peach halves. Spoon
hot sour cream sauce over each chop. Yield:
6 servings.

Veal Marengo

3 *tablespoons oil*
3 *pounds lean shoulder of veal, cubed*
1 *onion, finely chopped*
½ *cup tomato puree*
1 *tablespoon potato flour*
2 *cups veal or chicken stock*
1 *cup white wine*
1 *clove garlic, crushed*
2 *bay leaves*
¼ *teaspoon thyme*
Dash Worcestershire sauce
Dash liquid red pepper seasoning
Salt and pepper to taste
4 *tablespoons butter or margarine*
12 *small white onions*
1 *tablespoon sugar*
2 *tablespoons butter or margarine*
12 *mushrooms*
3 *tomatoes*

In deep, heavy kettle or Dutch oven heat oil
over medium heat. Add veal and cook until
brown. Add onion and tomato puree, and
cook 2 minutes; then stir in potato flour.
Gradually add the veal or chicken stock and
white wine. Add garlic, bay leaves, thyme,
Worcestershire sauce, red pepper seasoning,

salt and pepper to taste; cover and simmer over low heat 1 hour.

Melt butter or margarine in skillet over medium heat. Add white onions and sauté until almost tender. Sprinkle with sugar and continue cooking until brown and glazed.

Melt 2 tablespoons butter or margarine in skillet over medium heat, add mushrooms, and sauté 3 or 4 minutes. Peel tomatoes, cut in wedges, and remove seed. Add onions, mushrooms, and tomatoes to veal. Continue cooking 30 minutes or until meat is tender. Yield: 6 servings.

Peter Ponderosa Beef Rolls

   3 *slices boiled ham, cut in halves*
   6 *slices round of beef (about*
        3½ pounds)
   3 *tablespoons butter*
   1 *medium onion, chopped*
   1 *clove garlic*
   1 *cup tomato juice*
  ½ *teaspoon salt*
  ¼ *teaspoon pepper*
  ½ *teaspoon chili powder*
  ¼ *teaspoon basil*
  ⅓ *cup smooth peanut butter*
  ½ *green pepper, sliced*
  ⅛ *cup sliced pimiento-stuffed olives*
     Hot cooked rice

Place ham on beef slices pounded thin; roll up and secure with toothpick or string. In large skillet, brown meat in butter; drain off drippings. Stir in onion, garlic, tomato juice, salt, pepper, chili powder, and basil. Simmer 1 hour (add more liquid if needed). Spread peanut butter over beef rolls and add green pepper and olives. Cook 30 minutes longer or until tender, stirring occasionally. Serve in dish bordered with rice. Yield: 6 servings.

Barbecue Pork

Build a 20-briquette fire, add hickory, and get a good smoke going. Place fresh, whole Boston butt pork roasts on foil sheets on the grill. Close hood. Do not add any sauce or salt to the meat. Add 6 to 8 briquettes and hickory every 2 hours to assure steady heat and smoke. A 5-pound roast will cook in 6 to 7 hours. Remove the bone and either slice or chip the pork as you desire. Now add your favorite barbecue sauce and serve.

To freeze: The average covered grill will hold about 20 pounds of pork, all of which can be barbecued in one cooking. After removing from the grill, let the pork cool overnight. Slice or chip as desired, add sauce, put in freezer containers, and freeze in meal-size portions. To serve, simply thaw and heat in a double boiler.

Savory Pork Chops en Casserole

   2 *large onions, sliced*
  ¼ *cup butter or margarine*
   1 *(20-ounce) can tomatoes*
   2 *teaspoons sugar*
   1 *teaspoon salt*
  ¼ *teaspoon pepper*
     Pinch of oregano
   1 *cup soft breadcrumbs*
   2 *cups canned applesauce*
  ¼ *cup prepared horseradish*
   1 *(20-ounce) can sauerkraut, drained*
   6 *(1-inch) pork chops*
     Salt and pepper

Sauté onions in butter or margarine; add tomatoes, sugar, salt, pepper, oregano, and breadcrumbs. Combine applesauce and horseradish; mix well. Combine tomato mixture, applesauce mixture, and sauerkraut. Pour into covered casserole. Sauté pork chops until golden brown. Lay chops on sauerkraut mixture and sprinkle with salt and pepper. Cover; bake at 375 degrees F. for 1 hour and 40 minutes or until chops are tender. Yield: 6 servings.

Hobo Breakfast

Start a 25-briquette fire. While it is burning down to a cooking glow, prepare the main course. Use a 12-inch glass baking dish about 2 inches deep. Take 1½ pounds of pork sausage and press into the dish as if you were making a piecrust. Avoid thin spots in the sausage. Break 8 eggs and stir lightly to break yolks. Pour on top of sausage, taking care not to overfill. Add hickory wood to the coals and place the dish on the grill. Close hood. About 45 minutes later, place desired number of canned biscuits on cookie sheet and put onto grill, well away from the fire. Add more hickory to assure smoke. After 10 minutes, sprinkle shredded cheese over eggs, and let it melt while biscuits get done. Slice the sausage and eggs as you would a pie, and serve. Smoked biscuits with your favorite jellies or preserves are unbelievably delicious!

Pork Chops and Apples

  2 *teaspoons salt*
 ½ *teaspoon pepper*
  4 *pork chops (¾ inch thick)*
  2 *apples, cored and cut in half*
 ¼ *cup brown sugar*
 ½ *teaspoon caraway seeds*
 ½ *cup water*

Sprinkle half the salt and pepper on chops. Brown chops in skillet; then place in 1½-quart casserole. Place apples, skin side down, on top of chops. Sprinkle with sugar. Add caraway seeds and remaining salt and pepper to water and pour over chops and apples. Cover. Bake at 350 degrees F. for 30 to 40 minutes. Yield: 4 servings.

Cranberry Pork Chops

  4 *loin pork chops (1 inch thick)*
    Salt and pepper
  2 *cups ground or chopped cranberries*
 ½ *cup orange blossom honey*
 ¼ *teaspoon ground cloves*
 ¼ *teaspoon ground nutmeg*

Brown the chops in a skillet. Season with salt and pepper. Mix cranberries, honey, cloves, and nutmeg. Pour over the browned chops. Cover and bake at 300 degrees F. about 1 hour until tender. Serve with bowls of hot soup. Yield: 4 servings.

Pork Chop Bake

  1 *pound dry lima beans*
  8 *rib or center-cut pork chops*
  2 *cups molasses*

Soak lima beans overnight. The next morning, drain and rinse beans and cover them with salted water and cook for 1½ hours. In a Dutch oven, place a layer of cooked lima beans, and put 4 of the pork chops on top of the beans. Pour 1 cup of molasses over pork chops. Repeat with another layer of the beans, pork chops, and molasses. Cover and bake at 375 degrees F. for about 1 hour. Yield: 8 servings.

Baked Pork Chops
With Apple Stuffing

  6 *double loin pork chops*
  3 *medium apples, finely chopped*
 ½ *cup brown sugar*
  1 *teaspoon ground cinnamon*
 ½ *teaspoon ground nutmeg*
  3 *cups hot water*
  1 *carrot, finely chopped*
  1 *medium onion, finely chopped*
  2 *stalks celery, finely chopped*
  1 *teaspoon salt*
    Few grains pepper

Cut deep pockets in chops. Combine apples, brown sugar, cinnamon, and nutmeg; fill pockets with apple mixture. Place, stuffing side up, in baking pan. Pour water around chops; add carrot, onion, celery, salt, and pepper to water. Bake in moderate oven, 350 degrees F., for 1½ hours. Thicken gravy, if desired. Yield: 6 servings.

Spicy Glazed Pork Chops With Apricots

1 *(1-pound 14-ounce) can whole apricots*
1 *tablespoon bottled steak sauce*
1 *teaspoon salt*
6 *rib or loin pork chops, cut ½ inch thick*
1 *teaspoon whole cloves*

Drain syrup from apricots into medium-size saucepan; stir in steak sauce and salt. Heat to boiling; cook, uncovered, 15 minutes or until syrup thickens slightly. Save apricots for use later.

Brush chops on both sides with half of syrup; arrange in single layer in shallow baking pan. Do not cover.

Bake at 400 degrees F. for 45 minutes; turn chops. Stud apricots with cloves; arrange around chops; brush all with remaining syrup. Bake 30 minutes longer or until chops are tender and richly glazed. Yield: 6 servings.

Fried Pork Chops

Pour boiling water over pork chops and let stand for about 5 minutes. Remove chops and beat with edge of a saucer or add a meat tenderizer. Add salt and pepper, roll in flour, and fry in deep, hot fat.

Dixie Casserole

1½ *cups dried lima beans*
4 *cups water*
4 *teaspoons salt*
6 *pork chops*
2 *tablespoons flour*
⅓ *cup catsup*
2 *tablespoons brown sugar*
2 *tablespoons instant minced onion*
½ *teaspoon powdered mustard*
¼ *teaspoon ground black pepper*
⅛ *teaspoon instant garlic powder*
1 *bay leaf*

Soak lima beans overnight in water. Add 3 teaspoons of the salt. Bring to boiling point and simmer 1 hour or until beans are almost soft. Drain off water and save. Place beans in a 2½-quart casserole. Rub remaining salt on both sides of pork chops. Sprinkle chops with flour, and brown them on both sides. Place over beans. Mix 1½ cups of the bean water, catsup, sugar, instant minced onion, mustard, black pepper, garlic powder, and bay leaf. Pour over beans and pork chops. Cover and bake in preheated oven at 325 degrees F. for 1 hour or until done. Remove cover and bake an additional 30 minutes. Yield: 6 servings.

One-Pot Pork Chop Supper

4 *pork chops (about 1 pound)*
1 *(10¾-ounce) can condensed tomato soup*
½ *cup water*
1 *teaspoon Worcestershire sauce*
½ *teaspoon salt*
6 *to 8 small whole potatoes, or 3 medium, quartered*
4 *small carrots, split lengthwise and cut in 2-inch pieces*

In skillet, brown chops. Pour off fat. Add remaining ingredients. Cover; cook over low heat 45 minutes or until tender. Yield: 4 servings.

Variations: If desired, add ½ teaspoon caraway seed or ½ teaspoon leaf oregano, crushed.

Orange Pork Chops

6 *pork chops*
½ *cup orange juice*
1 *teaspoon salt*
¼ *teaspoon pepper*
½ *teaspoon dry mustard*
¼ *cup brown sugar*

Place chops in roasting pan. Mix other ingredients and pour on top. Bake at 350 degrees F. for 1 hour, basting occasionally.

Orange-Pork Chop Bake

6 *pork chops, ¾ to 1 inch thick*
Salt and pepper
¼ *cup flour*
1 *large onion, sliced*
2 *tablespoons molasses or honey*
1 *tablespoon prepared mustard*
¼ *teaspoon ground cloves*
½ *cup water*
1 *(3-ounce) can sliced broiled*
mushrooms, undrained
2 *oranges, peeled, sliced into*
cartwheels

Trim excess fat from pork chops. Heat the pieces of fat in large skillet; then remove. Salt, pepper, and flour the pork chops. Brown chops well on both sides in skillet. Remove chops to large baking dish. Top each chop with slice of onion. Drain fat from skillet. To skillet, add molasses, mustard, cloves, water, and mushrooms with liquid, stirring until well blended. Spoon sauce from skillet over meat. Cover with lid or foil. Bake at 350 degrees F. for 1 hour or until tender. The last 15 minutes of cooking, arrange orange slices over meat, spooning liquid in bottom of baking dish over orange slices. Yield: 6 servings.

Pork Chop and Potato Scallop

1 *can condensed Cheddar cheese soup*
½ *cup commercial sour cream*
¼ *cup water*
3 *tablespoons finely chopped parsley*
4 *cups thinly sliced potatoes*
2 *medium onions, sliced*
¾ *cup coarsely chopped green pepper*
Salt and pepper
6 *center-cut pork chops (¾ inch thick)*
¼ *cup flour*
2 *tablespoons vegetable oil*
6 *green pepper rings*
6 *canned crabapples*

Combine undiluted soup, sour cream, water, and parsley. In a 2-quart shallow dish alternate layers of potatoes, onion slices, chopped pepper, and cheese soup mixture. Sprinkle each layer of potatoes with salt and pepper. Place uncovered in a 375-degree F. oven and bake for 30 minutes.

Trim fat from pork chops; roll in flour, and brown in vegetable oil in a skillet. Place drained pork chops atop casserole. Cover and bake for 1 hour. Uncover; place green pepper rings and crabapples on pork chops and cook an additional 20 minutes. Yield: 6 ample servings.

Pork Chop-Rice Casserole

3 *or 4 pork chops*
2 *tablespoons shortening*
1 *cup uncooked rice*
1 *(No. 303) can tomatoes*
1 *onion, sliced*
1 *can beef consommé*
Salt and pepper
1 *teaspoon thyme*

Brown pork chops in small amount of shortening. In a greased 1½-quart casserole, place uncooked rice. Lay cooked pork chops on rice. Add the other ingredients and cook at 350 degrees F. for about 1 hour. Yield: 3 to 4 servings.

Stuffed Pork Chops

2 *thick pork chops*
½ *cup breadcrumbs*
¼ *teaspoon salt*
Dash pepper
1 *teaspoon minced parsley*
⅛ *teaspoon grated onion*
¼ *cup diced apple*
3 *tablespoons milk*

Have butcher cut a pocket on the bone side of each chop. Combine remaining ingredients and mix well. Stuff each chop with this mixture. Place in shallow greased pan and bake at 350 degrees F. about 1 hour or until tender. Yield: 2 servings.

Smoked Pork Chops

Lay single layer of smoked pork chops in shallow pan. Don't overlap. Bake at 350 degrees F. for 25 to 30 minutes.

Chopped Ham
With Mushrooms and Egg

> 1 *(12-ounce) can chopped ham*
> 1 *(4-ounce) can mushroom pieces and stems, drained*
> ¼ *teaspoon onion salt*
> 4 *eggs*
> *Salt and pepper to taste*

Cut ham into strips 1¼ x ¼ inches. Heat ham strips and drained mushrooms in skillet; stir in onion salt. Spread ham mixture evenly over bottom of skillet. Break eggs on top of ham; season with salt and pepper. Cover and cook, without stirring, until eggs are done. Yield: 4 servings.

Ham-Squash-Onion Casserole

> 6 *medium yellow squash*
> ½ *to 1 cup canned ham (cut in cubes)*
> 6 *to 8 small white onions, cooked and drained*
> 4 *hard-cooked eggs, sliced crosswise*
> ½ *cup shredded American cheese*
> ⅓ *cup canned mushrooms, drained*
> 2 *cups medium white sauce*
> ½ *cup breadcrumbs*

Cut stems from squash and slice crosswise in 1-inch slices. Cook in boiling water for 10 minutes or until just tender. Drain slices, being careful not to mash them, and place in bottom of deep casserole dish or deep piepan.
  Place ham cubes over squash and then place drained onions in border around squash and ham. Top ham with eggs. Add cheese and mushrooms to hot white sauce and stir until cheese is melted. Pour sauce over contents of casserole. Sprinkle breadcrumbs over sauce. Bake at 350 degrees F. for 20 minutes.

Ham Casserole

> 1 *cup cracker crumbs*
> ¾ *cup mushroom soup*
> ¼ *cup milk*
> ½ *cup shredded American cheese*
> 1 *cup chopped ham*
> 3 *diced pimientos*
> 2 *hard-cooked eggs, grated*
> *Black pepper*

In a buttered 9-inch baking dish sprinkle ¼-inch layer of cracker crumbs. Follow with layers of ingredients as listed; repeat to fill dish, and top with buttered cracker crumbs. Bake at 375 degrees F. for about 25 minutes or until bubbly and crusty. Yield: about 6 to 8 servings.

Apple-Ham Casserole

> 3 *cups cooked, diced ham*
> 2 *tablespoons prepared mustard*
> 2 *apples, cored and sliced*
> 2 *tablespoons lemon juice*
> ½ *cup brown sugar*
> 1 *teaspoon grated orange rind*
> 2 *tablespoons flour*

Arrange cooked, diced ham in 1½-quart casserole. Spread with mustard. Arrange cored and sliced apples over ham. Sprinkle with lemon juice. Combine brown sugar, orange rind, and flour and sprinkle over ham. Bake at 350 degrees F. for 30 to 35 minutes. Yield: 4 servings.

Ham and Corn Casserole

> ½ *cup diced cooked ham*
> 1 *(8-ounce) can cream-style corn*
> 2 *tablespoons shredded Cheddar cheese*
> 1 *egg, beaten*
> ½ *cup milk*
> ½ *cup cracker crumbs*

Mix all ingredients together. Put in a 1½-quart casserole dish and bake at 325 degrees F. about 45 minutes or until firm. Yield: 2 servings.

Ham and Noodles

    2 *cups diced baked ham*
    4 *hard-cooked eggs, chopped*
    2 *cups cream sauce*
    3 *cups cooked flat noodles*
   ¼ *pound New York cheese, diced*
   ¼ *teaspoon seasoning salt*
    2 *tablespoons margarine*

Mix all ingredients and place in casserole. Bake at 350 degrees F. for 30 minutes.

Plantation Casserole

    2 *cups cooked, chopped ham, chicken, or beef*
 1½ *cups cooked peas, drained*
    1 *(1-pound) can cream-style corn*
   ¼ *pound processed American cheese*
    1 *cup evaporated milk, divided*
   ¼ *cup chopped onion*
    1 *tablespoon Worcestershire sauce*
    1 *cup biscuit mix*
   ½ *cup cornmeal*
    2 *tablespoons sugar*
   ½ *teaspoon salt*
    1 *egg, beaten*

Mix meat, peas, corn, cubed cheese, ⅓ cup evaporated milk, onion, and Worcestershire sauce. Pour into greased 12- x 8-inch baking dish. Bake at 400 degrees F. for 10 minutes or until mixture is bubbly around edges. Combine biscuit mix, cornmeal, sugar, salt, and beaten egg. Add remaining milk and mix well. Pour around edges of hot meat mixture, leaving center uncovered. Bake 20 minutes longer. Yield: 6 servings.

Cheese-Ham Casserole

    2 *tablespoons butter*
 1½ *tablespoons flour*
    1 *cup milk*
    1 *cup shredded American cheese*
    2 *cups cooked macaroni*
   ½ *teaspoon salt*
 1½ *cups cooked, chopped ham*
    2 *tablespoons horseradish*
    2 *teaspoons prepared mustard*

Make white sauce with first three ingredients. Add cheese, macaroni, and salt; mix well. Pour into buttered casserole. Combine remaining ingredients; sprinkle over top of macaroni, pressing into mixture lightly. Bake at 350 degrees F. about 20 minutes.

Country Ham, Yokley Style

Put ham in can of hot water (just below the boiling point). Let boil for 10 or 15 minutes. This step gives the ham a good cleaning and removes excess salt from outside. Remove ham and discard water.

Place ham in can and fill can half full with hot water. Add 4 quarts ginger ale and put top loosely on can. Bring to a full rolling boil and boil for 30 minutes. The ginger ale helps to bring out the flavor of the ham.

At the end of 30 minutes, call for help. No, it's not ready to eat now, but you're ready for the third step. Place about four thicknesses of newspaper on the floor and set ham (still in can) on papers. Press can lid on tightly, pull papers around sides and top of can, and tie with string. Cover with quilts or blankets, or a heavy hunting coat! Let sit for 10 to 14 hours according to size of ham. A 12- to 13-pound ham requires about 10 hours.

Ham will still be slightly warm after uncovering. Remove bone. This is not a big job, but it is easier done if ham is still warm. The aitchbone and knuckle can be wiggled out easily. Slit along top of leg bone from knuckle to knuckle; loosen bone and pull out. The hock bone can be removed the same way.

Remove skin, but do not cut any of fat from ham. After bones have been removed, pack cavity with brown sugar. Tie ham tightly with twine, using enough to hold securely. Score fat lightly.

Place ham in heavy roasting pan with the fat side up. The purpose of the heavy roasting pan is to prevent overcooking of the lean part of the ham. Place pan in preheated 400-degree F. oven and cook for 15 to 20 minutes. Baste often with sweet wine. Do not overcook; the purpose of this step is to make the fat sizzle and get crisp. Remove from oven and cool. Place in refrigerator to cool thoroughly. Have butcher cut it in thin slices. Serve as main dish for a meal or with biscuits for a party.

Miss Nancy's Ham

Remove all skin and fat from outside of a sugar-cured or country ham before baking. Also saw off knuckle bone. If it is a very large ham, or a dry country ham, boil it in a large container for 50 to 60 minutes.

Stick whole cloves and whole allspice in ham to completely cover. Cover with drained crushed pineapple and place ham in a very heavy brown paper bag. Close bag tightly and bake at 300 to 350 degrees F. about 20 minutes per pound. This requires about 3½ to 4 hours for a family-size ham. Reduce baking time if ham has been boiled.

Virginia Ham

The ham should be at least two years old, cured by the old method of smoking over hardwood, such as hickory, with fruit woods for additional fine flavor. Soak it in cold water, overnight, after scrubbing and washing it well. A brush must be used as the ham is often moldy and flecked with wood ashes. Scrub it again after soaking.

Cover with cold water completely and let it simmer slowly, allowing 20 minutes per pound. In the old days the ham was cooked in a wash boiler or a lard can. We have found that an electric roaster set at about 220 degrees does admirably. The ham must cool in the water in which it has cooked.

Remove the ham. Peel off the fat, carefully. (Save the fat to use over the exposed portions after the ham is sliced as this keeps the flavor better and the ham moist when not at the table.)

Brush the ham with a slightly beaten egg to which has been added about 1 tablespoon of cold water. Sprinkle it with about 2 cups fine breadcrumbs, moistened lightly with sherry and flavored with brown sugar.

Put in a 425-degree F. oven and let it remain there until the crumbs brown. The ham must be completely cold before it is sliced. Slice paper thin and serve as desired.

Ham With Red Gravy

    4 *slices Smithfield country-cured ham*
       (½ inch thick)
 1½ *cups boiling water*

Soak ham slices in cold water at least 6 hours (it is very salty). Dry on paper toweling. Remove hard black rind. Put slice into ungreased heavy skillet at fairly high heat. Fry each side 5 to 7 minutes to a good brown, but do not burn.

Remove slices to platter, pour off all but 3 tablespoons of fat. Put pan back on stove so it is smoking hot. Add boiling water. Let boil up and be sure to scrape all "fry" from the bottom to blend into the gravy. Pour over the ham slices and serve with grits.

Creamed Ham and Sweetbreads With Ripe Olives

    6 *pairs sweetbreads*
      Juice of 4 lemons
    3 *pounds cooked, diced ham*
    6 *cups sliced ripe olives*
 1½ *cups melted butter*
 1½ *cups flour*
    4 *quarts light cream*
    3 *tablespoons salt*
 10 *peppercorns, crushed*
    3 *tablespoons Worcestershire sauce*

Soak sweetbreads in salted water for 1 hour. Cook 20 minutes in salted water with the juice of 4 lemons added. Remove sweetbreads and plunge into ice water; leave until cold. Remove from ice water and remove tubing and membrane. Cut sweetbreads into small pieces and mix with diced ham and sliced olives.

Melt butter; stir in flour and mix well. Add cream and put in top of double boiler. Add seasonings, then sweetbread mixture. Heat thoroughly.

Ham in Aluminum Foil

Place ham lengthwise on a long sheet of heavy aluminum foil. Pad bone ends with a fold of foil. Bring foil from both ends up over ham, overlapping 3 to 4 inches. Press foil down along sides of ham, then mold bottom foil up along sides, letting it extend up to hold juices. No need to seal. Place in shallow pan and bake at 400 degrees F. If it's a "cook-before-eating" type, allow 16 minutes per pound if whole; 18 minutes per pound if half. Bake fully cooked ham for 1¾ hours if whole; 1 hour if half.

Remove from oven, open wrap, lift out ham. Pour fat from foil, then smooth foil to form liner for pan. Remove rind from ham; return ham to lined pan. Score fat and stud with whole cloves. Spread with mixture of 1 cup brown sugar, 1 teaspoon dry mustard, and 3 tablespoons fruit juice. Decorate with pineapple slices and return to oven 15 minutes to brown.

Ham Loaf and Gravy

 ½ *cup firmly packed brown sugar*
 1 *flat can sliced pineapple*
 6 *whole maraschino cherries, drained*
 1 *pound ham, ground*
 ½ *pound fresh pork, ground*
 1 *cup fine soft breadcrumbs*
 1 *egg, unbeaten*
 1 *cup milk*
 ¼ *cup minced onion*
 ¼ *cup minced celery*
 ½ *teaspoon salt*
 ¼ *teaspoon pepper*
  Juice from pineapple, meat liquor, and water to make 1 cup
 ⅛ *teaspoon bottled brown seasoning sauce*
 1 *cup water*
 3 *tablespoons all-purpose flour*

Spread brown sugar in bottom of greased 9½- x 5¼- x 2¾-inch pan. Remove and drain 2 slices of pineapple (reserving remainder for making gravy); cut the two pineapple slices in 3 pieces. Arrange pineapple and cherries on brown sugar so some of each can be served with each serving of meat.

Mix ham, pork, breadcrumbs, egg, milk, onion, celery, salt, and pepper. Pack meat mixture firmly in loafpan over pineapple and cherries. Bake at 400 degrees F. for 1 hour. Remove from oven; pour juice from pan and reserve for gravy. Invert ham loaf onto serving platter and keep warm while making gravy.

Put pineapple juice, meat liquor, water, seasoning sauce, and remainder of pineapple, diced, into 1-quart saucepan. Shake water and flour vigorously in covered jar until thoroughly blended. Add to liquid in saucepan. Bring to boil over high heat, stirring constantly. Switch to a low heat and boil 1 minute. Yield: 6 servings.

Ham Loaf

 10 *pounds ground smoked ham*
 6 *pounds ground veal*
 1½ *cups chopped onion*
 1½ *cups minced green pepper*
 4 *teaspoons salt*
 1 *teaspoon pepper*
 16 *eggs, beaten*
 2 *quarts canned tomato soup*
 2 *quarts breadcrumbs*

Mix all ingredients and shape into loaves. Bake at 350 degrees F. for 1½ hours. Let cool. Slice with a very sharp knife. Yield: 100 servings.

Red Ham Loaf

 1½ *pounds ground ham*
 1 *pound ground pork shoulder*
 ⅛ *teaspoon black pepper*
 2 *eggs*
 ½ *cup canned tomatoes*
 ⅔ *cup milk*
 ⅔ *cup cracker crumbs*
  Salt to taste
 1 *cup brown sugar*
 2 *teaspoons powdered mustard*
 ⅓ *cup vinegar*
 ½ *cup water*

Mix ham, pork, pepper, eggs, tomatoes, milk, cracker crumbs, and salt. Shape into a loaf and place in loaf baking pan. Make basting sauce by combining brown sugar, mustard, vinegar, and water. Bring to a boil and boil for 2 minutes. Baste with this sauce every 15 minutes until done. Bake at 350 degrees F. for 1 hour. Yield: 6 to 8 servings.

Candied Ham Loaf

      2 *cups whole wheat breadcrumbs*
      1 *cup milk*
      2 *eggs, slightly beaten*
      2 *pounds ground ham*
      1 *pound ground beef*
      1 *teaspoon dry mustard*
    ½ *teaspoon salt*
    ½ *cup brown sugar*
    ½ *teaspoon ground cloves*

Soak breadcrumbs in milk; add eggs. Combine ham, beef, mustard, and salt; add to crumb mixture and mix well.

Combine brown sugar and cloves; spread in bottom of 9- x 5-inch loafpan. Pack meat mixture in pan. Bake at 350 degrees F. for 1½ hours. Yield: 6 servings.

Harlequin Ham-Cheese Loaf

      1 *pound boiled ham, thinly sliced*
    ½ *cup catsup*
      2 *tablespoons prepared mustard*
      1 *pound American cheese, shredded*

In a baking dish or breadpan place a slice of ham. Mix catsup and mustard. Spread thinly on ham slice. Sprinkle with shredded cheese. Add another slice of ham, spread with cat-sup-mustard mixture and sprinkle with cheese. Repeat and build up loaf, pressing firmly as each slice of ham is added until all ham, cheese, and sauce are used. Insert toothpick in each corner of loaf to keep it in shape. Bake at 350 degrees F. for 30 minutes. Remove from oven and chill the

loaf for about 4 hours. Serve in ¼-inch slices. Yield: 4 to 6 servings.

Ham Loaf Supreme

      1 *pound ground smoked ham*
      1 *pound ground lean pork*
      2 *eggs*
    ¾ *cup round buttery cracker crumbs*
    ¾ *cup milk*
         Salt to taste
         Pepper (optional)

Mix all ingredients and bake in a loafpan at 325 degrees F. until done (about 1½ to 2 hours). Yield: 6 servings.

Relish-Glazed Ham

      1 *(4-pound) canned ham*
         Whole cloves
    ¾ *cup brown sugar, firmly packed*
      1 *tablespoon prepared mustard*
      3 *tablespoons pickle relish*

Score ham and stud with cloves; put on rack in a shallow baking pan. Mix brown sugar, mustard, and pickle relish. Spread over top and sides of ham. Heat in a slow oven (325 degrees F.) 20 minutes per pound, about 1 hour and 20 minutes. Baste with glaze once or twice during heating. Yield: 12 to 16 servings.

Upside-Down Ham Loaf

    1½ *pounds ground ham*
      1 *pound ground pork*
    1½ *cups milk*
    ⅛ *teaspoon pepper*
      2 *eggs, beaten*
      1 *cup breadcrumbs*
         Sliced pineapple rings

Combine all ingredients except pineapple, and mix thoroughly. Arrange pineapple rings in well-greased loafpan. Spoon ham mixture over pineapple, and bake at 350 degrees F. for 1½ hours. Yield: 6 servings.

Deluxe Raisin-Ham Mousse

  1 *envelope unflavored gelatin*
1¼ *cups water*
1½ *teaspoons prepared mustard*
  ¼ *teaspoon salt*
  1 *cup dark or golden raisins*
  1 *teaspoon prepared horseradish*
  ¾ *cup whipping cream, whipped*
  ⅓ *cup mayonnaise*
  3 *cups ground cooked ham*
  1 *cup finely chopped celery*
    Pineapple slices
    Canned jellied cranberry sauce

Sprinkle gelatin on ½ cup of the water to soften. Place over low heat and stir until gelatin is dissolved. Remove from heat and stir in remaining ¾ cup water, mustard, and salt. Chill to consistency of unbeaten egg white. Meanwhile, cover raisins with water and boil 5 minutes. Drain and cool. Fold into gelatin mixture with horseradish, whipped cream, mayonnaise, ham, and celery. Turn into 8½- x 4½- x 2½-inch loafpan with waxed paper in the bottom. Chill until firm. Loosen edges with spatula and turn out onto serving plate. Garnish with pineapple rings and slices of jellied cranberry sauce. Yield: 8 to 10 servings.

Ham Pie

  3 *tablespoons chopped onion*
  ¼ *cup chopped green pepper*
  ¼ *cup shortening*
  6 *tablespoons flour*
  2 *cups milk*
  1 *can cream of chicken soup*
  2 *cups diced ham*
  1 *tablespoon lemon juice*
    Cheese Biscuits

Cook onions and peppers in hot shortening until brown; add flour, milk, and soup. Place diced ham in a 1½-quart casserole; add lemon juice. Pour creamed mixture over ham. Place Cheese Biscuits over top. Bake at 375 degrees F. for 30 minutes or until done. Yield: 4 servings.

Cheese Biscuits:

  1 *cup flour*
1½ *teaspoons baking powder*
  ½ *teaspoon salt*
  ½ *teaspoon shortening*
  ¾ *cup shredded cheese*
  1 *pimiento, chopped*
  ⅓ *cup milk*

Mix dry ingredients; cut in shortening and cheese. Add pimiento and milk and mix well. Roll dough and cut into small biscuits.

Ham Mousse Pie

  1 *cup sifted all-purpose flour*
  ¼ *teaspoon salt*
  ⅓ *cup shortening*
  ⅓ *cup finely crushed potato chips*
2½ *to 3 tablespoons cold water*
  1 *envelope unflavored gelatin*
  ¼ *cup cold chicken broth*
1¼ *cups hot chicken broth*
  2 *tablespoons vinegar*
  2 *teaspoons grated onion*
    Dash of pepper
1½ *cups ground cooked ham*
  ¼ *cup finely chopped celery*
  2 *tablespoons chopped green pepper*
  2 *hard-cooked eggs, chopped*
  1 *teaspoon dry mustard*
  ½ *cup heavy cream*
    Sliced stuffed olives, parsley (optional)

Sift flour and salt into a bowl; cut in shortening until mixture is the size of small peas. Stir in crushed potato chips. Add water slowly, stirring with a fork until dough forms a ball. Roll out ⅛ inch thick to a 12-inch circle; fit into a 9-inch piepan; flute edge; prick well. Bake at 425 degrees F. for 10 to 12 minutes or until golden. Cool.

Soak gelatin in cold chicken broth; dissolve in hot chicken broth. Add vinegar, onion, and pepper; mix well. Stir in ham, celery, green pepper, and eggs; chill until mixture begins to set. Combine mustard and cream; beat until stiff; fold into ham mixture and turn into cooled pie shell. Chill 2 hours or until firm. Garnish with sliced stuffed olives and parsley. Yield: 6 servings.

Ham and Apple Scallop

3 *cups diced, cooked ham*
4 *medium apples, peeled and sliced*
¼ *cup firmly packed brown sugar*
¼ *teaspoon ground nutmeg*
¼ *teaspoon black pepper*
¼ *cup apple juice or water*
1 *cup pancake mix*
1 *cup milk*
2 *tablespoons melted butter*

Make a layer of half the ham and apples in an 8-cup baking dish. Combine sugar, nutmeg, and pepper and sprinkle over layer. Repeat with remaining ham, apples, and sugar mixture. Pour apple juice or water over the mixture. Cover dish and bake at 350 degrees F. for 40 minutes or until apples are tender. Blend pancake mix, milk, and melted butter to make a batter. Pour over hot ham-apple mixture. Bake uncovered 20 minutes longer or until topping is puffed and golden. Yield: 6 servings.

Ham and Cheese Scramble

1 *cup cubed cooked ham*
1 *tablespoon chopped green onion*
3 *tablespoons butter or margarine*
1 *cup cream-style cottage cheese*
6 *eggs*
Dash pepper
1 *cup canned shoestring potatoes*

In medium skillet, cook ham and green onion in butter or margarine until lightly browned. Drain cottage cheese, reserving liquid. Add liquid to eggs with a dash of pepper; beat until blended. Pour egg mixture into skillet with ham and onions. Begin cooking over low heat. When mixture begins to set at bottom and sides, lift cooked portions with a wide spatula so uncooked portion goes to the bottom of the skillet. Continue cooking 5 to 8 minutes or until eggs

are cooked throughout, but are still glossy and moist. Fold in cottage cheese and remove from skillet immediately. Spoon onto shoestring potatoes. Yield: 4 servings.

Spicy Ham Roll-Ups

1 *cup cottage cheese*
1 *tablespoon dehydrated onion soup mix*
1 *tablespoon bottled mustard sauce*
1 *tablespoon finely chopped parsley*
½ *pound thinly sliced boiled ham (about 8 slices)*
Parsley sprigs

Combine all ingredients except ham and parsley. Cut each slice of ham in half crosswise. Spread some of cheese mixture on each ham slice. Roll up each slice tightly; secure with toothpick. Garnish roll-ups with a parsley sprig. Refrigerate until served. Yield: 8 servings.

Ham and Shrimp

¼ *cup (½ stick) butter*
¼ *cup chopped onion*
¼ *cup chopped celery*
¼ *cup all-purpose flour*
½ *teaspoon salt*
⅛ *teaspoon pepper*
2 *cups milk*
1 *(4-ounce) can sliced mushrooms, drained*
1½ *cups diced, cooked ham*
2 *(5-ounce) cans shrimp, drained and deveined*
Rice ring

Melt butter in saucepan; add onion and celery, and heat until transparent. Do not brown. Combine flour, salt, and pepper. Blend into butter. Add milk, stirring constantly. Stir until sauce is smooth and thickened. Blend mushrooms, ham, and shrimp into sauce. Cook, stirring gently, until ham and shrimp are heated. Place in center of a rice ring. Yield: 6 servings.

Ham Steak

1½ -pound ham steak (¾ inch
        thick)
½ teaspoon dry mustard
1 cup cooking sherry
1 (16-ounce) can whole-berry
        cranberry sauce
¼ cup granulated brown sugar

Put ham in shallow baking dish and dust
with mustard. Mix sherry, whole cranberry
sauce, and sugar, and spread over meat.
Bake uncovered at 350 degrees F. for 1 hour.
Yield: 4 servings.

Ham With Sweet Potatoes

1½ pounds sliced ham or shoulder
3 cups raw sliced sweet potatoes
2 tablespoons sugar
1 cup hot water
1 tablespoon drippings or other fat

Cut the ham or shoulder into pieces for serving. If the meat is very salty, parboil it in
water and drain. Brown the meat lightly on
both sides and arrange the pieces to cover
the bottom of a 2-quart baking dish. Spread
the sliced sweet potatoes over the meat and
sprinkle with sugar. Add the hot water to
the drippings in the frypan and pour over the
sweet potatoes and meat. Cover and bake at
325 degrees F. until the meat and sweet potatoes are tender, basting the potatoes occasionally with the gravy. Toward the last,
remove the lid and let the top brown well.
Yield: 5 or 6 servings.

Country-Style Ribs

1 (3-pound) side of spareribs
1 cup catsup
⅓ cup cider vinegar
2 tablespoons dark corn syrup
1 envelope golden onion soup mix
1 clove garlic, minced
⅛ teaspoon chili powder
Dash pepper
1¼ cups hot water

Set meat in one piece in a shallow baking
pan or broiler pan without rack. Roast in
450-degree oven for 30 minutes. Reset oven
temperature control at 350 degrees. Continue cooking ribs 30 minutes longer.
Meanwhile, combine catsup, vinegar, corn
syrup, soup mix, garlic, chili powder, and
pepper in quart jar. Add hot water; cover
and shake well. Remove meat from oven and
drain off fat. Pour sauce over ribs. Bake,
basting occasionally, until ribs are tender
and browned and sauce is thickened, about
35 minutes. (Do not let sauce become too
brown.) Yield: 4 to 6 servings.

Pork Loin Roast With Yam-Stuffed Apples

1 pork loin roast (about 6 pounds)
Salt, pepper, and sage (optional)
6 to 8 large tart baking apples
1 large can sweet potatoes
¼ cup brown sugar
1 teaspoon salt
¼ teaspoon cinnamon
½ cup slivered almonds
¼ cup melted butter
¼ cup maple syrup

Rub pork with ½ teaspoon salt per pound.
Sprinkle with pepper and sage. Place roast,
fat side up, on rack in an open pan. Do not
add water. Roast uncovered at 300 degrees
F. for 4 to 4½ hours or until well done.

Wash and core apples. Remove enough
pulp to make core opening about 1¼ inches
wide. Mash sweet potatoes, combine with
apple pulp, brown sugar, salt, cinnamon,
and one-half of the almonds. Blend butter
and syrup in saucepan and spoon a little of
the syrup mixture into apple cavities. Fill
cavities with sweet potato mixture; mound a
spoonful on top of each apple. Stud stuffing
with remaining almonds. Place apples
around roast or in separate dish the last 1½
hours of baking time. Baste apples occasionally with remaining syrup. When
roast is done, arrange apples and roast on
heated serving platter. Garnish with greens.

Pork Polynesian

    3½ pounds fresh pork loin
        Salt and pepper
    ¼   cup water
    ¼   teaspoon ground nutmeg
    ½   teaspoon ground cinnamon
    1   cup crushed pineapple
    2   (No. 303) cans sweet potatoes,
            drained
    1   tablespoon butter
    6   slices canned pineapple, cut in halves

Rub pork loin with salt and pepper; place pork, with fat side up, in a shallow rectangular glass baking dish. Pour water in dish and bake at 300 degrees F. for 1 hour and 45 minutes.

Combine spices and crushed pineapple with the drained sweet potatoes. The last 45 minutes of baking time for the roast, arrange the sweet potatoes around roast and spoon pineapple and spices over; dot with butter. Garnish with halved pineapple slices. Yield: 4 servings.

Oriental Ribs

    3   pounds lean pork ribs
        Salt and pepper
    1   (7¾-ounce) jar strained peaches
            (Junior babyfood)
    ⅓   cup catsup
    ⅓   cup vinegar
    2   tablespoons soy sauce
        Dash pepper sauce
    ½   cup brown sugar
    2   teaspoons ground ginger
    1   teaspoon salt
        Dash coarse ground black pepper

Rub ribs on both sides with salt and pepper. Place meat side up in foil-lined shallow pan and bake at 400 degrees F. for 45 minutes.

Combine other ingredients to make sauce. At the end of the 45-minute baking period, spoon off excess fat and cover ribs with half the sauce. Lower temperature to 325 degrees F. and bake for 1¾ hours, spooning additional sauce on ribs from time to time until all sauce has been used. Cut ribs into serving-size pieces. Yield: 4 servings.

Baked Spareribs Aloha

    3   pounds (2 strips) lean spareribs
        Salt and pepper to taste
    ½   cup diced onion
    ¼   cup diced green pepper
    2   (8-ounce) cans tomato sauce
    1   tablespoon Worcestershire sauce
    ⅓   cup cider or wine vinegar
    1   small can pineapple tidbits
    ¼   cup brown sugar
    ½   teaspoon dry mustard

Sprinkle spareribs with salt and pepper and place in shallow pan. Bake at 350 degrees F. for 1 hour and 15 minutes. Drain off all excess fat. While ribs are baking, mix remaining ingredients and let stand to blend flavors. Pour over ribs after they have been drained and bake an additional 45 to 50 minutes, basting frequently. Yield: 4 servings.

Easy Sausage Casserole

    24 small sausage links (about 2 pounds)
    2   tablespoons drippings
    2   tablespoons flour
    1   cup milk
    1   large can hominy, drained
        Salt and pepper to taste
    ½   teaspoon marjoram
    ½   cup chopped celery
        Paprika

Fry sausage links until deep golden brown. Remove; drain all but 2 tablespoons drippings from skillet. To this add flour and stir well. Add milk and liquid from the can of hominy and make a gravy. Add the hominy, salt, pepper, marjoram, celery, and sausage. Mix and pour into a 3-quart casserole; sprinkle with paprika. Cover and bake at 400 degrees F. about 10 minutes. Yield: 4 to 6 servings.

Chorizo Mexicano

1 *pound lean pork*
1 *or 2 cloves garlic*
1 *teaspoon oregano*
4 *chili anchos (seeds removed) or 1¾*
  to 2 tablespoons chili powder
⅛ *to ¼ teaspoon salt*
1 *tablespoon vinegar*

Grind together lean pork, garlic, oregano, and chiles. Add salt and vinegar. Place mixture in a covered nonmetallic container and store in a cool place for 2 or 3 days to allow flavors to blend. Fry as you would other sausage. Yield: 1 pound.

Sausage Links in Spiced Apple Rings

Small sausage links
Canned spiced apple rings

The amount you buy will have to be left up to the hostess, but you might allow 3 to 4 apple-sausages per person—depending on how hearty your guests eat. Pan-fry small sausages or oven-fry. Pour grease off and blot on paper towels. Put one sausage through the hole in center of apple rings.

Sausage Scramble

1 *pound bulk sausage*
3 *tablespoons butter*
2 *tablespoons flour*
½ *cup chopped onion*
2 *cups boiled, diced potatoes*
1¼ *cups milk*

Put sausage in heavy skillet and brown. Break up with fork while cooking. Drain off all fat. Add butter and blend in flour. Add onions and potatoes. Cook slowly for 10 minutes. Add milk and continue cooking for 5 minutes, or until mixture thickens, stirring constantly. Yield: 6 servings.

Tagliarini

1 *pound country sausage*
1 *pound lean ground beef*
1 *large green pepper, chopped*
1 *(No. 2) can tomatoes*
2 *(12-ounce) cans niblet corn*
1 *jar pimientos, chopped*
1 *(13½-ounce) can mushrooms (stems*
  and pieces)
1 *jar stuffed olives, sliced*
1 *cup catsup*
1 *teaspoon chili powder*
1 *teaspoon oregano*
Salt, pepper, and paprika to taste
½ *cup sherry*
1½ *packages (or 1 large and 1 small)*
  wide noodles
Slices of sharp cheese
Mozzarella cheese

Cook sausage and beef in a large skillet until done. Add green pepper and cook until pepper is partially done. Add other ingredients (except noodles and cheese) and bring to a boil. Cook noodles (not lasagna noodles) according to package directions. Drain and add to meat mixture. Stir well and put into fairly shallow baking dishes or the broiler pan. Cover with slices of sharp cheese and sprinkle with shredded mozzarella, if desired. Bake at 325 degrees F. about 20 minutes or until cheese is melted. Yield: 20 to 25 servings.

This may be placed in smaller baking dishes and frozen. Omit cheese until time to heat for serving.

Zesty Kabobs

2 *pounds lean, boneless pork shoulder*
3 *medium green peppers*
12 *small white onions*
Marinade for Kabobs
6 *to 8 large mushroom caps*
6 *to 8 firm tomato wedges*
6 *to 8 chunks (1-inch wide) peeled*
  summer squash
Salt

Cut meat into 12 large cubes. Place in saucepan and cover with salted water. Cover saucepan and bring to a boil. Reduce heat and simmer 15 minutes. Meanwhile, cut green peppers lengthwise in half, then crosswise in quarters. Remove cores and seed. Add green pepper quarters and onions to meat in saucepan and simmer 5 minutes. Drain.

Place meat in marinade. Let stand 1 hour. Drain, reserving marinade. Alternate meat, green pepper, and onions on 4 long skewers (about 12 inches each). Arrange mushrooms, tomatoes, and squash *separately* on 3 additional skewers. Sprinkle each kabob with salt. Place on a cookie sheet. Measure 1½ cups marinade, set aside, and keep warm. Liberally brush kabobs with half of the unmeasured marinade. Place kabobs 4 to 5 inches from heat and grill meat, green pepper, and onions about 20 minutes, or until tender; mushrooms 5 to 10 minutes, or until lightly browned; tomatoes 3 minutes, or until tender; and squash 10 minutes, or until tender. Turn and brush kabobs with remaining unmeasured marinade during cooking. Yield: 7 servings.

Marinade for Kabobs:

1½ *cups minced onion*
⅔ *cup oil*
3 *cups all-purpose barbecue sauce*
⅔ *cup red wine*
⅔ *cup minced parsley*

Sauté onion in oil until tender, but not browned. Add remaining ingredients and mix well. Bring to a boil over medium heat. Then reduce heat and simmer gently about 5 minutes to blend flavors, stirring occasionally. Yield: 5 cups sauce, or enough for 7 or 8 kabobs (about 12 inches each).

Glorified Pork Suey

1½ *pounds pork shoulder*
2 *tablespoons fat*
½ *cup chopped celery leaves*
¼ *cup soy sauce*
2 *teaspoons sugar*
1 *cup water*
1 *package frozen green beans, thawed*
1 *cup sliced celery*
2 *tablespoons sherry (optional)*
Salt and pepper
Hot cooked rice

Cut pork into 1-inch cubes. Brown in hot fat; drain off any excess fat. Add celery leaves, soy sauce, sugar, and water. Cover and cook over low heat until the meat is almost tender, about 1½ hours. Add green beans and celery and cook until beans are tender, adding more water if necessary. Add sherry and season with salt and pepper. Serve over hot rice. Yield: 4 to 6 servings.

Roast Pork With Apples and Potatoes

3-pound boned pork loin
2 *to 3 teaspoons salt*
½ *teaspoon pepper*
½ *teaspoon thyme*
½ *teaspoon rosemary*
Pinch ground allspice
½ *clove garlic, mashed*
4 *to 8 rather small potatoes*
2 *tart apples*

Remove most of fat from roast. Combine salt and spices and rub over surface of roast. Cover and refrigerate 12 hours before roasting. Wipe off seasonings. Roll and tie roast. Bake at 325 degrees F. about 35 to 40 minutes per pound, or until meat thermometer registers 185 degrees F. Add a small amount of hot water to pan juices and baste often.

Peel potatoes and slice lengthwise; add to roast when roast is about half-cooked. Fifteen minutes later, add the apples which have been peeled and quartered. Skim fat from pan juices; serve juices with roast. Yield: 8 servings.

Pork and Sweet Potato Pie

2 *cups cubed cooked pork*
1 *cup sliced tart apples*
1 *cup cooked peas*
Salt and pepper
1½ *cups gravy or brown sauce*
5 *medium-size cooked sweet potatoes*
2 *tablespoons butter or margarine*
¼ *teaspoon ground cinnamon*

Place pork in 2-quart casserole. Add apples and peas. Season. Add hot gravy. Top with sliced potatoes. Dot with butter and sprinkle with cinnamon. Bake at 350 degrees F. about 45 minutes. Yield: 5 servings.

Sloppy Joe

Ground pork
Salt and pepper
Hamburger buns
Sauce

Add salt and pepper to the ground pork and make into hamburger-size patties. Brown and cook almost done. Cool, wrap in heavy foil, and place in freezer. Defrost, heat slowly until well done, and serve on slightly toasted buns with a sauce concocted of the following ingredients combined to taste: chopped onion, green pepper, celery, chili sauce, garlic, and onion salt.

Pineapple Porkettes

8 *slices canned pineapple*
1 *pound ground pork*
1 *egg, beaten*
Salt and pepper
3 *cups cooked mashed sweet potatoes*
16 *thin slices bacon*

With a sharp knife, split each slice of pineapple into 2 thin slices. Mix the pork with the beaten egg and form into 8 round patties the size of the pineapple slices. Season the sweet potatoes and shape into similar patties. On a thin slice of pineapple place a pork patty, a potato patty on top of the pork, and top with thin slice of pineapple.

Wrap 2 slices of bacon around each patty, crisscross fashion, fastening in place with toothpicks. Place in a baking pan, and bake at 350 degrees F. for 1¼ hours. Yield: 6 to 8 servings.

Barbecued Lamb Shanks

4 *lamb shanks*
2 *tablespoons shortening*
1 *cup sliced onion*
1 *cup catsup*
1 *cup water*
2 *teaspoons salt*
2 *tablespoons Worcestershire sauce*
½ *cup vinegar*
¼ *cup brown sugar*
2 *teaspoons dry mustard*

Brown lamb shanks in shortening in heavy skillet. Combine remaining ingredients and pour over lamb shanks. Then cover and bake at 350 degrees F. or simmer on top of range for 1 hour and 45 minutes or until tender.

Baste sauce over shanks two or three times during cooking period. Uncover and continue cooking for 15 minutes. Serve hot. Yield: 4 servings.

Casserole of Rice and Lamb

2 *cups cooked rice*
2 *cups chopped cooked lamb*
½ *teaspoon salt*
1 *egg, slightly beaten*
⅛ *teaspoon celery salt*
⅛ *teaspoon paprika*
1 *cup breadcrumbs*
Butter
Milk to moisten

Line loafpan or 1½-quart casserole dish with cooked rice. To the lamb add seasonings, egg, crumbs, and milk; pack into the pan. Cover the meat with rice. Place bits of butter over top of dish. Place cover on dish, and place dish in pan of water. Bake at 325 degrees F. for 45 minutes.

Curried Lamb

2 -pound shoulder of lamb
3 tablespoons flour
3 tablespoons shortening
1 small onion, sliced
1 teaspoon curry powder
1 teaspoon lemon juice
½ cup boiling water
½ cup tomato juice
1 teaspoon salt
Cooked rice

Cut lamb in 1-inch cubes. Dredge with flour and brown in shortening in a heavy Dutch oven. Add all other ingredients except the rice and simmer slowly until the meat is tender. Serve over hot, cooked rice. Yield: 6 servings.

Lamb Chops, Durban

⅔ cup tomato sauce
⅔ cup vinegar
½ cup Worcestershire sauce
1 onion, grated
1 teaspoon dry mustard
1 teaspoon salt
12 lamb chops

Combine the tomato sauce, vinegar, Worcestershire sauce, onion, mustard, and salt in a bowl. Mix well. Marinate the chops at room temperature for 1 hour. Drain. Take the sauce and put in a saucepan. Meanwhile, pan-fry the chops, turning them over and over until well done. Now heat the sauce until hot. Pour over the lamb chops and serve hot. Yield: 6 servings.

Loin Lamb Chop Grill

4 loin lamb chops
8 link sausages
2 cups cooked peas
4 bananas
4 pineapple spears
4 bacon slices

Have loin lamb chops cut ¾ to 1 inch thick. Using broil setting, let oven preheat thoroughly. Place cooked peas in bottom of broiler pan. Put chops on rack and broil. When chops are browned on one side, turn them, and add to grill little link sausages and bananas which have been split in half lengthwise, a pineapple spear inserted in each, and a slice of bacon wrapped over the outside. Turn sausages and banana rolls once so that they will be evenly cooked. By the time the chops are browned on the second side, the bacon should be cooked, the sausages done, and the peas heated through. This requires from 10 to 12 minutes. Yield: 4 to 6 servings.

Parsley Lamb Patties

1 pound ground lamb
1 teaspoon salt
¼ teaspoon pepper
½ cup chopped parsley
1 teaspoon ground allspice

Combine ingredients, form into patties, and pan-fry or broil. Yield: 4 to 6 servings.

Savory Lamb Shanks

4 small lamb shanks
3 tablespoons shortening
1 cup meat stock or water
2 teaspoons Worcestershire sauce
1½ teaspoons horseradish
1 tablespoon vinegar
½ teaspoon salt
Few grains of pepper

Roll lamb shanks in flour and brown in hot fat in a skillet. Remove to a large casserole. Stir 1 tablespoon flour into remaining fat in skillet, add 1 cup of water gradually, and stir until thickened. Add horseradish, Worcestershire sauce, vinegar, salt, and pepper. Pour over lamb shanks and cover casserole. Bake at 325 degrees F. for about 2 hours or until tender. Yield: 4 servings.

Lamb Shish Kabobs
With Wine Marinade

    4 -pound lamb shoulder, boned
    2 *teaspoons seasoned meat tenderizer*
    ½ *cup salad oil*
    ⅓ *cup lemon juice*
    1 *tablespoon tarragon vinegar*
    1 *clove garlic, minced or crushed*
    ½ *teaspoon crushed mint leaves*
    ¼ *teaspoon thyme*
    ½ *cup dry white wine*
    ¼ *cup honey*
    1 *cup tomato sauce*
    1 *tablespoon brown sugar*
    ⅛ *teaspoon Tabasco sauce*
    1 *(3-ounce) can mushroom stems and*
        pieces

Cut lamb in 1½-inch cubes. Trim off excess fat, and sprinkle cubes with seasoned meat tenderizer (do not add additional salt). Leave meat at room temperature for 30 to 40 minutes.

Combine salad oil, lemon juice, vinegar, garlic, mint, thyme, wine, and honey. Mix well; then place in bowl that can be covered. At the end of 30 to 40 minutes, add meat to marinade, stirring well so that each cube is well coated with marinade. Cover bowl and place in refrigerator overnight.

At cooking time, drain meat, saving marinade. Put meat cubes on skewers. Pour marinade into saucepan and add tomato sauce, brown sugar, Tabasco, and mushrooms. Simmer this mixture while meat cooks and serve as a sauce over the shish kabobs. Yield: about 8 servings.

Boned Shoulder of Lamb

    Shoulder of lamb
    2 *cloves garlic*
    1 *teaspoon rosemary*
    2 *teaspoons salt*
    6 *peppercorns, crushed*
    ½ *glass Burgundy*

Have your butcher bone and roll a shoulder of lamb. Insert cloves of garlic in meat.

Roast at 450 degrees F. until brown on all sides. After browning, add rosemary, salt, peppercorns, and Burgundy. Reduce heat to medium and cook 2 hours longer. Refrigerate overnight and serve the next day.

Flavorful Lamb Roast

    6- to 7-pound leg of lamb
    Flour
    Seasoned salt
    Pepper
    1 *medium onion, sliced*
    ¼ *teaspoon rosemary*
    1 *(8-ounch) can tomato sauce*

Rub lamb well with flour. Sprinkle with salt and pepper. Place roast in pan with onion and rosemary around meat. Roast, uncovered, at 325 degrees F. allowing 30 minutes per pound. During the last 45 minutes, baste with tomato sauce. Yield: 4 servings.

Crown Lamb Roast
With Potato Dressing

    Crown of lamb
    Salt pork or bacon strips
    4 *slices bacon, diced*
    1 *tablespoon chopped onion*
    4 *cups bread cubes*
    1 *teaspoon chopped parsley*
    1 *teaspoon salt*
    ⅛ *teaspoon ground ginger*
    ¼ *teaspoon ground poultry seasoning*
    ⅛ *teaspoon pepper*
    1 *egg, beaten*
    2 *cups mashed potatoes*

Two or more rib sections are shaped into a crown. Allow two or three ribs per serving. Have crown of lamb prepared at your market. Season with salt and pepper. Wrap rib ends with salt pork or bacon to prevent charring of bone ends. Place crown right side up in an open roasting pan.

To make the dressing, brown the bacon

and the onion and the cubed bread, then add seasonings and mix well. Combine with the beaten egg and the mashed potatoes. Add enough water for desirable moisture, then use to fill center of lamb crown.

Place the roast on a rack in an open pan and into a slow oven (300 degrees F.). A lamb crown requires 30 to 35 minutes per pound for roasting. A meat thermometer, if used, will register 170 degrees F. when the roast is done.

To serve: Remove crown from pan to hot platter. Cover rib ends with small glazed white onions, large ripe or green olives with stuffing removed, butter-browned mushrooms, small potatoes, or just paper frills. This festive roast needs little more than a few sprigs of parsley to garnish it on the platter.

The Crown Roast is especially good served with butter-topped broccoli, a plate of crisp relishes, hot rolls, and beverage. Crown Roast should be served hot.

Save-Your-Marriage Supper

    1 *large baking potato*
    2 *lamb shoulder chops*
    2 *large or 4 small carrots*
    1 *medium onion, sliced*
    1 *medium green pepper, quartered*
    Salt and pepper to taste

Cut two pieces of foil (about 12 x 18 inches). Split potato in half and put in center of foil. Place chop on top, stack with other vegetables, and add salt and pepper. Fold foil, sealing packages tightly. Bake at 400 degrees F. for 1½ hours. Yield: 2 servings.

Lamb Supreme

    2 *pounds boneless lamb shoulder, cut in cubes*
    2 *tablespoons shortening*
    Water to cover
    ½ *teaspoon salt*
    ½ *teaspoon dill seed*
    ½ *cup fresh or canned mushrooms*
    1 *cup commercial sour cream*
    ½ *teaspoon vinegar*
    Flour

Brown meat in shortening. Cover with water. Season with salt and add dill seed. Cover and simmer 1½ hours or until tender. Remove meat. Add mushrooms, sour cream, and vinegar to liquid remaining in pan. Thicken with flour to gravy consistency. Add meat to gravy. Yield: 6 servings.

Creamed Chipped Dried Beef

    1 *small jar dried beef*
    1 *tablespoon flour*
    1 *tablespoon butter or margarine*
  1½ *cups milk*
    4 *or 6 well-buttered toasted slices of bread*

Put shredded beef in pan, sprinkle with flour, add butter, and slightly brown. Add milk and stir until thick. Serve on toast. Yield: 4 servings.

Corned Beef Hash Patties

    1 *(1-pound) can corned beef hash*
    4 *slices pineapple*
    2 *tablespoons melted butter*

Cut corned beef hash into 4 slices. Place pineapple slices in a 1½-quart flat casserole dish. Place slice of corned beef hash on top of pineapple slices; brush with melted butter. Bake at 350 degrees F. for 15 minutes. Yield: 4 servings.

Corned Beef Pâté Elégante

1   *(12-ounce) can corned beef,*
      unchilled
1   *(8-ounce) roll Braunschweiger*
      sausage
3   *tablespoons instant minced onion*
½   *cup mayonnaise*
3   *tablespoons vinegar*
1½ *teaspoons dry mustard, if desired*
      Sieved hard-cooked egg white, garnish

Flake corned beef with fork until meat is well broken up, Combine with remaining ingredients, except sieved egg white garnish, blending until the mixture is very smooth.

Refrigerate the pâté for several hours before serving. When serving, garnish with sieved egg white and accompany with crisp crackers or toast slices. Yield: 3½ cups.

Spicy Corned Beef

4   *pounds corned beef brisket*
    Water to cover
1   *orange, sliced*
1   *rib celery*
8   *whole cloves*
2   *bay leaves*
1   *clove garlic (optional)*

Cover brisket with water; add other ingredients. Simmer covered for 4 to 5 hours or until meat is tender. Let cool in water it is cooked in. If served whole, glaze top in any manner desired. (Suggestion: Brown sugar softened to a paste with mustard. Run in oven until lightly browned.) Yield: 8 to 10 servings.

Lunch-in-a-Hurry

1   *tablespoon butter*
2   *cups canned cream-style corn*
    Salt and pepper
1   *(12-ounce) can luncheon meat*

Melt butter in saucepan. Add corn and salt and pepper to taste. Pour into 2-quart baking dish. Cut luncheon meat into eight slices. Stand each slice up in the corn. Place in 350-degree F. oven until heated through. Serve with a green salad. Yield: about 4 to 6 servings.

Lunchtime Treat

1   *(12-ounce) can luncheon meat*
2   *tablespoons brown sugar*
⅛   *teaspoon ground nutmeg*
⅛   *teaspoon ground cinnamon*
2   *tablespoons water*
1   *(17-ounce) can sweet potatoes,*
      drained
2   *tablespoons butter or margarine*
½   *teaspoon salt*
2   *pineapple slices, cut in half*
8   *whole cloves*

Cut luncheon meat into 8 slices. Combine brown sugar, nutmeg, cinnamon, and water. Place 4 meat slices in 2-quart casserole dish; spread with half the sugar mixture. Mash sweet potatoes and add butter and salt; mix well. Place ¼ cup mashed sweet potatoes on each slice of luncheon meat. Spread with remaining sugar mixture. Top with other 4 meat slices and the pineapple slices decorated with 2 cloves each. Bake at 350 degrees F. for 20 minutes. Yield: 4 servings.

Broiled Luncheon Loaf

1   *(12-ounce) can luncheon meat*
1   *(5-ounce) jar blue cheese spread*
2   *tablespoons prepared mustard*

Cut luncheon meat into 4 slices. Place in pan and broil 3 inches from heat. Turn and cook on other side. Cover top with blue cheese spread, which has been mixed with prepared mustard. Continue to broil until cheese bubbles and browns slightly. Yield: 4 servings.

Meat and Corn au Gratin

1 *(12-ounce) can luncheon meat*
1 *(4-ounce) can or jar pimiento*
1 *medium onion, diced*
1 *(12- or 16-ounce) can whole-kernel corn, drained*
¼ *cup diced green pepper*
1 *can condensed cream of celery soup*
½ *cup light cream*
1 *teaspoon Worcestershire sauce*
½ *cup shredded Cheddar cheese*
½ *cup soft breadcrumbs*
2 *tablespoons butter or margarine, melted*
Paprika

Cut luncheon meat into 1-inch cubes. Cut pimiento in ½-inch pieces. Arrange the luncheon meat, pimiento, and onion with drained corn and green pepper in layers in a greased 2-quart casserole. Mix soup, cream, and Worcestershire sauce and pour over the meat-corn mixture. Top with shredded cheese and breadcrumbs, which have been mixed with melted butter. Sprinkle with paprika. Bake at 375 degrees F. about 30 minutes or until browned. Yield: 6 servings.

Canned Corned Beef Pie

3 *tablespoons chopped green pepper*
1 *small onion, chopped*
1 *tablespoon butter*
2 *(12-ounce) cans corned beef, unchilled*
1 *(8-ounce) can tomato sauce*
1 *baked 9-inch pie shell*
2 *slices sharp Cheddar cheese, quartered lengthwise*

Cook green pepper and onion in butter until onion is soft. Flake meat with fork and blend with vegetables. Stir in tomato sauce.

Pour into pie shell. Arrange cheese, spoke-fashion, on top of pie and then bake at 400 degrees F. for about 15 minutes. Yield: 6 to 8 servings.

notes

Pies and Pastry

Chess pies, of English descent, are definitely Southern in adaptation. Some hold to the theory that they are derivations of "cheese pies." Others prefer to believe they came about during plantation days.

When unexpected company dropped in, it is said that the cook of the house was sometimes hard-pressed to find a dessert. Therefore, she often made a pastry and filled it with a mixture of butter, eggs, and flavoring. The result was such a hit that when asked for the name of the pie, she modestly replied it was "jes pie."

Pecan pie recipes are almost as varied as the people of the South. Some cooks prefer molasses for the sweetening; others like corn syrup or white or brown sugar. No matter which is used, a pecan pie, its top covered with toasted halves, is sure to be well received in spite of its calorie-laden sweetness.

Sweet potato, fresh berry, pumpkin, and apple pies all vie for honors in the dessert field, but this doesn't lessen by one whit the popularity of pies such as caramel, buttermilk, lemon, lime, or raisin.

Blackberry Pie

    4 cups fresh blackberries
    1 cup sugar
    2 tablespoons flour
    4 tablespoons sugar
       Pastry for 9-inch, double-crust pie

Wash and cap berries. Cover with 1 cup sugar and allow to sit for about 30 minutes. Combine flour with 4 tablespoons sugar and gently stir into the berry-sugar mixture. Spoon into prepared pastry-lined pie plate. Cover with lattice strips of pastry and bake at 400 degrees F. until crust is golden brown. Dewberries and boysenberries can be substituted for blackberries, if desired.

From roadside markets beside Southern highways and byways, pails of freshly picked blackberries are taken home to be made into succulent cobblers or pies.

Fresh Blueberry Pie

       1 cup sugar
    3½ tablespoons quick-cooking tapioca
       ½ teaspoon ground cinnamon
       ¼ teaspoon salt
       ¼ teaspoon grated lemon peel
    ¹⁄₁₆ teaspoon ground cloves
       1 tablespoon fresh lemon juice
       4 cups fresh blueberries
          Pastry for 9-inch, double-crust pie
       2 tablespoons butter or margarine

Combine sugar, tapioca, cinnamon, salt, lemon peel, and cloves. Mix with lemon juice and blueberries. Turn into pastry-lined 9-inch pie plate. Dot with butter. Top with pastry rolled to ⅛-inch thickness. Cut 2 or 3 gashes in top of crust to allow escape of steam (or top with pastry cut into ½-inch strips arranged in lattice fashion). Bake at 425 degrees F. about 40 minutes or until crust is brown. Remove from oven; cool before serving.

Blueberry Pie

2 *cups fresh blueberries*
Pastry for 8-inch, double-crust pie,
  unbaked
1 *cup sugar*
2 *tablespoons tapioca*
1 *tablespoon flour*
¼ *teaspoon ground cinnamon*
1 *tablespoon butter*

Pour washed berries into unbaked pie shell. Mix sugar, tapioca, flour, and cinnamon; spread evenly over berries, and dot with butter. Put top crust on pie, make slits in top, and bake at 400 degrees F. for 30 minutes.

Blueberry Marble Pie

1½ *cups graham cracker crumbs*
¼ *cup melted butter*
¼ *cup sugar*
2 *cups washed, drained fresh*
  blueberries
⅓ *cup sugar*
1 *cup heavy cream*
⅓ *cup light corn syrup*

Combine graham cracker crumbs, melted butter, and ¼ cup sugar. Blend well and press on bottom and sides of a 9-inch pie plate.

Put blueberries through sieve or food mill; sweeten with ⅓ cup sugar. Let stand while whipping the cream with corn syrup until mixture holds its shape. Turn cream into piecrust and pour blueberry mixture in a thin stream over top to create a marbled effect. Freeze. Cut into wedges to serve.

Blueberry Meringue Pie

1 *quart blueberries*
½ *cup sugar*
⅓ *cup cornstarch*
1 *cup water*
2 *tablespoons lemon juice*
Baked 9-inch pastry
2 *egg whites*
¼ *cup sugar*

Pick over berries; then wash them. Crush 1 cup of berries, reserving remainder. Blend ½ cup sugar and cornstarch. Add crushed berries and water, and cook slowly, stirring constantly, until mixture thickens and bubbles. Remove from heat; add lemon juice and reserved whole berries. Pour into baked pie shell.

Beat egg whites until foamy; add sugar, a tablespoon at a time, and continue beating until meringue stands in stiff peaks. Spoon meringue over top of hot filling, pressing against inner edge of crust to seal. Bake at 350 degrees F. for 15 to 20 minutes or until meringue is lightly tipped with a golden brown. Cool before serving.

Baked Alaska Pie

Baked 8- or 9-inch pie shell
2 *cups fresh strawberries*
3 *egg whites*
6 *tablespoons sugar*
¼ *teaspoon cream of tartar*
1 *pint vanilla ice cream*

Bake pie shell and cool. Wash, cap, and cut strawberries in halves; chill. Make a meringue, using egg whites, sugar, and cream of tartar.

Place chilled berries in pie shell. Spoon ice cream over berries and spread meringue over ice cream. Be very careful to seal meringue to edge of crust. Bake at 500 degrees F. about 3 to 5 minutes, or until browned.

Apple Pie

Pastry for 9-inch, double-crust pie
¼ *cup sugar*
1 *tablespoon flour*
½ *teaspoon ground cinnamon*
Dash of salt
1 *(No. 2) can sliced pie apples or 6*
  medium-size tart, fresh apples
¼ *cup butter*
¾ *cup brown sugar*
½ *cup flour*

Blend together the ¼ cup sugar, 1 tablespoon flour, cinnamon, and salt. Toss lightly with apples. Spoon into pastry-lined pan. Combine butter, brown sugar, and ½ cup flour and sprinkle over pie filling. Cover with top crust and cut slits in top of crust. Bake at 425 degrees F. about 35 to 40 minutes.

Cheese-Apple Pie

Pastry:

¼ cup shortening
1 cup flour
½ teaspoon salt
¼ cup shredded sharp cheese
3 tablespoons cold water

Cut shortening into flour. Add other ingredients and press into a ball. Roll to fit a 9-inch piepan.

Filling:

⅔ cup sugar
½ cup flour
¾ teaspoon ground cinnamon
Dash salt
5 cups sliced, tart apples

Mix all ingredients and put into unbaked piecrust.

Streusel Topping:

½ cup sugar
½ cup flour
¼ teaspoon salt
⅓ cup butter or margarine
1 cup shredded sharp cheese

Combine sugar, flour, and salt. Cut in butter and cheese and sprinkle over apples. Bake at 425 degrees F. for 30 to 35 minutes.

Deep-Dish Apple Pie

5 cups sliced apples
1 cup sugar
1 teaspoon ground cinnamon
2 tablespoons butter or margarine
2 tablespoons water
2 teaspoons lemon juice, if desired
Pastry or biscuit dough

Place the sliced apples in a deep baking dish (about 1 quart), sprinkling sugar and cinnamon throughout the layers. Dot the top with butter and add water and lemon juice. Cover the apples with the crust and press it firmly against the edge of the dish to seal. Make an opening in the crust to permit the steam to escape. Bake at 425 degrees F. for about 30 to 40 minutes or until the apples are tender and the crust is brown. Yield: 6 servings.

Fresh Apple Cobbler

2 cups thinly sliced apples
½ cup brown sugar
½ teaspoon ground cinnamon
½ teaspoon ground nutmeg
1 tablespoon grated lemon peel
1 tablespoon lemon juice
1½ cups sifted enriched flour
3 teaspoons baking powder
1 tablespoon sugar
½ teaspoon salt
⅓ cup shortening
½ cup milk
1 egg, well beaten
2 tablespoons sugar

Arrange apples in greased 8- x 8- x 2-inch pan. Sprinkle with mixture of sugar, cinnamon, nutmeg, lemon peel, and lemon juice. Heat in oven (400 degrees) while preparing shortcake.

Sift together flour, baking powder, 1 tablespoon sugar, and salt. Cut in shortening until mixture is like coarse crumbs. Add milk and egg at once. Stir until flour is just moistened.

Spread dough over hot apples. Sprinkle with 2 tablespoons sugar. Bake at 400 degrees F. for 35 to 40 minutes.

Apple-Honey Crisp

    4 *cups sliced apples*
    ¼ *cup sugar*
    1 *tablespoon lemon juice*
    ½ *cup honey*
    ½ *cup flour*
    ¼ *cup brown sugar*
    ¼ *teaspoon salt*
    ¼ *cup walnuts or pecans*
    ¼ *cup butter*

Spread sliced apples in a shallow baking dish, sprinkle with sugar and lemon juice, and pour honey over all. Into a bowl put the flour, brown sugar, salt, and nuts. Work in the butter as for biscuits, making a crumbly mixture. Spread crumbs evenly over the apples and bake at 375 degrees F. for 30 to 40 minutes. Crust should be brown. Serve warm with plain cream or with whipped topping, or whipped cream topped with a dash of cinnamon.

Old World Apple Pie

    2 *cups finely chopped tart apples*
    ¾ *cup sugar*
    2 *tablespoons flour*
    ⅓ *teaspoon salt*
    1 *egg, beaten*
    ½ *teaspoon vanilla extract*
    1 *cup commercial sour cream*
       Unbaked pie shell

    Topping:

    ⅓ *cup flour*
    ¼ *cup butter*
    ⅓ *cup brown sugar*

Chop apples and set aside. Combine sugar, flour, and salt; add egg, vanilla, and cream. Beat until smooth. Add apples, mix well, and pour into pastry-lined piepan. Bake at 375 degrees F. for 15 minutes; reduce heat to 325 degrees F. and bake 30 minutes. Remove from oven and sprinkle with Topping made by combining flour, butter, and brown sugar. Return to oven and bake 20 minutes longer.

American Glory Apple-Cheese Pie

       Pastry for two-crust pie
    6 *cups sliced fresh apples*
    2 *teaspoons lemon juice*
    ¾ *cup sugar*
    2 *tablespoons flour*
    ½ *teaspoon ground cinnamon*
    ½ *teaspoon ground nutmeg*
    ⅛ *teaspoon salt*
    ⅓ *cup graham cracker crumbs*
    1 *cup shredded sharp Cheddar cheese*
    2 *tablespoons butter*

Prepare pastry; line a 9-inch piepan with half the pastry and set aside.

Prepare apples; sprinkle with lemon juice. Make a mixture of sugar, flour, cinnamon, nutmeg, and salt, and toss gently with apples.

Sprinkle graham cracker crumbs over bottom of pie shell. Spoon one-third of apples over pie shell. Top with half the cheese. Beginning with apples, repeat layers and end with apples. Slightly heap last layer of apples in the center. Dot with butter.

Place top crust over mixture and bake at 450 degrees F. for 10 minutes. Reduce heat to 350 degrees F. and bake 40 minutes.

Apple Macaroon Pie

       Unbaked 9-inch pie shell
    4 *cups apples, sliced thin*
    ½ *cup sugar*
    1 *tablespoon flour*
    ½ *teaspoon salt*
    1 *tablespoon butter or margarine*
    ½ *cup sugar*
    1 *tablespoon butter or margarine*
    1 *egg*
    ¼ *cup milk*
    1 *cup coconut*

Line piepan with pastry. Place apples in pan. Mix ½ cup sugar, flour, salt and sprinkle over apples. Dot with 1 tablespoon butter. Bake at 350 degrees F. for 20 minutes. Combine ½ cup sugar, 1 tablespoon butter, egg, milk, and coconut. Sprinkle over hot pie. Bake 30 minutes more.

Apple-Cheese Crisp

    3 cups chopped apples
    ⅛ teaspoon ground cinnamon
    ¼ cup water
    2 teaspoons lemon juice
    ¾ cup sugar
    ½ cup flour
    ¼ teaspoon salt
    4 tablespoons butter
    ¾ cup shredded cheese

Arrange the apples in a shallow 9-inch baking dish and sprinkle with cinnamon; add water and lemon juice. Combine sugar, flour, and salt. Work in butter to form a crumbly mixture. Lightly stir in shredded cheese. Spread mixture over apples and bake at 350 degrees F. about 30 to 40 minutes or until apples are tender and crust is brown and crisp. Yield: 6 servings.

Apple Charlotte

Kuchen Dough:

    1 cup sifted flour
    ½ teaspoon baking powder
    ¼ teaspoon salt
    2 tablespoons sugar
    2½ tablespoons butter
    2 eggs, beaten
    2 tablespoons milk

Combine flour, baking powder, salt, and sugar. Work butter into mix with a wooden spoon. Add eggs and beat well. Stir in milk. Grease an 8-inch springform pan, and with a rubber spatula spread dough on bottom of pan and part way up side of pan.

Apple Filling:

    5 cups sliced raw apples
    ½ cup golden seedless raisins
    ⅔ cup sugar
    1 teaspoon ground cinnamon
    1 tablespoon grated lemon peel

Put apple slices and raisins in enough water to cover, then cook until apples are just tender but have not lost their shape. Drain.

Combine sugar, cinnamon, and lemon peel and stir gently into apples and raisins. Spoon into dough-lined pan and bake at 425 degrees F. for 50 to 60 minutes. Serve hot with almond-flavored whipped cream.

Peanut Crunch Apple Pie

    5½ cups sliced apples
        Unbaked 9-inch pie shell
    ½ cup sugar
    ½ cup graham cracker crumbs
    ½ cup chopped dry-roasted peanuts
    ¼ cup unsifted flour
    ½ teaspoon ground cinnamon
    ⅛ teaspoon salt
    ½ cup margarine, melted

Arrange sliced apples in pie shell. Combine sugar, graham cracker crumbs, chopped peanuts, flour, cinnamon, and salt; mix thoroughly and sprinkle over apples. Pour melted margarine over peanut topping. Bake at 350 degrees F. about 1 hour or until apples are tender. Yield: one 9-inch pie.

Apricot Cream Dream Pie

    1 tablespoon unflavored gelatin
    ¼ cup cold water
    2 tablespoons lemon juice
    ¼ teaspoon salt
    ½ cup plus 2 tablespoons sugar
    1½ cups apricot puree
    1 cup whipping cream
    1 deep 9-inch graham cracker crust
    1 cup commercial sour cream

Sprinkle gelatin over water; let stand about 5 minutes. Add softened gelatin, lemon juice, salt, and ½ cup sugar to apricot puree. Heat at 175 degrees on thermostatically controlled top burner, stirring constantly, until gelatin is dissolved, about 8 to 10 minutes. Cool thoroughly. When mixture begins to thicken, fold in cream that has been whipped and sweetened with 2 tablespoons sugar. Pour apricot mixture into graham cracker crust: chill in refrigerator 4 to 6 hours. When firm, spread a thin layer of sour cream over pie.

Apricot-Raisin Pie

Pastry for two-crust pie
1 *cup dried apricots*
2 *cups water*
1 *cup golden raisins*
1 *scant cup sugar*
¾ *cup liquid from fruit*
2 *tablespoons quick-cooking tapioca*
Pinch of salt
2 *teaspoons grated orange peel*
1 *tablespoon orange juice*
2 *tablespoons butter*

Make pastry for two-crust pie. Place bottom pastry in pan, but do not bake. Cook dried apricots in water over medium heat until tender. Add raisins and cook about 7 to 8 minutes longer. Drain and save liquid. Spread fruit over pastry.

Mix sugar, juice from fruit (add orange juice if liquid does not measure ¾ cup), tapioca, salt, orange peel, and orange juice. Pour liquid over fruit in pastry shell. Dot with butter. Place pastry strips over top. Bake at 425 degrees F. for 10 minutes. Reduce heat to 350 degrees F. and bake an additional 25 to 30 minutes. Remove from oven and brush top with butter.

Banana Pie Supreme

6 *tablespoons cake flour*
⅔ *cup sugar*
¼ *teaspoon salt*
1¾ *cups milk*
2 *slightly beaten egg yolks*
1¼ *teaspoons vanilla extract*
½ *cup whipped cream*
3 *bananas*
Baked 9-inch pie shell

Mix together flour, sugar, and salt in top of double boiler. Add milk and cook over hot water, stirring constantly, until mixture thickens. Pour a small amount of mixture over egg yolks, beating vigorously. Return to double boiler and cook 2 minutes longer, stirring constantly. Remove from heat; cool and add vanilla. Chill. Fold in whipped cream. Arrange sliced bananas in pie shell;

cover with cooked custard; continue making layers until all is used, with custard as the top layer. Garnish with sliced bananas and whipped cream.

Black Bottom Pie

4 *cups corn flakes*
¼ *cup soft butter or margarine*
2 *tablespoons sugar*
1 *tablespoon unflavored gelatin*
¼ *cup cold water*
¾ *cup sugar*
4 *teaspoons cornstarch*
4 *egg yolks*
2 *cups scalded milk*
2 *squares unsweetened chocolate*
½ *teaspoon vanilla extract*
½ *teaspoon rum flavoring*
4 *egg whites*
¼ *teaspoon salt*
¼ *teaspoon cream of tartar*
1 *cup heavy cream*
2 *tablespoons powdered sugar*
½ *square unsweetened chocolate,*
    shaved

Crush corn flakes into fine crumbs. Blend butter and 2 tablespoons sugar; stir in corn-flake crumbs; mix well. Press evenly and firmly around sides and bottom of a 9-inch piepan. Chill.

Soften gelatin in cold water. Combine ½ cup sugar with cornstarch. Beat egg yolks until light; stir in scalded milk slowly. Gradually stir in sugar mixture. Cook over hot water, stirring occasionally, about 20 minutes until custard coats a metal spoon heavily. Take out 1½ cups of the custard; keep remainder hot. Melt chocolate over hot but not boiling water; add to the 1½ cups custard, beating until well blended and cool. Stir in vanilla. Pour into chilled pie shell.

To remainder of hot custard, add softened gelatin, stirring until dissolved. Cool until mixture is ready to set. Stir in rum flavoring. Beat egg whites with salt until foamy. Add cream of tartar and beat until stiff but not dry. Gradually beat in remaining ¼ cup sugar. Fold into custard mixture. Spread gently over chocolate filling. Chill until set.

Whip cream; fold in powdered sugar. Spread over pie; sprinkle with shaved chocolate. Serve at once.

Black Bottom Pie

Crust:

    14 gingersnaps
     5 tablespoons melted butter

Crush gingersnaps. Roll out fine, add melted butter, and pat into 9-inch piepan. Bake at 350 degrees F. for 10 minutes and allow to cool.

Filling:

     4 egg yolks, well beaten
     2 cups scalded milk
    ½ cup sugar
    1½ tablespoons cornstarch
    1½ squares bitter chocolate
     1 teaspoon vanilla extract

Add egg yolks slowly to hot milk. Combine and stir into sugar and cornstarch that has been mixed. Cook in top of double boiler for 20 minutes, stirring occasionally, until mixture coats spoon. Remove from heat and take out 1 cup, reserving the remainder. Add bitter chocolate to cup of custard you have taken out. Beat well as it cools. Add vanilla extract; then pour this mixture into piecrust. Chill.

Second Mixture:

     1 tablespoon unflavored gelatin
     2 tablespoons cold water
     4 egg whites
    ½ cup sugar
    ¼ teaspoon cream of tartar
     2 tablespoons whiskey
    ½ pint whipping cream
    ½ square bitter chocolate

Dissolve gelatin in cold water; add remaining custard, and cool. Beat egg whites until stiff, gradually adding sugar and cream of tartar. Add whiskey to egg mixture; fold

into plain custard mixture and spread over chocolate mixture. Chill. Cover the top of pie with the whipped cream and then add shavings of bitter chocolate. Yield: about 6 to 8 servings.

Bourbon Pie

Crust:

     1 box chocolate-snap cookies, crushed
    ½ cup margarine

Crush chocolate snaps and add melted margarine. Pat into 9-inch piepan and bake at 350 degrees F. until crust hardens (about 10 minutes). Remove from oven. Cool before adding chilled filling.

Filling:

    21 marshmallows
     1 (13-ounce) can evaporated milk
    ½ pint whipping cream
     2 tablespoons bourbon

Melt marshmallows and evaporated milk in saucepan. Do not boil. Cool and add whipped cream and bourbon. Pour into chocolate crust; chill. When ready to serve, top with whipped cream and chocolate crumbs.

Old Virginia Caramel Pie

    ¼ cup butter
    ½ cup granulated sugar
     3 eggs, well beaten
     1 teaspoon cornmeal
     1 cup seeded damson preserves
    ¾ cup milk
        Unbaked pastry shell
     1 tablespoon lemon juice (optional)

Cream butter, and add sugar gradually. Add eggs and meal and the preserves which have been blended well with the milk. Bake in a pastry-lined pie shell at 350 degrees F. for 25 minutes. One tablespoon of lemon juice improves the flavor of this pie.

Virginia Cheese Pie

Unbaked pie shell
1 *pound sharp Cheddar cheese, diced*
2 *eggs*
1 *tablespoon granulated sugar*
2 *tablespoons butter*

Preheat oven to 350 degrees F. Bake pie shell filled with diced Cheddar until cheese is soft and partially melted and pie shell is beginning to brown. Remove from oven and add eggs, blending with fork gently so as not to break pie shell. Sprinkle with sugar and dot with butter. Bake until shell is golden brown and filling slightly firm (about 15 minutes).

Dutch Cupboard Cheese Pie

1 *quart half-inch bread squares, toasted*
2 *tomatoes, sliced*
Salt and pepper
2 *cups (½ pound) natural Swiss cheese, shredded*
2 *eggs*
¾ *teaspoon salt*
½ *teaspoon paprika*
½ *teaspoon dry mustard*
⅛ *teaspoon pepper*
1½ *cups milk*

Arrange bread squares in 9-inch piepan. Top with tomatoes, salt, pepper, and Swiss cheese. Combine other ingredients; mix well. Pour over cheese. Bake in 350-degree oven for 40 minutes. Yield: 4 servings.

Party Cherry-Cheese Pie

Baked 11-inch pastry shell or graham cracker crust
1 *envelope unflavored gelatin*
½ *cup cold water*
⅓ *cup sugar*
¼ *teaspoon salt*
1 *teaspoon grated lemon rind*
2 *teaspoons lemon juice*
2 *cups creamed cottage cheese*
1 *cup heavy cream, whipped*

Prepare pastry shell. Sprinkle gelatin on cold water to soften; dissolve over boiling water or over direct low heat. Stir in sugar, salt, grated lemon rind, and lemon juice. Put cottage cheese through sieve or beat on high speed of electric mixer 3 minutes. Stir in gelatin. Fold in whipped cream. Turn into baked pastry shell. Chill. Then add the Cherry Glaze.

Cherry Glaze:

2 *(1-pound) cans red sour pitted cherries (water pack)*
1 *cup cherry liquid*
1 *envelope unflavored gelatin*
⅔ *cup sugar*
⅛ *teaspoon salt*
1 *tablespoon lemon juice*
⅛ *teaspoon red food coloring*

Drain cherries; reserve 1 cup liquid. Sprinkle gelatin on ½ cup of the cherry liquid; dissolve over boiling water or direct low heat. Stir in remaining ½ cup cherry liquid, sugar, salt, lemon juice, and food coloring. Chill until gelatin mixture mounds slightly when dropped from a spoon. While gelatin is chilling, arrange the drained cherries on top of pie. Spoon gelatin over cherries. Chill until firm. Yield: 10 to 12 servings.

Note: This recipe can be used for two 8-inch pies. If frozen cherries are substituted for canned cherries, thaw and drain; reduce sugar to ¼ cup.

Cherry Delight Pie

½ *pound graham crackers*
1 *stick butter, softened*
1 *(8-ounce) package cream cheese*
1 *cup powdered sugar*
1 *cup whipping cream or 2 cups frozen whipped topping*
1 *(1-pound 6-ounce) can cherry pie filling, chilled*

Crush crackers very fine, mix with butter, and press in bottom of 10-inch piepan.

Whip cream cheese, powdered sugar, and whipping cream until fluffy. Spoon into crust and chill at least 2 hours. Before serving, top with cherry pie filling. Yield: 8 servings.

Cherry Crumb Pie

Pastry for two-crust pie
4 *cups cherries, drained (use two 1-pound 3-ounce cans)*
2 *cups cherry juice and water*
2 *cups sugar, divided*
4 *tablespoons quick-cooking tapioca*
1½ *teaspoons salt, divided*
½ *teaspoon almond extract*
1 *tablespoon butter or margarine, melted*
4 *drops red food coloring*
1½ *cups sifted all-purpose flour*
½ *cup butter or margarine*

Line two 9-inch pie plates with pastry; make high fluted edges.

Combine cherries, juice and water, 1½ cups sugar, tapioca, ½ teaspoon salt, almond flavoring, butter or margarine, and food coloring. Divide evenly into the two pie shells.

Combine flour, 1 teaspoon salt, and ½ cup sugar in small mixing bowl. Cut in butter or margarine with pastry blender until mixture resembles fine meal. Sprinkle one-half of crumb mixture evenly over each pie. Bake at 400 degrees F. for 40 to 50 minutes. Yield: 6 to 8 servings from each pie.

Party Cherry Pie

3 *egg whites*
Dash salt
1 *teaspoon vanilla extract*
1 *cup sugar*
½ *cup saltine cracker crumbs*
½ *cup chopped pecans*
1 *teaspoon baking powder*
½ *pint heavy cream*
1 *can cherry pie filling*

Beat egg whites with dash of salt and teaspoon vanilla until foamy. Gradually add sugar and beat until stiff peaks form. In another bowl, mix cracker crumbs (10 single crackers), chopped pecans, and baking powder. Fold this mixture into egg white mixture. Put in well-greased 9-inch pie plate, building up sides. Bake at 275 degrees F. for

45 minutes. Cool. Whip ½ pint heavy cream. Put thin layer over cooled pie shell, then add cherry pie filling. Put remaining cream over filling. Garnish with a few cherries. Chill.

Kiss Pie

3 *egg whites*
1¼ *cups sugar*
3 *tablespoons water*
Dash of salt
½ *teaspoon vanilla extract*
1 *teaspoon vinegar*
Whipped cream
Grated bitter chocolate

Combine egg whites, sugar, water, salt, vanilla, and vinegar and beat for 30 minutes. Pour into pie plate lined with waxed paper, bringing mixture up the sides of the plate. Bake at 225 degrees F. for 45 minutes. Cool. Fill with whipped cream and sprinkle with the grated bitter chocolate.

Lemon Chess Pie

½ *cup butter, softened*
1 *cup sugar*
3 *or 4 eggs*
1 *tablespoon cornmeal*
Juice and rind of one lemon
Unbaked pastry shell

Cream the butter, which should have softened at room temperature, with the sugar until the granules of sugar have disappeared. Add the eggs, one at a time, beating well after each addition. Blend in the cornmeal and add the lemon juice and grated rind. (You should have at least ⅓ cup of lemon juice as the pie should taste lemony.) Pour into an unbaked pastry shell. Bake at 375 degrees F. until the pie is firm. Oldtimers shook the pie slightly and if the center trembled a little, a few more minutes were needed.

This recipe is enough to fill six pastry-lined tart shells which will need only about 25 minutes at 350 degrees F. Serve cold, but not ice-cold.

Lemon Chess Pie

1⅔ *cups sugar*
  1 *tablespoon flour*
  1 *tablespoon cornmeal*
  4 *eggs, unbeaten*
  4 *tablespoons melted butter*
  4 *tablespoons milk*
  4 *tablespoons lemon juice*
  1 *grated lemon rind*
    Unbaked 9-inch pie shell

Combine sugar, flour, cornmeal; toss lightly with a fork. Add next 5 ingredients; beat with rotary or electric mixer until smooth and blended. Pour into pie shell. Bake at 375 degrees F. about 35 minutes, or until top is golden brown. Cut while warm.

Lemon Chess Pie

  2 *cups sugar*
  1 *tablespoon flour*
  1 *tablespoon cornmeal*
  4 *eggs*
 ¼ *cup butter, melted*
 ¼ *cup milk*
  4 *tablespoons grated lemon rind*
 ¼ *cup lemon juice*
    Unbaked 9-inch pastry shell

Put sugar, flour, and cornmeal in bowl. Toss lightly with fork; then add eggs, butter, milk, lemon rind, and lemon juice. Beat until smooth and thoroughly blended. Pour into pie shell. Bake at 375 degrees F. about 35 to 45 minutes, or until golden brown.

Never-Fail Chess Pie

  4 *eggs, beaten*
1½ *cups sugar*
  2 *teaspoons cornmeal*
    Pinch of salt
 ¼ *cup melted butter*
  4 *tablespoons cream*
  1 *teaspoon vanilla extract*
    Unbaked 10-inch pie shell

Combine eggs, sugar, cornmeal, salt, butter, cream, and vanilla. Blend well before pouring into unbaked pie shell. Bake at 350 degrees F. for 30 minutes. Yield: one 10-inch pie.

Old Talbott Tavern Chess Pie

  2 *cups sugar*
  2 *tablespoons flour*
  2 *tablespoons cornmeal*
 ½ *cup margarine, softened*
  5 *egg yolks*
  1 *cup half-and-half*
    Unbaked 9-inch pie shell

Mix the sugar with the flour and cornmeal; then cream well with the margarine. Blend in egg yolks, beating well, and add the half-and-half gradually.

Pour into an unbaked pie shell and bake at 425 degrees F. for 15 minutes. Reduce heat to 375 degrees and bake 30 minutes or longer until done.

Orange Chess Pie

 ¼ *pound butter (part margarine may be used)*
  1 *cup sugar*
  6 *egg yolks or 3 whole eggs*
  3 *tablespoons white cornmeal*
  1 *cup orange juice*
  1 *tablespoon lemon juice*
    Grated rind of 1 orange (optional)
    Unbaked pastry shell

Cream the butter, and add sugar gradually. Add egg yolks, beaten until lemon colored, or the whole eggs, one at a time. Add cornmeal and juices of orange and lemon. You may also add the grated rind of 1 orange, if desired.

Pour into an unbaked shell or two smaller pie shells and bake at 350 degrees F. until firm.

You may add coconut to this recipe or make it into 8 or 10 tarts.

Chocolate Pie

    2 *cups sugar*
    6 *egg yolks, beaten*
    2 *egg whites, beaten*
    3 *tablespoons flour*
    3 *tablespoons cocoa*
    1 *quart milk*
    1 *small can evaporated milk*
    1 *teaspoon vanilla extract*
    2 *unbaked 9-inch pie shells*
    4 *egg whites*
    8 *tablespoons sugar*

Combine first 8 ingredients; mix well. Cook in top of double boiler until thickened. Pour into unbaked pie shells and bake at 375 degrees F. until filling is firm in center. Beat 4 egg whites and 8 tablespoons sugar to make meringue. Spread over filling; reduce heat to 325 degrees F. Return pies to oven; bake until meringue is browned. Yield: two 9-inch pies.

Chocolate Pie

    2 *cups sugar*
    6 *tablespoons flour*
    5 *squares melted chocolate*
    4 *egg yolks, beaten*
    4 *cups milk*
    4 *tablespoons butter or margarine*
    2 *baked 9-inch piecrusts*
    4 *egg whites, beaten stiff*
    6 *tablespoons sugar*
    1 *teaspoon vanilla extract*

Combine 2 cups sugar, flour, melted chocolate, egg yolks, and milk in a large saucepan. Cook over low heat until thick, stirring constantly. Remove from heat and stir in butter. When cool, spoon into baked piecrusts. Beat

egg whites until stiff. Fold in 6 tablespoons sugar and vanilla. Bake at 350 degrees F. until brown, about 12 to 15 minutes.

Chocolate Chip-Almond Pie

    6 *small chocolate bars with almonds*
    17 *marshmallows*
    ½ *cup milk*
    1 *cup whipping cream, whipped*
    ½ *cup chocolate chips*
    ½ *cup slivered almonds*
    1 *baked graham cracker crust*

Melt chocolate bars and marshmallows in milk in top of double boiler; cool. Fold in whipped cream, chocolate chips, and slivered almonds. Pour into graham cracker crust. Garnish with additional chocolate chips. Refrigerate for at least 4 hours.

Chocolate Angel Strata

    2 *egg whites*
    ½ *cup sugar*
       Baked 9-inch pie shell
    2 *egg yolks, slightly beaten*
    ¼ *cup water*
    1 *(6-ounce) package semisweet
         chocolate, melted*
    ¼ *cup sugar*
    1 *cup whipping cream*

Beat egg whites until soft mounds are formed. Add sugar gradually and continue beating until meringue stands in soft glossy peaks. Spread over bottom of baked pie shell. Bake at 325 degrees F. for 15 to 18 minutes or until lightly browned. Cool.

Mix egg yolks and water and add to melted chocolate. Mix well and spread 3 tablespoons over cooled meringue pie shell. Chill remainder of filling. Combine sugar and whipping cream; beat until thick. Spread half over chocolate in pie shell. Combine remaining whipped cream with chilled chocolate mixture. Spread over whipped cream in pie shell. Chill for 4 hours.

Rich Chocolate-Nut Pie

    Pastry for 9-inch pie
  ½ *cup butter or margarine*
  1 *teaspoon vanilla extract*
  1 *cup sugar*
  ⅓ *cup cocoa*
  ½ *teaspoon salt*
  ¼ *cup flour*
  3 *eggs, well beaten*
  ¾ *cup dark corn syrup*
  ¾ *cup milk*
  ¾ *cup pecan halves*

Line piepan with pastry. Cream the butter or margarine with vanilla. Gradually add sugar, cocoa, salt, flour, and eggs, creaming well. Beat in syrup and milk until well blended. Stir in pecans. Pour filling into prepared pastry. Bake at 450 degrees F. for 10 minutes and then reduce heat to 325 degrees F. and bake 40 to 45 minutes or until filling is set. This pie may be topped with whipped cream, if desired.

Chocolate Fudge Pie

  1 *stick butter or margarine*
  3 *squares unsweetened baking*
     chocolate
  4 *eggs, well beaten*
  3 *tablespoons white corn syrup*
1½ *cups sugar*
  ¼ *teaspoon salt*
  ¼ *cup milk*
  1 *teaspoon vanilla extract*
    Unbaked 10-inch pie shell

Melt butter and chocolate in top of double boiler. Beat eggs well and add other ingredients; add chocolate and butter. Mix well and pour into 10-inch crust. Bake at 350 degrees F. for 30 to 35 minutes or until top is crusty and filling is set. Do not overbake.

    This pie does not need meringue; may be served with ice cream or whipped cream. It is a very rich pie.

Chocolate Fudge Pie

  4 *eggs*
  2 *cups sugar*
  3 *squares bitter chocolate*
  1 *cup chopped nuts*
  ⅓ *cup melted butter or margarine*
  1 *teaspoon vanilla extract*
  1 *Unbaked 9-inch pie shell*

Beat eggs until thick and lemon colored. Gradually add sugar, beating continually. Combine melted chocolate and butter. Cool slightly. Pour into egg mixture. Stir to combine. Add nuts and vanilla. Pour mixture into pastry-lined pan. Bake at 350 degrees F. for 40 minutes. Serve with whipped cream or ice cream.

French Silk Chocolate Pie

  ½ *cup butter*
  ¾ *cup sugar*
  1 *square unsweetened chocolate,*
     melted and cooled
  1 *teaspoon vanilla extract*
  2 *eggs*
    Baked 8-inch pastry shell or graham
     cracker crust

Cream butter and sugar; blend in chocolate. Add vanilla. Add eggs, one at a time, beating for 4 to 5 minutes after each addition. Pour into pie shell. Chill thoroughly. If desired, top with whipped cream and sprinkle with shaved chocolate or walnuts. Yield: 6 servings.

Buttermilk-Coconut Pie

  5 *eggs*
  1 *stick melted butter or margarine*
  ¾ *cup buttermilk*
  2 *cups sugar*
  1 *cup coconut*
    Unbaked 9-inch pie shell

Mix all ingredients well. Pour mixture into pie shell. Bake at 350 degrees F. about 30 minutes, or until pie is done.

Coconut-Apple Pie

  ¾ cup white sugar
  1 tablespoon flour
  1 teaspoon ground cinnamon
  ¼ teaspoon ground nutmeg
  5 cups thinly sliced apples
    Unbaked 9-inch piecrust
  ½ cup flaked coconut
  ⅓ cup cornflake crumbs
  2 tablespoons melted butter or
      margarine
  2 tablespoons brown sugar

Mix together white sugar, flour, cinnamon, and nutmeg. Combine sugar mixture with apples. Pour into piecrust. Combine coconut, cornflake crumbs, butter, and brown sugar. Sprinkle over apple mixture. Bake in 400-degree oven about 45 to 50 minutes.

French Coconut Pie

  4 eggs, beaten
  1 cup plus 1 tablespoon sugar
  ¼ cup flour
  ½ cup margarine, melted
  ¼ cup white corn syrup
  ½ teaspoon vanilla extract
  ½ teaspoon coconut flavoring
  1¼ cups milk, scalded
  1 (16-ounce) package cookie coconut
  2 unbaked 9-inch pie shells

Beat eggs. Add sugar, flour, margarine, corn syrup, vanilla, and coconut flavoring. Beat until well blended. Stir in scalded milk and coconut. Pour into unbaked pie shells. Bake at 450 degrees F. for 10 minutes; reduce heat and bake 15 minutes. Yield: 2 pies.

Toasted Coconut Pie

  3 eggs
  1½ cups sugar
  ½ cup melted butter
  4 teaspoons lemon juice
  1 teaspoon vanilla extract
  1⅓ cups flaked coconut
    Unbaked 9-inch pie shell

Thoroughly beat eggs and combine with sugar, butter, lemon juice, and vanilla. Stir in coconut and pour filling into unbaked pie shell. Bake at 350 degrees F. for about 40 to 45 minutes.

French Coconut Pie

    Unbaked 9-inch pie shell
  3 eggs
  1½ cups sugar
  1 teaspoon vanilla extract
  ½ cup melted butter or margarine
  1 cup flaked coconut

Brush a little egg white on unbaked pie shell and bake at 400 degrees F. about 1 minute. This prevents a soggy crust. Beat eggs slightly; add other ingredients. Pour into pie shell. Bake at 400 degrees F. 10 minutes; at 375 degrees F. 15 minutes; at 350 degrees F. 15 to 20 minutes.

Coconut-Pineapple Pie

    Unbaked 9- or 10-inch piecrust
  ½ stick butter or margarine, softened
  1¾ cups sugar
  1 tablespoon cornmeal
  4 eggs
  1 (8¼-ounce) can crushed pineapple
  1 (3½-ounce) can flaked coconut

Prepare piecrust. Mix softened butter, sugar, and cornmeal. Add eggs, one at a time, mixing well after each addition. Add pineapple and coconut and mix well. Spoon mixture into piecrust. Bake at 450 degrees F. for 10 minutes; reduce heat to 325 degrees F. and bake 30 to 40 minutes or until center is firm.

Cornmeal Pie

1½ cups sugar
1½ cups brown sugar
 ½ cup butter, melted
  3 eggs, separated
1½ teaspoons vanilla extract
 ½ cup coffee cream
 ½ cup cornmeal
  1 cup pecans or 1 cup coconut
Unbaked 10-inch piecrust

Blend sugars and butter; add beaten egg yolks, vanilla, cream, and cornmeal. Add nuts or coconut. Add lightly beaten egg whites and blend. Pour into unbaked pie shell. Bake at 350 degrees F. about 35 minutes.

Frozen Lemon Pie

  3 eggs, separated
 ½ cup sugar
 ¼ cup lemon juice
  1 tablespoon grated lemon peel
 ¼ teaspoon salt
  1 cup heavy cream, whipped
  1 crumb crust

Combine beaten egg yolks, sugar, lemon juice, lemon peel, and salt; cook in double boiler, stirring constantly, till mixture coats spoon. Cool; fold in stiffly beaten egg whites. Fold in whipped cream. Pour filling into crust of wafer crumbs or graham cracker crumbs. Place in freezing unit and freeze firm. Serve frozen.

Frozen Lemon Pie

(Pirate's House, Savannah, Georgia)

  4 egg yolks
  1 can sweetened condensed milk
  1 (6-ounce) can frozen lemonade or
       juice of 4 lemons
  1 cup whipped cream
  4 egg whites, stiffly beaten
8- or 9-inch almond-flavored graham
       cracker crust

Beat egg yolks; add milk, then lemonade (undiluted) or lemon juice. Place in refrigerator while beating whipping cream and beating egg whites. Fold the whipped cream into lemon mixture; then fold in the beaten egg whites. Spoon into graham cracker crust, cover, and freeze overnight. Serve topped with whipped cream. Yield: about 6 to 8 servings.

Southern-Style Lemon Pie

  5 eggs
1⅓ cups white corn syrup
 ¾ cup sugar
 ⅓ cup lemon juice
     Grated rind of one lemon
 ¼ cup butter or margarine, melted
     Unbaked 9- or 10-inch pie shell

Beat eggs well. Add corn syrup, sugar, lemon juice, and grated lemon rind. Add melted butter or margarine; beat to mix well. Pour into unbaked pie shell. Bake at 375 degrees F. for 10 minutes; then reduce heat to 350 degrees and bake 25 to 35 minutes longer. Yield: 6 servings.

Mile-High Lemon Chiffon Pie

  1 envelope unflavored gelatin
 ½ cup cold water
  5 egg yolks
 ½ cup sugar
  1 teaspoon grated lemon rind
 ½ cup lemon juice
  5 egg whites, beaten
 ½ cup sugar
     Baked 9-inch pie shell (or crumb crust)

Mix gelatin and water in top of double boiler. Beat egg yolks; add sugar and mix well. Add egg yolks to gelatin mixture; cook in top of double boiler, stirring constantly, until gelatin is dissolved and mixture is slightly thickened (about 6 minutes). Add lemon rind and juice. Chill until mixture mounds slightly when dropped from spoon.

Beat egg whites until stiff, but not dry. Gradually add ½ cup sugar and beat until very stiff. Fold into gelatin mixture; spoon mixture into prepared pie shell. Chill until firm. Serve cold.

Egg Custard Pie

1 *cup sugar*
4 *egg yolks, beaten slightly*
2 *tablespoons flour*
1 *cup milk*
1 *tablespoon melted butter*
1 *teaspoon vanilla extract*
Unbaked 9-inch piecrust, chilled
4 *egg whites*
8 *tablespoons sugar*

Mix 1 cup sugar, egg yolks, flour, milk, butter, and vanilla. Pour into unbaked piecrust and bake at 450 degrees F. for 10 minutes; reduce heat and cook at 325 degrees F. about 25 minutes or until knife inserted in center of pie comes out clean. Remove from oven and top with Meringue.

Meringue: To make meringue, beat egg whites; add sugar gradually and continue beating until meringue holds in peaks. Spread lightly on slightly cooled pie. Be careful to spread all the way to the edges so that filling will be sealed. Bake at 325 degrees F. for 15 minutes. Cool slowly.

Fruit Cocktail Pie

1 *can fruit cocktail, drained*
1 *can sweetened condensed milk*
¼ *cup lemon juice*
Baked 9-inch pie shell
½ *pint whipping cream*
2 *tablespoons sugar*

Combine first 3 ingredients; pour into baked pie shell. Whip cream with sugar; spread on top of pie filling. Let stand in refrigerator until serving time.

Florida Key Lime Pie

1 *envelope (1 tablespoon) unflavored gelatin*
¼ *cup cold water*
4 *eggs, separated*
1 *cup sugar, divided*
⅓ *cup lime juice*
½ *teaspoon salt*
2 *teaspoons grated lime peel*
Green food coloring

Soften gelatin in cold water. Beat egg yolks; add ½ cup sugar, lime juice, and salt. Cook over hot water, stirring constantly until thickened. Add grated peel and gelatin; stir until gelatin is dissolved. Tint pale green with food coloring. Cool. Beat egg whites stiff but not dry; add remaining sugar slowly, beating after each addition; fold into lime mixture. Pour into baked 9-inch pie shell; chill until firm. Garnish top with halved white grapes and mint sprigs to resemble grape clusters.

Mod-Molasses Pie

1½ *cups unsulphured molasses*
3 *eggs, beaten*
½ *teaspoon ground nutmeg*
½ *teaspoon ground cinnamon*
½ *teaspoon salt*
2 *tablespoons melted butter or margarine*
½ *cup brown sugar*
1 *tablespoon cornstarch*
Unbaked 9-inch pie shell
½ *cup crushed corn chips*

Add molasses to beaten eggs and stir well. Add nutmeg, cinnamon, salt, and melted butter or margarine and mix well. Combine brown sugar and cornstarch and add to molasses mixture. Pour into unbaked pie shell, and sprinkle top with crushed corn chips. Bake at 400 degrees F. for 15 minutes; reduce heat to 350 degrees F. and bake an additional 30 minutes. Yield: one 9-inch pie.

French Macaroon Pie

15 *saltine crackers*
14 *dates, cut very fine*
1 *cup sugar*
½ *cup chopped pecans*
1 *teaspoon almond extract*
3 *egg whites, beaten*

Crush crackers until very fine. Add dates, sugar, pecans, and almond extract. Mix well; then fold in stiffly beaten egg whites. Put into a buttered 8-inch piepan. Bake at 300 degrees F. for 45 minutes. Serve cold with whipped cream.

Mystery Pie

3 *egg whites*
1 *cup sugar*
¼ *teaspoon baking powder*
1 *teaspoon vanilla extract*
20 *round buttery crackers, rolled fine*
1 *cup finely chopped pecans*
Whipped cream

Grease a 9-inch glass piepan. Beat egg whites until stiff; then fold in sugar, baking powder, and vanilla extract. Beat until stiff. Fold in cracker crumbs and chopped pecans. Pour mixture into piepan. Bake at 350 degrees F. for 20 minutes. To serve, top with whipped cream. Yield: 6 to 8 servings.

Oatmeal Pie

2 *eggs, beaten*
⅔ *cup melted margarine*
⅔ *cup sugar*
⅔ *cup white corn syrup*
⅔ *cup uncooked oatmeal (regular or quick-cooking)*
¼ *teaspoon salt*
1 *teaspoon vanilla extract*
Unbaked 8-inch pie shell

Mix all ingredients together and pour into uncooked pie shell. Bake at 350 degrees F. about 1 hour.

Osgood Pie

3 *egg yolks*
1¼ *cups sugar*
½ *teaspoon ground cinnamon*
½ *teaspoon ground cloves*
½ *cup raisins*
½ *cup pecans*
3 *egg whites, stiffly beaten*
Unbaked 9-inch pie shell

Beat egg yolks until light; fold in sugar and spices; add raisins and nuts. Fold stiffly beaten egg whites into first mixture. Pour into unbaked pie shell and bake at 350 degrees F. for 30 to 35 minutes.

Orange -Coconut Pie

1½ *cups sugar*
1 *stick soft butter or margarine*
3 *whole eggs*
¼ *cup orange juice*
Grated rind of one orange
1 *can flaked coconut*
Unbaked 9-inch pie shell

Cream the sugar and butter together. Then add the eggs one at a time, beating well after each addition. Add orange juice, grated orange rind, and coconut. Pour into an unbaked pie shell and bake at 350 degrees F. for 45 minutes or until the filling is firm.

Crusty Peach Cobbler

3 *cups sliced peaches, canned or fresh*
¼ *cup sugar*
1 *tablespoon lemon juice*
1 *teaspoon grated lemon peel*
1 *teaspoon almond extract*
1½ *cups flour*
½ *teaspoon salt*
3 *teaspoons baking powder*
1 *tablespoon sugar*
⅓ *cup shortening*
½ *cup milk*
1 *well-beaten egg*
2 *tablespoons sugar*

Arrange peaches in a greased, 8-inch square pan. Sprinkle with mixture of ¼ cup sugar, lemon juice, lemon peel, and almond extract. Heat in oven while preparing shortcake. Sift together flour, salt, baking powder, and sugar; cut in shortening until mixture is like coarse crumbs. Add milk and egg at once, and stir just until flour is moistened. Spread dough over hot peaches. Sprinkle with 2 tablespoons sugar. Bake at 375 degrees F. for 40 minutes.

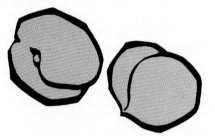

Peach Carousel Pie

  1½ cups flour
   1 teaspoon salt
   ½ cup shortening
   ¼ cup shredded Cheddar cheese
   4 tablespoons water
   1 (6-ounce) package butterscotch morsels
   2 tablespoons evaporated milk
   2 (No. 2) cans sliced peaches, drained
   1 tablespoon lemon juice
   ½ cup brown sugar
   1 tablespoon cornstarch
   ½ cup chopped pecans
   ½ teaspoon ground cinnamon
   8 maraschino cherries
   ½ pint whipping cream

Sift together flour and salt and cut in shortening. Add cheese and water and mix to a dough. Roll thin and place on a 14-inch pizza pan. Melt the butterscotch morsels in the milk in a double boiler; spread while hot over crust. Add lemon juice to the drained peaches and arrange on crust. Mix brown sugar, cornstarch, pecans, and cinnamon and sprinkle over peaches. Cut cherries and place on pie. Bake at 350 degrees F. for 30 minutes. Cool. When ready to serve, decorate with mounds of whipped cream.

Glazed Peach Pie or Tarts

   4 cups sliced fresh peaches, or canned peaches
   ¾ cup sugar
   1 package orange-flavored gelatin
   1 cup boiling water
  Dash of salt
   4 teaspoons lemon juice
  Baked 9-inch pie shell or 6 tart shells

Combine fresh peaches and sugar; let stand 10 minutes (or drain canned peaches and add sugar if desired). Dissolve gelatin in boiling water. Add salt and lemon juice. Cool. Add peaches and chill until slightly thickened. Turn into cold pie shell or tart shells, arranging fruit as desired. Garnish with whipped cream rosettes and peach slices in an attractive design.

Simonsen's Peanut Butter Pie

  Baked pie shell
   1 cup powdered sugar
   ½ cup peanut butter
   ¼ cup cornstarch
   ⅔ cup sugar
   ¼ teaspoon salt
   2 cups scalded milk
   3 egg yolks, beaten
   2 tablespoons butter
   ¼ teaspoon vanilla extract
   3 egg whites for meringue

Combine powdered sugar and peanut butter. Blend until the appearance of biscuit mix. Spread half of this mixture on pie shell.

Combine cornstarch, sugar, and salt; add scalded milk and mix well. Pour small amount over beaten egg yolks, mix well, then return to milk mixture. Cook in top of double boiler until mixture thickens. Add butter and vanilla extract; then pour into prepared pie shell. Top with meringue made from 3 beaten egg whites. Sprinkle the remainder of peanut butter mixture over meringue. Bake at 325 degrees F. until the meringue is brown.

Peanut Butter-
Ice Cream Pie

    4 *tablespoons peanut butter*
    4 *tablespoons light brown sugar*
    1 *pint vanilla ice cream*
    Crushed peanuts or graham cracker
        crumbs

Melt peanut butter and brown sugar in saucepan. Add ice cream and stir until mixture is well blended. Pour into Graham Cracker Crust. Sprinkle crushed peanuts or bits of graham cracker crumbs on top. Return to freezer.

Graham Cracker Crust:

1¼ *cups graham cracker crumbs*
 ¼ *cup butter or margarine*
 ¼ *cup sugar*

Roll crackers to fine, even crumbs. Pour into medium-size bowl. Add soft butter or margarine and sugar. Mix well. Pour mixture into piepan; press firmly with the back of a tablespoon to make an even layer of crumbs on the bottom and sides. To firm, bake at 350 degrees F. for 6 to 8 minutes. Cool before adding ice cream mixture. Yield: one 8-inch pie.

Pecan Pie

1¾ *cups sugar*
 ¼ *cup dark corn syrup*
 ¼ *cup butter or margarine*
  3 *eggs, beaten*
  1 *cup chopped pecans*
    Few grains salt
  1 *teaspoon vanilla extract*
    Unbaked 9-inch pie shell

Mix sugar, corn syrup, and margarine; bring to a boil. Beat eggs thoroughly. Gradually add boiling mixture to eggs; stir in pecans, salt, and vanilla. Pour into unbaked pie shell. Bake at 375 degrees F. for about 35 to 40 minutes. Yield: one 9-inch pie.

Pecan Pie

  3 *eggs*
 ¾ *cup granulated sugar*
  1 *cup dark corn syrup*
  1 *teaspoon vanilla extract*
 ¼ *cup melted butter*
  1 *cup pecans*
    Unbaked 9-inch pie shell

Beat eggs. Add sugar and beat well. Stir in syrup, vanilla, and butter. Put pecans in bottom of pie shell pan and pour in syrup mixture. Pecans will come to the top. Bake at 350 degrees F. for about 40 to 45 minutes.

Blender Pecan Pie

  2 *eggs*
 ⅔ *cup sugar*
 ½ *teaspoon salt*
 ½ *cup white corn syrup*
  2 *tablespoons melted butter*
  1 *teaspoon vanilla extract*
  1 *cup pecans*
    Unbaked 9-inch pie shell
    Pecan halves

Put eggs, sugar, salt, corn syrup, butter, and vanilla extract in blender and blend well. Add 1 cup pecans and blend just enough to chop nuts coarsely. Pour into pie shell and place pecan halves on top. Bake at 425 degrees F. for 15 minutes. Reduce heat to 350 degrees and bake an additional 30 minutes.

Pecan Custard Pie

   3 *eggs*
   1 *cup granulated sugar*
   2 *tablespoons flour*
1½ *cups milk*
   1 *tablespoon melted butter*
   ½ *cup white corn syrup*
   ¼ *teaspoon salt*
   1 *teaspoon vanilla extract*
   1 *cup chopped pecans*
    Unbaked 10-inch pie shell

Beat eggs well. Combine sugar and flour and stir into eggs. Heat milk and butter until butter is melted; add to eggs with corn syrup, salt, and vanilla; mix well. Stir in pecans. Pour into pie shell. Bake at 350 degrees F. about 30 minutes or until filling is firm.

Georgia Pecan Pie

½ cup granulated sugar
1 cup white corn syrup
3 eggs
4 tablespoons margarine
Dash salt
1 tablespoon vanilla extract
1 cup broken pecan meats
Unbaked 9-inch piecrust

Cook sugar and syrup until it thickens. Beat eggs; slowly add hot syrup to eggs, beating constantly. Add margarine, salt, vanilla, and pecans and pour into unbaked piecrust. Bake in a preheated 450-degree F. oven for 10 minutes. Lower temperature to 300 degrees F.; bake 35 minutes.

Meringue Pecan Pie

2 egg yolks
1 cup granulated sugar
4 tablespoons flour
1 cup commercial sour cream
¼ teaspoon lemon extract
⅛ teaspoon salt
Baked 9-inch piecrust
2 egg whites, beaten
1 cup brown sugar
1 cup broken pecans

Combine egg yolks, granulated sugar, flour, sour cream, lemon extract, and salt in top of double boiler. Cook over hot water until thickened, stirring constantly. Cool. Spoon cooled mixture into baked piecrust. Beat egg whites until stiff; gradually beat in brown sugar. Stir in pecans and spread over filling. Bake at 325 degrees F. about 15 minutes to brown meringue.

Mock Pecan Pie

1 cup Grape Nuts cereal
¾ cup lukewarm water
1 cup light brown sugar, firmly packed
1 cup dark corn syrup
¼ cup melted butter
⅛ teaspoon salt
3 eggs, beaten
1 teaspoon vanilla extract
Unbaked 9-inch piecrust

Soak Grape Nuts in water until water is absorbed. Combine sugar, corn syrup, butter, and salt in saucepan. Bring to a boil, stirring until sugar is dissolved. Remove from heat. Beat eggs until foamy. Add a small amount of hot syrup mixture to eggs, mixing well. Stir in rest of syrup mixture; add Grape Nuts mixture and vanilla. Pour into unbaked piecrust and bake at 375 degrees F. for 40 to 50 minutes.

Sour Cream-Pecan Pie

Pastry for 9-inch piepan
1 cup broken pecans
2 teaspoons flour
¼ teaspoon salt
1 cup sugar
1 cup commercial sour cream
2 eggs, well beaten
½ teaspoon grated lemon rind

Line piepan with pastry and sprinkle it with pecans. Combine flour, salt, and sugar in top of double boiler. Add sour cream and cook until slightly thickened. Add eggs; heat. Remove from heat and add lemon rind; then pour mixture over pecans in pastry shell. Place in a 425-degree F. oven and cook about 10 minutes. Reduce heat to 325 degrees F. and bake until filling is firm.

Southern Pecan Pie

    3 eggs
    ¾ cup granulated sugar
    ¾ cup white corn syrup
       Dash salt
    ¼ cup melted butter or margarine
    1 teaspoon vanilla extract
    1 cup chopped pecans
       Unbaked 9-inch pastry shell

Beat eggs thoroughly; add sugar, syrup, and salt and mix well. Add butter and vanilla; beat well. Put pecans in bottom of pie shell. Pour mixture over nuts. Bake at 400 degrees F. for 10 minutes; lower temperature to 300 degrees F. and cook 35 minutes longer.

Yam-Pecan Pie

    1 cup cooked sweet potatoes, mashed
    ½ cup sugar
    ¾ teaspoon ground cinnamon
    ¾ teaspoon ground ginger
       Dash salt
    ¾ cup undiluted evaporated milk
    2 eggs, well beaten
       Unbaked 9-inch pie shell
    ¼ cup butter or margarine
    ½ cup light brown sugar
    ¾ cup finely chopped pecans

Combine sweet potatoes, sugar, spices, salt, milk, and eggs. Pour into pie shell and bake at 375 degrees F. for 20 minutes. Remove from oven and sprinkle with topping made by combining butter, sugar, and pecans. Return to oven and bake an additional 25 minutes.

Party Rice-Pineapple Pie

    1 can sweetened condensed milk
    ½ cup lemon juice
       Grated rind of lemon
    2 egg yolks
    1 cup cooked rice
    ½ cup crushed pineapple
    1 graham cracker crust (9-inch pan)
    2 egg whites, beaten
    2 tablespoons sugar

Blend milk, juice, rind, and egg yolks. Fold in rice and pineapple. Pour into graham cracker crust or pastry pie shell. Cover with meringue made by beating egg whites until foamy, then adding sugar gradually. Beat until stiff but not dry. Bake at 350 degrees F. for 10 minutes or until brown. Chill. This pie is also good with whipped cream instead of meringue.

Sour Cream-Pineapple Pie

    1   cup sugar
    ⅓   cup flour
    1   (13½-ounce) can crushed pineapple
    1   cup commercial sour cream
    ¼   teaspoon salt
    1½   tablespoons lemon juice
    3   egg yolks, slightly beaten
         Baked 9-inch pie shell

Combine first six ingredients and cook over low heat until thickened. Pour a small amount over egg yolks; return to hot mixture and cook and stir for 2 minutes. Cool, stirring frequently. Pour into baked pie shell.

    Meringue:

    3 egg whites, beaten
    ¼ teaspoon salt
    ⅓ cup sugar
    ¼ teaspoon cream of tartar

Beat egg whites until foamy, then add salt, sugar, and cream of tartar and continue beating until stiff peaks form. Put meringue on top of pie, being careful to seal all edges. Bake at 350 degrees F. about 12 to 15 minutes, or until delicately browned. Watch meringue carefully as it bakes.

Pixie Pie

    1 *stick butter*
    4 *cups berries (dewberries, blueberries,*
         huckleberries, or blackberries)
    1 *cup sugar*
    1 *cup flour*
 1½ *teaspoons baking powder*
    1 *cup sugar*
    1 *cup milk*

Melt the butter in a 10-inch baking dish. Coat berries with 1 cup sugar (in case you are using sweetened frozen berries, omit the sugar).

Mix dry ingredients, stir in milk gradually, and beat well. Pour batter into melted butter and mix lightly. Pour berries in pan, spreading them evenly over batter. Bake at 375 degrees F. for 45 minutes. Berries will sink into batter while baking. Yield: 6 to 8 servings.

Pumpkin Pie

    Pastry for 10-inch pie shell
    3 *cups cooked or canned pumpkin,*
         mashed
    1 *cup sugar*
    1 *cup brown sugar*
    1 *teaspoon salt*
    1 *teaspoon ground cinnamon*
    1 *teaspoon ground nutmeg*
    1 *teaspoon ground ginger*
  ¼ *teaspoon ground cloves*
  ¼ *teaspoon ground allspice*
    4 *eggs, slightly beaten*
  ¼ *cup butter or margarine, melted*

Mix together the mashed pumpkin, sugar, brown sugar, salt, cinnamon, nutmeg, ginger, cloves, and allspice. Add the slightly beaten

eggs and the melted butter. Mix well and pour into prepared pie shell. Bake at 450 degrees F. for 10 minutes, then reduce heat to 325 degrees F. and cook until the center is set.

"Frost on the Pumpkin" Pie

 1½ *cups crushed gingersnaps or graham*
         crackers
  ¼ *cup melted butter or margarine*
  ½ *cup powdered sugar*
    1 *cup whipping cream*
 1¼ *cups sifted powdered sugar*
  ½ *teaspoon ground cinnamon*
  ½ *teaspoon vanilla extract*
    3 *egg yolks*
  ⅓ *cup sugar*
 1¼ *cups cooked, mashed pumpkin*
  ½ *cup milk*
  ½ *teaspoon each salt, ground allspice,*
         ginger, nutmeg, and cinnamon
    1 *tablespoon unflavored gelatin*
  ¼ *cup cold water*
    3 *egg whites*
  ¼ *cup powdered sugar*

Mix crushed gingersnaps, butter, and powdered sugar. Press into a 10-inch pie plate. Bake at 325 degrees F. for 10 minutes.

Whip cream until it stands in peaks. Add 1¼ cups sifted powdered sugar, ½ teaspoon cinnamon, ½ teaspoon vanilla extract. Beat until stiff peaks form, and chill until ready to use.

Beat egg yolks; add sugar, pumpkin, milk, salt, and spices. Mix well and cook over medium heat until it boils. Cook 2 minutes longer, stirring constantly. Remove from heat and add gelatin which has been dissolved in cold water; cool.

Beat egg whites until stiff; fold in ¼ cup powdered sugar. Fold in the cooled pumpkin mixture.

Fill crust with a layer of pumpkin mixture, a layer of whipped cream mixture (using about half of it), and another layer of pumpkin. Chill 2 hours to set. Before serving, top with remaining whipped cream. Yield: 8 servings.

Raisin Pie

2 *eggs*
1 *cup sugar*
2 *tablespoons butter, softened*
½ *cup milk*
1½ *cups raisins*
½ *cup chopped nuts*
Unbaked 9-inch pie shell

Beat eggs until fluffy; gradually add sugar and beat well. Beat in softened butter. Add milk, raisins, and nuts. Pour into unbaked pie shell and bake at 350 degrees F. for 30 to 35 minutes.

Sour Cream-Raisin Pie

¾ *cup sugar*
½ *teaspoon ground cinnamon*
¼ *teaspoon ground cloves*
¼ *teaspoon ground nutmeg*
¼ *teaspoon salt*
¼ *cup flour*
1½ *cups commercial sour cream*
2 *eggs, well beaten*
1 *cup chopped raisins*
1 *teaspoon vanilla extract*
Baked 9-inch pie shell

Mix sugar, spices, salt, and flour in top of double boiler. Add sour cream; stir and heat over hot water until thickened. Cover and cook for 15 minutes. Pour the hot mixture slowly into the well-beaten eggs; add raisins and cook over hot water for a few minutes. Stir in vanilla. Pour into baked pie shell. Let cool before serving.

Rum Pie

12 *egg yolks*
1 *cup sugar*
2½ *envelopes unflavored gelatin*
½ *cup water*
½ *cup rum*
1 *quart cream*
1 *(6-ounce) package chocolate morsels*

Cream egg yolks and sugar. Dissolve gelatin in water over hot water. Add rum and gelatin to the egg mixture. Whip cream and add to egg mixture. Pour into Graham Cracker Crusts (page 271). Cover with chocolate morsels. Yield: 5 pies.

Rum Cream Pie

5 *egg yolks*
¾ *cup sugar*
2½ *tablespoons plain gelatin*
½ *cup cold water*
¾ *cup cream*
3 *tablespoons dark rum (or to taste)*
Crumb pie shell (10-inch)

Beat egg yolks until light and add sugar. Soak gelatin in cold water; put over low heat, until dissolved. Pour over sugar and egg mixture, stirring briskly. Whip cream until stiff, fold into the egg mixture, and flavor with rum. Cool until the mixture begins to set; then pour into pie shell. Chill until firm. Sprinkle top generously with shaved bittersweet chocolate curls. Garnish with whipped cream, if desired, and serve cold. Yield: 1 pie.

Sour Cream Pie

1 *cup commercial sour cream*
¾ *cup sugar*
2 *eggs, slightly beaten*
Pinch of salt
1 *teaspoon ground cinnamon*
½ *teaspoon ground nutmeg*
½ *teaspoon ground cloves*
½ *cup pecans*
Unbaked 8- or 9-inch piecrust

Mix cream and sugar together; add slightly beaten eggs and the remaining ingredients. Pour into unbaked pie shell and bake at 425 degrees F. for 20 minutes. Reduce heat to 325 degrees F. and bake another 20 minutes. Sweetened whipped cream and pecans may be put on top of cooled pie when serving, if desired.

Note: 1 cup evaporated milk plus 1 tablespoon vinegar may be used in place of sour cream.

Butternut Squash Pie

   ¾ *cup sugar*
   1 *tablespoon flour*
   ¼ *teaspoon salt*
   1 *teaspoon ground cinnamon*
   ½ *teaspoon ground nutmeg*
   ½ *teaspoon ground ginger*
   ¼ *teaspoon ground mace*
   1½ *cups cooked, mashed butternut squash*
   1 *egg, slightly beaten*
   1½ *cups milk*
   2 *tablespoons melted butter*
   Unbaked 9-inch pie shell
   Whipped cream (optional)

Mix together sugar, flour, salt, and spices. Add to cooked mashed squash. Add egg, milk, and melted butter and put in pastry shell. Bake at 450 degrees F. for 15 minutes. Reduce heat to 325 degrees F. and bake until firm (about 40 minutes). Serve warm.

Strawberry Pie

   Vanilla pudding mix
   Milk
   Baked 9-inch pie shell
   1 *quart fresh strawberries*
   ¾ *cup sugar*
   ⅓ *cup water*
   2 *tablespoons cornstarch*
   ⅓ *cup water*
   Sweetened whipped cream
   Sliced bananas, for garnish

Mix vanilla pudding according to package directions. Cool, then put into baked pie shell. Wash and cap strawberries. Crush only 1 cup of berries and slice those remaining. To the 1 cup of crushed berries add the sugar and ⅓ cup water. Bring to a boil; cook and stir for 5 minutes. Mix the cornstarch with ⅓ cup water and add to cooked strawberries; cook until thick and clear.

Cool, then add remaining berries, spooning them over the pie. Chill. Just before serving, garnish with whipped cream and bananas.

Strawberry Pie

   1 *cup sugar*
   3½ *tablespoons cornstarch*
   Few grains salt
   1 *cup crushed strawberries*
   ½ *stick butter or margarine*
   ¼ *cup water*
   Baked 9-inch pie shell
   1 *(3-ounce) package cream cheese*
   1 *cup whole strawberries*
   1 *cup whipped cream*
   ¼ *teaspoon almond extract*
   2 *tablespoons powdered sugar*

Combine first 6 ingredients in saucepan; cook until thick and transparent, stirring constantly. Cool. Spread pie shell with softened cream cheese. Stand whole strawberries in cream cheese to completely cover pie shell. Spread cooled sauce over strawberries. Cover with whipped cream to which almond extract and powdered sugar have been added. Chill. Yield: 6 servings.

Strawberry-Banana Pie

   3 *cups fresh or frozen strawberries*
   1 *cup sugar*
   ½ *teaspoon red food coloring*
   Pinch of salt
   4 *tablespoons cornstarch*
   ½ *cup cold water*
   Baked 9-inch pastry
   3 *bananas, sliced*
   1 *cup whipping cream*

Slice strawberries; add sugar. Stir and let stand long enough to make juice. Drain off juice and add enough water to make 2 cups liquid. Add red coloring and salt to liquid. Bring to a boil. Mix cornstarch in ½ cup cold water and stir in boiling liquid. Let cool. Add berries. In cooled piecrust, put bananas. Spoon on berries; top with whipped cream. Yield: 6 servings.

Glazed Strawberry Pie

> Baked 9-inch pastry shell
> 1 quart fresh strawberries or 2 pints
>   frozen whole strawberries
> Strawberry Glaze
> Whipped cream, sweetened

Prepare pastry for one-crust pie; bake. Wash, drain, and hull fresh strawberries or thaw frozen berries. Place berries in cooled, baked shell. Spoon Strawberry Glaze over all; be sure that all berries are covered. Cool. Just before serving, spread with sweetened cream. Yield: 6 to 8 servings.

> Strawberry Glaze:
>   1 pint strawberries
>   ½ cup water
>   1 cup sugar
> 2½ tablespoons cornstarch
>   1 tablespoon butter
>   Red food coloring

Crush berries well; combine with water and cook about 5 minutes. Strain and add sugar and cornstarch. Bring to a boil, and cook until mixture is clear. Add butter and enough food coloring for an attractive red color. Cool slightly; spoon over strawberries in pie shell.

Strawberry-Ice Cream Pie

>   2 cups sliced fresh strawberries
>   1 cup sugar
>   1 box strawberry-flavored gelatin
>   1 pint vanilla ice cream
>   Baked pie shell, or graham cracker
>   crust

Combine strawberries and sugar and let stand until sugar is dissolved. Drain off liquid and measure. Add more water if liquid does not measure 1 cup. Heat the liquid to boiling and pour over gelatin; stir until dissolved. Add ice cream and stir until melted. Add the drained berries and put mixture in baked pie shell or graham cracker crust. Chill and serve with whipped cream or ice cream, if desired.

If frozen strawberries are used, thaw them and drain off syrup. Then proceed as with fresh strawberries.

Kentucky Mint Julep Strawberry Chiffon Pie

>   3 cups fresh strawberries
> 1½ tablespoons unflavored gelatin
>   ¼ cup cold water
> 1½ cups sugar
> 1½ cups water
>   ½ teaspoon mint extract
>   ⅛ teaspoon salt
>   Baked 9-inch pie shell
>   1 cup heavy cream, whipped
>   6 fresh mint leaves

Wash, hull, and drain strawberries. Sprinkle gelatin in ¼ cup cold water. Combine sugar and the 1½ cups water, mint extract, and salt. Bring the mixture to a boil and simmer for 10 minutes. Add gelatin and stir until dissolved. Pour hot syrup over 2½ cups of the strawberries, stirring gently so they will hold shape. Cool mixture until it begins to thicken; then pour into cooled pie shell. Chill until filling is firm; then cover with whipped cream. Garnish top with the remaining ½ cup strawberries and the mint leaves. Serve pie very cold.

Frozen Strawberry-Rice Pie

>   ½ pint heavy cream, whipped
>   1 (8-ounce) package cream cheese,
>   softened
>   ½ cup sugar
> 1½ cups frozen strawberries, drained
> 1½ tablespoons unflavored gelatin
>   4 tablespoons juice from berries
>   1 cup cooked rice
>   Baked 9-inch pie shell

Whip cream and set aside. In a mixing bowl, whip cream cheese with sugar until light and fluffy. Add strawberries. Put gelatin in juice from berries. Heat until gelatin is dissolved. Combine with cream cheese mixture. Add cooked rice and mix well. Fold in whipped cream. Turn into baked 9-inch pie shell. Chill and serve. Yield: 6 servings.

Fresh Strawberry-Rhubarb Pie

Rhubarb Layer:

2½ tablespoons cornstarch
⅔ cup sugar
¾ cup water
2 cups fresh rhubarb, cut in ¾-inch pieces

Combine cornstarch and sugar in small saucepan. Gradually blend in water, and mix until smooth. Add ½ cup rhubarb cut into ¾-inch pieces. Bring to a boil, and boil 3 to 5 minutes. Cool; then stir in remaining rhubarb.

Strawberry Layer:

1½ tablespoons cornstarch
⅓ cup sugar
¼ cup water
1½ cups fresh strawberries, whole or sliced
Pastry for 8-inch double-crust pie

Combine cornstarch and sugar in a small saucepan. Blend in water and mix until smooth. Add ½ cup strawberries and bring to a boil. Boil 3 to 5 minutes. Cool and stir in remaining strawberries.

Line an 8-inch piepan with pastry. Pour rhubarb mixture into shell. Cover rhubarb mixture with strawberry mixture and top with pastry. Bake at 400 degrees F. for 15 to 20 minutes or until crust is browned. Yield: 6 servings.

Sweet Potato Pie

2 cups cooked sweet potatoes
¼ cup butter
3 eggs
1 cup milk
1¼ cups sugar
¼ teaspoon salt
¼ teaspoon ground nutmeg
1 teaspoon vanilla extract
¼ cup bourbon
Unbaked 9-inch pie shell

Boil sweet potatoes in jackets until tender. Peel and cream potatoes until smooth. Then combine with other ingredients and place in unbaked pie shell.

Bake at 425 degrees F. for 15 minutes; then reduce heat to 350 degrees F. and cook an additional 1 hour and 20 minutes. Yield: one 9-inch pie.

Glazed Sweet Potato Pie

1 cup sugar
2 teaspoons cornstarch
½ teaspoon salt
¼ teaspoon ground cinnamon
¼ teaspoon ground nutmeg
⅛ teaspoon ground cloves
¾ cup dark corn syrup
3 tablespoons butter or margarine
1 cup cooked sweet potatoes, mashed
3 eggs, slightly beaten
Unbaked 9-inch pie shell
¼ cup pecans (optional)

Mix sugar, cornstarch, salt, and spices in a heavy saucepan. Stir in corn syrup, butter, and sweet potatoes. Bring to a boil over medium heat, stirring occasionally. Boil for 3 minutes or until slightly thickened. Remove from heat and stir gradually into slightly beaten eggs. Pour into unbaked pie shell. Sprinkle pecans over top. Bake at 400 degrees F. for 10 minutes; reduce heat to 350 degrees F. and cook 35 to 40 minutes longer. Yield: one 9-inch pie.

Sweet Potato Custard Pie

>   2 cups cooked sweet potatoes, mashed
>   3 egg yolks, well beaten
>   2 tablespoons melted butter
>   ½ cup sugar
>   1 teaspoon salt
>   ¼ cup finely grated coconut
>   1 cup milk
>   ½ teaspoon ground nutmeg
>   Unbaked 9-inch pie shell
>   3 egg whites
>   6 tablespoons sugar

Combine sweet potatoes and egg yolks; add butter, ½ cup sugar, salt, coconut, milk, and nutmeg. Pour into pie shell and bake at 325 degrees F. until set, about 30 to 40 minutes. Beat egg whites until stiff, but not dry. Add sugar and mix well. Spread on top of pie and continue baking until meringue is brown.

Yummy Yam Pie

>   4 eggs
>   1½ cups cooked yams, mashed
>   ⅓ cup sugar
>   2 tablespoons guava jelly
>   ½ cup finely chopped pecans
>   1 cup milk
>   ½ teaspoon ground nutmeg
>   Pinch of salt
>   Unbaked 9-inch pie shell

Beat eggs until light. Add yams, sugar, and jelly. Beat thoroughly. Blend in pecans, milk, nutmeg, and salt, beating well after each addition.

Pour into pie shell and bake at 450 degrees F. for 10 minutes. Reduce heat to 350 degrees F. and bake for 30 minutes.

Sweet Potato Pie

>   1 heaping cup of cooked sweet
>   potatoes, mashed
>   ¼ cup butter or margarine
>   2 eggs
>   1 cup sugar
>   1 cup cream (or half-and-half)
>   3 tablespoons brandy
>   Unbaked 9-inch pie shell

Cream together sweet potatoes and butter. Beat eggs, add sugar, and beat until light. Then add the potatoes and butter. Thin with cream and brandy. Pour into pie shell and bake at 350 degrees F. for 45 minutes.

Sweet Potato Pie

>   ¼ teaspoon ground allspice
>   ¼ teaspoon ground nutmeg
>   ½ cup boiling water
>   1¼ cups cooked sweet potatoes, mashed
>   ½ cup sugar
>   2 eggs, beaten
>   ½ teaspoon salt
>   3 tablespoons butter
>   1 cup evaporated milk, undiluted
>   Unbaked 9-inch pie shell

Mix spices with boiling water and stir into sweet potatoes. Add sugar, eggs, salt, and butter; blend thoroughly. Stir in milk and heat mixture over hot water about 5 minutes, stirring constantly. Pour into pie shell and bake at 425 degrees F. until filling is set, about 20 minutes. Cool. Serve with Whipped Orange Topping.

Whipped Orange Topping:

>   ¼ teaspoon unflavored gelatin
>   1 tablespoon orange juice
>   ½ cup evaporated milk, chilled
>   ½ teaspoon grated orange rind
>   2 tablespoons powdered sugar

Soften gelatin in orange juice. Place milk over heat until it steams, but don't boil. Remove from heat, add gelatin, and stir to dissolve gelatin. Stir in orange rind and sugar. Cool; then chill until set. Whip milk until stiff. Spoon over pie.

Southern Transparent Pie

>   1 box light brown sugar
>   1 stick butter or margarine, melted
>   5 eggs
>   1 teaspoon vanilla extract
>   2 unbaked 8-inch pie shells

Blend sugar and butter. Add eggs, one at a time, blending well after each addition. Add vanilla. Pour into two unbaked piecrust shells and bake at 400 degrees F. for 10 minutes. Reduce heat to 300 degrees F. and bake until firm, about 35 to 40 minutes. Center should be slightly shaky. Yield: two 8-inch pies.

Three Story Pie

Unbaked 9-inch pie shell
1 cup or more cooked dried fruit
   (peaches or apricots)
2 tablespoons flour
1 cup sugar
1 cup milk
3 egg yolks, beaten
1 teaspoon vanilla extract
2 tablespoons butter or margarine

Line piepan with pastry. Mash cooked fruit until smooth and add sugar if desired. Spread fruit on prepared crust. Mix flour and sugar. In top of double boiler heat the milk. Gradually add small amount of milk to yolks; mix well, then add to hot milk. Stir in sugar and flour mixture; cook over low heat, stirring constantly until mixture is thick enough to coat a spoon. Add vanilla and butter. Pour mixture over fruit. Bake at 350 degrees F. about 25 minutes.

Meringue:

3 egg whites, beaten
Pinch of cream of tartar
6 tablespoons sugar

Beat egg whites, with cream of tartar added, until foamy. Add sugar, a small amount at a time, and continue beating until egg whites are stiff. Spread on pie and bake at 350 degrees F. until brown.

Graham Cracker Crust

20 or more graham crackers
¼ cup butter or margarine, at room
   temperature
½ cup sugar

Roll crackers to fine, even crumbs. Pour crumbs into bowl. Add soft butter or margarine and sugar. Blend these ingredients well. Pour mixture into piepan; press firmly to make an even layer of crumbs on bottom and sides. Put into freezer to get firm before adding filling. Yield: 1 crust.

Graham Cracker Crumb Shell

2¼ cups graham cracker crumbs
1¼ teaspoons cinnamon (or to taste)
2 tablespoons sugar
½ cup soft butter or oleo

Blend together graham cracker crumbs, cinnamon, and sugar. Using soft butter or oleo as a binder, mix together and press firmly and evenly into 10-inch pie plate.

Hot Water Pastry

¾ cup shortening
¼ cup boiling water
1 teaspoon cold milk
2 cups flour
½ teaspoon salt (optional)

Scald a mixing bowl with hot water. Put shortening in hot bowl and add boiling water. Beat until blended. Add milk, flour, and salt and stir until well mixed. Divide into two balls. Roll on floured board and fit into piepans. Yield: two 8- or 9-inch crusts.

Magic Piecrust

3 cups flour
1 teaspoon salt
1¼ cups shortening
1 egg, slightly beaten
6 tablespoons water
1 teaspoon vinegar

Combine flour and salt; cut in shortening until mixture resembles coarse cornmeal. Combine egg and water; sprinkle over flour mixture. Add vinegar and lightly stir until mixture forms a ball. Wrap in waxed paper and chill until ready to use. Yield: enough crust for 5 single pies.

Poultry and Dressing

If it's chicken, Southerners are bound to like it. Wrap a crust around it, put dumplings with it, fry it in deep fat, mix it with spaghetti, slather it with barbecue sauce, or bake it to a golden brown, and guests will ask for second helpings.

The odds are great that turkey and dressing will appear on tables for Thanksgiving, but it wouldn't be wise to bet on the kind of dressing that will be used.

Seashore sections will use oyster dressing (Southerners call it "dressing" rather than "stuffing"). Rice dressing is a favorite in Louisiana and Texas. And in some sections of Maryland the turkey is stuffed with kraut.

The most Southwide preference for dressing is for one made with cornbread. Some bakery bread or biscuits may be added to the crumbled cornbread, but not enough to make it soft or gummy. It is to this basic mixture that oysters, or chestnuts, or pecans, or sausage are added along with celery, onions, eggs, and seasonings.

Cornish hens are gaining in popularity. Their flavor is similar to that of chicken and turkey; their small size makes them ideal for a family meal or for gourmet dining.

Foil-Baked Turkey

Line a shallow roasting pan with aluminum foil and place turkey on a rack in the pan. Brush all over with soft butter or margarine. Bake turkey in a 325-degree F. oven.

When turkey is lightly browned, cover with a "tent" of foil. To make tent, tear off a sheet of heavy-duty aluminum foil 5 to 10 inches longer than the bird. Crease through center and place over bird. Hold in place by crimping it lightly at breast and over drumsticks. This will keep turkey moist without basting and will prevent overbrowning.

A 6- to 8-pound turkey should cook in 3½ to 4 hours; a 12- to 16-pound turkey in 4½ to 5½ hours. Turkeys differ in tenderness and it may be necessary to increase or decrease the cooking time. Test for doneness by moving the drumstick and thigh joint. If it moves easily, turkey is done. Toward the end of roasting time, insert a meat thermometer in the thickest part of the thigh. It will read 185 degrees F. when the turkey is done.

Turkey Luncheon Dish

1 *cup milk*
1 *can cream of mushroom soup*
2 *tablespoons cornstarch*
2 *chopped pimientos*
1 *cup turkey dressing*
2 *cups cooked, chopped turkey*

Heat milk, reserving 2 tablespoons; add soup. Moisten cornstarch with 2 tablespoons milk and add to first mixture, stirring until slightly thickened. Add pimientos, turkey dressing, and chopped turkey. Heat thoroughly and serve over squares of hot cornbread.

Roast Turkey with Cornbread Dressing is standard fare for Thanksgiving and Christmas dinner.

Roast Turkey

Wash turkey in cold running water and pat inside dry with paper towels; leave outside of bird moist. Stuff turkey (wrap any leftover stuffing in foil and place in oven during last hour turkey is roasted). Fasten neck skin to body with skewer. Push legs under band of skin at tail, or tie to tail. Place turkey, breast side up, on rack in shallow open roasting pan. Insert meat thermometer in thigh muscle or in thickest part of breast; thermometer must not touch bone. Place loose covering or "tent" of aluminum foil over turkey. Roast in slow oven (325 degrees F.) according to timetable. Remove foil last half hour to brown turkey. When turkey is done, the thermometer should read 180 degrees F. to 190 degrees F.

Basic Roast Turkey Timetable

Ready-To-Cook Weight (Lbs.)	Approximate Time (Hrs.)
6 to 8	3½ to 4
8 to 12	4 to 4½
12 to 16	4½ to 5½
16 to 20	5½ to 6½
20 to 24	6½ to 7

Since turkeys vary in type, roasting periods are approximate. You may have to decrease or increase indicated times.

Turkey Royale

2 *tablespoons butter*
½ *pound fresh mushrooms, sliced*
¼ *cup butter*
3 *tablespoons flour*
  Dash cayenne pepper
½ *teaspoon dry mustard*
¾ *cup turkey or chicken broth*
¾ *cup light cream*
½ *cup dry white wine*
1 *(3-ounce) can pimiento, drained and chopped*
1 *cup shredded sharp Cheddar cheese, divided*
  About 5 cups sliced, cooked turkey

Melt the 2 tablespoons butter in saucepan; add mushrooms and sauté over medium heat for 10 minutes. Set aside.

In another pan melt the ¼ cup butter and stir in flour, cayenne, and dry mustard; stir until blended. Stir in broth, light cream, and wine. Add pimiento and ½ cup shredded cheese. Cook over low heat until cheese is melted.

Butter a 2-quart casserole and in bottom arrange a layer of sliced, cooked turkey, using about 2½ cups meat. Top turkey layer with half of the mushrooms; pour half the sauce over the top. Top with second half of turkey, mushrooms, and remaining sauce. Sprinkle with ½ cup shredded cheese and bake at 300 degrees F. for about 1 hour. Serve over hot buttered cornbread. Yield: 6 to 8 servings.

Turkey-in-the-Sack

1 *teaspoon pepper*
2 *teaspoons salt*
3 *teaspoons paprika*
4 *teaspoons hot water*
1 *cup peanut oil*
1 *turkey, 14 to 16 pounds*

Combine pepper, salt, paprika, and hot water. Let stand at least 10 minutes. Add peanut oil and mix thoroughly. Select turkey carefully. It should not exceed 14 to 16 pounds. Wash and dry. Rub peanut oil mixture into inside and outside of turkey. Truss as desired. Pour remaining oil into large paper sack (type used in grocery stores). Rub oil inside sack until every pore in every inch of the sack is sealed. Add additional oil if needed.

Place turkey in sack, breast up. Fold over end of sack and tie securely with string. Bake at 325 degrees F. approximately 10 minutes per pound. Since the sack is airtight, the turkey is cooked by live steam; therefore, when sack is opened, be careful! With no basting, no careful watching, the turkey comes out tender to the bone and golden brown!

Turkey With Mushroom Sauce

½ cup chopped green onions
¼ cup chopped green pepper
1 cup chopped celery
½ cup margarine or bacon drippings
1 (10½-ounce) can undiluted cream of
   mushroom soup
1 (10½-ounce) can golden mushroom
   soup
2 soup cans water
4 cups cooked, chopped turkey
1 tablespoon Worcestershire sauce
½ teaspoon Kitchen Bouquet
Salt and pepper to taste
2 tablespoons chopped pimiento
1 tablespoon minced parsley
½ cup Sauterne wine (optional)
20 individual tart shells

Sauté green onions, pepper, and celery in margarine or bacon drippings until tender. Add soups and water. Add turkey and all other ingredients except wine. Cook slowly for 30 minutes. Stir in wine and pour in chafing dish. Serve hot in tart shells. Yield: 20 servings.

Turkey Casserole

2 tablespoons butter or margarine
2 tablespoons flour
1 cup milk
½ cup orange juice
1 cup commercial sour cream
¼ cup sherry or fruit juice
2 cups cooked, parslied rice
2 oranges, peeled and sliced
4 cups cooked, chopped turkey
½ cup slivered almonds

In medium saucepan melt butter or margarine. Stir in flour and cook until smooth. Slowly add milk a little at a time and continue cooking until mixture is smooth and has thickened. Do not boil. Add orange juice and sour cream. Remove from heat. Stir in sherry.

Arrange rice in 6-cup casserole; cover with layer of orange slices. Add a layer of cooked turkey. Pour sauce over all and garnish with remaining orange slices. Sprinkle with almonds. Bake at 350 degrees F. for 25 to 30 minutes. Yield: 6 servings.

Five-Can Casserole

1 small can boned turkey or chicken
   (or your favorite fish)
1 small can evaporated milk
1 can cream of chicken soup
1 can cream of mushroom soup
1 (5-ounce) can Chinese noodles

Mix all ingredients together. Bake in buttered 1-quart casserole for 25 minutes at 350 degrees F., or heat and serve from chafing dish. It may also be served plain or in patty shells. Although the recipe sounds as if the dish would be thin, the Chinese noodles take up some of the moisture. Don't dilute soups.

Superb Turkey Hash

1 large onion, finely chopped
2 green peppers, diced
5 tablespoons butter or margarine
2 tablespoons cooking oil
4 cups diced, cold, cooked turkey
Hot pepper sauce
2 cups cold leftover turkey dressing
Salt and pepper
1½ teaspoons tarragon
½ cup blanched almonds or walnut
   meats
8 eggs, slightly beaten
¾ cup grated Parmesan cheese

Sauté the onion and green pepper in butter and oil until just wilted. Add the turkey and dressing and mix well. Add seasonings and almonds and toss. Press the turkey down well in the skillet. Cover for just 2 or 3 minutes. When the turkey is thoroughly heated, pour in the beaten eggs, mixed with the grated cheese, and cook over low heat until set. If practicable, run the skillet under the broiler for just 2 or 3 minutes to brown the egg and cheese.

Turkey Hash

      2 *cups leftover turkey gravy or cream*
          sauce
     ¼ *cup finely diced onion*
      3 *cups finely diced cooked turkey*
      1 *cup cooked diced celery, drained*
      3 *tablespoons chopped green pepper*
      1 *tablespoon chopped parsley*
     Salt and pepper
      2 *teaspoons sherry, if desired*

Heat gravy or cream sauce with onions until it comes to a boil. Stir in other ingredients and heat through, adjusting seasoning to taste. Stir in sherry if desired. Yield: 5 cups.

Turkey Hash

     ½ *cup butter*
      1 *cup flour*
      2 *cups milk*
      2 *cups stock*
      2 *cups chopped celery*
     ½ *cup grated onion*
      1 *teaspoon white pepper*
     Salt to taste
      8 *cups turkey, cut into bite-size pieces*

Melt butter in large saucepan. Add flour and stir over medium heat until butter takes up all the flour. Let brown very slightly. Add milk, stock, celery, onion, and white pepper. Salt to taste. Cook on low heat, about 20 minutes. Add turkey and simmer 30 minutes. Yield: 25 servings.

Holiday Buffet Turkey Loaf

   Green Layer:

      1 *package lime-flavored gelatin*
      1 *cup boiling water*
     ¾ *cup ice water*
      1 *teaspoon salt*
      3 *tablespoons vinegar*
      1 *cup grated cucumber*
     ¼ *cup chopped green pepper*
     ½ *cup chopped celery*

Dissolve gelatin in hot water. Add cold water, salt, and vinegar. Chill until slightly

thickened. Add vegetables and pour into mold. Chill until firm.

   Red Layer:

    1½ *tablespoons unflavored gelatin*
     ½ *cup cold water*
      1 *cup tomato juice*
      1 *teaspoon onion juice*
      1 *teaspoon salt*
      2 *cups ground, cooked turkey*

Soak gelatin in cold water. Heat tomato juice; add gelatin and stir until completely dissolved. Chill until slightly thickened. Fold in seasonings and turkey. Put mixture over green layer and chill until firm. Unmold and garnish with poinsettia flowers of pimiento and green pepper.

Turkey or Chicken Loaf

      1 *envelope unflavored gelatin*
     ½ *cup cold turkey stock or chicken*
          bouillon
      1 *cup boiling turkey stock or chicken*
          bouillon
     ½ *teaspoon salt*
      2 *tablespoons lemon juice*
     ¼ *cup pineapple juice*
    1½ *cups diced cooked turkey or chicken*
     ½ *cup well-drained crushed pineapple*
     ½ *cup diced celery*
     Mayonnaise or salad dressing

Soften gelatin in cold stock; add boiling stock with salt, and stir until gelatin has softened. Add lemon juice and pineapple juice and chill until consistency of egg white. Fold in turkey or chicken, pineapple, and celery. Put in a 3-cup mold and chill until firm. Unmold and serve with mayonnaise or salad dressing. Yield: 6 servings.

Herb-Baked Chicken
(4-ounce serving, 140 calories)

   Use 1½ to 3 pounds of tender broiler-fryer pieces. Brush chicken pieces lightly with soft margarine or salad oil. Sprinkle with salt, pepper, and a pinch of dried thyme. Place pieces skin side down on a rack in a shallow open pan.

Bake 30 minutes at 400 degrees F. Turn chicken pieces; brush lightly with drippings in pan. Sprinkle with salt, pepper, and thyme. Bake 30 minutes longer, or until golden and fork-tender.

Chicken à la King

    ½ cup chopped green pepper
    ⅔ cup butter or margarine
    ⅔ cup flour
    4 cups chicken broth
    2 cups milk
    2 teaspoons salt
    1 teaspoon pepper
    2 teaspoons paprika
    1 egg yolk, slightly beaten
    2 (4-ounce) cans pimientos, chopped
    2 cups cooked, diced chicken
    Toasted breadcrumbs

Lightly brown green pepper in butter or margarine; add flour and mix until smooth. Add chicken broth, milk, salt, pepper, and paprika. Cook slowly, stirring constantly, until slightly thickened. Add egg yolk gradually and stir for 1 minute. Add pimientos and chicken; simmer until all ingredients are heated thoroughly and mixture is thick. Top with toasted breadcrumbs.

Bill Long's Barbecued Chicken

Allow ½ chicken per person, planning in terms of 6 servings. Place chicken halves on broiling rack, skin side down, about 5 inches from the heat. Broil a few minutes, turn, brush with melted butter, and broil other side the same length of time. Turn chicken pieces at regular intervals, allowing 45 minutes to 1 hour cooking time. Baste frequently with Barbecue Sauce.

Barbecue Sauce:

    ½ cup vinegar
    ⅓ cup salad oil
    1 teaspoon Worcestershire sauce
    ½ teaspoon grated onion
    ½ clove garlic, minced
    ¾ teaspoon salt
    ¼ teaspoon paprika
    1½ tablespoons tomato paste
       Few drops Tabasco sauce
    ¼ teaspoon dry mustard

Mix all ingredients and use as a baste for broiling chicken. Yield: enough for 6 chicken halves.

Barbecued Chicken

    ½ cup soy sauce
    ½ cup brown sugar
    3 drops Tabasco sauce
    1½ teaspoons ground ginger
    ½ teaspoon paprika
    1 clove garlic, chopped
    1 cup pineapple juice
    ¼ cup melted butter
    ½ cup water
    2 or 3 fryers, halved

Mix all ingredients. Cut chickens in half and soak in sauce mixture for 3 hours, turning every 30 minutes. Cook chickens on grill or barbecue pit.

Lemon Barbecue Chicken

2 (2½- to 3-pound) broilers
1 cup salad oil
½ cup fresh lemon juice
1 tablespoon salt
1 teaspoon paprika
2 teaspoons crushed basil
2 teaspoons onion powder
½ teaspoon crushed thyme
½ teaspoon garlic powder

Split chickens in halves or quarters; place in shallow baking pans. Combine other ingredients in a jar and shake well to blend. Pour sauce over chicken; cover tightly and marinate in refrigerator for 6 to 8 hours or overnight, turning chicken occasionally.

Remove chicken from refrigerator about an hour before grilling. Place chicken on grill, skin side up, and cook about 20 to 25 minutes, brushing often with sauce. Turn chicken and cook an additional 20 minutes.

Chicken may be cooked in oven. Place 8 inches from broiler; brush often with sauce. Yield: 4 to 8 servings.

Grilled Chicken and Scalloped Potatoes

2½-pound frying-size chicken, cut in
    pieces for serving
Salt
Melted butter
Potatoes, cut in slices or strips
Salt and pepper
Milk
Cubes of Cheddar cheese

Sprinkle chicken pieces with salt. Place on grill over hot coals to cook. Set a pan of melted butter on grill and baste chicken as it cooks; turn the chicken to cook on all sides.

While chicken is cooking, prepare potatoes. Put potatoes in a shallow pan; sprinkle with salt and pepper. Pour a little milk over potatoes and dot with cubes of cheese. Cover pan with aluminum foil and cook until potatoes are tender. Potatoes should be done when chicken is tender. Yield: 6 servings.

Brandied Chicken Anise

⅓ stick butter
1 clove garlic, minced
1 small onion, chopped
4 whole chicken breasts
Salt to taste
1 chicken bouillon cube
½ cup water
½ cup brandy
¼ teaspoon anise seed

Melt butter in heavy skillet; add garlic and onion and sauté until transparent. Remove from skillet and brown chicken breasts in the butter. When chicken is brown on all sides, return garlic and onion to the skillet. Add salt, bouillon cube, water, brandy, and anise seed.

Cover the skillet and cook over low heat until the chicken is tender (about 45 minutes). Yield: 4 servings.

Chicken Breasts Riviera

4 boned chicken breasts
½ cup buttermilk
¼ pound butter
¾ teaspoon salt
⅔ cup grated Parmesan cheese
1 tablespoon minced parsley
1 cup cooking sherry
1 (4-ounce) can sliced mushrooms

Place chicken breasts in buttermilk while preparing fire. Line firebox of grill with aluminum foil. Allow coals to burn down until covered with a gray ash. Place butter in a frypan and place on grill. (Pan may be made by doubling foil and folding around sides to make a shallow edge.)

Remove chicken breasts from buttermilk and sprinkle with salt. Combine Parmesan cheese and parsley and coat both sides of chicken with this mixture. Place in frypan when butter is hot. After 5 minutes and when chicken breasts are well coated with butter, place the breasts on the open grill until they are a golden brown. Then place them back in frypan.

Pour the sherry over chicken and simmer about 1 hour, basting frequently with sherry and butter from the pan. During the last 30 minutes, add the mushrooms. Remove chicken to hot platter and spoon the remaining sauce over it. Garnish with parsley and whole preserved kumquats, if desired. Yield: 4 to 8 servings.

Chicken Breasts Supreme

    6 large broiler-fryer chicken breasts,
        boned
    Salt and pepper
    ¾ cup butter or margarine, divided
    ¼ cup finely chopped onion
    2 tablespoons finely chopped parsley
    ½ teaspoon each rosemary and basil
    1½ cups packaged stuffing mix
    ½ cup boiling water

Halve breasts. Cut through thickest part of each half breast to form a pocket. Sprinkle with salt, and pepper. Melt ½ cup butter in saucepan. Add onion and cook until tender but not brown. Stir in herbs and stuffing mix. Add boiling water; mix well. Fill breast pockets with stuffing; secure with skewers. Place on rack in shallow baking pan. Brush with remaining ¼ cup butter, melted. Bake at 350 degrees F. for 1 hour. Serve with Supreme Sauce. Yield: 6 servings.

    Supreme Sauce:

    3 tablespoons butter or margarine
    3 tablespoons flour
    2 chicken bouillon cubes
    1¾ cups boiling water
    ½ cup heavy cream
    2 egg yolks
    ½ teaspoon paprika
    2 teaspoons lemon juice

Melt butter in saucepan. Blend in flour. Add bouillon cubes to boiling water; stir slowly into blended flour and butter. Cook, stirring constantly, until mixture thickens and comes to a boil. Beat together heavy cream and egg yolks. Add to bouillon mixture and heat to serving temperature, stirring constantly. Stir in paprika and lemon juice.

Chicken Cornelia

    7 whole chicken breasts, split, boned,
        and skinned (making 14 portions)
    Salt, pepper, and paprika
    1 can cream of mushroom soup
    1 can cream of chicken soup
    1 pint whipping cream
    1 cup Noilly Prat vermouth
    Mushrooms, sautéed in butter
    Parsley, finely chopped

Sprinkle chicken breasts with salt, pepper, and paprika. Lay them, not touching, in a well-greased broiler pan of oven. Mix together the two soups, whipping cream, and vermouth. Pour this mixture over the chicken. Bake, uncovered, at 350 degrees F. for 1 hour. The sauce turns into a luscious golden gravy.

Just before serving, get out a large skillet and in it sauté as many mushrooms as desired. When they are nicely browned (about 7 minutes), spoon them over the chicken breasts and gravy, which have been placed on a large serving platter. Garnish with a drift of finely chopped parsley. Yield: 14 servings.

Creamed Chicken

    ½ pound butter or chicken fat
    2 cups flour
    1½ teaspoons salt
    Pepper to taste
    4 cups hot milk
    2½ cups chicken broth
    1 cup cream
    8 cups shredded, cooked chicken
    1 can mushroom soup
    8 egg yolks, diced
    Patty shells, bread cases, or thin toast

Melt butter or chicken fat; smooth in the flour, salt, and pepper. Add the hot milk gradually, stirring constantly. Add chicken broth, cream, and chicken. Heat well, and add mushroom soup and diced egg yolks. Serve in patty shells, in bread cases, or on thin, crisp toast. Yield: 40 servings.

Chicken Casserole

    4 *cups diced, cooked chicken*
    4 *cups chicken broth*
 1½ *cups diced celery*
    1 *cup diced processed cheese*
    1 *large onion, diced*
    2 *eggs, beaten*
    1 *can mushroom soup*
    ½ *teaspoon pepper*
    2 *teaspoons salt*
    1 *cup water chestnuts (optional)*
    4 *cups cracker crumbs*

Combine all ingredients except 1 cup cracker crumbs saved to sprinkle on top of casserole. Bake uncovered at 350 degrees F. for 45 minutes. Yield: 8 to 10 servings.

Chicken-Rice Casserole

    1 *cup uncooked rice*
    1 *can cream of celery soup*
    1 *can cream of chicken soup*
    1 *cup water*
    6 *chicken breasts*
    ½ *stick melted butter*

Put rice in the bottom of a 2-quart casserole. Mix soup with water and pour over rice. Dip chicken breasts in melted butter, then lay on top of the rice. Bake at 325 degrees F. for about 45 minutes. Yield: 6 to 8 servings.

Chicken and Ham Bake

    ¼ *cup chopped onion*
    ¼ *cup margarine*
    2 *tablespoons parsley flakes*
    ½ *teaspoon poultry seasoning*
    ¼ *teaspoon pepper*
    1 *cup cracker crumbs*
    ¼ *cup water*
    1 *egg*
 1½ *cups chopped, cooked chicken*
    ¼ *pound American cheese, shredded*
    6 *slices boiled ham*
    ¼ *pound sliced American cheese*

Sauté onion in margarine until tender. Add parsley, seasonings, cracker crumbs, water, egg, chicken, and ¼ pound shredded cheese; mix well. Place a large spoonful of stuffing in center of each ham slice. Fold ham over stuffing. Secure with toothpicks. Place in a 10- x 6- x 2-inch baking dish and cover with foil. Bake at 350 degrees F. for 20 or 30 minutes. Remove foil and lay slices of cheese on centers of ham rolls. Bake 5 minutes more until cheese melts. Yield: 6 servings.

Chicken Continental

    3-pound frying chicken, cut in pieces
    ⅓ *cup seasoned flour*
    ¼ *cup butter*
    1 *(10½-ounce) can condensed cream of chicken soup*
 2½ *tablespoons grated onion*
    1 *teaspoon salt*
    Dash pepper
    1 *tablespoon chopped parsley*
    ½ *teaspoon celery flakes*
    ½ *teaspoon thyme*
 1⅓ *cups water*
 1⅓ *cups instant-cooking rice*

Roll chicken in flour; brown in butter. Remove chicken. Stir soup, onion, seasonings, and water into drippings. Cook and stir to a boil. Spread instant rice in 1½-quart shallow casserole. Pour all but ⅓ cup soup mixture over rice. Stir to moisten. Top with chicken and rest of soup mixture. Bake, covered, at 375 degrees F. for 30 minutes. Yield: 4 servings.

Chicken Excelsior House

    6 *chicken breasts*
    Garlic salt
    ¼ *pound butter or margarine*
    1 *teaspoon paprika*
    3 *tablespoons lemon juice*
    1 *cup commercial sour cream*
    ¼ *cup sherry wine*
    1 *(8-ounce) can mushrooms and stems*
    Generous dash cayenne pepper

If chicken breasts are whole, cut them in half and sprinkle generously with garlic salt. Melt butter or margarine; add paprika and lemon juice. Roll chicken breasts in the melted butter mixture and place on baking sheet. Bake at 375 degrees F. for 1 hour or until tender. Make a sauce of sour cream, wine, mushrooms, and pepper. Pour it over the chicken and bake an additional 15 minutes. Yield: 12 servings.

Fried Chicken

6 chicken breasts (or 1 fryer cut into pieces)
2 eggs
1 teaspoon paprika
1 teaspoon salt
½ teaspoon pepper
2 cups flour
Corn oil (enough for 12-inch frying pan)

Prepare chicken. Beat eggs thoroughly. Mix dry ingredients well in a medium-size paper bag. Dip each piece of chicken in egg and then shake it thoroughly in the bag of dry ingredients. Fry in very hot oil about 12 minutes on each side. Yield: 6 servings.

Gâteau de Foies de Poularde

10 to 12 chicken livers
1 tablespoon butter
2 tablespoons consommé
2 whole eggs
2 egg yolks

Mix all ingredients in a blender. Add cream if needed to make a liquid puree. Pour mixture in a mold or pan which has been oiled and lined with waxed paper. Cover with foil and set in a pan of cold water. Bake at 300 degrees F. for 1½ hours. Do not let water in pan boil. Turn out on a plate and slice about ½ inch thick.

Serve on thin buttered toast rounds with chopped lobster or crabmeat covered with a rich white sauce.

Hunter's Chicken
(Family size)

2 fryers, cut in serving-size pieces
½ cup flour
½ teaspoon marjoram
Dash thyme
1 teaspoon salt
½ teaspoon pepper
½ cup cooking oil
1 large onion, finely chopped
1 large green pepper, finely chopped
1 (8-ounce) can mushrooms
1 (No. 303) can tomatoes
1 pint stuffed olives
1 tablespoon chopped parsley
½ cup Sauterne
½ cup sherry

Shake chicken pieces in flour with seasonings added. Put cooking oil in electric skillet and heat; cook chicken slowly until brown. Add onion and green pepper and cook until browned. Add mushrooms, tomatoes, olives, and parsley. Cover and simmer for 20 minutes. Add Sauterne and cook 45 minutes. At the last, add one-half cup sherry, or less, and simmer a few minutes longer.

Chicken Livers and Rice

¼ cup butter or margarine
3 tablespoons minced onions
1⅓ cups packaged precooked rice
½ pound frozen or fresh chicken livers, cut into 1-inch pieces
Seasoned flour
1 can cream of chicken soup, undiluted
½ cup milk
1 tablespoon chopped parsley

Melt 1 tablespoon butter in saucepan, add onions, and cook until tender. Add to rice; cook as package directs. Meanwhile, roll chicken livers lightly in flour; sauté in remaining butter in skillet until browned on each side. In 1½-quart casserole, combine livers, rice, soup, and rest of ingredients. Bake at 375 degrees F. for 30 minutes until hot and bubbly. Yield: 5 to 6 servings.

Bacon-Wrapped Chicken Livers

Chicken livers
Butter
Salt and pepper
Water chestnuts, sliced
Lean streaked bacon

Sauté chicken livers in butter. Salt and pepper generously. This takes about 5 minutes. Cool enough to handle. Place a slice of water chestnut on each side of each chicken liver. Wrap in one-half strip of bacon, and fasten with round toothpick. Place on a shallow sheet pan. Put in oven and cook at 350 degrees F. until bacon is brown. Do not overcook, as livers are already cooked. Drain fat from livers and put in chafing dish for serving, using burner to keep hot.

Paella

6 *ounces Spanish olive oil*
3 *buttons minced garlic*
¼ *pound lean pork, cut in chunks*
½ *frying-size chicken, cut in chunks*
1 *onion, chopped*
1 *green pepper, chopped*
½ *cup canned tomatoes*
½ *pound crawfish or Florida lobster,*
     cut in chunks
¼ *pound oysters*
¼ *pound scallops*
½ *pound shrimp*
½ *pound red snapper*
2 *quarts seafood stock*
2½ *cups rice*
2 *bay leaves*
Pinch of saffron
Dash yellow food coloring
1 *tablespoon salt*
Petits pois
Parsley
Hard-cooked eggs, quartered
Pimiento
Cold, cooked asparagus
White wine

Heat olive oil in a large casserole. Add garlic, pork, and chicken; cook until meat is tender. Then add onion, green pepper, tomatoes, crawfish, oysters, scallops, shrimp, and red snapper (other seafood could be used). When seafood is almost done, add seafood stock and rice. Bring to a boil; then add bay leaves, saffron, food coloring, and salt. When rice begins to thicken, cover and bake at 350 degrees F. for 15 minutes. Serve from casserole; garnish with petits pois, parsley, eggs, pimiento, and asparagus. Sprinkle with white wine. Yield: about 4 servings.

Chicken Korma

2 *(3½-pound) frying-size chickens, cut*
     into serving-size pieces
Salt and pepper
1 *cup buttermilk (or yogurt if you*
     prefer to be fancy)
4 *cloves garlic, minced*
4 *tablespoons butter or margarine*
2 *onions, finely chopped*
½ *teaspoon ground ginger*
2 *whole cloves*
2 *teaspoons salt*
2 *teaspoons ground coriander*
2 *teaspoons ground almonds*
¾ *teaspoon ground turmeric*
¾ *teaspoon ground cumin seeds*
¼ *teaspoon ground pepper*
¼ *teaspoon ground chili peppers or*
     cayenne pepper

Sprinkle chicken pieces with salt and pepper. Place in a large bowl; pour buttermilk or yogurt mixed with half the garlic over the chicken. Marinate at room temperature for 2 hours or longer, basting frequently.

Melt butter in a 3-quart casserole or heavy saucepan or skillet. Add onions, remainder of the garlic, ginger, cloves, and salt. Sauté over low heat for 5 minutes, stirring frequently.

Mix other ingredients together and add to sautéed mixture. Cook for 5 minutes, stirring constantly. Add chicken and marinade and stir well. Cover and cook over low heat (or in 350-degree oven) for 1½ to 2 hours or until chicken is tender. Stir occasionally. Yield: 4 servings.

Party-Special Chicken

  2 *pounds chicken parts*
  2 *cups diagonally sliced celery (1 inch)*
  ½ *cup chopped onion*
  ½ *teaspoon ground ginger*
  2 *tablespoons butter or margarine*
  1 *(10½-ounce) can condensed cream*
      of chicken soup
  1 *(11-ounce) can mandarin oranges,*
      drained
  ¼ *cup shredded coconut*

In skillet, brown chicken and cook celery, onion, and ginger in butter until vegetables are tender. Remove chicken and place skin side down in shallow baking dish (12 x 8 x 2 inches). Stir soup into skillet to loosen brown bits; pour over chicken. Bake at 375 degrees F. for 30 minutes. Turn chicken; bake 30 minutes longer. Top with oranges and coconut the last 10 minutes. Yield: about 4 servings.

Bertha's Dishpan Pie

  1 *broiler-fryer (about 3 pounds), cut-up*
Salt
  5 *cups (about) self-rising flour*
  1 *cup shortening*
  2 *cups buttermilk*
  ½ *pound butter or margarine*
Pepper
  2 *quarts (about) hot water*

Cut chicken into serving pieces; salt and let sit 30 minutes. Make biscuit dough of self-rising flour, shortening, and buttermilk. Be sure to knead harder than for biscuits.

Roll part of dough very thin and cut into strips; use to line bottom and sides of buttered 6-quart roasting pan or any large casserole. Place about half of the chicken pieces (raw) over the strips in pan; add lumps of butter between pieces and sprinkle with pepper to taste. Place strips of pastry (or dumplings) on the chicken until it is completely covered; then place remaining chicken on this pastry and repeat the butter and pepper. Save enough butter to butter two crusts.

Roll piece of dough large enough to cover the chicken in pan, and seal it to the side crusts by pressing with the fingertips. Dampen crust well with water. Make a small hole in the center of the crust and pour in enough boiling water to barely float the crust. Place in 450-degree F. oven and cook until crust is brown, about 25 minutes. Remove from oven and brush crust well with butter. Roll out another top crust and place on top of the other cooked crust; return to oven to brown, about 10 minutes; then butter top crust.

Reduce oven heat to very low, and continue cooking until chicken is very tender when tested with a fork. Or the pie may be completed on top of the range, over very low heat. Add more water if the pie gets too dry. Overall cooking time is about 1 hour and 45 minutes. Yield: 4 to 6 servings.

Chicken Pie

    Pastry for two-crust pie
  6 *tablespoons butter or chicken fat*
  6 *tablespoons flour*
  ½ *teaspoon salt*
  ¼ *teaspoon pepper*
1¾ *cups chicken broth*
  ⅔ *cup rich milk*
  2 *cups chopped, cooked chicken*

Prepare pastry; divide in two parts, two-thirds in one part and one-third in other. Roll out and place two-thirds in 10- x 6- x 1½-inch baking pan.

Melt butter; add flour and seasonings. Let bubble. Add liquids and cook slowly until thickened. Add chicken. Pour into pastry-lined pan. Top with rest of pastry. Pinch edges together. Bake at 425 degrees F. for 35 minutes. Yield: 6 servings.

Chicken Pie Deluxe

1¼ *cups packaged prepared herb-*
seasoned stuffing
½ *cup butter or margarine*
½ *cup milk*
1 *(10½-ounce) can condensed cream*
of celery soup
1½ *cups cooked, boned chicken in pieces*
¾ *cup cooked peas*
1 *tablespoon minced onion*
Dash of pepper
¾ *cup prepared packaged herb-*
seasoned stuffing, finely crumbled
Parsley

Mix 1¼ cups stuffing with butter. Press
mixture to bottom and sides of 9-inch
pie plate. In saucepan, stir milk into soup;
add chicken, peas, onion, pepper. Heat and
turn into pie shell.

Bake at 425 degrees F. about 10 minutes
or until bubbly. Then on top of pie arrange
border of the ¾ cup stuffing. Sprinkle center
with parsley. Yield: 6 servings.

Fried Meat Pies

2 *(6½-ounce) cans boned chicken*
½ *small green pepper*
1 *medium jalapeño pepper*
2 *sticks celery*
½ *medium onion*
Cooking oil
2 *tablespoons water*
Salt and pepper to taste
1 *tube ready-to-cook biscuits or pie*
dough

Shred chicken or put through food chopper.
Chop pepper, jalapeño, and celery into fine
pieces and grate the onion. Sauté vegetables
in cooking oil. Add chicken and water. Add
salt and pepper to taste. Cook until just
enough water remains to keep the meat
moist. Do not let chicken get dry.

Roll biscuits or pie dough to approximately ¹⁄₁₆ inch thickness. Keep biscuits
round as you would for a piecrust. If pie
dough is used, cut round pieces 6 inches in
diameter.

Place 3 tablespoons of the meat mixture
on the dough, spreading it over one-half the
circle to within ½ inch of the edge. Fold the
other half over to form a half-moon-shaped
pie. Flute the edges with a fork.

Drop the pies into hot cooking oil. If biscuit dough is used, cook until a light brown.
Serve hot with frozen fruit or gelatin salad.

Variation: Cooked ground meat, left-over
roast, turkey, or chicken may be substituted
for the boned chicken.

Flaky Crust Chicken Pie

1 *teaspoon salt*
1 *broiler-fryer (2 ½ to 3 pounds),*
chopped
2 *tablespoons butter or margarine*
2 *cups water*
1 *cup milk*
Flour
Pastry
3 *hard-cooked eggs, sliced*

Broil salted chicken in butter; turn and add
2 cups water; cover and simmer until
chicken is tender. Remove meat from bones.
Add milk to chicken broth, and thicken with
a little flour.

Roll one-fourth of the Pastry (see below)
⅛ inch thick, and cut to fit sides of 3-quart
baking pan, having one strip higher than
pan to form edge. Place chicken and sliced
hard-cooked eggs in layers in pan and pour
in the broth.

Roll out remaining pastry, and place on
top of pie, folding under around edge; flute
with fingers. Cut a cross in center of pastry,
and fold triangles back to allow steam to escape while pie bakes.

Bake at 450 degrees F. for 10 minutes;
then reduce heat to 350 degrees F. and bake
15 minutes or until pastry is a delicate
brown. Yield: 4 to 6 servings.

Pastry:

1 *cup plus 2 tablespoons plain flour*
½ *teaspoon salt*
6 *tablespoons shortening*
2½ *tablespoons (about) cold water*

Measure flour, add salt, and sift together into bowl. Cut in 4 tablespoons shortening very thoroughly; add remaining shortening and cut into size of large peas. Sprinkle with water, a little at a time. When all particles are moistened, press into ball.

Chicken Party Pie

Pastry:

1½ cups flour
⅛ teaspoon salt
½ cup shortening
¼ cup water or milk
⅓ cup shredded sharp American cheese

Combine dry ingredients; cut in shortening. Add liquid, blend in cheese, and mix lightly. Roll out on floured board. Place pastry in 9-inch piepan and prick with a fork. Bake at 425 degrees F. for 12 to 15 minutes or until pastry is delicately browned.

Filling:

1½ cups chopped, cooked chicken
1 cup pineapple tidbits, drained
1 cup chopped pecans or walnuts
½ cup chopped celery
1 cup commercial sour cream
⅔ cup mayonnaise
3 tablespoons shredded sharp
　　American cheese
Stuffed olives, sliced

Combine chicken, pineapple, nuts, and celery. Combine sour cream and mayonnaise; add ⅛ cup to chicken mixture and blend. Pour mixture into baked pie shell, top with remaining sour cream mixture, and garnish with shredded cheese and olive slices. Yield: 6 big servings.

Speedy Chicken Pie

2½- to 3- pound broiler-fryer, cut-up
3 cups salted boiling water
3 hard-cooked eggs, sliced
⅛ teaspoon pepper
1 cup self-rising flour
1 cup milk
Butter or margarine

Simmer chicken in salted boiling water until tender. Cool. Save 1½ cups of broth. Remove chicken from bones.

Combine the 1½ cups broth, chicken, eggs, and pepper. Mix flour and milk. Dot bottom of 3- to 4-quart baking dish generously with butter or margarine; pour in batter. Spoon chicken mixture over batter. Bake at 350 degrees F. about 40 minutes or until done. (Part of the batter will rise to surface during cooking.) Yield: 6 servings.

Sour Dough Chicken Pie

2 recipes plain biscuit dough
2 chickens (3 pounds each), cooked,
　　boned, and cut in bite-size pieces
1 pound butter
1 recipe sour dough*
Pepper
10 eggs
2½ to 3 cups chicken stock
2 tablespoons flour
2 cups milk

*Sour dough as the term applies here refers to a recipe of biscuit dough (2 cups flour) covered and left in the refrigerator for 3 days.

Line bottom and sides of large baking pan with one-half of the plain biscuit dough, rolled thin. Place about one-third of the cooked and boned chicken over the pastry and dot with butter. Roll sour dough very thin and cut into dumplings; place layer over chicken and sprinkle with pepper. Over this break 6 whole raw eggs to make a layer; dot with butter. Cover with another layer of sour dough dumplings. Repeat layer of chicken, butter, and dumplings. Add the remaining 4 whole raw eggs and remainder of chicken. Dot with butter and cover with chicken stock seasoned to taste. Sprinkle 2 tablespoons flour over the top and add 2 cups milk.

Roll out remainder of biscuit dough and cut into four equal pieces. Place on top of pie, trim off excess, and press edges of dough together to seal. Dot with butter. Bake at 300 degrees F. for about 2 hours. Yield: 15 servings.

Biscuit-Topped Chicken Pie

Bony pieces of chicken
Boiling water
1 cup chicken broth
2 tablespoons flour
Salt and pepper to taste
2 hard-cooked eggs, sliced
Recipe biscuits

Cover pieces of chicken with boiling water and cook until tender. Remove meat from bones and place in 4-quart casserole. Thicken broth with flour and season to taste; pour over the chicken. Add sliced hard-cooked eggs to casserole. Top with small biscuits and bake at 425 degrees F. for 15 to 20 minutes. Yield: 4 servings.

Poulet Elégante

1 (9-ounce) package frozen artichoke
  hearts
12 small new potatoes, peeled
3 fryer chicken breasts, halved
¼ cup flour
½ cup butter
2 tablespoons chopped green onion
1 (6-ounce) jar mushrooms, undrained
¼ cup dry red wine
½ teaspoon seasoned salt
¼ teaspoon seasoned pepper
½ cup commercial sour cream
1 tablespoon flour

Thaw artichoke hearts. Arrange in buttered 2½-quart casserole with potatoes. Coat chicken pieces with ¼ cup flour. Brown carefully in butter. Place on top of vegetables in casserole. Cook green onion until tender in same skillet used for browning chicken. Add mushrooms with liquid and wine. Pour over chicken.

Next sprinkle with salt and pepper. Cover. Bake at 350 degrees F. for 1½ hours.

Remove the chicken and vegetables to warm serving platter. Blend together sour cream and 1 tablespoon flour. Add to juices in casserole. Heat this gravy through and serve with the chicken. Yield: 6 servings.

Chicken-Noodle Tetrazzini

1 (4-pound) chicken or 8 whole
  chicken breasts
1 teaspoon salt
2 quarts water
1 (10-ounce) package noodles
1 quart chicken broth
½ pound butter or margarine
1 medium green pepper, chopped
1 medium onion, minced
1 (4-ounce) can sliced mushrooms
⅔ cup flour
1 pint milk
2 cups chicken broth
½ pound shredded American cheese
½ pound shredded sharp Cheddar cheese
Salt and pepper to taste

Cook chicken in salted water until tender. Remove from broth, cool, bone, and cut into pieces. Strain broth, cool, and remove fat.

Cook noodles in 1 quart chicken broth. Make sauce by melting butter and adding chopped pepper, minced onion, and sliced mushrooms. Cook until tender; add flour and blend well. Add milk and 2 cups broth and cook until sauce is thick. Stir in shredded cheese and cook over low heat until it melts.

Combine chicken, noodles, and cheese sauce. Add salt and pepper. Place in a 2½- or 3-quart casserole; bake at 350 degrees F. for 40 minutes. Yield: 12 servings.

Rolled Chicken Elégante

1 (3-ounce) can broiled chopped
  mushrooms, drained
2 tablespoons margarine
2 tablespoons all-purpose flour
½ cup light cream
¼ teaspoon salt
Dash cayenne pepper
1¼ cups shredded sharp Cheddar cheese
6 or 7 boned whole chicken breasts
All-purpose flour
2 eggs, slightly beaten
¾ cup fine, dry breadcrumbs

Cook mushrooms in margarine about 5 minutes. Blend in flour; stir in cream. Add salt and cayenne; cook and stir until mixture becomes very thick. Stir in cheese; cook over very low heat, stirring constantly, until cheese is melted. Turn mixture into pie plate. Cover; chill thoroughly, about 1 hour. Cut the firm cheese mixture into six or seven equal portions; shape into short sticks.

If not already done, remove skin from chicken breasts. To make cutlets, place each piece of chicken, boned side up, between two pieces of plastic wrap. (Overlap where chicken breast is split.) Working out from the center, pound with wooden mallet to form cutlets not quite ¼ inch thick. Peel off plastic wrap. Sprinkle meat with salt.

Place a cheese stick on each chicken breast. Tucking in the sides, roll chicken as for jellyroll. Press to seal well.

Dust the chicken rolls with flour, dip in slightly beaten egg, then roll in fine, dry breadcrumbs. Cover and chill chicken rolls thoroughly, at least 1 hour. (Or prepare ahead when entertaining; the rolls can chill all afternoon or overnight.) About an hour before serving time, fry rolls in deep, hot fat 5 minutes or until crisp and golden brown; drain on paper towels. Place rolls in shallow baking dish and bake in slow oven, 325 degrees F. about 30 to 45 minutes. Yield: 6 to 7 servings.

Chicken Soufflé

    8 *slices day-old bread*
    2 *cups chopped, cooked chicken*
    ½ *cup mayonnaise*
    1 *cup diced celery*
    ¾ *cup finely chopped onion*
    ¾ *cup finely chopped green pepper*
       Salt and pepper to taste
    4 *eggs, beaten*
    3 *cups milk*
    1 *can cream of mushroom soup*
    1 *cup shredded cheese*

Cut 4 slices of the bread into cubes; remove crusts from the other 4 slices. Line bottom of a 10½- x 7- x 1½-inch baking dish with the bread cubes.

Combine chicken, mayonnaise, celery, chopped onion, and pepper; season to taste. Spread this mixture over bread cubes. Cover with bread slices. Combine beaten eggs and milk and pour over bread slices; cover and place in refrigerator overnight.

One hour before serving time, preheat oven to 350 degrees F., and bake soufflé for 15 minutes. Pour undiluted soup over mixture and bake 30 minutes. Sprinkle top with shredded cheese and bake an additional 15 minutes. Yield: 10 to 12 servings.

Scalloped Chicken and Rice

    1 *(4- or 5-pound) chicken, cooked and*
       boned
    2 *cups cooked rice*
    3 *cups chicken broth*
    2 *cups dry breadcrumbs*
    3 *large eggs, well beaten*
    ½ *cup finely diced green pepper*
    ½ *cup chopped pimiento*
    1 *can cream of mushroom soup*

Mix all ingredients except soup. Place mixture in large, buttered baking dish. Spread soup over top and bake, covered, at 325 degrees F. for 45 minutes. Garnish as desired. Yield: 6 to 8 servings.

Chicken Vermouth

    4 *chicken breasts*
       Salt and pepper
    ¼ *pound butter or margarine, melted*
    ½ *cup honey*
    ¼ *cup lemon juice*
    ¼ *cup dry vermouth*

Place chicken breasts in heavy flat pan. Season with salt and pepper. Broil chicken just enough to brown lightly; remove from oven and cover with melted butter to which has been added the honey, lemon juice, and vermouth. Cover with aluminum foil and bake at 325 degrees F. for about 1 hour. Yield: 4 to 8 servings.

Country Captain

3½- pound young, tender hen
⅓ cup flour
½ teaspoon salt
¼ teaspoon pepper
½ cup shortening
1 cup finely chopped onion
1½ cups finely chopped green pepper
1 clove garlic, finely chopped
1 teaspoon salt
½ teaspoon white pepper
2 teaspoons curry powder
4¾ cups canned tomatoes
1 teaspoon chopped parsley
½ teaspoon powdered thyme
¼ pound (1 cup) shelled almonds, blanched, or 1 cup canned toasted almonds
2 cups hot cooked rice
¼ cup currants
Parsley for garnish, if desired

Cut chicken into frying-size pieces; remove skin. Combine flour, salt, and pepper. Roll chicken in flour mixture, coating evenly. Brown on all sides in hot shortening. Remove from skillet; put chicken in a pan and keep warm.

Into the drippings put onion, green pepper, and garlic. Cook very slowly, stirring constantly, until vegetables are tender. Add salt, pepper, and curry powder toward the end of this step. Add the tomatoes, parsley, and thyme.

Put warm chicken pieces in roaster; pour tomato mixture over. If it does not cover the chicken, add a little water to the skillet and rinse it out over the chicken. Cover and bake at 350 degrees F. for 45 minutes or until chicken is tender.

Split blanched almonds in halves; brown lightly in a little melted butter. (Reheat canned almonds a few minutes in small frying pan or in oven.)

To serve, put chicken in center of large heated platter; pile rice around it. Drop currants into hot sauce to plump them; pour over chicken. Scatter toasted almonds on top. Garnish with parsley, if desired. Yield: 6 to 8 servings.

Poulet Marengo·

6 large chicken breasts, split and skinned
1 stick margarine
1 teaspoon salt
2 tablespoons chopped chives
1 tablespoon tomato paste
1½ cups chicken stock
1 (4-ounce) can sliced mushrooms
2 packages frozen lobster tails
3 ripe tomatoes, cut in wedges

Brown chicken breasts in margarine. Sprinkle with salt and chives; place, meat side down, in skillet. Mix tomato paste, chicken stock, and mushrooms and pour over chicken. Cover and let simmer until tender, about 45 minutes. Cook lobster according to package directions. Remove meat from shell and cut into bite-size pieces. About 5 minutes before serving, add lobster to chicken mixture. Remove to platter, using tomato wedges as a garnish. Pour sauce over mixture. Yield: 12 servings.

Chicken á la Vinson

1 large fryer or medium-size hen
5 tablespoons flour
Salt and pepper
Paprika
8 ounces olive oil
2 medium onions, chopped
5 small green onions, chopped
3 branches celery, chopped
1 large clove garlic, minced
3 tablespoons chopped parsley
1 large green pepper, chopped
1 (4-ounce) can mushrooms
1 jar marinated artichokes
Italian seasoning
Wine to taste

Prepare the fryer or hen as for frying. Disjoint and clean carefully. Place the chicken in a paper bag in which the flour, salt, pepper, and paprika have been combined. Shake until chicken is coated with the mixture. Remove the chicken from the bag and place in an iron pot in which the olive oil has been heated. Brown the pieces of chicken; then remove from the pot and place on brown paper to drain. Pour off part of the olive oil—leave just enough to cover the bottom of the pot. Sauté the chopped onion, celery, garlic, parsley, and pepper in the oil remaining in the pot.

Add the juice from a can of mushrooms and the oil from a jar of marinated artichokes to the sautéed mixture. Return the chicken to the pot. Simmer until the chicken is tender. Add a small amount of Italian seasoning to the mixture. Add the mushrooms, artichokes, and several tablespoons of wine (if desired) to the chicken just before serving.

Serve over long-grain rice, or for a special treat serve over wild rice. Yield: 6 servings.

Chicken Breasts in White Wine

    8 *chicken breasts*
    4 *tablespoons butter*
    ½ *cup white wine*
      Seasoning to taste
    3 *cups rich white sauce or 2 cups white*
        sauce and 1 can mushroom soup
    1 *cup sliced button mushrooms*
    ½ *cup slivered toasted almonds*

Sauté chicken breasts in butter to a light brown. Arrange in a glass baking dish or casserole. Add wine and seasoning to white sauce. Add mushrooms and pour over chicken. Bake at 350 degrees F. for 1 hour. Sprinkle with almonds 10 minutes before removing from oven. Yield: 8 servings.

Chicken in Wine

    2 *frying-size chickens*
      Flour
      Approximately 1 cup cooking oil
    1 *clove garlic, minced*
    1 *(8-ounce) can sliced mushrooms*
      Salt and pepper
      Garlic salt
    1 *bottle white wine*

Cut chicken into serving-size pieces, and coat with flour. Put ½ inch cooking oil in frying pan; brown garlic and remove from oil. Fry chicken until brown; remove from frying pan and place in large flat baking dish.

Empty the mushrooms, juice and all, into frying pan and brown thoroughly. Over the chicken pour the garlic, mushrooms, and oil. Add salt, pepper, and a little garlic salt. Pour wine over chicken and bake in the oven at 325 degrees F. for 1 hour. Serve the gravy over wild rice. Yield: 8 servings.

Rock Cornish Game Hen With Orange, Nut, Rice Stuffing

    6 *Rock Cornish game hens,*
        approximately 1 pound each
    ¼ *cup butter or margarine*
    ¼ *cup chopped onion*
 1⅓ *cups packaged precooked rice*
    1 *cup water*
    ½ *cup orange juice*
    2 *teaspoons grated orange rind*
    2 *tablespoons chopped parsley*
    1 *cup chopped pecans*
    ½ *teaspoon sugar*
    ¼ *teaspoon poultry seasoning*
 1½ *teaspoons salt*
      Melted butter or margarine

Thaw hens, rinse, and pat dry. Melt butter or margarine in saucepan; add onion and sauté until tender, but not browned. Add rice, water, orange juice, orange rind, parsley, nuts, and sugar. Mix just to moisten rice. Bring to a boil quickly over high heat. Cover, remove from heat, and let stand 5 minutes. Add poultry seasoning and salt and mix lightly with a fork.

Lightly salt inside cavity of each hen. Use approximately 1 cup of dressing for each hen, packing lightly.

Place hens breast side up in uncovered pan; bake at 425 degrees F. about 1 hour, or until tender, basting frequently with melted butter or margarine. Yield: 6 servings.

Hen-in-Wine Cornish Casserole

1 *tablespoon rosemary leaves*
1 *cup dry white wine*
4 *Rock Cornish hens, quartered*
¼ *cup flour*
1 *teaspoon salt*
½ *teaspoon black pepper*
1 *teaspoon fresh parsley, cut up*
1 *clove garlic*
½ *cup butter*
1 *pound mushrooms*

Soak rosemary leaves in wine for 30 minutes to 1 hour. Place pieces of hen in paper bag containing mixture of flour, salt, pepper, and parsley. Shake well to coat thoroughly. Brown garlic clove in melted butter in skillet and remove. Add pieces of hen, brown quickly, and remove to casserole dish. Sauté mushrooms in butter remaining in skillet and add to casserole. Pour wine mixture over this and bake in 350-degree F. oven 30 to 45 minutes. Yield: 4 servings.

Rock Cornish Game Hens With Oyster Dressing

4 *Rock Cornish game hens*
2 *small onions, chopped*
2 *tablespoons cooking oil*
3 *dozen oysters, drained and cut in halves*
4 *tablespoons butter*
4 *cups packaged breadcrumbs with herbs*
1 *cup hot oyster liquid (or hot water)*
Salt and pepper

Thaw hens, wash, and pat dry. Fry onions in oil; add drained oysters and cook until edges curl (about 10 minutes). Add 2 tablespoons butter and combine with breadcrumbs. Add hot oyster liquid (or hot water) to mixture to make consistency desired (do not have mixture too dry). Rub Cornish hens inside and outside with remaining butter and season with salt and pepper. Stuff hens, wrap individually in aluminum foil, and bake at 400 degrees F. approximately 1 hour. Fold back foil and let hens brown. Yield: 4 servings.

Batter-Fried Cornish Hens

2 *Rock Cornish game hens*
1 *egg*
¾ *cup milk*
1 *cup sifted flour*
1½ *teaspoons salt*
Corn oil or shortening for frying

Thaw Rock Cornish hens and quarter. Beat egg slightly and combine with milk. Gradually add to flour mixed with salt; stir to a smooth batter. Heat enough fat in deep pan to just cover hen. Fat should be hot enough to brown a bread cube in 60 seconds or 350 degrees F. on frying thermometer. Dip hen in batter and then in hot fat. Hens should be thoroughly cooked to a golden brown in approximately 15 minutes. Drain on unglazed paper. Yield: 2 servings.

Harvest Cornish Hens

3 *Rock Cornish game hens, halved*
1½ *teaspoons salt*
½ *cup butter or margarine*
1½ *cups orange juice*
2 *tablespoons slivered orange peel*
2 *teaspoons instant minced onion*
½ *teaspoon ground ginger*
¼ *teaspoon hot pepper sauce*
4 *teaspoons cornstarch*
½ *cup toasted slivered almonds*
2 *oranges, cut in quarters*
2 *cups seedless grape clusters, if desired*

Thaw hens, rinse, and pat dry. Sprinkle halves on both sides with salt. Heat butter in large skillet. Add halves three at a time; brown on both sides, removing as browned. Return all halves to skillet; add orange juice and peel, onion, ginger, and hot pepper sauce. Simmer, covered, for 20 to 25 minutes or until tender. Arrange halves on heated platter; keep warm.

Blend cornstarch with a little cold water; stir into sauce in skillet. Cook, stirring constantly, until mixture thickens and comes to a boil. Add almonds, orange sections, and grapes, if desired. Heat gently. Pour a little sauce over hens. Serve remaining sauce separately. Surround with hot mashed potatoes or rice. Garnish with parsley, orange sections, and grapes. Yield: 6 servings.

Rock Cornish Hens Imperial

   3 *Rock Cornish game hens, halved*
    Cooking sherry
   3 *cups breadcrumbs*
1¼ *cups Parmesan cheese*
1½ *cloves garlic, crushed*
  ¼ *teaspoon pepper*
   3 *teaspoons salt*
   1 *teaspoon parsley flakes*
  ¾ *cup chopped blanched almonds*
1½ *sticks butter, melted*
    Parsley for garnish

Thaw hens, rinse, and pat dry. Soak the halved Cornish hens in cooking sherry for 2 hours. Combine breadcrumbs, Parmesan cheese, garlic, pepper, salt, parsley flakes, and almonds. Mix well; add two-thirds of the melted butter and stir. Drain the hens and dip each piece in the remaining third of the melted butter; then roll in the breadcrumb mixture. Place the pieces in an uncovered metal pan (13- x 9-inch pan will hold hens). Put a small amount of butter on each piece. Bake at 350 degrees F. for 1 hour. Garnish with parsley; serve warm. Yield: 6 servings.

Cornish Hen—Brown Apple Stuffing

  ¼ *cup butter*
   4 *Rock Cornish game hen livers*
   1 *apple, peeled and sliced*
   1 *medium onion, peeled and sliced*
   3 *slices white bread*
   3 *slices whole wheat bread*
  ½ *teaspoon brown sugar*
   1 *teaspoon salt*
  ½ *teaspoon pepper*
  ½ *teaspoon poultry seasoning*

Melt butter in skillet. Sauté livers, apple, and onion until slightly brown. Meanwhile, slightly moisten bread under tap and break pieces quickly into bowl. Add brown sugar and seasonings to bread and mix lightly. Cut up hen livers and add with onions and apples to bread mixture. Mix well; adjust seasonings to taste. Brown stuffing quickly in remaining butter in skillet, adding more if needed. Stuff lightly into cavities of birds.

Basic Dressing and Variations

  ½ *cup butter or margarine*
   1 *cup chopped celery with leaves*
  ½ *cup chopped onion*
   2 *cups turkey or chicken broth*
   6 *to 8 cups cornbread and white bread, crumbled*
  ¼ *cup chopped parsley*
  ¼ *teaspoon each basil, rosemary, and thyme*

Melt butter in large skillet; add celery and onion and cook until tender but not brown. Add broth; bring to a boil. Add crumbled bread, parsley, and herbs; mix lightly. Add water or more broth if dressing is too dry. Yield: approximately 3 quarts, enough for 12- to 16-pound turkey.

Oyster Dressing: Substitute liquid from 1 pint oysters for part of broth; add ½ teaspoon Tabasco. Coarsely chop oysters and add to dressing mixture.

Orange Dressing: Add 1 tablespoon grated orange rind and 2 cups diced orange sections to basic dressing.

Mushroom Dressing: Cook ½ pound mushrooms, sliced, with onion and celery. Or substitute liquid from 6-ounce can mushrooms for part of water; add mushrooms to stuffing mixture.

Cornbread-Bacon Dressing

½ cup butter or margarine
1 cup diced bacon
1 cup minced onion
2 cups diced celery
2 teaspoons salt
½ teaspoon pepper
2 teaspoons poultry seasoning
4 cups crumbled cornbread
2 cups white dry breadcrumbs

Heat butter in heavy skillet over low heat. Add bacon, onion, celery, and seasonings and sauté until tender. Combine with cornbread and white bread in bowl. Mix thoroughly and stuff loosely in turkey. Yield: enough for 10-pound turkey.

Cornbread Dressing

1½ cups crumbled cornbread
3 slices dry toast, diced
1 stem celery, chopped
1 small onion, diced
2 or 3 sprigs parsley, chopped
1½ to 1¾ cups orange juice
3- to 5-pound hen

Mix ingredients for dressing together in a large bowl. Amount of orange juice is determined by preference. Stuff hen, and bake at 325 degrees F. for 30 to 40 minutes per pound. As a side dish, dressing may be baked in a buttered casserole dish at 350 degrees F. about 30 minutes or until crust forms on top. Yield: 6 servings.

Cornmeal Mush Turkey Stuffing

3 cups cornmeal
2 cups cold water
6 tablespoons bacon drippings or other shortening
1½ quarts boiling water
1 tablespoon sage
½ teaspoon pepper
1 medium onion, grated fine
6 whole eggs, beaten
1 pound hamburger meat
6 slices dried bread (soaked in water, with water squeezed out)

Make cornmeal mush by adding cold water to the cornmeal until it is nearly moist enough to pour. Put the bacon drippings in the boiling water and slowly add the cornmeal, stirring constantly to avoid lumping. Cook over high heat, stirring continuously to keep from scorching, until the mush tastes done and is very thick. Cool slightly.

Add other ingredients, one at a time, mixing after each addition. Stuff turkey with as much of stuffing as needed. During last hour of baking, place remaining stuffing around turkey. Yield: 8 or 9 cups.

Cornbread Dressing

3½ cups cornbread crumbs
3½ cups white breadcrumbs
¼ cup butter, melted
3 tablespoons minced onion
1 cup chopped celery
2 teaspoons salt
½ teaspoon pepper
½ teaspoon savory seasoning
2 or 3 teaspoons sage
1 egg, beaten slightly
½ cup milk
2 cups hot chicken broth

Crumble bread in large bowl. Melt butter and lightly sauté onion and celery. Add to crumb mixture; add other ingredients and mix well. If dressing seems too dry, add more broth. Bake in shallow pans at 400 degrees F. about 15 to 25 minutes. Yield: 8 servings.

Celery Dressing

¾ pound day-old white bread
3 tablespoons shortening
1¾ cups diced celery
¼ cup chopped onion
¾ teaspoon poultry seasoning
½ teaspoon salt
1 teaspoon celery salt
⅛ teaspoon pepper
½ cup cold chicken broth

Break bread into small pieces after removing crusts. (There should be about 6 cups of coarse crumbs.) Melt shortening in skillet; add celery and onion, and cook over low heat until tender, stirring often. Add bread and seasonings and toss together until well mixed. Cool.

Add the cold broth and mix well. Spoon lightly into cavity of turkey, or bake at 350 degrees F. for 30 to 35 minutes in a separate pan. Yield: about 7 cups dressing.

Madeira Dressing

½ cup butter or margarine
1¼ cups diced onion
1 cup diced celery
½ cup chopped celery tops
1½ teaspoons thyme
1 pound bulk sausage, lightly browned
1 tablespoon salt
1½ teaspoons black pepper
6 to 8 cups coarse breadcrumbs (part white bread; part cornbread)
¾ cup Madeira wine

Melt butter; add onion, celery, celery tops, and thyme; cook until onion and celery are tender. Add to sausage; add salt, pepper, and breadcrumbs. Add Madeira and mix lightly. Stuff the turkey lightly. Yield: enough for a 10-pound turkey.

Rice Dressing

3½ cups rice
1 pint oysters
½ pound bacon
2 large onions, chopped
1 green pepper, chopped
5 stems celery, chopped
3 eggs, beaten slightly
3 teaspoons poultry seasoning
Salt and pepper
2 bay leaves, chipped into slivers
Worcestershire sauce
Dash Tabasco sauce

Boil rice in well-salted water. Do not over-cook. Drain. Boil oysters for 1 minute in their own juice. Fry and crumble bacon. Mix all ingredients together. Add bacon drippings. Add a little of the oyster water if dressing seems too dry. Stuff and bake as usual. Yield: enough for a 12- to 15-pound turkey.

Toasted Rice-Oyster Dressing

1½ cups uncooked rice
3 cups water
1½ teaspoons salt
⅓ cup chopped onion
1 cup chopped celery
3 tablespoons minced parsley
½ cup melted butter or margarine
1½ quarts oysters
3 cups toasted dry breadcrumbs
3 teaspoons poultry seasoning
Salt and pepper to taste
3 eggs, well beaten

Spread rice in shallow baking pan. Toast at 400 degrees F. until golden brown, about 20 minutes, shaking pan occasionally so rice will toast evenly. Combine rice, water, and salt in a 4-quart saucepan.

Heat to boiling; lower heat; cover and cook for 14 minutes or until rice is tender. Cook onion, celery, and parsley in butter until soft. Add oysters and cook until edges curl. Remove from heat and stir in breadcrumbs, poultry seasoning, salt, pepper, eggs, and rice. Toss lightly.

Spread in pan and bake at 450 degrees F. for 20 minutes or stuff loosely in turkey. Yield: enough for 12- to 16- pound turkey.

Oyster Dressing

5 to 6 cups breadcrumbs
½ cup melted butter
½ cup chopped onion
⅛ teaspoon black pepper
1 egg, beaten
1 teaspoon salt
½ cup cold water to moisten
¼ teaspoon thyme
1 teaspoon sage
½ to 1 pint oysters

Combine all ingredients. Pour into greased 3-quart casserole. Bake at 350 degrees F. for 1 hour. Yield: 8 to 10 servings.

Salads and Salad Dressings

Colonial settlers called all greens "sallet," and this included cooked kale, mustard, and poke. Wilted lettuce was also a favorite in early households: the fresh, tender "sallet" leaves were made more palatable by tossing them with hot bacon drippings. Slaw, or coleslaw, a salad made of cabbage, is another alltime Southern favorite.

When we consider the large number of ways and the frequency with which tomatoes are used, it is surprising to learn that early American colonists thought this versatile vegetable was poisonous.

The popularity of fruits in salads is due in part to their abundance in the South's marketplaces. Fruit salad plates are popular fare in all restaurants.

The importance of congealed salads cannot be overlooked. Meats, fruits, and vegetables are mixed with flavored or unflavored gelatin to make an attractive and palatable addition to the meal.

Festive Congealed Salad

- 4 envelopes unflavored gelatin
- 2 cups cold water
- 1½ cups sugar
- 1 tablespoon whole cloves
- 2 cups boiling water
- 1 (20-ounce) can sliced pineapple, cut in bite-size pieces
- 1 (1-pound) bottle maraschino cherries, cut in quarters
- ½ cup vinegar
- 12 to 14 sweet midget gherkins, cut in thin slices
- 1 cup chopped nuts

Soak gelatin in 2 cups cold water. Combine sugar, whole cloves tied in a bag, and 2 cups boiling water; boil for 3 minutes; then remove cloves. Add to gelatin and stir until dissolved. Cool; then add pineapple and cherries (with juice), vinegar, sliced gherkins, and chopped nuts. Spoon into individual molds and chill until firm, or place in a 13- x 9-inch pan. To serve, unmold individual molds onto lettuce or cut into squares from large pan. Yield: 14 to 16 servings.

Congealed Carrot Salad

- 2 (3-ounce) packages lemon-flavored gelatin
- 2 cups boiling water
- 1 (No. 2) can crushed pineapple, drained
- 1 cup grated carrots
- 1 cup shredded Cheddar cheese
- ¾ cup chopped pecans

Dissolve gelatin in boiling water. Drain pineapple; add enough water to liquid drained from pineapple to make 2 cups and stir into the gelatin. Refrigerate until partially congealed; then stir in pineapple, carrots, cheese, and pecans and chill until firm.

Clockwise from the top: Congealed Carrot, Layered Aspic, Congealed Chicken, Strawberry-Cheese, Avocado-Buttermilk Salads.

Heavenly Ambrosia

6 *large and juicy oranges*
4 *ripe bananas*
1 *apple, diced*
½ *cup maraschino cherries, cut in halves*
½ *cup flaked coconut*
Dash salt

Cut oranges first. When peeling orange, hold over bowl so all juice will remain in bowl. Be sure to cut sections deep enough to remove all membrane from orange. Remove sections by cutting along the side of each, dividing membrane from outside to center.

Peel bananas, and slice over oranges. Dice the apple in very small pieces and add to mixture. Add cherries, coconut, and salt. Toss lightly and garnish with additional coconut and a few chopped pecans. This is much better if made several hours ahead of time. Yield: 6 to 8 servings.

Angel Salad

2 *(3-ounce) packages lime-flavored gelatin*
2 *cups hot water*
1 *teaspoon unflavored gelatin*
2 *teaspoons cold water*
2 *(3-ounce) packages cream cheese*
1 *small can crushed pineapple, drained*
1 *cup celery, chopped*
1 *(2-ounce) jar pimientos, chopped*
1 *cup chopped pecans*
½ *pint whipping cream, whipped until stiff*

Mix lime gelatin and hot water. Soften unflavored gelatin in cold water; add to hot gelatin. Soften cheese and blend in pineapple; add celery, pimientos, and pecans. Fold into cooled gelatin and refrigerate until thick, but not firmly jelled. Fold in the whipped cream. Pour into mold that has been rinsed in cold water and chill until firm. Yield: 12 generous servings.

Apple-Walnut Salad

⅔ *cup mayonnaise*
1 *tablespoon lemon juice*
1 *tablespoon sugar*
⅛ *teaspoon salt*
3 *red apples*
1 *cup diced celery*
⅓ *cup chopped walnuts*
Salad greens
Sliced oranges, grapes

Combine mayonnaise, lemon juice, sugar, and salt. Peel and dice apples (leave skin on half an apple to add color to salad). Stir into mayonnaise. Add celery and walnuts. Serve on salad greens, and garnish with sliced oranges and grapes. Yield: about 6 servings.

Cooked Apple Salad

6 *apples*
½ *cup cream cheese, softened*
Mayonnaise or cream
¼ *cup chopped nuts*

Core apples, but do not remove peel. Cook in a covered pan in small amount of water until apples are tender but not mushy. Remove from water and remove peel. Combine cream cheese, a small amount of mayonnaise, and nuts and fill apples with this mixture. Chill and serve with additional mayonnaise. Yield: 6 servings.

Apricot Salad

1 *(17-ounce) can apricots, drained*
¼ *pound Cheddar cheese, shredded*
1 *cup chopped pecans*
Juice from canned apricots
½ *cup sugar*
2 *tablespoons flour*
1 *egg*

In a large, flat dish place a layer of apricots, a layer of cheese, and a layer of pecans. Combine juice from apricots with sugar, flour, and egg. Cook the mixture until thick. Pour over fruit-cheese mixture and chill before serving. Yield: 6 servings.

Apricot Salad

2 (3-ounce) packages orange-flavored gelatin
2 cups boiling water
1 (No. 2) can apricots
1 (6¼-ounce) package miniature marshmallows
1 cup whipped cream (or 1 can evaporated milk, chilled and beaten until thick)

Dissolve gelatin in boiling water and allow to cool and partly set; beat with electric mixer. Add juice and mashed pulp of apricots. Add marshmallows and beat on low speed, then add whipped cream and beat slowly. Pour into bowl and place in refrigerator until congealed. Yield: 12 to 16 servings.

Apricot-Cheese Salad

2 (3-ounce) packages orange-flavored gelatin
2 cups boiling water
1 (No. 303) can apricots, drained
1 (No. 2) can crushed pineapple, drained
1 cup miniature marshmallows
1 cup combined apricot and pineapple juices

Dissolve gelatin in boiling water. Drain apricots and cut each one into three pieces. Mix drained fruits and marshmallows. (Save juice from apricots and pineapple.) Put into refrigerator. Add 1 cup of combined juices to gelatin. Chill until thickened and fold in fruits and marshmallows. Pour into a lightly oiled 12- x 8-inch pan and spread with Topping.

Topping:

1 envelope unflavored gelatin
¼ cup cold water
½ cup sugar
3 tablespoons flour
1 egg, slightly beaten
1 cup combined apricot and pineapple juices
2 tablespoons butter
1 lemon, juice and grated rind
1 cup whipped cream
1 cup shredded cheese

Dissolve gelatin in cold water. In double boiler combine sugar, flour, egg, and juices. Stir in butter, gelatin, lemon juice, and rind. Continue cooking and stirring to blend. When cool, fold in whipped cream and spread over salad. Sprinkle top with shredded cheese and serve in squares on lettuce. Salad is best if made day before serving. Yield: 12 servings.

Apricot Ring Salad

1 pound dried apricots, washed and drained
½ cup water
½ cup sugar
3 (3-ounce) packages lemon- or lime-flavored gelatin
5 cups boiling water
1 (No. 2) can crushed pineapple
1 cup shredded or slivered almonds

Simmer the apricots in the water until very tender. Remove from heat; add the sugar and mash and whip with a fork until it is pureed. Set aside ½ cup.

Dissolve gelatin in boiling water and set aside to cool. Add the reserved apricot puree, pineapple, and almonds. Pour into a 3-quart ring mold or individual molds. Place in refrigerator to harden. Yield: 12 to 16 servings.

Apricot-Cheese Delight Salad

> 1 *(17-ounce) can apricots, drained and chopped fine*
> 1 *large can crushed pineapple, drained*
> 2 *(3-ounce) packages orange-flavored gelatin*
> 2 *cups hot water*
> 1 *cup apricot juice*
> 1 *cup miniature marshmallows*

Drain fruit; keep apricot and pineapple juice separate. Chill fruit. Dissolve gelatin in hot water. Add the apricot juice. Fold in apricots, pineapple, and marshmallows. Chill until firm. Then add Topping.

Topping:

> ½ *cup sugar*
> 3 *tablespoons flour*
> 1 *egg, slightly beaten*
> 2 *tablespoons butter*
> 1 *cup pineapple juice*
> 1 *cup whipping cream, whipped*
> ¾ *cup shredded Cheddar cheese*

Combine sugar and flour. Blend in egg and butter. Add pineapple juice and cook over low heat, stirring constantly until thickened. Let cool thoroughly. Fold in whipped cream and spread over congealed salad. Sprinkle with cheese and chill. Cut in squares and serve on lettuce. Yield: 12 servings.

Frosted Apricot Salad

> 2 *(3-ounce) packages orange-flavored gelatin*
> 2 *cups boiling water*
> 1 *(No. 2) can apricots, drained and mashed*
> 1 *(No. 2) can chunk pineapple, drained*
> 1 *cup fruit juice*
> ½ *cup sugar*
> 2 *tablespoons flour*
> 2 *tablespoons butter*
> 1 *egg, well beaten*
> 1 *cup cream, whipped*

Dissolve gelatin in boiling water. Add 1 cup of the fruit juice to gelatin mixture. Reserve

rest of juice. Add apricots and pineapple. Chill until firm.

Combine 1 cup of fruit juice with sugar, flour, butter, and beaten egg. Cook over low heat until smooth, stirring constantly. Cool. Whip the cream and add to cooked mixture. Frost gelatin mixture with cooked mixture. Garnish with slices of apricots and mandarin oranges, if desired. Nuts may be added to gelatin mixture. Yield: 12 servings.

Banana-Peanut Salad

> 6 *bananas, peeled and cut in half*
> 1 *teaspoon flour*
> 1 *tablespoon sugar*
> ½ *teaspoon ground mustard*
> 1 *tablespoon butter*
> 1 *egg, well beaten*
> 2 *tablespoons vinegar*
> *Crushed or ground peanuts*

Prepare salad dressing before slicing bananas. Mix flour, sugar, and mustard. Add butter, egg, and vinegar and cook over medium heat until mixture thickens.

Slice bananas, roll in salad dressing then in ground peanuts. Serve on lettuce leaf.

Cheeseberry Salad

> 1 *(3-ounce) package cherry-flavored gelatin*
> 1 *cup boiling water*
> 1 *(1-pound) can whole-berry cranberry sauce*
> 2 *tablespoons lemon juice*
> 1 *(8-ounce) package cream cheese*
> 1 *cup cream, whipped*
> 1 *(8¼-ounce) can crushed pineapple or ½ cup chopped nuts*

Dissolve gelatin in boiling water. Add cranberry sauce and lemon juice. When cool, pour into oiled loafpan and chill until thickened. Soften cream cheese; whip until light and fluffy. Fold in whipped cream and pineapple or nuts. Spoon this mixture over thickened gelatin mixture. Freeze, unwrapped, about 3 hours.

Let stand at room temperature about 10 minutes; then slip salad onto sheet of plastic wrap. Cover with moisture- and vapor-proof wrap. Label and freeze until needed.

To serve without freezing, let first layer chill thoroughly, add topping, and chill at least 3 hours before serving. Yield: 6 to 8 servings.

Bing Cherry Salad

　1　(No. 303) can pitted bing cherries, cut in half
　1　(8¼-ounce) can crushed pineapple
　2　(3-ounce) packages cherry-flavored gelatin

Drain juices from cherries and pineapple. Measure 1½ cups, bring to a boil and pour over gelatin. Stir until dissolved. Measure remainder of juice and add water to make 1½ cups. Add to gelatin. Add fruits and stir well. Pour into mold and chill until firm.

Bing Cherry Salad With Wine

　2　(No. 2) cans pitted bing cherries in heavy syrup, chopped
　2　(3-ounce) packages cherry-flavored gelatin
　1　envelope unflavored gelatin, dissolved in cold water
　2　cups boiling water
　½　cup port wine
　4　teaspoons lemon juice
　Dash of salt
　Lettuce
　Mayonnaise

Drain cherries and save 1⅓ cups syrup. Put gelatin into 2-quart bowl. Add boiling water and stir until gelatin dissolves. Cool slightly. Add cherry juice, wine, lemon juice, and salt. Cool until syrupy. Add cherries. Turn into ring mold and chill until firm. Serve on lettuce leaf and top with mayonnaise.

Black Cherry-Wine Mold

　2　(No. 303) cans dark sweet cherries, pitted
　Water
　2　(3-ounce) packages cherry-flavored gelatin
　1　cup red wine

Drain cherries, saving syrup. Add enough water to make 2½ cups liquid. Bring to boil. Add to gelatin, stirring until gelatin is dissolved. Add wine. Chill and when slightly thickened, add cherries. Mold. Serve with sour cream dressing. Yield: 8 servings.

Cherry-Cola Salad

　1　(No. 303) can bing cherries, pitted
　½　cup cola drink
　½　cup chopped pecans
　1　(3-ounce) package black cherry- or raspberry-flavored gelatin

Drain cherries; pour juice into measuring cup and add water to make 1 cup. (Do not use full 2 cups liquid per package of gelatin, as cherries are quite juicy and salad may not be firm enough.) Bring juice to a boil and dissolve gelatin in it. Add cola drink, drained cherries, and pecans. Let sit in refrigerator until firm. Yield: 8 servings.

Deluxe Cheese Mold

　1　(3-ounce) package orange-pineapple-flavored gelatin
　1　cup boiling water
　1　cup orange sherbet
1½　cups cottage cheese
　½　cup crushed pineapple, drained

Dissolve gelatin in boiling water. Blend in sherbet. Chill until very thick. Stir in cottage cheese and pineapple. Spoon into 8 individual molds or a 1-quart mold. Chill until firm.

Celery and Apple Salad

2 *eggs, separated*
½ *cup milk*
½ *cup sugar*
2 *tablespoons cornstarch*
Juice of 3 lemons
Pinch of salt
2 *cups chopped apples*
¾ *to 1 cup chopped celery*
¾ *cup white raisins*

Beat whites of eggs; add yolks and beat again. Add milk and mix well. In top of double boiler combine sugar and cornstarch. Add egg-milk mixture and stir well. Add lemon juice and pinch of salt and cook until it thickens. Cool. Combine apples, celery, and raisins. Add cooled dressing and mix well. Yield: 8 servings.

Chiffon Fruit Salad

1½ *cups canned peach slices, drained*
1 *cup hot peach syrup (or peach syrup and water)*
1 *(3-ounce) package lemon-flavored gelatin*
½ *cup diced celery*
½ *cup chopped nuts*
½ *cup miniature marshmallows*
⅓ *cup mayonnaise*
1 *cup frozen whipped topping*

Line bottom of 1½-quart mold with 8 peach slices for garnish. Chop remaining peach slices. Mix hot peach syrup with gelatin and stir until gelatin dissolves. Chill until thickened. Add celery, nuts, marshmallows, mayonnaise, and chopped peach slices; mix well. Blend with frozen whipped topping. Spoon into salad mold. Chill until firm. Yield: 8 to 12 servings.

Citrus Salad

Crisp salad greens
Orange sections
Grapefruit sections
Maraschino cherries, if desired

Line salad bowl or individual plates with salad greens. Arrange orange and grapefruit sections on greens. Garnish with cherries, if desired. Serve Orange French Dressing (page 329) with salad.

Cola Congealed Salad

1 *(No. 303) can bing cherries, drained*
1 *(No. 2) can crushed pineapple, drained*
1 *(3-ounce) package cherry-flavored gelatin*
1 *(3-ounce) package strawberry-flavored gelatin*
1 *(8-ounce) package cream cheese*
1 *cup chopped pecans*
2 *small bottles cola drink*

Drain cherries and pineapple. Heat liquid to boiling and pour over gelatin; stir until dissolved. Stir in softened cream cheese and mix until smooth. Add pecans, cola, and drained fruits and mix well. Pour into a 13- x 9- x 2-inch pan, or into individual molds, and chill until firm. Yield: 10 servings.

Cranberry-Sour Cream Salad

1 *(3-ounce) package cherry-flavored gelatin*
1 *cup hot water*
1 *can whole-berry cranberry sauce*
½ *cup chopped celery*
¼ *cup chopped nuts*
1 *cup commercial sour cream*

Combine gelatin and hot water and let congeal slightly. Mix cranberry sauce, celery, nuts, and sour cream and stir into gelatin mix. Pour into molds and refrigerate. Serve on lettuce, with mayonnaise, if desired. Yield: 6 to 8 servings.

Cranberry Salad

  1 *(3-ounce) package strawberry-*
     flavored gelatin
  1 *cup boiling water*
  1 *cup cold water*
 ½ *teaspoon salt*
 ½ *cup chopped walnuts*
  1 *cup raw sliced cranberries*
 ½ *cup diced celery*
 ½ *cup chopped apple*
 ½ *cup sliced purple grapes*

Dissolve gelatin in boiling water; add cold water and salt. Place in refrigerator and allow to thicken slightly. Remove from refrigerator and stir in remaining ingredients. Return to refrigerator and chill for about 2 hours. Yield: 6 to 8 servings.

Frozen Cranberry Salad

  2 *(3-ounce) packages cream cheese*
  2 *tablespoons mayonnaise*
  2 *tablespoons sugar*
  1 *flat can crushed pineapple*
  1 *(1-pound) can whole cranberries*
 ½ *cup chopped nuts*
 ½ *pint (1 cup) cream, whipped*

Whip the cream cheese; add mayonnaise, sugar, and crushed pineapple, then cranberries and nuts. Fold in whipped cream. Freeze. Yield: 8 to 10 servings.

Jellied Cranberry Relish

   2 *oranges, quartered and seeded*
   1 *quart cranberries*
1½ *cups sugar*
   2 *envelopes unflavored gelatin*
1½ *cups bottled cranberry juice cocktail*

Put orange quarters and cranberries through food chopper using medium blade. Add sugar; mix well. In saucepan sprinkle gelatin on the cranberry juice cocktail to soften.

Place over low heat, stirring constantly, until gelatin is dissolved. Remove from heat; stir into orange-cranberry relish. Turn into a 6-cup mold and then chill until firm. Yield: 12 servings.

Molded Cranberry Salad

  1 *(8½-ounce) can crushed pineapple*
   Boiling water
  1 *(3-ounce) package raspberry-*
    flavored gelatin
  1 *(1-pound) can whole-berry cranberry*
    sauce
  1 *cup drained mandarin orange*
    sections
  1 *teaspoon grated orange peel*
   Whipped cream dressing

Drain syrup from pineapple. Measure syrup and add boiling water to make 1¼ cups. Dissolve gelatin in hot liquid; chill until partially set. Fold in cranberry sauce, orange sections, grated orange peel, and crushed pineapple. Pour into molds and chill until set. Serve with a whipped cream dressing. Yield: 6 to 8 servings.

Molded Cranberry Salad

  1 *(1-pound) can cranberry sauce*
  1 *cup commercial sour cream*
   Dash salt
  1 *cup diced marshmallows*
  1 *tablespoon unflavored gelatin*
 ½ *cup juice from canned plums*
 ¾ *cup diced canned plums, drained*
 ½ *cup diced celery*
 ½ *cup diced or chopped walnuts*

Beat cranberry sauce, sour cream, and salt with rotary beater; add marshmallows. Soften gelatin in juice from plums.

Dissolve this over hot water and add to cranberry mixture. Chill until partially thickened. Fold in plums, celery, and walnuts. Pour into individual molds and chill until firm. Yield: 6 servings.

Cranberry Mold

  2 *(3-ounce) packages cherry-flavored gelatin*
  1 *envelope unflavored gelatin*
  1 *(No. 2) can pitted bing cherries*
  1 *can whole-berry cranberry sauce*
  ½ *cup chopped apples*
  ½ *cup chopped celery*
  ½ *cup chopped English walnuts*
  ½ *teaspoon salt*

Combine flavored gelatin and unflavored gelatin in a bowl. Drain cherries and measure juice. Add water to make 1½ cups. Heat to boiling; pour over gelatin and stir until dissolved. Add all ingredients and mix well. Pour into large mold and chill in refrigerator until firm. Yield: 12 servings.

Cranberry Salad

  1 *(6-ounce) package cherry-flavored gelatin*
  2 *cups boiling water*
  1 *(1-pound) can cranberry sauce*
  1 *(No. 2) can crushed pineapple, drained*
  2 *cups chopped nuts*

Dissolve gelatin in boiling water. Add cranberry sauce and stir to dissolve. Add drained pineapple. Put in a shallow dish about 1 inch deep and sprinkle nuts on top. Chill overnight or several hours before serving. Yield: 10 to 12 servings.

Cranberry Salad Mold

  2 *(3-ounce) packages raspberry-flavored gelatin*
  1 *teaspoon salt*
  2 *cups hot water*
  1 *cup cold water*
  3 *teaspoons lemon juice*
  2 *cups whole-berry cranberry sauce*
  1 *cup canned crushed pineapple, drained*
  ½ *cup chopped nuts*

Dissolve gelatin and salt in hot water; add cold water and lemon juice and chill. When slightly thickened, add remainder of ingredients. Spoon into mold and chill until firm. Yield: 12 servings.

Creamy Fruit Salad Mold

  1 *cup commercial sour cream*
  ½ *cup salad dressing or mayonnaise*
  ⅓ *cup peanut butter*
  ½ *cup flaked coconut*
  2 *(3-ounce) packages lemon-flavored gelatin*
  1 *cup boiling water*
  1 *(1-pound) can orange and grapefruit sections (about 2 cups)*
  1 *(No. 2½) can pineapple tidbits (about 1½ cups)*
  Water
  1 *cup seeded, halved red grapes*

Stir together sour cream, salad dressing or mayonnaise, and peanut butter until evenly blended. Stir in coconut. Dissolve gelatin in 1 cup boiling water. Drain and measure juices from orange and grapefruit sections and pineapple tidbits; then add enough water to make 2 cups. Stir into gelatin mixture. Add the fruits. Chill gelatin-fruit mixture until partially set, stirring occasionally. Stir the sour cream-peanut butter mixture into the gelatin-fruit mixture. Pour into one 2-quart mold or eight 1-cup individual molds. Chill until set. Unmold on lettuce and garnish with additional fruits, if desired. Yield: 8 servings.

Fruit Delight Salad

  1 *(1-pound) can white grapes, drained*
  1 *can mandarin oranges, drained*
  1 *cup pineapple chunks*
  1 *cup miniature marshmallows*
  1 *cup coconut*
  1 *cup commercial sour cream*
 10 *maraschino cherries*

Combine all ingredients, garnish with cherries, and chill several hours. Yield: 8 servings.

Date Salad

    2 *(3-ounce) packages cream cheese*
  ½ *pint whipping cream, whipped*
    1 *(8-ounce) box dates, chopped*
    1 *small can crushed pineapple, drained*
    1 *cup chopped pecans*
  ½ *teaspoon vanilla extract*

Mix cream cheese and whipped cream. Add dates, pineapple, nuts, and vanilla. Mix and put in refrigerator at least 1 hour before serving. Yield: 8 to 10 servings.

Frozen Date Salad

    1 *(8-ounce) package cream cheese, softened*
    1 *(8½-ounce) can crushed pineapple, undrained*
    1 *cup chopped pitted dates*
    8 *maraschino cherries, chopped*
    1 *tablespoon lemon juice*
  ⅛ *teaspoon salt*
  ½ *pint heavy cream, whipped, or packaged whipped topping*
    2 *tablespoons chopped nuts*

Blend cheese and pineapple. Add dates, cherries, lemon juice, and salt. Fold in whipped cream and nuts. Pour into a 1-quart or individual molds. Freeze until firm. Unmold on lettuce leaves. Yield: 8 servings.

Easy Summer Salad

    1 *(8½-ounce) can crushed pineapple*
    1 *(3-ounce) package mixed-fruit-flavor gelatin*
    1 *envelope whipped topping mix*
    1 *(12-ounce) carton cottage cheese*

Put pineapple in small saucepan; cook for 2 minutes. Add gelatin and cook 2 minutes longer. Set aside to cool. Prepare whipped topping according to package directions. Add cottage cheese and stir well; add to gelatin mixture. Pour into mold or shallow dish and chill until firm enough to cut into squares. Yield: 8 servings.

Dot's Salad

    1 *(3-ounce) package lemon-flavored gelatin*
    1 *cup boiling water*
    1 *(No. 2) can crushed pineapple*
    1 *(3-ounce) package cream cheese*
  ⅓ *cup mayonnaise or salad dressing*
    1 *medium carrot, grated*
    1 *cup finely chopped celery*
  ½ *cup chopped nuts*

Combine gelatin with 1 cup boiling water. Drain pineapple, measure juice, and add water to make 1 cup; then add to gelatin. Chill until partially set. Soften cream cheese and add mayonnaise or salad dressing. Add to gelatin and stir well; add other ingredients. Pour into mold and chill until firm. Yield: 10 to 12 servings.

Frozen Fruit Salad

    2 *(3-ounce) packages cream cheese, at room temperature*
  ⅓ *cup mayonnaise or salad dressing*
    2 *tablespoons lemon juice*
  ¼ *cup sugar*
    1 *teaspoon salt*
 1½ *cups miniature marshmallows*
    1 *(13½-ounce) can pineapple chunks, well drained*
  ½ *cup coarsely chopped walnuts*
    1 *medium orange, peeled and cubed*
  ¼ *cup red maraschino cherries, halved*
  ¼ *cup green maraschino cherries, halved*
    1 *cup heavy cream, whipped*
    Salad greens

Combine cream cheese, mayonnaise, lemon juice, sugar, and salt. Beat with rotary beater until well blended. Stir in rest of ingredients except cream; then gently fold in cream. Spoon mixture into 2 ice cube trays and place in freezer overnight. To serve, let stand at room temperature several minutes; slice and serve on crisp salad greens. Yield: 10 or 12 servings.

Fruited Cream Salad

1 *(3-ounce) package orange-flavored*
  gelatin
1 *cup boiling water*
1 *pint vanilla ice cream*
1 *jar maraschino cherries, halved*
1 *large can crushed pineapple, drained*
1 *cup chopped pecans*

Dissolve gelatin in boiling water. Add ice cream and stir until melted. Add cherries pineapple, and pecans. Place in 2-quart mold and refrigerate. Yield: 8 to 10 servings.

Fruited Cheese Salad

1 *(3-ounce) package cream cheese*
¼ *cup mayonnaise*
2 *teaspoons lemon juice*
⅛ *teaspoon salt*
2 *tablespoons chopped maraschino*
  cherries
1 *(13½-ounce) can pineapple chunks,*
  drained
1 *cup diced bananas*
⅓ *cup chopped walnuts*
½ *cup heavy cream*

Soften cheese; add mayonnaise, lemon juice, and salt. Mix well. Add fruits and nuts. Whip cream until slightly thickened; fold in. Pour into tray and freeze until firm. Cut into squares and serve. Yield: 6 servings.

Green Salad

1 *(3-ounce) package lime-flavored*
  gelatin
1 *(3-ounce) package lemon-flavored*
  gelatin
1½ *cups boiling water*
1 *cup cottage cheese*
1 *flat can crushed pineapple*
1 *can sweetened condensed milk*
½ *cup salad dressing*
½ *cup chopped peanuts*

Dissolve gelatin in boiling water. Cool slightly and add other ingredients. Mix well and chill until firm. Yield: 8 servings.

Golden Glow Salad

1 *head lettuce*
6 *oranges*
3 *grapefruit*
3 *bananas*
5 *small grape clusters*

Arrange lettuce in salad bowl. Peel and section oranges and grapefruit; peel and slice bananas. Mix fruits and arrange in bowl. Garnish with grape clusters. Serve with Lemon French Dressing (page 329).

Grape Salad

1 *(8-ounce) package cream cheese*
½ *cup pineapple juice*
1 *large can crushed pineapple, drained*
4 *cups seedless white grapes*
⅔ *cup chopped nuts*
1 *(6-ounce) package miniature*
  marshmallows

Cream the cheese with pineapple juice. Add pineapple, grapes, nuts, and marshmallows. Mix well and refrigerate for several hours. Serve on lettuce leaves. Yield: About 6 to 8 servings.

Frozen Fruit Salad Delight

1 *(3-ounce) package cream cheese,*
  softened
½ *cup mayonnaise*
2 *tablespoons milk*
2 *tablespoons fresh or bottled lemon*
  juice
2 *tablespoons sugar*
1 *(11-ounce) can mandarin oranges,*
  drained
1 *(1-pound) can dark sweet cherries,*
  drained
½ *cup chopped pecans*
1 *cup whipping cream, whipped*

Blend cream cheese with mayonnaise and milk; add lemon juice and sugar. Add oranges, cherries, and pecans. Fold in whipped cream.

Place 8 fluted paper muffin liners in muffin cups. Spoon salad mixture into each. Freeze until firm, at least 3 hours.

To serve, peel off muffin liners and place individual salads on crisp lettuce. Serve frozen. Yield: 8 servings

Ginger Ale Salad

    2 tablespoons unflavored gelatin
    4 tablespoons cold water
    ¼ cup boiling water
    ¼ cup sugar
    ⅛ teaspoon salt
    1 pint ginger ale
       Juice of 1 lemon
    ½ pound grapes, seeded and skinned
    1 orange, peeled and sliced
    1 grapefruit, peeled and sectioned
   12 maraschino cherries, cut in halves
    6 slices pineapple, cut in chunks
    ¼ pound preserved ginger, chopped

Soak gelatin in cold water; then dissolve in boiling water. Add sugar, salt, ginger ale, and lemon juice. Chill until nearly set and combine with grapes, orange, grapefruit, cherries, pineapple, and ginger. Place in a wet mold and chill. When firm, serve on lettuce with salad dressing. Yield: 14 servings.

Ginger Ale Salad

    1 (3-ounce) package lime-flavored
          gelatin
    1 cup boiling water
    1 cup ginger ale
    1 cup drained, diced canned peaches
    ¼ cup chopped walnuts or pecans
    ¼ cup finely diced celery
       Lettuce leaves
       Whipped cream or mayonnaise

Dissolve gelatin in boiling water. Add ginger ale and blend well. Chill until slightly thickened; then fold in fruit, nuts, and celery. Turn into 1-quart or individual oiled molds; chill until firm. Turn out on lettuce leaves and serve with whipped cream or mayonnaise. Yield: 6 to 8 servings.

Harvest Bowl Salad

    2 eggs
    ¼ cup sugar
       Dash of salt
    2 tablespoons lemon juice
    ⅔ cup whipping cream
    2 cups chopped apples
    1 cup pineapple chunks
    1 cup grapes, cut in halves
    2 bananas, sliced
    ½ cup chopped pecans
    ½ cup chopped celery

Beat eggs slightly; add sugar, salt, and lemon juice and cook in top of double boiler until thick, stirring constantly. Cool. Whip cream and fold into cooled egg mixture. Combine fruits, pecans, and celery and fold in dressing. Yield: 6 servings.

Red and Green Salad

    1 (3-ounce) package lime-flavored
          gelatin
    1 cup boiling water
    1 (2-ounce) jar pimientos, chopped or
          sieved.
    1 (3-ounce) package cream cheese
    1 (8¼-ounce) can crushed pineapple,
          undrained
    1 cup finely chopped celery
    ½ pint cream, stiffly whipped

Dissolve gelatin in boiling water. Let cool. Drain pimiento and chop or sieve; mix with cream cheese until smooth. Beat gelatin when partially thickened and add cream cheese mixture. Fold in pineapple and celery. Have cream very stiff before folding into gelatin mixture. Chill until firm. Serve on salad greens and garnish as desired. Yield: 12 servings.

Lime 'n Pine Salad Ring

  2 *eggs, slightly beaten*
 ⅓ *cup powdered sugar*
 ¼ *cup lime juice*
 ⅓ *teaspoon salt*
  1 *tablespoon butter*
  2 *cups miniature marshmallows*
  1 *(15¼-ounce) can pineapple tidbits,*
     well drained
  1 *(16-ounce) can peaches, well drained*
  1 *cup whipping cream, whipped*
     Green food coloring
     Cottage cheese or salad greens

Combine eggs, sugar, lime juice, salt, butter, and marshmallows. Cook in top of double boiler, over low heat, stirring constantly until thickened. Cool. Fold pineapple, diced peaches, and cooled lime mixture into whipped cream. Blend in a few drops of food coloring. Turn into 5-cup ring mold. Freeze until firm. To serve, unmold on chilled platter and fill center of ring with cottage cheese or salad greens. Garnish with lime slices around ring. Yield: 8 servings.

Heavenly Lime Salad

  2 *small or 1 large package lime-*
     flavored gelatin
  2 *cups boiling water*
  1 *(8-ounce) package cream cheese,*
     softened
 18 *large marshmallows*
 ¼ *cup boiling water*
1½ *cups cold water*
 ½ *cup whipping cream, whipped*
  1 *(No. 2) can crushed pineapple*
  1 *cup chopped pecans or English*
     walnuts

Dissolve the gelatin in 2 cups boiling water in large mixing bowl. Mash cream cheese in small bowl; add hot gelatin mixture and stir until dissolved. Melt marshmallows in ¼ cup boiling water in top of double boiler and add to gelatin mixture. Add 1½ cups cold water. Add whipped cream and beat mixture until it is smooth. Add pineapple and nuts. Pour into greased mold, large baking dish, or individual molds. Yield: 18 to 20 servings.

Lime-Pine Ring Salad

  1 *(3-ounce) package lime-flavored*
     gelatin
  1 *cup boiling water*
  1 *(No. 2) can crushed pineapple*
 ½ *pint commercial sour cream*
  1 *cup chopped nuts*
     Green food coloring, if desired

Dissolve gelatin in boiling water. Drain pineapple and add ½ cup pineapple juice to the gelatin mixture. Put in refrigerator and leave until the consistency of egg whites. Put in a large mixing bowl; add sour cream and beat well. Add crushed pineapple (drained), nuts, and coloring. Pour into salad mold and chill until firm. Yield: 8 servings.

Make-Ahead Fruit Salad

 ½ *cup mayonnaise*
 ½ *cup heavy cream, whipped*
  1 *tablespoon lemon juice*
  2 *cups (1-pound 13-ounce can) drained*
     peach slices
  1 *cup miniature marshmallows*
 ½ *cup halved maraschino cherries*
  1 *banana, sliced*
 ¼ *cup chopped nuts*

Combine mayonnaise, whipped cream, and lemon juice. Mix until well blended. Fold in remaining ingredients; chill. This salad may be made hours ahead; it tastes even better when the fruit flavors mingle longer with the marshmallows and whipped cream. Serve on lettuce leaves with finger sandwiches. Yield: 8 servings.

Frosty Nesselrode Mountain

  1 *(8-ounce) package cream cheese*
 ½ *cup mayonnaise*
 ½ *cup pineapple preserves*
 ½ *cup raisins*
 ½ *cup chopped nuts*
 ½ *cup halved candied cherries*
  1 *cup heavy cream, whipped*

Soften cheese, blend with mayonnaise, and add pineapple preserves, raisins, nuts, and cherries. Fold in whipped cream. Pour into refrigerator trays or individual molds and freeze. Serve either as salad or as a dessert. Yield: 8 servings.

Orange Mandarin Salad

3 (3-ounce) packages orange-flavored gelatin
2 cups boiling water
1 pint orange sherbet
1 large can mandarin oranges or 3 small cans

Dissolve the gelatin in boiling water. Stir well, add orange sherbet. Stir until melted. Add oranges and juice. Pour in mold and refrigerate. Serve with Topping. Yield: 10 servings.

Topping:

1 pint whipping cream
1 (3-ounce) package cream cheese
½ cup marshmallow whip

Whip cream. Add softened cream cheese and marshmallow whip. Use green food coloring, if desired.

Orange Sherbet Salad

2 (3-ounce) packages orange-flavored gelatin
1 cup boiling water
1 pint orange sherbet
1 (8¼-ounce) can crushed pineapple
1 cup miniature marshmallows
1 (11-ounce) can mandarin orange sections, drained
½ pint whipping cream, whipped

Dissolve gelatin in boiling water. Add orange sherbet. When partially set, add other ingredients, folding in the whipped cream last. Chill until firm. Yield: About 12 servings.

Peach Congealed Salad

1 (3-ounce) package lemon-flavored gelatin
1 cup boiling water
1 (3-ounce) package cream cheese, softened
2 tablespoons mayonnaise
1 (No. 303) can sliced peaches, drained
1 small can crushed pineapple
1 cup chopped nuts (optional)
1 (6-ounce) package miniature marshmallows (optional)

Dissolve gelatin in boiling water and let stand until cool. Mix cream cheese and mayonnaise until smooth. Drain peaches and cut into small pieces. Add pineapple. Nuts or marshmallows, or both, may be added. Add cooled gelatin to fruit mixture and refrigerate until firm. Yield: 10 servings.

Peach-Cottage Cheese Salad

⅔ cup orange juice
2 tablespoons flour
2 tablespoons sugar
Few grains salt
¼ teaspoon powdered mustard
½ teaspoon grated orange rind
1 to 2 teaspoons vinegar
4 tablespoons mayonnaise
2 tablespoons whole milk
8 canned peach halves, drained
Lettuce
1 cup cottage cheese
¼ cup sliced dates
¼ cup slivered toasted almonds
1 tablespoon coarsely grated orange rind

To make sauce: heat orange juice. Mix flour, sugar, salt, and mustard, and stir to blend. Add to hot juice, and cook and stir until mixture thickens. Remove from heat and blend in ½ teaspoon grated orange rind and vinegar. Cool; stir in mayonnaise and milk.

Place each peach half on lettuce leaf. Combine cottage cheese, dates, almonds, and orange rind. Mound this mixture on peach halves, and top with sauce. Yield: 8 servings.

Frozen Peach Salad

   3 *cups peeled, crushed peaches*
   2 *cups miniature marshmallows*
  ½ *cup drained, crushed pineapple*
  ½ *cup slivered almonds*
  ¼ *cup maraschino cherries,*
      quartered
  ½ *teaspoon almond extract*
  ⅛ *teaspoon salt*
   2 *cups commercial sour cream*
    Few drops red food coloring

Mix all ingredients in a 2-quart bowl. Pour into an 8-inch square pan. Cover with foil and freeze before time to serve; then cut into squares. Yield: 6 to 8 servings.

Pink Arctic Freeze

   2 *(3-ounce) packages cream cheese*
   2 *tablespoons sugar*
   2 *tablespoons mayonnaise*
   1 *(1-pound) can jellied cranberry sauce*
   1 *cup drained, crushed pineapple*
  ½ *cup chopped pecans*
  ½ *cup heavy cream, whipped*

Cream together cheese and sugar; stir in mayonnaise. Fold in cranberry sauce, pineapple, nuts, and whipped cream. Turn into a 9- x 5- x 3-inch loafpan. Freeze until firm. Cut in slices and serve on lettuce. (May also be frozen in round cans, unmolded, and served in attractive slices.) Yield: 8 servings.

Pineapple-Carrot Salad Ring

   1 *cup boiling water*
   1 *(3-ounce) package lemon-flavored*
      gelatin
   1 *cup cold pineapple juice*
   4 *or 5 grated carrots*
   1 *cup pineapple tidbits*
    Lettuce or endive
    Mayonnaise or French dressing

Pour boiling water over gelatin. Add 1 cup cold pineapple juice and mix well. Set aside to cool. Add grated carrots and pineapple tidbits. Place in individual molds or in a large ring mold. Place in refrigerator to congeal. Turn out on bed of lettuce or endive and garnish with French dressing or mayonnaise. If a large mold is used, the outside can be garnished with fruit, such as sliced pineapple, sliced orange and apricot, and slices of avocado. Yield: 6 servings.

Pineapple-Cherry Salad

   1 *(No. 2) can water-packed red sour*
      cherries
   2 *(3-ounce) packages cherry-flavored*
      gelatin
   1 *cup boiling water*
   1 *(20-ounce) can crushed pineapple*
  ½ *cup chopped nuts*
   1 *cup cherry liquid*
   1 *cup sugar*
    Juice of 1 lemon
    Red food coloring, if desired

Drain cherries; reserve liquid. Dissolve gelatin in boiling water; cool. Stir in pineapple, drained cherries, and nuts. Chill until mixture begins to thicken slightly.

Combine cherry liquid, sugar, lemon juice, and food coloring and boil 1 minute. Cool thoroughly; then add to gelatin mixture. Stir often until mixture is thick. Spoon into 2-quart mold or shallow pan and chill thoroughly. Yield: 10 to 12 servings.

Raspberry Salad

   2 *(10-ounce) packages frozen red*
      raspberries and juice
 3¾ *cups boiling water*
   3 *(3-ounce) packages red raspberry-*
      flavored gelatin
   1 *(No. 2½) can crushed pineapple and*
      juice
   1 *cup chopped walnuts or pecans*
   3 *bananas, diced*

Take raspberries out of freezer long enough to partially thaw. Pour boiling water over gelatin and stir to dissolve completely. Stir in crushed pineapple and juice. Refrigerate until just starting to set around edges. Fold in nuts, bananas, and frozen raspberries and juice. Put in large mold and set in refrigerator to congeal. To serve, immerse mold in very hot, not boiling, water and count to 15 at normal speed. Invert mold on large plate.

Raspberry-Rhubarb Salad

> 1 *package frozen rhubarb*
> ¼ *cup sugar or less*
> 2 *cups unsweetened pineapple juice*
> 1 *(6-ounce) package raspberry-*
>   *flavored gelatin*
> 2 *cups chopped tart apples*
> 1 *cup chopped pecans*

Cook rhubarb as directed on package. Sweeten to taste. Add pineapple juice and bring to a boil. Add gelatin and stir until dissolved. When cool and beginning to set, add finely chopped and peeled apples and nuts.

Mix well and pour into molds. Leave overnight in refrigerator before using. Yield: 12 servings.

Ribbon Salad

First Layer:

> 1 *(3-ounce) package lime-flavored*
>   *gelatin*
> 1 *cup boiling water*
> 1 *cup cold water*

Dissolve gelatin in boiling water. Add cold water and pour into loafpan. Let sit until firm before adding the second layer.

Second Layer:

> 1 *(3-ounce) package lemon-flavored*
>   *gelatin*
> 1 *cup boiling water*
> 1 *(3-ounce) package cream cheese,*
>   *softened*
> 1 *small can crushed pineapple*
> 1 *teaspoon vinegar*

Dissolve gelatin in boiling water. Add cream cheese and beat until smooth. Cool, then add crushed pineapple (not drained) and vinegar. Pour on top of first layer of gelatin. When firm, add third layer.

Third Layer:

> 1 *(3-ounce) package cherry-flavored*
>   *gelatin*
> 1 *cup boiling water*
> 1 *cup cold water*

Dissolve gelatin in boiling water, then add cold water. Let cool, then pour over second layer of gelatin. Let sit in refrigerator until firm. Yield: 12 servings.

Ribbon Salad

> 2 *(3-ounce) packages lime-flavored*
>   *gelatin*
> 2 *cups boiling water*
> 1½ *cups cold water*
> 2 *(3-ounce) packages lemon-flavored*
>   *gelatin*
> 1 *cup boiling water*
> 2 *cups miniature marshmallows*
> 1 *(8-ounce) package cream cheese*
> 1 *(1-pound 4-ounce) can crushed*
>   *pineapple, drained*
> 1 *cup pineapple juice*
> ½ *pint cream, whipped*
> 2 *(3-ounce) packages raspberry-*
>   *flavored gelatin*
> 2 *cups boiling water*
> 1½ *cups cold water*

Dissolve lime gelatin in 2 cups boiling water; add 1½ cups cold water. Pour into 14- x 10- x 2-inch pan. Chill until set.

Dissolve lemon gelatin in 1 cup boiling water in top of double boiler. Add marshmallows and cream cheese, which has been cut in small pieces. Beat until well blended. Remove from heat and stir in pineapple and pineapple juice. Cool; then fold in whipped cream. Spoon over top of chilled lime gelatin. Chill until lemon layer is firm.

Dissolve raspberry gelatin in 2 cups boiling water. Add 1½ cups cold water. Cool; then pour over chilled lemon layer. Chill until firm. Yield: 12 to 15 servings.

Twenty-Four-Hour Sour Cream Salad

1 *can spiced grapes, drained*
1 *can mandarin oranges, drained*
1 *can pineapple chunks, drained*
6 *or 8 maraschino cherries, sliced*
2 *cups miniature marshmallows*
½ *pint commercial sour cream*

Mix fruit and marshmallows. Let sit 1 hour. Fold in sour cream which has been well stirred. Place in covered bowl or casserole. Let sit in refrigerator 24 hours. Fruit cocktail may be substituted for grapes and oranges. Yield: 8 to 10 servings.

Spiced Fruit Salad Mold

2 *packages unflavored gelatin*
1 *cup cold water*
1 *(No. 2½) can crushed pineapple, drained*
3 *white grapefruit, peeled, separated into sections, and drained*
1¾ *cups sugar*
2 *cinnamon sticks*
½ *lemon, sliced*
Green food coloring, if desired

Soften gelatin in cold water. Combine juice from pineapple and grapefruit; add sugar, cinnamon sticks, and lemon slices. Bring to a boil and simmer for 5 minutes. Pour hot juice through a strainer into dissolved gelatin. Cool. Add a few drops of green food coloring, if desired. Add fruit and spoon into individual salad molds. Chill in refrigerator overnight. Serve in lettuce cups topped with mayonnaise. Yield: 10 servings.

Sunny Salad

1 *(1-pound) can pear halves*
1 *medium avocado*
Lemon juice
Lettuce
Mayonnaise

Drain pears. Slice peeled avocado into thin wedges; dip in lemon juice. Arrange pears and avocado on lettuce-lined plates. Top with mayonnaise, if desired. Yield: 4 to 6 servings.

Rose of Sharon Salad

½ *cup water*
½ *cup vinegar*
1 *cup sugar*
2 *(3-ounce) packages raspberry-flavored gelatin*
1 *package unflavored gelatin dissolved in 3 tablespoons water*
2 *cans tomato soup*
1 *green pepper, chopped*
2 *cups grated cabbage*
1 *onion, chopped*
1 *cup chopped celery*
Dash pepper
Salt to taste

Combine water, vinegar, and sugar, and bring to a boil. Add raspberry-flavored gelatin and stir until dissolved. Let cool. Add other ingredients and mix well. Refrigerate overnight. Yield: 6 servings.

Russian Salad

1 *(3-ounce) package lime-flavored gelatin*
¾ *cup boiling water*
¼ *cup pineapple juice (drained from crushed pineapple)*
1 *cup cream*
1 *(No. 2) can crushed pineapple*
2 *bananas, mashed*
24 *miniature marshmallows*
¼ *cup mayonnaise*
1 *(3-ounce) package cream cheese*
1 *cup chopped nuts*

Dissolve gelatin in boiling water. Add pineapple juice and allow to cool, then add cream. Chill in refrigerator until it reaches the mushy stage. Add other ingredients and mix well. Put into molds and keep in refrigerator until set. Yield: 10 servings.

Spring Salad

2 envelopes unflavored gelatin
1 cup cold orange juice
2 tablespoons sugar
2 cups very hot orange juice
Dash of salt
⅓ cup lemon juice
1 (9-ounce) can crushed pineapple,
   drained
½ cup seeded grapes, quartered
½ cup chopped nuts
½ cup chopped celery

Soften gelatin in 1 cup cold orange juice. Dissolve sugar in 2 cups very hot orange juice. Add gelatin mixture and stir until gelatin is dissolved. Add salt, lemon juice, and syrup drained from pineapple. Stir well and chill until mixture begins to thicken.

Fold crushed pineapple into the chilled gelatin mixture. Add grapes, nuts, and celery. Pour into a 1½-quart mold and chill until set. Yield: 12 servings.

White Congealed Salad

2 eggs, slightly beaten
2 tablespoons sugar
3 tablespoons vinegar
½ pound marshmallows, chopped
1 tablespoon unflavored gelatin
¼ cup cold water
1 (No. 2) can crushed pineapple
1 (No. 2) can Royal Anne cherries, cut
   in halves
1 cup chopped pecans
1 cup heavy cream, whipped

In top of double boiler, mix the eggs, sugar, and vinegar. Cook over boiling water, stirring constantly, until thickened. Add marshmallows and gelatin in ¼ cup water. Remove from heat as soon as marshmallows begin to melt and gelatin is dissolved. Cool slightly and add pineapple and cherries, plus juices in each. Add nuts and fold in whipped cream. Spoon into 1½-quart mold and chill until firm. Yield: 18 to 20 servings.

Williamsburg Inn Salad

2 envelopes unflavored gelatin
½ cup cold water
1 cup boiling water
½ cup cold water
½ cup vinegar
½ teaspoon salt
2 cups sugar
Few drops green food coloring
1 cup diced, blanched almonds
1 cup sliced sweet pickles
1 cup crushed pineapple, drained
1 cup sliced stuffed olives

Soften gelatin in ½ cup cold water. Add to boiling water and stir until dissolved. Add ½ cup cold water, vinegar, salt, sugar, and a few drops of green food coloring.

Chill until mixture thickens. Fold in other ingredients. Chill until ready to serve. Yield: 6 servings.

Wine Salad

2 (3-ounce) packages raspberry-
   flavored gelatin
2 cups boiling water
1 cup port wine
1 (No. 2) can crushed pineapple (do
   not drain)
1 can whole-berry cranberry sauce
½ cup chopped nut meats
1 cup finely chopped celery

Dissolve gelatin in boiling water. Cool slightly; then add wine and let cool until slightly thickened. Stir in other ingredients; place in oiled molds and chill until firm. Yield: 8 to 10 servings.

Strawberry Salad

    2 *(3-ounce) packages strawberry-*
       flavored gelatin
2½ *cups boiling water*
    1 *(10-ounce) package frozen*
      strawberries
    3 *bananas, sliced*
  ½ *cup chopped pecans*
  ½ *pint commercial sour cream*

Dissolve gelatin in boiling water. Add strawberries and stir until thawed. Add sliced bananas and chopped pecans. Pour half of mixture into 8- x 8- x 2-inch pan and hold in refrigerator until firm. Jell remaining half only to thick-pouring consistency. Spread sour cream on first mixture and pour remaining half on top. Refrigerate to jell.

Strawberry Gelatin Salad

    1 *(3-ounce) package strawberry-*
      flavored gelatin
  ¾ *cup boiling water*
    1 *(10-ounce) package frozen*
      strawberries
    1 *(8¼-ounce) can crushed pineapple*
      (not drained)
    1 *banana, mashed*
    1 *(8-ounce) carton commercial sour*
      cream

Dissolve gelatin in boiling water. Cool; then add slightly thawed strawberries and pineapple. Chill until thickness of honey. Stir in mashed banana. Spoon half this mixture into a loafpan, spread sour cream over this layer, and top with another layer of gelatin mixture. Chill. Yield: 8 to 10 servings.

Surprise Salad

    1 *small can crushed pineapple*
    1 *cup sugar*
    1 *(3-ounce) package raspberry-*
      flavored gelatin
    1 *cup boiling water*
    1 *cup shredded cheese*
    1 *cup whipping cream*

Put the pineapple and sugar in a small saucepan; bring to a boil. Dissolve gelatin in boiling water and add to pineapple mixture. Stir in shredded cheese. Chill until partially congealed. Fold in whipped cream and put into mold. Place in refrigerator until set.

Wonder Salad

    1 *(3-ounce) package lemon-flavored*
      gelatin
    1 *(3-ounce) package lime-flavored*
      gelatin
    4 *cups boiling water*
    1 *envelope unflavored gelatin*
  ¼ *cup cold water*
    2 *cups shredded cabbage*
    2 *medium cucumbers, cut fine*
    2 *tablespoons vinegar*
Juice 1 lemon
    1 *(No. 2) can crushed pineapple, well*
      drained
    1 *cup chopped almonds*
    1 *teaspoon salt*

Dissolve flavored gelatin in boiling water. Dissolve plain gelatin in cold water; add to hot gelatin and stir until dissolved. Add other ingredients and place in refrigerator to congeal. Yield: 6 to 8 servings.

Chicken Salad
With Avocado

    3 *cups diced cooked chicken*
  ½ *cup diced celery*
    1 *cup sliced pitted black olives*
  ⅓ *cup mayonnaise*
1½ *cups diced avocado (½-inch pieces)*
    1 *tablespoon lemon juice*
Dash cayenne pepper
Lettuce

Blend chicken, celery, and olives with mayonnaise. Cut the avocado just before serving and sprinkle lemon juice over it. Fold the avocado into the chicken mixture and season to taste, adding cayenne. Serve in lettuce cups and garnish with cut pieces of olive or slices of avocado. Yield: 6 servings.

Chicken Salad

1 *envelope unflavored gelatin*
¼ *cup cold water*
1 *cup mayonnaise*
1 *cup heavy cream, whipped*
½ *teaspoon salt*
2 *cups cooked, diced chicken*
¾ *cup blanched, toasted, and chopped almonds*
¾ *cup seedless green grapes*

Soak gelatin in cold water; dissolve over hot water. Cool mixture; then add mayonnaise, cream, and salt. Fold in remaining ingredients and chill. Yield: 8 servings.

Favorite Chicken Salad

½ *cup low-calorie salad dressing*
1 *tablespoon canned lemon juice*
1 *(5- to 6-ounce) can boned chicken*
1 *cup thinly sliced celery*
2 *tablespoons chopped pickles*
1 *small onion, chopped*
Salt and pepper

Mix salad dressing and lemon juice. Add chicken cut in bite-size pieces, celery, pickles, and chopped onion. Season to taste. Chill. Serve on lettuce. Yield: 4 servings.

Hot Chicken Or Seafood Salad

2 *cups cut-up chicken (or crab or shrimp)*
2 *cups thinly sliced celery*
½ *cup cashews*
½ *teaspoon salt*
1 *onion, grated*
1 *cup mayonnaise (not salad dressing)*
2 *tablespoons lemon juice*
½ *cup shredded sharp cheese*
1 *cup potato chips, crushed*

Combine all ingredients except cheese and potato chips. Pile lightly in casserole or individual baking dishes. Sprinkle with cheese and potato chips. Bake in preheated oven at 400 degrees F. about 20 minutes or until mixture is heated and cheese is melted.

Molded Chicken Salad

2 *tablespoons unflavored gelatin*
½ *cup cold water*
¾ *cup mayonnaise or salad dressing*
Salt, pepper, paprika, and vinegar to taste
1 *to* 1½ *cups diced cooked chicken*
1 *cup finely chopped celery*
½ *cup chopped olives*
½ *cup cooked, diced chestnuts*
3 *tablespoons chopped pimiento*
Several sprigs chopped parsley

Soak gelatin in cold water; dissolve by placing over hot water and stirring until completely dissolved. Cool slightly, then fold in mayonnaise, salt, pepper, paprika, and vinegar to taste. Add other ingredients and mix well. Turn into an oiled mold and refrigerate until congealed. Unmold on bed of lettuce or other greens. Garnish with carrot curls, radish roses, or other colorful vegetables. Yield: 6 servings.

Chicken and Pineapple Salad

1 *envelope unflavored gelatin*
1½ *cups chicken stock, divided*
½ *teaspoon salt*
2 *tablespoons lemon juice*
¼ *cup canned pineapple syrup*
1½ *cups diced cooked chicken*
½ *cup drained, canned crushed pineapple*
½ *cup diced celery*

Sprinkle gelatin on ½ cup of the chicken stock to soften. Place over low heat and stir until gelatin is dissolved. Remove from heat and stir in remaining chicken stock, salt, lemon juice, and pineapple syrup. Chill to consistency of unbeaten egg white.

Fold in chicken, pineapple, and celery. Turn into a 3-cup mold and chill until firm. Unmold on serving plate and garnish with salad greens. Yield: 4 to 6 servings.

Jellied Chicken Almond

1 tablespoon unflavored
    gelatin
¼ cup cold water
1 cup mayonnaise
1 cup heavy cream,
    whipped
½ teaspoon salt
1½ cups diced cooked
    chicken
¾ cup chopped blanched
    almonds, toasted
¾ cup halved green
    seedless grapes

Soften gelatin in cold water; dissolve over hot water. Cool slightly; then combine with mayonnaise, whipped cream, and salt. Fold in diced chicken, blanced almonds, and grapes. Spoon into 6 or 8 individual salad molds. Chill until firm. Unmold on lettuce leaves. Garnish with sliced stuffed olives and mayonnaise. Yield: 6 to 8 servings.

Chicken Pressed

1 (2½-to 3-pound) hen
1 cup chopped celery
5 hard-cooked eggs, diced
¼ teaspoon prepared
    mustard
Salt and red pepper to
    taste
1 envelope unflavored
    gelatin
2 tablespoons cold water
1 cup chicken broth

Boil hen in large quantity of water over low heat until meat cooks away from the bones. Remove meat from bones and chop fine. Add celery and diced eggs to chicken and mix well. Add seasonings. Soak gelatin in cold water. Dissolve in hot chicken broth. Add to chicken mixture. Place in mold and let sit until firm. Yield: 10 servings.

Hot Chicken Salad Casserole

4 cups diced, cooked chicken
2 cans cream of chicken soup
2 cups diced celery
4 tablespoons minced onion
2 cups slivered almonds
1 cup mayonnaise
¾ cup chicken stock
1 teaspoon salt
½ teaspoon black pepper
4 tablespoons lemon juice
6 hard-cooked eggs, chopped fine
1 cup cracker crumbs

Combine all the above ingredients except cracker crumbs and place in 3- to 4-quart casserole. Cover with cracker crumbs. Bake at 350 degrees F. for 40 minutes. Yield: 10 to 12 servings.

Chicken Mayonnaise

1 (3-pound) hen
4 envelopes unflavored
    gelatin
1 cup cold water
2 cups chopped celery
1 small bottle stuffed
    olives, sliced
1 pint mayonnaise
1 cup chopped almonds
    or pecans
2 cups cold chicken stock,
    free of fat
Salt and pepper to taste

Cook hen; remove from stock and cut meat from bone. Soften gelatin in cold water; dissolve over hot water. Combine remaining ingredients; add gelatin. Put into large mold or in individual molds. Serve on lettuce or watercress. Yield: 10 servings.

Summer Breeze Chicken Salad

  2 *(5-ounce) cans chicken, drained and diced*
  1 *(5-ounce) can water chestnuts, drained and chopped*
  2 *tablespoons chopped walnuts*
  ¼ *cup chopped green pepper*
  ¼ *teaspoon salt*
  ⅓ *cup French dressing*
    Sliced cucumbers
    Tomatoes, sliced ½ inch thick

Combine chicken, water chestnuts, walnuts, green pepper, salt, and French dressing. Mix well. To serve, place a cucumber slice on a tomato slice and top with a scoop of chicken salad. Yield: 4 to 6 servings.

Hot Crab Salad

  ½ *cup chopped green pepper*
  1 *small onion, chopped*
  ½ *cup diced celery*
  ¼ *cup toasted shredded almonds*
  1 *(6½-ounce) can crabmeat*
  ½ *cup mayonnaise*
  ½ *teaspoon Worcestershire sauce*
  ¼ *teaspoon salt*
    Dash pepper
  ½ *cup buttered breadcrumbs*

Chop green pepper, onion, and celery rather fine; combine with nuts, crabmeat, mayonnaise, and seasonings. Fill individual shells or baking dishes with mixture and top with buttered crumbs. Bake at 350 degrees F. for 30 minutes. Serve hot. Yield: 2 servings.

Patio Special Tuna Salad

  2 *(7-ounce) cans tuna, drained and flaked*
  ½ *cup chopped celery*
  ¼ *cup pickle relish, drained*
  ½ *teaspoon lemon juice*
  1 *teaspoon finely chopped onion*
  ⅓ *cup mayonnaise*
    Sliced cucumbers
    Tomatoes, sliced ½ inch thick

Combine tuna, celery, relish, lemon juice, onion, and mayonnaise. Mix well. To serve, place a cucumber slice on a tomato slice and top with a scoop of tuna salad. Yield: 4 to 6 servings.

Shrimp and Macaroni Salad

  2 *cups cooked macaroni*
  ½ *teaspoon salt*
  ½ *cup mayonnaise or salad dressing*
  2 *tablespoons finely chopped sweet pickles*
  5 *hard-cooked eggs, chopped*
  5 *finely chopped ripe olives*
  ½ *cup finely chopped onions*
  ½ *cup chopped celery (optional)*
  2 *pounds cooked, deveined shrimp*

Combine all ingredients except shrimp. Mix well and place in covered dish in refrigerator to chill. About 30 minutes before serving stir in cooked shrimp and toss lightly. Serve from lettuce-lined salad bowl. Yield: 10 to 12 servings.

Refreshing Shrimp Salad

  ¾ *pound cooked, peeled, and cleaned fresh or frozen shrimp*
  1 *quart shredded cabbage*
  ½ *cup sliced green pepper*
  1 *cup commercial sour cream*
  1 *tablespoon lemon juice*
  1 *teaspoon Worcestershire sauce*
  ¼ *teaspoon salt*
  ¼ *teaspoon dill weed (or dill seed)*
    Dash ground nutmeg
  ½ *cup toasted, blanched slivered almonds*
    Salad greens

Thaw frozen shrimp. Cut large shrimp in half. Combine cabbage, green pepper and shrimp; chill. Combine sour cream, lemon juice, Worcestershire sauce, and seasonings; chill. Add almonds and dressing to shrimp mixture; toss lightly. Serve on salad greens. Yield: 6 servings.

Hot Turkey Salad Soufflé

- 6 *slices white bread*
- 2 *cups diced, cooked turkey or chicken*
- ½ *cup chopped celery*
- ½ *cup chopped onion*
- ½ *cup mayonnaise*
- ¾ *teaspoon salt*
- *Pepper to taste*
- 2 *eggs, beaten*
- 1½ *cups milk*
- 1 *can cream of mushroom soup*
- ½ *cup shredded sharp cheese*

Cube 2 slices of bread and place in bottom of a greased 8- x 8- x 2-inch baking dish. Combine turkey, celery, onion, mayonnaise, salt, and pepper. Spoon over bread cubes. Trim crusts from remaining 4 slices of bread and arrange slices on top of turkey. Combine eggs and milk and pour over mixture. Cover and chill. Spoon soup over top of casserole. Bake at 325 degrees F. until set, or about 1 hour. Sprinkle cheese over top for the last few minutes of baking. Yield: 6 servings.

Wild Rice and Turkey Salad

- ½ *pound wild rice*
- 4 *cups cooked, chopped turkey or chicken*
- 1 *cup mayonnaise*
- ½ *cup French dressing*
- *Salt to taste*
- 1 *(5-ounce) can sliced almonds*
- 1 *cup diced celery*
- 2 *cans mandarin oranges*
- 1 *(No. 2) can pineapple tidbits*

Cook rice according to package directions. Cool. Add turkey, mayonnaise, French dressing, salt, almonds, and celery and put in refrigerator to chill. Just before serving, add oranges and pineapple. Serve on lettuce.

Corned Beef Salad

- 1 *envelope unflavored gelatin*
- 2 *tablespoons cold water*
- 1 *can beef consommé*
- 1 *(12-ounce) can corned beef*
- 1 *cup chopped celery*
- ¾ *cup mayonnaise*
- ¼ *cup salad dressing*

Dissolve gelatin in cold water. Heat consommé, add gelatin, and stir until dissolved. Set aside to cool. Break corned beef into bite-size pieces. Add celery, mayonnaise, and salad dressing and mix well. Add cooled consommé and mix well to blend. Refrigerate. Serve on salad greens. Yield: 6 servings.

Festive Tuna-Rice Salad

- 3 *cups cooked long-grain rice*
- 1 *(7-ounce) can light tuna, drained and flaked*
- 3 *hard-cooked eggs, chopped*
- 2 *tablespoons sweet pickle relish*
- 1½ *teaspoons fresh chives, minced, or frozen chives*
- ½ *cup chopped celery*
- 1 *large pimiento, drained and chopped*
- ½ *cup mayonnaise*
- 1 *teaspoon prepared mustard*
- ½ *teaspoon lemon juice*
- *Dash salt and pepper*
- *Paprika*

Cool cooked rice to room temperature. Combine rice, tuna, eggs, relish, chives, celery, and pimiento. In another bowl mix together the mayonnaise, mustard, lemon juice, salt, and pepper. Pour over rice mixture and toss. Chill thoroughly. Serve in a salad bowl and sprinkle with paprika. Yield: 8 servings.

Macaroni Salad

8 *ounces elbow or shell macaroni*
Tart French dressing
1½ *cups chopped celery*
1 *tablespoon minced sweet onion*
¼ *cup chopped tart cucumber pickle or*
stuffed green olives
¼ *cup minced green pepper*
1 *cup finely cubed cheese, ham, cooked*
meat, or fish
¾ *cup mayonnaise or other desired*
dressing
Salt

Cook macaroni; drain thoroughly and rinse with cold water. Add enough tart French dressing to coat the macaroni; chill thoroughly. Drain off any excess dressing and combine with the other ingredients, using enough mayonnaise to bind the ingredients together. Garnish with pepper rings, egg slices, or wedges of peeled tomato. Yield: 6 servings.

Crispy Salmon Salad

1 *(1-pound) can salmon*
4 *cups shredded cabbage*
¼ *cup chopped onion*
¼ *cup chopped parsley*
2 *hard-cooked eggs, chopped*
1 *teaspoon salt*
Dash cayenne pepper
¼ *teaspoon paprika*
3 *tablespoons vinegar*
½ *cup salad oil*
1 *tablespoon chopped pimiento, if*
desired
1 *tablespoon chopped sweet pickle*
1 *tablespoon chopped green pepper*

Drain and flake salmon. Combine cabbage, onion, parsley, eggs, and salmon. Set aside. Combine salt, cayenne, and paprika. Add vinegar and oil slowly, beating thoroughly. Add pimiento, sweet pickle, and green pepper. Add dressing to salmon mixture and mix thoroughly. Yield: 8 servings.

Hawaiian Tuna Party Salad

½ *cup mayonnaise*
¼ *cup chutney*
2 *teaspoons curry powder*
½ *teaspoon salt*
1 *cup chopped celery*
1 *(20-ounce) can pineapple tidbits,*
drained
3 *(7-ounce) cans tuna*
2 *cups cooked rice*
Slivered almonds for garnishing

Mix mayonnaise, chutney, curry, and salt. Combine celery, pineapple, tuna, and rice.

Combine the two mixtures and garnish with slivered almonds. Serve in lettuce cups. Yield: 8 servings.

Avocado Salad

1½ *medium, ripe but firm avocados*
1 *(3-ounce) package cream cheese*
½ *carton (about ½ cup) commercial*
sour cream
2 *tablespoons mayonnaise*
1½ *envelopes unflavored gelatin*
Juice small lemon
Green food coloring, if desired
Lettuce or endive
Coleslaw dressing

Mash avocados. Combine with cream cheese, sour cream, and mayonnaise (by hand or blender) until smooth. Add gelatin to lemon juice and place over warm water until gelatin melts. Blend well with avocado mixture.

Add food coloring to shade desired to make salad light or dark. Chill in 1-quart mold or in individual custard cups. Since this is a rich salad, smaller portions are suggested for individual molds.

When ready to serve, place on small salad plates in bed of lettuce or endive. Frost with coleslaw dressing over each salad. This salad may be made ahead of time, covered, and placed in freezer for a day or two. Yield: 6 to 8 servings.

Confetti Artichokes

1 *(9-ounce) package frozen artichoke
    hearts*
2 *tablespoons chopped pimiento*
¼ *cup Italian dressing*
⅛ *teaspoon salt*
   Dash pepper

Cook artichokes according to package directions; drain. Add remaining ingredients and toss to combine flavors. Chill. Yield: 4 to 6 servings.

Buttermilk Aspic

2 *envelopes unflavored gelatin*
½ *cup cold water*
½ *cup boiling water*
2 *cups buttermilk*
2 *teaspoons salt*
1 *tablespoon lemon juice*
2 *teaspoons sugar*
½ *teaspoon Worcestershire sauce*
1 *cup catsup*
1 *tablespoon grated onion*
1 *cup finely chopped celery*

Soften gelatin in cold water for 5 minutes. Add boiling water and stir until gelatin is dissolved; then cool to room temperature.
    Combine the buttermilk, salt, lemon juice, sugar, Worcestershire sauce, catsup, and onion. Add gelatin and blend well. Chill to consistency of honey; fold in chopped celery. Spoon into a 1½-quart ring mold; chill until firm.

Congealed Avocado Salad

1 *(3-ounce) package lime-flavored
    gelatin*
1 *cup boiling water*
1 *(3-ounce) package cream cheese*
1 *avocado, chopped*
1 *small onion, chopped very fine*
2 *stalks celery, chopped*
1 *pimiento, chopped*
½ *cup mayonnaise*

Dissolve gelatin in boiling water. Cool to syrupy stage. Combine softened cream cheese with other ingredients and add to cooled gelatin mixture. Spoon into 8 individual molds, and chill thoroughly. Serve on bed of lettuce. Yield: 8 servings.

Three-Bean Salad

1 *(1-pound) can cut green beans*
1 *(1-pound) can cut
    yellow wax beans*
1 *(1-pound) can red
    kidney beans*
¼ *cup chopped green pepper*
1 *medium onion, sliced very thin*
½ *cup cider vinegar*
⅓ *cup cooking oil*
½ *cup sugar*
1 *teaspoon salt*
1 *teaspoon pepper*

Drain beans, rinse well, and drain again. Add green pepper and sliced onion to beans. Mix other ingredients and add to bean mixture. Mix well and let sit overnight in the refrigerator. Yield: 12 to 15 servings.

Fresh Snap Bean Salad, Italian Style

2 *cups cooked fresh snap beans*
2 *cups diced cooked potatoes*
¼ *cup chopped onion*
⅛ *teaspoon minced fresh garlic*
1 *teaspoon salt*
⅛ *teaspoon ground black pepper*
2 *tablespoons salad oil*
1 *cup diced celery*
8 *anchovies, diced*
3 *tablespoons mayonnaise*
1 *tablespoon cider vinegar*
   Head lettuce
   Black olives

Combine the first 7 ingredients. Mix lightly. Cover and marinate in the refrigerator at least 1 hour. Just before serving, add celery, anchovies, mayonnaise, and vinegar. Mix lightly. Serve on lettuce and garnish with black olives. Yield: 8 servings.

Fresh Snap Bean and Tuna Fish Salad

    1 *pound (3½ cups, cut) young, tender fresh snap beans*
    1 *teaspoon salt*
    Boiling water
    ¼ *cup olive or salad oil*
    2 *teaspoons fresh lemon juice*
    ⅛ *teaspoon ground black pepper*
    1 *(6½-ounce) can tuna fish*

Wash beans, remove tips, and cut into 1½-inch lengths. Place in a saucepan with 1 teaspoon salt and ½ inch boiling water. Bring to boiling point and cook, uncovered, 5 minutes. Cover and continue cooking until beans are crisp-tender, about 10 minutes. Combine oil, lemon juice, and black pepper. Mix well. Drain beans and while hot add the oil mixture. Mix lightly. Turn into a serving dish. Break tuna fish into chunks; scatter over top. Serve hot or cold as a main dish salad. Yield: 4 servings.

Beet and Pineapple Salad Supreme

    1 *(3-ounce) package strawberry-flavored gelatin*
    1 *(3-ounce) package raspberry-flavored gelatin*
    1 *(3-ounce) package cherry-flavored gelatin*
    4 *cups boiling water*
    1 *(No. 2) can French-cut beets*
    1 *(No. 2) can crushed pineapple*
    ½ *cup sweet pickle juice (or vinegar)*

Dissolve all gelatin in boiling water. Drain liquid from beets and pineapple (about 1½ cups), and add with pickle juice to gelatin mixture. Chill until syrupy, then stir in drained beets and pineapple. Put into 3-quart mold and chill until firm. Serve with Dressing. Yield: 16 servings.

Dressing:

    1 *cup mayonnaise*
    1 *tablespoon chopped green onion and tops*
    1 *tablespoon diced celery*
    1 *tablespoon finely chopped green pepper*

Mix all ingredients and let stand several hours. Thin with light cream, if desired. Yield: 1¼ cups.

Beet and Horseradish Salad

    1 *(No. 2) can tiny whole beets*
    6 *tablespoons horseradish*
    4 *teaspoons sugar*
    4 *teaspoons vinegar*
    Salt and pepper

Drain beets. Heat juice with horseradish, sugar, vinegar, salt, and pepper. Pour over beets and set in refrigerator. Yield: 6 to 8 servings.

Twenty-Four-Hour Cabbage Salad

    4 *pounds cabbage, sliced thin*
    2 *green peppers, grated*
    2 *carrots, grated*
    1 *onion, grated*
    1 *tablespoon unflavored gelatin*
    ½ *cup cold water*
    1½ *cups sugar*
    1 *cup vinegar*
    1 *teaspoon celery seed*
    1 *teaspoon salt*
    ¼ *teaspoon pepper*
    1 *cup salad oil*

Combine cabbage, green pepper, carrot, and onion and put in a bag to drain. Dissolve gelatin in cold water. Heat sugar and vinegar. Add dissolved gelatin and stir. Cool and add celery seed, salt, and pepper. Allow to cool until mixture is thickness of cream. Add salad oil and sliced and grated vegetables. Chill for 24 hours. Yield: 8 servings.

Congealed Cabbage Salad

   1 *(3-ounce) package lime-flavored*
      gelatin
1½ *cups boiling water*
   1 *cup grated cabbage*
   1 *cup shredded American cheese*
   1 *cup chopped pecans*
   1 *cup mayonnaise*
     Dash salt

Dissolve gelatin in boiling water. Cool; then put in refrigerator. After gelatin has partially congealed, add grated cabbage, shredded cheese, pecans, mayonnaise, and salt, and mix well. Spoon into mold and put in refrigerator until firm. Yield: 8 servings.

Calico Slaw

Especially good served with fish or seafood.

   3 *cups shredded green cabbage*
   3 *cups shredded red cabbage*
   1 *large sweet pepper, shredded*
     Salt and pepper
   3 *tablespoons sweet pickle relish*
 ½ *cup mayonnaise*

Shred cabbage in large bowl. Add green pepper, salt, pepper, relish, and mayonnaise. Toss with a fork. Yield: 6 to 8 servings.

Ellen's Cabbage Salad

   2 *(3-ounce) packages lemon-flavored*
      gelatin
3¾ *cups boiling water*
   3 *cups shredded cabbage*
   1 *cup chopped celery*
   1 *cup chopped unpeeled red apples*
   2 *tablespoons lemon juice*

Dissolve gelatin in boiling water. Let sit in refrigerator until syrupy. Shred cabbage. (The secret of crisp cabbage is to chill in cold water before shredding.) Add chopped celery. Chop apples and cover with lemon juice to prevent discoloration; add to cab-

bage. Add cabbage, celery, and apples to gelatin and chill. Yield: 8 servings.

Cabbage and Peanut Salad

   1 *egg*
 ½ *cup vinegar*
 ½ *cup water*
   1 *teaspoon salt*
 ½ *teaspoon dry mustard*
   2 *tablespoons sugar*
   2 *cups finely shredded cabbage*
 ½ *cup chopped peanuts*
 ½ *teaspoon celery seed*

Beat egg in small saucepan. Add vinegar, water, salt, dry mustard, and sugar. Mix thoroughly and cook over low heat, beating constantly until mixture is slightly thickened. Cool. Pour dressing mixture over shredded cabbage, chopped peanuts, and celery seed. Yield: 4 to 6 servings.

Apple-Sour Cream Slaw

   1 *cup sliced celery*
   2 *cups shredded cabbage*
   1 *cup shredded carrots*
   2 *large red apples, diced*
 ⅓ *cup seedless raisins*
 ⅓ *cup chopped salted peanuts*
   1 *cup commercial sour cream*
   2 *tablespoons lemon juice*
   2 *tablespoons cider vinegar*
   2 *tablespoons sugar*
   1 *teaspoon salt*
 ¼ *teaspoon pepper*
   1 *teaspoon dry mustard*

In a large bowl combine the celery, cabbage, carrots, apples, raisins, and salted peanuts. Mix remaining ingredients to make a dressing and pour over vegetable mixture. Toss to mix well. Yield: 10 to 12 servings.

Club Coleslaw

  1 *(2-pound) head cabbage*
  1 *green pepper, diced*
  1 *red pepper, diced*
  1 *(13¼-ounce) can pineapple tidbits,*
     drained
  ¼ *cup sugar*
  1 *teaspoon salt*
  1 *cup mayonnaise*
  2 *tablespoons lemon, lime, or orange*
     juice
  ½ *teaspoon dry mustard*
  1 *teaspoon celery seed*

Finely shred the cabbage and combine with diced peppers and drained pineapple. Sprinkle with sugar and salt; stir to mix. Let stand about 30 minutes.

    Mix mayonnaise, lemon juice, and dry mustard; stir into cabbage mixture. At serving time, sprinkle with celery seed. Yield: 12 servings.

Hot Curried Slaw

This is wonderful with lamb.

  6 *cups shredded cabbage*
  1 *large shredded onion*
  2 *tablespoons butter*
  ½ *clove garlic*
  2 *teaspoons flour*
  2 *teaspoons curry powder*
  1 *can beef consommé*
  1 *can water*
1½ *cups commercial sour cream*
    Dash of pepper
  4 *whole cloves*

Shred cabbage and set aside. Brown onion in butter; add garlic and blend in flour and curry powder. Mix beef consommé and water; add 1 cup of this to onion mixture. Remove the clove of garlic and add sour cream. Simmer over low heat until mixture thickens. Add pepper and set aside.

    Heat beef consommé; add whole cloves and shredded cabbage. Cover pan and simmer for 5 minutes. Remove cloves. Turn the cabbage into a buttered casserole; add the onion and sauce mixture and mix well with a fork. Bake at 350 degrees F. for 20 minutes. Yield: 6 servings.

Cucumber Coleslaw

  4 *cups shredded cabbage*
  2 *cups peeled, diced cucumbers*
  1 *medium onion, sliced very thin and*
     soaked in vinegar
  1 *teaspoon sugar*
  ½ *teaspoon salt*
  ½ *teaspoon celery seed*
  1 *tablespoon tarragon vinegar*
  ½ *cup salad dressing*

Combine cabbage and cucumbers; add onion slices and toss. Sprinkle the sugar and salt over mixture. Add celery seed and tarragon vinegar and mix well. Add salad dressing just before serving and mix well. Yield: 6 servings.

Hawaiian Coleslaw

This slaw is marvelous with fried chicken or baked ham.

  4 *cups fresh, shredded green cabbage*
  1 *(11-ounce) can mandarin orange*
     slices
  1 *cup crushed pineapple, drained*
  ½ *teaspoon salt*
  ¼ *teaspoon ground ginger*
  ¼ *teaspoon ground nutmeg*
  1 *tablespoon orange juice*
  ¼ *teaspoon white pepper*
  ½ *cup mayonnaise or tart salad*
     dressing

Shred cabbage into large bowl. Drain orange sections, but reserve the juice. Drain and measure the pineapple. Add salt and spices to shredded cabbage. Add orange juice and pepper. Toss lightly. Add the drained fruit, tossing all with a fork. Stir in the mayonnaise. Chill well before serving. Yield: 6 servings.

Coleslaw

  1 *quart finely shredded cabbage*
 1½ *cups chopped celery*
  ½ *cup chopped green pepper*
  ¾ *teaspoon salt*
  ½ *cup mayonnaise*
  ¼ *teaspoon Tabasco sauce*
  ½ *teaspoon sugar*
  ⅛ *teaspoon paprika*
  1 *tablespoon lemon juice*
  1 *tablespoon milk*
    Tomato wedges

Place cabbage, celery, and green pepper in large bowl. Sprinkle salt over vegetables; toss lightly. Measure mayonnaise into cup; stir in Tabasco, sugar, paprika, lemon juice, and milk; add to vegetables; toss lightly. Turn into bowl; garnish with tomato wedges. Yield: 6 servings.

Crunchy Slaw Salad

  4 *cups shredded green cabbage*
  ¾ *teaspoon salt*
  1 *teaspoon sugar*
  1 *cup diced celery*
  ½ *cup chopped salted peanuts*
  2 *cups homemade salad dressing*
    Dash of paprika

Wash and drain the firm cabbage head. Shred into a large bowl. Sprinkle with salt and sugar; add the diced celery and toss with a fork. Add chopped peanuts and salad dressing and mix well. Add paprika for color and flavor. Yield: 6 servings.

Red and Green Slaw

  4 *cups shredded green cabbage*
  2 *cups drained sweet red or dark
      cherries, pitted*
  2 *cups miniature marshmallows*
  1 *cup orange sections*
    Coleslaw dressing

Combine cabbage, cherries, marshmallows, and orange sections with enough commer-

cial coleslaw dressing to moisten. Chill. Yield: 6 to 8 servings.

Hot Fresh Apple Slaw

  3 *cups finely shredded cabbage*
  2 *tablespoons cider vinegar*
  2 *teaspoons sugar*
  2 *tablespoons butter or margarine*
  1 *teaspoon tarragon leaves*
  ¼ *teaspoon salt*
 ¹⁄₁₆ *teaspoon ground black pepper*
  2 *cups (2 medium) grated raw apples*

Place cabbage in a saucepan with vinegar, sugar, butter, and seasonings. Bring to boiling point. Stir in apples and cook only to heat apples. Serve as meat accompaniment. This dish is especially good when served with pork, ham, corned beef, or tongue. Yield: 4 generous servings.

Chinese Slaw

  1 *medium can French-cut green beans*
  1 *small can mushrooms*
  1 *diced pimiento*
  1 *medium can Chinese vegetables*
  1 *small can English peas*
  1 *can water chestnuts, sliced*
 1½ *cups diced celery*
  1 *onion, sliced and ringed*
  ¾ *cup sugar*
  ¾ *cup vinegar*
    Salt and pepper

Drain all vegetables and combine in glass container. Heat sugar and vinegar and pour over vegetables. Add salt and pepper to taste. Yield: 8 to 10 servings.

Marinated Carrot Sticks

  5 *small carrots*
  2 *tablespoons vinegar*
  2 *tablespoons salad oil*
  ½ *clove garlic, crushed*
  ½ *teaspoon seasoned salt*
  ¼ *teaspoon salt*
    Minced fresh parsley

Cut carrots into thin, short sticks. Mix other ingredients except parsley. Place carrots in marinade so they are at least partially covered, and chill overnight, turning sticks occasionally. Drain and sprinkle with parsley before serving. Yield: 4 servings.

Captain's Salad

    1 quart leaf lettuce or romaine
    1 quart spinach leaves
    ½ cup small sweet onion rings
    3 tablespoons toasted sesame seed
    1 teaspoon salt
    ¼ teaspoon pepper
    ½ teaspoon dry mustard
    3 tablespoons vinegar
    1 tablespoon honey
    ½ cup vegetable oil
    3 tomatoes, peeled and cut in wedges
    2 cups herbed, seasoned croutons

Trim and wash greens. Drain well and tear into bite-size pieces before measuring. Add onion rings and sesame seed; toss and refrigerate until just before ready to serve.

Make salad dressing by combining salt, pepper, and mustard in small mixing bowl; stir in vinegar and honey. Slowly add vegetable oil while beating with rotary beater or electric mixer; refrigerate.

Just before serving, combine greens, tomato wedges, salad dressing, and herbed, seasoned croutons and toss lightly. Serve immediately from chilled salad bowl. Yield: 8 to 10 servings.

Cottage Cheese Salad

    1 package lime-flavored gelatin
    1 package lemon-flavored gelatin
    2 cups boiling water
    ½ cup chopped celery
    ¼ cup chopped green pepper
    1 (12-ounce) package cottage cheese
    1 small can crushed pineapple, drained
    ½ cup mayonnaise or salad dressing
    1 teaspoon minced onion

Dissolve gelatin in boiling water. Chill until slightly thick. Fold in celery, green pepper, cottage cheese, pineapple, salad dressing, and onion. Chill. Yield: 10 servings.

Cracker Salad

    1 stack saltine crackers
    1 cup chopped onion
    1 cup sweet pickles, chopped
    1 medium green pepper, chopped
    1 small jar pimientos, drained
    5 hard-cooked eggs, chopped
    1 pint salad dressing

Crush crackers and put in large mixing bowl. Add all ingredients and mix well. This salad is especially good if put in a covered plastic container and chilled for a couple of hours before serving. Yield: 6 servings.

Cool-as-a-Cucumber Ring

    1 envelope unflavored gelatin
    ½ cup cold water
    ½ teaspoon salt
    1 large cucumber, pared
    ½ small onion
    3 cups creamed cottage cheese
    1 (8-ounce) package cream cheese
    ½ cup mayonnaise
    ⅔ cup chopped celery
    ⅓ cup nuts

Soften gelatin in water; add salt, and heat and stir over low heat until gelatin is dissolved.

Cut the cucumber in half and remove seeds; grate cucumber with onion and set aside. Beat the cheeses, and stir in gelatin. Add the remaining ingredients. Pour into a 1-quart ring mold and chill overnight. This is good served with cucumber slices, radishes, cold cuts. Yield: 8 servings.

Cucumber Salad

　1 *(3-ounce) package lime-flavored*
　　　gelatin
　¾ *cup hot water*
　¼ *cup lemon juice*
　1 *teaspoon onion juice*
　1 *cup commercial sour cream*
　1 *cup chopped cucumber*

Dissolve gelatin in hot water. Add lemon juice and onion juice. Chill until partially set. Fold in sour cream and cucumber. Pour in oiled mold and chill until firm. Garnish with tomato wedges. Serve on lettuce. Yield: 4 to 6 servings.

Pat's Dilled Cucumber Salad

　Cucumbers
　Mayonnaise
　Juice from jar of garlic dill pickles
　Salt and pepper to taste
　Dill seed

Peel the cucumbers or not, depending on their freshness and your taste. Slice very thin. Combine equal parts mayonnaise and juice from garlic dills. Pour over sliced cucumbers. Sprinkle with salt and pepper to taste; then add dill seed, in the proportion of ¼ teaspoon per serving. Elegant with any fish or ham dish.

Dill Pickle Salad

　1½ *tablespoons unflavored gelatin*
　1 *cup cold water*
　1 *cup sugar*
　¼ *cup lemon juice*
　¼ *teaspoon salt*
　¼ *cup dill pickle juice*
　¼ *cup pineapple juice*
　¼ *cup pimiento juice*
　2 *dill pickles, chopped*
　½ *cup chopped pimientos*
　1 *cup chopped pecans*
　1 *cup crushed pineapple, drained*

Dissolve gelatin in cold water. Bring sugar, lemon juice, salt, dill pickle juice, pineapple juice, and pimiento juice to a boil and pour over gelatin. Cool. Place in refrigerator until slightly congealed. Then add pickles, pimientos, pecans, and pineapple. Pour into ring mold. Yield: 8 servings.

Louis Pappas's Famous Greek Salad

　6 *boiling-size potatoes*
　2 *medium onions, or 4 green onions,*
　　　sliced
　½ *cup thinly sliced green pepper*
　¼ *cup finely chopped parsley*
　Salt
　½ *cup salad dressing*
　1 *large head lettuce*
　12 *roka leaves or 12 sprigs watercress*
　2 *tomatoes, cut into 6 wedges each*
　1 *peeled cucumber, cut lengthwise into*
　　　8 fingers
　1 *avocado, peeled and cut into wedges*
　4 *portions of feta (Greek cheese)*
　1 *green pepper, cut into 8 rings*
　4 *slices canned, cooked beets*
　4 *cooked and peeled shrimp*
　4 *anchovy fillets*
　12 *black olives (Greek style preferred)*
　12 *medium-hot Salonika peppers*
　4 *fancy-cut radishes*
　4 *whole green onions*
　½ *cup distilled white vinegar*
　¼ *cup each olive and salad oil blended*
　　　Oregano

Boil the potatoes in their jackets for about 30 minutes, or until tender but not soft. Drain, cool, and peel the potatoes; when cool, slice into a bowl. Add sliced onion and pepper and chopped parsley; sprinkle lightly with salt. Fold in the salad dressing, using more if necessary to hold salad together lightly.

　Line a large platter with outside lettuce leaves and place 3 cups of the potato salad in a mound in the center of the platter. Cover with the remaining lettuce, which has been shredded. Arrange the roka or watercress on top of this. Place the tomato wedges around the outer edges of the salad, with a few on top. Add the cucumber fingers in between the tomatoes, making a solid base of the salad. Place the avocado wedges around the outside of the mound.

Arrange slices of feta cheese on top of the salad, with the green pepper rings over all. On the very top, place the sliced beets with a shrimp on each beet slice and an anchovy fillet on the shrimp. The olives, peppers, radishes, and green onions can be arranged as desired. Sprinkle vinegar over top; then sprinkle with the blended oil. Sprinkle oregano over all. Yield: 4 servings.

Tossed Lettuce and Fruit Salad

To serve with slices of cold turkey for supper or lunch: Toss iceberg lettuce with sections of grapefruit, oranges, grapes, sliced pears, and unpeeled apples with your favorite French dressing.

Luncheon Salad Romanoff

½ cup cooked asparagus
½ cup cooked string beans
½ cup cooked green peas
4 radishes, sliced
2 hearts of artichoke, chopped
2 hard-cooked eggs, chopped
1 teaspoon fresh mixed herbs
⅓ cup French dressing
¼ cup mayonnaise

Toss lightly all ingredients except mayonnaise, and marinate for at least 30 minutes. Before serving, blend in mayonnaise.

Wilted Lettuce

1 large head lettuce
6 slices crisp bacon
¼ cup bacon fat
¼ cup tarragon vinegar
⅛ teaspoon salt
¼ teaspoon ground black pepper
¼ teaspoon sugar

Wash lettuce, pat dry, tear into bite-size pieces. Put in a salad bowl. Break bacon into 1-inch pieces and add to lettuce. Heat together the remaining ingredients. Pour over lettuce, tossing as you pour. Serve at once. Yield: 6 servings.

Tossed Lettuce and Mushroom Salad

1 medium head lettuce
½ small bunch watercress
¼ pound (1 cup) very small whole white mushroom caps
French dressing

Wash lettuce and watercress and pat dry. Break into bite-size pieces and place in a salad bowl. Wash mushrooms and add along with French dressing. Toss lightly, but thoroughly, to coat each piece of lettuce and watercress. Serve at once. Yield: 6 servings.

Head Lettuce and Anchovy Salad

1 clove garlic
1 head lettuce
1 (2-ounce) can anchovy fillets
4 hard-cooked eggs, sliced
⅛ teaspoon ground black pepper
2 tablespoons salad oil
2 tablespoons fresh lemon juice

Rub salad bowl with clove of garlic. Cut head lettuce into chunks and anchovies into pieces. Add remaining ingredients. Toss lightly. Yield: 6 servings.

Wilted Lettuce Salad

Select very fresh spring lettuce leaves. Wash carefully and chop about 4 cups of it into a large bowl. Add 3 finely chopped young onions and tops, and toss mixture lightly. Fry about 5 slices bacon; drain. In the hot bacon drippings, add about ½ to 1 teaspoon salt, 1 teaspoon sugar, and 2 tablespoons vinegar. Stir well, heat, and pour immediately over lettuce; toss lightly to coat all leaves. Crumble cooked bacon over top. Yield: 3 or 4 servings.

Mexican Salad

    4 cups shredded lettuce
    ½ cup sliced green onion
    1 pound ground beef
    ¼ cup chopped onion
    1 can ranch-style beans, drained
    ½ cup French dressing
    ½ cup water
    1 tablespoon chili powder
    1 (8-ounce) wedge Cheddar cheese,
         shredded

Shred lettuce and slice green onions into large salad bowl; let stand. Brown ground beef in skillet; add chopped onion and cook until tender. Stir in beans, dressing, water; and chili powder; simmer 15 minutes.

Add meat and 1½ cups cheese to lettuce and green onions. Toss lightly. Sprinkle with remaining cheese and serve immediately with tortilla chips. Yield: 6 to 8 servings.

German Potato Salad

    12 potatoes, boiled
    ½ cup salad oil
    1 cup cider vinegar
    1½ cups water
    1 heaping teaspoon flour
    1 teaspoon salt
    1 tablespoon sugar
    2 tablespoons celery seed
    2 onions, cut fine

Peel potatoes. Cool; then slice into large bowl. Combine salad oil, vinegar, water, and flour in saucepan. Boil until slightly thick. Remove from heat and add salt, sugar, celery seed, and chopped onion. Spoon this mixture over sliced potatoes. Serve either hot or cold. Let sit overnight in covered dish in refrigerator. Garnish with hard-cooked eggs. Yield: 10 to 12 servings.

Potato Salad Mold

    20 medium potatoes
    1 envelope unflavored gelatin
    ¼ cup cold water
    ½ cup olive juice
    ½ cup vinegar
    ¼ cup dill pickle juice
    2 medium onions, chopped
    2 large peppers, chopped
    2 celery stalks, chopped
    1 large bottle olives, chopped
    1 cup chopped pickles
    ¾ cup mayonnaise

Boil potatoes in jackets. Peel when cool, and chop in large bowl. Dissolve gelatin in cold water. Bring olive juice, vinegar, and dill pickle juice to a boil and pour over gelatin. Cool. Place in refrigerator until slightly congealed. Add onions, peppers, celery stalks, olives, and chopped pickles to potatoes. Add gelatin preparation and blend in mayonnaise. Put salad in mold and refrigerate overnight. Yield: 20 servings.

Deviled Potato Salad

    8 hard-cooked eggs
    2 tablespoons vinegar
    1 tablespoon prepared horseradish
         sauce
    2½ tablespoons prepared mustard
    1 cup mayonnaise or salad dressing
    1 cup commercial sour cream
    ½ teaspoon celery salt
    1 teaspoon salt
    6 medium potatoes, cooked in jackets,
         peeled and cubed (4½ cups)
    1 cup chopped celery
    ¼ cup chopped onion
    2 tablespoons chopped green pepper
    2 tablespoons chopped pimiento

Cut eggs in half and remove yolk. Mash and blend yolks with vinegar, horseradish, and mustard. Add mayonnaise, sour cream, celery salt, and salt; mix well. Chop egg white; combine with potatoes, celery, onion, green pepper, and pimiento. Fold in egg yolk mixture; chill. Garnish with tomato wedges and cucumber slices. Yield: 6 to 8 servings.

Piquant Mushrooms

  1 *(4-ounce) can whole button*
     mushrooms, drained
  2 *tablespoons chopped onion*
  2 *tablespoons salad oil*
  1 *teaspoon vinegar*
  ½ *teaspoon lemon juice*
  ½ *teaspoon sugar*
    Dash salt

Combine mushrooms and onion. To make dressing, combine remaining ingredients and mix well. Pour dressing over mushrooms. Chill. Yield: 4 to 6 servings.

Plantation Salad

  4 *tablespoons unflavored gelatin*
  1 *cup cold water*
  ½ *cup vinegar*
  4 *tablespoons lemon juice*
  ½ *cup sugar*
  ½ *teaspoon salt*
 4½ *cups boiling water*
  4 *cups shredded cabbage*
  3 *cups diced pineapple*
  ½ *cup chopped green pepper*
  ½ *cup chopped pimiento*

Soak gelatin in cold water; add vinegar, lemon juice, sugar, salt, and boiling water. Stir until gelatin is dissolved; chill until syrupy. Combine the cabbage, pineapple, green pepper, and pimiento. Mix with the gelatin mixture. Pour into two 2-quart ring molds, first rinsed in cold water. Chill until firm. Yield: 25 servings.

Sauerkraut Salad

  1 *(No. 2½) can chopped sauerkraut*
  1 *large onion, chopped*
  1 *cup chopped celery*
  1 *green pepper, chopped*
  1 *(4-ounce) can pimiento, chopped*
 1¼ *cups sugar*

Mix all ingredients except sugar, then sprinkle the sugar over top of mixture. Cover container and refrigerate for 24 hours. Mix well and serve. Yield: 8 servings.

Scandinavian Salad

  1 *(No. 2) can cut green beans*
  1 *(No. 2) can English peas*
  1 *(No. 2) can whole-kernel corn*
  2 *cups chopped celery*
  1 *(4-ounce) jar pimientos, chopped*
  ½ *cup chopped onion*
    Salt
  1 *cup sugar*
 1½ *tablespoons salt*
  1 *cup vinegar*
  ½ *cup cooking oil*
  1 *teaspoon paprika*

Drain vegetables, mix together, and add salt. Stir well and chill for 1 hour. Remove from refrigerator and drain. Add remaining ingredients and stir until sugar is dissolved. Pour into a large dish, cover, and refrigerate several hours. Yield: 8 to 10 servings.

Dilled Tomato Molds

  1 *(3-ounce) package salad gelatin,*
    tomato flavored
  1 *teaspoon salt*
  1 *cup boiling water*
  2 *teaspoons vinegar*
  ½ *tray (7 to 10) ice cubes*
  ½ *cup chopped celery*
  2 *tablespoons chopped capers*
  1 *tablespoon chopped onion*
  ½ *teaspoon dill seed*
  ⅛ *teaspoon coarsely ground pepper*
    Mayonnaise Dressing

Dissolve gelatin and salt in boiling water. Add vinegar and ice cubes; stir constantly until thickened—about 3 minutes. Remove any unmelted ice.

Stir remaining ingredients into gelatin. Spoon into a 3-cup mold or individual molds. Chill until firm.

Serve with crisp salad greens. Yield: 2⅓ cups, or 4 servings.

Tomato Aspic

> 1 *envelope unflavored gelatin*
> 1½ *cups canned tomato juice*
> ¼ *cup chili sauce*
> 1 *teaspoon grated onion*

Soak gelatin in ½ cup cold tomato juice for 5 minutes. Heat rest of tomato juice (1 cup) and add to softened gelatin; stir until dissolved. Add chili sauce and onion. Pour into mold and chill. Unmold on crisp greens. Yield: 4 servings.

Tropical Salad and Dressing

> 4 *cups palm hearts (lettuce may be substituted)*
> 1 *cup cubed pineapple*
> ¼ *cup chopped dates*
> ¼ *cup chopped candied or preserved ginger*

> *Dressing:*

> 4 *tablespoons vanilla ice cream*
> 2 *tablespoons mayonnaise*
> 2 *tablespoons crunchy peanut butter*
> *Pineapple juice or preserved ginger juice*

Combine ingredients for salad. Mix ice cream, mayonnaise, and peanut butter thoroughly. Thin with either pineapple or ginger juice, pour over salad, and serve.

Vegetable Salad Mold

> 1 *tablespoon unflavored gelatin*
> ¼ *cup cold water*
> 1 *(3-ounce) package lime-flavored gelatin*
> 1 *cup boiling water*
> ½ *cup cold water*
> 2 *tablespoons vinegar*
> 2 *teaspoons grated onion*
> 1 *cup finely shredded sharp cheese*
> ¼ *cup diced celery*
> ½ *cup sliced stuffed olives*
> *Dash salt*

Dissolve unflavored gelatin in ¼ cup cold water. Dissolve lime gelatin in boiling water; add unflavored gelatin and stir until dissolved. Add ½ cup cold water and vinegar; put in refrigerator until partially set. Stir in other ingredients and spoon into 1-quart mold. Yield: 6 servings.

Creamy Blue Cheese Dressing

> ½ *cup commercial sour cream*
> 2 *tablespoons mayonnaise*
> *Juice of ½ lemon*
> *Tops of 2 green onions, chopped*
> ¾ *cup crumbled American blue cheese (about 4 ounces)*
> ½ *teaspoon Worcestershire sauce*

Mix all ingredients together well. Add a pinch of salt and a little sugar, if desired. Yield: 1 cup.

Cooked Salad Dressing

(total calories, 300; per tablespoon, 15)

> 2 *teaspoons dry mustard*
> 1 *teaspoon salt*
> *Dash paprika*
> 2 *tablespoons sugar*
> ½ *tablespoon unflavored gelatin*
> 4 *teaspoons cold water*
> ¾ *cup hot water*
> 1 *tablespoon butter or margarine*
> 1 *egg, well beaten*
> ¼ *cup cider vinegar*

Mix seasonings. Soften gelatin in cold water. Add hot water to mustard mixture; stir until blended. To this add gelatin and butter; stir until gelatin dissolves. Stir hot mixture slowly into beaten egg. Cook, stirring constantly, until mixture begins to thicken. Remove from heat; stir in vinegar. Pour into jar; set aside to cool and thicken. Yield: 1¼ cups.

Chiffonade French Dressing

1½ *teaspoons salt*
¼ *teaspoon pepper*
¼ *teaspoon dry mustard*
1 *cup salad oil*
⅓ *cup vinegar*
1 *hard-cooked egg, chopped*
1 *teaspoon grated onion*
2 *tablespoons chopped green pepper*
1 *tablespoon chopped celery*
1 *tablespoon chopped parsley*

Combine salt, pepper, and mustard. Stir in oil and vinegar. Add remaining ingredients. Pour into jar and shake well. Yield: 1 pint.

Lemon French Dressing

2 *teaspoons salt*
4 *teaspoons sugar*
Dash pepper
Dash paprika
1⅓ *cups salad oil*
8 *tablespoons vinegar*
8 *teaspoons lemon juice*
1 *teaspoon grated lemon rind*

Combine all ingredients and shake, beat, or blend. Refrigerate. Yield: 1½ cups.

Low-Calorie French Dressing

3 *tablespoons salad oil*
¾ *teaspoon salt*
1 *teaspoon sugar*
⅛ *teaspoon paprika*
½ *teaspoon dry mustard*
¼ *teaspoon Tabasco sauce*
1 *cup grapefruit juice, divided*
2 *teaspoons cornstarch*

Combine salad oil, salt, sugar, paprika, dry mustard, and Tabasco in small mixing bowl. Blend together ½ cup of the grapefruit juice and 2 teaspoons cornstarch in small saucepan. Cook over low heat, stirring constantly until mixture thickens and comes to boil.

Add to salad oil mixture; beat with rotary beater until smooth. Beat in remaining ½ cup of grapefruit juice. Yield: 1 cup. (About 35 calories per tablespoon.)

Orange French Dressing

1 *(6-ounce) can orange juice concentrate*
¾ *cup salad oil*
¼ *cup vinegar*
3 *tablespoons sugar*
½ *teaspoon dry mustard*
¼ *teaspoon salt*
¼ *teaspoon Tabasco sauce*

Mix the ingredients together. Put in a jar and chill. Yield: 1¾ cups.

Special Fruit Salad Dressing

½ *cup sugar*
1 *teaspoon salt*
3 *tablespoons flour*
2 *eggs*
¼ *cup vinegar*
1½ *cups pineapple juice*

Combine dry ingredients in saucepan. Add eggs and mix well. Add vinegar and pineapple juice. Cook over low heat until thick and smooth, stirring constantly. Chill thoroughly. Serve on molded, frozen, or fresh fruit salad. Yield: 2 cups.

Mayonnaise Dressing

¼ *cup vinegar*
2 *tablespoons mayonnaise*
1 *envelope onion salad dressing mix*
⅔ *cup salad oil*

Mix vinegar and mayonnaise in cruet or jar with tight-fitting cover. Add salad dressing mix. Cover and shake well. Add salad oil; cover and shake again. Yield: 1 cup.

Mayonnaise-Scallion Dressing

½ *cup mayonnaise*
2 *tablespoons minced fresh scallions*
½ *teaspoon Worcestershire sauce*
⅛ *teaspoon cayenne pepper*

Combine mayonnaise, scallions, Worcestershire, and cayenne. Serve in separate bowl with stuffed peppers, if desired. Yield: 4 servings.

Green Goddess Salad Dressing

1 *cup mayonnaise*
½ *cup commercial sour cream*
¼ *teaspoon garlic powder*
2 *coarsely cut green onions with tops*
2 *tablespoons lemon juice*
¼ *cup chopped parsley*
¼ *teaspoon black pepper*
¼ *cup coarsely cut green pepper*
3 *anchovy fillets*
Dash Worcestershire sauce

Place all ingredients in blender. Cover and blend 10 seconds on high speed or until pale green and smooth. Yield: about 2 cups.

Poppyseed Dressing for Fruit Salad

⅓ *cup honey*
1 *teaspoon salt*
2 *tablespoons vinegar*
1 *tablespoon prepared mustard*
¾ *cup salad oil*
2 *to 3 teaspoons poppy seed*

In a small bowl combine the honey, salt, vinegar, and prepared mustard. Gradually add the salad oil, beating thoroughly until the mixture is well blended. Stir in the poppy seed. Put into a pint jar; cover and chill for several hours before serving.
Shake well each time before using. Yield: 1 cup.

Poppyseed Dressing

1 *teaspoon salt*
1 *teaspoon dry mustard*
1 *teaspoon paprika*
1 *teaspoon poppy seed*
½ *cup white corn syrup*
¼ *to ⅓ cup vinegar*
1 *cup corn oil*

Place all ingredients in a small bowl. Beat until well blended and thickened. Place in a covered container and chill several hours. Shake before serving. Yield: 1¾ cups.

Poppyseed Dressing

1½ *cups sugar*
2 *teaspoons dry mustard*
2 *cups salad oil*
3 *tablespoons poppy seed*
2 *teaspoons salt*
¾ *cup vinegar*
3 *tablespoons onion juice*

Combine all ingredients. Shake vigorously before using. Yield: 2½ cups.

Tomato Dressing

1 *cup salad oil*
⅓ *cup vinegar*
1 *(8-ounce) can tomato sauce*
2 *tablespoons bottled lemon juice*
1 *small onion, grated*
1 *clove garlic, minced or crushed*
3 *tablespoons sugar*
¼ *teaspoon pepper*
1 *teaspoon salt*

Combine ingredients; shake or beat to blend thoroughly. Chill several hours to blend flavors. Beat well before using. Serve over lettuce wedges. Yield: about 2½ cups.

Salad Dressing for Slaw

⅓ *cup finely chopped onion*
⅓ *cup French dressing*
¼ *cup sugar*

Combine all the ingredients and let sit in refrigerator. It will be better if allowed to sit for three days before using. To make a creamier dressing, 3 tablespoons mayonnaise may be added. Yield: 1 cup.

Riverside Dressing

> 1 can tomato soup
> ½ cup salad oil
> ½ cup vinegar
> ½ cup sugar
> 1 teaspoon Worcestershire sauce
> 1 teaspoon dry mustard
> 1 teaspoon salt
> 1 medium onion, grated, and juice
> 1 clove garlic, split

Combine all ingredients, except clove of garlic, and beat together. Add garlic and store in a glass jar. Keep in refrigerator and shake well before using. Yield: 3 cups.

Wilted Lettuce Dressing

> 2 tablespoons bacon drippings
> ½ teaspoon salt
> ¼ teaspoon dry mustard
> 1 teaspoon sugar
> 1 tablespoon vinegar

Mix ingredients in saucepan and heat to sizzling. Pour over leaf lettuce. Yield: ¼ cup.

Tomato Salad Dressing

> 1 (10½-ounce) can tomato soup
> ¾ cup vinegar
> ½ cup salad oil
> ¼ cup sugar
> 1 tablespoon Worcestershire sauce
> 3 tablespoons grated onion
> 1 teaspoon salt
> 1 tablespoon dry mustard
> 1 teaspoon paprika
> 2 cloves garlic

Mix all ingredients together, except for the two cloves garlic, in a quart jar. Shake well.

Add the garlic and let stand awhile for a garlic flavor to develop. Chill. Remove garlic before serving. Yield: 1 quart.

Rotisserie Salad Dressing

> 2 garlic cloves, chopped very fine
> 1 cup mayonnaise
> ¼ cup chili sauce
> ¼ cup catsup
> 1 teaspoon prepared mustard
> ½ cup cooking oil
> 1 tablespoon Worcestershire sauce
> 1 teaspoon black pepper
> Dash Tabasco sauce
> Juice and pulp of one finely grated
>   onion
> 2 tablespoons water

Put all ingredients in a quart jar and shake till well mixed; then keep refrigerated. Serve on head lettuce salad. Yield: 2¼ cups.

notes

Sauces

It would be difficult to give a "typical" barbecue sauce for the entire South. Texans add a few ground hot peppers and a dash of chili powder, while other sections prefer to get their flavor from lemon juice or cider vinegar and a few milder spices.

Cocktail sauce is used by the gallons in restaurants, particularly those specializing in seafoods. Steamed shrimp depends on this sauce, heavily seasoned with horseradish, to bring out its flavor.

Dessert sauces take many forms, with citrus sauces very popular as toppings for puddings, pound cakes, and ice creams.

Vegetables, too, come to the table in a new dress with hollandaise and other sauces added.

Barbecue Sauce for Chicken or Pork

    1 *small onion, chopped fine*
    2 *tablespoons bacon drippings*
    1 *tablespoon Worcestershire sauce*
    ⅔ *cup tomato catsup*
    1 *tablespoon vinegar*
    3 *tablespoons lemon juice*
    2 *tablespoons prepared mustard*
    1 *cup beef, pork, or chicken broth*

Fry onion in bacon drippings until soft and light yellow. Add remaining ingredients and simmer slowly for 15 minutes or until fairly thick. Serve hot on roasted meats.

Sauce for Ribs and Burgers

    1 *cup water*
    ½ *cup white vinegar*
    2 *teaspoons salt*
    1 *teaspoon pepper*
    2 *tablespoons Worcestershire sauce*
    1 *clove minced garlic (optional)*
    ¼ *pound butter or margarine*

It's easy to start an argument by suggesting that any particular barbecue sauce is "typical." Some Southern cooks have different sauces for sausage, chicken, beef, and pork.

Combine all ingredients and bring to a boil. The sauce can then be sealed in a jar and stored in the refrigerator or used at once. Yield: enough sauce for three chickens, halved, or for 5 to 6 pounds of ribs.

Barbecue Sauce For Chicken

    ½ *cup honey*
    ½ *cup catsup*
    1 *tablespoon candied ginger, chopped fine*
    1 *tablespoon finely chopped onion*
    1 *clove garlic, minced*
    1 *frying-size chicken*
    ½ *to 1 cup cracker meal*

Combine first 5 ingredients and cook over low heat about 5 minutes. Do not overcook. Store in refrigerator until ready to use.

Cut chicken in serving-size pieces. Place in baking pan and brush with chicken barbecue sauce. Sprinkle generously with cracker meal. Bake at 300 degrees F. for 90 minutes.

Barbecue Sauce

 2 *sticks margarine, melted*
 Juice of 3 lemons
 ¼ *cup horseradish*
 ½ *teaspoon Tabasco (or other hot*
   sauce)
 ¼ *cup wine vinegar*
 ½ *cup catsup*
 1 *tablespoon Worcestershire sauce*
 4 *teaspoons salt*

Combine all ingredients in heavy pan and bring to a boil. Mixture is better if removed from heat and allowed to sit for several hours before using on chickens. Yield: enough for 4 small chickens. This sauce is also good on barbecued spareribs.

Barbecue Sauce for Pork

 1 *tablespoon sugar*
 2 *tablespoons flour*
 2 *teaspoons dry mustard*
 2 *teaspoons celery salt*
 2 *teaspoons salt*
 ⅛ *teaspoon cayenne pepper*
 2 *cloves garlic, minced*
 2 *medium onions, chopped*
 ½ *cup Worcestershire sauce*
 2 *cups catsup*
 2 *cups water*
 ½ *cup vinegar*

Combine all ingredients and simmer for 15 minutes. Strain through a coarse strainer to remove onion bits. Yield: about 1 quart.

Celia Emmerich's Citrus Sauce

 Juice and grated rind of 1 orange
 Juice and grated rind of 1 lemon
 Juice and grated rind of 1 lime
 ½ *cup sugar*
 1 *egg, beaten lightly*

Put all ingredients in the top of a double boiler. Beat the mixture well, and cook over hot water until thickened slightly.

Celery Sauce

Combine 2 cups well-seasoned white sauce with 1 cup chopped, cooked celery.

Cocktail Sauce

 2 *tablespoons lemon juice*
 1 *cup catsup*
 1 *tablespoon finely chopped celery*
 1 *tablespoon horseradish*
 1 *tablespoon finely chopped onion*
 1 *teaspoon Worcestershire sauce*
 ½ *teaspoon salt*
 3 *drops Tabasco sauce*

Combine all ingredients and mix thoroughly. Chill. Yield: 1¼ cups.

Cocktail Sauce

 2 *cups catsup*
 2 *cups chili sauce*
 ¼ *cup cider vinegar*
 6 *drops Tabasco sauce*
 ½ *cup prepared horseradish*
 ¼ *cup finely minced celery*
 ¼ *cup finely minced onion*
 2 *teaspoons Worcestershire sauce*

Mix together and refrigerate. Use for all seafood cocktails. Yield: 4½ cups.

Blender Hollandaise Sauce

Heat ½ cup butter until it begins to bubble. Into the container of a blender put 3 egg yolks, 2 teaspoons lemon juice, ½ teaspoon salt, and a few grains of cayenne. Turn the blender on and off to combine the ingredients; then turn it to high and gradually pour the hot butter into the mixture. The sauce will thicken almost immediately. It can be kept warm by putting the container in a bowl or pan of hot water.

Mustard Hollandaise Sauce

1½ *teaspoons powdered mustard*
1 *tablespoon water*
¾ *cup butter or margarine*
1½ *tablespoons fresh lemon juice*
3 *large egg yolks, well beaten*
¹⁄₁₆ *teaspoon salt*
¹⁄₁₆ *teaspoon ground black pepper*

Combine mustard and water; let stand 10 minutes for flavor to develop. Divide butter or margarine into three pieces. Place one piece in the top of a small double boiler and melt. Add lemon juice and egg yolks. Cook slowly over hot water (not boiling), beating constantly with a rotary beater until butter has melted. Add second piece of butter or margarine and continue beating. As the mixture thickens, add the third piece. Remove from water at once. Stir in salt, ground black pepper, and mustard. Serve over cooked vegetables, fish, or meats. Yield: 1⅓ cups.

Kumquat Sauce

Wash kumquats and cut away any blemishes in peel. Slice thinly across width of fruit, removing seeds. Cover with hot water in large kettle and boil from 1 to 3 minutes. Drain.

To 1½ cups of the scalded peel and pulp add 1½ cups hot water. Bring to a boil and simmer for 10 minutes. Add ⅓ cup sugar (or equivalent in honey, desired proportions of honey and sugar, or other sweetener proportionately). Use less sugar if greater tartness and characteristic flavor is preferred. Yield: a generous pint.

Kumquat Sauce

Wash kumquats and cut blemishes from peels. Slice thinly into heavy saucepan, removing seed as you slice. Cover with hot water and boil 1 to 3 minutes; drain.

To 1½ cups of this scalded peel and pulp, add 1½ cups hot water. Bring to a boil and add ⅓ cup sugar and simmer for 30 minutes. Less sugar may be used if greater tartness is desired. This makes a generous pint of sauce.

Spicy Dunk Sauce

½ *cup chili sauce*
¼ *cup well-drained bottled horseradish*
1 *teaspoon Worcestershire sauce*
1 *teaspoon minced onion*
¼ *teaspoon garlic salt*
½ *teaspoon salt*
⅛ *teaspoon pepper*
1 *tablespoon vinegar*
2 *dashes Tabasco sauce*
¼ *teaspoon bottled meat sauce*
1 *teaspoon celery seeds*
2 *tablespoons granulated sugar*
1 *teaspoon celery salt*

Combine all ingredients. Keep in covered jar in refrigerator 2 or 3 days before using. Yield: ¾ cup.

Tahitian Ice Cream Sauce

Mix 1 tablespoon of pineapple and apricot preserves with ¾ ounce of rum for each serving. Warm the mixture before pouring over vanilla or coconut ice cream.

Simple Plum Sauce

Gather orange-colored plums from roadside clumps or buy the larger red ones. Wash thoroughly and lift gently from the water. Add 1 cup of sugar for each cup of fruit. Less sugar will produce a thinner and sharper sauce. Add no water, as that clinging to the fruit will suffice. Slow cooking will necessitate only occasional stirring and little attention. When the mixture has thickened, put through a colander for removal of seeds and skins. The sauce may be sealed, but it will keep well refrigerated for a long period.

Game Sauce

Warm a glass of currant jelly in half as much port wine and serve hot.

Hot Orange Sauce

  ¼ *cup butter*
  ¼ *cup flour*
  ½ *teaspoon salt*
     Dash cayenne pepper
1½ *cups brown stock*
 ⅔ *cup orange juice*
  2 *tablespoons sherry or port wine*
     Grated rind of 1 orange

Melt butter; add flour, salt, and cayenne, stirring until well browned. Slowly add stock. Just before serving, add orange juice, wine, and grated orange rind.

Cold Orange Sauce

6 *tablespoons currant jelly*
3 *tablespoons sugar*
   Grated rind of 2 oranges
2 *tablespoons port wine*
2 *tablespoons orange juice*
2 *tablespoons lemon juice*
¼ *teaspoon salt*
   Dash of cayenne pepper

Put jelly, sugar, and grated orange rind in bowl and beat well. Add other ingredients and stir until blended thoroughly.

Orange Mayonnaise

1 *cup mayonnaise*
⅓ *cup frozen concentrated orange juice, undiluted*

Combine mayonnaise and undiluted orange concentrate and mix well. Use for coleslaw, Waldorf salad, or mixed fruit salad. Yield: 1⅓ cups.

Fresh Orange Sauce

½ *cup butter or margarine*
2 *egg yolks*
1 *tablespoon boiling water*
2 *tablespoons fresh lemon juice*
½ *cup fresh orange juice*
¼ *teaspoon salt*
¼ *teaspoon paprika*
2 *tablespoons grated orange rind*

Place butter in a 3-cup saucepan and mix until soft and fluffy. Beat in egg yolks, one at a time. Stir in boiling water; then add lemon juice. Stir and cook ½ minute over low heat. Add orange juice, salt, and paprika. Mix well. Cook over low heat until sauce is the consistency of heavy cream. Remove from heat and blend in orange rind. Serve with ham, pork, lamb, duck, turkey, or asparagus. Yield: 1¼ cups.

Pineapple-Almond Sauce

¼ *pound butter*
½ *bell pepper, diced fine*
1 *cup chopped, blanched almonds*
¼ *cup soy sauce*
⅛ *cup Worcestershire sauce*
5 *drops Tabasco sauce*
1 *teaspoon garlic salt*
1 *(No. 1½) can chunk pineapple and juice*
½ *cup white corn syrup*
½ *cup white vinegar*

Melt butter in a skillet and sauté bell pepper and almonds until pepper is soft, then stir in other ingredients. Simmer for a few minutes until mixture becomes rather thick. Yield: 4 servings.

Roux

It has been exaggeratedly said that all savory Creole dishes begin . . . "First, you make a roux." Most people, unfamiliar with Creole recipes, have as much difficulty pronouncing it as making it. Roux (pronounced roo) is a thickening agent used in gumbos, jambalayas, stews, and other Creole dishes to impart a distinctive roasted flavor. According to Creole cooks, roux is best made in an iron pot (a heavy skillet can be used) in which is melted 2 tablespoons butter, shortening, or bacon drippings. Add 2 tablespoons flour and stir until brown, being very careful not to burn the mixture. Overbrowning will destroy the subtle taste needed to enhance the roux. For this amount a medium-size, chopped onion may be added. Continue to stir until onion is golden brown.

Salsa Verde

    2 (8-ounce) cans tomato sauce or
        2 cups tomato puree
    2 hot green chiles, finely chopped
    1 small clove garlic, minced
    1 medium onion, chopped
    Salt to taste

Combine all of the above ingredients in a saucepan and cook over low heat for several minutes. Serve in a bowl and let each person take as much as desired. For those who prefer really "hot" enchiladas, Salsa Verde may be substituted for cream mixture and poured over the enchiladas after they are rolled and filled. If you wish to do this, double the Salsa Verde recipe. Salsa Verde is very hot. Treat it with respect.

Tartar Sauce Supreme

    1 cup mayonnaise
    1½ tablespoons minced or grated pickles
    1½ tablespoons minced parsley
    1½ tablespoons capers
    1½ tablespoons minced or grated onion
    1½ tablespoons minced green olives

Combine all ingredients and let sit several hours prior to serving. Yield: 1 cup.

Horseradish Sauce

    4 tablespoons heavy cream
    1 tablespoon vinegar
    Salt and paprika
    3 tablespoons horseradish, grated

Whip cream stiff. Mix the other ingredients; beat gradually into the cream.

Versatile Vegetable Sauce

    1 stick butter
    ½ cup grated Parmesan cheese
    1 teaspoon salt
    2 cups commercial sour cream
    ¼ cup chopped chives
    ⅓ cup chopped cucumber

Cream together butter, Parmesan cheese, and salt. Blend in sour cream, chives, and cucumber. Spoon over vegetables. Yield: approximately 3 cups.

notes

Soups, Stews, And Chowders

Soups and stews to a Southerner mean a hearty concoction of meat, fish, or poultry (sometimes the combination of all) with vegetables.

The most notable soup using seafood as a base is gumbo, as only the Creoles can make it. Time-consuming in its preparation, gumbo may have chicken and ham added with the crab, shrimp, and oysters. Louisianians claim the secret of making a good gumbo lies in the roux, or flour browned in shortening.

Both Virginia and Georgia claim Brunswick stew. Adaptations have been made from original recipes, which used squirrel for the main meat in this thick stew, filled with fresh garden vegetables.

Texas' contribution is chili, and whether it's classed as a soup or a stew is debatable. Not limited to that section of the South, this food may be hot or mild according to the heavy (or light) hand of the cook dispensing the chili powder and hot pepper seasoning.

North Carolina claims peanut butter soup, which has to be tasted to be appreciated. South Carolina is noted for its she-crab soup, and fine restaurants in the area serve the dish with pride.

Okra Gumbo

1 *frying-size chicken*
2 *thick slices ham*
3 *tablespoons margarine*
1 *onion, chopped*
6 *large fresh tomatoes*
1 *pod red pepper*
1 *tablespoon chopped parsley*
20 *pods fresh, sliced okra or 1 package frozen, sliced okra*
1 *sprig thyme or bay leaf*
3 *quarts water*
Salt and pepper to taste
2 *to 3 tablespoons flour*

Gumbo is alternately classed as a stew or as a soup. When a real Southern gumbo is made with chicken, seafood, or in combination, it's a meal in itself.

Cut up chicken; cut ham in small squares. Put margarine into soup kettle; when hot, add the chicken and ham. Cover closely and let cook for about 10 minutes. Add chopped onion. Peel tomatoes and chop fine, straining off and reserving the juice. Remove seed from red pepper and shred. Add parsley, tomatoes, pepper, okra, and thyme. Let cook until chicken is browned, stirring often. When well browned, add the juice from tomatoes. Be careful not to let okra scorch.

When chicken is well fried and browned, add water and let simmer for about an hour. Add salt and pepper to taste. Remove from heat, remove chicken from bone, and return meat to okra mixture. Mix flour with small amount of cold water; add to soup mixture. Stir well and heat until mixture thickens. Serve over hot, fluffy rice. Yield: about 12 to 14 servings.

Duck Gumbo

2 or 3 ducks
Salt and pepper
¼ cup flour
¼ cup bacon drippings or cooking oil
1 large onion, chopped fine
1 large green pepper, chopped fine
4 tablespoons flour
2 to 3 cups water (from cooking giblets)

Cut up ducks for frying. Boil giblets in a large amount of water and set aside. Season ducks with salt and pepper and roll each piece in flour; brown in hot bacon drippings or cooking oil. Remove from oil. Add chopped onion and green pepper and cook until soft; remove from oil. Make a roux by adding 4 tablespoons flour to the oil and cooking until very dark brown. Add water from giblets. Return onion, pepper, and duck to this and cook at very low temperature for about 2 hours. Serve hot over rice or potatoes. Yield: 6 to 8 servings.

Seafood Gumbo

1½ to 2 pounds fresh shrimp
½ teaspoon crab boil
2 tablespoons bacon drippings
2 tablespoons flour
1 large onion, chopped medium fine
1 cup cooked, chopped ham
2 pounds fresh okra, washed, stemmed, and chopped or 1 box frozen okra, chopped
3 stalks celery, chopped
2 tablespoons chopped parsley
1 (No. 2) can tomatoes
1 large green pepper, chopped
1 pound crabmeat, fresh or frozen, picked from the shell
1 clove garlic, mashed
1 teaspoon salt
½ teaspoon freshly ground pepper
¼ teaspoon dried thyme
¼ teaspoon ground oregano
2 bay leaves

Cover well-washed shrimp with water and add crab boil. Cook until shrimp are tender, about 10 minutes. Drain and save the water. Peel shrimp and reserve. In an iron pot or Dutch oven, make a roux with bacon drippings and flour. Add the chopped onion and sauté until transparent. Add ham and okra. Cook about 10 minutes over medium heat, stirring constantly. Add the shrimp water, celery, parsley, tomatoes, green pepper, crabmeat, garlic, salt, and pepper. Simmer mixture for an hour. Add thyme, oregano, bay leaves, and peeled shrimp. Cook for an additional 20 minutes. Serve over fluffy rice. This can be frozen. Yield: 8 to 10 servings.

Filé Gumbo: Filé can be substituted for the okra. Add 1 teaspoon filé just before serving. Do not reheat!

Tuna-Cheddar Chowder

¼ cup thinly sliced green onions
1 tablespoon butter or margarine
1 (10¾-ounce) can condensed Cheddar cheese soup
½ soup can milk
½ soup can water
2 teaspoons lemon juice
1 (7-ounce) can tuna, drained and flaked

Cook onion in butter until tender. Stir in soup; gradually blend in milk, water, and juice. Add tuna. Heat, stirring now and then. Yield: 2 to 3 servings.

Grouper Chowder

A first-class chowder cannot be built with a fish that has been on ice more than an hour or two. After that time the oils become strong and distasteful and dominate the flavor of the dish.

Water used in boiling the heads and back should be held at a minimum so that the liquid will have a heavy consistency when the chowder is completed.

Clean the head, backbone, and throat of an 8- to 10-pound grouper or two 4- to 5-pound groupers (preferably the gray grouper or gag). The rest of fish may be frozen. Place in a large pot with 2 or 3 bay leaves, 1 clove garlic, 2 or 3 medium-size Spanish onions, and the tops of a bunch of celery. Add 1 or 2 tablespoons Worcestershire sauce, salt and pepper to taste, and about 3 pints water. Cover and boil until meat falls off bone. Remove fish and pick out all bones. Return fish to pot with remaining liquid.

Cut ½ pound of salt pork into ½-inch squares, and brown in small frying pan.

Put into the pot: 1 can garbanzo beans (or, if not available, 4 medium-size diced Irish potatoes), 1 can tomato paste, 1 can tomatoes, ¼ pound butter (or ⅛ pound if on a diet), and the remaining celery cut fairly fine. If green datyl peppers are available, add 1 or 2 cut in half. When the celery is nearly done (slightly crisp) add about 2 pounds diced grouper fillet and the salt pork and as much of the grease as desired. Remove from fire and allow about 10 minutes for diced fillet to cook.

In addition to the fish fillets, there may be added crabmeat, scallops, or clams in such amounts as may be desirable. This usually adds not only flavor but incentive for much conversation.

A couple of tablespoons of sherry to each serving is also acceptable.

Potato and Corn Chowder

6 or 7 medium potatoes
2 chicken bouillon cubes
1 onion bouillon cube
1½ tablespoons dried onion
1 teaspoon salt
¼ teaspoon coarse ground black pepper
1 stick butter or margarine
2 tablespoons flour
¾ cup chopped cooked ham or Canadian bacon
3 cups whole milk
1 can white "shoe peg" corn (cream style will not do as well)
3 drops Tabasco sauce

Peel and quarter potatoes; place potatoes, bouillon cubes, dried onion, salt, and pepper in pot and cover with water. Boil potatoes until soft; drain, reserving 1½ cups of water in which potatoes were boiled. Mash the potatoes in pot.

Melt the butter in a small frying pan; add flour and ham, cooking for a few minutes over low heat, stirring well. Pour over the mashed potatoes.

Add the reserved 1½ cups water, the milk, and the corn; stir well. Bring almost to a boil to allow to thicken, but *do not boil* or milk will curdle. Add a sprinkling of coarse ground black pepper and the Tabasco sauce.

Add salt and then more salt to taste, making additions carefully (it is easy to get too much salt). This should be done while allowing the chowder to mellow. Keep on very low heat about 1 hour before serving. This chowder is best when made one-half day ahead of serving and then slowly warmed at serving time. Yield: about 4 to 6 servings.

Captain "Bo's" Fish Chowder

2 cups diced potatoes
1 large green pepper, chopped fine
1 large onion, chopped fine
1 large clove garlic, minced
½ cup chopped celery
1 cup salad oil
1 (No. 303) can tomatoes
1 (6-ounce) can tomato paste
2 cups water
2 bay leaves
2 tablespoons Worcestershire sauce
Salt and pepper to taste
3 large carrots, cleaned and sliced
3 pounds fillet of flounder (or fish of your choice)
2 cups shrimp
1 small lemon, sliced
3 hard-cooked eggs, sliced
2 tablespoons chopped parsley

Brown potatoes, green pepper, onion, garlic, and celery in salad oil. Add tomatoes, tomato paste, water, bay leaves, Worcestershire sauce, salt, pepper, and carrots. Simmer for at least 30 minutes. Add fish, shrimp, lemon, eggs, and parsley and cook an additional 15 minutes or until fish and shrimp are done. Yield: 8 to 10 servings.

Cream of Tomato Soup

> 2 *tablespoons butter or margarine*
> 3 *tablespoons flour*
> 1½ *teaspoons salt*
> ⅛ *teaspoon pepper*
> 2 *cups milk*
> 1 *(No. 2) can tomatoes*
> 1 *tablespoon minced onion*
> ¼ *teaspoon celery seed*
> ½ *teaspoon salt*
> ½ *teaspoon sugar*
> ½ *bay leaf*
> 1 *whole clove*
> *Pinch soda*

Melt butter in top of double boiler. Stir in flour, 1½ teaspoons salt, pepper, and milk. Cook, stirring constantly, until smooth and thickened.

In a saucepan, combine tomatoes, onion, celery seed, salt, sugar, bay leaf, and whole clove. Simmer, uncovered, for 5 minutes. Remove bay leaf and whole clove and put remainder through food mill or in blender. Stir in soda. Just before serving, stir tomato mixture into milk mixture. Heat, stirring constantly. If soup curdles, beat with egg beater. Yield: 4 to 6 servings.

Southern Bean Soup

> 1 *pound navy beans*
> *Water*
> *Ham hock (smoked and meaty)*
> 3 *medium potatoes, cut in cubes*
> 1 *cup chopped onion*
> 1 *cup chopped celery*
> 2 *cloves garlic, minced*
> *Salt and pepper*

Wash beans and soak overnight in enough water to cover. The next morning add enough water to make 5 quarts. Add ham hock and simmer for about 2 hours or until beans reach the mushy stage. Add potatoes, onion, celery, and garlic; simmer for 1 hour. Remove ham hock; add meat from bone to soup. Season to taste with salt and pepper. Yield: about 4 to 4½ quarts.

Holiday Sweet Soup

This is one of the delicious, famous sweet soups of the Scandinavian countries. It is especially compatible with turkey because of this bird's bland flavor.

> 1 *cup dried apricots*
> 1 *cup dried prunes*
> 1 *quart apple cider*
> 2 *tablespoons sugar*
> *Juice of one lemon*
> ¼ *teaspoon ground cinnamon*
> ¼ *teaspoon ground nutmeg*
> *Dash ground cloves*
> *Pinch of salt*
> 6 *lemons for garnish*
> 6 *whole cloves for garnish*

Wash apricots and prunes; dry. Combine fruit with cider in a kettle and heat to boiling. Lower heat and simmer for 30 minutes or until fruit is tender. Add sugar, lemon juice, spices, and salt. Serve soup chilled or hot and garnish with a lemon slice with a whole clove in the center. Yield: 6 servings.

Gazpacho

> 1 *large green pepper, seeded and*
>   *chopped*
> 2 *cucumbers, peeled, seeded, and*
>   *chopped*
> 8 *ripe tomatoes, peeled and mashed*
> 3 *teaspoons salt*
> 1½ *teaspoons paprika*
> 1 *clove garlic, peeled and mashed*
> 1 *small, mild onion, peeled and*
>   *chopped*
> ¼ *cup olive oil*
> 9 *tablespoons wine vinegar*
> 1½ *cups cold tomato juice*

Combine half the vegetables with salt and paprika. Vegetables must be chopped extremely fine. Mix the garlic, onion, oil, vinegar, and tomato juice. Put half in the blender with half of the vegetables. Run the blender until vegetables are smoothly blended. Repeat the process with the remaining chopped vegetables and remaining liquid. Combine the two batches. Chill until very cold, but not so cold that the oil hardens. Taste for seasoning and add more, if desired.

Pour into chilled bouillon cups. At the table, offer toasted croutons, chopped cucumbers, chopped scallions, and chopped green pepper with Gazpacho.

Vegetable Soup

    1½ pounds stew meat
     3 quarts water
    2½ tablespoons salt
     ½ teaspoon pepper
        Celery leaves
     1 large onion, chopped
     2 bay leaves, crushed
     ¼ teaspoon oregano
     ¼ teaspoon thyme
    1½ cups diced potatoes
     1 cup diced carrots
     ½ pound green beans, cut in 1½-inch
          pieces
     4 cups shredded cabbage
     1 large onion, chopped
     2 (No. 303) cans tomatoes
     1 teaspoon sugar
     1 (No. 303) can whole-kernel corn
     1 package frozen green peas
     1 package frozen green lima beans

Place the beef in soup kettle with 2½ quarts water. Add 1 tablespoon of the salt, pepper, celery leaves, and 1 chopped onion. Combine bay leaves, oregano, and thyme; tie in a cheesecloth bag and drop into kettle with meat. Cover and simmer for at least 3 hours. Remove celery leaves. Remove meat from bones, cut into bite-size pieces, and add to stock. Then add potatoes, carrots, green beans, cabbage, 1 chopped onion, and 1 tablespoon salt. Simmer for an hour.

Add 2 cups water, tomatoes, sugar, corn, peas, and lima beans and ½ tablespoon salt. Cook for an hour longer. Remove cheesecloth spice bag before serving. Yield: about 6 quarts.

She-Crab Soup

     1 medium onion, chopped
     3 tablespoons butter
     2 teaspoons flour
     1 quart whole milk
     1 pound (or 2 cups) flaked, white
          crabmeat
     ¼ pound crab roe
     ⅛ teaspoon white pepper
     ⅛ teaspoon ground mace
     1 pint milk
     ½ cup sherry wine

Sauté onion in half the butter, over low heat. Melt rest of the butter in top of double boiler and blend in the flour. Stir in the onion and add 1 quart milk, stirring constantly. Add the crab meat and roe and stir well; add pepper and mace and cook slowly for 20 minutes. Add the pint of milk and stir well. Remove from heat and add wine. Serve in soup bowls which have been heated, top with a dollop of cream, and garnish with parsley sprigs or a sprinkle of paprika. Serve with crackers. Yield: 6 to 8 servings.

Perdita's Onion Soup

    1½ ounces butter
     1 tablespoon cooking oil
     1 pound Spanish onions (thinly sliced)
     2 level teaspoons sugar
     5 cups boiling beef stock
        Salt and pepper to taste
     4 or more bread croutons, each serving
        Grated Grúyere or Parmesan cheese

Bread Croutons: Slice bread, ¼ inch thick, on slant. Bake in slow oven until dry and pale brown, about 30 minutes.

Preparation of Soup: Heat butter and oil in heavy pan. Add onions and stir. Cover and cook over low heat until soft (10 to 12 minutes). Sprinkle with sugar and stir over moderate heat until pale gold. Add the stock and seasonings to taste. Cover and simmer gently 20 to 30 minutes. Put the bread croutons into bowls and add the boiling soup. Serve cheese separately. Yield: 4 servings.

French Onion Soup Escoffier

¼ *pound butter*
2½ *pounds onions, sliced*
1 *quart beef stock*
1 *quart chicken stock*
2 *tablespoons Worcestershire sauce*
1 *bay leaf*
1½ *teaspoons celery salt*
1 *teaspoon black pepper or 12*
peppercorns, crushed
Salt to taste
French garlic croutons
1 *cup grated Parmesan cheese*

Heat butter in a heavy kettle. Add sliced onions and brown well, stirring constantly. Add beef and chicken stock, Worcestershire sauce, bay leaf, celery salt, and pepper. Allow to simmer 40 minutes. Remove bay leaf, and salt to the dictates of your own taste. Serve soup at once in heated tureen and float croutons and grated cheese on top. Yield: 2 quarts.

Onion Soup

9 *to 10 onions, sliced thin*
¼ *stick butter*
1 *tablespoon olive oil*
1 *heaping tablespoon flour*
½ *teaspoon prepared mustard*
Chicken Stock
¼ *cup dry sherry*
Salt to taste

In a 6-quart Dutch oven slowly stir onions in butter and olive oil over medium to low heat until they are browned. This will take about an hour. (Hint: You may need to put the pan in cold water from time to time to cool the butter in order not to cook onions too brown.)

When onions are browned to color of hazelnuts, add flour, prepared mustard, and Chicken Stock. (Add water if soup is too thick.) Add dry sherry and salt to taste. Serve hot with croutons and grated Parmesan cheese. This soup can be made ahead of time and frozen. Yield: about 2 quarts.

Chicken Stock:

Chicken necks and backs
½ *bay leaf*
1 *whole clove*
1 *onion, chopped*
1 *carrot, sliced*
1 *large stalk celery, chopped*
Parsley
½ *cup dry vermouth*

Put ingredients in a 4-quart kettle and fill with water. Cook for about 2 hours. Strain through cheesecloth. Use this chicken stock as the base for Onion Soup.

Beef Soup

1 *pound ground round baby beef*
Salt and pepper
½ *teaspoon Italian seasoning*
8 *cups water*
1 *large onion, chopped*
1½ *cups sliced carrots*
1½ *cups sliced celery*
⅓ *cup chopped parsley*
1 *teaspoon Italian seasoning*
Romano cheese

Season ground beef with salt and pepper and ½ teaspoon Italian seasoning. Mix well and shape into small balls about the size of marbles. Put into a heavy pot with 8 cups water and bring to a boil. Add all vegetables, parsley, and an additional teaspoon Italian seasoning. Add more salt and pepper if needed. Cover and cook over slow heat for about 2 hours. Serve sprinkled with Romano cheese. Yield: 8 to 10 servings.

Jellied Consommé

The consommé (canned variety for the sake of convenience—and because it is excellent) is placed in the refrigerator 4 to 6 hours before it is to be used. Just before serving, remove the jellied consommé from can, break the jelly (or cut into cubes or diamond shapes), and spoon into chilled serving dishes. For garnish, allow thin, transparent lemon slices—sliver thin—to gleam golden against the rich, brown transparency of the consommé.

Split-Pea Soup

   2 *cups split peas*
   6 *cups water*
 12 *cups water*
     Ham bone or 2-inch cube of salt pork
 ½ *cup chopped onion*
  1 *cup chopped celery*
 ½ *cup chopped carrots*
  2 *cups soup stock or milk*
  2 *tablespoons butter*
  2 *tablespoons flour*
     Salt to taste

Soak peas for 12 hours in 6 cups water. Drain the peas and put in a large kettle. Add water and ham bone or salt pork and simmer, covered, for 3 hours. Add chopped onion, celery, and carrots; simmer one hour longer. Put soup through a food mill or in blender. Chill and remove all fat. Add soup stock or milk, if desired.

    Melt butter; stir in flour until mixture is smooth. Add to soup stock and stir until it boils. Taste and add salt as desired. Yield: 12 servings.

Peanut Butter Soup

  1 *quart milk*
  1 *cup smooth peanut butter*
 ½ *teaspoon salt*
 ⅛ *teaspoon pepper*

Scald milk. Add a few spoonfuls at a time to peanut butter. Mix until well blended, then add to milk. Stir in salt and pepper.

Cold Soup Serendipity

    Put several very ripe tomatoes through a sieve until you have the desired amount of smooth pulp and juice. To this add grated onion, grated cucumber, and lemon juice to taste. Season with salt and cayenne. This is best made early in the day so that it will be thoroughly chilled.

Chilled Cream Vichyssoise

  4 *leeks (white part), finely sliced*
 ¼ *cup finely chopped onion*
 ¼ *cup butter or margarine*
  5 *medium potatoes, cut in*
      quarters
  1 *carrot, sliced*
  1 *quart chicken stock*
  1 *teaspoon salt*
  2 *cups milk*
  3 *cups cream*

Sauté leeks and onion in butter or margarine until yellow. Add potatoes, carrot, chicken stock, and salt. Bring to a rapid boil; cover. Reduce heat and simmer until potatoes and carrots are soft. Mash and rub through a fine strainer or put in blender. Return to heat and add milk. Season to taste; cool. Add cream and chill thoroughly. Serve in very cold cups. Yield: 8 servings.

Brunswick Stew

3 *large hens*
2 *pounds calf liver*
12 *large onions*
5 *pounds potatoes*
2 *gallons canned tomatoes*
2 *gallons canned corn*
1 *gallon chicken stock*
2 *quarts milk*
2 *pounds butter*
2 *bottles chili sauce*
Worcestershire sauce
Tabasco sauce
Salt and pepper

Boil hens several hours; save stock. Remove meat from bones and cut it into small pieces as for hash. Boil and grind liver. Cut onions fairly fine and dice potatoes; mix all together in a large pot (preferably iron). Add tomatoes, corn, chicken stock, milk, and butter. Cook slowly, and after stew begins to simmer, stir constantly for several hours (6 hours as a minimum) or until it thickens well. Season liberally with chili sauce, Worcestershire, Tabasco, salt, and pepper. Yield: 5 gallons.

Mother's Stew

2 *to 2½ pounds very lean beef stew meat*
2 *tablespoons bacon drippings or shortening*
2 *large onions, diced*
5 *large potatoes, cut in eighths*
4 *or 5 large carrots, cut in 2-inch slices*
Salt and pepper to taste
Garlic flakes or garlic salt (optional)
Diced celery (optional)
1 *can condensed tomato soup*

Brown stew meat in bacon drippings or shortening. Add diced onions and cook until browned. Add vegetables and seasonings. Add soup and a soup can of water. Simmer (at 250 degrees F.) for about 3 hours, or until meat and vegetables are tender. Add more water as needed. Yield: 6 servings.

Beef With Burgundy

½ *pound fresh mushrooms, sliced*
½ *clove garlic, minced*
2 *onions, sliced or chopped*
2 *tablespoons butter*
1 *teaspoon mixed salad herbs*
¾ *cup Burgundy*
2 *(12-ounce) cans roast beef with gravy*
2 *tablespoons chopped parsley*
1 *tablespoon flour*
3 *tablespoons water*

Sauté mushrooms, garlic, and onion in butter. Add herbs, wine, and roast beef with gravy. Add parsley and bring to a boil. Thicken liquid with 1 tablespoon flour blended with 3 tablespoons water. Serve over buttered noodles or with potatoes or steamed rice. Yield: 6 generous servings.

Louisiana Stew

2 *pounds beef chuck, cut in about 1½-inch pieces*
4 *cups boiling water*
1 *teaspoon lemon juice*
1 *clove garlic, minced*
2 *bay leaves*
1 *teaspoon salt*
½ *teaspoon thyme*
½ *teaspoon red pepper*
4 *small carrots, cut in fourths*
4 *medium potatoes, cut in thirds*
8 *or 9 small white onions*
1 *cup celery, cut in ½- or 1-inch lengths*

Thoroughly brown meat on all sides in a little hot fat. Add water, lemon juice, garlic, bay leaves, and seasonings. Cover and simmer 2 hours, stirring occasionally to keep from sticking. Remove bay leaves; add carrots, potatoes, onions, and celery. Continue cooking 30 minutes or until vegetables are done. Do not overcook vegetables. Remove meat and vegetables; thicken liquid by adding 1 tablespoon flour to 1 tablespoon water and cook gently a few minutes. Pour over meat and vegetables. Yield: 8 servings.

Carolina Stew

6 *ounces salt pork, cut in cubes*
3 *pounds lean beef, cut in 2-inch cubes*
2 *teaspoons salt*
1 *teaspoon black pepper*
2 *tablespoons flour*
2 *tablespoons butter or bacon fat*
2 *large carrots, cut in ½-inch pieces*
3 *medium onions, cut in quarters*
1 *bay leaf, crumbled*
¼ *teaspoon marjoram*
¼ *teaspoon thyme*
1 *pinch ground cloves*
2 *cloves garlic, finely chopped*
1 *tablespoon tomato paste*
2 *cups beef bouillon or beef stock*
Fifth red Burgundy wine
18 *to* 24 *small white onions*
Beef bouillon
1 *pound quartered fresh mushrooms*
2 *tablespoons butter*

Fry salt pork until brown in a 4-quart Dutch oven. Remove browned meat from fat and set aside. Dry beef cubes thoroughly and coat with mixture of salt, pepper, and flour.

Add 2 tablespoons butter or bacon fat and brown beef cubes in this. Remove from pan and set aside. Brown carrots and onions in fat. Add bay leaf, marjoram, thyme, cloves, garlic, and tomato paste; stir well.

Return salt pork and beef cubes to pan and toss lightly. Add beef bouillon or beef stock and bring to a low boil, being careful not to burn. Remove mixture to a 4- to 6-quart casserole from which stew will be served. Pour wine over mixture. Liquid should barely cover; more beef stock or bouillon may be added if needed.

Cover the casserole dish and set on lower shelf of oven. Bake at 325 degrees F. for 1 hour; reduce heat to 250 degrees F. and cook 4 to 5 hours longer. Mixture should barely simmer, so regulate heat accordingly.

The meat is done when a fork pierces it easily (a meat thermometer can also be used).

While stew is simmering, cook small onions 5 minutes in beef bouillon. Sauté mushrooms in butter and set aside. When meat is cooked, drain liquid from casserole into colander over large saucepan, reserving liquid for the sauce. Wash out casserole; then return stew to it.

Place cooked, drained onions and mushrooms over meat. Skim fat from drained liquid; simmer liquid for a minute or two, removing fat as it rises. About 2 cups of sauce should remain. If too thin, it can be boiled down rapidly; if too thick, add beef stock or bouillon. Taste sauce and add more seasoning if desired.

Pour sauce over stew in casserole. Cover and simmer for about 2 to 3 minutes, basting meat with sauce. Place on a heating tray and keep covered until time to serve. Yield: about 6 servings.

Baked Beef Stew

1½ *pounds round steak cut in 1-inch cubes*
2 *tablespoons shortening*
2 *(10½-ounce) cans condensed golden mushroom soup*
½ *cup water*
½ *cup sliced onion*
¼ *teaspoon savory*
1 *pound peas, shelled*
3 *medium carrots, halved lengthwise and cut in 2-inch pieces*
1½ *cups biscuit mix*
½ *cup milk*
½ *cup chopped parsley*
2 *tablespoons melted butter or margarine*

In skillet, brown beef in shortening; pour off fat. Add soup, water, onion, and savory. Pour into 2-quart casserole. Cover; bake at 350 degrees F. for 1 hour. Add peas and carrots. Cover; bake 1 hour longer. Meanwhile, combine biscuit mix and milk. Stir 20 times; knead on floured board 10 times. Roll into 12- x 8-inch rectangle; sprinkle with parsley. Roll in jellyroll fashion starting at long edge. Seal ends; cut into 8 slices. Top stew with biscuits and brush with butter. Bake uncovered 20 minutes or until biscuits are done. Yield: 6 servings.

Beef Stew

      1 *pound stew meat*
     ½ *teaspoon salt*
     ½ *cup brown rice*
      2 *cups boiling water*
     ½ *teaspoon salt*
      1 *bunch carrots (about 8), diced*
      1 *teaspoon salt*
      1 *large potato, diced*
      2 *tablespoons dry onion soup mix*
      3 *beef bouillon cubes*
      2 *tablespoons flour*
     ⅓ *cup water*

Cut stew meat into ¾- to 1-inch cubes. Brown in skillet; add water just to cover and ½ teaspoon salt; cover and cook over low heat for 2 hours. Add more water if needed. When meat is tender remove from heat, separate meat from broth. Chill broth and remove surface fat.

In a 4-quart kettle put the brown rice, 2 cups boiling water, and ½ teaspoon salt; boil slowly for 30 minutes. Add diced carrots, 1 teaspoon salt, and enough water just to barely cover. Cook 20 minutes, or until carrots are tender. Add diced potato and cook 5 minutes.

Add soup mix and bouillon cubes which have been dissolved in boiling water or hot broth. Add meat and broth in which meat was cooked. Add water to cover and let simmer for 1 hour. Just before serving, add flour to water and stir until dissolved, then add to stew. Stir well and serve hot.

Tahoma Stew

     2½ *pounds chuck steak cut in large
          cubes*
      3 *onions, chopped*
      3 *carrots, diced*
      3 *potatoes, diced*
      2 *stalks celery, chopped*
      1 *large can tomatoes*
         Oregano, onion, and garlic salt to taste

Flour beef cubes and brown in pan with onions. Add all other ingredients. Place in pressure cooker and let simmer for about ½ hour on 15 pounds pressure. Thicken gravy if necessary.

Teriyaki Stew

      2 *pounds lean stew beef, cut in 2-inch
          cubes*
     ¼ *cup cooking oil*
         Boiling water
      2 *bay leaves*
         Salt and pepper to taste
      1 *teaspoon bottled brown bouquet
          sauce or soy sauce*
      1 *whole stalk celery*
      1 *carrot*
      1 *onion*
      1 *bunch celery, cut in 2-inch
          strips*
      1 *bunch small carrots, cut in 2-inch
          lengths*
      4 *medium potatoes, cut in quarters*
     12 *whole small onions*
      4 *tablespoons Worcestershire sauce*
      1 *tablespoon cooking sherry, if desired*
      1 *pound fresh mushrooms, cut in
          halves*
      1 *box frozen peas (or 1 pound fresh
          peas)*
      3 *tablespoons instant blending flour for
          thickening*

Brown beef in cooking oil in skillet. Put in deep pot and cover with boiling water; add seasonings, whole stalk celery, carrot, and onion. Cook slowly until meat is tender (at least 1 hour).

Remove bay leaves, celery, and carrot. Add cut celery, carrots, potatoes, and small onions. Cook about 20 minutes or until onions are tender. Additional water may be added with the vegetables if necessary. Add Worcestershire sauce, sherry, mushrooms, and frozen peas and then cook several minutes. Mix flour with enough water to make a thin and fairly clear gravy; add to mixture and stir until thickened. Serve hot over a bed of hot, fluffy rice. Yield: 6 to 8 servings.

Tasty Oven Stew

 1 *pound cubed beef stew meat*
1½ *cups beef broth*
 1 *teaspoon Worcestershire sauce*
 ½ *cup onion, chopped*
 1 *teaspoon salt*
 1 *teaspoon pepper*
 1 *cup instant rice*
 ½ *cup crumbled American cheese*

Cook stew meat until tender. Drain off 1½ cups of the beef broth and add the Worcestershire sauce, onion, salt, and pepper; bring to a boil. Add the meat and rice and turn into a 1½-quart casserole. Freeze, if desired. To serve, dot the top with the pieces of cheese and bake at 350 degrees F. until cheese is bubbly and brown.

Oven Stew

 2 *pounds beef stew meat*
 ¼ *cup flour*
 4 *teaspoons salt*
 1 *clove garlic, chopped fine*
 3 *tablespoons shortening*
1½ *cups water*
 5 *medium green peppers*
 2 *cups sliced onion*
 2 *cups diced tomato*
 ¼ *cup chopped parsley*
 ½ *teaspoon ground black pepper*

Trim and discard excess fat from meat. Cut meat into 1-inch cubes. Blend flour with salt and mix with the meat. Brown with garlic in hot shortening. Turn into a 2-quart casserole. Add water. Cover and cook in a preheated slow oven at 325 degrees F. for 1¼ hours. Wash green peppers, cut out the stems, and remove seeds and pulp. Cut peppers into 1½-inch pieces. Add to beef along with onion, tomato, parsley, and pepper. Cover, return to oven, and cook 20 minutes or until vegetables are tender. Serve hot. This stew should be eaten the day it is made because the green pepper has a tendency to fade. Yield: 6 servings.

Burgundy Stew

 2 *to 4 pounds stewing meat*
 Onions
 Carrot slices
 Red wine
 Whole pepper
 Parsley roots
 Thyme
 Bay leaf
 Butter and oil
 3 *to 4 cloves garlic*
 1 *tablespoon flour*
 Juice from roast
 Bouquet garni
 Pepper and salt to taste

Cut a piece of your favorite stewing meat (the French use the *gite* or *aiguilette* from the shank) into large cubes. Two pounds will take care of 4 to 6 persons. Let the meat marinate or not (according to taste) with onions, carrot slices, red wine, whole pepper, parsley roots, thyme, and bay leaf.

If you let the meat marinate, dry well. Brown on all sides in butter and oil, add the vegetables from the marinade along with 3 or 4 cloves of garlic, and let meat give off its own liquid over slow heat for 10 to 15 minutes. Do not boil mixture.

Sprinkle a tablespoon of flour over the preparation; mix with wooden spoon until flour darkens. Add wine from marinade, which you have reduced and strained. (If you have not marinated beforehand, simply add straight red wine.) Add some juice from a roast, or water if the juice is lacking, a bouquet garni, and pepper and salt to taste. Cover and cook over low heat for 2 to 2½ hours. Yield: 4 to 6 servings.

Brown October Stew

1½   pounds beef chuck, shank, or round,
         cut in large cubes
1½ -pound lamb shoulder, cut in small
         cubes
   3   tablespoons flour
   2   teaspoons salt
   ½   teaspoon pepper
   ¼   teaspoon ground ginger
   3   tablespoons olive or salad oil
   1   cup chopped onion
   2   cloves garlic, minced
   4   cups mixed vegetable juice
   1   (1-inch) stick cinnamon
   4   medium carrots, scraped and
         quartered
   1   medium eggplant, cut in large
         cubes (do not pare)
   4   stalks celery, cut in 3-inch sticks
   8   large dried prunes, split and pitted
   8   large dried apricot halves

Trim all fat from beef and lamb; shake cubes
(a few at a time) in mixture of flour, salt,
pepper, and ginger in paper bag to coat
evenly. Brown quickly in oil in large heavy
kettle or Dutch oven. Stir in onion, garlic,
mixed vegetable juice, and stick cinnamon.
Arrange carrots, eggplant, and celery around
meat. Cover and simmer for 1 hour. Stuff
each prune with apricot half. Place on stew.
Cover and simmer 1 hour or until meat is
tender. Yield: 6 to 8 servings.

Starving Campers' Stew for Six

2½   to 3 pounds stew beef, cut in cubes
      Salt and pepper to taste
      Flour to dredge meat
      Bacon drippings or oil
   1   tablespoon paprika, or more to taste
   2   cups water
   6   medium onions
   6   carrots
   2   or 3 stalks celery
   6   potatoes
   ½   cup commercial sour cream

Salt and pepper the meat and dredge it
lightly with flour. Heat drippings or oil very

hot in Dutch oven and brown the meat.
Don't crowd the meat, or it will steam instead of browning. Add paprika and see that
each piece of meat is coated with it. Add
water, cover closely, and simmer 1 hour.

Meanwhile, pare and cut the vegetables in
chunks. Add vegetables to meat, add more
water as needed, and cook, covered, until all
is tender. Stir in sour cream just before serving and adjust seasonings.

Note: If there's a vegetable you think in-
dispensable in stew, but the children don't
particularly enjoy, try cutting that vegetable
very small and cooking it with the meat. It
will impart its flavor, then disappear.

Cape Town Bredee
(Meat Stew, South African Style)

1½   cups dried white beans
   2   tablespoons salad oil or butter
   3   onions, chopped
   4   pounds mutton or lamb, cut into
         2-inch cubes
   9   tomatoes, peeled and chopped
   2   teaspoons salt
   ¼   teaspoon dried ground chili peppers
   2   tablespoons curry powder
   1   tablespoon sugar
   ¼   cup water
   2   tablespoons vinegar
   1   cup chopped sour apples
   ½   cup seedless raisins

Place the beans in a saucepan with water
to cover and soak overnight. Drain, cover
with water again, and boil for at least 1
hour.

Heat oil in a heavy saucepan that has a
tight-fitting lid. Add the onion. Sauté for 5
to 10 minutes. Add the meat and brown well
on all sides. Add the tomatoes, salt, and
chili peppers. Cover and cook over very low
heat for 30 minutes. Combine the curry
powder, sugar, water, and vinegar; stir until
blended smooth. Add to the meat and onion
mixture and stir until all ingredients are well
blended. Drain the beans and add. Now add
the apples and raisins. Stir well and cover

tightly. Cook over a very low heat for 2½ hours, or until meat is very tender. Small amounts of water may be added if required.

The bredee should be thick and smooth and rich. Serve with boiled rice.

Georgia Chili

1 *pound ground beef*
Salt and pepper
1 *onion, chopped*
3 *tablespoons chili powder, divided*
1 *tablespoon shortening*
2 *cups tomato juice or water*
2 *stalks celery, diced*
1 *green pepper, diced*
1 *medium can tomatoes*
1 *medium can kidney beans*

Season ground beef with salt and pepper. Brown beef and onion, mixed with 1 tablespoon chili powder, in the shortening. Add tomato juice, celery, green pepper, and remaining 2 tablespoons chili powder. Simmer slowly for 45 minutes, or until vegetables are tender. (If mixture cooks down, add more tomato juice or water.) Add tomatoes and simmer 15 minutes longer; then add kidney beans and simmer a few minutes more. Yield: 6 generous servings.

Creole Game Stew

3 *ducks (teal, butterball, or mallards*
  are best)
4 *tablespoons flour*
Salt and pepper to taste
4 *tablespoons peanut oil*
½ *cup chopped onion*
¾ *cup chopped green pepper*
¼ *cup flour*
3 *chicken bouillon cubes*
3 *cups hot water*

Cut ducks into serving-size pieces. Dredge with 4 tablespoons flour, salt, and pepper. Brown in peanut oil in a heavy skillet. Remove ducks. Add onion and green pepper and cook until onions are transparent;

remove. Put ¼ cup flour into skillet and stir and cook until flour is browned. Add bouillon cubes to hot water and stir until dissolved. Add to browned flour mixture in skillet, along with ducks and vegetables. Cook over low heat for 1½ to 2 hours.

Serve with hot fluffy rice tossed with chopped parsley or chopped green pepper. Yield: 3 to 6 servings.

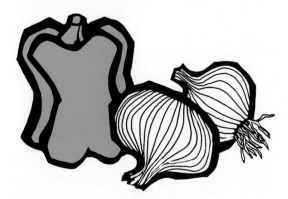

Wayne's Venison Stew

3 *or 4 pounds venison (shoulder or*
  neck cuts)
¼ *cup flour*
3 *tablespoons bacon drippings*
1½ *to 2 cups hot water*
1½ *cups red wine*
1 *teaspoon mixed dried herbs (thyme,*
  marjoram, basil)
1 *teaspoon dried parsley*
1 *large onion, sliced*
1½ *teaspoons salt*
½ *teaspoon pepper*
4 *carrots, scraped and quartered*
4 *potatoes, pared and quartered*

Cut sinews and bones from venison. Cut meat into bite-size pieces; roll in flour. In a large deep kettle heat bacon drippings; then brown floured venison. Add hot water, wine, herbs, parsley, onion, salt, and pepper. Cover kettle and bring mixture to a boil. Reduce heat and simmer about 2 hours. Add carrots and potatoes. Cover and simmer for 1 hour; add a little more water if needed. When meat is tender and vegetables done, serve hot with thick slices of French bread. Yield: 8 servings.

Lamb Stew With Parsley Dumplings

2 *pounds boneless lamb*
Water
6 *carrots, diced*
3 *medium onions, diced*
2 *stalks celery, cut in 2-inch pieces*
6 *medium potatoes, quartered*
Salt and pepper
Parsley Dumplings

Cut lamb into 1-inch squares. Cover with water, cover tightly, and cook slowly for 1 hour. Add carrots, onions, celery, and potatoes. Season to taste with salt and pepper. Cover and continue cooking slowly until lamb and vegetables are done, about 1 hour. About 15 minutes before end of cooking time, bring mixture to boiling point and drop Parsley Dumplings by tablespoonfuls on meat and vegetables. Cover tightly and cook until done. Yield: 6 servings.

Parsley Dumplings:

1 *cup flour*
1½ *teaspoons baking powder*
½ *teaspoon salt*
1 *tablespoon minced parsley*
1 *egg, beaten*
⅓ *cup milk*
2 *tablespoons melted margarine*

Sift dry ingredients together. Add minced parsley. Combine egg, milk, and melted margarine; add to dry ingredients, stirring only until flour is moistened. Drop by spoonfuls on meat mixture.

Caesar Stew

2 *pounds boneless shoulder of lamb*
1½ *cups boiling water*
3 *tablespoons onion flakes*
1 *bay leaf*
3 *pounds spinach*
3 *cups diced tomatoes*
1½ *teaspoons salt*
1 *teaspoon rosemary leaves*
½ *teaspoon ground black pepper*
2 *tablespoons flour*
2 *tablespoons cold water*

Trim excess fat from lamb and cut into 1-inch cubes. Brown on all sides in fat trimmed from lamb. Add boiling water, onion flakes, and bay leaf. Cover and cook 1 hour or until meat is tender. Add spinach to lamb with tomatoes, salt, rosemary, and pepper. Cook about 10 minutes or until spinach is done. Blend flour with cold water and add to stew. Cook 1 minute or only until slightly thickened. Serve as a one-dish meal. Yield: 6 servings.

Curried Lamb Stew

2 *pounds lamb shank, neck, or shoulder*
3 *tablespoons flour*
2 *tablespoons chopped onion*
2 *tablespoons cooking oil*
1½ *cups boiling water*
1 *(8-ounce) can tomato sauce*
1½ *cups 1-inch celery strips*
1 *to 1½ teaspoons curry powder*
1 *teaspoon salt*
1 *medium green pepper, cut in strips*
3 *cups cooked rice*

Cut meat into 1-inch cubes. Trim off excess fat. Roll meat in flour and cook very slowly with onion in cooking oil until meat is browned on all sides. Add water slowly. Add tomato sauce, celery, curry, and salt, and then cover and simmer for about 1½ hours. Add green pepper strips; cover and continue cooking until the vegetables and meat are tender. Serve on hot cooked rice. Yield: 6 servings.

Camper's Stew

4 *slices bacon*
2 *pounds shoulder of lamb, cut in pieces*
Salt and pepper
2 *onions, sliced*
2 *large potatoes, sliced*
3 *tomatoes, peeled and sliced, or ½ cup canned tomatoes, well drained*
4 *tablespoons coarse breadcrumbs*
1 *tablespoon butter, melted*
1 *teaspoon Worcestershire sauce*

Fry bacon. Rub pieces of lamb with salt and pepper; fry until brown with sliced onions in a little bacon fat.

Line bottom of 2-quart baking dish with bacon slices. Put in pieces of lamb, well drained. Cover with layer of fried onions, then a layer of sliced potatoes. Put in sliced or canned tomatoes. Season lightly with salt and pepper. Sprinkle with crumbs. Moisten with butter mixed with Worcestershire sauce. Cover and bake at 350 degrees F. for 2 hours. Uncover, increase temperature, and cook until brown. Yield: 4 servings.

Southern Stew

    2 *pounds smoked ham*
1½ *cups chopped onion*
    2 *cloves garlic, minced*
    3 *tablespoons shortening*
  ½ *cup minced green pepper*
  ½ *lemon, cut in 2 wedges*
  ½ *teaspoon pepper*
  ¼ *teaspoon thyme*
    1 *(16-ounce) can tomatoes*
    1 *cup uncooked rice*
1½ *cups hot water*

Cut ham into ½-inch cubes and set aside. Cook onion and garlic in shortening until tender. Add ham and brown lightly; pour off drippings. Add green pepper, lemon, pepper, thyme, tomatoes, rice, and water. Cover tightly and simmer 25 to 30 minutes or until rice is fluffy. Yield: 10 servings.

Mississippi Catfish Stew

    2 *pounds catfish fillets or other fish*
        fillets, fresh or frozen
  ½ *cup chopped bacon*
    1 *cup chopped onion*
    2 *(1-pound 13-ounce) cans tomatoes*
    2 *cups diced potatoes*
    1 *cup catsup*
    2 *tablespoons Worcestershire sauce*
    2 *teaspoons salt*
  ½ *teaspoon pepper*

Thaw frozen fillets and remove skin. Cut fillets into 1-inch pieces. Fry bacon until lightly browned in a large kettle over low heat. Add onion and cook until tender. Add tomatoes, potatoes, catsup, and seasonings. Bring to the boiling point. Reduce heat and cook, covered, for 30 minutes, stirring occasionally. Add fish and continue cooking for 40 to 45 minutes or until potatoes are tender. Yield: 6 servings.

notes

Vegetables

Southerners have an affinity for vegetables, and their preferences run the gamut from artichokes to zucchini. We are well known for our use of greens (collard, turnip, and mustard), black-eyed peas, and sweet potatoes. But few realize that the South is the Okra Belt. This spiny vegetable is served fried, boiled, and in mixtures of regional foods such as gumbo. Tomatoes team up well with okra in soups and stews.

Sweet potatoes are served in breads and pies and can be candied and baked.

For good luck all year, it's a safe bet that most Southerners will have a serving of black-eyed peas, preferably cooked with ham hocks or salt pork, on New Year's Day. Hopping John is another regional favorite, combining rice and black-eyed peas.

Corn comes to the table barbecued, on the cob, baked, or in casseroles. But in no other dish does it reach such acceptance as in corn pudding, a light, fluffy baked dish of corn scraped from the cob and cooked in a suspension of eggs and milk.

Artichoke Bottoms With Shrimp

    1 jar artichoke bottoms
    3 tablespoons olive oil
 1½ tablespoons wine vinegar
      Salt and pepper to taste
    1 cup cooked shrimp, cut into
         small pieces
  ½ green pepper, finely diced
  ⅓ cup mayonnaise
    2 teaspoons lemon juice
      Paprika to taste
    6 cooked whole shrimp

Marinate the artichoke bottoms in a mixture of olive oil, wine vinegar, and salt and pepper for about 1 hour. Mix the cut-up shrimp, green pepper, and mayonnaise seasoned with lemon juice and paprika. Drain the artichoke bottoms and place on serving plates. Pile the shrimp mixture on top of each artichoke bottom, cover with a thin layer of mayonnaise, and garnish each with a whole shrimp. Yield: 6 servings.

Fresh vegetables are available every month of the year, with most of them coming from commercial gardens in the Southern region.

Artichokes Vinaigrette

    2 (10-ounce) packages frozen artichoke
         hearts
    1 (4-ounce) can pimiento, drained and
         chopped
  ½ cup olive oil
  ½ cup white wine vinegar (or half
         vinegar and half dry white wine)
    2 tablespoons chopped sweet pickle
    1 tablespoon sweet pickle liquid
  ½ teaspoon crumbled oregano
  ½ teaspoon crumbled basil

Cook artichoke hearts in boiling salted water according to package directions. Drain and place in an earthenware or glass bowl. Add pimiento. Combine remaining ingredients in jar or bowl; shake or beat until well mixed. Pour over artichoke hearts. Toss lightly to coat evenly. Let stand at room temperature at least 30 minutes, stirring occasionally. Serve immediately or refrigerate until ready to serve. Yield: 8 servings.

Creamed Artichokes

2 *cups artichokes*
2 *tablespoons butter*
2 *tablespoons flour*
1 *cup milk*
Salt and pepper to taste

Scrub artichokes well. Steam or cook in small amount of water until tender. Make a cream sauce of the remaining ingredients. Pour over the hot, whole artichokes just before serving. Yield: 4 servings.

Asparagus-Pork Barbecue

2 *tablespoons butter*
2 *tablespoons flour*
1 *cup milk*
⅛ *teaspoon salt*
Pepper to taste
¼ *cup sharp shredded cheese*
1½ *cups cooked asparagus cuts and tips, drained*
4 *smoked pork chops*
1 *(8-ounce) package herb dressing*

Make white sauce with first 5 ingredients. Before removing from heat, add shredded cheese. When slightly cool, add asparagus. Make a double-thick foil square. Place a smoked pork chop on half of foil, spoon cheese-asparagus mixture on top, and sprinkle lightly with herb dressing. Fold package over and seal tight. Place on barbecue grill and bake approximately ½ hour (or bake on cookie sheet in oven at 325 degrees F. for 1 hour). Yield: 4 servings.

Asparagus Parmesan

1½ *pounds fresh asparagus*
1 *cup dry white wine*
½ *cup water*
¼ *cup melted butter or margarine*
½ *teaspoon salt*
¼ *teaspoon pepper*
¼ *cup Parmesan cheese*

Wash asparagus and snap off less tender ends of stalk. Simmer asparagus, covered, in white wine and water until crisp-tender (about 10 minutes). Drain and place on heatproof platter. Pour the melted butter over the asparagus and sprinkle with salt, pepper, and Parmesan cheese. Place under broiler for 2 to 3 minutes. Yield: 4 servings.

Asparagus Pie

Piecrust mix
2 *tablespoons grated Parmesan cheese*
2 *egg yolks*
½ *teaspoon salt*
Pinch cayenne pepper
½ *cup melted butter*
1 *tablespoon lemon juice*
1 *envelope unflavored gelatin*
½ *cup cold water*
½ *cup boiling water*
2 *cups cooked or canned asparagus, drained*

To your favorite piecrust mix, add grated Parmesan cheese before rolling out crust. Line ungreased 9-inch piepan with crust, crimp, and bake at 350 degrees F. until light golden color.

Beat egg yolks in bowl until thick and lemon colored; add salt and a pinch of cayenne pepper. Melt butter in saucepan. Add 3 tablespoons of the melted butter, a little at a time, to the egg mixture. Then add remaining butter alternately with lemon juice, beating all the while. Sprinkle 1 envelope unflavored gelatin over ½ cup cold water to soften; add ½ cup boiling water. Cool slightly; add to egg mixture. Put asparagus in pie shell; cover with egg mixture. Chill. Serve plain or garnish with sour cream. Yield: 6 servings.

Asparagus Roll-Ups

  1 *can green asparagus spears, drained*
    well
  1 *(3-ounce) package cream cheese,*
    softened
  8 *to 10 slices sandwich bread*

Drain asparagus well and pat dry with paper towels. Mix softened cream cheese with small amount of liquid drained from asparagus. Do not add too much liquid.

Remove crusts from slices of bread, and roll slices with rolling pin. Spread each slice with cream cheese. Add a spear of asparagus to each slice and roll lengthwise in jellyroll fashion. Before serving, cut each sandwich in half. These sandwiches become soggy if made the day before. Yield: 16 to 20 sandwiches.

Asparagus Vinaigrette

  1 *(10-ounce) package frozen asparagus*
    cuts
  1 *cup water*
  3 *tablespoons chopped onion*
  2 *tablespoons chopped dill pickle*
  1 *tablespoon capers*
  ½ *teaspoon salt*
  1 *(3-ounce) package celery-flavored*
    salad gelatin
  1 *teaspoon salt*
  1 *tablespoon tarragon vinegar*
  ½ *tray (7 to 10) ice cubes*
  1 *tablespoon chopped pimiento*
  1 *teaspoon chopped parsley*
  ⅛ *teaspoon coarsely ground black*
    pepper
  1 *hard-cooked egg, diced*

Place asparagus, water, onion, pickle, capers, and ½ teaspoon salt in saucepan; cover. Bring to boil quickly, separating asparagus with fork. Reduce heat, and simmer just until tender (about 8 to 10 minutes). Drain, measuring liquid; add water to liquid to make 1 cup. Cool asparagus mixture.

Bring measured liquid to a boil; then remove from heat. Add gelatin and 1 teaspoon salt; stir until gelatin is completely dissolved. Add vinegar and ice cubes. Stir constantly until thickened (about 3 minutes). Remove any unmelted ice. Add cooled asparagus mixture, pimiento, parsley, and pepper. Fold in egg. Spoon into individual molds or a 1-quart mold. Chill until firm. Yield: 6 to 8 servings.

Asparagus-Water
Chestnut Casserole

  2 *(14½-ounce) cans cut asparagus,*
    drained
  1 *can water chestnuts, finely sliced*
  1 *can cream of mushroom soup*
  Buttered breadcrumbs

Place alternate layers of asparagus and water chestnuts in glass baking dish. Pour soup over layers. Top with buttered breadcrumbs. Bake in 350-degree F. oven for 30 minutes. Yield: 4 to 6 servings.

Asparagus and Lamb Chops

  1 *can asparagus soup, undiluted*
  ½ *cup evaporated milk*
  1 *tablespoon butter*
  ¼ *teaspoon white pepper*
  1½ *cups cooked asparagus spears,*
    drained
  6 *lamb chops*
  2 *teaspoons salt*
  ½ *teaspoon pepper*
  ½ *teaspoon basil*
  6 *pimiento strips*

Combine soup, milk, butter, and pepper in saucepan; heat. Warm asparagus spears. Sprinkle chops liberally with salt, pepper, and basil; then broil.

Pour all but ¼ cup of sauce into heated chafing dish. Arrange lamb chops in dish, with asparagus spears in center. Pour remaining sauce over asparagus and garnish with pimiento strips. Serve immediately. Yield: 6 servings.

Asparagus à la India

1½ pounds fresh asparagus
3 tablespoons butter or margarine
1 teaspoon salt
¼ teaspoon ground cardamom
¼ teaspoon freshly ground black
    pepper
1 cup cooked rice

Wash asparagus and snap off tough part of the stalk. Cut in 1-inch diagonal chunks. Melt butter in saucepan or electric skillet; add asparagus and salt. Cover and cook on medium heat. Add cardamom and pepper to asparagus, along with cooked rice. Cook 8 minutes or until asparagus is just tender. Yield: 4 servings.

Asparagus-Turkey Divan

½ cup butter or margarine, divided
½ cup flour
1 cup light cream
1¾ cups milk
¼ cup sherry
¼ cup grated Parmesan cheese
1 egg yolk
1½ teaspoons salt
¼ teaspoon pepper
6 to 12 slices cooked turkey
2 bunches fresh asparagus, cooked
¼ cup grated Parmesan cheese

Melt 6 tablespoons butter or margarine in top of double boiler and blend in flour. Add cream and milk, stirring well. Cook until mixture thickens, stirring frequently. Add sherry and ¼ cup grated cheese; cook 2 minutes longer. Remove from heat. Combine egg yolk, salt, and pepper; add small amount of sauce to egg yolk, beat until smooth, and add to sauce in double boiler. Cover and simmer. Melt remaining butter or margarine. Arrange turkey in shallow baking dish, place asparagus over turkey, pour melted butter over, and top with the cream sauce. Sprinkle with ¼ cup cheese. Bake at 350 degrees F. for 12 to 15 minutes or until lightly browned. Yield: 6 servings.

Asparagus Soufflé in Tomatoes

½ stick butter
¼ cup flour
1 teaspoon celery salt
1 teaspoon white pepper
1 teaspoon salt
¼ teaspoon ground nutmeg
1½ cups milk
6 eggs
2 (No. 300) cans cut asparagus,
    drained
Tomatoes (one per person)

Melt butter in saucepan. Add the flour, blending well. Add celery salt, white pepper, salt, nutmeg, and milk. Cook, stirring constantly, over low heat until sauce is very thick. Set aside to cool slightly.

Separate eggs. Beat yolks until light and lemon colored. Beat egg whites until stiff but not dry. Fold white sauce into beaten yolks; then fold in egg whites. Add the asparagus; mix well. Pour into 2-quart baking dish, set dish in pan of hot water, and bake at 350 degrees F. for 45 minutes.

Select tomatoes of even size; slice stem off. With a grapefruit knife cut out half of tomato and fill with baked soufflé. Return to oven for 10 minutes or until skin looks popped. Yield: 10 to 12 servings.

Asparagus With Horseradish Sauce

1½ pounds fresh asparagus
1 cup commercial sour cream
2 tablespoons horseradish, drained
2 teaspoons sugar
Dash seasoned salt
¾ cup dry breadcrumbs
1 tablespoon butter or margarine,
    melted

Cook asparagus in salted water until slightly tender; drain and place in hot serving dish. Heat sour cream in a double boiler over hot, not boiling, water. Add horseradish, sugar, and seasoned salt. Pour over hot asparagus. Top with buttered breadcrumbs and serve hot. Yield: 4 to 6 servings.

Creole Butter Beans

1 *tablespoon butter*
½ *cup thin onion slices*
½ *cup diced celery*
1 *(10½-ounce) can*
   tomato soup
½ *teaspoon Worcestershire sauce*
1 *teaspoon prepared*
   horseradish
1 *tablespoon pickle*
   relish
2 *(1-pound) cans butter beans*

Melt butter over low direct heat. Add thinly sliced onions and cook about 7 minutes, until tender. Stir in diced celery, tomato soup, Worcestershire sauce, prepared horseradish, pickle relish, and butter beans. Continue cooking 30 minutes. Stir gently occasionally. Yield: 6 servings.

Best-Yet Baked Beans

2 *pounds navy beans*
  Salt and pepper to taste
½ *pound fresh pork side meat, sliced*
1 *small onion, minced*
1 *can cream of tomato soup*
1 *can water*
1 *cup light brown sugar*
¼ *cup molasses*
1 *teaspoon dry mustard*
2 *tablespoons vinegar*

Wash and pick beans. Soak overnight in water to cover. Drain, cover with fresh water, and cook very slowly until just tender. Drain well; add salt and pepper to taste.

While beans are cooking, fry the pork slowly, but do not brown. Remove slices and set aside. Add onion to cooking fat and cook slowly. Add other ingredients and let simmer a few minutes. Put in beans; let stand overnight to blend flavors and give better color.

Put beans in heavy Dutch oven or chicken fryer; bake at 300 degrees F. for 3 hours; stir once or twice. Remove cover, place pork slices on top, and bake 30 minutes longer or until meat is brown. Yield: 8 to 10 servings.

Creole Beans

1 *cup thinly sliced*
   onion
⅔ *cup chopped green*
   pepper
⅔ *cup diced celery*
2 *tablespoons margarine*
1½ *teaspoons salt*
¼ *teaspoon pepper*
2 *cups diced fresh or*
   drained canned tomatoes
2 *cups cooked or*
   canned green beans

Cook onion, green pepper, and celery in margarine until tender. Mix in remaining ingredients and cook until beans are heated thoroughly. Yield: 6 servings.

Mexican Beans

5 *slices bacon*
1 *onion, minced*
¼ *cup chopped green pepper*
2 *(1-pound 11-ounce) cans red kidney*
   beans (unseasoned)
2 *cups cooked or canned tomatoes,*
   drained
1 *(4-ounce) can deviled ham*
¾ *teaspoon dry mustard*
1 *teaspoon curry powder dissolved in a*
   teaspoon hot water
3 *tablespoons molasses*
  Salt to taste

Dice 3 bacon slices and fry with onion and green pepper. Mix kidney beans, tomatoes, deviled ham, mustard, curry powder, molasses, and salt. Add the onion mixture and mix well. Put into a 2-quart casserole. Top with the remaining strips of bacon and bake at 350 degrees F. for 2 or 3 hours. Yield: 6 generous servings.

Easy Baked Beans

   1 *(16-ounce) can pork and beans with*
       tomato sauce
   1 *small onion, chopped*
   1 *green pepper, chopped*
   1 *teaspoon prepared mustard*
   1 *teaspoon chili powder*
   3 *to 4 tablespoons molasses (or more,*
       if you like beans sweeter)
   Catsup or tomato sauce to taste
   2 *slices bacon*

Combine all ingredients except bacon slices. Place in a greased 2-quart casserole and lay bacon slices on top. Bake, uncovered, at 350 degrees F. about 30 to 40 minutes or until mixture thickens and bacon is thoroughly cooked. Yield: 4 to 6 servings.

Texas Red Beans

   2 *pounds pinto beans*
   1 *onion, minced*
   Small strip salt pork
   Large clove garlic, minced
   Water
   Salt to taste

Place beans, onion, salt pork, and garlic in large, heavy kettle. Add water to cover beans by 3 inches. Cook slowly until beans are very soft. This will probably take 3 to 4 hours. Add salt to taste before beans are done. A small amount of chili powder may be added, if desired.

Mashed Beans

   1 *tablespoon bacon drippings*
   2 *jalapeño peppers, chopped*
   ½ *pound shredded Cheddar cheese*
   4 *to 6 cups cooked, mashed Texas Red*
       Beans (see above)

Put bacon drippings in large skillet. Combine other ingredients, add to drippings, and cook until crisp; turn and brown beans on all sides. If too dry, add a small amount of cooking liquid while beans are cooking.

Scalloped Green Beans And Celery

   2 *cups cooked green beans, fresh or*
       canned
   2 *cups cooked celery*
   4 *tablespoons butter, divided*
   2 *tablespoons flour*
   1½ *cups milk*
   ½ *cup vegetable liquid*
   ½ *teaspoon salt*
   ½ *cup shredded cheese*
   2 *cups breadcrumbs*

Cook beans and celery. Make a white sauce of 2 tablespoons of butter, flour, milk, vegetable liquid, and salt. When thickened, add the shredded cheese to melt. In a greased 1½-quart baking dish, place half the cooked beans and celery, half the breadcrumbs, then the remainder of the beans and celery. Pour the cheese sauce over all, and top with remaining crumbs which have been mixed with 2 tablespoons melted butter. Bake at 350 degrees F. about 15 to 20 minutes. Yield: 6 to 8 servings.

Green Beans With Hot Mustard Sauce

   ½ *teaspoon powdered mustard*
   ½ *teaspoon water*
   1 *teaspoon butter or margarine*
   1 *teaspoon flour*
   ⅛ *teaspoon salt*
   ⅛ *teaspoon ground black pepper*
   2 *large egg yolks, beaten*
   ¾ *cup milk*
   2 *teaspoons fresh lemon juice*
   1 *pound (3 cups) hot cooked green*
       beans
   Chopped pimiento

Combine powdered mustard and water; let stand 10 minutes for flavor to develop. Melt butter or margarine. Stir in flour, mustard, salt, and ground black pepper; blend well. Mix egg yolks with milk and stir into the mixture. Cook until slightly thickened, stirring constantly. Do not boil. Add lemon juice and pour over beans. Garnish with chopped pimiento. Yield: 6 servings.

Green Beans With Almonds

    2 *pounds fresh green beans, cut or left*
      whole
    2 *cups boiling water*
    ¾ *teaspoon salt*
    1 *teaspoon sugar*
    ½ *cup blanched slivered almonds*
    ¼ *to ½ cup butter*

Place green beans in kettle of salted water, with sugar added. Cook, covered, until barely tender (from 10 to 25 minutes). Drain, but keep hot for serving.

Lightly sauté almonds in butter and sprinkle over green beans in serving dish. Yield: 6 servings.

Green Beans With Toasted Almonds

    2 *(1-pound) cans French-style green*
      beans
      Salt and pepper to taste
    2 *tablespoons bacon drippings*
    ½ *of 5-ounce can slivered almonds,*
      toasted

Cook beans with salt, pepper, and bacon drippings about 8 to 10 minutes. Toast the almonds in a little butter and set aside. When ready to serve, toss the toasted almonds over the hot beans. If you want to be fancy with these beans, add a little shredded cheese before you sprinkle with almonds. This is a good dish to serve with baked chicken and herbed rice. Yield: 6 servings.

Fresh Snap Beans With Fresh Lemon-Chive Dressing

    ¼ *cup fresh lemon juice*
    ¼ *cup melted butter*
    1 *tablespoon chopped chives*
    3 *cups cooked fresh snap beans*

Mix the lemon juice, butter, and chives together. Pour over cooked snap beans and heat. Serve immediately. Yield: 6 servings.

Green Bean Casserole

    1 *medium onion, diced*
    2 *tablespoons margarine*
    2 *tablespoons flour*
    2 *tablespoons water*
    1 *teaspoon salt*
    ½ *teaspoon black pepper*
    2 *tablespoons lemon juice*
    2 *(No. 303) cans green*
      beans, drained
    1 *cup commercial sour cream*
    ½ *cup shredded*
      Cheddar cheese
    ½ *cup dry breadcrumbs*

Sauté onion in margarine. Gradually stir in flour, water, salt, pepper, and lemon juice; simmer for 3 minutes. Add beans and sour cream; place in a 2-quart casserole. Sprinkle with cheese and crumbs. Bake at 350 degrees F. for 30 minutes. Yield: 8 servings.

Snap Beans With Egg Sauce

    1 *pound young string beans, wax*
      beans, or green beans
   1¼ *cups boiling water*
   1½ *tablespoons butter*
    1 *tablespoon flour*
    1 *cup fresh skim milk or soup stock*
    2 *egg yolks*
    ¼ *teaspoon salt*
    ⅛ *teaspoon paprika*
    1 *tablespoon lemon juice*

Prepare beans and tie loosely in small bunches. Cook, covered, in boiling water for 20 minutes. Drain, untie, and place on warm platter. Melt butter and stir in flour until blended. Stir in skim milk or stock. When sauce is smooth and boiling, remove from heat and beat in egg yolks. Over low heat, stir the sauce for a minute more, while eggs thicken. Add the salt, paprika, and lemon juice. Pour the sauce down the center of the stack of beans. Yield: 4 servings.

Swedish Mushrooms and Green Beans

    1 *pound fresh mushrooms*
    2 *tablespoons butter*
  ½ *cup top milk*
    2 *teaspoons salt, divided*
  ⅛ *teaspoon pepper*
    1 *pound small green string beans*
    1 *cup boiling water*

Clean and slice the mushrooms. Melt butter; add mushrooms and cook slowly, stirring occasionally, until the mushrooms are slightly browned. Place them in a 2-quart heat-resistant glass casserole; add the top milk, 1 teaspoon salt, and pepper. Cover and bake in a moderate oven, 350 degrees F., about 15 minutes or until the mushrooms are tender.

Wash the string beans and snip off the ends. Place in boiling water to which 1 teaspoon salt is added and cook about 30 minutes or until tender. Drain the beans well and pile lightly into the center of the mushroom casserole. Serve at once. Yield: 6 servings.

String Beans, Mushrooms, and Cashews

    2 *pounds string beans*
  ½ *pound fresh mushrooms*
    3 *tablespoons butter*
    1 *teaspoon salt*
  ½ *cup cashew nuts*

Steam green beans in salted water until tender. Sauté mushrooms in butter with 1 teaspoon salt. Add to drained beans; add cashews and serve hot.

Green Beans

    1 *(No. 303) can whole beans*
    Salt and pepper to taste
    2 *cloves garlic, minced*
    2 *tablespoons salad oil*

Put green beans in casserole dish; add salt and pepper and minced garlic. Drizzle salad oil over beans (do not mix) and bake at 350 degrees F. about 30 minutes.

Green Beans

Find a market where the beans are in large bins, not packaged. Get the tenderest, leanest, greenest beans. When you get home, divest the beans of strings, if any, and slice them in two the long way. To cook, bring to a boil, in a large skillet, enough water to float beans. Before adding beans, add several drops of green vegetable coloring, a teaspoon salt, a dash of sugar, and a pinch of soda. When water is at full boil, add the beans. When the water returns to a boil, cover and cook for about 8 minutes or until beans are almost tender. Drain the beans and add a couple of tablespoons of butter and return them to the skillet to stand until time to reheat them for dinner. Don't make the mistake of adding lemon juice. It gives them a bleach job, and what you're after is the *haricots verts* look.

Green Beans and Cheese

    1 *pint or 1 package*
         frozen green beans
    Boiling water
    1 *teaspoon salt*
  ¼ *cup margarine*
  ½ *cup shredded American*
      cheese

Cook beans in boiling, salted water until tender; drain. Add margarine and cheese. Stir gently until the margarine and cheese have melted. Add more salt if it is needed and serve hot. Yield: 4 servings.

Harvard Beets

    12 *small beets or 1 (No. 2) can, drained*
    ½ *cup sugar*
     2 *teaspoons cornstarch*
    ½ *cup vinegar*
     2 *tablespoons butter*

Mix sugar, vinegar, and cornstarch together. Boil for 5 minutes. Pour over prepared beets in saucepan and let stand on back of range 30 minutes. If not warm enough, they may be put on a low burner for a few minutes before serving. Yield: 6 servings.

Beets With Pineapple

     2 *tablespoons brown sugar*
     1 *tablespoon cornstarch*
    ¼ *teaspoon salt*
     1 *(8½-ounce) can pineapple tidbits*
     1 *tablespoon butter or margarine*
     1 *tablespoon lemon juice*
     1 *(1-pound) can sliced beets, drained*

Combine brown sugar, cornstarch, and salt in saucepan. Stir in pineapple and its juice. Cook, stirring constantly, till mixture thickens and bubbles. Add butter, lemon juice, and beets. Heat 5 minutes. Yield: 4 servings.

Celebrity Broccoli

     2 *packages frozen broccoli*
     2 *tablespoons butter*
     2 *tablespoons minced onion*
    1½ *cups commercial sour cream*
     2 *teaspoons sugar*
     2 *teaspoons vinegar*
     1 *teaspoon poppy seed*
     1 *teaspoon paprika*
    ½ *teaspoon salt*
    ⅛ *teaspoon cayenne pepper*
    ¼ *cup chopped pecans*

Cook broccoli, according to package directions, until tender; drain. Melt the butter in a small saucepan. Put in the onion and brown lightly. Remove from heat and stir in the sour cream, sugar, vinegar, poppy seed, paprika, salt, and cayenne pepper. Arrange broccoli on heated platter. Pour sour cream sauce over it. Sprinkle with pecans. Yield: 6 to 8 servings.

Broccoli-Cheese Sauce

     1 *package frozen broccoli*
     1 *medium onion*
     2 *tablespoons cooking oil*
     1 *can cream of chicken soup*
    ½ *cup cubed processed cheese*
    ½ *cup milk*
     1 *teaspoon salt*

Thaw the package of frozen broccoli and chop into small pieces. Chop onion fine.

   Heat cooking oil in a saucepan; toss in chopped vegetables and fry for 5 minutes. Add can of soup and heat to bubbling. Reduce heat; stir in the cheese, milk, and salt. Cook until bubbly. Serve over flaky rice. Yield: 6 to 8 servings.

Broccoli Casserole

     2 *packages frozen broccoli*
     2 *tablespoons butter*
     2 *tablespoons flour*
     1 *teaspoon salt*
     2 *cups milk*
    ¼ *teaspoon pepper*
    ¾ *cup shredded cheese*
    ¼ *cup chopped almonds*
    ½ *cup buttered breadcrumbs*
     4 *slices bacon*

Cook broccoli until just tender. Drain and place in greased casserole. Make a sauce of the butter, flour, salt, milk, pepper, and cheese. Sprinkle almonds over broccoli; then pour sauce over all. Sprinkle top with breadcrumbs and bacon. Bake at 350 degrees F. for 20 minutes or until bubbling hot and browned on top. Yield: 8 servings.

Baked Broccoli

(58 calories each serving)

1 *medium bunch broccoli, cooked*
⅔ *cup stewed tomatoes*
2 *tablespoons grated Parmesan cheese*
1 *scant tablespoon chopped parsley*

Break up broccoli into flowerets, or chop coarsely. Mix with tomatoes and pour into baking dish. Cover with cheese and parsley. Bake, uncovered, at 350 degrees F. for 35 to 40 minutes. Yield: 4 servings.

Cabbage With Cream Cheese

3 *cups shredded cabbage*
1 *(3-ounce) package cream cheese, softened*
Dash pepper
¼ *teaspoon celery seed*

Cook cabbage in ½ inch boiling, salted water in a covered container for about 5 minutes or until cabbage is crispy tender. Stir in cream cheese and stir until cheese melts. Add pepper and celery seed. Serve hot. Yield: 4 servings.

Baked Creamed Cabbage

1 *medium head cabbage*
½ *cup boiling salted water*
3 *tablespoons butter*
3 *tablespoons flour*
½ *teaspoon salt*
1½ *cups milk*
¼ *cup breadcrumbs*

Shred cabbage very fine and cook 9 minutes in boiling salted water. Remove cabbage, drain well, and place in a buttered 1½-quart casserole. Melt butter in saucepan; stir in flour and salt until smooth. Add milk gradually. Continue stirring until mixture thickens. Pour this sauce over cabbage and sprinkle breadcrumbs over top. Bake at 325 degrees F. about 15 minutes or until crumbs are browned. Yield: 6 servings.

Cabbage Roll

10 *large cabbage leaves*
1 *pound ground beef*
1 *cup breadcrumbs*
1 *can tomatoes, well drained*
1 *large onion, chopped fine*
1 *teaspoon salt*

Cook 10 cabbage leaves for 2 minutes in enough water to cover. Drain off water and set aside.

Mix other ingredients together. Place mixture on cabbage leaves and roll. Wrap rolls in foil and bake at 300 degrees F. for 40 minutes. Yield: 4 to 6 servings.

Sausage-Stuffed Cabbage

6 *cups bread cubes*
1 *pound (2 cups) sausage*
2 *eggs, beaten*
1 *large head cabbage*
Salt and pepper
Parsley
½ *cup buttered dry breadcrumbs*
1 *can condensed mushroom soup*
Milk

Arrange bread cubes on a baking sheet. Toast at 325 degrees F., turning occasionally, until bread cubes are golden brown on all sides. Remove from oven and set aside. Brown the sausage thoroughly in a frying pan. Remove pan from heat. Drain fat from pan. Cool sausage and stir in toasted bread cubes and beaten eggs. Slice the top off the head of cabbage. Scoop out the center, leaving a firm shell. The scooped-out part can be served later. Sprinkle with salt and pepper. Stuff the sausage mixture into the cabbage. Replace cabbage top and secure with toothpicks. Tie cabbage in a cheesecloth. Cover the bottom of a large kettle with water about 1½ inches deep and bring to a boil. Place the cabbage on a rack in the boiler; cover kettle and let cabbage steam until tender, about 40 to 60 minutes, depending on the size. Remove the cabbage and take off cheesecloth. Remove toothpicks and garnish with parsley and a sprinkling of buttered crumbs. To serve, cut into wedges and spoon mushroom sauce over each wedge. To make sauce, use condensed mushroom soup thinned with milk, seasoned to taste, and heated thoroughly. Yield: 6 to 8 servings.

Note: Plan to have coleslaw the following day, using the center white cabbage. Store the cabbage in a covered dish, or refrigerator bag, in the refrigerator until used.

Creamed Cabbage

  1 *small head cabbage*
  6 *tablespoons butter*
  4 *tablespoons flour*
  2 *cups milk*
 ½ *teaspoon salt*
 ½ *cup breadcrumbs*
  4 *tablespoons melted butter*

Chop cabbage into fourths and parboil in salted water for 10 minutes. Drain. Make a white sauce by melting the 6 tablespoons butter, then adding flour, and cooking until it bubbles. Slowly add milk and salt; cook, stirring, until sauce thickens. Put a layer of cabbage into an ovenproof casserole, then a layer of white sauce. Repeat and cover with the crumbs which have been mixed with the 4 tablespoons melted butter. Bake at 350 degrees F. for 30 to 35 minutes.

Colorful Cabbage

 ½ *stick (¼ cup) butter or margarine*
  2 *tablespoons chopped onion*
  2 *tablespoons chopped green pepper*
 ½ *teaspoon salt*
  4 *cups (1 quart) shredded cabbage*
  1 *tablespoon flour*
 ½ *cup milk*
  2 *tablespoons chopped pimiento*
   Shredded sharp Cheddar cheese,
     if desired

Melt butter. Add onion and green pepper. Cook about 5 minutes. Stir in salt and cabbage. Cover and cook over low heat about 10 minutes. Sprinkle flour evenly over cab-

bage mixture. Gradually stir in milk. Cook 3 to 5 minutes, stirring occasionally. Blend in pimiento. Sprinkle with cheese and serve at once. Yield: 4 to 6 servings.

Pan-Creamed Cabbage

 ½ *cup butter or margarine*
  2 *quarts shredded cabbage*
  1 *cup light cream*
  1 *teaspoon seasoned salt*
   Nutmeg
 ½ *cup California Sauterne or other*
    white dinner wine

Melt butter in a large skillet or saucepan; add cabbage. Cook over moderate heat, stirring frequently, until cabbage is wilted. Cover and cook about 5 minutes. Stir in cream, salt, and a light sprinkling of nutmeg. Cover and cook until almost tender. Add wine and simmer a few minutes or until cabbage is tender. Yield: 5 to 6 servings.

Orange-Glazed Carrots

  5 *medium carrots*
 ¼ *cup boiling, salted water*
  1 *tablespoon sugar*
  1 *teaspoon cornstarch*
 ¼ *teaspoon salt*
 ¼ *to ½ teaspoon ground ginger*
 ¼ *cup orange juice*
  2 *tablespoons butter or margarine*

Slice carrots crosswise at an angle, about 1 inch thick. Cook, covered, in the boiling, salted water about 15 minutes, or until just tender. Mix sugar, cornstarch, salt, ginger, orange juice, and butter and pour over carrots. Cook, stirring occasionally, for about 8 minutes. Yield: 4 servings.

Carrot Ring

      9 carrots
      1 green pepper, chopped
   ¾ cup blanched almonds
      4 eggs, beaten
   1¼ cups homogenized milk
   1½ teaspoons salt

Scrape carrots and grate coarsely. Add chopped pepper, almonds, beaten eggs, milk, and salt. Put in well-greased ring mold.

Set mold in pan of hot water and bake at 350 degrees F. for 1¼ hours. Turn out on platter and serve any cooked green vegetable in middle of circle. Peas or French-style string beans blend well with the ring. Yield: 4 generous servings.

Carrot Casserole

   2 cans of diced or shoestring carrots
   1 can cream of mushroom soup
   ½ onion, finely chopped
   1 small bag potato chips, crushed

Alternate layers of carrots with soup and onion mixture in a greased 1-quart casserole. Bake at 325 degrees F. for 20 to 25 minutes or until thoroughly heated. Just before removing from oven, sprinkle with crushed potato chips and brown slightly.

Carrots With Celery Seed Sauce

      4 medium carrots
   ¼ cup water
      2 tablespoons butter or margarine
      1 teaspoon flour
   ½ teaspoon celery seed
   ¼ teaspoon salt

Scrape carrots and cut in crosswise slices. Cook carrots with ¼ cup water for 12 to 15 minutes in a tightly covered 2-quart saucepan over low heat. Brown butter in a small frypan or saucepan. Stir in flour, cooking liquid from the carrots, celery seed, and salt. Cook over low heat 1 minute, stirring constantly. Mix sauce with carrots. Yield: 2 to 4 servings.

Carrot-Cheese Ring

   ½ stick butter or margarine
      2 cups cooked, mashed carrots
      2 cups shredded cheese
      3 eggs, beaten
   ½ cup milk
      Salt and pepper to taste

Add butter to hot, mashed carrots. Combine all other ingredients. Mix well and pour into a greased ring mold. Set in pan of hot water. Bake at 325 degrees F. about 40 minutes or until firm. Turn onto hot platter. Fill center with cooked, buttered peas.

Beaumont Inn Corn Pudding

   2 cups whole-kernel corn
   8 tablespoons flour
   1 teaspoon salt
   4 rounded teaspoons sugar
   4 tablespoons melted butter
   4 eggs, well beaten
   2 pints milk

Stir into the corn the flour, salt, sugar, and butter. Add well-beaten eggs to milk, and stir into the corn. Place in a 1½-quart shallow pan and bake at 325 degrees F. for 40 to 45 minutes. Stir from bottom 3 times while baking. Yield: 6 servings.

Dutch Baked Corn

   4 ears fresh corn or 1 (No. 2) can corn
   1 tablespoon butter
   2 tablespoons flour
   1 cup milk
   2 teaspoons sugar
   1 teaspoon salt
      Dash paprika
   2 eggs, separated

Cut corn from cob. Melt butter; mix with flour and pour in milk gradually. Bring to a boil, stirring constantly. Add the corn, seasonings, and yolks of eggs, well beaten; then fold in stiffly beaten egg whites. Put in a buttered casserole. Bake 30 minutes in moderate oven. Yield: 4 servings.

Barbecued Corn

   8 *ears corn*
   ½ *cup soft-type margarine*
   ⅛ *teaspoon Tabasco sauce*
   ½ *teaspoon chili powder (optional)*

Remove husks and silk from ears of corn. Place each ear on a piece of heavy-duty aluminum foil. Blend remaining ingredients; spread each ear with 1 tablespoon of the mixture. Wrap in foil, double wrapping if fire is very hot or if corn is to be placed directly on the coals. Roast 20 to 25 minutes, turning two or three times. Yield: 8 delicious servings.

Corn and Green Bean Casserole

   1 *(4½-ounce) can deviled ham*
   ¾ *teaspoon paprika*
   2 *teaspoons flour*
 1¾ *cups light cream*
   1 *teaspoon grated onion*
   ¾ *teaspoon salt*
   ¼ *teaspoon pepper*
   2 *(No. 2) cans green beans*
   1 *(No. 2) can whole-kernel corn*
   ½ *cup commercial sour cream*

Heat deviled ham in skillet. Add paprika, flour, cream, onion, and seasonings. Heat and stir until thickened. Heat and drain green beans and corn. Add to sauce, along with sour cream. Serve immediately. Yield: 6 servings.

Herbed Roasting Ears

   ½ *cup soft butter or margarine*
   1 *teaspoon dried, crushed rosemary*
   ½ *teaspoon dried, crushed marjoram*
   6 *ears sweet corn*
   1 *head romaine*

Blend butter with herbs; spread on corn. Wrap each ear of corn in two or three leaves of romaine. Place in shallow baking dish. Cover tightly with foil. Bake at 450 degrees F. for 20 to 25 minutes. Yield: 6 servings.

Corn Pudding

   2 *eggs, well beaten*
   1 *cup milk*
   2 *tablespoons flour*
   1 *tablespoon butter*
   2 *cups fresh corn cut from cob*
     Salt and pepper to taste

Beat eggs well and mix with other ingredients. Place in buttered casserole. Set in pan of water. Bake 30 to 40 minutes at 350 degrees F. Yield: 4 servings.

Baked Corn Pudding

   6 *to 8 ears tender corn*
 1½ *cups milk*
   2 *eggs, beaten*
   ½ *teaspoon salt*
   ⅛ *teaspoon pepper*
   2 *tablespoons sugar (optional)*
   ¼ *stick butter or margarine*

Cut and scrape corn from cob. Add remaining ingredients. Place in a well-greased shallow baking dish. Butter should be dotted on top. Bake at 375 degrees F. for 30 to 35 minutes. Serve hot. Yield: 4 to 6 servings.

Cherokee Corn-Rice Casserole

   1 *pound ground beef*
   1 *teaspoon cooking oil*
   ¾ *cup chopped onion*
 1½ *teaspoons salt*
   ⅛ *teaspoon pepper*
     Dash garlic powder
   ⅛ *teaspoon thyme*
   ⅛ *teaspoon oregano*
   ½ *small bay leaf, crushed*
   1 *pint cooked tomatoes*
   1 *can cream of mushroom soup*
   ½ *cup regular rice*
   1 *(No. 2) can corn*
   3 *tablespoons melted butter or margarine*
   ½ *cup shredded cheese*
   4 *stuffed olives, sliced*

Cook beef in oil until light colored. Add onion and cook until onion is transparent. Add remaining ingredients except cheese and olives. Mix well and spoon into a 3-quart baking dish. Top with shredded cheese and cook, covered, at 350 degrees F. for 45 minutes. Remove from oven and garnish with olives. Yield: 6 to 8 servings.

Corn on the Grill

Use fresh sweet corn and prepare for cooking. Salt and pepper generously. (Coarse ground pepper is best.) Brush generously with melted margarine. Wrap individual ears of corn in aluminum foil and cook for 20 minutes (medium-size ears).

Corn on a Grill

Soak corn in shucks in water for 10 minutes. Drain and place on grill over hot coals. Roast on all sides. Corn will be done in about 10 minutes. When ready to serve, remove shucks and serve corn with plenty of butter. Allow one ear per person.

Creamy Fresh Corn

    6 to 8 ears fresh corn
    3 strips bacon, halved
    ⅔ cup water
    1 teaspoon salt
    ½ teaspoon sugar
    ¼ cup milk
    2 teaspoons flour
    ⅛ teaspoon pepper
    1 tablespoon butter or margarine

Husk corn and cut the kernels from the cob. Scrape cob well with a tablespoon to remove all the pulp and milk (there should be 3 cups). Cook bacon slowly until crisp in an 8-inch skillet; remove and drain on paper towel. Stir corn into hot bacon fat and then add water, salt, and sugar. Stir and cook 5 minutes, uncovered. Stir milk gradually into flour; mix until smooth. Add to corn and

stir constantly for a few minutes, or until thickened. Mix in pepper and butter. Serve hot, garnished with bacon. Yield: 6 servings.

Southern Corn Pudding

    3 cups canned yellow corn
    3 eggs, beaten well
    3 tablespoons sifted flour
    2 teaspoons salt
    1 tablespoon sugar
    1 tablespoon melted butter
    1 pint milk, scalded

Grind corn using a medium-coarse grinder. To beaten eggs add flour, salt, sugar, and melted butter. Mix well. Next add the milk and ground corn, mixing well. Pour into a well-buttered casserole and bake at 350 degrees F. until firm, approximately 40 minutes.

Variation: This recipe can also be used to make a hominy pudding by omitting flour, salt, sugar, and butter. And, instead of corn, use 3 cups canned yellow hominy.

Maque Choux
(Stewed Corn and Tomatoes)

    12 ears fresh corn
     2 tablespoons shortening
     1 medium onion, minced
     ½ to ¾ cup canned whole tomatoes
     ½ medium green pepper, minced
     ¼ cup chopped celery
     ⅓ teaspoon sugar
        Salt and pepper to taste
        Several dashes Tabasco sauce

With a sharp knife, shave the kernels from the cob, cutting the kernels about half their depth. Use the back of the knife and scrape cob for the rest of pulp and milk of the corn.

In a heavy skillet, sauté corn in shortening until corn turns golden brown. Add remaining ingredients and cook for about 20 minutes. Stir often and add a little milk if mixture becomes too dry. Yield: 8 to 10 servings.

Okra and Fresh Corn Casserole

    3 *cups cut okra*
    2 *tablespoons butter or margarine*
    6 *ears fresh corn*
    Salt and pepper to taste
    2 *tablespoons butter or margarine*
    2 *tablespoons flour*
    1 *cup milk*
  ¼ *pound sharp cheese, shredded*
    1 *cup bread or cracker crumbs*

Wash the okra and drain well. Place in skillet with 2 tablespoons of butter or margarine and let it cook slowly, stirring frequently, until the sticky substance has disappeared. Cut corn from cob. Put okra and corn in alternate layers in a greased casserole, sprinkling with salt and pepper as you go along. Make a sauce with 2 tablespoons of butter or margarine, flour, and milk. Stir well; do not let it get brown. Add cheese and stir until melted. Pour over okra and corn and cover with crumbs. Bake at 350 degrees F. for about 30 minutes or until the top is slightly brown. Yield: 6 servings.

Cucumbers in Sour Cream

    2 *medium cucumbers, peeled and*
        sliced
  ¾ *teaspoon salt*
  ½ *cup commercial sour cream*
    2 *teaspoons minced onion*
    1 *tablespoon lemon juice*
    1 *teaspoon chopped dill pickle*
  ⅛ *teaspoon salt*
  ⅛ *teaspoon pepper*
    3 *radishes, minced*

Place cucumber slices in a bowl. Sprinkle with salt, cover bowl, and chill for one hour; drain.

Mix other ingredients together and stir into cucumber slices. To serve, sprinkle sliced radishes over the top. Yield: 3 to 4 servings.

Pleasant Hill Baked Eggplant

    1 *large eggplant*
  ½ *medium onion, chopped*
    3 *tablespoons butter*
    3 *tablespoons chopped parsley*
    1 *can cream of mushroom soup*
      Worcestershire sauce to taste
      Salt and pepper to taste
  20 *to 24 round buttery crackers,*
        crumbled

Cut off eggplant top, lengthwise, and scrape out inside, leaving a ¼-inch shell intact. Parboil the eggplant meat in a little salt water until it is tender. Drain thoroughly.

Sauté the onion in butter, stir in parsley, then add to the cooked eggplant. Add mushroom soup and the seasonings. Add crackers, broken up, and pile mixture into the eggplant shell. Sprinkle additional crumbled crackers on top. Bake at 375 degrees F. for 30 to 35 minutes. Yield: 4 servings.

Eggplant Casserole

    1 *medium or large eggplant*
      Salt and pepper
    1 *small onion, diced*
    2 *tablespoons butter*
  ¾ *cup milk*
    3 *tablespoons shredded sharp cheese*
    1 *cup crushed crackers*
    4 *slices American cheese, if desired*

Pare and slice eggplant; cook in salted water until tender. Drain and mash. Add other ingredients except cheese slices. Place in a greased, 1-quart casserole dish. Bake at 350 degrees F. for 40 minutes. Arrange cheese slices on top and bake an additional 20 minutes. Yield: 4 servings.

Eggplant Casserole

  1 *medium eggplant*
  1 *teaspoon salt*
  2 *tablespoons chopped green pepper*
  1 *egg, beaten*
  1 *medium onion, chopped*
 ¾ *cup breadcrumbs*
  1 *cup cream-style corn*
 ½ *teaspoon pepper*
 ½ *cup shredded cheese*

Cook eggplant until tender. Drain and mash, then add all ingredients except cheese and mix well. Put in a 1½-quart baking dish and sprinkle cheese on top. Bake at 350 degrees F. for 30 minutes. Yield: 6 servings.

Eggplant Casserole

  2 *cups ground beef*
  1 *tablespoon butter*
  2 *cups cooked, mashed eggplant*
  2 *cups cooked rice*
  1 *can cream of mushroom soup*
   Salt and pepper to taste
 ½ *cup crushed salty crackers*

Sauté ground beef in butter until it changes color. Add other ingredients except cracker crumbs. Put in buttered casserole and top with cracker crumbs. Bake at 350 degrees F. for 25 or 30 minutes. Serve hot. Yield: 4 to 6 servings.

Sautéed Eggplant

  2 *medium eggplant*
  1 *egg*
  1 *tablespoon evaporated milk*
 ¼ *teaspoon black pepper*
  1 *teaspoon salt*
   Flour (about ½ cup)

Peel eggplant and slice lengthwise in ¼-inch slices. Beat egg; add milk, pepper, and salt. Dip eggplant slices in this mixture, then in flour. Fry in hot fat, turning once to brown sides. Serve hot. Yield: 6 servings.

Eggplant Stuffed With Ham

  1 *large eggplant*
   Salted water
  1 *small onion, minced*
  1 *green pepper, chopped fine*
  2 *tomatoes, quartered*
  2 *tablespoons butter*
 ½ *teaspoon salt*
 ⅛ *teaspoon black pepper*
  1 *cup diced boiled ham*
   Breadcrumbs

Wash and dry eggplant and cut a slice from the top. Scoop out inside to within ½ inch of skin. Cover shell and top with salted water and set aside. Chop eggplant pulp and combine with onion, pepper, and tomatoes. Cover and cook in a small amount of boiling salted water until tender. Drain and mash. Add butter, salt, black pepper, and ham. Drain shell and top slice; fill with mixture. Place in shallow baking dish, sprinkle with breadcrumbs, and bake at 350 degrees F. for 25 minutes. Yield: 4 to 6 servings.

Smothered Lettuce
(Mountain Spring Salad)

    Select fresh spring lettuce before it heads. Chop enough lettuce to fill bowl. Add 3 young onion heads and onion tops, chopped fine. Add a teaspoon sugar and salt to taste. Pour 2 tablespoons vinegar over this. Cook 5 slices cured country bacon until crisp, and place strips over lettuce. Pour hot bacon drippings over all. Serve immediately.

Lettuce in Cream

 ⅓ *cup top milk or light cream*
  3 *tablespoons cider vinegar*
 ¾ *teaspoon sugar*
 ⅛ *teaspoon ground black pepper*
 ¾ *teaspoon salt*
  1 *medium head lettuce*
  1 *cup chopped green onions*
    (scallions)

Combine first 5 ingredients and set aside. Wash and dry lettuce, tear into bite-size pieces, and place in a salad bowl. Add green onions and cream mixture. Toss lightly. Yield: 6 servings.

Healthy Iceberg Lettuce

1½ heads iceberg lettuce, cut from stem end into 6 wedges
½ fresh lemon, juiced and strained
1 fresh ripe tomato, peeled, diced, and sieved
½ small onion, minced
1 clove garlic, minced
1 ripe avocado, peeled and mashed
1 teaspoon salt
1/16 teaspoon cayenne pepper
1 tablespoon salad oil

Wash iceberg lettuce and shake to dry. Gently bounce on board on stem end to loosen leaves a bit. With sharp knife cut into wedges, about 4 to a head, depending on size serving. Set aside to keep chilled. Strain lemon juice into a small bowl, adding sieved tomato, minced onion and garlic, and mashed avocado. Stir in salt, cayenne, and salad oil and blend well.

Arrange iceberg lettuce wedges on platter and serve dressing in an accompanying bowl. Excess dressing may be refrigerated. Yield: 6 servings.

French-Fried Mushrooms

1 pound medium, fresh mushrooms (approximately 20)
¼ cup all-purpose flour
1 teaspoon salt
Dash ground black pepper
2 eggs, beaten
¾ cup fine dry breadcrumbs

Wash mushrooms and leave stems attached. Dip in flour mixed with salt and pepper, then into beaten eggs. Roll in breadcrumbs.

Fry until golden brown in deep fat heated to 365 degrees. Drain on paper towels.

Ten-Minute Chicken-Mushroom Dinner

¾ cup sliced fresh mushrooms or 1 (3- or 4-ounce) can sliced mushrooms
1 (10½-ounce) can cream of chicken soup
½ cup milk
2 (5-ounce) cans boned chicken
¾ teaspoon poultry seasoning
¼ teaspoon salt
Dash ground black pepper
Cooked rice

If using fresh mushrooms, use approximately ⅛ pound. If using canned mushrooms, drain. Place all ingredients except rice in 1½-quart saucepan. Stir and cook 10 minutes or only until hot. Serve over hot cooked rice. Garnish, if desired, with paprika. Yield: 6 servings.

Mushrooms à la Grecque

2 (10-ounce) packages frozen whole mushrooms
½ cup olive oil
½ cup cider vinegar
1 teaspoon salt
¼ teaspoon freshly ground pepper
¼ teaspoon crumbled chervil
1 bay leaf
1 clove garlic, cut into quarters
1 hard-cooked egg yolk, sieved
2 tablespoons drained capers

Defrost mushrooms and place in an earthenware or glass bowl. Combine remaining ingredients, except egg yolk and capers, in saucepan; bring to boil. Pour hot mixture over mushrooms. Let stand at room temperature at least 30 minutes, stirring occasionally. Remove garlic and bay leaf. Refrigerate until ready to serve. Just before serving, stir in sieved egg yolk and capers. Yield: 6 servings.

Creamed Onions

 3 *pounds small white onions*
 1 *teaspoon salt, divided*
 4 *tablespoons butter or margarine*
 5 *tablespoons flour*
 2 *cups milk*
 ⅛ *teaspoon Tabasco sauce*

Peel onions; place in saucepan. Add ½ teaspoon of the salt and enough water to cover. Bring to a boil; cover and cook 20 to 25 minutes. While onions are cooking, melt butter in saucepan; blend in flour and remaining ½ teaspoon salt. Gradually add milk; cook, stirring constantly, until mixture thickens and comes to a boil. Stir in Tabasco. Add drained onions; heat to serving temperature. If desired, sprinkle with toasted almonds. Yield: 12 servings.

Sweet and Sour Onions

 4 *large onions*
 ¼ *cup cider vinegar*
 ¼ *cup melted butter or margarine*
 ¼ *cup boiling water*
 ¼ *cup sugar*

Slice the onions and arrange in a 1-quart baking dish. Mix the rest of the ingredients and pour over the onions. Bake at 300 degrees F. for 1 hour. Yield: 4 to 6 servings.

Onions Unbelievable

 This requires one large white onion per serving. Remove any dry skin and stem. Working from the top, core the onion generously, leaving a cavity 1 inch across and almost through the onion. Salt and pepper the cavity. Then fill with butter, and salt and pepper the entire onion. Wrap in foil, making a twist at the top. Cook in closed grill in about 1½ hours over a steady medium fire. Open foil 10 minutes before serving and leave on the smoking grill for a scrumptious smoked onion.

Swiss Onion Squares

 1 *egg, well beaten*
 ¾ *cup milk*
 2 *cups biscuit mix*
 2 *tablespoons poppy seeds*
 2 *cups chopped sweet onion*
 2 *tablespoons butter*
 1 *egg*
 ¾ *cup commercial sour cream*
 ½ *teaspoon salt*
 ¼ *teaspoon pepper*
  Paprika

Blend egg and milk with biscuit mix and poppy seeds. Turn into greased 9- x 9-inch pan. Fry onions in butter until tender and lightly browned. Spread on dough. Beat egg with sour cream and season with salt and pepper. Spread over onions. Bake at 400 degrees F. for 25 minutes. Cut into squares, sprinkle with paprika, and serve very hot. Yield: 6 to 8 servings.

Peas and Corn in Sour Cream

 1 *small onion, minced*
 1 *stalk celery, chopped*
  Few sprigs of parsley, chopped
 2 *tablespoons butter or margarine*
 2 *cups cooked peas, drained*
 1 *(No. 2) can whole-kernel corn or 2 cups cooked fresh corn*
  Salt and pepper to taste
 ½ *teaspoon basil*
 ½ *cup commercial sour cream*
 1 *teaspoon lemon or lime juice*

Cook onion, celery, and parsley in melted butter until tender. Add drained peas and corn, salt, pepper, and basil. Heat and blend gently. Just before serving add sour cream and lemon juice. Yield: 6 to 8 servings.

Peas—French Style

>   3 *to 4 outer leaves of lettuce*
>   2 *pounds green peas*
>   1 *teaspoon sugar*
>   2 *to 4 tablespoons water*
>   *Salt*
>   *Butter, as desired*
>   *Milk or cream, as desired*

Line heavy saucepan with wet lettuce leaves. Place peas in lettuce, then add sugar and water. Cover pan tightly, and cook until tender (about 20 minutes). Add salt to taste; add butter and milk or cream to the liquid left. Serve the peas on the lettuce leaves.

Patio Black-Eyed Peas

>   2 *cups cooked, diced ham*
>   1 *onion, sliced*
>   1 *green pepper, chopped*
>   ¼ *cup bacon drippings*
>   ½ *cup hot water*
>   2 *(1-pound) cans black-eyed peas*
>   2 *cups elbow macaroni, cooked and drained*
>   *Salt and pepper*
>   ¼ *cup crumbled corn chips*

Brown ham, onion, and pepper in bacon drippings. Add ½ cup hot water and simmer 1 minute. Combine with peas and macaroni; add salt and pepper to taste. Turn into 2-quart casserole and bake uncovered at 350 degrees F. for 25 minutes. Top with corn chips and return to oven for 5 minutes. Yield: 6 servings.

Egg-Green Peas in Sauce

>   2 *tablespoons butter or margarine*
>   ½ *cup nonfat dry milk solids*
>   2 *tablespoons flour*
>   ½ *teaspoon salt*
>   ¼ *teaspoon pepper*
>   1 *cup warm water*
>   3 *hard-cooked eggs*
>   2 *cups cooked green peas*

Melt butter in heavy saucepan. Remove from heat. Add nonfat dry milk, flour, salt, and pepper. Stir until well mixed. Gradually add warm water. Stir until smooth. Cook until thick, stirring constantly. Add chopped eggs and peas. Yield: 6 servings.

Fresh Corn-Stuffed Sweet Peppers

>   6 *medium, sweet peppers*
>   3 *cups fresh corn, cut off the cob*
>   1 *cup diced fresh tomato*
>   1 *tablespoon chopped fresh onion*
>   3 *tablespoons flour*
>   1 *teaspoon salt*
>   1 *teaspoon chili powder*
>   ¼ *teaspoon ground black pepper*
>   2 *tablespoons butter or margarine, melted*

Slice tops from peppers. Carefully remove seeds and membranes. In covered saucepan parboil in boiling salted water to cover for 5 minutes. Drain. Combine remaining ingredients and spoon into drained green peppers. Place in baking pan and bake in a preheated moderate oven (375 degrees F.) for 35 minutes or until done. Yield: 6 tasty servings.

Oriental Stuffed Sweet Peppers

>   4 *medium, fresh sweet peppers*
>   1 *cup (½ pound) cooked diced shrimp*
>   2 *tablespoons French dressing*
>   1 *cup diced fresh pineapple*
>   ½ *cup diced fresh celery*
>   ¼ *teaspoon salt*
>   ⅛ *teaspoon ground black pepper*
>   ¼ *cup diced fresh sweet pepper*
>   *Paprika*

Cut stem ends from peppers; remove seeds and membrane; wash and drain. Combine shrimp, French dressing, pineapple, celery, salt, pepper, and diced sweet pepper. Fill pepper shells with shrimp mixture. Garnish with whole shrimp dusted with paprika.

Beef-Stuffed Sweet Peppers

  1 *pound ground beef*
  ¼ *cup shortening*
  2 *cups diced fresh tomatoes*
  1 *cup diced cooked potatoes*
  ½ *teaspoon minced fresh onion*
1½ *teaspoons chili powder*
  1 *teaspoon salt*
  ⅛ *teaspoon ground black pepper*
  4 *large sweet peppers*
  ¼ *cup buttered soft breadcrumbs*

Sauté beef in hot shortening. Add tomatoes and cook 5 minutes. Remove from heat. Stir in potatoes, onion, and seasonings. Meantime, cut off pepper tops, remove seeds, and parboil in boiling water for 5 minutes. Drain. Fill with meat mixture. Top with buttered breadcrumbs. Turn into greased baking dish and bake in preheated moderate oven (375 degrees F.) for 35 minutes or until crumbs are brown. Yield: 4 servings.

Oven Meal

2 *cups raw diced potatoes*
2 *cups chopped celery*
2 *cups raw hamburger*
1 *cup finely chopped green pepper*
2 *cups canned tomatoes*
1 *cup raw sliced onions*
Salt and pepper to taste

Place ingredients in baking dish in order given. Sprinkle each layer with salt and pepper. Bake at 375 degrees F. for 1½ hours. Yield: 6 servings.

Butter-Browned Potatoes

2 *(1-pound) cans whole white*
   potatoes, drained
Salt and pepper
Paprika
¼ *cup butter or margarine*

Sprinkle drained potatoes lightly with salt, pepper, and paprika. Cook in butter until browned, turning often. Yield: 6 servings.

Barbecue-Fried Potatoes

6 *medium potatoes, peeled and*
  sliced thin
Hot bacon drippings or oil for frying
Salt and pepper to taste
2 *teaspoons chili powder, more or less*
  to taste
1 *small onion, chopped*

Prepare potatoes. Heat drippings or oil in skillet; add potatoes and sprinkle with salt and pepper. Cover and fry over medium heat, turning occasionally, until almost tender and lightly browned. Remove lid, sprinkle with chili powder, and add the chopped onion. Increase heat and finish cooking, turning as needed, until potatoes are good and brown. Drain well on paper towels before serving. Yield: 6 servings.

Potatoes and Carrots au Gratin

2½ *cups coarsely grated raw potatoes*
1½ *cups coarsely grated raw carrots*
  ½ *cup coarsely grated onion*
  1 *can cream of celery soup, undiluted*
  ½ *cup milk*
  ½ *teaspoon salt*
   Dash pepper
  ½ *cup shredded American cheese*

Heat oven to 375 degrees F. Combine potatoes, carrots, and onion in buttered 2-quart baking dish. Blend soup, milk, salt, and pepper and pour over vegetables. Cover. Bake 1 hour. Uncover, sprinkle with cheese, and bake 15 minutes. Yield: 8 servings.

Party Potatoes

8 *to 10 medium potatoes*
1 *(8-ounce) package cream cheese*
1 *cup commercial sour cream*
Salt and pepper to taste
2 *tablespoons butter*
Touch of paprika

Pare potatoes. Boil until tender; drain. Beat softened cheese and sour cream at medium speed until well blended. Add hot potatoes gradually, beating constantly until light and fluffy. Season to taste with salt and pepper. Put in 2-quart casserole. Dot casserole with butter and sprinkle with paprika. Bake at 325 degrees F. for 25 minutes. Yield: 6 servings.

Stuffed Potatoes

    6 *large potatoes*
    ½ *pound sausage*
    1 *teaspoon salt*
    ¼ *teaspoon pepper*
    4 *tablespoons butter*
    1 *large onion, diced*

Bake the potatoes in a 400-degree F. oven until well done (about 1 hour). While the potatoes are baking, brown the sausage lightly, add the diced onion, and leave on low heat until ready for use. Split the potatoes in half, remove the inside, and mash thoroughly. Add the salt, pepper, and butter and mix thoroughly. More seasoning may be added to suit taste. Drain excess fat from sausage and discard fat. Add the sausage mixture, mix thoroughly, and return to potato shells. Return to the 400-degree F. oven for about 30 minutes. Yield: 6 servings.

Pumpkin Fritters

    5 *eggs*
    1½ *cups sugar*
    ½ *teaspoon salt*
    2¼ *teaspoons nutmeg*
    1¼ *teaspoons cinnamon*
    3 *cups bread flour*
    1 *(No. 2½) can pumpkin*
    8 *teaspoons vanilla extract*
    2 *teaspoons baking powder*
    Melted butter

Beat eggs; mix with sugar, salt, spices, and flour. Beat until mixture becomes smooth and fluffy. Add pumpkin, vanilla, and baking powder. Whip until thoroughly mixed. Fry in skillet in melted butter until fritter becomes brown on both sides. Don't fry too fast; otherwise, fritter will not be done in middle. Yield: about 4 dozen.

Sauerkraut au Gratin

    3 *tablespoons flour*
    ½ *teaspoon salt*
    ⅛ *teaspoon pepper*
    1 *teaspoon dry mustard*
    1 *teaspoon Worcestershire sauce*
    ¼ *cup melted butter or margarine*
    1⅓ *cups milk*
    1½ *cups shredded Cheddar cheese,*
        divided
    1 *(1-pound 11-ounce) can sauerkraut,*
        drained
    ⅔ *cup fine dry breadcrumbs or*
        cornflake crumbs

Stir flour, salt, pepper, mustard, and Worcestershire sauce into melted butter. Slowly add milk and cook until thickened, stirring constantly. To this add 1 cup of the cheese and the well-drained sauerkraut; mix well. Pour into a 1½-quart casserole. Mix crumbs with remaining ½ cup cheese; sprinkle over sauerkraut. Bake at 375 degrees F. about 30 minutes. Yield: 6 to 8 servings.

Baked Spinach With Bacon

    3 *cups cooked, drained spinach*
    2 *cups drained canned tomatoes*
    1 *medium onion, chopped*
    ¼ *cup chili sauce*
    1 *cup cracker crumbs*
    1 *teaspoon salt*
    ¼ *teaspoon paprika*
    ½ *pound American cheese, sliced thin*
    6 *slices bacon*

Place a layer of spinach in a buttered 2-quart baking dish, next a layer of tomatoes, a sprinkling of onion, small amount chili sauce, crumbs, salt, and paprika. Then make a layer of cheese. Repeat until all the ingredients are used, and sprinkle more crumbs on the top. Arrange the slices of bacon over the top of the dish and bake at 350 degrees F. for 25 minutes or until the cheese melts and the bacon is crisp. Serve hot. Yield: 6 servings.

Spinach Deluxe

   3 *tablespoons butter*
   3 *tablespoons flour*
   1 *cup milk*
   ½ *pound processed American cheese,*
     cut in cubes
   1 *cup finely chopped cooked spinach,*
     drained
  1½ *cups breadcrumbs*
   3 *eggs, beaten*
    Salt and pepper to taste
    Hot mashed potatoes, seasoned
    Hot buttered whole beets

Melt butter in skillet. Add flour and stir until smooth. Gradually add milk and stir until mixture begins to thicken. Add cheese; remove from heat and stir until cheese has melted. Add well-drained cooked spinach, breadcrumbs, beaten eggs, and seasonings. Put mixture into a well-buttered 1-quart ring mold, and bake at 325 degrees F. for 50 minutes or until mixture is firm. Unmold on platter, fill center with seasoned mashed potatoes and garnish with tiny whole beets. Yield: 4 to 6 servings.

Acorn Squash With Spiced Brazil Nut Filling

   3 *acorn squash*
   ¼ *cup sugar*
   2 *tablespoons flour*
   ¼ *teaspoon salt*
   ½ *teaspoon ground cinnamon*
   ¼ *teaspoon ground nutmeg*
   ¾ *cup chopped Brazil nuts*
   1 *tablespoon grated orange rind*
   3 *tablespoons butter or margarine*

Cut acorn squash in half lengthwise; then scrape out seeds and stringy portions. Put dry ingredients, nuts, and grated rind in mixing bowl. Cut in butter with two knives or pastry blender until mixture resembles coarse meal. Place squash halves in baking pan and fill with crumbly mixture. Set the bottom of the baking pan in hot water; cover and bake at 400 degrees F. for 30

minutes; then uncover and bake 30 minutes longer. Yield: 6 servings.

Orange-Stuffed Squash

   3 *medium acorn squash*
   ¼ *cup brown sugar*
   2 *tablespoons butter or margarine*
   1 *teaspoon salt*
   1 *teaspoon orange peel*
   ¼ *cup orange juice*
   ¼ *cup chopped pecans*

Cut squash in half; remove seeds and stringy section. Place cut side down on baking sheet and bake at 350 degrees F. about 30 minutes. Scoop out pulp, leaving ¼ inch in shell. Combine pulp with sugar, butter, salt, and orange peel. Add orange juice (add more if mixture is too dry); fold in chopped pecans. Fill shells with this mixture. Broil until lightly browned. Yield: 6 servings.

Acorn Squash With Cranberries

   2 *acorn squash*
   ½ *cup fresh cranberries*
   ½ *cup brown sugar*
   2 *tablespoons melted butter or*
     margarine
   ½ *teaspoon ground cinnamon*

Cut squash in half lengthwise; remove seed. Combine cranberries, brown sugar, butter, and cinnamon; fill squash halves with this mixture. Place in a shallow baking dish and surround with ½ inch water. Bake at 350 degrees F. for 50 minutes or until squash is done. Yield: 4 servings.

Acorn Squash With Sausage Balls

   3 *medium acorn squash*
   ½ *teaspoon salt*
  1½ *pounds sausage*
   3 *tablespoons butter or margarine*
   6 *tablespoons brown sugar*

Wash acorn squash; cut in half and remove seeds and membrane. Sprinkle with salt and place cut side down in oiled baking pan. Bake at 350 degrees F. for 30 minutes. Form sausage into 18 small balls and brown on all sides. Pour off excess fat. Turn squash and place butter and sugar in cavities; add sausage balls and continue baking for 30 minutes or until tender. Yield: 6 servings.

Baked Acorn Squash With Pineapple

3 *medium acorn squash*
1 *small can crushed pineapple*
½ *cup brown sugar*
1 *teaspoon mixed spices*
¼ *cup chopped pecans*
4 *tablespoons soft margarine*
½ *cup water*

Cut squash in half; remove seed. Place squash halves in baking dish. Drain pineapple and combine with brown sugar, spices, pecans, and margarine. Spoon mixture into squash halves. Pour water into dish. Cover. Bake at 375 degrees F. for 45 minutes. Remove cover; bake 15 minutes longer, or until slightly brown. Yield: 6 servings.

Glazed Squash With Pineapple

4 to 6 *acorn squash*
2 *tablespoons butter*
½ *teaspoon salt*
Few grains pepper
1 *tablespoon sugar*
¼ to ½ *cup crushed pineapple*
Marshmallows
Brown sugar

Cut squash in half; remove seed and boil until tender. Remove pulp and set shells aside. To 2 cups cooked mashed squash, add next 5 ingredients. Mix well and refill shells. Top with marshmallows and sprinkle with brown sugar. Place under broiler to glaze. Yield: 4 to 6 servings.

Saint Pete Squash

3 *acorn squash*
2 *tablespoons melted butter*
½ *teaspoon salt*
½ *cup orange juice*
½ *cup fig bar cookies, cut into small pieces*
¼ *cup salted cashew nuts*

Cut squash in halves, lengthwise; remove seeds and brush with butter. Sprinkle with salt. Place squash cut side down in baking pan and bake at 400 degrees F. for 30 minutes. Turn cut side up. Fill centers of squash with mixture of orange juice, fig bar pieces, and cashews. Bake about 25 minutes longer, or until tender. Yield: 6 servings.

Squash and Carrot Casserole

8 *yellow squash, cooked and drained*
6 *carrots, cooked and drained*
2 *eggs*
3 *tablespoons chopped onion*
½ *stick butter or margarine*
2 *tablespoons flour*

Beat the cooked squash and carrots together. Then beat in all other ingredients. Turn into greased shallow casserole dish. Bake at 350 degrees F. for 1 hour. This can be prepared in the morning and refrigerated until time to bake. Yield: 4 to 5 servings.

Squash-Onion Casserole

Cut yellow squash crosswise into ¼-inch slices. Slice an equal quantity of onions the same way. Cut heavy-duty aluminum foil into 8- x 10-inch pieces, one for each serving. Alternate squash and onion slices in the center of the foil. Bend ends of foil up to hold vegetables in place. Add liberal amount of butter or margarine and salt and pepper. Fold foil to make an envelope. Close hood and cook for 1¼ hours over medium fire. Open top of envelope 10 minutes before serving, but keep on the smoking grill.

Squash Casserole

1 *pound squash*
1 *large onion, grated*
1 *cup shredded Cheddar cheese*
¼ *cup cream*
2 *tablespoons butter*
1 *egg, beaten*
Dash ground nutmeg
Salt and pepper to taste
½ *cup cracker crumbs*
Paprika

Cook squash and onion in small amount of salted water. Drain and add cheese, cream, butter, egg, nutmeg, salt, and pepper. Mix well. Pour into a buttered casserole. Top with cracker crumbs and paprika. Bake at 350 degrees F. until mixture bubbles and crumbs are brown, about 25 minutes. Yield: 4 to 6 servings.

Squash Casserole

2 *cups cooked squash*
¾ *stick butter or margarine*
2 *eggs*
1 *teaspoon salt*
½ *teaspoon pepper*
1 *cup chopped onion*
1 *cup shredded cheese*
1 *cup evaporated milk*
2 *cups cracker crumbs*

Mash cooked squash. Add other ingredients and mix well. Pour into a greased 1-quart casserole and bake at 375 degrees F. for about 40 minutes. Yield: 6 servings.

Baked Squash

2 *pounds yellow squash*
3 *strips bacon*
1 *small white onion, finely chopped*
Salt and pepper
1 *egg, beaten*
Breadcrumbs

Chop squash into chunks. Cut up bacon into small pieces. Place pieces of bacon in large saucepan and cook slowly over low heat until crisp. Add onion and cook until the pieces begin to brown. Add salt and pepper. Add chopped squash to onion and bacon mixture. Cover and cook until soft. Take from heat; stir well and mash slightly. Put into 1½-quart baking dish; flatten out until smooth on top. Pour beaten egg over all and sprinkle with breadcrumbs. Bake at 375 degrees F. until egg is done and breadcrumbs are browned. Yield: 6 servings.

Candied Summer Squash

2 *medium, yellow squash or 3*
pattypan squash
1 *cup dark corn syrup*
2 *tablespoons butter or margarine*
Ground cinnamon

Wash squash; cut in pieces. (If yellow summer squash are used, slice crosswise ½ inch thick; if pattypan are used, slice up and down ½ inch thick.) Arrange squash slices in oiled 1½-quart baking dish. Pour corn syrup over squash. Bake at 325 degrees F. for 35 to 45 minutes. Uncover; dot with butter or margarine, and sprinkle with cinnamon. Bake 5 to 10 minutes longer. Yield: 6 servings.

Country Club Squash

6 or 8 *tender, small squash*
Salt and pepper to taste
2 *tablespoons butter*
1 *bouillon cube*
1 *tablespoon grated onion*
1 *egg, well beaten*
1 *cup commercial sour cream*
½ *cup breadcrumbs*
½ *cup shredded cheese*
Dash of paprika

Cut and cook squash until tender. Mash and add salt, pepper, butter, bouillon cube, and onion. Add well-beaten egg and sour cream. Pour into 1-quart casserole dish. Combine breadcrumbs, shredded cheese, and paprika. Sprinkle over top of squash. Bake at 350 degrees F. for 30 minutes.

Stuffed Butternut Squash

    3 *butternut squash*
    3 *tablespoons butter or margarine*
    ¼ *teaspoon salt*
    1 *tablespoon brown sugar*
    2 *tablespoons raisins*
    ½ *cup chopped walnuts*
    3 *tablespoons brown sugar*
    1 *tablespoon butter or margarine*
    ¼ *cup light corn syrup*

Cut squash in halves; remove seeds. Bake at 400 degrees F. about 50 minutes or until done. Remove from oven; scrape out pulp down to skin (getting about 3¾ cups pulp). Add 3 tablespoons butter, ¼ teaspoon salt, 1 tablespoon brown sugar, and beat until smooth. Fold in raisins and ½ cup chopped walnuts.

   Put filling back into butternut shells; place in shallow baking dish. Combine the 3 tablespoons brown sugar, 1 tablespoon butter or margarine, and the corn syrup. Drizzle syrup over top of squash. Bake at 450 degrees F. about 15 minutes or until top is crusty. Yield: 6 servings.

Butternut Squash And Pineapple

    2 *small butternut squash*
    2 *cups sugar*
    ½ *stick margarine*
    1 *cup chunk pineapple*

Peel squash; remove seeds and cut into cubes. Cook in boiling water until tender. Remove from water; drain. Combine cooked squash with sugar, margarine, and pineapple. Cook over low heat until mixture has a candied appearance. Yield: 4 to 6 servings.

Zucchini Bake Corn

    1 *(16-ounce) can cream-style corn*
    ⅓ *cup crushed salted crackers*
    ⅛ *teaspoon ground sage*
    1 *cup sliced zucchini*
    1 *small onion, chopped*
    ½ *teaspoon salt*
       Pepper
    2 *tablespoons butter or margarine*

Combine corn, crushed crackers, and sage; put into a 2-quart baking dish. Arrange zucchini over corn. Sprinkle with chopped onion, salt, and pepper; dot with butter. Cover and bake at 375 degrees F. about 40 minutes. Yield: 6 servings.

Zucchini With Parmesan Cheese

    4 *small zucchini squash*
    ¾ *cup water*
    ½ *cup milk*
    ¼ *cup butter*
       Salt and pepper
    ¼ *cup Parmesan cheese*

Peel zucchini and slice. Cook in water until tender. Drain and add milk, butter, and seasonings. Put in baking dish. Top with Parmesan cheese. Bake at 350 degrees F. 20 minutes. Yield: 4 servings.

French-Fried Zucchini

    6 *small zucchini squash, pared*
    ¼ *cup milk*
    ½ *cup flour*
       Hot shortening
       Salt

Cut zucchini in lengthwise strips (as for French-fried potatoes). Dip in milk, roll in flour, and drop into hot shortening (375 degrees F.). Cook about 5 minutes or until tender and golden brown. Drain on paper towels; sprinkle with salt and serve hot. Yield: 4 servings.

Squash and Cheese Casserole

    4 *pounds yellow squash*
    2 *pounds zucchini squash*
    1 *large onion, chopped*
    2 *tablespoons sugar*
    1 *teaspoon salt*
    2 *cups water*
    1 *cup shredded Cheddar cheese*
    1 *cup processed American cheese,*
      shredded
    1 *stick butter*
    1 *cup half-and-half cream*

Slice squash; peel and chop onion. Add sugar, salt, and water and simmer until squash is tender, about 20 minutes. Drain and mash. In a buttered 2-quart casserole dish, alternate layers of squash and mixed cheeses. Dot with butter. Pour half-and-half cream over the top and bake at 300 degrees F. for 15 minutes. Yield: 8 servings.

Zucchini and Cucumbers In Sour Cream

    2 *zucchini squash, about 8 inches long*
    1 *cucumber, 8 inches long*
    Boiling water
    ¾ *teaspoon salt*
    ½ *cup chopped green onions*
    2 *tablespoons butter or margarine*
    ½ *cup commercial sour cream*
    ⅛ *teaspoon coarsely ground black*
      pepper
    Chopped parsley

Wash squash and cucumber. Cut into crosswise slices ¼ inch long. Place squash in a saucepan with about ½ inch boiling, salted water. Cover, bring to boiling point, reduce heat, and cook 15 minutes or until almost tender. Add cucumber and cook only until crisp-tender, about 3 minutes. Drain if necessary. In the meantime, sauté green onions in butter or margarine. Add to squash and cucumbers along with sour cream and black pepper. Mix lightly. Heat, but do not boil. Garnish with parsley. Yield: 6 servings.

Tuna-Stuffed Zucchini

    3 *large zucchini squash*
    2 *tablespoons butter or margarine*
    Salt and pepper
    1 *cup packaged, seasoned bread*
      dressing
    ½ *teaspoon seasoned salt*
    ⅔ *cup hot water*
    ¼ *cup mayonnaise*
    1 *tablespoon green onion flakes*
    2 *(6½- or 7-ounce) cans tuna*

Cut cleaned zucchini squash in half lengthwise. Brown cut side in butter. Arrange browned squash cut side up in shallow baking dish. Sprinkle lightly with salt and pepper. Combine bread dressing, seasoned salt, hot water, mayonnaise, and onion flakes; mix well. Add tuna broken into chunks with the oil, mixing lightly.

    Mound tuna mixture on the squash. Bake at 350 degrees F. about 30 minutes, until squash is tender and tuna is browned. Yield: 6 servings.

Tuna-Stuffed Zucchini

    3 *zucchini squash*
    1 *can tuna, drained*
    ¼ *cup chopped onion*
    ½ *cup coarse breadcrumbs*
    ½ *teaspoon salt*
    ½ *teaspoon pepper*
    4 *tablespoons melted butter*

Cut zucchini in halves, lengthwise. Carefully scoop out centers, leaving outer rim thick enough that it will not break. Combine scooped-out zucchini with tuna, onion, breadcrumbs, salt, and pepper. Add melted butter and mix well. Spoon into zucchini shells.

    Place in a shallow casserole dish; cover and bake at 350 degrees F. about 25 minutes. Remove cover and bake an additional 10 minutes for stuffing to brown. Yield: 4 to 6 servings.

Miss Sallie's Candied Yams

    4 *or 5 large sweet potatoes*
    ¾ *cup water*
    1 *cup sugar*
    ½ *teaspoon salt*
    ½ *teaspoon ground nutmeg*
    ½ *cup butter*

Wash and peel yams; cut lengthwise in ¼-inch-thick slices. Place in baking pan. Cover with ¾ cup water and boil until tender, but not soft. Sprinkle slices with sugar, salt, and nutmeg. Dot with butter and bake until syrup is formed (about 20 to 30 minutes).

Frozen Candied Sweet Potatoes

    Peel and slice sweet potatoes into a heavy skillet. Two or three large potatoes may be cooked at a time. Add sugar to suit taste (from ¼ to ½ cup per large potato). Add ¾ stick of margarine and about ¼ cup hot water. Cook until tender, but not mushy. Cool, then put into freezer cartons. To serve, remove from freezer and put into casserole dish. Bake at 300 degrees F. about 20 minutes. Marshmallows may be placed on top of potatoes if desired.

Orange-Glazed Sweet Potatoes

    A favorite with all folks is the yam or sweet potato. This attractive way of serving them is especially good for a festive occasion like Thanksgiving. Giving a little color and because they have a little handle (orange rind), it adds height to the serving plate, making a basket effect.

    2 *pounds sweet potatoes or 2 (1-pound*
          10-ounce) cans
    3 *large navel oranges*
    2 *(6-ounce) cans concentrated orange*
          juice, undiluted
    ½ *cup butter or margarine*
    ½ *cup sugar*

Cook potatoes in jackets in salted boiling water until tender; drain and peel. Cut potatoes in ½-inch-wide sticks. (For canned ones, drain and cut in sticks.) Slice oranges; select 8 large slices. Remove rind from remaining slices.

    Arrange the potato sticks on the 8 orange slices; place in shallow baking dish; loop rind pieces over top. Heat orange juice concentrate, butter, and sugar in small saucepan until blended and heated through. Spoon one-third of mixture over potatoes.

    Bake at 350 degrees F. for 30 minutes, basting with remaining sauce until the potatoes are richly glazed. Yield: 8 generous servings.

Sweet Potato Balls

    2 *cups hot mashed sweet potatoes*
    ¼ *cup pineapple juice*
        Crushed corn flakes

Measure cooked potatoes, add pineapple juice to potatoes, and beat until smooth. Then form into balls the size of small eggs. Roll these in crushed corn flakes. Place in a buttered shallow 2-quart baking dish and bake at 325 degrees F. for 25 minutes. Yield: 4 to 6 servings.

Sweet Potato Soufflé

    6 *medium sweet potatoes*
    3 *tablespoons butter*
    1 *egg, beaten*
    2 *tablespoons sherry*
        Salt and pepper, to taste
    ⅛ *teaspoon ground nutmeg*
    1 *tablespoon butter*

Bake sweet potatoes at 450 degrees F. until soft. Remove, peel, and combine with 3 tablespoons butter. Mash potatoes well. Add egg to potatoes. Add sherry and beat until light and fluffy. Season with salt and pepper, and place in buttered 2-quart casserole dish. Sprinkle with nutmeg and dot with additional butter. Bake at 350 degrees F. about 30 minutes. Yield: 6 servings.

Yummy Yams

4 *large yams*
⅔ *to ¾ cup sugar*
   Pinch salt
4 *tablespoons margarine*
⅓ *cup thick cream*
   Ground cinnamon, if desired

Butter a 13- x 9- x 2-inch baking dish. Peel yams and cut into strips like French fries. Add sugar, salt, and thick cream. (Amount of sugar will vary according to size of yams.) Bake at 450 degrees F. for about 45 minutes. Shredded cheese or marshmallows may be used as a topping. Yield: 6 servings.

Sweet Potatoes

1 *(No. 303) can small whole sweet*
   potatoes
¼ *cup butter or margarine*
1 *to 2 teaspoons ground cinnamon*
¼ *cup brown sugar*
½ *cup crushed pineapple*

Drain potatoes and place in greased casserole. Dot butter over tops of potatoes, and add cinnamon and brown sugar. Add crushed pineapple. Cover and let sit in refrigerator overnight or bake at once at 350 degrees F. about 30 minutes.

Shredded Yams

(New Perry Hotel, Perry, Georgia)

2 *pounds raw sweet potatoes*
1 *gallon water*
1 *tablespoon salt*
1 *cup sugar*
½ *cup white corn syrup*
½ *cup water*
1 *cup pineapple juice*
4 *tablespoons butter or margarine*

Shred yams into a gallon of water with salt added. Combine sugar, syrup, and water in a heavy saucepan and cook until it forms a light syrup. Drain potatoes, rinse, and pat dry. Place in heat-resistant 12- x 6- x 3-inch glass baking dish. Pour pineapple juice over potatoes, then the cooked syrup. Dot with butter. Bake, uncovered, at 350 degrees F. about 35 minutes or until potatoes are translucent. Yield: 12 servings.

The Parson's Tipsy 'Taters

1 *cup chopped pecans*
1 *cup flaked coconut*
2 *tablespoons sugar*
1 *cup dark seedless raisins*
½ *cup peach or apricot brandy (or*
   cream sherry)
2 *packages instant sweet potato flakes*
1 *dozen regular-size marshmallows*
1 *(4-ounce) bottle maraschino cherries,*
   drained
2 *tablespoons liquid from drained*
   cherries

The night before preparing the dish, mix pecans, coconut, sugar, raisins, and brandy; cover and let sit in refrigerator overnight.

One hour before time to serve, prepare the instant sweet potatoes according to package directions. Taste mixture and add a little brown sugar, if desired. Add fruit mixture and stir well.

Butter a large casserole dish and place one-half of sweet potato mixture in casserole. Distribute marshmallows over top of potatoes; cover with remainder of potatoes. Distribute cherries over top and sprinkle the cherry juice over cherries. If desired, sprinkle a little flaked coconut over top. Bake at 325 degrees F. for 20 to 25 minutes. Serve warm with roast beef at home, or wrap in heavy-duty aluminum foil and carry to a church supper or to a cookout to serve with barbecued chicken or pork. Yield: about 8 to 10 servings.

Candied Sweet Potatoes

4 *medium sweet potatoes*
½ *cup butter or margarine*
½ *cup brown sugar*
¼ *cup hot water*

Wash and bake sweet potatoes. Peel and cut in lengthwise slices about ½ inch thick. Place in shallow 2-quart dish. Pour a syrup made of butter or margarine, brown sugar, and hot water over potatoes. Bake at 375 degrees F. for 1 hour. Yield: 4 to 6 servings.

Brandied Sweet Potatoes

   6 *large sweet potatoes*
   2 *teaspoons cornstarch*
  ½ *teaspoon ground nutmeg*
   2 *teaspoons salt*
  ½ *cup granulated sugar*
   1 *cup water*
   1 *tablespoon lemon juice*
  ⅓ *cup brandy*
    Miniature marshmallows

About 1¼ hours before serving put 6 large scrubbed, unpared sweet potatoes or yams in boiling salted water to cover. Cover pan and cook about 25 minutes or until tender; drain and cool. In 1-quart saucepan mix cornstarch, nutmeg, salt, and sugar. Gradually stir in water; cook over low heat, stirring constantly until clear. Stir in lemon juice and brandy.

Start heating oven to 375 degrees F. Peel potatoes; slice crosswise, ¼ to ½ inch thick, into buttered shallow baking dish. Pour on sauce; cover and bake for 30 minutes or until glazed, basting occasionally. When glazed, sprinkle a few miniature marshmallows over potatoes and broil just until golden. Yield: about 8 servings.

Candied Yams

  ½ *cup butter or margarine*
  ½ *cup unsulphured molasses*
   3 *(1-pound) cans yams*

Melt butter in skillet; stir in unsulphured molasses and syrup drained from yams. Boil rapidly about 2 minutes. Place yams in skillet. Cook over very low heat until glazed, about 20 minutes, turning and basting occasionally. Yield: 12 servings.

Orange Candied Sweet Potatoes

   6 *medium sweet potatoes*
   1 *cup orange juice*
   1 *cup sugar*
  ½ *teaspoon grated orange rind*
   1 *cup water*
  ¼ *cup butter*
  ½ *teaspoon salt*

Peel uncooked potatoes and slice in ¼-inch slices; arrange in a buttered baking dish. Make a syrup of the remaining ingredients and pour over the potatoes. Cover and bake at 350 degrees F. until tender. Baste occasionally. Remove the lid the last 10 minutes and allow to brown. If desired, a layer of marshmallows may be added and browned just before removing dish from the oven.

Sweet Potatoes Southern Style

   2 *cups mashed canned or freshly*
     cooked sweet potatoes
  ½ *stick margarine, melted*
   2 *tablespoons grated orange peel*
  ½ *cup orange juice*
   1 *cup white corn syrup*
   4 *egg yolks, slightly beaten*
   4 *egg whites*
   3 *tablespoons sugar*

Mix potatoes, margarine, grated orange peel, orange juice, syrup, and egg yolks. Stir until smooth. Beat egg whites until stiff. Add sugar; stir and fold into potato mixture. Pour into buttered 1-quart casserole; bake at 400 degrees F. for 20 minutes. Reduce heat to 300 degrees; bake 15 minutes. Yield: 6 servings.

Peachyam Oven Side Dish

> 1 *(No. 303) can yams, drained*
> 1 *(No. 303) can sliced peaches, drained*
> ¼ *cup brown sugar*
> 1 *teaspoon ground cinnamon*
> ½ *stick margarine*
> ½ *cup chopped nuts*

Drain yams and peaches and reserve liquid. Cut the yams in slices about the size of the peach slices. Place the yam and peach slices in neat arrangement in a large, shallow, glass baking dish that has been buttered. Mix the juice from the yams and from the peaches and pour over the top, barely to cover. Sprinkle mixture of brown sugar and cinnamon over the top. Dot with margarine and sprinkle with chopped nuts. Bake at 350 degrees F. for 30 minutes.

Sweet Potato Puffs

These are made with cooked, mashed sweet potatoes (canned ones may be used but should be thoroughly drained before mashing or they will be soggy). An easy way to form balls is with an ice cream scoop. Roll balls in chopped peanuts and place on a greased baking sheet, brush with melted butter or margarine, and bake at 375 degrees F. for 15 to 30 minutes, or until golden brown. For a really sweet "puff," the ball may be formed around a marshmallow.

Tomatoes-Eggplant Casserole

> 2 *eggplant*
> *Salt*
> 3 *tablespoons vegetable oil*
> 2 *pounds tomatoes*
> 1 *clove garlic*
> 1 *cup breadcrumbs*

Peel the eggplant and cut lengthwise into ⅜-inch-thick slices. Salt the slices and place on paper towels to drain; then fry them slowly in vegetable oil. Peel and chop the tomatoes fine. Cook them with 1 clove garlic in the vegetable oil or shortening over low heat until tender. Add about half of the breadcrumbs to thicken the tomatoes.

Place eggplant slices in a baking dish, cover with tomatoes, and sprinkle remainder of breadcrumbs over this mixture. Baste lightly with oil and cook at 400 degrees F. for 45 minutes. Yield: 4 to 6 servings.

Turnip Greens With Pot Liquor Dumplings

> 2 *pounds fresh young turnip greens*
> ¼ *pound salt pork or desired amount of bacon drippings*
> *Salt to taste*
> *Enough water to have 3 cups liquid when done*
> *Dumplings*

Clean and wash greens thoroughly. In a 3-quart saucepan combine salt pork, salt, and water. Cover pan and bring to simmering. Add washed greens, cover, and cook gently until greens are tender. Lift greens from liquid, drain, and arrange on serving platter that can be kept warm. Arrange Dumplings as desired on dish with greens; pour liquid over to keep them moist and hot. Serve at once. Yield: 3 to 4 servings.

Dumplings:

> 1 *cup cornmeal*
> ½ *teaspoon salt*
> ⅔ *cup boiling water*
> *Pot liquor*

Combine cornmeal and salt in a mixing bowl. Stir boiling water into cornmeal mixture and stir to blend well. Using a heaping tablespoon for each portion, shape into balls and place gently in boiling pot liquor from cooked greens. Replace cover; simmer slowly until dumplings are done (20 to 30 minutes). Remove from heat and let stand 10 minutes.

Baked Vegetable Casserole

1½ cups milk, scalded
1 cup dry breadcrumbs
¼ cup melted butter or margarine
½ teaspoon salt
1 tablespoon chopped parsley
2 pimientos, chopped
Dash paprika
1½ tablespoons chopped onion
3 eggs, beaten
1 to 2 cups frozen, mixed vegetables
1½ cups shredded cheese

Pour scalded milk over breadcrumbs; stir to moisten. Add butter, salt, parsley, pimiento, paprika, onion, and beaten eggs. Mix well. Place thawed vegetables in a quart-sized baking dish. Pour sauce over vegetables. Sprinkle shredded cheese on top. Place dish in a pan of water and bake at 325 degrees F. for 1 to 1¼ hours. Yield: 4 to 6 servings.

Vegetable Scramble With Potato Chip-Bacon Crumbles

3 slices bacon
1 (10-ounce) package frozen French-cut green beans
1 tablespoon bacon drippings
¼ cup water
3 tablespoons chopped onion
3 cups coarsely shredded cabbage
½ teaspoon salt
2 tablespoons cider vinegar
1 tablespoon sugar
1 cup crumbled potato chips

Cook bacon until crisp; remove to paper towels, blot dry, and crumble. Add beans to 1 tablespoon bacon drippings left in skillet. Add water and chopped onion; cover and bring to a boil. Reduce heat and simmer for 5 minutes. Add cabbage and sprinkle with salt; cover and bring to a boil. Reduce heat and simmer 5 minutes longer. Do not overcook. Add vinegar and sugar and toss to blend well. Remove to serving dish and top with bacon and potato chip crumbles. Yield: 4 to 6 servings.

Vegetable Crème

2 (10-ounce) packages frozen broccoli
1 tablespoon chopped green pepper
1 tablespoon chopped pimiento
1¾ cups Cheddar cheese sauce
4 tablespoons butter or margarine, melted
½ cup dry breadcrumbs
Grated Parmesan and Romano cheese

Cook broccoli according to package directions. Arrange broccoli, green pepper, and pimiento in buttered 2-quart casserole; pour the cheese sauce over the vegetables.

Mix together the butter and breadcrumbs. Sprinkle buttered breadcrumbs and grated cheese on top of vegetable-cheese mixture. Bake at 350 degrees F. for 30 minutes or until sauce bubbles. Yield: 6 to 8 servings.

Variations: Any one of the following (cooked according to package directions) may be substituted for the broccoli in the above recipe.

2 (10-ounce) packages frozen cauliflower
2 (10-ounce) packages frozen brussels sprouts
2 (10-ounce) packages frozen lima beans*

*If lima beans are used, increase the quantity of cheese sauce to 2 cups.

notes

INDEX